The
BOOKER T. WASHINGTON
Papers

The
BOOKER T. WASHINGTON
Papers

VOLUME 5
1899–1900

Louis R. Harlan
and
Raymond W. Smock
EDITORS

Barbara S. Kraft
ASSISTANT EDITOR

University of Illinois Press
URBANA · CHICAGO · LONDON

© 1976 BY THE BOARD OF TRUSTEES OF THE UNIVERSITY OF ILLINOIS
MANUFACTURED IN THE UNITED STATES OF AMERICA

Library of Congress Cataloging in Publication Data (Revised)

Washington, Booker Taliaferro, 1856–1915.
  The Booker T. Washington papers.

  Includes bibliographies.
  CONTENTS: v. 1. The autobiographical writings.
—v. 2. 1860–89.—v. 3. 1889–95.—v. 4. 1895–98.
—v. 5. 1899–1900.
  1. Washington, Booker Taliaferro, 1856–1915.
2. Afro-Americans—Biography. 3. Afro-Americans—
History—1863–1877—Sources. 4. Afro-Americans—
History—1877–1964—Sources.
E185.97.W274   301.45′19′6073024   75–186345
ISBN 0–252–00627–5 (v. 5)

To Phyllis

EDITOR'S FOREWORD

THIS VOLUME IS, in essence, the work of Raymond W. Smock. He selected, proofread, and annotated the documents from September 1899 through March 1901 under the editor's direction as his doctoral dissertation at the University of Maryland. Thus, he bears primary responsibility for most of this volume and a portion of Volume 6. Beginning with this volume he has been named coeditor of the series.

CONTENTS

CONTENTS

CONTENTS

CONTENTS

xv

CONTENTS

CONTENTS

INTRODUCTION

During the period of this volume Booker T. Washington continued to rise in prestige and power as the black spokesman without equal in America. Washington's paradox, although he seldom admitted it publicly or privately, was that his fortunes continued to rise while those of the race he represented declined. Washington believed, however, that his life did not represent an exception to the black experience; rather, it was a model that others could follow. His public optimism about the advancement of the race was partly an attempt to convince himself, and the world, that racial harmony was possible in America. In the tradition of American boosterism, Washington advertised and promoted Tuskegee Institute as the example of what blacks were capable of doing on their own. He always tried to look on the bright side, even when reports of the most virulent racism reached him. Washington heeded the advice of his friend Timothy Thomas Fortune, who cautioned him in 1899: "Others may get discouraged, but you can't without inviting disaster."

Washington's racial philosophy remained consistent with the formula of his Atlanta Compromise of 1895. His public utterances were always sanguine and conventional. For this reason many of his speeches are repetitive. He often used the same speech, slightly modified to fit the particular audience, many times in the course of his arduous speaking schedule. In 1913 Washington compared his speeches with the sermons of a minister. "I sometimes change my text," he wrote, "but usually preach the same sermon." Even when forced to deal with an emotional question such as lynching, Washington minimized the evil and turned his response into clichés and stock phrases by stressing that lynching would cease when all blacks had secured an education and a bank account.

Criticism of Washington's leadership in the late 1890s was mild when compared to the opposition he would face later. Few blacks or whites were thinking of repudiation of Washington's leadership at this time. Criticism of his conservative approach grew as he became powerful enough to make his leadership monolithic, and as worsening racial conditions in American life called for new approaches. Critics such as the black physician Nathan F. Mossell and the black clergyman Reverdy C. Ransom, for example, chastised Washington for his attempt to stand aloof from controversial issues such as black civil rights. They could not understand how he could be hailed as the Moses of his race when he refused to take a bold stand on political issues. Others, especially college-trained blacks, criticized Washington for his failure to promote higher education. At the turn of the century, however, few blacks were completely polarized on this issue, and there was general praise by both blacks and whites for Washington's work at Tuskegee Institute.

Washington's civil rights activities were usually carried out secretly. He helped finance the search for a case to test the Louisiana Constitution of 1900, and, using friends as intermediaries, he sought to check Jim Crow practices on railroads. In 1900 he successfully lobbied against disfranchisement of black voters in Georgia. Despite all of this, however, Washington's secret militancy never balanced his public conservatism. His power as a race leader grew from his accommodationist public image and his strong following among whites, not from his secret activities. His secret life can be explained in part by his attempt to be all things to all men. Washington tried to dominate all aspects of racial leadership, and this included an attempt to control the direction of civil rights activities.

In 1900 Washington founded the National Negro Business League to help promote black business and to advertise the economic success some blacks had achieved. The league reflected Washington's belief that black advancement depended on integration into the American economy. It served a more important function for Washington, however, by providing him with a corps of loyal supporters in every major American city. It became an important basis of Washington's political influence with black Americans.

Though he publicly eschewed political activity, Washington often used the meetings of the National Negro Business League as a front for secret political activity. Money raised at league meetings sometimes found its way into the hands of lawyers handling civil rights cases. Washington claimed that the National Negro Business League was strictly a business organization, and often told reporters that political activity was the domain of the National Afro-American Council. While Washington kept his public association with the council to a minimum, he wielded a strong influence on its program through his good friend T. Thomas Fortune, one of the vice-presidents and a power on the executive committee of the council.

This volume contains documents relating to the beginnings of important movements among whites concerned with black advancement in America. The organized philanthropy of the Southern Education Movement had its origin in the excursions of Robert Curtis Ogden and other northerners in the late 1890s. Edgar Gardner Murphy's letters concerning his Montgomery Race Conference and the reform movement that the conference was intended to initiate reveal the limitations of the racial thought of the "best South" and their northern counterparts, who debated the merits of repealing the Fifteenth Amendment while about two hundred "safe" blacks, including Washington, watched from a Jim Crow gallery.

Among the most revealing letters in this volume are those to and from T. Thomas Fortune, the leading black journalist of the time. From these letters are gleaned some of the best insights into Washington's actions, both public and private. Fortune was deeply involved with Washington as an adviser, ghost-writer, and friend. He was a key factor in Washington's elaborate web of power and influence that became known as the Tuskegee Machine. The two men corresponded almost daily during the period of this volume, but many of the letters are repetitive. When important new information occasionally appears in an otherwise routine letter, the editors have used passages to annotate other documents, thus presenting the useful information without the mundane material.

Because of the efficiency of Washington's private secretary, Emmett Jay Scott, the Booker T. Washington Papers after 1898 are much more voluminous than in earlier years, although not until about 1904 was sufficient care taken to preserve fully Washington's outgoing correspondence. This poses problems for the editors of a selective edition. This volume, for example, contains less about the development of Tuskegee Institute than earlier volumes of the series. This important aspect of Washington's life has not been neglected, but it must take second place to other emerging themes, such as Washington's growing role as a national political figure. Tuskegee Institute, however, remains central to an understanding of Washington, and the story of the school and its people is among the richest legacies of the Washington Papers. By 1899, however, the main process of institution-building was over. Less space, therefore, will be devoted to matters at the school except those that are especially revealing of social and educational history.

This volume also contains the full text of Washington's first book, *The Future of the American Negro*, published in December 1899. His first autobiography, *The Story of My Life and Work*, which also appeared during the period covered in this volume, can be found in its entirety in Volume 1 of *The Booker T. Washington Papers*.

In this and subsequent volumes, letters from W. E. B. Du Bois are published with the permission of Mrs. Shirley Graham Du Bois and the University of Massachusetts Press, publishers of *The Correspondence of W. E. B. Du Bois*, Vol. I (1973). No further publication of these letters is authorized without their consent.

In addition to persons whose help was acknowledged in earlier volumes, the editors would like to express their appreciation to the following: Thomas C. Barringer, Dennis A. Burton, Pete Daniel, John Duffy, Lawrence Foust, Patricia Carter Ives, Sara D. Jackson, Stuart Kaufman, Charles McLaughlin, Sylvia L. Render, Chalmers M. Roberts, Walter Rundell, Jr., and Jerry Thornbery. The editors could not do their work without the contribution of the staff of the Booker T. Washington Papers project: Janet P. Benham, Patricia A. Cooper, Sadie M. Harlan, Sharyn Mitchell, Denise P. Moore, and Judy A. Reardon. Pete Daniel, a former assistant editor of the project, who has continued to be of valuable assistance to the editors, has been named to the board of editorial advisors.

We are grateful to the National Endowment for the Humanities, the National Historical Publications and Records Commission, and the University of Maryland for their continued support of this project.

CHRONOLOGY

1899   May 10–Aug. 5: Vacation in Europe.

Aug. 31: Reception in Charleston, W.Va.

November: Washington opposes disfranchisement in Georgia.

December: Publication of *The Future of the American Negro*.

1900   May 8–10: The Montgomery Race Conference.

May: Publication of *The Story of My Life and Work*.

July 19: Washington appointed chief commissioner of the Negro Department of the Charleston, S.C., Interstate Exposition.

Aug. 23–24: First convention of the National Negro Business League in Boston.

September: German government requests Washington's help in establishing a cotton-growing experiment in Togo.

Oct. 12: Address before the Southern Industrial Convention in Huntsville, Ala.

Nov. 3: Serialization of *Up from Slavery* begins in the *Outlook*.

SYMBOLS AND ABBREVIATIONS

STANDARD ABBREVIATIONS for dates, months, and states are used by the editors only in footnotes and endnotes; textual abbreviations are reproduced as found.

DOCUMENT SYMBOLS

1. A — autograph; written in author's hand
    H — handwritten by other than signator
    P — printed
    T — typed

2. C — postcard
    D — document
    E — endorsement
    L — letter
    M — manuscript
    W — wire (telegram)

3. c — carbon
    d — draft
    f — fragment
    p — letterpress
    t — transcript or copy made at much later date

4. I — initialed by author
    r — representation; signed or initialed in author's name
    S — signed by author

Among the more common endnote abbreviations are: ALS — autograph letter, signed by author; TLpI — typed letter, letterpress copy, initialed by author.

REPOSITORY SYMBOLS

Symbols used for repositories are the standard ones used in *Symbols of American Libraries Used in the National Union Catalog of the Library of Congress,* 10th ed. (Washington, D.C., 1969).

A-Ar	Alabama Department of Archives and History, Montgomery, Ala.
ATT	Tuskegee Institute, Tuskegee, Ala.
CtY	Yale University, New Haven, Conn.
DHU	Howard University, Washington, D.C.
DLC	Library of Congress, Washington, D.C.
DNA	National Archives, Washington, D.C.
MH	Harvard University, Cambridge, Mass.
MNS	Smith College, Northampton, Mass.
MU	University of Massachusetts, Amherst, Mass.
MdBMC	Morgan State College, Baltimore, Md.
NN	New York Public Library, NYC
NN-Sc	Schomburg Collection, New York Public Library, NYC
NRU	University of Rochester, Rochester, N.Y.
NcD	Duke University, Durham, N.C.
ViHaI	Hampton Institute, Hampton, Va.

OTHER ABBREVIATIONS

BTW	Booker T. Washington
Con.	Container
NNBL	National Negro Business League
RG	Record Group
Ser.	Series

Documents, 1899-1900

From Timothy Thomas Fortune

Washington, D.C., Jan 1, 1899

My Dear Mr Washington: Your letter of the 29th ult was received today, with check for $30. I thank you so much. It came in the nick of time. But I grieve to worry you when you have so many worries of your own.

Scott left today.

He will tell you of what transpired here. It was a terrible fight and I am a shade sick as a result of it and the tremendous victory I won.[1]

I shall wait for you here. *My return ticket is over the B & O.* Don't buy your New York ticket until we meet. Yours sincerely

T Thomas Fortune

ALS   Con. 154   BTW Papers   DLC.

[1] Fortune considerably overstated his "victory." Going to Washington in late December for the national meeting of the Afro-American Council, a few days before the meeting he was the principal speaker at a gathering in a black church. In a candid speech he sharply criticized President McKinley's silence on voting rights and lynching during his recent tour of the South. "I want the man whom I fought for to fight for me," he was reported to have said, "and if he don't I feel like stabbing him." The next day Fortune claimed he had been misquoted and misconstrued by the white press, but even the black newspapers were critical of his "rash and ill-judged utterances." Nevertheless, he was chairman of a committee to draft a statement of the Afro-American Council addressed to President McKinley. The moderation of the statement was in marked contrast to Fortune's earlier utterances, and this ensured BTW's approval. Fortune signed the address but would not accompany the delegation that presented it to McKinley. (Thornbrough, *Fortune*, 181-88.)

From Robert Lloyd Smith

Oakland, Texas, Jan 2 1899

Dear Friend, Yours of 28 ult. came to me to day. I wrote you a long time ahead in order that you might arrange your affairs so as to give us the inspiration of your presence and the good of your advice at our next annual convocation and fair which will be held the 2nd Wednesday in Oct 1899. The executive committee of our organization authorized me to communicate with you and as we are all your children and followers, we thought you would honor us with your presence and give us your benediction. Our movement has grown so much and our annual gatherings are getting to be such events that we long to enlarge its sphere so that every body that will may come, hear and learn. Acting upon the plans and in the lines promulgated at the last Tuskegee Conference we decided at our annual convocation to have a *fair* and we want you to come and see what we are doing and to tell us how to do better.[1] In one of the Dec issues of the student[2] I saw your plan how to lengthen the school term by planting and gathering a crop for the teacher. I laid this before the body and we were unanimous in resolving to put this in operation. I think we're going to win. We are all united and determined to succeed and I believe and feel that God Almighty is with us as he is with you. We are after the mudsillers. We want to teach the common people — those who never went a day to school in their lives industry economy thrift perseverance self control and develop higher ideas of *home* and its functions.

I have had a straight out struggle this year. Ive had to fight every inch of my way in everything but thank God I am still on gaining ground and am enabled by his help to say "Hitherto hath the Lord helped us." Now then we must have you. Our folks here will defray the expense unless its more than they can raise. But I must have you and it is absolutely necessary that you be with us and we have the faith that takes no denial. I think honestly if you'll come you'll be in better heart for your own special work. Regards to Mrs W Mr & Mrs Scott and other friends.

R. L. Smith

ALS Con. 162 BTW Papers DLC. Written on stationery of the Farmers' Improvement Society of Texas, R. L. Smith, president. The letterhead also contains the following description: "WHAT WE ARE FIGHTING FOR: The Abolition of the Credit System. Better Methods of Farming. Cooperation. Proper Care of the Sick and Dead. Improvement and Beautifying of our Homes."

[1] Smith wrote to BTW: "Each visit I have made [to Tuskegee] has been worth thousands of dollars to the people of Texas and I have often wished that I could inspire them as you all inspire me." He said that his Farmers' Improvement Society was organizing black women to raise poultry for market and wanted to expand the operation to include other livestock such as hogs and cattle. (Jan. 19, 1899, Con. 162, BTW Papers, DLC.)

[2] BTW, "How to Build Up a Good School in the South," *Tuskegee Student*, 12 (Dec. 1, 1898), 3-4.

From Edward Henry Clement[1]

[Boston, Mass.] January 2, 1898 [1899]

My Dear Mr. Washington: I am going to print the letter sent me regarding your position in the political troubles of the blacks, by Mr. Emmett J. Scott, but I wish I could have a signed article by you on the whole question, both general and going into particulars. I should not ask you to contribute it free, but would pay you our best rates for contributions. Any time soon for an article of, say, 2,000 words.

I was shocked the other night to hear a reference to your policy in a meeting of colored men, hissed. Turning to my next neighbor in the pew I asked, "Is he not hitting at Washington?" and the answer was, "Yes; there is much and growing opposition to his counsels among blacks." In any candid editorial comment on the situation this surely cannot be ignored with safety.

I confess that I wonder at, and admire, your reserve and am not at all sure that yours is not the course of wisdom in the thickening difficulties which beset the upward path of your race. I am much impressed with the protests of such men as Dubois and Dunbar against the new outburst of intolerance in the South. The indifference in the North that is settling down over the whole problem is one of the most serious phenomena and it seems to me that it must be rudely shaken up once in a while to prevent the crust forming from hardening into solid substance. I wish you would write us an article. That would mark an epoch in the new year for the development of the question. Very truly yours,

E H Clement

TLS Con. 138 BTW Papers DLC.

[1] Edward Henry Clement (1843-1920) was editor-in-chief of the Boston *Transcript* from 1881 to 1906. Though his editorials often took a more militant position than that of BTW on the franchise and civil rights, Clement was a consistent defender of the Tuskegean in a city where he had many critics.

To Frank E. Saffold[1]

[Tuskegee, Ala.] Jan. 3, 1899

Mr. Saffold: In speaking to you last night about the unsatisfactory condition of the boarding department I refrained from telling you that it has been rather apparent to me and others for some time that I fear the bottom of the weakness is this. You have been led into the temptation of spending entirely too much of your time and giving too much of your thought and activity to your insurance and other private business. Your department is a very responsible one and I realized that when I appointed you to that position that it was a great risk to put a person so young as yourself in so responsible a position. I thought, however, that you would recognize this fact and make an extra effort to give satisfaction. I fear you have made the mistake that many young people make, you want to get hold of money, which is [a] right and proper desire, but you will find that you will help yourself financially much quicker and in a much more satisfactory way by devoting yourself so fully and wholly in thought and activity to your school work that you would make your department so successful and praiseworthy that the school will feel willing to increase your salary and would be obliged to do it rather than let you leave your present position. This would not only give you more money here but would give you a reputation that would put your services in demand at a high salary elsewhere. I give you two examples of teachers who have themselves made such reputations, the two I have in mind are Dr. Kenniebrew and Mr. Gibson;[2] they have devoted themselves wholly to their work to such an extent that they have made reputations that placed their services in wide demand. It might be that after one has been in a position like yours for eight or ten years and has established himself and made a reputation in it that he could afford to divide his time between regular business and private affairs, but I do not believe that you can afford to without running the risk of succeeding in neither enterprise.

You cannot succeed in your present position unless you make up your mind to go into the department, into every corner of your work daily, and you will also have to leave your home early in the morning, often going to the department before and after the students' breakfast. I impress upon you especially the importance of seeing that everything is made clean, systematic and orderly in the students' kitchen.

Booker T. Washington

TLpS Con. 282A BTW Papers DLC.

[1] Frank E. Saffold was BTW's private secretary and stenographer from 1892 to 1896, when he was transfered to the boarding department. He served there as business agent from 1897 to 1899.

[2] Charles H. Gibson joined the Tuskegee staff in the mid-1890s and served for many years as head bookkeeper and accountant.

To Emmett Jay Scott

Crawford House, Boston, Mass. 1, 10, 1899

Dear Mr. Scott: Please tell Mrs. Washington and Mr. Logan that it is very possible that Mrs. Barrows[1] and Mrs. Johnson,[2] who is Supt. of the Woman's Prison in this state, will stop at Tuskegee the latter part of this month. They will be going to or from New Orleans to attend the meeting of the prison association. I hope things will be in good condition and that they will receive a hearty welcome there.

We had I think what was by far the largest and most enthusiastic meeting for Tuskegee Sunday evening that we have ever had in Boston.[3] The house was packed from door to pulpit and hundreds of people went away who could not get in. The colored brethren were represented in good numbers. I find that the matter to which Mr. Clement referred in his letter has been a good deal exaggerated. I send you a marked copy of the Courant which sets the matter about right. The sensible, sober, thinking colored people are with me here. I also send marked copies of the Herald, Journal, Globe and Record. Yours truly,

Booker T. Washington

TLS Con. 165 BTW Papers DLC.

[1] Isabel Hayes Chapin Barrows. She wrote to BTW on Jan. 8, 1899, urging his public endorsement of William E. Benson and Kowaliga Academic and Industrial Institute, and describing her plan to visit Tuskegee. (Con. 149, BTW Papers, DLC.)

[2] Ellen Cheney Johnson (1829-99), born in Athol, Mass., and reared in New Hamp-

shire, took a leading part in the work of the U.S. Sanitary Commission during the Civil War. After the war she turned her attention to prison reform, which resulted in the establishment of the Massachusetts Reformatory Prison for Women at Sherborn in 1877. Ellen Johnson was superintendent of the prison for fifteen years, and her work was in the vanguard of prison reform of the late nineteenth century. She thought that women prisoners should be given the chance for education, and she established a series of stages to be mastered on the way to their rehabilitation.

3 At a meeting in the Old South Church on Jan. 8, 1899, BTW defended himself against charges that he "sold out" his fellow blacks to their oppressors for his own aggrandizement. These charges had been made earlier that week at a meeting of the Colored National League of Boston, a civil rights group. BTW also answered those who had attacked his policy of patience instead of retaliation for the murders of blacks committed in the South in recent months. Though he condemned lynching, he said: "It has been equally unfortunate that the negro has so long retained the idea that any member of his own race who sought in a manly, independent and unselfish manner to thus encourage the Southerner to enter into active sympathy with the negro, must necessarily be a trimmer or a traitor to the highest interest of his race." He urged his listeners to recognize that "there are native Southern white men whose hearts beat in just as earnest sympathy for all that concerns the highest and permanent interest of the negro as is true of any found in any section of our country." (Boston *Transcript*, Jan. 4, 1899, 14; Jan. 9, 1899, 9.)

An Endowment Campaign Pamphlet

[Boston, Mass., ca. Jan. 13, 1899]

A PLAN TO HELP TUSKEGEE

TEMPORARY ENDOWMENT OF $25,000 FOR THE INSTITUTE

BUSINESS MEN OF BOSTON INTERESTED IN PROJECT —
IT WILL RELIEVE PRINCIPAL BOOKER T. WASH-
INGTON AND GIVE HIM TIME FOR THE EXEC-
UTIVE WORK OF THE SCHOOL

From the Boston Herald, January 13, 1899.

A few business men in Boston and elsewhere have proposed a plan to raise $25,000 for the temporary endowment of the Tuskegee Normal and Industrial Institute, at Tuskegee, Ala., for each of two years, so as to relieve the principal, Booker T. Washington, somewhat of the constant daily strain of collecting the money for the daily life of the institution and give him time for the executive work of the school.

It does seem that, in the midst of the tremendous seriousness of the race problem in the South, when all thinking people North and South acknowledge that the Tuskegee school is doing just the work which will eventually solve our great race problem, that there ought to be hundreds who will count it a privilege to help Tuskegee in this larger way just now.

The plan is to secure persons who will agree to give either $1,000, $750, $500 or $250 for a period of two years, with the understanding that such gifts are not to interfere with any other gifts which are already being annually given to Tuskegee. Such gifts will only be called for when the full $25,000 is secured. Several gentlemen have already agreed to give $1,000, and to get their friends to give additional amounts. It is earnestly hoped that many new friends, as well as old ones, will feel moved to make contributions or pledges at once.

This is a temporary relief fund and the understanding is that the principal can be expended. Pledges or contributions to this fund can be sent direct to Principal Booker T. Washington, Tuskegee, Alabama, or to any of the Trustees of the school. $15,000 of the $25,000 has already been pledged or given.

From the Boston Herald, January 13, 1899.

We print in another column an appeal for the Tuskegee Normal and Industrial Institute, which, we trust, will commend itself to the relatively few well-to-do people in this community whose cooperation is needed to make the plan successful. We believe that it is generally recognized that Principal Booker T. Washington of the Tuskegee Institute is a man who better appreciates the conditions of the race problem at the South, and the manner in which this should be solved, than any other living man. The work which he is carrying on, when its possible effect upon the future of our country is taken into account, is of inestimable value. It is something which rises to the magnitude of a public calamity that a man who has it in him to do work which will act as a beacon light for the guidance for hundreds of thousands, and perhaps millions, of people, should be compelled to turn for a large part of his time from his tremendous and essential labors, for the purpose of carrying it on. There should be inspiration enough in what he is doing to lead men of wealth to individually agree to make the pledge of $25,000 for the next two years. It is not an infrequent occurrence for a man of wealth to pay that sum, or twice that sum, for a race horse, or four times that sum for a steam yacht. Yet the sum which it is now proposed to raise represents a fund which at this critical period in the race problem is to be devoted to the exposition of a practical method of forever settling this vexed contention. We certainly trust that Mr. Washington will not have to wait a week before he has the money guaranteed, not for the next two, but for the next four years.

PD Con. 217 BTW Papers DLC.

From Edgar Webber

Tuskegee, Ala., Jan 16, 1899

Dear Sir: I enclose you a letter from Mr. Hertel in answer to one of mine in which I expressed to him the importance of not being in too big a hurry in the matter of getting out this publication. I called his attention to the criticisms with which their book "Progress of A Race"[1] is meeting with on account of the ev[id]ently hasty manner in which it was compiled which caused it to be inacurate in many respects, and to be confined in an undue proportion to *Georgia* men and matters when it purports to be *national* in its scope. I, however, offered to furnish material for a prospectus, explaining to him the nature or character of the material which I could furnish.

After reading my letter he has come to the conclusion to make haste a little more slowly as you will see by the inclosed letter, and prefers to wait for the manuscript before making up a prospectus.

He still clings to the idea of getting President McKinley to write the introduction, a preface or an indorsement of some kind. Not knowing exactly how you feel about that I send his letter.

I shall continue to give my attention to the collection of photographs and to the outlining of the work so as [to] make it as easy as possible for you to write. To do this latter successfully I am of course compelled to study your life from every source of information I can discover. As I have remarked once or twice before, there seems to be no written record obtainable in regard to the events of your life from about 1885 to 1894. There was no scrap book kept during this period which was undoubtedly a very busy period of your life and a period in which the school was growing and becoming known. By dilligent searching, I find now a[nd] then a little something concerning the events of this period.

Mr. Hertel suggest[s] that I should be on hand when the manuscript is being typewritten to suggest and mark where each illustration is to come in, and I think I could give you some valuable suggestions, if I were present or near at hand when you write. Many of these suggestions can not be incorporated in the outline or Memorandum. I think I have enough before me now to engage my attention until you return here, and will hardly need to refer any more letters to you until you come back.

I need a little money and would be glad if you could send me at once $25 or $30 or arrange for me to get it here. Very truly yours,

Edgar Webber

ALS Con. 153 BTW Papers DLC.

1 John William Gibson, *Progress of a Race; or The Remarkable Advancement of the American Negro . . . with an Introduction by Booker T. Washington.* Atlanta, Ga., and Naperville, Ill.: J. L. Nichols and Co., 1897. Six revisions of this work, with varying subtitles and different editors, appeared between 1898 and 1929. Henry F. Kletzing and William H. Crogman did the first revision in 1898, and later J. L. Nichols and W. H. Crogman did several revisions. The book was a typical product of the J. L. Nichols firm. It was designed to be a race history and Who's Who sold largely by subscription among blacks throughout the country.

From Charles G. Harris[1]

Montgomery, Ala., January 16, 1899

Dear Mr. Washington: You remember no doubt that during my recent visit to Tuskegee I began a conversation with you relative to William E. Bolden,[2] recently a student of the school. You were so greatly in demand on that day that I could not finish my conversation with you. It is to continue that subject that I now write you.

Mr. Washington, I claim that Bolden was cruelly if not criminally treated by some one in authority at the school. There are facts in the case of which I feel sure that you know nothing, and I intend to make those facts known to you to-day.

During my visit to Tuskegee in the month of October, 1898, Bolden was complaining. To my personal knowledge he made three unsuccessful attempts to see the school physician and each time he had the best possible excuse for being tardy. You know what the rule is with reference to this matter.

Previous to this time the doctor had been treating him for indigestion. He told Bolden that he had only stomach trouble.

After my return here (about the middle of October) Bolden wrote me that he had improved somewhat but was not entirely well. I wrote him telling him to get an excuse and come and stay with me until his condition grew better. He promptly applied to Mr. Palmer for an excuse from school, telling him that his physical condition was bad, and that he did not think it safe for him to remain in school. Mr. Palmer told him that he would have to bring him a written statement from the doctor to verify what he had said regarding his health. Bolden asked the doctor to give him the statement required by Mr. Palmer: this he refused to do. He told Bolden that if the food did not agree with him to find work in some family. This he tried to do but failed.

Now on the same day that Bolden had applied to the doctor for an excuse, the doctor told Mr. Palmer (while sitting at the dinner table) that there was nothing the matter with Bolden of a nature serious enough to secure him an excuse from school. He said that Bolden was affected with a little indigestion.

Bolden very promptly wrote me and told me of the predicament into which he was placed and asked my advice. He stated that if he should leave the school without being excused, he would be expelled and he felt that he would get no better if he remained there. Now, what could I say to him? I could not advise him to disregard the rules of the institution and have his name brought to disgrace, so I advised him to apply for better food.

I did not hear from Bolden immediately and feeling somewhat uneasy, I called the doctor to the telephone and asked about him. He told me in response to my question that Bolden was well. He seemed to catch something of my astonishment for he immediately modified his statement by saying "Bolden will be all right in a day or two." I then asked him why he did not excuse him when he applied for an excuse. He said "I have been thinking lately that a change would do him good." He then promised that he would excuse Bolden to come to Montgomery and remain awhile. I told him that I would send Bolden his fare and asked the Dr. to let him know that he might be excused. He did not tell me that at that very moment the young man was confined to his bed, a hopeless dying consumptive but left me under the impression that he was convalescent from a case of indigestion. Bolden was never told by the physician to leave his room and go to the hospital but after having several hemmorrhages at different times in his room he went to the hospital of his own accord. The doctor had assured him that his lungs were "as sound as a dollar." The doctor accounted for the blood in quite a different way and said that it did not come from the lungs.

At the time of the death of Dr. K.'s father, the doctor left word that Bolden must get out of the hospital — "he must go home or *some* place" he could not stay *there*.

On Sunday evening Nov. 20, Bolden, being excused from the hospital, came directly to my house. He had not sat up a whole day for three weeks. I had my physician to examine him and learned for the first time that he had consumption. His fever was then 103. The doctor advised me that it was exceedingly dangerous for the invalid to remain in my house with my family; I did what I could to have him accommodated at Hale Infirmary. The expense of keeping him at that place was so great that I could not afford to maintain him there. I could do nothing but get him the proper medicine, buy him some warm underclothes and send him back to Tuskegee. He remained at my house until Tuesday, noon.

I understand that the doctor (Kennebrew) was not pleased with my "sending him back upon the school." He would allow no other patient to stay in the same room with Bolden that night and compelled him to leave the hospital the following day to go to South Carolina. He begged that he might be allowed to remain there until he might be able to travel. When he found that he had to go, he begged that I be informed of the matter. In spite of all protest I am told that he was started away from the school, without a lunch or without any one to accompany him to his destination.

He left Tuskegee on Wednesday, Nov. 23. Remember he had not sat up an entire day for three weeks. The train between Chehaw and Atlanta was not heated although the weather was quite cold. Owing to the out-of-the-way place in which his father lives, Bolden did not reach his home until Sunday. He died the following Monday.

Here is the shameful part of Dr. Kennebrew's conduct: When I arrived at Tuskegee to assist with the music for the entertainment of the President, I was asked by some student — "How is Bolden?" I answered "I do not know, but since I have not heard from him I suppose that he is dead." Out of this grew the rumor that Bolden was dead. On Dec. 8, this rumor grew so obnoxious to Dr. Kennebrew that he had Mr. Logan to announce publicly in the pavilion that the rumor was untrue and that he (Dr.) had had a letter from

Bolden's home stating that he was getting along very well. According to the letter that I received from Bolden's father Bolden was in his grave at the time that Mr. Logan made the announcement for Dr. Kennebrew.

The morning after the announcement had been made, I saw Dr. K. on his way to the hospital and asked him to let me see the letter that he had received. He told me that he had left it at his office. He did not offer to get it for me so I asked him if the letter were from Bolden's father; this he did not know; he could not even remember the initials of the Bolden who wrote the letter. He gave me the details as to how the young man reached his home so far in the country. This account however does not agree with the account which is contained in the letter I received from Bolden's father on Dec. 29. Somebody has certainly departed from the truth. In my mind there is no doubt as to the guilty party.

I do not write this letter thinking that it will do Bolden any good. I write it hoping that you look into the matter. Miss Hilyer[3] and Mr. Palmer, as well as Mr. Logan can attest to a part of the matter contained herein. I will never believe that you ever intended an excellent young man like William Bolden to fare as he did.

I claim that Dr. K. is in a great measure responsible for that young man's misfortunes. Whether it is the result of ignorance, negligence or a desire to lessen the actual number of deaths *at the school,* I do not know. This I do know — It would not take many cases parallel to this, to seriously injure the reputation of the school. Yours very sincerely,

Chas. G. Harris

TLS Con. 155 BTW Papers DLC. Written on stationery of the U.S. Land Office, Department of the Interior.

[1] Charles G. Harris, formerly and later choir director at Tuskegee, in 1899 was a clerk in the U.S. Land Office in Montgomery.

[2] William Edgar Bolden of Greenville, S.C., entered the Tuskegee junior class in 1896 and advanced to the A middle class during the 1898-99 school year.

[3] Jennie F. Hilyer taught nurse training and physiology at Tuskegee from 1896 to 1899.

From George Washington Henderson

New Orleans, La., Jan. 19 1899

My dear Mr. Washington: Your letter of Jan. 2 is at hand. No, I was not aware of your wish or of any action on your part to test the constitutionality of the recently made Louisiana Election Law. I hardly need to say that I rejoice in your interest in the matter.

My expectation has been from the first that the law would be tested in the U.S. Court at no very distant day. The Times-Democrat openly advised it, and I have cherished the hope that honorable white democrats would take up the matter out of patriotism and self-respect.

This hope may prove delusive, and yet I would be glad if by some sort of wise management, it could be realized.

My idea has been that no case can be made till there is an election. Meanwhile I will make inquiries and set some plan in motion if possible to bring a test case as soon as circumstances will permit. I will write you from time to time, and shall be glad of any counsel or help you can give us. Very truly Yours,

Geo. W. Henderson

ALS   Con. 155   BTW Papers   DLC.   Docketed: "Returned from Mr. Fortune."

From Warren Logan

Tuskegee, Ala., 1-21-99

Dear Mr. Washington: Mr. Taylor resumed the drawing a few days ago after being in doors for a week with a bad toe.

I have received your letter notifying me of the intended visit of Mrs. Barrows and asking me to have the school put in good condition. I have already addressed myself to this matter and trust Mrs. Barrows will find things in fairly good order when she comes. I shall do every thing I can to have her get as good [an] impression as possible of the school. The question of entertainment has come up. I have thought it would be best to have her stay at your house and take her meals in the Teachers' Home. I do not know whether Mrs. Washington is intending to be at home within the next few days or not; if she is, it will of course be very easy to provide for Mrs. Barrows.

We have had quite a religious awakening in the school since you left. More than one hundred students have professed christianity and many of the teachers have been spiritually refreshed. The meetings have been in progress for the past two weeks.

We have had some trouble during the last few days with the Cuban students. Dr. Kenniebrew recommended that they be given the students' diet, except for breakfast, and they have objected to it and up to this time, have refused to take their meals from the students' boarding department. I think however they will come 'round to it all right in a day or two. They seem to regard that they are conferring a great favor upon the institution by being here. Gomez[1] and Pedro[2] are the leaders in the trouble.

I trust your health keeps good and that all goes well with you.

I have been very much interested in the project as stated in the Transcript, for raising funds for the school, and trust it may be a complete success. Very truly,

Warren Logan

TLS   Con. 157   BTW Papers   DLC.

1 Juan E. Gomez.
2 Pedro Salina.

From George H. McDaniel[1]

Springfield, Ill., Jan 23rd 1899

Dear Sir: We have recently had John Temple Graves[2] of Atlanta Ga. in our midsts lecturing upon his hobby — "The Last Hope of The Negro." He represented you as holding his wholesale colonization scheme in favor next to your own great work i.e. He says you say that should your "experiment" fail you will endorse his scheme as the next best thing.

As we value your opinions you will do us a favor by informing us if Mr. Graves has fairly represented you[r] views. Very Kindly

G. H. McDaniel

ALS Con. 158 BTW Papers DLC. Docketed: "Told him I have often heard you ridicule Graves' proposition — but that you'd reply yourself to his letter. EJS."

[1] George H. McDaniel was pastor of the Union Baptist Church in Springfield, Ill., and editor and owner of the *National Standard-Enterprise*, a weekly founded in 1887.

[2] John Temple Graves (1856-1925), a Georgia newspaperman and lecturer, was an anti-black extremist. During his career he edited the Atlanta *Journal*, Rome (Ga.) *Tribune*, Atlanta *News*, Atlanta *Georgian*, and New York *American*.

From Timothy Thomas Fortune

New York, Jan 25, 1899

My Dear Mr. Washington: I have your favor of the 24th instant. I have read with interest Mr. Henderson's letter. It seems to me that instead of hoping that some white friend would go ahead and test the law, Mr. Henderson and others in Louisiana should go ahead and do it. We seem to be a race of "Micawbers," always waiting for something to turn up instead of going ahead and turning something up.

My stomach still bothers me a great deal, but I hope it will soon get regulated. I am very glad that you are so well satisfied with my stay in Boston.[1] I had my compensation in the pleasure of being with you.

I will look up the Independent's offer of the "Diamonds." We manage to keep the ball rolling in one direction or another.

My folks are all well, and send regards to you and Mrs. Washington. Several of the daily newspapers have used Fred's[2] article on "Race War in a Lot." He is very proud of his performance. Yours truly,

T. Thomas Fortune

ALS Con. 154 BTW Papers DLC.

[1] On Jan. 17, the Colored National League of Boston held a rally at the Charles Street A.M.E. Church supporting BTW, who had been attacked by the local black

opposition. Both Ida Wells-Barnett and Fortune spoke at the gathering. Fortune also gave enthusiastic support to the proposal that blacks end their unquestioning loyalty to the Republican party, in view of McKinley's refusal to take steps to counter southern disfranchisement and lynching.

2 Frederick Randolph Moore (1857-1943) was born in Prince William County, Va., and moved at a young age to Washington, D.C. In 1875 he became a messenger in the U.S. Treasury Department and two years later was assigned to the Secretary of the Treasury's office. His new position put him in close proximity to cabinet members and presidents, and he was with President Garfield when the latter was assassinated. Moore resigned in 1887, after several months in Europe on department business, and moved to New York. Former Secretary of the Treasury Daniel Manning gave him a job as clerk in the Western National Bank (later merged with the National Bank of Commerce), which he held for eighteen years. After the failure of the Negro Protective League, which he had organized the year before, Moore founded the Afro-American Investment Building Company in Brooklyn, in 1893. In 1904 Moore became an officer of the short-lived Afro-American Realty Company in Harlem. The following year, Moore was appointed on BTW's recommendation as deputy collector of internal revenue for the second district of New York, but he resigned a few months later when he became an organizer for the NNBL.

In 1904 BTW bought the Boston-based *Colored American Magazine* and made Moore editor. Three years later, after BTW clashed with Fortune over the Brownsville incident, BTW furnished money to buy the *Age* and installed Moore as editor and part-owner. Washington kept his investment secret, and was careful to hold stock in Emmett J. Scott's name, but he kept a close watch on both the business and editorial aspects of Moore's paper. BTW and Scott sent many editorials and repeated proposals for increasing circulation and management of the enterprise. Moore, however, did not endorse the Tuskegee line completely, and his political militancy often distressed his benefactor. Moore helped found the National Urban League in 1911 and served on its first board. Toward the end of Taft's administration, Moore was confirmed as minister of Liberia, but he resigned the appointment in three months without having visited the country. Moving from Brooklyn to Harlem in the early 1920s, Moore was elected an alderman from a Harlem district in 1927, serving until 1931. In 1929 he and other black residents succeeded in ousting the white incumbent assemblyman, Abraham Grendthal, in an election signifying the new black majority in Harlem.

From Warren Logan

Tuskegee, Ala., 1-27-99

Dear Mr. Washington: I have yours enclosing letter from Thomas Austin in reference to the Cubans. On recommendation of Dr. Kenniebrew, the Cubans' meals excepting breakfast, were changed from the Teachers' Home to the students' boarding department. The breakfast is still gotten from the Teachers' Home. Naturally, the boys objected to the change and I believe are eating very little, if any, of the food from the students' dining room. As I wrote you a few days ago, Pedro and Gomez are showing a very ugly spirit in the matter and have influenced the other boys not to eat the students' food. The first day this was given them, Pedro kicked the vessels over which contained it.

Under the circumstances, the question is, whether changing to the teachers' diet will not do more harm than good to the boys. Before making any change, I shall wait to hear from you further in regard to the matter.[1]

A young man by the name of Harrison died at the school yesterday of pneumonia. He had been here only about three weeks and as he came from Choctaw county, remote from the rail-road, it was impossible to send his remains home or even to communicate by telegraph with his people. The interment will be made in the school cemetery this morning.

Mrs. Barrows, Mrs. Johnson and Mr. Joseph F. Scott[2] of the Boys' Reformatory at Concord, reached the school night before last from New Orleans and spent yesterday inspecting the industrial departments. I think they were much pleased with the school as a whole. Mrs. Johnson and Mr. Scott left for the North last night and Mrs. Barrows went to Kowaliga this morning, Mr. Benson carrying her through the country.

Albert Johnson[3] has been quite ill for the past week. The Doctor tells me that he is not certain what his trouble is but it is stomach trouble of some kind. He is much better at this time and I think will be alright in a few days, if his trouble does not take an unfavorable turn. Trusting you keep well, Very truly,

Warren Logan

TLS Con. 160 BTW Papers DLC.

1 Three days later Logan wrote BTW that he believed the Cuban students would eat the food from the students' department if they were not interfered with. He believed the Cubans were "prejudiced against" the food. Logan told Major Ramsey, the school disciplinarian, "to see that they go to their meals regularly." Logan urged BTW not to make a change in the food until the Cuban students had complied with the order to eat with the other students. "I think in order to help these boys we have got to be firm as well as kind in our treatment of them," he wrote BTW. Logan blamed some of the teachers for encouraging the Cubans to demand better food. (Jan. 30, 1899, Con. 160, BTW Papers, DLC.)

2 Joseph F. Scott (1860-1918) was from 1880 until 1913 associated with various re-

formatories in Massachusetts and New York. In 1900 he was elected president of the National Prison Association. He was a leading opponent of capital punishment.

[3] George Washington Albert Johnston.

From Julius Daniel Dreher

Columbia, S.C. Jan. 31, 1899

Personal.

Dear Professor Washington, I had a long spell of grippe and bronchitis and I am now on my way to my mother's at Selwood, S.C., to take some rest. While there I wish to do some work on my article on the Negro Problem. It will be a plea for justice and forbearance in dealing with the colored people of the South. I shall be glad to have any suggestions from you on the subject. Tell me plainly what *you think* it best for a man in my position to say *to help the Negro.* Our correspondence, of course, must be mutually confidential. The editor of *The Forum* gave me very little encouragement to write for that review: but Mr. Munro[1] of the *North American* wishes me to write and assures me that my article will receive "friendly consideration."

As you have studied the situation carefully and have had so many opportunities to get the facts, I wish you to tell me how the new constitutions of South Carolina, Louisiana and Mississippi affects the Negro as a voter. If I am not mistaken, these are the only States in the South which have restricted the right of suffrage by an educational qualification. In my opinion it will injure the ignorant white to let him vote *simply because he is white.* The poorer whites need a stimulus to acquire education, for they are less interested generally in schools than the Negroes; at least that is my opinion and, so far as I know, the general opinion in the South. Am I correct?

I would like to have copies of any of your addresses which have been published. I heard you in the Broadway Tabernacle, N.Y., several years ago, when, referring to the action of the Constitutional Convention in this State, you said something like this: "I am sometimes asked whether such action does not discourage me? I reply that my race is a patient and long-suffering people and they

21

can better afford to be wronged than the white people can afford to wrong them." Where can I find that sentiment in one of your printed addresses?

To what extent and in what manner are the Negroes defrauded in business dealings? Are they not generally becoming sufficiently intelligent to protect themselves in having contracts for labor (especially on farms) enforced?

Is it your opinion that intercourse of white men with colored women has appreciably (or greatly) decreased in the last 30 years? Is intercourse between colored men and white women, which has always been somewhat rare, increasing or decreasing? Do you hear of such intercourse in various parts of the South as you travel around? I shall refer to this incidentally in writing about lynching.

I wish to read articles, pamphlets, and books bearing on this general subject, and will thank you for any information or suggestions.

I received the papers you sent me. It may interest you to know that Mrs. W. W. St. Clair (whose husband died a few weeks ago) lives in my house in Salem, and that her mother, Mrs. Price,[2] whose mother owned your mother (strange language that seems to be now), was at my house when the paper came and that they both read the account of the President's visit to Tuskegee and your speech in Boston with much interest.

Please address me at *Selwood, S.C.*

I have written this at two places while waiting for a belated train. With all good wishes, Very sincerely yours

Julius D. Dreher

ALS Con. 152 BTW Papers DLC.

1 David Alexander Munro (1872-1910), after many years with the publishing house of Harper & Brothers, became general manager in 1889 and editor in 1896 of the *North American Review.*

2 Lucinda Katherine Burroughs Price (1831-1912), daughter of James and Elizabeth Burroughs. After marrying a farmer, Ferdinand Price, in 1860, she lived near Dillon's Mill in southeastern Franklin County, Va. (Mackintosh, *Burroughs Plantation*, 10, 25, 27.)

A Circular of the Tuskegee Negro Conference

Tuskegee, Alabama [ca. January 1899]

OUT OF THE OLD INTO THE NEW

From a Photograph, showing the influence of the
Tuskegee Negro Conference.

THE TUSKEGEE NEGRO CONFERENCE

The usual yearly Tuskegee Negro Conference will be held in connection with the Tuskegee Normal and Industrial Institute, Wednesday, February 22nd, 1899, and the Workers' Educational Conference, composed of the officers and teachers of the various schools for the education of the black youth of the South, on Thursday, February 23, 1899. You and your friends are invited to attend. You will be at no expense while in Tuskegee as the school desires you to be its guest while here. If you find it more convenient to come Tuesday and remain over night we shall be glad to have you do so.

The Conference will begin at 9 A. M. and all should be present at that hour.

We hope to make this the largest and most profitable Conference we have ever held.

Each community should be represented. In order to encourage

23

the diversifying of crops, all kinds of garden seeds will be given without charge to all who attend the Conference and are not able to buy seeds.

The main object of these Conferences is to help and encourage the colored people in the buying of homes, the diversifying of crops, building school houses, lengthening school terms, and the improvement of their moral and religious condition.

Each community should organize a local Negro Conference. Mr. Thomas J. Jackson,[1] one of the teachers at Tuskegee, will be glad to help organize local Conferences if sent for. He will also be glad to supply reading matter telling how to organize local Conferences.

Reduced rates will be given on all the Railroads.

Further information about the Conference can be secured from . . .

Booker T. Washington, Principal,

Tuskegee Normal and Industrial Institute,

Tuskegee, Alabama.

To . . . .

PD   BTW Folder   ViHaI

[1] Thomas J. Jackson taught mathematics at Tuskegee during the 1897-98 school year and then became Tuskegee Negro Conference agent from 1898 to 1901.

From Timothy Thomas Fortune

New York, Feb 1, 1899

Dear Mr. Washington: Your letter of the 29th ult., dated at De-Kalb, Ill. was received, and I am very glad to hear from you, as I had begun to get a shade uneasy over your silence.

I agree with you that some good may result from our Boston campaign. From all I can hear from there a very healthy *counter* sentiment was created. Councilor Isaac Allen[1] was in here Monday and he took that view of it, and numbers of others. What they need most in Boston is somebody who will go ahead and do something.

I am glad to say my gastritis is much better, but it gave me a fearful razzle for six days. I can't imagine what brought it on.

I hope you may have a successful time of it in St. Louis and Kansas City, and of course I shall be very glad to see you again.

I had a note from Mr. Scott yesterday and he was anxious to know if I was going to attend the Conference and I told him I was not in a position to answer the question at this time. With kind regards, Yours truly

T. Thomas Fortune

ALS   Con. 154   BTW Papers   DLC.

[1] Isaac B. Allen was a member of the executive committee of the Colored National League of Boston.

From Emmett Jay Scott

Tuskegee, Ala., Feb. 3, 1899

Dear Mr. Washington: Our friends at Montgomery fear that Leftwich is bent upon hurting the session of the Tuskegee Negro Conference. You will note that his Conference is called to meet Feb. 18th just 4 days before ours. You will note also that he says that it is the purpose to form a district Conference to be composed of the following counties, Autauga, Crenshaw, Butler, Elmore, Lowndes and Montgomery. I do not know whether he has advertised the fact that you are to supply seed or not, but a letter received from Mr. Adams[1] advises against your influence being given this Conference in any way whatever and also against any seed being sent there through your influence. I have instructed Mr. Jackson who is working in that section this week to very carefully emphasize the fact that the Tuskegee Negro Conference has no relation whatever to this affair of Leftwich's. Yours very truly,

E J Scott

TLS   Con. 161   BTW Papers   DLC.

[1] Probably Lewis Adams of Tuskegee or J. W. Adams of Montgomery, both trustees of Tuskegee Institute.

From Isabel Hayes Chapin Barrows

Washington, D.C. Feb. 4, 1899

My dear Mr. Washington, Your kind note of Jan. 20, 1899, was received since my return from the south. I thank you and the scores of others who have written such warm words about my husband, but none of them seem to prevail upon the President to make him make up his mind.[1]

I had a pleasant time at Tuskegee, but it was forlorn without either you or Mrs. Washington. Mrs. Johnson, of the Sherborn Prison, and Mr. Scott of the Concord reformatory, went with me and were immensely interested. They both want you to visit their prisons and speak to their people and I hope you can do it sometime.

I was delighted to see your house going up and to know that you are to have such a substantial abode.[2]

Mrs. Johnson and I were both quite shocked with the publicity and lack of proper care of the sanitary closets for the young ladies and the teachers. To our northern ideas the lack of privacy is extremely disagreeable. That large, ill-smelling, brick establishment, just under the dining-room windows, is a monstrosity. How much would it cost to have a neat wooden structure, that can be better ventilated, put in some less conspicuous place and with an approach shielded by a vine-covered lattice work? (I think every such house on the place should be so shielded). If it were not *too* much I think we would like to raise the money and have it done. I talked with some of the young ladies and some of the teachers and one and all agreed that it was a great trial to them to use the present structure. One young lady told me that she avoided going there till she was fairly sick. She says she can never get hardened to it. A teacher told me the same. Another young lady said she tried to get used to it, because one of the teachers told her she was prudish about it, but she said it was always embarrassing and always would be, to go to that place in daylight, when she was sure to meet some of the male students or teachers in the vicinity. Still another young lady told me of being taken ill in the night, a stormy night, and rushing in there in the dark, in haste, found a night watchman there, who had taken advantage of the night and the storm to go there himself! I think that one experience was quite enough to make a change of some kind necessary.

It seems to me there ought to be a building with twenty separate partitions, the building to stand high, so that it can be well ventilated; it should also be kept well supplied with earth and below should be what we in the north call a "farm-box," a large box on runners, the runners furnished at the front end with strong hooks. To these a horse is attached and the whole thing drawn off weekly or oftener, and used on the land. We have such arrangements in our camp and our closets are as sweet as our dining room, no odor and nothing unsightly about it, while the farmer is glad of the fertilizer. Of course we have but a family of 25 or 30, but what we can do for 30 can be done on a larger scale for a thousand. Of course the whole school ought to be provided, but I had in mind only the ladies' department in what I have said.

Your admirable scientific man[3] ought to be able to help in suggestions. We enjoyed meeting him very much, especially Mrs. Johnson who runs a 400 acre farm, and who declares that she is going down there to take lessons from him.

I drove to Kowaliga and had a most interesting time there and brought back with me the white fellow, McInnish,[4] who is now in my family in Dorchester.

I hope that Mrs. Washington is better. Yours sincerely,

Isabel C. Barrows

TLS Con. 153 BTW Papers DLC.

[1] BTW recommended to President McKinley that Samuel J. Barrows be appointed librarian of Congress. (J. A. Porter to BTW, Feb. 10, 1899, McKinley Papers, DLC; S. J. Barrows to BTW, Feb. 27, 1899, Con. 149, BTW Papers, DLC.)

[2] BTW's residence along Old Montgomery Highway on the edge of the Tuskegee campus, known as The Oaks, was completed in the spring of 1900. The two-and-a-half-story brick house contained fourteen rooms and was the center of social life at the school. It was not an overly pretentious house but BTW and the Tuskegee trustees had to move gingerly in the matter to avoid having the house become a source of controversy. (See W. P. Bancroft to BTW, Mar. 27, 1899, Baldwin to Bancroft, Apr. 6, 1899, and Baldwin to BTW, Jan. 28, 1900, below.)

[3] George Washington Carver.

[4] Barrows wrote to BTW: "The white fellow, McInnish, whom I brought up from Kowaliga is doing admirably in school at the bench and in his drawing. He is still in my own family. Mr. Benson writes that nothing ever helped his school so much among the whites. Everybody talked about it, that any one interested enough in the

colored people to come there to visit a school, should carry off a *white* man to help him. The leading white man there who had up to that time utterly refused to come near them, got them at once to overhaul a wagon and to make a dining-room table for him, 'paying in spot-cash.' Half a dozen other white men brought work, that they might have a chance to talk over this wonderful occurrence and they say his letters home are full of the interesting things he sees and the kindness he receives. I never dreamed of it having such a result." (Mar. 3, 1899, Con. 153, BTW Papers, DLC.)

From William Farrington Aldrich

Washington, D.C. 2-6 1899

Your School land bill passed house today. Lac[e]y and Underwood were active in its favor.

W. F. Aldrich

HWSr Con. 540 BTW Papers DLC. The telegram was addressed to BTW in "city," indicating his presence in Washington.

From Warren Logan

Tuskegee, Ala., 2-9-99

Dear Mr. Washington: Your telegram instructing me to send Mr. Calloway to Boston, was duly received and Mr. Calloway started on the evening train day before yesterday. He ought to have reached Boston this, Thursday morning.

I suppose that you wanted to consult with Mr. Calloway in reference to the land bill. I presume there is no doubt of the President's signing the bill and of our getting the land. The thing to be looked after is the selection of the land. This I believe the bill provides, is to be made by the Governor of the State. I trust the fair thing will be done by the school and that we will not have to accept land that is of very little value.

Much of the public land in the Southern part of the State is practically worthless, having had much of the timber cut off of it, or being in swamps.

Our friends here seem to be glad that we have gotten the land.

I have arranged for Mr. Carver to go to Montgomery tonight

and make his exhibition before the Committee on Agriculture, tomorrow. Major Culver[1] has kindly allowed space in his office for the exhibition. Mr. Carver will carry down some butter and a number of farm products, including some canned fruits. His plan will be to show these and explain to the members of the Legislature, his methods of teaching Agriculture and Dairying.

I had seen Mr. Hare before your telegram was received, in reference to the bill affecting the colored Agricultural schools. I find this bill was introduced at the instance of Patterson, and made an appropriation for the teaching of Horticulture in his school. Mr. Hare had Major Culver to go before the Committee, tell them about the agricultural work which Patterson has done, or rather, that he has not done and the Committee decided unanimously to make an adverse report on the bill. I do not know any thing that equals the "cheek" of this man.

Mr. Hare states that some of the members of the Legislature to whom he talked, proposed to undertake to withdraw the appropriation from Patterson's school and give it to us, but he was advised by some of them, if this were done, Governor Johnston would veto the bill making the change. Major Culver is in favor of doing this. Mr. Hare thinks that it will be best not to make any effort to get an increased appropriation from this Legislature, as there is a prejudice against the Agricultural schools and a disposition to change the system, if not abolish it all-together.

I trust the work of raising the special fund, goes encouragingly on and that you will be able to complete the fund before returning to Tuskegee. Very truly,

Warren Logan

TLS Con. 160 BTW Papers DLC. Addressed to BTW at Crawford House, Boston.

[1] Isaac Franklin Culver, state commissioner of agriculture.

From Mary Caroline Moore

Framingham [Mass.] Feb. 10, 1899

My dear Mr. Washington   Your letter and the one addressed to you by Bishop Lawrence[1] came to-night.

We certainly shall want after the confirmation service[2] to speak to the Bishop.

Of course we are sorry not to see you *now*, but hope nothing will prevent seeing and hearing you March 21st.

As for me, many thanks for the invitation.

Portia's cup of happiness would be full indeed if you could be with her on the 24th; but of course she never dreamed of the possibility, and it was a great thing to have Mrs. Washington here at the baptism.

Portia would like the letter from Bishop Lawrence so I venture not to return it, unless therefore you write me within a day or two that you want it, I will hand it over to your little girl.

Portia is well. Sincerely yours

Mary C. Moore

ALS   Con. 158   BTW Papers   DLC.

1 William Lawrence (1850-1941) was Episcopal bishop of Massachusetts from 1893 to 1926. The son of Amos Lawrence, a wealthy wool manufacturer, Bishop Lawrence viewed the swollen fortunes of the late nineteenth-century industrialists with enthusiasm, declaring that "Godliness is in league with riches."

2 Portia Washington, influenced by her teacher Mary C. Moore, left the Baptist faith and was confirmed as an Episcopalian.

From Henry Bradley Plant[1]

Tampa, Fla., February 11th. 1899

Dear Sir: I received a letter some days since, from Mr. R. R. Wright, President of the Georgia State Industrial College, College, Georgia, making request on me for an Annual Pass in order to help build up his school. Mr. Wright says in his letter: "The Railroads of Alabama, I understand, grant to Mr. Booker T. Washington passes over their Systems." I find that we did not issue you a pass over the Plant System, but that upon your request we have in the past issued transportation to one or two of your representatives. I should regret very much if the parties to whom such passes have been issued in the past had informed outsiders that they held same or had made any exhibition whatever, other than to the Conductors of our trains. You will appreciate the necessity for a strict compliance in all ways with the rulings of the Interstate and various State Railroad Commissions in regard to issuance of free transportation and the impracticability of our granting free transportation to all who might make request on us for the purpose of building up institutions of an educational nature, and I hope that you will issue instructions to whomsoever may hold passes on any part of our System at the present or in the future, to be very careful and not let it be known that your institution is so favored. Yours respectfully,

H. B. Plant

TLS Con. 159 BTW Papers DLC.

1 Henry Bradley Plant (1819-99), founder of the Plant System of railroads, steamship lines, and hotels in the Gulf states.

From George Washington Carver

Tuskegee, Ala., 2-13 1899

My dear Mr. Washington The Ther. stands now (8:30) zero, at 7 a m 4° below zero. Stock is suffering badly for want of shelter. I am doing the best I can for them. I sincerely hope we will never let another winter pass without the propper sheds for them.

I went to Montgom. on Fri. last and returned Sat. Both Houses viewed the exhibit and showed intense interest. I never met a more cordial body, not a thing passed during the whole time to remind me of my *color*. They regretted very much that we did not exhibit for a whole week. Many farmers came in and asked many questions, took Buls. ect.

Secy. Culver & staff took special pains to make everything very pleasant and all complimented the exhibit very highly. I took grasses in variety[,] sheep diseases, sweet potatoes in var.[,] butter, cheese, soils, some chem. aparatus, roots of peas, clovers ect. milk testing aparatus, pictures of growing crops, Bul. 1-2 also nature studies, maps, charts ect. swine diseases. I met most all the body by introduction as they came in from time to time during the two days I was there. A number of ladies came also.

They all expressed the warmest feeling for the school. And the

Com. (Culver) says he is ready to do anything possible for us at any time. It would be nice Mr Washington if you would write to Mr. Culver personally, and thank him for his unusual kindness.

Mr Callahan[1] said to tell you that he captured a pound of the butter, I took down 3 and 1/4 pounds and gave it all away of course and the sweetpotatoes also. I never saw such a scramble for the butter, and the cheese was a marvel to them.

This cold wave is going to be very damageing to our crops.

Hope you are well. Best wishes

Geo. W. Carver

ALS   Con. 153   BTW Papers   DLC.

1 Possibly William Washington Callahan, then the Decatur city attorney.

An Abraham Lincoln Memorial Address in Philadelphia[1]

[Philadelphia, Pa.] February 14, 1899

Gentlemen: You ask one whom the Great Emancipator found a piece of property and left an American citizen to speak of Abraham Lincoln. My first acquaintance with our hero and benefactor is this: Night after night, before the dawn of day, on an old slave plantation in Virginia, I recall the form of my sainted mother, bending over a batch of rags that enveloped my body, on a dirt floor, breathing a fervent prayer to Heaven that "Marsa Lincoln" might succeed, and that one day she and I might be free; and so, on your invitation, I come here to-night to celebrate with you the answer to those prayers. But be it far from me to revive the bitter memories of the past, nor would I narrow the work of Abraham Lincoln to the black race of this country; rather would I call him the Emancipator of America — the liberator of the white man North, of the white man South; the one who, in unshackling the chains of the Negro, has turned loose the enslaved forces of nature in the South, and has knit all sections of our country together by the indissoluble bonds of commerce. To the man in the North who cherished hatred against the South, Lincoln brought freedom. To the white man who landed at Jamestown years ago, with hopes as bright and prospects as cheering as those who stepped ashore on Plymouth Rock, Lincoln, for the first time, gave an opportunity to breathe the air of unfettered freedom — a freedom from dependence on others' labor to the independence of self-labor; freedom to transform unused and dwarfed hands into skilled and productive hands; to change labor from drudgery into that which is dignified and glorified; to change local commerce into trade with the world; to change the Negro from an ignorant man into an intelligent man; to change sympathies that were local and narrow into love and good-will for all mankind; freedom to change stagnation into growth, weakness into power; yea, to us all, your race and mine, Lincoln has been a great emancipator. Even the treasures of nature in our Southland, that seemed to hide themselves from the hand of man, have felt the inspiring hand of freedom; and coal and iron and marble have leaped forth, and where there was once the overseer's lash, steam and electricity make go the shop, the factory, and the furnace.

But all is not done, and it remains for us, the living, to finish the work that Lincoln left uncompleted. You of the great and prosperous North still owe a serious and uncompleted duty to your less fortunate brothers of the white race South, who suffered and are still suffering the consequence of American slavery. What was the task you asked them to perform? Returning to their destitute homes after years of war, to face blasted hopes, devastation, a shattered industrial system, you ask them to add to their burdens that of preparing in education, politics, and economics, in a few short years, for citizenship, four or five millions of former slaves. That the South, staggering under the burden, made blunders, that in some measure there has been disappointment, no one need be surprised.

The four million slaves that Lincoln freed are now nearly ten million freemen. That which was three hundred years in doing can hardly be undone in thirty years. How can you help the South and the Negro in the completion of Lincoln's work? A large majority of the people Lincoln freed are still ignorant, without proper food, or property, or skill, or correct habits — are without the requisites for intelligent and independent citizenship. The mere fiat of law could not make a dependent man independent; it could not make an ignorant voter an intelligent voter; it could not make one man respect another man. These results come by beginning at the bottom and working upward; by recognizing our weakness as well as our strength; by tangible evidences of our worthiness to occupy the highest positions. Unfortunately, too many of my people, because of ignorance, began at the top instead of the bottom; grasped for the shadow instead of the substance. I come to your State and say the German is ignorant; you point to the best paying truck-farm, operated by a German. I say the German is without skill; you point to the largest machine-shop in your city, owned and operated by a German. I say the German is lazy; you point to the most magnificent dwelling on your avenue, that is the result of the savings of the German, who began in poverty. I say the German can not be trusted; you point to the German who is the president of the largest bank. I say the German is not fitted for citizenship; you point me to the German who is the chief executive of your magnificent city — these are the kind of arguments that kill prejudice by the acre. When you come to Alabama and ask has the Negro executive ability, I want to show you, as I can at Tuskegee, Alabama, an institution of learning, originated and controlled by Negroes, where there are more than 1000 students, 88 officers, 26 industries, 42 buildings, 2267 acres of land, $300,000 worth of property. When you ask has the Negro mechanical skill, I want to show you the finest house in a county, planned and constructed by a Negro. When you ask is the Negro lazy, I want to show you the finest farm, owned and operated by a Negro. When you ask is the Negro honest, I want to show you a Negro whose note is acceptable at the bank for $5000. When you ask is the Negro economical, I want to show you a Negro with $50,000 in the bank. When you ask is the Negro fit for citizenship, I want to show you a Negro paying taxes on a cotton factory. I want to show you Negroes who stand at the front in the affairs of State, religion, education, mechanics, commerce, and household economy. "By this sign we shall conquer." By this method we shall so knit our civil and business interests into that of the white man's, that when he prospers we shall prosper; when we fail, he fails. By this method we shall crawl up, pull up, or burst up.

Yes, in answer to your proclamation, Father Abraham, we are coming, ten million strong — we are coming by the way of the college, by the way of agriculture, the shop, the factory, the trades, the household arts. With this foundation, if God is right and the Bible is true, there is no power that can permanently stay our progress.

You can not graft a fifteenth century civilization onto a twentieth century civilization by the mere performance of mental gymnastics. You can not convert a man by abusing him. The mere pushing of knowledge into the heads of a people, without providing a medium through the hands for its use, is not always wise. The educated man is more dangerous than the ignorant, idle man. An educated man standing on the corners of your streets with his hands in his pockets is not one whit more benefit to society than an ignorant man in the streets with his hands in his pockets. It is only as the black man produces something that makes the markets of the world dependent on him for something, will he secure his rightful place.

Eight years ago I could have shown you a colored community in Alabama that was in debt, mortgaging crops; living from hand to mouth on rented land; paying fifteen to forty percent. interest on advances for food; school lasting three months, taught in a wreck of a log cabin; people of all ages and sexes huddled together, often to the number of six or eight in one room, and without habits of thrift or economy. A little more than a dozen years ago, four teachers — one a carpenter and blacksmith, one trained in agriculture, one in cookery, another in sewing, combined with literary education — went to this community. Go with me to that community today, and I will show you a large modern school-house, with school lasting eight months; farms well cultivated and owned by colored people, who live in homes with two or three rooms. I will show you a people almost free from debt, and a gin, and a store, and a wheelwright and a blacksmith shop operated by Negroes; a community that has been revolutionized in religion, education, and industry. Let us multiply these communities in every part of the South. By this way we are coming; by this way we are proving ourselves worthy of the confidence of our great emancipator. We mean to prove our worth — not by mere talk or complaints of, or faultfinding — and the rest, in a large measure, we leave with you.

And, may I say, you do well to keep the name of Abraham Lincoln permanently linked with the highest interests of the Negro race. His was the hand, the brain, and the conscience that gave us the first opportunity to make the attempt to be men instead of property. What Lincoln so nobly began, the philanthropy and wealth of this nation, aided by our own efforts, should complete. The character of the father who has a half dozen children is determined by the manner that he treats all of those children. He may rear with care and love five of them, yet the neglect, the abandonment of one will serve to blight his standing with his neighbors. The character of this nation will very largely be judged by the help and encouragement which it renders to the ten millions of Negroes who constitute so large a proportion of the American family. So long as these people are down, so long as they are fettered with ignorance, poverty, and lack of opportunity, so long will the reputation and character of the whole nation suffer.

The struggle of Abraham Lincoln up from the lowest poverty and ignorance to the highest usefulness gives hope and inspiration to the Negro. Like Lincoln, he is gathering strength from the very obstacles he is mastering and overcoming. No race in history has ever grown strong and useful except as it has had to battle against tremendous odds; except as it has been tried year by year in a crucible of fire. Like Lincoln, the Negro knows the meaning of the one-room cabin; he knows the bed of rags and hay; he knows what it is to be minus books and school-house; he has tasted the lowliest poverty, but through them all he is making his way to the top. In the effort he is slowly but surely learning that the highest character of citizenship is in the possession of virtue, intelligence, simplicity, the spirit of self-denial, economy, thrift, and the ownership of property: these elements of strength will give him that manhood without which no race can permanently stand, and which no adverse influence can take from him.

One might as well talk of stopping the flow of the Mississippi River as the progress of a race that is securing property, education, and Christian character.

Let us never forget that we are one people in this country, and that which helps the Negro helps the white man; and that which hinders the Negro hinders the white man. Show me a Negro who hates a white man on account of his race, and I will show you a weak and undeveloped Negro. Show me a white man who hates a Negro on account of his race, and I will show you a weak and undeveloped white man.

"The laws of changeless justice bind
Oppressor with oppressed;
And close as sin and suffering joined
We march to fate abreast."

No member of your race in any part of this country can harm the weakest or meanest member of my race without the proudest and bluest blood in our civilization being degraded.

Gentlemen, friends of humanity, raise yourselves above yourselves, above race, above party, above everything, if you can; subserve the highest welfare of ten millions of people, whose interests are permanently interwoven by decree of God with those of sixty millions of yours, and seek with me a way out of this great problem, which hangs over our country like a blighting shadow. Find any method of escape save that of patiently, wisely, bravely, manfully, bringing the Southern white man and the Negro into closer sympathetic and friendly relations through education, industrial and business development, and that touch of high Christian sympathy which makes the whole world kin — find any way out of our present condition save this, and I am ready to follow where you lead.

It seems to me that the highest duty which the generous and patriotic people of this country owe to themselves and their country is to give willingly the means for the support of such institutions which are, without doubt, solving this serious and perplexing problem. If we had the means of Tuskegee alone we could make our work tell in a hundredfold larger degree in the settlement of this great question. You of the North have, in a large measure, the money for education which is to settle this problem.

No individual or race that makes itself permanently felt in the building-up of the country is long left without proper reward or recognition. The most important problem that is now confronting the Negro and his friends is the turning of the force of his education in the direction that it will contribute most effectively to the betterment of the country and the Negro himself.

I do not want to be misunderstood. I favor the highest and most thorough development of the Negro's mind. No race can accomplish anything until its mind is awakened. But the weak point in the past has been, in too many cases, that there has been no connection between the Negro's educated brain and the opportunity or manner of earning his daily living. There has been almost no thought of connecting the educated brain with the educated hand.

Industrial education is not meant to teach one to work so much as to teach him how to make the forces of nature — horse-power, steam, and electricity — work for him. It is the ignorant, unskilled man who toils from day to day with his hands, while the man with education and trained hands makes the forces of nature do work for him. The masses of the colored people work hard, but by reason of their want of skill and intelligence, some one else receives the profits. There is little profit in the raising of the raw material that enters into cotton fabrics; the profit comes in the higher forms of manufacturing. By reason of the Negro's lack of skill he is at present at the bottom, so far as the matter of profit-sharing is concerned. At the Tuskegee Institute in Alabama we seek to give such an education as will put the Negro on the upper tier in the matter of production and profit-sharing.

It is said that we will be hewers of wood and drawers of water, but we will be more. We will turn the wood into machinery; into implements of agriculture. We will turn the water into steam; into dairy and agricultural products, and thus knit our life about that of the white man in a way to make us realize anew that "God made from one blood all people to dwell and prosper on the face of the earth."

PD Con. 978 BTW Papers DLC. Published by the Union League Club for distribution to its membership.

1 This address was prepared for delivery at the Union League Club's Lincoln Dinner on Feb. 12, 1899, but BTW was snowbound on a train between New York and Philadelphia. He did deliver the address, however, on Feb. 14 at a public reception at the home of Henry C. Davis in Philadelphia.

To Henry Bradley Plant

Tuskegee, Ala., Feb. 15, 1899

My dear Sir: Replying to your favor of Feb. 11th I beg to say that I have at no time whatever, to Mr. R. R. Wright or any one else, given any intimation of the courtesies extended representatives of this institution by you. We have been too grateful to you for your kindness to have told any one of these favors after being especially admonished not to do so. I regret very much that any occasion has arisen for you to write us in this connection, but the assurance is candidly given that we in every way respect not only your wishes, but appreciate your interest in the work of this institution. Yours very truly,

Booker T. Washington

TLSr Copy   Con. 159   BTW Papers   DLC.

An Act of Congress

Washington, D.C., Feb. 18, 1899

Be it enacted by the Senate and House of Representatives of the United States of America in Congress assembled, That the governor of the State of Alabama be, and he is hereby, authorized to select, out of the unoccupied and uninhabited lands of the United States within the said State, twenty-five thousand acres of land, and shall certify the same to the Secretary of the Interior, who shall forthwith, upon receipt of said certificate, issue to the State of Alabama patents for said lands: *Provided,* that the proceeds of said lands when sold or leased shall forever remain a fund for the use of the Industrial School for Girls of Alabama, located at Montevallo, Alabama.

Sec. 2. That the governor of the State of Alabama be, and he is hereby, authorized to select, out of the unoccupied and uninhabited lands of the United States within the said State, twenty-five thousand acres of land, and shall certify the same to the Secretary of the Interior, who shall forthwith, upon receipt of said certificate, issue to the State of Alabama patents for said lands: *Provided,* That the proceeds of said lands when sold or leased shall forever remain a fund for the use of the Tuskegee Normal and Industrial Institute.

Approved, February 18, 1899.

U.S. Statutes at Large, 55th Cong., 3rd sess., 1899, 837.

From William Jonathan Northen

Atlanta, Ga. Feb. 24th./99

Dear Sir: I have a letter from Mr. Hazard, of Boston, inviting me to make an address before the Congregational Club of that city, on Monday evening, May 22nd., relative to the conditions of the colored people of the South. He asked that I speak upon the "White man's views," informing me, at the same time, that you have accepted an invitation to speak, on the same occasion, upon "the black man's views."

I am inclined to accept this invitation. I have so written Mr. Hazard, this morning. I have told him I would take the matter under consideration and inform him definitely, in a few days.

I would be especially glad to make this speech before the same audience that you make yours. There is very much involved in the question, and it would, of course, be unfortunate and hurtful if we should pursue different lines and become, in the least, antagonistic. If you will kindly give me the outline of what you propose, I will then be in very much better position to reply definitely to Mr. Hazard.

Your early attention will greatly oblige, Yours truly,

W. J. Northen

TLS Con. 159 BTW Papers DLC. Written on stationery of the Georgia Immigration & Investment Bureau, ex-Gov. W. J. Northen, manager.

From Henry Clay Reynolds

Montevallo, Alabama, Feb. 25, 1899

Dear Sir, Your letter of the 21st, enclosing copy of letter from Dr. Mosely has been received.[1] I think he is mistaken in regard to your making him any promise whatever as to the $100 matter. The facts connected with the whole affair, are as follows: before I went to Washington, and took Dr. Mosely, I wrote him a letter stating that if he would go there with me, and get the Bill through, that I thought I could get him in the neighborhood of $750. Of course when I made this promise I knew that you would pay your pro rata share of the amount. After I went to Washington I became convinced that he would work as well for $500 as he would for $750; so while there in a conference with you and my son, we agreed to offer him $500 and his expenses; you agreed to pay half of this amount, but stated to me that you would prefer that I make arrangements with Mosely, as you did not wish your name connected with it in any way. I went immediately and saw Mosely, and told him exactly what we had agreed on; I told him furthermore that I would be personally responsible for this amount, and would see to it that all his expenses were paid while there. You remember you gave me some money to pay him, I believe about $20 or $25, I do not remember exact amount. I gave him while there and before I left, money amounting to about $75. Of course we cannot, as honorable men afford to ignore him and his assistance and I know you will do whatever is right in the matter.

He is writing me daily, wanting the $500, but I have put him off, on account of press of business in the Legislature. He did everything in his power, and between us, was virtually the cause of the Bill passing, when he secured an interview with Reid for me; from that time our success was certain. I have never told Mosely even how much we were indebted to him for this interview and his assistance. Legally I don't suppose he could force us to pay it, but of course this does not enter into it with me. We are honor bound to see he gets the $500, and I hope you will send me [a] check for half of it by return mail.

I am very much afraid the Florence people will get their Bill through during the last six days of Congress, which is suspension of rules, and it is of the utmost importance that we have a Commissioner appointed, and let him get to work. Of course we prefer Plowman, as I know he is a most capable man. But the Commissioner ought to be appointed and at work selecting our lands.

The Governor informed me himself last week that he knew of [a] considerable body of lands that would sell easily for the cash at $12.50 per acre. Of course if the Florence Bill passes, they will in all probability find these lands themselves.

In regard to Mosely I would advise that you write him that you left the matter with me as to his Fee, and I will see that it is settled agreeable to him. If you would prefer, we can go to see him together. He is soon to leave for Singapore, and has been very unfortunate, and needs the money. We have derived great benefit, and of course I know you will pay your part in the matter. Yours &c

H. C. Reynolds

TLS Con. 160 BTW Papers DLC.

1 R. A. Moseley, Jr., wrote BTW on Feb. 15 requesting that BTW meet his promise to pay him $100. He went on to add: "I wish for your abundant success in all of your undertakings." (Con. 158, BTW Papers, DLC.)

To Henry Clay Reynolds

[Tuskegee, Ala.] Feb. 27, 1899

Dear Sir: I did not reply to your telegram[1] which was received several days ago for the reason that I knew you were not well when you left Montgomery and were very much worried, and I had the feeling that your telegram was sent in haste in the midst of your worry. I am exceedingly sorry that any seeming disagreement has sprung up between the two institutions, I think, however, if you will review the matter calmly you will find that we are not at fault. I think you will agree with me that we worked together in the most complete harmony and in the greatest good faith while we were getting our bill through Congress. If you had let me know about the plans which you had in mind about the appointment of a commissioner I should have been willing to have acted with you and there need not have been any disagreement as to who was to be appointed. You will also remember that when I first wrote you about the bill to be introduced in the Alabama Legislature that I made a special request that a copy of the bill be sent here; I received no copy of the bill and hence did not know the provisions of the bill [until] I went to Montgomery on Saturday a week ago. If I had known what the provisions of the bill were and had known you were going to have Mr. Plowman appointed I would have had our trustees endorse Mr. Plowman and there would have been no trouble or disagreement whatever. It was to avoid trouble that I had Mr. Calloway go to Montevallo to see you so that we could find out what your plans were and to put ourselves in position to act with you. The whole trouble was caused by our not knowing what your plans were. After our Executive Committee had endorsed Mr. Thompson there was nothing left for me to do but to support him according to the decision of our Executive Committee. After I returned from Montgomery we had another meeting of the Committee and the decision of the Committee at the second meeting was still to support Mr. Thompson and of course I had to act accordingly. Now I feel that unless there is something in connection with the selection of these lands that I do not know about that there is little need for the intense feeling that now seems to exist in regard to the appointment of a commissioner. I do not know at this time who the Governor is going to appoint. The last time I saw Mr. Plowman he told me the Governor had promised to give him the position; Mr. Thompson now tells me that the Governor has promised him the position. I shall be satisfied with any action that the Governor may take in this matter. I feel very sure, and I would not have endorsed Mr. Thompson if I had not known it, in case that he gets the position that your school will be treated [with] entire fairness. His present plan is to meet you and other representatives of your school in connection with representatives from this institution as soon as he is appointed — that is in case he is appointed — and get suggestions as to the wishes of the two schools and as far as possible he will carry out these wishes. He assures me that he means to select the land just as fast as possible, in fact says he wants to get through with the work within three or four months and is going to work to that end. He will be very anxious to have the help of any one connected with your school who can assist him in securing the most valuable lands for the two schools. I have known Mr. Thompson ever since I have been here and I feel sure that in the end there will be no cause for complaint by reason of his selection. He is full of energy and will work night and day to make a success of his mission. I had an occasion during the time that we were planning for the visit of President McKinley here to come in close daily contact with Mr. Thompson for a number of days and I found him at all times reliable and unselfish in his wish to serve the highest interests of this institution. When you know Mr. Thompson I do not believe that you will have any cause to feel dissatisfied with his appointment. I very much wish that you and I could meet and talk the whole matter over with Mr. Thompson without the presence of any one else, I think this would accomplish good. All this of course is based on the assumption that Mr. Thompson will receive the appointment.

It is probable that two ladies from the North, Miss Hyde[2] and Miss Breed, will visit your school sometime within the next few days. They are very excellent ladies. Your truly,

Booker T. Washington

TLpS Con. 282A BTW Papers DLC.

1 Reynolds wired BTW from Montevallo on Feb. 20, 1899: "I could never have believed your doing this." (Con. 540, BTW Papers, DLC.) Presumably he referred to differences on the choice of land agent.

2 Possibly Ellen Hyde.

To Timothy Thomas Fortune

Tuskegee, Ala., Feb. 27, 1899

My dear Mr. Fortune: I have your letter of Feb. 22d. I have been thinking about you a good deal during the last few days but could not possibly find time to write you. I am very much pleased with the proof of the cut which you sent me and shall be glad to see how it looks in your paper. I have not had time yet to read your editorial in the Age which has just come, I shall read it carefully, however, and shall give you my opinion afterwards. Smith[1] has made a desperate effort to get this matter before the public but there is nothing in it to do us any harm. I think it just as well that you published it.[2] I am anxious to see you again. It is my present plan to be in New York very soon after the 10th of March and shall perhaps linger about there until sometime in April.

Our Conference has closed and I was exceedingly busy from start to finish. It was an excellent meeting. The numbers were somewhat reduced by reason of the condition of the roads but the enthusiasm was at a high pitch and results of substantial progress were most gratifying. The Workers' Conference was also good. Among other notables we had Bishop Turner. He conducted himself very well and made a good impression. Bishop Turner, Silas X. Floyd and numbers of that class of people told me frankly before leaving that they were completely won over to my support; they said they came here expecting not to be given freedom of speech and action and the treatment which they received they said took all the wind out of their position. I send you a marked copy of the Montgomery Advertiser containing a report of the meeting. Mr. Scott will also send you an article.

I hardly know what to say about Alexander.[3] He is a good fellow and I want to give him employment if I can. I wish he were a little stronger mentally. It is pretty hard for us to use an individual now here unless he has a pretty strong mental equipment.

I hope your health is still improving. Yours truly,

Booker T. Washington

TLS Con. 160 BTW Papers DLC.

1 Charles Spencer Smith (1852-1922) was a leading A.M.E. minister soon to become a bishop (1900). Born in Canada, he taught school in Kentucky and Mississippi during Reconstruction. In 1871 he was licensed as an A.M.E. deacon and became a pastor in Union Springs, Ala. He served one term (1874-76) in the Alabama legislature. Moving as a pastor to Tennessee, he attended Central Tennessee College and graduated from its medical department (later Meharry Medical College) in 1880. After several years as a traveling agent for the David C. Cook Sunday School Publishing House, Smith founded the A.M.E. Sunday School Union and edited its paper, *Our Sunday*. He aided Bishop Daniel A. Payne in the preparation of the second volume of Payne's *History of the African Methodist Episcopal Church* (1891) and was on the title page as editor. After becoming bishop, Smith served in eastern Canada, the West Indies, South Africa, and West Africa until 1908.

2 Charles Spencer Smith's letter, published in the New York *Age*, Feb. 23, 1899, criticized BTW and said of industrial education that the Negro "has graduated long since in . . . hoeing cotton and corn." Smith's central argument was that not until trade unions ceased to draw the color line would it be wise to increase the number of Negro mechanics. W. H. Baldwin, Jr., protested to Fortune that "the writer is hardly a competent person to appreciate the modesty and simple strength of the man who impresses the world with his greatness." Fortune replied that it was best "to print the opinions of the Doctor Smiths and then rip 'em up the back." (Baldwin to Fortune, Feb. 24, 1899, Con. 153, Fortune to Baldwin, Feb. 25, 1899, Con. 154, copies, BTW Papers, DLC.) Reprinting Smith's article, the Atlanta *Constitution* commented: "The truth is, as all who have indorsed Booker Washington's views clearly understand, the mechanical and industrial training which he advocates with so much power and truth are mere elements in his plan. They are to go hand in hand with other forms of education, and they fit in with the highest." (Atlanta *Constitution*, Mar. 12, 1899, 16, 18.)

3 Charles Alexander.

From Viola Knapp Ruffner

[Charleston, S.C.?] Feb 27/99

Dear Booker   I am sick in bed & can only see the marks I make & suffer all the time. Will you write the name of the gentleman from Mass. who called on me at the time you & your wife were here. You said he was a Professor in some College near Boston. He gave me his card but I cannot find it. Will you & your wife, both write it so I shall be sure to see it plain. I think he has been writing an article upon your school which I shall get the family to read to me. You have had a great gift this time from Mr Huntington. You can almost educate the race, if they will make an effort themselves, but they are still too much influenced by the past & make little effort to be independent by their own efforts. Those about the house are still under the influence of slavery. Write me on receipt will you? Kind regards to your wife & yourself from your old friend

Viola Ruffner

ALS   Con. 153   BTW Papers   DLC.

To Timothy Thomas Fortune

Tuskegee, Ala., Mar. 1, 1899

My dear Mr. Fortune: I have read two or three times your editorial based on Smith's letter. I would have more patience with this matter if I did not know that Smith is not in earnest, is most hypocritical and is simply trying to draw me into a newspaper contention and thus attract attention to himself. It is impossible that any man with common sense should not see the folly of many of the statements made by Smith. Now in regard to your editorial, I think it covers the ground most completely. The extract from Buckle[1] is especially effective. I had never seen this before. If you will tell me where I can secure this book I should like to get it. This extract[2] covers my view of the case in a most satisfactory manner. We must keep hammering away at these fellows until a fellow can feel that he can go to Harvard and Yale and graduate and still go into the South or elsewhere and do business just as a white man does. There is no need why every colored man who graduates at college should go to teaching or preaching. If we do not through the instrumentality of the stronger brain in the race, lay hold of the business and industrial openings in the South during the next 10 years these opportunities will pass beyond our recall.

My present plan is to be in New York on the 12th or 13th and I shall see you.

I am expecting a visit from Mr. Walter H. Page, editor of the Atlantic Monthly, this week. Yours truly,

Booker T. Washington

I am very glad indeed to see Mr. Baldwin's letter and I thank you for sending it.

B. T. W.

TLS Con. 161 BTW Papers DLC.

[1] Henry Thomas Buckle (1821-62), author of *History of Civilization in England* (2 vols., 1857-61).

[2] BTW used both Fortune's quotation from Buckle and a speech by Walter Hines Page in an unsigned article in the *Tuskegee Student*, Mar. 16, 1899. Page said: "To my mind, it is money and labor wasted in what is called education, if men and women are not taught to do things. An education that does not teach a man to do something and do it well, is not an education, whether that thing be the building of a house or a steam engine, becoming a great scholar or whatever it may be. Now, if that is true in general, it is true of every white man, it is true of every colored man."

The *Tuskegee Student* noted that the quotation from Buckle's *History of Civilization* had appeared in the New York *Age* earlier. Buckle said:

"Of all the results which are produced among a people by their climate, food and soil, the accumulation of wealth is the earliest and in many respects the most important. For although the progress of knowledge accelerates the increase of wealth, it is nevertheless certain that, in the first formation of society, the wealth must accumulate before the knowledge can begin. As long as every man is engaged in collecting the materials necessary for his own subsistence, there will be neither leisure nor taste for higher pursuits; no science can possibly be created, and the utmost that can be effected will be an attempt to economize labor by the contrivance of such rude and imperfect instruments as even the most barbarous people are able to invent.

"In a state of society like this, the accumulation of wealth is the first great step that can be taken, because without wealth there can be no leisure, and without leisure there can be no knowledge."

The *Tuskegee Student* commented: "No amount of misrepresentation, nor of sophistry, nor of rodomontade, will shake from their faith those who believe with all their might that the Negro, that every race, must have a firm, a secure footing, in the basic, industrial avocations, if prosperity is to be assured him and those who are to come after him." (*Tuskegee Student*, 8 [Mar. 16, 1899], 2, 3.)

From Richard W. Thompson[1]

Washington, March 1, 1899

My Dear Sir — I am a candidate for an humble position in the Census Bureau that of clerk. Having reason to believe that you are a friend of mine, and that my course in journalism for the past few years has met your approval to the extent of convincing you that I am deserving of recognition. I appreciate the fact that I ask a great deal in urging you to depart from your policy of non-interference in matters of this kind, but as this is an exceptional case, and need not be made a matter of public notoriety, I feel warranted in asking this favor at your hands. I have no doubt that a hearty indorsement from you, testifying to capabilities, character and especial fitness for the duties required, would result in my appointment among the very first. A letter along the lines indicated, sent to me, in care of the Colored American, will place me under everlasting obligations to you.

Wishing you continued success in the great work to which you are devoting your life, I am   Very truly yours,

R. W. Thompson

TLS   Con. 162   BTW Papers   DLC.

1 Richard W. Thompson was born in Brandenburg, Ky., in 1865. While serving as a mailman from 1888 to 1893, he was managing editor of the Indianapolis *Freeman* and the Indianapolis *World*. In 1894 he moved to Washington, D.C., where he was a government clerk for many years. Thompson was managing editor of the Washington *Colored American* for several years until 1903 and ran the National Negro Press Bureau, a syndicated news service to about a dozen black newspapers, which BTW secretly subsidized and which was one of his prime agencies for influencing black editors.

From Timothy Thomas Fortune

New York, March 2, 1899

My dear Mr. Washington: Your letter of the 27th Feb was received this morning and I am very glad to hear from you, as it has been quite a long time since your last letter was received. We [have] been looking for a report of the Conference ever since it took place, but aside from some personal notes sent by Silas Floyd too late for use last week, your letter and the Advertiser, which came this morning, is the first mention I have seen any where. The papers donot seem to have paid the usual attention to it this year — I mean the New York newspapers. But it appears to me that the newspapers all along the line have entered into a conspiracy of silence or misrepresentation of our case. I don't seem to get published anything I want published in them. They practically ignored the Federation convention here as they did the Council convention at Washington. The Boston Transcript last Saturday had an article of mine[1] in good shape, which I dare say you have seen. But they are slow pokes, and hold matter until it gets sour.

Mr. Baldwin expressed my views of Smith's article in the letter I sent you. He made a brave effort to get his matter, which he had plated, in a lot of our newspapers, but only three have carried it, as far as I have seen.

Of course you are the best judge about Alexander.

Did Mr. Page get to the Conference? I see no mention of his name in Mr. Bedford's article. I am glad you had Bishop Turner and a lot of people it is worth while to convince, and there are lots of them. They seem to be growing.

I see Barnett[2] ran in the Courant[3] his long letter to me and my answer on the Youngs Hotel dinner,[4] which I [thought] was an unwise thing to do. I am very glad that my answer was guardedly reserved.

Dr. Frissell will injure Hampton and the industrial educational interests if he does not muzzle Kelly Miller and Hugh Browne[5] on the political phase of the situation, and unless they are muzzled I am going to open up on them and Hampton in the Age and Independent. It is not necessary to give [a]way the *whole* political case in order to propagate the industrial idea.

My health is passably fair.

I am very glad to hear you may be here about the 10th and remain until April. Yours truly

T Thomas Fortune

ALS Con. 154 BTW Papers DLC.

[1] Fortune probably refers here to his article in the Boston *Transcript* on Thurs-

day, Feb. 25, 1899, on the resolutions of the Afro-American Council meeting.

2 Isaiah D. Barnett, a black Bostonian.

3 The Boston *Courant*, a black weekly newspaper.

4 In an effort to still the growing criticism of his racial policies among northern blacks, BTW through Fortune about 1898 arranged to meet a Boston group at dinner at Young's Hotel. According to Fortune's later account he told the diners, as the coffee and cigars were passed out, that BTW would welcome their free expression of opinion as to how the race could best be served in the current crisis. "Each of the speakers launched into a tirade against Dr. Washington and his policies and methods, many of them in lofty flights of speech they had learned at Harvard University. The atmosphere was dense with discontent and denunciation." The climactic speech was that of William H. Lewis, the black lawyer and Harvard football coach, who told BTW to go back South to his educational work and "leave to us the matters political affecting the race." Washington listened to the criticism, but in his address of half an hour he spoke unruffled of his work at Tuskegee, "without once alluding to anything that had been said in heat and anger by those to whom he spoke." (Fortune, quoted in Scott and Stowe, *Booker T. Washington*, 314-15.)

5 Hugh Mason Browne was educated in the Washington, D.C., public schools and Howard University, graduating in 1875. After receiving A.M. and D.D. degrees from Princeton Theological Seminary in 1878, Browne did additional graduate work in Scotland and Germany. He taught at Liberia College for a year and a half and returned to Washington in 1886 as head of the physics department of the M Street High School. BTW cited Browne's talk at a Thanksgiving Day service in 1893 at the Lincoln Memorial Church in Washington as the source for the "cast down your bucket" metaphor of his Atlanta Exposition address. (See above, 3:410, 413.) In 1898 Browne became head of the physics department at Hampton Institute, and in 1901 he was appointed principal of the newly organized Baltimore High School. One year later Browne was recommended by BTW as the best man to reorganize the Institute for Colored Youth in Philadelphia (later called Cheyney State College).

A strong supporter of BTW, Browne attended the Washington–Du Bois Conference that met in New York in Jan. 1904 to effect a rapprochement between the two factions. BTW, Du Bois, and Browne were designated a committee to select what became the Committee of Twelve for the Advancement of the Negro Race to serve as a clearinghouse and advisory service. But Du Bois finally resigned, charging that BTW and Browne voted two to one to pack the Committee of Twelve with pro-BTW men. The committee published a number of pamphlets but never served as a means of unifying the black factions.

From Henry McNeal Turner

Atlanta, Ga. Mar. 3, 1899

Dear Doctor: Have the kindness please to hand this little package to your agricultural chemist, with whom I had a talk, and promised to send a few grape seed which I brought from Africa, I expected to have sent him more, but I had given out to six different parties, some of the seed to see who could succeed in getting them to grow in this Country. These are all I had left, and if he can get one or two of these to sprout and grow, we can get cuttings and establish their growth in this Country. It makes a large beautiful grape that has the flavor of honey. They are known as the honey grape of South Africa. If he succeeds in having them to sprout and grow I am sure he will inform me. I lost the name of the chmesist [chemist]. If you have more than one, I want you to give these seed, to the one I had a talk with. He will remember our conversation, he was a small dark gentleman, be very particular, as I want him to get the seed by all means, Respectfully,

H. M. Turner

ALS Con. 165 BTW Papers DLC. Docketed: "Mr. Carver — If you are the one these seed are intended for — Keep them — otherwise advise, if you know, who they are for — Return letter. BTW." Carver replied on the letter: "Yes I am He. G.W.C. I will plant them at once and give them the best care."

From Timothy Thomas Fortune

New York, March 4, 1899

My Dear Friend: I am glad to have your letter of the 1st instant. I donot believe you will allow yourself to be drawn into a newspaper controversy with Smith. I think his whole yawp has died a-borning. I am glad that you think I covered the ground in my editorial reply.

I am glad you want to read "Buckle's History of Civilization." *It is the key to history*. We can secure it for you at publishers' price if you want to have us do so. I donot know the publisher, but we can locate it. It is in two volumes, and I think it will cost $6.00. You should also read in connection with it Malthus' theory of "Population." You would find your intelligence greatly illuminated by reading these two works.

We have made an article on the conference and carry Floyd's Personal Notes, with your cut, in the coming issue.

I have declined to have any thing to do with the National Biographical Cyclopedia of Eminent and Progressive Colored men, edited by E. E. Cooper, for which you are to write the introduction.

What the deuce can Cooper edit? He can't parse a simple sentence, and he thinks every humbug at a cross roads who can write his name is a great negro. You are in bad company.

Take Cook's article in the current Hampton Southern Workman, it is vile, and if Frissell keeps it up I shall open my batteries on him.

My health is fair.

I am glad you are coming on the 12th. Your friend,

T Thomas Fortune

ALS   Con. 153   BTW Papers   DLC.

To Timothy Thomas Fortune

Tuskegee, Ala., Mar. 7, 1899

My dear Mr. Fortune: I am glad to have your letter of March 2d. Mr. Page is now here and is spending the day very pleasantly and I hope mutually profitable. He spoke to the students Sunday evening with a great deal of earnestness and I have asked Mr. Scott to send you some extracts from his address which I thought perhaps you might like to use.

By this time I think you must have received some report of our Conference. There was a very aggravating blunder made in the sending out of the Associated Press dispatches; the fault was our own tho of course I cannot say how widely the press would have published the dispatches had they been sent from here at the proper time and in the proper manner. I think you will find that a little later on the weekly press will have a pretty full report of the Conference, but owing to the serious mistake I have mentioned little got into the daily press as compared with last year. The N.Y. Commercial Advertiser had a very good article last week.

There is no way for us to get the white press to give us attention except by continual hammering. I think you ought to congratulate yourself that the press all over the country has taken up the idea which you first gave life to of cutting off the Southern representation in Congress. It is especially noticeable in the strong weekly papers.

I am surprised that I have not seen your Transcript article; if I do not receive it soon in the press clippings I shall send for it.

I notice that a good many of the colored papers are going for the C. S. Smith editorial. Charles Stewart[1] has been here several days and has sent off some good articles. He has become thoroughly won over to our side.

I have noted for some time with a great deal of sadness the harm which Brown and Kelly Miller are likely to do to the cause of industrial education. I think it was a great blunder for Kelly Miller to have spoken in Boston at that Hampton meeting. His political opinions have no concern whatever with the cause of industrial education. If such influences are to control the Hampton Conference I fear that it will do me and you little good to go there. I shall speak to Dr. Frissell about both of these men when I see him. Yours truly,

Booker T. Washington

TLS Con. 161 BTW Papers DLC.

1 Charles Stewart was born in Frankfort, Ky., in 1869. As a young man he worked on the Louisville *Courier-Journal* and the Chicago *Inter Ocean* before attending a state school in Louisville and a business school in Chicago. After graduation from Alabama A & M College, Stewart worked as a Chicago newspaperman. He was general correspondent of the National Baptist Convention, president and manager of Stewart's General Press Bureau in Chicago, and a member of the National Negro Press Association.

From Charles Young

Wilberforce University, Ohio, March 9, 1899

Dear Mr. Washington: I have mailed you herewith two photos of myself one in civilian dress of last May, the other taken out of doors in our last camp at Marion, Summerville, S.C. Of course I shall expect yours according to promise in return.

Thank you for your last letter. If Lieut. Ramsey does not succeed in his undertaking (and I hope with all my heart he may because his success is mine and yours) if you wish to get your boys under my training for the purposes of discipline and the moral and mental benefits accruing from obedience etc. get guns from the Gov't and ask the President of the U.S. for me.

This [is] confidential as it appears they are trying to fix me at Howard and at Wilberforce and in Hayti.

With high regard. Very truly yours,

Chas Young

ALS Con. 165 BTW Papers DLC.

Extracts from an Address at the Hollis Street Theater[1]

[Boston, Mass.] March 21, 1899

THE INFLUENCE OF OBJECT-LESSONS IN THE SOLUTION OF THE RACE PROBLEM

In the heart of the Black Belt of the South in ante bellum days there was a large estate, with a palatial mansion surrounded by a beautiful grove in which grew flowers and shrubbery of every description. Magnificent specimens of animal life grazed in the fields, and in grain and all manner of plant growth this estate was a model. In a word, it was the highest type of the product of slave labor.

Then came the long years of war, then freedom, then the trying years of reconstruction. The master returned from the war to find the faithful slaves who had been the bulwark of this household in possession of their freedom. Then there began that social and industrial revolution in the South which it is hard for any one who was not really a part of it to appreciate or understand. Gradually day by day this ex-master began to realize, with a feeling almost indescribable, to what an extent he and his family had grown to be dependent upon the activity and faithfulness of their slaves; began to appreciate to what an extent slavery had sapped the sinews of strength and independence, how the dependence upon slave labor had deprived him and his offspring of the benefit of technical and industrial training, and worst of all had unconsciously led them to see in labor drudgery and degradation instead of beauty, dignity and civilizing power. At first there was a halt in this man's life. He cursed the North and he cursed the Negro. Then there was despair, almost utter hopelessness, over his weak and childlike condition. The temptation was to forget all in drink and to this temptation there was a gradual yielding. With the loss of physical vigor came the loss of mental grasp and pride in surroundings. There was the falling of a piece of plaster from the walls of the house which was not replaced, then another and still another. Gradually the window panes began to disappear, then the door knobs. Touches of paint and whitewash which once helped to give life were no more to be seen. The hinges disappeared from the gate, then a board from the fence, then others in quick succession. Weeds and unmown grass covered the once well kept lawn. Sometimes there were servants for domestic duties and sometimes there were none. In the absence of servants the unsatisfactory condition of the food told that it was being prepared by hands unschooled to such duties. As the years passed by, debts were accumulating in every direction. The education of the children was neglected. Lower and lower sank the industrial, financial and spiritual condition of the household. For the first time the awful truth of scripture, "Whatsoever a man soweth that shall he also reap," seemed to dawn upon them with a reality that is hard for mortals to appreciate. Within a few months the whole mistake of slavery seemed to have concentrated itself upon this household.

If there was proof wanting that slavery wrought almost as much permanent injury upon the Southern white man as upon the black man, it was furnished in the case of this family. And further, those who would understand conditions as they exist today in the South, must be led to see and feel that so long as the rank and file of my own people are in ignorance and poverty, so long will this ignorance and poverty prove a millstone about the neck of your brothers and sisters in the South. If the ignorance and poverty of the Negro prove a temptation to the white man to deprive the Negro of his legal rights by unholy methods, let us remember that the wrong to the Negro is but temporary, but upon those committing the crimes the results are eternal. The Negro can afford to be wronged, the white man can not afford to wrong him without the proudest and bluest blood in your civilization being degraded. And so, my

friends, though myself born in the slavery of the South, let me entreat you that it is in that broader and deeper and more generous
attitude we want to view the South — that of helping to remove
the burden from the entire people regardless of race or color. And
just here may I mention that one of the chief charms and compen-
sations of the efforts put forth at Tuskegee is in the abundant
evidence that we are not assisting in lightening the burdens of one
race but two — in helping to put that spirit into men that will make
them forget race and color in efforts to lift up an unfortunate
brother.

In this spirit let us return for a moment to the life of the family
to whom I have been referring. As the years went by the night
seemed to grow darker till all seemed hopeless and lost. At this
point relief and strength came from an unexpected source. The
idea of this Southern white man of Negro education had been that
it merely meant a parrot-like absorbtion of Anglo-Saxon civilization
with a special tendency to imitate the weaker elements of the white
man; that Negro education meant merely the high hat, kid gloves,
a showy walking cane, patent leather shoes and all the rest of it.
To this ex-master it seemed impossible that the education of the
Negro could produce any other result. And so last of all did he expect help or encouragement from an educated black man, but it
was just from this source that help came. Soon after the process of
decay began in this white man's estate the education of a certain
black man began — began on a logical sensible basis. It was an
education that would fit him to see and appreciate the physical and
moral conditions that existed in his own family and neighborhood,
and in the present generation, and would fit him to apply himself
to their relief. By chance this educated Negro strayed into the employ of this white man. His employer soon learned that this Negro
had not only a knowledge of science, mathematics and literature
in his head but in his hands as well. This black man applied his
knowledge of agricultural chemistry to the redemption of the soil
and soon the washes and gullies began to disappear and the waste
places began to bloom. New and improved machinery in a few
months began to rob labor of its toil and drudgery. The animals
were given systematic and kindly attention. Fences were repaired
and rebuilded, whitewash and paint were made to do duty. Everywhere order slowly began to replace confusion, and hope despair

and profits losses. As he observed day by day new life and strength being imparted to every department of his property this white son of the South began revising his own creed regarding the wisdom of educating Negroes. Hitherto his creed regarding the value of an educated Negro had been rather a plain and simple one and read: "The only end that could be accomplished by educating a black man was to enable him to talk proper to the mule, and he contended that the Negro's education did great injustice to the mule since the new language tended to confuse the mule and make him 'balky.'"

We need not continue the story except to add that today the grasp of the hand of this ex-slaveholder and the listening to his words of hearty gratitude and commendation for the education of the Negro is enough to compensate those who have given and those who have worked and sacrificed for the elevation of my people through all these years. If we are patient, wise, unselfish and courageous such examples will multiply as the years pass by.

A missionary traveling in the heart of Africa was surprised to find an African chief who was living the Christian life. When the missionary asked the African where and when he had heard of the Christian religion, the old chief replied that he had not heard of it but he had seen it for two years by daily contact with a man who had lived the Christ life. Object lessons that shall bring the Southern white man into daily, visible, tangible contact with the benefits of Negro education will go much further towards the solution of present problems than all the mere abstract argument and theories that can be evolved from the human brain. In proportion as the Negro learns to do something as well or better than a white man he will find his place in our economic and political life and his place, like that of every being possessing real worth, will be that of a man, "a man for a' that and a' that." It is not our duty to set metes and bounds upon the aspirations and ambitions of any individual or race, but it is our duty to see that the foundation is wisely and firmly laid. A race that plants itself in the ownership of the soil, the industries, the domestic arts of a country, in intelligence and religion and in the confidence of the people among whom it lives, is the race that will win regardless of all temporary makeshifts, obstacles and discouragements. Man may ruffle the surface but the permanent flow of the river can he not stop.

We of this generation in the South must lay the foundation for those that are to come. I would not advocate that the end of every Negro's education should be to excel in the ownership of property, skill in agriculture, mechanic and industrial arts, but I would with all the emphasis of my soul, remind my race over and over again that if we of this generation lay the foundation well in these, our children and children's children will find through them the surest way to recognition and success in letters, arts and statesmanship. Then will the sacred story repeat itself: "The rain descended, and the floods came, and the winds blew, and beat upon that house; and it fell not; for it was founded upon a rock."

TM   Con. 955   BTW Papers   DLC.

1 BTW considered this "a rather notable meeting." He arranged to have both Paul Laurence Dunbar and W. E. B. Du Bois on the same program. This was the first time that these men had appeared before a Boston audience. (See above, 1:144.) BTW's real motivation for having Dunbar and Du Bois on the same platform with him was to avoid competition, since Horace Bumstead of Atlanta University had scheduled to have Du Bois and Dunbar appear in several cities near Boston just a few days before the Hollis Street Theater meeting. (Bumstead to BTW, Mar. 3, 1899, Con. 150, BTW Papers, DLC.) BTW wrote Bumstead that such an arrangement would detract from his own meeting. (Mar. 10, 1899, MH.)

The program was designed to launch a campaign for large contributions to Tuskegee that would free BTW of the necessity of constant fund-raising. Francis J. Garrison and the Boston banker Henry Lee Higginson were the principal organizers. "The theatre was filled," BTW recalled, "with representatives of the most cultured and wealthy men and women in Boston, and was said to be the most successful meeting of the kind that had been held for a good while." (1:144.) Others felt, however, that BTW, who was clearly exhausted, came off a rather poor third in the oratorical competition, and BTW's fund-raising sponsors decided also to raise a sum to send him to Europe for a rest. (Du Bois, *Autobiography*, 237.)

From Oliver F. Gray

Washington, D.C. 3-21st 1899

Dear Sir: Believing that the Negro must forget the past if he would win for himself a place in future events I think nothing would do more to inspire confidence in us or to weaken race predujice than for our public schools in the southland to join with the southern people on memorial day and each Negro pupil place a flower on some dead confederate soldier's grave. Please give your ideas on above plan and oblige   Yours Res'y

Oliver F Gray

ALS Con. 154 BTW Papers DLC. Docketed: "This is a monumental proposition! E J Scott."

To Margaret James Murray Washington

Boston Mass. Mch 23rd 1899

Meeting great success too busy to write.

B. T. W.

HWIr Con. 540 BTW Papers DLC.

A Contract with Max Bennett Thrasher

[Boston, Mass., Mar. 23, 1899]

This agreement entered into between Booker T. Washington, representing the Tuskegee Normal and Industrial Institute, on the one part, and M. B. Thrasher, on the other, contracts:

That for the sum of fifty dollars a month, to be paid on the 10th day of the following month, by the said Booker T. Washington, the said M. B. Thrasher is to furnish newspaper and magazine articles, pertaining to Tuskegee and its work, of the same general nature, length and number as he has furnished heretofore, examples being articles published in Success, the National Magazine, Sabbath Reading, Frank Leslie's, and an article published through the S. S. McClure newspaper syndicate, any pay received for such articles to be the property of the said M. B. Thrasher.

That the said Thrasher is to spend two months of each winter at or near Tuskegee, in the study of the conditions there and among the graduates of the Institute. Traveling expenses to & from Boston to be paid by Mr. Washington.

That the said Thrasher shall hold himself in readiness to travel with or for Mr. Washington at the latter's request for the purpose of collecting material for such articles as have been described, all traveling expenses to be paid by Mr. Washington.

That this contract shall hold in force from the first day of May, 1899, to the first day of May, 1901.

TMd Con. 160 BTW Papers DLC. Thrasher drafted the agreement and enclosed it in a letter to BTW on Mar. 23.

From the Diary of Helen Tufts Bailie[1]

[Boston, Mass.] March 23, 1899

Booker T. Washington is downstairs (BO) talking with Mr. Garrison.[2] Have had a good look at him — not very significant looking man until you see into his face, then you feel his purposeness.

Sophia Smith Collection MNS. Courtesy of Katherine H. Sawyer, curator of the Sophia Smith Collection.

[1] Helen Tufts Bailie (1874-1962) was descended from one of the rebellious founders of the Unitarian Church in Boston and was herself a lifelong activist in the Unitarian movement, serving as an officer of the Alliance of Unitarian Women. Mrs. Bailie was deeply involved in the liberal movements of her time, and during the Red Scare of the 1920s was tried and ousted from the D.A.R.

[2] Probably Francis Jackson Garrison.

From Francis Jackson Garrison

Boston, March 23, 1899

Dear Mr. Washington: I saw Miss Gray this morning, and she agrees with me that you ought, if possible, to arrange your plans so as to go abroad as near the first of May as possible, if you are to have a month's rest in Paris before going to England. I think that you ought to allow not less than six weeks for England, and that means that you should practically arrange to be absent from this country for three months. It will be time well spent, and I trust that you will make no engagements on this side to interfere with that plan. If you are back by the 1st of August, will it not practically serve your purpose? Please do not forget to send Miss Mason[1] the list of the contributors to the special guarantee fund which is now being raised for Tuskegee. If Mrs. Washington can go with you, I hope she will. There will be no trouble in raising the funds, I am sure. Yours very truly,

Francis J. Garrison

TLS   Con. 154   BTW Papers   DLC.

[1] Ellen Frances Mason of Boston was one of the principal contributors to the fund for Tuskegee's operating expenses and to another fund to pay BTW's travel expenses to Europe.

From William P. Bancroft[1]

Wilmington, Delaware, 3rd Mo., 27th, 1899

Dear friend: I hope I am not doing what is impertinent, or what may seem so to thee. If so, I will be content — if thou should think such best — with a very short answer.

When at Tuskeegee lately I noticed that a *very large house* was being built. In walking around the place by myself I went into it. I was told that it belonged to thee personally. If it is for thy use, and if thy private means are not very different from what I suppose them to be, this seems hard to reconcile with thy position and the needs of the school. This matter has stood in the way of my speaking of the institution as freely as I would have liked to have done. I feel very confident there is some explanation which would relieve me from my difficulties; and I have thought it best to write in this way freely to thee and state them.

I believe I have only mentioned the matter in one instance, except in speaking to the members of my family who were with me at Tuskegee. Perhaps I should not have mentioned it in that one instance. Respectfully,

Wm. P. Bancroft

TLS   Con. 149   BTW Papers   DLC.

[1] William P. Bancroft was a prominent Quaker business and civic leader in Wilmington, Del. He was a benefactor of the Friends School there and took an active

interest in matters pertaining to education, such as helping develop a public library. He was a partner in Joseph Bancroft & Sons Co., a cotton-goods factory at Rockford, near Wilmington.

Extracts from an Address before the Birmingham Lyceum[1]

[Birmingham, Ala., Mar. 30, 1899]

I thank you most earnestly for the privilege of speaking to you concerning the education of my race. I feel sure that I come here in a spirit which neither you nor I misunderstand. Surely no people should have a more vital interest in the elevation of the half million of negroes in Alabama than the most enlightened white people in Alabama. No people have so much to lose by the negro's ignorance and degradation; no people have so much to gain by his education and industry being made useful. Since the old days of slavery I very much fear that, for reasons which I need not explain, in sympathy and mutual interest we have gotten too far apart from each other. In saying this I do not want to be misunderstood, and would repeat what I have said on another occasion, that "in all things that are purely social we can be as separate as the fingers yet one as the hand in all things that pertain to our mutual interest."

INTERESTED IN THE NEGRO

No people were more deeply interested in our fathers and mothers than you and your fathers and mothers. Between you and those who were in slavery there was a bond of sympathy which few have ever understood. Between us today that bond of sympathy exists, though at times it may have seemed strained and warped. Considering what you have been to us and what you are today, it doesn't seem strange that you should inquire after our methods of elevation and our progress in education. We are not unmindful nor ungrateful for what you are helping us to do as a race; we recall with deepest gratitude that from the first year that we were made a free people that you have shared with us the few dollars which the state has been able to devote to education, and it is with special pride that we point to the fact that here in the city of Birmingham you seem to have taken special pride through your efficient system of public schools in promoting the education of my people.

At Tuskegee it has been our aim to give the students intelligence, Christian character, to teach them how to make a living by becoming skilled in some industry — to do a common thing in an uncommon way — and to teach them the beauty, dignity and civilizing power that there is in intelligent labor.

It has also been our endeavor in every manly way to teach them how to gain the respect and confidence of the white people among whom they are to live for all time. To do this we constantly remind them that they must learn to do something as well or better than any one else.

When I first began this work at Tuskegee and the idea got spread among our people that the students were to be taught industry in connection with their academic studies, I got a great many verbal messages and letters from parents to the effect that they wanted their children taught books, but not how to work. This protest went on for three or four years, but I am glad to say that our people have gradually been educated to the point where they see their own condition and needs so clearly that it has been eight years since we have had a single protest from parents against the teaching of industry, and there is a positive enthusiasm over it, in fact the public sentiment among the students is so strong that it would not permit a student to remain on the grounds who was unwilling to labor.

GROWTH OF SCHOOL

Starting in 1881 in a little house with one teacher and 30 students, the institution at Tuskegee has gradually grown in the number of students until we have at present 1,047 students, two-thirds of them being young men and the remaining number girls. The average age of these students is eighteen and one-half years. None are admitted until they are fourteen years of age. These students come from twenty-four states and territories and from three foreign countries. The average attendance this year is about 900. All except a small number board and sleep upon the school grounds. In all of the departments — academic, industrial and religious — eighty-eight officers and teachers are employed. Counting students, teachers and families, there is a population upon the school grounds at all times of about 1,200 persons.

Twenty-six different industries are in constant operation in connection with our students' academic training, and each student is taught some trade or industry. These are all industries at which the students can find immediate employment as soon as they finish our course of training. In fact we have many times more applications for our graduates each year than we can possibly fill. The demand this year for students to take charge of dairies and farms in different parts of the south has been very great.

When we started we had absolutely nothing in the way of property except an appropriation of $2,000, since increased to $4,500, from the state of Alabama, to be used in the payment of teachers. Since 1881, while friends in different parts of the country have given us money to help pay the teachers and to buy material which we could not produce, still very largely by the labor of the students themselves we have gradually built up a property that is now valued at $300,000. In all we have 2,267 acres of land. Counting large and small, there are forty-two buildings upon the grounds, and all of these buildings except four have been almost wholly built by the labor of the students. There is no mortgage upon any of this property. The annual expense of carrying on this work is now about $75,000. About 2,000 of our graduates and ex-students are now at work in every southern state, mainly in Alabama, as school teachers, farmers, mechanics, housekeepers and leaders along other lines.

INSTRUCTION IN COOKING

It has been surprising to me how the negro's education has been overlooked in the very matters that any individual should know most about. Let us take the matter of intelligent, cleanly, healthy cooking. Here is something that directly concerns the whole race three times a day every day in the year. Cooking not only concerns the whole colored race in this state, but the health and happiness of the white race, for you will agree with me that a large proportion of you depend upon the negro for the preparation of your food.

How often has my heart been made to sink as I have gone through the south and into the homes of the people and found women who could converse intelligently on Grecian history, who had studied geometry, could analyze the most complex sentences

64

in grammar, and yet know nothing of the composition and proper proportion of the poorly cooked and still more poorly served corn bread and fat meat that they and their families were eating three times a day. It is little trouble to find girls who can locate Pekin or the Desert of Sahara on an artificial globe, but it is hard to find girls who can find on the dinner table the proper place for the carving knife and fork, or the meat and vegetables.

SOLUTION OF CHEAP COTTON

It will pay the white people of the south, if for no other reason than to increase their own material wealth, to take the deepest interest in the negro's education. We hear a prolonged moan going up from all portions of the south because of 4 cents and 5 cents cotton. The explanation of this low price of cotton, I think all will agree, is to be found largely in over-production. Efforts are made each year to reduce the acreage in cotton, and year by year the amount produced increases. Is not the explanation to be found in the fact that the black man produces the larger proportion of the cotton? As a rule the black man is ignorant and knows not how to produce anything else except cotton. Is it not true that in all the history of the world an ignorant farming class produces but a single crop? Is it not true that you can only have a diversified crop where you have an intelligent farming class? The only way for the south to save itself from the depressing influence of the low price of cotton — of a one-crop system in farming — is in part to educate the black man so as to make him intelligent in all matters of agriculture. When the black man prospers as a farmer the white man prospers. It is impossible for a black man to be worth twenty thousand dollars without all his neighbors sharing in the benefits of that twenty thousand dollars.

In the economy of God, there is but one standard by which an individual can succeed — there is but one standard for a race. This country requires that every race shall measure itself by the American standard. By it a race must rise or fall, succeed or fail, and in the last analysis mere sentiment counts for little. During the next half a century and more my race must continue passing through the severe American crucible. We are to be tested in our patience, our forbearance, our perseverance, our power to withstand temptations, to economize, to acquire and use skill and industry, in our ability to compete, to succeed in commerce, to disregard the super-ficial for the real, the shadow for the substance, to be great and yet small, learned and yet simple. This is the passport to all that is best in the life of our republic, and the negro must possess it or be de-barred.

PROF. WASHINGTON'S HUMOR

I once met a young colored medical student in the north who said he was making a specialty of nervous diseases and after com-pleting his education he intended going to the Mississippi bottoms to practice among his race.

"Don't you know, young man," I said to him, "that the negroes in the Mississippi bottoms haven't advanced to that degree of civ-ilization where they can have the blessings of nervous prostration? You'd better learn all you can about chills and fever."

"The gospel of the toothbrush" is one of the most important and one of the hardest things we have to teach in Tuskegee. When we have succeeded in teaching a student to use a toothbrush of his own accord, we consider him on the highroad to civilization and enlightenment.

An education which increases the negro's wants and require-ments without giving him the means of supplying them is hurtful, and is all a mistake.

The white man is by his education taking from the negro many of those occupations which a generation ago were confined almost exclusively to the colored man. After the war nearly every barber shop in the south and north was filled with colored barbers. But the white man came along, fixed up a shop with fans, periodicals and other attractions, until now he has control of nearly every first-class barber shop in the north, anyhow. The negro didn't know enough to keep up with the procession. You will notice that when-ever a white man takes a negro's occupation, he changes the name. Old Uncle Sam used to be known as "barber," but the white man is called "tonsorial artist."

It is mighty hard to make a good Christian out of a hungry man. A negro goes home from church, where he has been shouting and praying, as a negro so loves to do, and if he finds nothing to eat at home, he very generally goes out and finds something to eat be-fore morning.[2]

Birmingham *Age-Herald*, Mar. 31, 1899, 8. Subheadings were supplied by the newspaper.

1 BTW spoke at the Birmingham Lyceum to about 250 persons. He began by giving an account of his early life and how he founded Tuskegee Institute. Since white women were present in the audience there had been some opposition to BTW speaking by the racist Regents of the White Shields, but Emmett J. Scott, acting as advance man for BTW, assured Birmingham citizens that BTW's speech had nothing to do with social equality and that he often spoke before audiences containing white women. (Birmingham *Age-Herald*, Mar. 30, 1899, 3; Mar. 31, 1899, 8.)

2 The Birmingham *Age-Herald*, Mar. 31, 1899, 8, reported that the audience applauded BTW for over a minute when he told the story of an old black woman in Mississippi who went into an Episcopal church, took a seat in the rear, and began to moan and clap her hands as the rector began his sermon. "Her demonstration practically broke up the services, and one of the officers of the church went back to stop her. 'What's the matter with you, aunty, are you sick?' 'No, sir; I'se happy; I'se got religion. Yes, sir, I'se got religion!' 'Why, don't you know,' said the officer, without thinking, 'that this isn't the place to get religion?'"

From Francis Jackson Garrison

Boston, March 31, 1899

Dear Mr. Washington: I duly received your favor of the 28th from New York, and am glad to know that you and Mrs. Washington can probably be ready to go to Europe by the first of May. I have already taken the refusal of a stateroom for you, and it only remains to decide by which line it may be best, on the whole, for you to go, but if you take the Atlantic Transport Line to London, the steamer will leave New York on the 29th of April, while if you go by the Red Star Line to Antwerp, the steamer will sail on the 3d of May.[1] I am assuming that you will probably wish to leave England about the 20th or 27th of July, but of course you can arrange the date to suit your convenience when you get on the other side. The amount required to cover all your expenses is already assured, and you must prepare to drop all cares and have a good time for at least three months. If you can stay longer, the expense will not interfere. Miss Mason and I think that it will be a capital idea for you to go first to Paris, for three or four weeks' recreation there before crossing to England, and in the meantime I shall notify the friends in England so that they can communicate with you and arrange for your visiting them. My own idea is that it will be well for you to spend the greater part of June in London, and then go north along the east coast (by way of York, Scarboro and Newcastle) to Edinburgh, returning by way of the Lake District, Oxford, Stratford, etc., but distances are so comparatively slight over there that it will be perfectly easy to vary the route as circumstances may dictate.

Please let me know if you think it will be practicable for you to sail as early as the 29th of April, or if the four days' difference to the 3d of May would be of essential value to you. We can get better rates on a steamer of the earlier date, and I should think better accommodation also, but I shall be governed by your decision.

I hear that Mr. Higginson[2] has received about $2500. more towards the guarantee fund, and believe the committee means to make a push to finish that up very soon now. Yours very truly,

Francis J. Garrison

TLS Con. 154 BTW Papers DLC.

[1] Garrison made these arrangements with the help of his nephew, Oswald Garrison Villard of New York. He wrote Villard on Apr. 1, 1899, that the Atlantic Transport Line offered very favorable rates, but added: "When the agent learned that I was inquiring for colored passengers, however, he promptly said that the line would not take them. This may be so, but I prefer to know it from headquarters, & so I drop this line to ask if you can kindly go down there for me & ask if the Line actually refuses to take such an eminent man & public character because he is (partly) colored. I have also quotations from the Red Star & American Lines — to go out by the *Noordland* May 3 & return by the *Paris* or *St. Louis*, July 22 or 27 — of $216 or $225, — all first cabin, & am asking the Boston agent (who thinks there will be no prejudice against color) to make sure that there will be no discrimination, for I am bound that no indignity shall be put upon Booker Washington & his wife. It will be an honor to any line to have them as passengers." (Oswald Garrison Villard Papers, MH.) Apparently Villard found that the Atlantic Transport Line would not accommodate the Washingtons, for Garrison wrote him on Apr. 6, 1899, thanking him for his trouble. "The Washingtons must sail on the 3d or 10th of May," he added, "and as the A.T.L. profess to be full up to the 20th, I shall not trouble you further; and in view of the animus of the agents, I do not care to subject our friends to any possible slights or annoyances on the steamers, even though they could get passage by them." (Oswald Garrison Villard Papers, MH.) The Washingtons sailed on a Red Star steamer, the *Friesland*, on May 10, and returned on the *St. Louis*.

[2] Henry Lee Higginson (1834-1919) was a Boston investment banker in the firm of Lee, Higginson and Co. In 1866-67 he and two other Bostonians engaged in an experiment with the employment of black labor on a Georgia cotton plantation. They lost heavily, and Higginson reluctantly returned to Boston and a banking career. He gave money generously to Radcliffe College, Harvard, the University of Virginia, and other schools, and was a patron of the Boston Symphony Orchestra.

From Timothy Thomas Fortune

New York, March 31 1899

Dear Friend: After going into the matter I find that it would cost
$130 to get the people to go to the Governor[1] — 5 from here, 4
from central New York and 5 from Western New York. It might
accomplish something, but it costs too much as things stand, and
so I abandon it. *We fail always because we are too poor to do things
as other men do them.* Yours truly

T Thomas Fortune

ALS Con. 154 BTW Papers DLC.

[1] Theodore Roosevelt.

From Charles Young

Wilberforce, Ohio, March 31, 1899

Dear Sir: Replying to your communication of recent date and telegram of to-day, I wish in the first place to thank you for your kindly
interest in the matter of detail to your Institution. When I spoke
to you or (rather wrote) of this matter I thought that your boys
were supplied with guns. Very valuable things when backed by
common sense and very harmless when the student has been educated to know their use and how not to abuse this use. If they are
not properly taught in future wars of this country we shall see re-
enacted upon the part of our people the disgraceful soldier dis-
orders of a month ago. I refer to the muster out of the colored
Volunteer. But your institution is doing too great a work to be
handicapped by taking up this phase of the problem, perhaps. I did
not expect to meet any obstacle when I made you the offer.

It would be impossible, however, for me to do creditable work
with the boys without the General Government would with your
permission furnish guns and equipment for them. This I would
not have you do unless you could see your way perfectly clear to it.
The boys at Wilberforce have had such equipment and arms in
their possession for 5 years with the best results. The pride and

manliness, the self-respect and obedience, the strong virtues of promptness, reverence, neatness, and command — things consequent of this training — are not to be had without a gun, a uniform, and authority at the back of the whole department. Do not think that this would turn your institution into a military camp. My work at colleges is common-sensical and along the line of helpfulness.

I am very well situated here and this is my mother's home; my sole reason for wishing to change was to come into contact with a greater number of the youth of our race. But you know far better than I whether the South is ready or will with friendliness encourage and countenance its colored youth in the acquirement of the qualities I have enumerated.

Your photograph (unautographed) reached me safe. Thank you for it.

Wishing every success to your great work and blessing you in my heart for your kindness in this military matter, I am sincerely Yours,

Chas Young

ALS   Con. 165   BTW Papers   DLC.

To Timothy Thomas Fortune

Tuskegee, Ala., Apr. 4, 1899

Dear Mr. Fortune: I have read with interest the letters from Mr. Shepard[1] and Mr. Hunter,[2] of North Carolina and thank you for sending them to me. Mr. Hunter's letter has some good suggestions in it and I see no reason why many of them might not be made practical. He or some other man would have to take hold of the matter and push it as an individual.

I confess to you that I see no hope for any permanent change in our present condition by reason of anything that Congress or any National Convention will do. Congress by reducing some of the representation[3] will have some effect but even that will not cure the present evil. I have been asking myself lately some rather serious questions and I want to put one or two of them to you. Is there any reason why the Negro in the South should continue to oppose the Southern white man in his politics? Is not this the source of nearly all our trouble? Unconsciously we seem to have gotten the idea into our blood and bones that we are only acting in a manly way when we oppose Southern white men[4]

· · · ·

[Booker T. Washington]

TLf Con. 154 BTW Papers DLC. The first paragraph was penciled out in this draft.

[1] James Edward Shepard was later a leading North Carolina black educator. Born at Raleigh, N.C., in 1875, he graduated from Shaw University in 1894. After a minor position in the recorder of deeds office in Washington in 1899, Shepard was deputy internal revenue collector at Raleigh from 1900 to 1906. Long interested in the better training of black ministers, Shepard in 1910 founded the National Religious Training School and Chautauqua in Durham, N.C., of which he was president from its founding until 1947. The school is now North Carolina Central University.

[2] Aaron Burtis Hunter was the principal of St. Augustine School (later College), an Episcopal school for blacks in Raleigh, N.C. Born in Philadelphia in 1854, he was a graduate of Amherst and of Union Theological Seminary. Though he conceded the need for liberal arts study, Hunter gradually introduced bricklaying, stone masonry, and other industrial subjects patterned after the Hampton Institute curriculum. In 1898 he was one of the founders of the Capon Springs Conference for Christian Education in the South, and served as its secretary-treasurer.

[3] Edgar Dean Crumpacker (1851-1920), an Indiana Republican congressman, revived the idea of the Lodge Force Bill of 1890, which sought to reduce the representation in Congress of southern states denying suffrage rights on account of race. The movement, known as Crumpackerism, was opposed by BTW and Fortune from the beginning. (Crumpacker to BTW, Nov. 7, 1899, Con. 151, Fortune to BTW, Nov. 20, 1898, Con. 153, Feb. 20, 1900, Con. 172, BTW Papers, DLC.) When the conservative Supreme Court failed to act against the disfranchisement provisions of southern state constitutions, however, public pressure for congressional action mounted. In 1904 the more militant black delegates slipped past BTW and the Roosevelt lieutenants a plank in the Republican platform favoring the reduction of representation, but Roosevelt's refusal to endorse it, on BTW's advice, caused the plank to become a dead letter. (Merrill and Merrill, *Republican Command*, 115, 176, 183.)

[4] Fortune apparently forwarded BTW's letter to the Associated Press. (See A Report of a Letter in the New Orleans *Picayune*, Apr. 9, 1899, below.) It also appeared in the New York *World*, Apr. 11, 1899, 6. BTW later denied that this letter was for publication. (See To the Editor of the Chicago *Tribune*, Apr. 10, 1899, below.)

To Emily Howland

Tuskegee, Ala., Apr. 4, 1899

My dear Miss Howland: I meant to have answered your kind letter of March 15th earlier but was uncertain as to your address. In that letter you stated you would be at home after the 1st of April so I waited until that time.

I agree with you that it would help our cause if there could be some reliable source from which information could be gotten in regard to schools in the South. There is a movement on foot by some parties in New York to bring about this result tho I do not know how much practical good it will amount to. The Charity Organization Society in New York is also doing some good work along this line. The great trouble now is that almost every little school that starts up in the South calls itself an industrial school because they find that the matter of industrial education has become popular in the North and in the South. You would be surprised if you made a careful examination, to find how few of these schools are doing anything along industrial lines. Many who have the name industrial are doing nothing along industrial lines. This you see deceives the public. In a few years people in the North will be saying that they have been giving money for industrial education for such a length of time and now we ought to see some of the results, when the truth is very few of the institutions are really doing industrial work. I do not claim that all institutions should be industrial but it is important that the public know which are industrial and which are not. A friend of mine has recently made a personal examination into schools in North Carolina; many of these schools in their publications claim to be industrial but in almost no case did he find these schools coming up to their claims and in fact in most of the instances there was no industrial work at all.

I am glad that you have written Lizzie Wright in regard to her trustees. She is a good woman but needs to be guided.

Enclosed I send you a little slip giving some account of my recent visit to Birmingham, Ala.

Friends in Boston have arranged for Mrs. Washington and myself to take a trip to Europe, going the first of May. It is very hard now to tear ourselves away from this work but these friends insist that we do so and have provided for the expenses for the trip. Under the circumstances I do not see that there is anything left for us to do but go. My present plan is to spend a good portion of the months of June and July in working for the school in England. We shall spend the month of May in Paris. Yours truly,

Booker T. Washington

The contribution which you made sometime ago has been devoted to another purse and could not now be applied to the aid of the two young men [in] whom Miss Morton is interested. These two young men are in our night school and I think will get through school some way.

B. T. W.

TLS   Emily Howland Papers   NN-Sc.

To Lavinia Euphemia De Vaughn[1]

[Tuskegee, Ala.] Apr. 5, 1899

Miss De Vaughn: I think on the whole your division is being conducted in a satisfactory way, but there are some matters which I think you should give attention to and if you do I am sure that you will find it very much to your personal advantage as well as to the advantage of your division and the school. Many of the persons on that place who have sewing to do have the feeling that the work is not carefully finished, that it is not rigidly inspected after it is finished. You should see that there is no room for criticism on this point. You should inspect carefully each garment and be sure that it is all right before it is turned out. Then the feeling prevails among some that you do not like to have work returned to you to be altered or changed in any respect. I hope you will be very sure to give no persons cause to criticise you in this respect. If you want to be successful in your work I would advise you to encourage people to make suggestions or criticisms of your work. For example, after you have sent out a garment to one of the lady teachers you should follow that garment up and ask the teacher personally if the garment is all right and if she has any criticism to offer. In case she returns the garment for alteration or makes criticisms you should thank her heartily for giving you opportunity to do it. Some of the teachers also have the feeling that you take criticisms made upon your work in a personal way. You should try to get to the point as soon as possible where you will not let your personal feelings have anything to do with your work. Every person who patronizes you should be treated courteously and kindly, and even if you do have any personal feeling in regard to a teacher it should never show itself in your business dealings. The best way to succeed in your business is to cultivate attention and politeness.

I am very anxious to have you extend the scope of the work in your division. Do not be content to merely take work that is brought to you but seek work from persons on the school grounds and off the school grounds. At the Montevallo Industrial School for white girls in this state, the Principal tells me that his dressmaker sends all through the county and gets dresses from people to be made by the students. You can do something of that kind here. We are very anxious to have the industrial room work go forward each year. If there is anything that your division needs to make it more successful I wish you would let me know.

I do not write this to criticise you unnecessarily or discourage you, but I feel sure that if you pay attention to these points it will help you in every respect.

In setting prices on your work you must bear in mind that people are not willing to pay as much for work done by students as by professional dressmakers.

[Booker T. Washington]

TL Copy   Con. 152   BTW Papers   DLC.

1 Lavinia Euphemia De Vaughn of Union Springs, Ala., graduated from Tuskegee in 1895. She taught school in Bullock County, Ala., after graduation and then studied dressmaking at the Pratt Institute in Brooklyn. In 1898 she joined the Tuskegee faculty and taught dressmaking until 1900. In 1901 she was in charge of dressmaking at Georgia State Industrial College.

From Timothy Thomas Fortune

Washington, D.C. April 6 [1899]

My dear Mr Washington: I have your favors of the 4th instant and I am very glad to hear from you. I am particularly delighted to learn that the Birmingham visit was such a pronounced success. It is a beautiful article that Mrs. Washington wrote on the visit, and I have this day sent it on to The Age with a short editorial.

As to the Roosevelt article[1] I think that it is a criminal indiscretion, intended to disparage the assistance that our men gave the precious Rough Riders and that the main point of the article as to our men is based in a premeditated lie, *which cannot be refuted,* because the retreating troops are not localized as to their Regiment and company, which could have been done if the truth had been intended to be conveyed. As to the statement that our men fight all right when led by white officers, well I expected better things of Roosevelt, who seems bent on proving willy-nilly that the Rough Riders were not saved from annihilation by the black troopers. But I am very sorry that Roosevelt has placed himself on record in such a way as to detract from the courage of our men.

As to the matter of the Georgia troops I will submit it as my proposition to the committee tomorrow. But I question if your point is well taken, *as no State militia receives any assistance of any sort from the Government in time of peace.* The militia of the States is absolutely under the control of the States and supported in all its departments by the States. Yours truly

T. Thomas Fortune

ALS   Con. 153   BTW Papers   DLC.

[1] The article mentioned by Fortune was chap. 4 of Theodore Roosevelt's book, *The Rough Riders* (1899), serialized in *Scribner's*, 25 (Apr. 1899), 520-40. Roosevelt at first praised the black regulars for their gallantry at San Juan Hill, though he never quite conceded that it was their conquest of the top of the hill with high casualties that drove the Spanish troops down the hill into the Rough Riders. In his book, Roosevelt first praised the black troops as having "behaved very well," but added later that they were "peculiarly dependent upon their white officers." He intimated that black soldiers did well because of the leadership qualities of the white officers. At one point in the battle, according to his account, black troops mixed with his own were "uneasy" and "began to drift to the rear." When he threatened them with his pistol, he said, they "flashed their white teeth at one another, as they broke into

broad grins, and I had no more trouble with them." (Roosevelt, *The Rough Riders*, 103, 143-45.) It was this bombast in exaggerating his own role that caused the comic writer Mr. Dooley (Finley Peter Dunne) to write in a review of the book: "An' if Tiddy done it all he ought to say so an' relieve th' suspinse. But if I was him I'd call th' book 'Alone in Cubia.'" (Filler, ed., *Mr. Dooley, Now and Forever*, 107.) According-ing to one of the black soldiers involved in the pistol-pulling incident, they had been *ordered* to help in the rear, and the next day Roosevelt conceded that he had made a mistake and apologized. (Gatewood, *Smoked Yankees*, 92.)

William Henry Baldwin, Jr., to William P. Bancroft

New York. April 6, 1899

My dear Sir: Mr. Booker T. Washington has sent me your letter of the 27th. ultimo, in which you refer to the house being built for him, and he has also sent me a copy of his reply to you.

I beg to assure you on my part that I appreciate your great kindness in writing so frankly to Mr. Washington, and I am sure you will not feel that I am in any way impertinent if I write further to you on this subject.

As a Trustee of Tuskegee and one whose constant thought is upon the work of that Institution, you will I trust permit me to give you another point of view of Mr. Washington's house.

Mr. Washington has been living with his family in a house belonging to the Institute. Mrs. Walter Baker gave to his children the sum of $3,000., and Mrs. Baker's friends thought that it would be well for the children to have this money invested in a house. Mr. Washington therefore arranged to build a house for the use of his own family, to give up the house belonging to the Institute for the purpose of a library, and, further, to provide that the construction of the house should be made by the students of the Institute.

As every brick and every bit of wood work will be done by the students the money will have a three fold use. First: It will permit his present house to be used for a library; Second: Every dollar of the money will be paid to the students for work done on the building; Third: It will give a comfortable house to Mr. Washington for his own family and a place where friends of the Institute may be entertained while visiting Tuskegee.

I have often times publicly referred to the wise use of this personal legacy and I think it deserves much commendation.

There is another side to this also. Few know the enormous physical and mental work that Mr. and Mrs. Washington have been doing for many years. It is imperative that if we expect Booker Washington to live and to do good work, for him to have comfortable surroundings. The pressure of his work during the last few years has told much on his health and we are anxious to have him comfortably cared for, so that his health may be preserved for many years.

The great charm and strength of Booker Washington lies in his extreme modesty. His simple tastes and habits and the quiet strength of his modesty appeal very strongly to me.

I hope that this explanation coming from me will be well taken on your part, and that you will be able to agree with me that the building of his house, although, for Tuskegee, a large house, is very much to be commended.

I wish also to say that all funds contributed to this Institution are carefully audited and accounted for with detailed report to the Trustees; and that I have seen to it personally that a public accountant from New York shall keep in constant touch with the accounts and make audit of them to me each thirty days. Yours very truly,

[William H. Baldwin, Jr.]

TL Copy   Con. 792   BTW Papers   DLC.

A Report of a Letter in the New Orleans *Picayune*

New Orleans, La., April 9, 1899

BOOKER T. WASHINGTON

Advises the Negroes How to Avoid the Terrible Race Wars
They Should Cease Opposing the Southern Whites
And Help Build Up the States

Tuskegee, Ala., April 8. Prof. Booker Washington, answering the request of a prominent colored man in North Carolina as to what should be done to allay the present conflict between the races, clearly advises him to make alliance with the triumphant Democracy. Says the letter:

"I have been asking myself lately some rather serious questions, and I want to put one or two of them to you. Is there any reason why the negro in the south should continue to oppose the southern white man in his politics?

"Is not this the source of nearly all our troubles?

"Unconsciously we seem to have gotten the idea into our blood and bones that we are only acting in a manly way when we oppose southern white men with our votes.

"I believe that Governor Johnston, of Alabama, is just as good a friend to the black man as Hon. Wm. Youngblood, of Alabama. Hon. Wm. Youngblood has about 400 white followers. Hon. Joseph F. Johnston has 500,000 white followers in Alabama. Why should we longer follow Mr. Youngblood, with his 400 white followers, rather than Governor Jos. F. Johnston, with his 500,000 followers, when no principle is at stake?

"Why is it that the negro in Cuba has surpassed us in settling his race problem? Is it not because the negro in Cuba has made the white man's interest there his own?

"For example, suppose during the agitation of the freedom of Cuba, the negro had continued to espouse the cause of Spain, instead of the cause of the white man in Cuba, would not the white Cubans have grown furious against the black man in Cuba?

"In some way, by some method, we must bring the race to the point where it will cease to feel that the only way for it to succeed is to oppose everything suggested or put forth by the southern white men. This I consider one of our real problems. I confess that personally I have not brought myself wholly to the point that I should like to see the whole race get to, but I merely ask these questions to put you to thinking along these lines, if you have not already begun to do so.

"I believe that there are thousands of white Democrats in North Carolina who are 50 per cent better friends to the negro than Governor Russell,[1] and I see no necessity in continuing to follow Governor Russell, who has no power to protect, or if he has the power, does not exercise it, rather than these other white men who can protect us if we cease to continually and forever oppose them."

New Orleans *Picayune*, Apr. 9, 1899, 12.

1 Daniel L. Russell, Republican governor of North Carolina from 1897 to 1901. Russell was elected on a fusion ticket of Populists and Republicans, but he accomplished little for either blacks or white farmers.

To William McKinley

Tuskegee, Ala., Apr. 10, 1899

Dear Sir: Complying with your very kind request to submit some suggestions regarding the appointment of Census Supervisors in the South I would suggest that since it is your intention to make the Census taking non-partisan;

First, that two or three Democrats of high standing be appointed in each state;

Second, that two or three colored men who have business standing in their neighborhoods be appointed;

Third, that the remainder be white Republicans.

Some such plan in my opinion would avoid trouble and secure the cooperation of the South, and at the same time enable you to stand by those who have stood by your administration in the South. Yours respectfully,

[Booker T. Washington]

TL Copy   Con. 160   BTW Papers   DLC.

To the Editor of the Chicago *Tribune*

Tuskegee, Ala., April 10, 1899

I am not in politics and do not intend to enter politics. Matter reported by Associated Press related to what I wrote in a private letter not intended for publication.

Booker T. Washington

Chicago *Tribune*, Apr. 11, 1899, 9.

From John William Griggs[1]

Washington, D.C. April 13, 1899

Dear Sir: The President has referred to me your letter of the 8th inst. relative to the trial of the persons accused of lynching the colored postmaster[2] and his family at Lake City, South Carolina.

I am glad to inform you that this Department, in connection with the Postoffice Department, has spared no expense and devoted all possible time to ferret out the evidence that would justify the conviction of the guilty parties. I have employed as special counsel for the United States, one of the ablest lawyers in Charleston, and a man having a wider influence at the bar and among the better class of the people than any other I could find. The special inspectors and detectives have worked night and day for months to secure the evidence. If the prosecution fails, it will only be because the jury will not convict in the face of clear evidence. I assure you that the Government has done all in its power to punish these men. Respectfully yours,

John W. Griggs
Attorney-General

TLS Con. 154 BTW Papers DLC.

1 John William Griggs (1849-1927), former governor of New Jersey, was Attorney General under McKinley. Later he was a director of the Radio Corporation of America and other firms.

2 Frazier B. Baker of Florence, S.C., a black Republican, in 1898 was appointed postmaster at Lake City in Williamsburg County. White citizens objected to his appointment, and on Feb. 21, 1898, a mob of several hundred people set Baker's house on fire. As his family tried to escape the flames, they were gunned down. Baker was killed inside the burning house. His wife was shot in the arm, and the bullet killed the twelve-month-old baby she was carrying. Three other children were wounded.

In Apr. 1899 eleven men stood trial for murder in federal court, two turned state's evidence, three were acquitted, and the rest were freed because of hung juries. (Tindall, *South Carolina Negroes*, 255-56.)

From Samuel Laing Williams

Chicago, Apl 14 1899

My Dear Mr Washington   The enclosed is from the Chicago Tribune. I suppose the quotation is from your Birmingham Address.
I fail to see anything in any way different from that part of the address to the public by the Afro American Council in reference to
the politics. Some of the colored folks seem to be quite stirred up
by what they seem to think is a surrender on your part to all the
meaner forces in the South that are just now aiming at our disfranchisement.

I insist that your reference to politics is misread, misunderstood
and misinterpreted.

It may not be your policy to take notice of these things, but I
think a letter from you to the Tribune explaining your position
would clarify the fears suspicions and disappointments of some of
your would be friends. Yours truly

S. Laing Williams

ALS   Con. 164   BTW Papers   DLC.

From Francis Jackson Garrison

Boston, April 17, 1899

Dear Mr. Washington: I enclose herewith a check for $100. to
cover the expenses of yourself and Mrs. Washington to New York,
and also to enable you to procure such special clothing or baggage
as you may need for the journey. I also enclose three letters of introduction for your use in Paris, and think you will find all of them
serviceable to you.

The first is to M. Auguste Laugel, a French gentleman who was
long the secretary of the Duc d'Aumale, one of the sons of King
Louis Philippe. Mr. Laugel married a daughter of Mrs. Maria
Weston Chapman, one of the most prominent and able supporters
of my father in the anti-slavery movement. He is also the regular
Paris correspondent (about literary topics) of the New York Nation.

Mr. & Mrs. Laugel live in apartments in the Rue d'Anjou, and will certainly be glad to receive a call from you and your wife.

Mr. Theodore Stanton is the son of Mrs. Elizabeth Cady Stanton,[1] whose name is of course well known to you as one of the prominent leaders of the woman suffrage movement in this country, and is the correspondent of several American newspapers.

Theodore Tilton was for several years the editor of the New York Independent, but has lived in Paris for the last 25 years. He was a warm friend of Frederick Douglass, and will be heartily glad to become acquainted with you. Both he and Mr. Stanton can be of much help to you in telling you what to see in Paris and how to see it.

I shall send you other letters for your use in London before you sail. Yours very truly,

Francis J. Garrison

P.S. Mr. Tilton is the same whose name was so unpleasantly notorious in the Beecher-Tilton scandal in 1874, but that is a matter of the dim distant past. He was a warm anti-slavery man, & used to be an intimate visitor at my father's house in the war days.

TLS Con. 154 BTW Papers DLC.

1 Elizabeth Cady Stanton (1815-1902) was a pioneer of the women's rights movement. She was president of the National Woman Suffrage Association from 1869 to 1890 and co-editor of a prodigious *History of Woman Suffrage,* the first three volumes of which were published from 1881 to 1886.

From Timothy Thomas Fortune

Washington, D.C. April 18, 1899

My dear Mr. Washington: Cooper was here last night and said he had your interview in type, but had forgotten to bring me a proof as he had promised. He said he would fetch it around today.

Pledger is much better.

Please send me the title of the book by Helen Gardiner you said was so good.

I understand that the President has decided to give the white Democrats of the South half of the Census Supervisors in the Southern States. I am very much surprised, as I supposed he would give them all of them. I also understand that he intends to take care of the 14 regulars of ours promoted for gallantry at Santiago. If you can brace him up on this point it would be a great service for the race. Call his attention to the fact that you heard he was going to do it and thank him.

I am not sure that I can go to New York this week. Yours truly

T. Thomas Fortune

ALS Con. 154 BTW Papers DLC.

An Interview in the *Christian Endeavor World*

[Boston, Mass., Apr. 20, 1899]

A WASHINGTON OF TO-DAY

From Slave Boy to Race Leader

Character Has No Complexion

The interviewer of Booker T. Washington, the man who is destined to be "first in the hearts of his Afro-American countrymen," must be nimble of foot, and prepared to utilize every second of his allotted time like grains of precious gold, for the famous promoter of industrial education for Africans is as busy as a beaver. He travels from ten to twenty thousand miles in a year, and visits all the great cities of the land, making friends for his educational enterprise, besides supervising its operations.

My first question was the inevitable one, "When and where were you born?"

"I don't know when I was born. In the old slavery days they didn't think it worth while to record the day and hour when another negro baby was born. The earliest recollection I have is of clinging wonderingly to my mother's skirts and hearing her shout hallelujah because we were free. A picture of my ancestral home? Ha-ha! It was a common log cabin with a clay floor, down in Franklin County, Va. I remember the clay floor because I used to tumble around on it a great deal. It had no windows, but it had a door — that's about all it did have."

The story of his first-aroused thirst for knowledge is one that surely will inspire all of us.

"The thing that first led me to study," he said, "was, soon after slavery was ended, seeing a young colored man reading a newspaper to a group of colored people who surrounded him with gaping mouths and wondering eyes. He was almost a god to them. When I realized the power which this ability to read gave, I began to feel an ambition to know, too."

"And so you entered school?"

"Yes; such as it was. The teachers for colored children were sometimes almost as illiterate as their pupils."

THE EVOLUTION OF A NAME

There's an exceedingly picquant bit of boyish conceit connected with his registration at that school. He tells it charmingly.

"I soon noticed that the other boys had more than one name apiece. I had never known but the one — 'Booker.' So I told the teacher that I wanted two names, like the rest of the boys. Then she asked what my other name was, and, after scratching my head a second, I told her to put it down 'Washington.' Yes; I think I realized whose name I was taking."

Now comes a chapter of heroic struggles against odds. The lad worked in a coal-mine in West Virginia during the day and studied at night. Having outstripped the public-school teachers in knowledge, he hired private teachers. Sometimes he would walk miles to be taught, only to find that the teacher knew less than he himself did.

"How did you first hear of Hampton?" I asked.

"I overheard a man talking about it one day in the coal-mine. He said it was a school where one could work for his education. As soon as I heard that, I made up my mind it was just the place for me, and began, as far as I could, to make preparations to go. I had no money to amount to anything. When I started, I had no definite idea where it was, or how I was going to get there. I walked a good share of the way, rode a part of the distance on the train, and begged some rides. When I got as far as Richmond I had no money left, and I slept under the sidewalk for a number of nights, working during the day, unloading vessels or wherever I could get a job, until I earned enough money to pay my way to the Hampton

Institute. When I reached there, I had only fifty cents left, and I went to work again."

At Hampton Institute, young Washington had to stand a unique entrance examination.

"Of course," he said, "they knew nothing of me, and I presume that, after my long tramp and hand-to-hand encounter with poverty, my appearance was not very prepossessing. They didn't know whether to admit me or not, but they gave me a room to sweep. I guess I swept that room three or four times before I was satisfied. Then a teacher came in and took her handkerchief and wiped the walls to see if she could find any dust. After that, they said I could be admitted."

He continued to wield that same broom, to pay expenses, varying this sometimes with farm work. He showed the same quickness of intellect which had carried him ahead of his teachers at home. He kept well toward the head of his classes, being one of three or four students chosen to represent the class on commencement day. But the aptitude which most strongly manifested itself was that which to-day makes him rank among the foremost public speakers. When asked about school honors, he replied:

"Perhaps I won more honors in the debating society than in the class-room. The first question I remember discussing was whether or not the United States should own Cuba. I took the view that we should."

One of the most interesting things which Mr. Washington told me in all that interesting interview was about the beginnings of Tuskegee Institute, with its now thirty-seven buildings and thousands of acres of land. It was born in a little abandoned negro hut. In answer to the question, "How in the world did you ever conceive of such an institution?" he said:

"In 1881, while I was still at Hampton, the colored people in the town of Tuskegee, Ala., wrote to General Armstrong to send them a teacher. He asked me to go, and I went. I expected to find something in the way of a school, or preparations for a school; but I found nothing. So I began teaching in a little shanty, that I fixed up the best I could to make it a fit place. I remember that during the first two or three months I taught in it, it was in such a condition that whenever it rained one of the students had to hold an umbrella over me while I heard the recitations.

"After teaching this way awhile, the impression began to grow upon me that I was largely throwing away my time, trying to give these students a book education, without getting hold of them in their home life, and without teaching them how to care for their bodies, and inculcating in them habits of neatness, order, and industry. Here it was that I conceived the idea of such a work as has followed. I saw, too, that I must give my scholars an opportunity to earn something so that they could remain in school. They were so poor when they first came to me that they could stay in school only a month or two; then they would have to go out and work for a while to get something to eat and wear."

"Had you any capital to start such a school with?"

"I had unbounded enthusiasm. I began looking around to see if I could get hold of some land. I found a farm near Tuskegee that I thought would answer the purpose, but I couldn't buy real estate with enthusiasm, and I hadn't a cent of money. But my boldness led me to write to General Marshall, the treasurer of Hampton, and ask him to loan me $500 to make a payment on that farm; and to my unbounded surprise he sent me a check for what I asked, and I wasn't long in getting the school moved.

"Then I taught the boys and girls a part of each day, after which we would go out on the farm and clear it up and get ready to raise crops. That was the beginning."

"But please tell me how you have since managed to get all your buildings and the other thousands of acres of land."

"It's a long story. I'll tell you how we got our first building, though. We pitched in and built it ourselves — yes, sir; people scoffed, but we even made our own bricks. The point at which we stuck was the burning of the bricks — none of us knew how to fire a kiln. We had no money to hire labor, but we had to have those bricks, and I owned a gold watch which I took to the pawn-shop and got enough money to employ an experienced brick-maker to burn the bricks."

"That was a heroic measure, sure. No doubt you cherish that watch as a ————."

"I have never got that watch out of pawn yet, but we are now manufacturing a million bricks a year. That was a pretty poor sort of building, but we builded self-respect and manhood into it, and when white people saw what we could do, we won their respect.

Now we can put up a building that no one need be ashamed of. In our last building the steam-heating apparatus and the electric-light fixtures were put in by our own steamfitters and electricians. The plans were by an architect from our own school."

"But you promised to tell me how you added to your lands?"

"The last 25,000 acres came as a donation from Congress."

"No doubt you had to do some lobbying."

"Yes, I worked at it about a year. I think President McKinley's visit to Tuskegee helped us very much in getting the bill through."

"How do you like lobbying?"

"I'd rather hoe corn. It's terrible work."

When questioned as to having any inclinations to enter politics, Mr. Washington replied: "I have been urged often, and have been offered all sorts of inducements, but have invariably refused. I think, now, that the best course is to give the major part of our strength to getting education and Christian character. Very few of our graduates take to politics."

In proof of his opinion that the respect of the white man is to be won by the black man demonstrating business ability and becoming a property-holder, he tells this pithy story: "In a Southern city was a colored man that owned two or three houses and a good bank account. He had acquired an education, and a reputation for gentlemanly conduct. One day two white men passed him on the street and one of them said to the other, 'It's all I can do to keep from calling that nigger "Mister"!' "

"That is just what we are after!" exclaims Mr. Washington. "It's the respect we want, and mean to have, by deserving it."

A striking experience of his own triumphantly demonstrates that

Character Has No Complexion

"I had rather an interesting experience in Georgia some days ago," he said to me, his fine face lighting up with a look of satisfaction. "I was travelling from Augusta to Atlanta in a Pullman car. Although they have a separate car-service for colored people in some sections of the South, as a rule I have no trouble in getting accommodations on a Pullman car. Just as I entered the door, two ladies from Boston happened to meet me, and, recognizing me, asked me to go and sit in their section. While I sat there, they ordered supper, and invited me to eat with them.

"The car was full of Southern white men, who began to eye us curiously. But, knowing that the ladies were innocently offending and that I couldn't well explain the situation, I sat down and ate with them, conscious that it was likely to raise a storm. Afterwards I excused myself and went to the other end of the car. Meanwhile it became noised about in the Pullman who I was.

"Then, to my great gratification, almost every white man in that car came to me personally and took occasion to cordially thank me for the work I am trying to do for my people. If a man is really trying to perform an unselfish service for his kind, sooner or later the most prejudiced must come to recognize it."

"In other words," I suggested as a last shot, "we are coming to recognize the fact that character has no complexion."

"Exactly!" responded he; "and it is character that I crave for my people. That granted, all proper recognition will follow."

Christian Endeavor World, 13 (Apr. 20, 1899), 589–90. John F. Cowan was the interviewer. A photograph of BTW and his family appeared on the cover of this issue and several illustrations accompanied the text.

To Walter Hines Page

Tuskegee, Ala., Apr. 21, 1899

Dear Mr. Page: Dr. H. B. Frissell, principal of the Hampton Institute, is very anxious to have you take part at a conference to be held at the Capon Springs, West Virginia.[1] He will write you fully about the object and scope of this conference. It is to be held during the summer months and is the only meeting that brings together Northern and Southern white people to discuss in a free, helpful manner the matter of education in the South for both white and colored people. I very much hope that you will accept Dr. Frissell's invitation if you can see your way clear to do so. Yours truly,

Booker T. Washington

TLS   Walter Hines Page Papers   MH.

[1] The Capon Springs Conference for Christian Education in the South, founded in 1898 by Edward Abbott, was taken over in 1899 by Robert C. Ogden and some twenty-five guests from the North who arrived in his private Pullman car. Most of

them were sympathetic to the Hampton-Tuskegee approach to black education. When in 1901 they began to meet in the principal southern cities and formed an alliance with progressive white southern educators, the so-called Ogden Movement was born. Out of the conferences grew the Southern Education Board and the Rockefeller-funded General Education Board of overlapping membership. Philanthropy became cartelized as the Slater, Peabody, and later Jeanes, Phelps-Stokes, and Rosenwald funds were brought into close collaboration. The Ogden Movement stressed white public educational growth through local taxation, with only token attention to black schools, though the allied philanthropic foundations aided black institutions to alleviate the inequalities that the educational campaigns produced. (Dabney, *Universal Education in the South*, 2:3-73; Harlan, *Separate and Unequal*.)

To Warren Logan

[Tuskegee, Ala.] 4, 22, 1899

Mr. Logan: Mr. Scott will tell you about an important visitor[1] that is likely to come to Tuskegee at any time to represent Mr. John D. Rockefeller. He may make his business known when he comes and he may not.

B. T. W.

TLI   Con. 17   BTW Papers   ATT.

1 Frederick Taylor Gates.

To Charles G. Harris

[Tuskegee, Ala.] Apr. 22, 1899

Dear Mr. Harris: I received your letter of Apr. 20th in which you accept the proposition of the Finance Committee for service in this institution next year. That is, your salary is to be $750 for the school year with a suitable house. What you say regarding your boy will be all right.

There are one or two other matters connected with this work which I deem it proper to put before you at this time. I have thought about the matter a good deal and have definitely decided that I want an effort made hereafter to make more of a feature of the singing of the school. I am convinced that we cannot do a better service for our cause in the line of music than to make a thorough study of the older and newer plantation songs and let Tuskegee be a place where these songs are kept alive. I do not mean of course that all the singing is to be those of the plantation songs, but I want at least ½ or ⅓ of the singing by the school or choir to be of that character, and then I want to cultivate the singing of such Southern songs as the Old Kentucky Home, Swanee River, etc., more than we have in the past. Next year I want the choir enlarged to a considerable extent. We should have to get effective music in the chapel, a choir containing at least 150 members. I see no reason why we might not have this. In that case the larger proportion of the difficult singing could be done by the choir instead of by the whole school. In order to allow you to make a thorough study of the plantation songs and other music I shall be willing to arrange for you to have plenty of time to devote to the choir and singing by the whole school. When you were here before I think you were too much crowded with other duties to enable you to devote as much time to the choir and congregational singing as should have been the case. And then I am anxious that a larger number of instruments be used in connection with the choir. I wish you to consider carefully all of these requests and write me by return mail if possible. I think it best to have all these matters thoroughly understood before we reach a final agreement. Yours truly,

Booker T. Washington

TLpS   Con. 282A   BTW Papers   DLC.

A Statement on Lynching in the
Birmingham *Age-Herald*

Philadelphia, April 25 [1899]

I would like to speak at length upon these Georgia occurrences[1] and others of a like nature, which have taken place in recent years, but in view of my position and hopes in the interest of the Tuskegee Institute and the education of our people, I feel constrained to keep silent and not engage in any controversy that might react on the work to which I am now lending my efforts.

I think I can be of more service to the race by giving my time and strength in helping to lay the foundation for an education which will be the permanent cure for such outrages.

I don't mind adding that I am opposed to mob violence under all circumstances. Those guilty of crime should be surely, swiftly and terribly punished, but by legal methods. As a rule the men guilty of these outrages are ignorant individuals who have had no opportunity to secure an education and moral restraint.

The solution of our present difficulties is to be found in the thorough mental, religious and industrial education of both races in the south. It is an encouraging fact to note that of the hundreds of colored men who have been educated in the higher institutions of the south not one has been guilty of the crime of assaulting a woman.

Birmingham *Age-Herald*, Apr. 26, 1899, 2.

[1] The newspapers on Apr. 24 reported one of the most gruesome lynchings in American history. At Palmetto, Ga., Lige Strickland, a preacher, and a man named in news stories as Sam Hose (also called Sam Holt and Tom Wilkes) were burned by a mob of about 2,000 men, women, and children. After Hose's body was burned, the mob cut it into pieces for souvenirs. The charge against Hose was murder of a white man and rape of his wife, and Strickland was said to be a fellow conspirator.

BTW apparently drafted a letter of protest to the governor of Georgia but T. Thomas Fortune prevented him from sending it. (Harlan, *BTW*, 262-63; New York *Times*, May 11, 1899, 2; Scott to BTW, May 16, 1899, below.)

From Anonymous

Opelika Ala   April 28/99

Dear Sir: As a friend of your race, and as one who sincerely desires your success in the laudable work in which you are engaged, in educating and Christianizing your race, and believing as I do, that, holding the position that you do, an expression from you, in regard to the duty of your people on occasions of this kind, (I mean when rape is committed) would effect a great deal of good, I send the enclosed views of Gov. Chandler[1] of Ga. for your quiet consideration.

Without desiring to make a defense of the numerous lynchings which have occurred of recent years, good judgment and a sense of justice would seem to indicate that it is as much the duty of the colored as the white race to apprehend the criminal after such occurrences, but have they shown such a disposition? I ask this of you in the light of justice. Ask yourself the question, "What would probably be the effect of the Colored people joining the whites in their efforts to apprehend & have punished perpetrators of this heinous crime?" In my humble opinion, if they would do this, it would do more towards the suppression of this particular crime than anything else. While there are a great many hot headed & unreasonable men in our Country, you are doubtless aware of the fact that there are a great many good Christian men here among us, and their restraining influence would soon be felt in case the Colored people should join in their efforts to bring law breakers to summary Justice. In regard to the burning at Newnan last Sunday, I will say that I have not heard a single expression of approval of it since the occurrence, but every one has spoken of it as a barbarous & inhuman act.

As far as I am personally concerned I am heartily in favor of the education (Christian education) of your race, and of the Colored people protecting the chastity of their race. They should watch with great care their daughters, and immediately demand justice for the infraction of any law for the protection of a man's family. If the Colored people would pay more attention to this thing, the white people would respect them more, & they would grow in self respect.

These views are submitted for your consideration with the kindliest interest,

X X X
Anonymous

ALSr   Con. 149   BTW Papers   DLC.

1 Allen Daniel Candler (1834-1910) served successively in the Georgia state legislature (1872-81), in the U.S. Congress (1882-93), as Georgia secretary of state (1894-97), and as governor of Georgia (1898-1901). He supported educational reform, including tax exemption of college endowments and prompt payment of teachers' salaries. When the northern philanthropist Robert C. Ogden and his colleagues, the organizers of the Conference for Education in the South dedicated to improving southern public education, made their first foray into Georgia in 1901, Candler refused to attend their meeting in a black church in Atlanta. Candler was reported as saying he did not

"think much of" the purpose of the meeting. He supposed that BTW, "a good negro . . . doing pretty good work," attended the meeting to placate his northern benefactors. (Harlan, *Separate and Unequal*, 216.)

From Peter Jefferson Smith, Jr.[1]

Boston, Apr 28th 1899

My dear Mr. Washington   I have seen both Mr Clement and Mr Plummer.[2] I found Mr Clement as sound and solid as they come and expressed his disgust in the most positive manner for George W. Forbes[3] and has promised to give me his speech on that occasion[4] that I may send it to you after reading it for myself, he said Col. Hallowell[5] was like himself simply disgusted, he also said that he expected an interview with Fortune on Monday afternoon. Plummer is just wild and until this time he says he did not know the friends you have in Boston and when you return from your trip abroad he will see to it that your friends extend you such a welcome as no colored man ever had given him in this city or country he denounced Forbes at the League[6] as did I. D. Barnett.[7] I will tell you all about it when I see you.   Plummer says he will try and be in New York so as to see you off. I send you the papers having matter of interest. Faithfully Yours

P. J. Smith Jr

ALS   Con. 162   BTW Papers   DLC.

[1] Peter Jefferson Smith, Jr., in 1899 was employed by Tuskegee as northern "advance agent," though his duties also included activities against William Monroe Trotter and other Boston critics of BTW. He became a job printer and, with money from BTW, established a black newspaper, the Boston *Advocate*, to compete with Trotter's Boston *Guardian*. When the *Advocate* failed, Smith founded the Boston *Colored Citizen*, which also soon failed. At this point BTW brought Charles Alexander to Boston to compete with Trotter for subscribers. Smith had been a janitor or contractor for cleaning Boston office buildings. He later practiced podiatry in Boston and Washington, and secured through BTW's intervention several minor government clerkships in Washington. Never a successful or particularly useful lieutenant of BTW, Smith was characterized by his uncritical loyalty. (Fox, *Guardian of Boston*, 42, 46, 70-72.)

[2] Clifford H. Plummer, born in Virginia in 1861, was a black Boston lawyer and one of BTW's staunchest supporters. His loyalty extended to secret activities to undermine BTW's detractors. Plummer, for example, was the attorney for Bernard Charles, one of the defendants in the celebrated Boston Riot in 1903. During the trial Plummer secretly maintained contact with Tuskegee. Later he infiltrated Trot-

ter's New England Suffrage League as a spy for BTW, despite his public image of being one of the "radicals" in Trotter's camp. Plummer observed the first meeting of the Niagara Movement in 1905 as a spy for BTW and was probably instrumental in blocking press coverage of the meeting. (Harlan, "Secret Life of BTW," 407; Fox, *Guardian of Boston*, 74-77; Meier, *Negro Thought*, 238.)

3 George W. Forbes, originally of Mississippi, had attended Wilberforce University and then Amherst College, where he was a classmate and good friend of William H. Lewis. For several years he edited the black weekly Boston *Courant*, and beginning in 1897 was assistant librarian of the west branch of the Boston Public Library. In the fall of 1901 he joined William Monroe Trotter in founding the Boston *Guardian*, which became the focus of the sharpest criticism of BTW. The Boston Riot of 1903 and its aftermath, which included an effort by BTW's Boston friends to oust Forbes from his library position, caused Forbes to dissolve the partnership in the *Guardian*. He drifted to the center, occasionally even doing service for BTW and his followers, including a pamphlet for the Committee of Twelve. (Fox, *Guardian of Boston*, 29-30, 64-66.)

4 On Apr. 24, 1899, a group of Boston blacks met at Young's Hotel to commemorate the forty-eighth anniversary of Charles Sumner's election to the Senate. They were aroused and angered by news of the Sam Hose lynching in the Boston papers of that day. President McKinley's name was hissed, and BTW was "severely criticized." Butler R. Wilson, who presided, said: "We can no longer, with safety, allow men, however honest and earnest they may be, to lead us along dangerous paths. We seek to obtain rights, not to surrender them." George W. Forbes and Clement G. Morgan joined in the criticism, the latter saying that rights had never been won by compromise and invoking the spirit of Sumner. Edward H. Clement made an effort to defend BTW, but the climax of the evening was the call by two black war veterans for violent resistance and retaliation for lynchings.

William H. Lewis gave the principal speech. He said of the Tuskegee program: "The gospel of industrial education has been declared to be the negro's only salvation. If it is meant by this that through some mysterious process a trade will give to the negro all his rights as a man and citizen, it is a sufficient refutation of the theory to say that the South would not stand for it a single moment." (Boston *Transcript*, Apr. 25, 1899, 7; Boston *Morning Journal*, Apr. 25, 1899, 10.) This dinner should not be confused with an earlier dinner at Young's Hotel at which Fortune presided and BTW spoke. (See Fortune to BTW, Mar. 2, 1899, above.)

5 Probably Richard Price Hallowell (1835-1904), who spoke at the meeting, rather than Col. Norwood Penrose Hallowell, commander of the 55th Colored Regiment, who was unable to attend. Richard P. Hallowell, born into a prominent Quaker family, was a commission merchant, first in Philadelphia and later in Boston. He was a director of banks in Boston and Medford, Mass., where he resided. He was an abolitionist and was active in the woman suffrage movement. During the Civil War he departed from his Quaker pacifism to recruit troops for the black 54th and 55th Massachusetts Volunteers. After the Civil War he was active in supporting black schools in the South and was a trustee of the Calhoun Colored School in Alabama. Hallowell was also a student of history and published, among other works, *The Quakers in New England, The Quaker Invasion of Massachusetts*, and a pamphlet, *Why the Negro Was Enfranchised*. BTW relied on Hallowell to contribute to his secret campaigns against disfranchisement, Jim Crow cars, and peonage.

6 The Colored National League.

7 Isaiah D. Barnett attended the dinner but was not one of the speakers.

From Roger Nash Baldwin[1]

Wellesley Hills, Massachusetts. April 30, 1899

Dear Sir, I received your circular and letter a few days ago, and I wish to say that I am very sorry that it was necessary for you to send it. I meant to send my contribution a month ago.

I am only a school boy, but that, however, instead of lessening my interest in Tuskeegee, has made me feel more for fellow school boys and girls of the South. Also, my uncle, Mr. Wm. H. Baldwin Jr.,[2] is one of your trustees, and that, of course, adds interest. And also, my meeting you at his house in Brooklyn a year ago has tended to arouse more interest. Since then, my feelings have grown, and those of the family also, so we decided to send you the enclosed $20. wishing you better and better success. I am — Yours truly —

Roger N. Baldwin

ALS   Con. 792   BTW Papers   DLC.

1 Roger Nash Baldwin (1884–) was the nephew of William H. Baldwin, Jr. After graduating from Harvard in 1905 with an M.A. in anthropology, Baldwin became a social worker in St. Louis. He was one of the early leaders of the National Urban League and also supported the NAACP. During World War I he became a pacifist and served a prison term as a conscientious objector. He joined the American Union against Militarism, out of which grew the American Civil Liberties Union, of which he was for many years a dominant figure.

2 Emmett J. Scott sent Roger's letter to William H. Baldwin, Jr., who wrote back: "Enclosed *Private* — Don't tell Roger — It is very interesting to me." He also wrote across Roger's letter: "Noted with pleasure   WHB Jr." W. H. Baldwin, Jr., then passed the letter on to his father, who wrote: "Glad enough to read this! Roger is a very bright, smart lad. Thanks, Father   May 14." (Scott to Baldwin, May 8, 1899, Con. 792, BTW Papers, DLC.)

An Article in the *A.M.E. Church Review*

[Tuskegee, Ala., April 1899]

How I Came to Call the First Negro Conference

Soon after the Tuskegee Normal and Industrial Institute was opened, it was impressed upon my mind in several ways that a great deal of good could be accomplished by starting some movement which would interest the older people to the extent of putting them to work for their own elevation in a way that had not been started before.

This was first called to my attention by noticing on more than one occasion the unusual amount of common-sense displayed by what is termed the ignorant colored man of the South. Just here I would remark that it will interest any one who chooses to make a comparison; that he will find that the uneducated black man in the South, especially the one living in the country district, has more natural sense than the uneducated ignorant class of almost any other race. It was this that led me to the conclusion that any people who could see so clearly into their own condition and describe their own condition so vividly as was and is true with the common farming class of colored people in the South, could be led to do a great deal towards their own elevation. This caused me to call what is now known as the Tuskegee Negro Conference.

At first, I sent invitations to about 75 farmers, mechanics, school teachers and ministers to come and spend a day at Tuskegee, talking over their condition and needs. I was very careful to tell all who were invited that I did not want them to come prepared with any address or cut-and-dried speech. I very often find that when the average man is asked to prepare an address, too much time is spent in giving attention to rhetoric, and little sense is put into the address; so I was very careful to impress upon all who were invited, that we wanted no formal address, but wanted them to come and talk about the conditions and needs very much in the same way as they would do around their own firesides.

To my surprise, there came to this first conference 400 men and women of all grades and conditions. Of course, the bulk of people were farmers, mechanics and a very few scattering ministers and teachers. The morning of the first day was spent in having told in a plain and simple manner what the conditions were along industrial lines. We had each delegate, as far as he could, tell the number who owned their farms, the number who rented land, the number who lived in one-room log cabins, the number who mortgaged their crops, and we also asked as to the educational condition of the people. We had them tell whether or not they had a school house in their community, how long the school lasted, how much money was given towards its support, the kind of teachers, whether good or bad, whether or not the people made any attempt to extend the school term, after the time provided by the State fund had expired. We also gave attention to the moral and religious life of the people, having them state what kind of minister they had, whether he was in all respects satisfactory. Taking up the life of the teacher, we would have them give facts about their churches and Sunday schools.

We were surprised at the frankness and directness of the reports made by those who came to this first conference. In the afternoon we spent the time in hearing from these people as to what, in their opinion, would bring about remedies for the evils which existed and this, by far, was the most gratifying part of the conference. It was satisfactory to see how those concerned saw into their own condition and suggested the needed remedies for the evils reported in the morning. It was found that in what was known as the "Black Belt" of the South at least four-fifths of the people in many counties were living on rented land, in small one-room cabins, and at least four-fifths mortgaged crops for food on which to live and were paying a rate of interest on these mortgages that ranged from 15 to 40 per cent. per annum. The schools in most cases extended but three months and were taught, as a rule, in the churches or broken down log cabins or under a bush arbor.

Many of the reports showed that the majority of the ministers were moral and upright. When we were discussing remedies, there seemed to be a universal agreement that the thing that was most needed was intelligent, unselfish ministers and teachers who would live among the people and teach them how to improve their industrial, educational and religious condition. I remember that during the discussion one man said that the Negro had too many Sundays, that while the white man only had one, the Negro had two, meaning that he kept Saturday and Sunday. In a number of such remarks illustrations were given showing how the Negro could improve his present condition.

It may prove interesting to give the declarations adopted by the first Tuskegee Negro Conference:

1. The seriousness of our condition lies in that, in the States where the colored people are most numerous, at least 90 per cent

of them are in the country, they are difficult to reach, and but little is being done for them. Their industrial, educational and moral condition is slowly improving, but among the masses there is still a great amount of poverty and ignorance and much need of moral and religious training.

2. We urge all to buy land and to cultivate it thoroughly; to raise more food supplies; to build houses with more than one room; to tax themselves to build better school houses, and to extend the school term to at least six months; to give more attention to the character of our leaders, especially ministers and teachers; to keep out of debt; to avoid lawsuits; to treat our women better; and that conferences similar in aim to this one be held in every community where practicable.

3. More can be accomplished by going forward than by complaining. With all our advantages, nowhere is there afforded us such business opportunities as are afforded in the South.

We would discourage the emigration agent. Self-respect will bring us many rights now denied us. Crime among us decreases as property increases.

From the first we have insisted that these conferences were to be confined, in discussion, to matters which the people themselves had in their power to remedy, rather than to matters which the nation, as a whole, or the entire race could remedy. In thus confining the scope of the conference it has not been our intention in these discussions to take up all that was vital to the Negro race. We have appreciated the fact that other organizations could better discuss outrages perpetrated upon the race, the political rights of the race, etc. We have also insisted from the beginning that these conferences must be simple in their organization; that there must be almost no machinery, few officers, and a very short constitution. In fact, I don't think that during the eight years these conferences have been held, we have spent more than forty minutes in electing officers. There is no constitution for the government of these conferences; the only constitution is common-sense, and the thing which we have insisted upon in these conferences is that the rank and file of the people themselves must be permitted to do the talking. I have never permitted any one to lecture at these conferences, as during the days of slavery the Negroes were not permitted to come together, touch elbows and get ideas and inspiration from each other; and the matter of laying plans for the future was almost unknown to them. These conferences seem to give them the opportunity that they most desire and they make the most of it.

One of the most interesting features of these conferences is to hear a man get up and tell how four or five years ago he used to mortgage his crop and how he has gotten out of debt, in a plain and simple manner. Such lessons are listened to attentively by the remaining portion of the conference and are more inspiring than any lecture could be from some one who is far from the ranks of the mass of people.

The second conference was attended by some 800 persons, representing almost every section of the South. The attendance has increased each year until now we have from 2,000 to 3,000 delegates. I think that the most interesting thing in our last conference was when we gave the people an opportunity to tell in what way these conferences were beneficial to the masses of people. One man said that in his community before these conferences began only two persons owned land, but since the organization there are fourteen persons who own land; few live in one-room cabins, and very few mortgage their crops. He said that they had not only built a schoolhouse, but had extended the school term from three to six months.

It is a very common thing to hear these men remark that they have long since gotten to the place where no man who is not morally upright can be a preacher or teacher in their community. These few facts indicate the importance of having the right kind of men among the rank and file of the people.

The day following what is known as the Negro Conference we have what is known as the Workers' Conference, which is composed of teachers in the institutions in the South for higher education for the Negro. This conference was called because many lessons can be gleaned from the Negro Conference which ought to be discussed and put into practice by those who compose the Workers' Conference. This latter conference is attended every year by the oldest and some of the most important workers among the colored people in the South. The larger institutions are well represented. It all illustrates the growth which is gradually taking place. The last

Workers' Conference was spent in discussing the relation existing between the white man and the black man in the South. This meeting was held in the heart of that section, and the discussions were very liberal and most helpful.

We have had during the eight years of these conferences, some very important and prominent visitors.

In his visit to Tuskegee and in speaking of these conferences, President McKinley said:

"One thing I like about this institution is that its policy has been generous and progressive; it has not been so self-centered or interested in its own pursuits and ambitions as to ignore what is going on in the rest of the country, or make it difficult for outsiders to share the local advantages. I allude especially to the spirit in which the annual conferences have been held by the leading colored citizens and educators, with the intention of improving the condition of their less fortunate brothers and sisters. Here we can see an immense field and one which cannot too soon or too carefully be utilized. The conferences have grown in popularity, and are well calculated not only to encourage colored men and colored women in their individual efforts, but to cultivate and promote an amicable relationship between the two races — a problem whose solution was never more needed than at the present time."

Out of this central conference at Tuskegee has grown a large number of local conferences which are organized in the various counties and which meet monthly for the improvement of the people from industrial, religious and moral standpoints. The most important meeting of a similar character is one in the State of Texas under the leadership of Hon. R. L. Smith. This movement in Texas, embracing very much the same idea as the one started at Tuskegee, is growing in its scope and importance each year, and one of the most interesting and valuable features of Tuskegee conferences is the report which Mr. Smith makes of the growth and spread of his work in Texas.

Aside from the direct benefit which the Negro is receiving from these conferences, it is very plain that they are having indirect influence in bringing about more satisfactory relations between the black man and the white man. A movement of any kind which assists in uplifting the Negro will receive the hearty support of the best class of white people of the South who are fast learning that they cannot go much higher than they can carry the Negro with them.

Booker T. Washington

A.M.E. Church Review, 15 (Apr. 1899), 802–8.

From Timothy Thomas Fortune

New York, May 2, 1899

My dear Friend: I got your telegram on returning from Washington and went to Boston Sunday night, and am just back. Monday morning I saw a great many of our men and tested them indirectly as to the prevailing sentiment, and I discovered that the course of the Young's Hotel banqueters was generally condemned and disproved.

I then went to see Barnett[1] and Plummer. They are both out for blood, and will renew the fight in the League next Monday night. I outlined the sort of resolution they should offer at the meeting and they are sure it will go through. They are both good friends of yours, as is also Addison of the Courant, with whom I spent an hour. I met Rev. C. S. Morris[2] in the Courant office, and he is also doing good work.

My appointment with Mr. Clement was for 3 o'clock. He was all smiles and graciousness and plunged right into the subject of the banquet. He said he was much grieved at the attitude of the speakers, but that he had unlimited faith in your wisdom and discretion and that he did not think the matter would hurt you in the least in Boston. He promised to publish anything I should write on you or any phase of the race question. P. J. Smith called while I was talking to Mr. Clement and remained with me until I left the depot at 5 o'clock for New Haven. Yours truly

T. Thomas Fortune

Our newspapers are still reading the riot act to you.

ALS Con. 154 BTW Papers DLC.

1 Isaiah D. Barnett.

2 Charles Satchell Morris was born in Louisville, Ky., in 1865. After attending Howard University from 1886 to 1889 and the University of Michigan Law School in 1893, he studied at Newton Theological Institution from 1895 to 1898. Simultaneously he was pastor of the Myrtle Baptist Church in West Newton, Mass., from the time of his ordination in 1896 until sometime in 1899. During 1899-1900 he was a missionary in Liberia and South Africa. He was pastor of the Abyssinian Baptist Church in New York City from 1901 to 1908 and of the Bank Street Baptist Church in Norfolk from 1911 to 1916. In the 1920s he was president of the Boydton Academic and Bible Institute in Virginia.

Like many other professional men of the period, Morris fluctuated between support of BTW and the more militant position of the Niagara Movement. At the Afro-American Council meeting in 1903, Morris said: "Samson slew the Philistines with the jawbone of an ass. The little crowd from Boston has the same weapon, but does not know how to use it. . . . The shallows may roar, but the great deeps of Negro manhood believe in Booker Washington and are proud to trust and follow him." (Extract from the Louisville *Evening Post*, July 3, 1903, quoted in Scott to BTW, July 7, 1906, Con. 327, BTW Papers, DLC.) In 1906, on the other hand, he said in an address at Faneuil Hall in Boston: "I believe Booker T. Washington's heart is right, but that in fawning, cringing and groveling before the white man he has cost his race their rights and that twenty years hence, as he looks back and sees the harm he has done his race, he will be brokenhearted over it." (Mathews, *BTW*, 282-83.) Later that year, however, Morris reversed himself, saying: "I have reached the point where I am through fighting black men. Hereafter I shall devote my energies and thought to the fighting of the enemies outside of the race." ("A Clarion Call from Dr. Charles S. Morris," news release, ca. Oct. 1906, Con. 327, BTW Papers, DLC.) Morris wrote Washington that his change of heart was the result of Washington's courage and leadership at the Atlanta Riot "in that supreme hour when leadership was imperative." (Morris to BTW, Nov. 7, 1906, Con. 327, BTW Papers, DLC.)

From George Bruce Cortelyou[1]

Executive Mansion   Washington, D.C. May 6, 1899

My dear Sir: I beg leave to acknowledge the receipt of your letter of the 3rd instant in behalf of the appointment of Prof. Jesse Lawson as a member of the United States Commission to the Paris Exposition, and to say that by direction of the President it has been brought to the attention of the Secretary of State. Very truly yours,

> Geo. B. Cortelyou
> Assistant Secretary
> to the President.

TLSr Con. 151 BTW Papers DLC.

1 George Bruce Cortelyou (1862-1940), of Hempstead, Long Island, rose from stenographer to cabinet member. After graduation from the Massachusetts State Normal School at Westfield, he worked as a stenographer in the New York customs house. In 1891 he moved to Washington to work in the Post Office Department, and in 1895 he became a White House secretary under presidents Cleveland, McKinley, and Roosevelt. In 1903 Roosevelt appointed him Secretary of Commerce and Labor, and in 1904 he managed Roosevelt's presidential campaign. After the election he became Postmaster General, and in 1907 Secretary of the Treasury. He returned to New York as head of the Consolidated Gas Company (1909-35).

From Josephine Redding[1]

New York City   7 May/99

Dear Sir: You may or may not know me as the editor of The Art Interchange and later as the editor of Vogue. I am still connected with the latter paper. Thus much for introduction. I am interested in the negro race, but heretofore have taken no active part in furthering its development.

Du Bois's article in the January *Atlantic* the Negro Schoolmaster in the South — was the subject. I dont recall whether that was exact title, made a great impression upon me and naturally the Hose[2] incident in Georgia has horrified me.

I have written an editorial on the cruel position of the negro, but of course that will not be remembered long enough after reading to be translated into action. I should like to demonstrate the negro's capacity for conscientiously performed needed work.

If I should start a laundry on a large scale, under social patronage here in New York and administer it myself, i.e. be its manager, would some girl graduates of Tuskegee be willing and capable of being book-keeper, shipping clerk, laundresses? The idea has just come to me and I have not as yet laid the scheme before capitalists.

Theres room for a well conducted, no-chemicals-used laundry and beside being a necessity the oddity of a laundry being run by a literary woman and the social influence I have would be additional reasons for its success.

I have a thorough training in the commercial side of life, and can keep books as well as I can correct copy or write editorials.

I want to start the laundry in any event and it occurred to me that I would ask you if I could make it an opportunity to practically aid the negro girl.

My idea would be to pay them a little above the usual wage and to give them annually a percentage of the profits, not very large perhaps, but still if the enterprise succeeded at all, it would be an appreciable am't. I want the best class of negro girl that I can obtain and the most capable and I want all the positions of every kind to be filled by negro girls — unless perhaps that of drivers.

As to the care of the girls here — you could probably give me the address of some educated negro preacher in New York whose wife and himself could confer with me as to the best environment to give the girls after working hours.

Please regard this letter as confidential and will you let me know at your earliest convenience whether you regard the scheme as feasible so far as the negro girls are concerned? The enterprise will be a business one not philanthropy so that no girl need feel patronized. Very truly yours

Josephine Redding

ALS   Con. 160   BTW Papers   DLC.

1 Mrs. Josephine Redding was the founder and first editor of *Vogue* from 1892 to 1907. She had earlier edited *Art Interchange* and *Home Decoration*. She was active in the Society for the Prevention of Cruelty to Animals. A colleague described her as "a violent little woman, square and dark, who in an era when everyone wore corsets, didn't." She was otherwise conventional, however, and had the support of the New York social elite. Her greatest coup was gaining permission to sketch Consuelo Vanderbilt's lingerie trousseau. Edna Woolman Chase wrote of her: "Mrs. Redding always wore a hat in or out of the office, and once when she was ill in bed, she received one of her staff in her nightgown and a hat. She would come bursting into the small office, indignant, a depressed cat in her arms, talking about how she had accosted a man beating a dray horse, how she had hauled him off to the police station." (Chase, "Fifty Years of *Vogue*.")

2 The Sam Hose lynching.

To William McKinley

Tuskegee, Alabama, May 9th, 1899

Sir: I very much hope that you can retain in the Regular Service as Paymaster, Major Manley B. Curry,[1] who is the son of Doctor J. L.

M. Curry, the Secretary of the Slater & Peabody Educational Fund.

Doctor Curry, his father, has given the last twenty years to this work, and my race has no truer or better friend. He stands for purity of elections and for all that is best in Southern life. Respectfully,

Booker T. Washington

TLS   Adjutant General's Office Document File   Con. 648   RG94   DNA.

1 Manly Bowie Curry (1857-1907) was born in Talladega, Ala. After three years' service as an additional paymaster of volunteers, Curry was appointed captain and paymaster in the U.S. Army. In 1905 he was promoted to major and in 1907 was killed in an automobile accident in Atlanta in the line of duty. BTW renewed his efforts for Manly Curry on his return from Europe in 1899, for which J. L. M. Curry warmly thanked him. (J. L. M. Curry to BTW, Aug. 15, 1899, Con. 151, BTW Papers, DLC.)

From Allen W. Turnage[1]

Philadelphia   May 9th, 1899

My Dear Sir: It is from a sense of profound respect for you and interest in my Race, that I take this opportunity to write you a few lines, the object of which is to endorse your policy and profound judgment in dealing with the Race Problem of the South. To my mind, you have found the channel, and the only one that will float the Negro's ship. Your policy appeals not only to the Duty of this Nation, but to the Negro himself, for without the Negro be the chief actor, outside aid can do him no more good than one man drinking medicine to save another; and what is true in financial aid is also true in moral and political aid. We have had the plainest evidence as to the result of his political gift, that was saddled on him many years before he had the faintest knowledge how to better his condition by its aid; or how to keep it from working against his children (thirty years later). Looking at man as human, and not as a saint, you know and I know that the actions of the Negro in politics toward his neighbors is the chief cause of his political downfall in the South. At no time in the history of our political career has the Negro ever been advised along lines of moral suasion by any of the political leaders (in fact it has not been to the interest of the leaders to take that course); as they were all in it for what they could get out of it, but no doubt many of them would have carried the interest of their Race with them, had it been possible to have done so by their policy. But, his first movements in politics are things of the past, never to be fastened on him again, without his actions — his political power is in his own hands, and those who desire to see him clothed with political power (which he ought to be) should point him to a natural fountain — just as you do as to his industrial development — that is to let the dead past bury the dead and deal with what is, by using our God given power more and looking to legislative power less. By so doing, legislative power will come far quicker, if not to us, to our children — in fact, legislative power will never come to us, we must go to it, and since we have no outward organized force to fight our way, the only thing at our command is moral suasion. Not in the sense of a slave, but in the sense that a merchant uses toward his patrons. In writing to you I call your special attention to the very important fact that while many of our Race in the North appreciate your attitude as to the general betterment of the Race in the South, and the manner in which you are trying to attract consideration toward the black man of the South, yet there is a large number of them, and I think I am safe in saying three fourths of them, do not agree with your course in bringing the Race out of their present condition, and when I state the facts to you, you will not be surprised at them, but wonder why any of them should agree with you. I have lived in this City twenty five years, and have been associated with many public movements, looking to or having for their object the betterment of the Race in this City, and in the South. I have attended nearly all of the large Race meetings, politically and otherwise. I have been a close investigator of the political, social and industrial movements of the Race in this City and my business as a tradesman has enabled me to have a wide knowledge of the Race, and when I speak of the Negro I speak of his production, which demonstrates what he really is, and not what he says he is. When I say that so far as an upward tendency toward a higher development in Civil Government, the educated Negro of the North is precisely in the same groove with the illiterate Negro of the South, and as to Race elevation by patronage of Race enterprise, he is behind the illiterate class in the Northern cities. We have had four changes in Municipal and State Government in this City and State in the past fifteen years, and these changes were the work of the better element of the white Republican and Democrats, while all of the colored men, almost to a man, voting against the Reform, for party reason only. A well educated colored man of respectability ran for Representative in a Ward of three thousand colored voters last fall, and failed to get three hundred voters, and the only excuse was the fact that he ran independent. This Ward contains the centre of education and wealth of the Race in this City. Of the three thousand only about fifty are employed in political jobs, and the majority of that number are laborers. Now, in this black belt known as the Seventh Ward, in which resides a large number of wealthy and well off men and women of the Race, outside of barber shops, undertakers, liquor saloons and gambling dens, there is not a single creditable retail store, or any other industry of note carried on by the Race. In this Ward I have seen more than fifty stores (some of them first class) set up only to fail in short order, for the want of Race patronage, and yet they will tell you that their political attitude is for the interest of the Race. Several years ago a rich philanthropist of the Episcopal Church organized a body of colored men and formed a Club,[2] which had for its object social, industrial and moral development of the Race in this City, and more especially the young colored men coming from the South, as an attraction against the influence of the slums — a higher Institution looking to the needs of the newly emancipated Negro never was organized. The membership of that Club contained the representative value of the Race in this City. It was composed of men coming from every station and grade — from laborers to men of thousands. Illiterates, educated and graduates from two and three colleges, and the best business men of the Race. It existed about twelve years, but seven years of that time it existed only in name, and would not have existed two years had it not been for the ardent zeal and money of that rich white man. When he saw that they would not pay their dues so as to keep the Club up, he bought the building and willed it to the Organization, but as soon as he died the Club went down, and the building sold for the Club's debt. Two of its Presidents were appointed diplomats to represent this Country in Foreign Courts, but had no ability to deal with a Court at home. This Club at one time was seven hundred members strong and four hundred were delinquent at one time, at only fifteen cents a month. During the existence of this Club we had some of the ablest instructors in the land to lecture to us in the needs of the Race present and future, in the line of industry and ethical culture, and the very thing that is taking place in the South now, was pointed out to us sixteen years ago. We were plainly told what would surely take place in the near future if the morals of the Race were neglected. Many of our Ministers were members of this Club and were at these Lectures. Our colored politicians were there, but what did they do, and what have they done since the Club went down? They were advised to send a number of our educated young men in the South to take up a line of useful work, and make a mark for themselves and help the Race. If that Organization had been kept up they would have been in a position to call a large number of the better element of whites together in this City and voice their own sentiments, instead of finding fault with you, because you were wise enough not to lay aside your cause and deal with criminality of the South; they not only oppose your attitude in not attacking the South while in this City, but a large number of them are opposed to your attitude in the South, for the same reason, the truth is, as I told you a few years ago that the true condition of the white and black man of the South has never been considered from a common sense standpoint along the line of political economy, ethical culture and natural laws, the fundamental structure upon which all Races and Nations must rise or fall. The Negro has never been directed toward these principles by his political nor christian advisers. The politicians have pointed him to prejudice and the cruel side of slavery; the clergy have pointed him to vicarious atonement, and he seeks no redress outside of those two channels. He will rise just in proportion as he gets out of these two grooves. I do not believe that he should not believe in God, but believing in vicarious atonement and miracles is one thing, and believing in the efficacy and universality of God is another. The Negro's religious views, and his idea of politics go hand in hand against his progress, and to my mind your idea of education is doing more to bring the Race near to God and political power in reality, than the whole Negro Clergy combined. I know that you cannot openly deal with the delusion of the clergy at this stage, and I hope and trust you will not allow the clergy nor the Negro politicians to move you one inch. Receive their help and encouragement, such as they are able to give along lines of common sense and political economy and natural law, but their folly never!

I have shown you the attitude, politically and industrially, of your Race in this City. Are they in a position to criticise your work, or to dictate what you should say, North or South? In the North they are free to vote and the vote counted. But do they act any different from the illiterate class in the cotton fields of the South? Can the South look to examples of the Negro of the North, and say if we give the Negro equal rights to vote, he will divide his vote and vote for whatever in his judgment benefits the community? The actions of the Negro all over this Country, is a City upon a hill, and he cannot hide. He may hide himself from his Race, who do not hunt him up along all lines, but he cannot hide his political and moral value when weighed in the public scales, and appealing to past conditions will not make the required weight. I am Respectfully yours

Allen W. Turnage

P.S. if your work is publicly attacked, there is a few of us that has not stooped to belive, stand Ready to meet the attack — the writer is a member of Rev. Jos. J. May's[3] Church 21ist and Chesnut st. May God help you to stand firm. Knowing that all the Reforms that have benefited mankind has been opposed at the start and that is one of the sureist evidence that you are in the Right.

supplement

in portra[y]ing the weaker side of the Race in this City I do so not from will but from a sense of Duty in doing what ever I can to prevent any thing that tends to Impede the only proper measure that has been started in the true interest of the black man of the South since the war. For every act and so called gift where the Negro has not been the chieft actor himself, has been a dark failure. The Negro's gifts has all been promissory notes, with no money in bank to pay them when due. In stating that $3/4$ of the Race in this city are a gainst your course in dealing with the Race problem of the South, I wd. not have you to understand that they are a gainst industrial training to that number ($3/4$) for more than half of them I think a gree with your course in that direction, but the larger number opposes your attitude in trying to bring the white and black man to gather in friendly Relation a long all lines by submission and moral suasion upon the part of the Negro. That to my mind is the greatest, grandest and most Godly part of your work, for all other stands for naught, if you leave behind you the spirit of hell to strike it down as you and every common sense man know has been the case with every so called Negro gift. Negro gifts has been weighed and found wanting, and the time has come for Negro creation or he must go down. Nearly all that has been done by the Race for good or evil has been the Result of the Ex-slave. The progress of the Race since the war has been held up by the vacilators and the dishonest thinking element as being entirely the out come of freedom. Now if the Race acquired no fitness in the 2 hundred and 45 years of slavery to an Able them to make that progress, how can slavery be charged with the present condition of the Race. Since slavery had no effect on the higher side of man, how could it have any on the lower side, except it be that the Negro had no quality to Rec'd only that which was low — and if that was true why should he of been set free to be come a public pest and a curse to himself. The truth is, that whole argument is vacilation upon the part of the educated thinker and profound Ignorance and desire, with them who are fed on delution. These arguments have all aimed at the white man of the South, but the effect has fell on the poor Negro. To tell the plain truth about how (this boasted progress) was made wd. Reflect credit on the South (and hence the sophistry) but has that course benefited the Race? To tell of the cruelty of slavery before the war, when it was for the object of destroying that institution was a Righteous act. But to tell down Rite lies to day for political ends for the Politicians and church popularity for the clergy is all wrong and hellish, and the eviel effect falls on the Negro, for every stone thrown at the white man of the South if it misses him, it will surely hit the Negro. The progress of the Race emanated largely from what they gained in slavery, and the evil condition of [the] Race to day is largely due to the neglect of the ex-slave who had neither the time nor knoledge to Raise their children with moral qualities So as to wholely a void the increase[d] Immorality that has sprung up with the children of the ex-slave. Man Reaps that which he sews, and not knowing the Seed is no excuse for natural law. From ever[y] quarter the Negro has been fed on delution. What can be exspected of his children. If he has been neglected the Result is sure.

TLS Con. 163 BTW Papers DLC. The postscript and supplement were autograph.

1 Allen W. Turnage, according to the 1900 census, was born in North Carolina in 1846. He was a stove-maker and dealer, married, with five children. He had lived in Philadelphia since the 1870s, and was still there in 1911.

2 The Civic Club of Philadelphia was organized about 1887 by a white philanthropist. It made a study of the work and wages of domestic servants and another of charity organizations that discriminated against blacks. (Du Bois, *Philadelphia Negro,* 356, 430, 445, 449.)

3 Joseph May (1836-1918) was pastor of the First Unitarian Congregational Society of Philadelphia from 1876 to 1901. The son of the Massachusetts abolitionist Samuel Joseph May, he graduated from Harvard College in 1857 and from Harvard Divinity School in 1865. Many years before the social gospel movement he sought to give religion a public as well as a personal application. He was active in the promotion of black education in Philadelphia.

From William H. Hurt

Montgomery, May 11th 1899

Dear Sir, Your telegram of date, yesterday, received. While your telegram is sent from N.Y. I send this letter to Tuskegee, not knowing how long you will remain in N.Y. and supposing this will be forwarded you from Tuskegee.

A Bill[1] has been introduced by Col Bulger[2] of Tallapoosa for an amendment to the constitution, having the object in view you mention in Telegram.

I have the honor to be on a Joint Committee of senate & House having this and other Amendment Bills under consideration, and I now state I shall do all in my power to prevent these Bills reported favorably, and am of the opinion that at least, the one you refer to will be defeated in the committee, and so far as I am concerned all of them.

I agree with you in this matter. Very truly

W H Hurt

ALS Con. 175 BTW Papers DLC.

¹ At a special session of the legislature, and again at the constitutional convention later in May, Col. Thomas L. Bulger introduced measures calling for separate elementary schools for black and white children, with only the taxes of black citizens to go to the support of black schools. Both measures were defeated.

² Thomas Lafayette Bulger (1855-1930), the son of a Confederate brigadier general, was born in Dadeville, Tallapoosa County, Ala., and practiced law there after attending Roanoke College and West Point. An active Democrat, Bulger was a state senator from 1886 to 1887 and in 1915, and a member of the state house of representatives from 1898 to 1902 and in 1908. In 1901 he represented Tallapoosa County at the state constitutional convention.

To Timothy Thomas Fortune

On Board *S.S. Friesland.* May 12[15], 1899

My dear Mr. Fortune: We are now five days out at sea¹ and have had a very smooth sail. Mrs. Washington has been somewhat sick, but I have been able to appear at meals three times a day. We are hoping to reach Antwerp, Belgium, Saturday.

I write just a line now to say that I very much hope that you will postpone the meeting of the National Council until some time in September. If it occurs in August I feel quite certain that I can be of almost no service to you. Besides, most of the people are out of Chicago in August, and it is a difficult time to get a proper hearing.

I cannot return to the United States before the 6th or 7th of August and then I have some immediate engagements which will take my time for nearly two weeks.

Please send the AGE to me at the address given below.

Mrs. Washington and I both desire to be remembered to Mrs. Fortune. Very sincerely,

Booker T. Washington

Address: c/o Brown Shipley & Co., London, England.

TLS   Con. 160   BTW Papers   DLC.

¹ In fact BTW sailed on May 10, according to the Red Star Line advertisement in the New York *Times,* May 10, 1899, 13.

To John Henry Washington

On Board *S.S. Friesland.* May 12[15], 1899

Dear Brother: We are now five days out at sea and have had, so far, an excellent passage. Mrs. Washington has been somewhat sick each day but nothing serious. We plan to reach Antwerp, Belgium, Friday night or Saturday morning, where I hope to mail this letter.

I suppose you have heard that the Misses Stokes have decided to give us the new industrial building for the girls? It is important that we take advantage of these new buildings as fast as possible. If we delay putting them up too long, people will be inclined not to help us this way and the way they otherwise would. Please see that no pains are spared to make all the brick this summer that it is possible to make. That is the most important thing. In case you could get enough men it might pay to have two sets of hands for the brick-yards during the summer. You will have to make a great deal of allowance for rainy weather. The only way out will be to push the brick-yard with a tremendous force while you do have good weather.

I think it well for you and Mr. Logan to arrange with Mr. Taylor in some way to draw the plans for the girls' Industrial building. This building should contain a large room for washing, one for ironing, one for drying, and it seems to me, a room for recitation. You understand that the old laundry is to be moved into this new building. With steam machinery, however, I am sure that half the space which the present laundry occupies will do for the new laundry.

This building should also contain rooms for two modern kitchens, two model dining-rooms, two model bed-rooms, two model sitting rooms, a large room for dressmaking, one for millinery, one for plain sewing, and small offices for the teachers in connection with these different divisions. It should also contain a small reception room, plenty of closets and pantries, etc. I do not want it to be more than two stories high, and should be so built that we can add to it at any time we see proper.

It will not be necessary to begin the erection of this building before I return home, but I want the plans to be all ready, as I wish to show them to the Misses Stokes in August. All told, this building must not cost more than twelve thousand dollars — less, if possible. It will therefore be necessary for Mr. Taylor to study how to make it cheap and plain, but good and substantial. It must, at the same time, contain plenty of room, that is, the rooms must not be too small. Just as far as possible, I want you to secure graduates to help work on these new buildings. Your brother,

Booker T. Washington

TLS Con. 17 BTW Papers ATT.

From Francis Jackson Garrison

Boston, May 15, 1899

Dear Mr. Washington: Miss Mason has just sent me the enclosed letter from Mr. Higginson, who sent it to her, not knowing your address. I hope you are having an enjoyable voyage, and that the sea has had no terrors or discomforts for you and Mrs. Washington. I had a call on Saturday from Peter Smith, who reported your going off and brought me your parting word.

I have a letter this morning from Mrs. Moore[1] of London, recommending Smith's West Central Hotel. I forgot to suggest that you write to London a week or two before you go there, or as soon as you know the date, and engage your room at the Hotel. Mrs. Moore speaks of her intention to bring you in contact with Mr. Fox Bourne,[2] the agent of the Aborigines Protection Society,[3] an English society which for many years has done excellent service in looking vigilantly after the interests of the weaker races of the British possessions in India, Africa, etc.

I mailed you on Friday the report of the Boston meeting to protest against the recent lynchings at the South. It was largely attended, and altogether successful. Grimke's[4] address, which was very good, is given in full.[5] With best regards to Mrs. Washington, Yours very truly,

Francis J. Garrison

TLS Con. 154 BTW Papers DLC.

1 Mrs. Rebecca Moore, then eighty years old, was a longtime friend of Frederick Douglass, whom she met in England in 1845 and visited in Washington in 1888.

2 Henry Richard Fox Bourne (1837-1909) was born in Jamaica, where his father, a fervent reformer, had been sent to oversee the freeing of former slaves. Bourne's family moved to British Guiana in 1841 and then to London in 1848. While a clerk in the war office, Bourne maintained an active journalistic and literary career, writing books and articles for radical journals. In 1870 he resigned his government position and for some years edited the radical working-class *Weekly Dispatch*. In 1889 he became the secretary of the Aborigines Protection Society and editor of its journal, *Aborigines Friend*, positions he held until his death twenty years later. At the society, Bourne worked for tribal rights, land ownership, and sharing local wealth equally with whites. He never opposed colonialism, but he was against its economic and social exploitation, arguing that the mother country was obliged to nurture and preserve native culture and institutions.

3 The Aborigines Protection Society was organized in 1837 by members of a parliamentary committee to investigate the condition of aboriginal peoples in British colonies. The society frequently worked with the British Anti-Slavery Society, also organized about this time.

4 Archibald Henry Grimké (1849-1930) was the son of a wealthy white planter, Henry Grimké, and a slave mother, Nancy Weston, near Charleston, S.C. Manumitted on the father's death in 1852, the family moved to Charleston, where a white half-brother, Montague Grimké, attempted to re-enslave them. Archibald and his brother Francis escaped in 1863 and hid with a free black family until the end of the Civil War brought their freedom. The two brothers attended Charleston schools and then entered Lincoln University in Pennsylvania. After their graduation in 1870, Archibald remained at Lincoln as librarian, earned a master's degree in 1872, and then attended Harvard Law School, graduating in 1872. He established a law practice in Boston.

In 1879 Archibald Grimké married Sarah Stanley, a white woman, who bore his only child, Angelina Weld Grimké, a writer and teacher. A versatile man, Grimké edited a black newspaper in Boston, the *Hub*, from 1883 to 1885, was president of the American Negro Academy from 1903 to 1916, wrote biographies of William Lloyd Garrison and Charles Sumner, and was consul in Santo Domingo in the second Cleveland administration.

On his return to the United States, Archibald Grimké took up the cause of black suffrage. He sent an open letter to President McKinley urging him to use federal authority to prevent disfranchisement. Through the Afro-American Council, the Committee of Twelve, the New England Suffrage League, the Niagara Movement, and finally the NAACP Grimké carried on his fight. He oscillated between the BTW conservative camp and the militants in search of an effective movement for black rights. He began to spend part of each year in Washington with his brother Francis, minister of the Fifteenth Street Presbyterian Church. After the Brownsville episode in 1906, Archibald Grimké made a definite break with BTW. He and his brother were among the founders of the NAACP. Archibald Grimké was president of the Washington branch of the NAACP in its first decade, leading the fight against segregation of federal office workers in the Wilson administration. He received in 1919 the Spingarn medal, awarded annually by the NAACP for "the highest and noblest achievement of an American Negro."

5 Archibald H. Grimké denounced southern outrages against the Negro in a protest meeting at the People's Temple in Boston on May 9, 1899. "A nation as an in-

dividual reaps exactly what it sows," he said. The South now, through the racial aggressions of the white masses, was reaping the violence that the aristocratic class had sown in the 1870s as a means of regaining political control of the South. "What is the life of a negro worth when the mob hounds are thirsting for negro blood?" Grimké asked. He urged his audience to turn from suicidal apathy, for otherwise the mob would eventually destroy civilization in the North as it was already doing in the South. In an impassioned utterance he warned: "O, my country, my country, every drop of blood drawn by southern mobs from the negro will be required at thy hands, and every groan, all the piled-up agony and wrongs of this simple and patient people will be exacted of thee in the coming years when thou shalt be judged and found wanting at the bar of some life and death crisis and emergency in thy history." (Boston *Transcript*, May 10, 1899, 4; Boston *Globe*, May 10, 1899, 7.)

From Emmett Jay Scott

Tuskegee, Ala., May 16, 1899

Dear Mr. Washington: I am back in Tuskegee this morning and much refreshed from the trip you were kind enough to give me to New York. I am very sorry, however, that in sailing out from the pier you and Mrs. Washington were not able to find us; we were standing in a bunch toward the center of the crowd frantically waving our hands and handkerchiefs. I trust you have crossed the ocean without much sickness and without unpleasant incident of any kind.

I find everything at the school in very satisfactory condition. Mr. Higginson sent a check for $7,296 to Mr. Logan together with a list of the donors and their addresses. I shall see that the Southern Letter is sent to each of these persons to whom it is not now going, and shall also send personal acknowledgment and receipt to each of them.

I beg to enclose herewith clipping from the N.Y. Sun of May 11th from the pen of Dr. Julius D. Dreher.[1] It is a very strong presentation of the case and will enlist your commendation I am sure. I also beg to hand you clipping of the speech made by Mr. Fortune at the Conference of the A.M.E.Z. Church in New York the [day] that you left.[2] Since it has been published I almost feel that it is a good thing to be delivered from one's friends. Mr. Fortune made a direct attempt to serve your cause by meeting the objection that you were too conservative and cited the instance of your having written a letter to the Governor of Georgia which he tore up, and mentioned that he had tore up other communications from you of a somewhat incendiary character. Of course it was done in all kindness, but I fear that the publication is not the very best.

The children are all well and happy. Hattie is greatly improved and I think that there is no occasion whatever for any worry on the part of yourself or Mrs. Washington. Portia left New York promptly Thursday morning so as to reach Boston that afternoon.

With all good wishes for a pleasant vacation, I am, Faithfully yours,

Emmett J. Scott

I enclose some clippings — picked out of the whole that I thought you might care to see.

TLS Con. 703 BTW Papers DLC.

1 Julius Daniel Dreher, president of Roanoke College, refuted a letter by a fellow southerner who had defended the Sam Hose lynching on the ground that blacks were lynched only in rape cases. The Chicago *Tribune*, Dreher wrote, reported that 103 of 127 lynchings in 1898 were for alleged crimes other than rape, including the case of one man who was lynched for stealing a Bible. Pleading for an end to mob violence, Dreher asked the white man to put himself in the black man's place and assume an attitude of "sympathy, encouragement, and helpfulness." (New York *Sun*, May 11, 1899, 6.)

2 After castigating McKinley as "the man who spread violets on the graves of ex-Confederates . . . a man of jelly, who would turn us all loose to the mob and not say a word," Fortune said that BTW, on the night after the lynchings, showed him a letter he had written to the governor of Georgia. "I read that letter and tore it up. I said 'Washington you are the only man that now stands between the whites and the colored man as a bond of sympathy. Don't send that letter. It will destroy the power we have!'" BTW did not send the letter, said Fortune, nor many others he had told him to destroy. (New York *Times*, May 11, 1899, 2.)

To the Editor of the Indianapolis *Freeman*

The Hague, Holland, May 23, 1899

Editor The Freeman, Indianapolis, Ind.: It has been a severe and trying ordeal for me to leave the United States just at this time when there is so much transpiring which concerns the interest of our people, but my friends insisted that I needed the rest and recreation which a trip through Europe would bring, and since they very kindly provided the means there was nothing for me to do but to accede to their wishes.

In a trip through Holland in company with Mrs. Washington, Mr. Edward Marshall[1] of the New York Journal and others, I have seen much which may prove of interest to your readers. It has been said many times that "God made the world but the Dutch made Holland." For one to realize the force of this he must see Holland for himself. One of the best ways to see the interior and peasant life of Holland is to take a trip as we have done, in one of the canal boats plying between Antwerp, Belgium, and Rotterdam, Holland.

It has been especially interesting for me to compare the rural life of Holland with that of the colored people in the South. Holland has been made very largely what it is by the unique system of dykes or levees which enables the people to use to advantage all of the land in this small country.

The great lesson which our colored farmers can learn from Holland is how to make a living from a small plot of land well cultivated instead of 40 or 50 acres poorly tilled. I have seen a whole family making a comfortable living by cultivating two acres of land, while our Southern farmers in too many cases try to till 50 or 100 acres and find themselves in debt at the end of the year. In all Holland I do not think one can find a hundred acres of waste land; every foot of land is covered with grass, vegetables, grain or fruit trees. Another advantage which our Southern colored farmers would have in trying to pattern after the farmers of Holland, would be that they would not be obliged to go to such additional expense for horse or mule power. Most of the farming is done here with the hoe and spade. I have seen these people on Sundays and during the week but I have not seen a single Dutchman, woman or child in rags. Here there are practically no beggars and very poor people. They owe their prosperity very largely to the thorough and intelligent cultivation of the soil.

Next to the thorough tilling of the soil, the thing of most interest from which our colored people in America may learn a valuable lesson, is the fine dairying which has made Holland famous throughout the world. Even the poorest family has its herd of Holstein cattle, and they are the finest specimens of cattle that it has been my pleasure to see. To see thousands of these cattle grazing on the fields is worth the trip to Holland. As the result of the attention which they have given to breeding Holstein cattle, Holland butter and cheese is in demand all through Europe and other countries as well. The most ordinary farmer has a cash income as the result of the sale of his milk and butter. Many of these people make more money out of the wind than our poor Southern people do out of the soil.

The old fashioned wind-mill is to be seen on every farm. This mill not only pumps the water for live stock, but in many cases is made to operate the dairy, to saw the wood, to grind the grain and to run the heavy machinery. These people are, however, not unlike our Southern colored people in one respect and that is in having their women and children work in the field. This I think is done in a measure even larger than in the South among the colored people.

Another element of strength in the farming and dairying interests of them is to be found in the fact that many of these farmers have received a college or university training. After this, they take a special course in Agriculture and Dairying. This is as it should be. Our people in the South will prosper in proportion as a large number of our university men take up agriculture and kindred callings after they have finished their academic education.

In the matter of physical appearance, including grace, beauty and general carriage of the body, I think our own people are far ahead of the Hollanders. I do not think I exaggerate to say that I have not seen in all Holland a single beautiful woman. But they are a hardy, rugged, industrious set of people. In our trip on the canal boat, we saw the men at the landings in large numbers in their wooden shoes and the women and girls in their beautiful old fashioned head dress, each community having its own style which has been handed down from one generation to the other.

We were in Rotterdam over Sunday. The free and rather boisterous co-mingling of the sexes on the streets was noteworthy. In this also our people in the United States could set an example to the Hollanders. It has also been our privilege to pass through Delft, where the finest pottery in the world is made and which was especially interesting to me because of its being the place from which the Pilgrim Fathers sailed.

Here in The Hague, we have had an opportunity to see something of the work of the Peace Conference which I believe is going to have an important and practical effect in the furthering of peace between the nations. President Seth Low, one of our American Commissioners, received me very kindly and cordially.

The foundation of the civilization of these people is in their respect for and observance of the law. This is the great lesson which the entire South must learn before it can hope to receive the respect and confidence of the world. Europeans do not know how to understand how the South can disregard its own laws in the manner it is too often doing. If you ask any man on this side of the Atlantic why he does not emigrate to the Southern part of the United States, he shrugs his shoulders and says, "No law," "they kill." I pray God that no part of our country may much longer have such a reputation in any part of the world.

Booker T. Washington

Indianapolis *Freeman*, June 17, 1899, 1. This also appeared in other newspapers and in the *Tuskegee Student*, 13 (June 22, 1899), 4.

1 Edward Davis Marshall (1869-1933) accompanied BTW to Europe as a correspondent for the New York *Journal*. It was Marshall's first assignment after recovering from severe wounds received on his first day as a war correspondent in the Spanish-American War.

From Joseph Sturge

Birmingham, [England] May 24 1899

Dear sir   I hear from Mr Garrison that this letter will probably find you in Paris — and I write to say that my sisters and I shall be pleased if it suits Mrs Washington and yourself to spend a day or two with us when you are in England. It would be a great pleasure to make your personal acquaintance, as I have heard a good deal that has interested me in your work.

I have just heard from our agent in Montserrat that he has had to part with the master who has had charge of our school there for a number of years. It would in some respects be advantageous if we could choose as his successor, instead of a West Indian, some one from the States, who has been inspired with a sense of the importance and honourable character of manual work, such as you inculcate at Tuskegee. It occurs to me to ask whether you have any man — upon whose character you can absolutely rely — whose qualifications as a teacher would satisfy our government inspector, and who would incline to apply for such a post. I doubt whether it would be judicious to appoint a man under 25, and he would have to go down almost at once.

The School is a mixed one, with about 200 children. The late teacher had I think about $400 and a house. The island is very healthy. I am yours very truly

Joseph Sturge

ALS Con. 162 BTW Papers DLC.

Charles Winston Thompson to Warren Logan

Tuskegee, Ala. May 30th. 99

Dear Sir: As an appreciation of the pleasant relations that have existed between us for several years past, and your check of recent date covering your account in full, as well as evidence of our good will and best wishes for the success of your School, I beg to hand you herewith our duplicate deposit ticket for Fifty Dollars, which I beg you to accept as a donation from The Bank of Tuskegee. Hoping for a continuation of your patronage and a more liberal share of your deposits, I am, Yours very truly,

Chas. W. Thompson
Prest.

TLS Con. 163 BTW Papers DLC.

From Timothy Thomas Fortune

New York, June 1, 1899

My dear Mr. Washington: Your card of the 22 May dated at the Hague got here three days before your letter of May 12, dated on the Friesland. Of course I am rejoiced to hear from you. I have been sick every day since you left on the 10th, sometimes in the bed and sometimes out. I am a shade better. While sick last week I spent five days on the soldier business (three chapters) and one on Education, making 70 pages of foolscap, about 18,000 words or 40 pages of the book print, as the Chicago people were howling for it, but the job did me up badly. I am glad it is done however, and Scott writes me that the job has been "done to the Queen's taste." I don't know. I hope so.

C. H. J. Taylor is dead. I have no rhetorical flowers to place on his grave, as I am no hypocrite and he was an unmitigated nuisance and disturbance and all the rest of it.

I send you one of the clippings of the Boston article I wrote before you left here but which did not appear until May 18.[1] I sent Clement an editorial note yesterday on your study of the peasants and agricultural conditions in the Netherlands. I send clipping because I prefer to keep the original for my scrap book.

I have broken connection entirely with the Hampton Conference, as I don't like the managing influences as they showed up last year and promise to this year and have written them I shall not be there. And then I must rest in the woods as much as I can this hot spell, as I am afraid of my health. I seem to go to smash on a moment's notice.

My family are well and wish to be remembered to you and Mrs. Washington.

As to the meeting of the Council, Bishop Walters[2] has already filed application for rates with the Traffic Association for August (late) to conform to the date for the Women's Convention, and the change could not be made to September without a row with the Association (Traffic) and a lot of red tape. I am sorry the word came so late from you on the subject. The bretheren are preparing to fast and prayer on June 2 and 4. I shall pray but eat, as a day's fasting would smash me up.

Pledger is preparing to give you a big send off in Atlanta when you return and wants me to be there. We shall see.

My Chicago trip had to be postponed for the present because of my sickness. And I am a bit afraid to go, as the whole West is yelling for me to speak for it from Indianapolis to Omaha, and I don't want to talk.

I am fighting your battles as the occasion requires. You will see that I have plugged Smith[3] of the Gazette by the clipping enclosed. Dancy[4] wants to make friends, but he is too small to bother with seriously.

The Country seems sorter empty without you. McKinley is still playing the sneak and ingrate.

With kind regards for you and Mrs. Washington, Yours truly

T. Thomas Fortune

ALS Con. 154 BTW Papers DLC.

[1] The article lauded BTW as the successor to Frederick Douglass. In defending BTW against W. Calvin Chase's charges that the Tuskegean was raised to his position by whites, Fortune wrote that BTW attained leadership through his own merits "by supreme devotion to his race, by persuasive eloquence, by a wisdom tempered with studied conservatism." (Boston *Transcript*, May 18, 1899, 8.)

[2] Alexander Walters (1858-1917) was born in Bardstown, Ky. At the age of twelve he joined the A.M.E. Zion Church and was licensed to preach five years later. During the next twenty years Walters's service took him to San Francisco, Chattanooga, Knoxville, and then to New York City, where he led one of the largest A.M.E. Zion congregations. In 1891 he received a D.D. degree from Livingstone College, and the following year he was elected bishop of his church. In 1898 Walters urged T. Thomas Fortune, whom he had helped to found the defunct Afro-American League, to revive their former organization in protest against the resurgence of lynchings and other outrages against blacks. Together they helped found the National Afro-American Council, which elected Walters its first president in 1898. Walters was also president of the Pan-African Association, which was organized in London in 1900. Walters and BTW maintained harmonious relations except for a brief time after the former sided with Fortune against BTW in the Brownsville affair.

[3] Harry C. Smith (1863-1941) of Cleveland, Ohio, was a leading black journalist, state legislator, and militant champion of civil rights. Born in Clarksburg, W.Va., he was taken by his widowed mother to Cleveland, where by her and his sister's efforts he secured a high school education in the city's public schools. While still in high school, Smith secured employment as a cornetist, and after graduation in 1882 he pursued a musical career, directing several vocal groups and bands and composing popular music.

In 1883 Smith founded the Cleveland *Gazette*, a black weekly, with the aid of John F. Lightfoot, John Holmes, and James H. Jackson. Within a few years Smith became sole owner. From its beginning the *Gazette* was a forthright opponent of the color line both locally and nationally.

Smith was active in Republican politics, and his paper championed Joseph B. Foraker's race for the governorship. After election Foraker appointed him deputy state oil inspector, a post he held from 1886 to 1890. Smith was a state legislator from 1894 to 1898 and 1900 to 1902. He introduced and helped secure passage of the Ohio civil rights law in 1894 and an anti-lynching law in 1896. He was also successful in getting the state railroad commission to bar the entry of Jim Crow cars into the state.

Though a loyal Republican, Smith was constantly critical of the southern policy of the party, and in the 1892 election he advised an opportunistic course, saying: "Let our newspapers tell the people . . . to stay in the ranks of the Republican Party, but act, politically, on election day, as did Hanna and his Republican followers in recent years here in Cleveland when they assisted in the election of Mayor John Farley and Mayor Tom L. Johnson, both Democrats." (Cleveland *Gazette*, Oct. 4, 1892, quoted in Meier, *Negro Thought*, 32.)

Smith was one of the few editors who held to the assimilationist ideas of the Reconstruction period and virtually ignored the racial pride and solidarity ideas ascendant in the BTW era. He urged blacks to participate in politics, to integrate the schools, and to press constantly for inclusion in the larger society. In this his attitudes were similar to those of his close white friend Albion W. Tourgée and of the black novelist Charles W. Chesnutt, though unlike Chesnutt he never personally befriended BTW.

An active member of the Niagara Movement, Smith was one of the founders of the NAACP and a member of its first executive committee. He was largely responsible for barring the racist film, "The Birth of a Nation," from Ohio for many years. He ran for Ohio secretary of state in 1920 and later for governor, but lost both bids. He remained editor of the *Gazette*.

4 John Campbell Dancy (1857-1920) had a highly successful political career in Edgecombe County, N.C., one of the solidly Republican southern "black counties," before coming to Washington as recorder of deeds in the District of Columbia during Harrison's second administration.

After three years at Howard University, which he attended with T. Thomas Fortune, Dancy returned home to Tarboro following his father's death and taught school. He was elected register of deeds in Edgecombe County in 1883 and served until 1889, when he received from Benjamin Harrison the lucrative appointment as collector of customs in Wilmington, N.C. McKinley reappointed Dancy to the post when the Republicans returned to power in 1896. During the 1880s Dancy was chief secretary of the state Republican conventions and was also a delegate to the national Republican conventions, seconding the nomination of John A. Logan for Vice-President in 1884. In 1902 Roosevelt appointed Dancy recorder of deeds in the District of Columbia, a position he held until 1910. He was removed by President Taft, who thought someone else should have an opportunity to fill the traditional black post, BTW's pleas to the contrary notwithstanding.

In the early 1880s Dancy edited the *North Carolina Sentinel* until he was elected editor of the A.M.E. Zion Church journal, the *Star of Zion*, a position he held until he became the editor of the *A.M.E. Zion Quarterly Review* in 1892. Through these publications and in his political life Dancy exemplified the policy of accommodation, and during their long association Dancy supported a number of BTW's projects, most notably the National Negro Business League. His son, John Campbell Dancy, Jr., was for many years head of the Detroit Urban League.

To Emmett Jay Scott

[Paris, ca. June 5th, 1899][1]

Dear Mr. Scott: I am a little late in sending the article about which I wrote you the other day but I am now sending it by this mail. Enclosed I send an article written upon Lynching in the South, which I have had in my mind to write for some time but I have only recently found time for it.[2] I have devoted considerable time and thought to it. I am anxious that it have a larger circulation than any other article I have written as yet. I want you to have it published as far as possible in all the leading Southern white daily papers, such as The Montg. Adver., The Age Herald, Constitution, Atlanta Journal, and one or two of the leading papers in all the Southern states. After it has been published in the Southern papers, send marked copies of these to all the leading Northern daily and religious papers, such as Boston Transcript, Boston Herald, Washington Post, Eve. Post, Independent, Outlook &c. Also send marked copies to all of the Colored papers published in the U.S. It might perhaps be only fair to the daily papers to let them know that it has been sent to other papers. Keep a good many on hand at the school. Send a half doz. to Mr. Francis J. Garrison, 4 Park st. Boston. Four copies to Mr. R. P. Hallowell, 526 Atlantic ave. Boston. One to Mrs. Ednah D. Cheney Jamaica Plain Mass. Please send one or two to those people in New Bedford who have recently been criticising me. A copy also to the New Bedford Standard. I am anxious that people both in the North and South shall see what I have said to both races, Colored and white. Some papers will publish what I have said to one race and will omit what I have said to the other. This will do me great injustice. Please lay aside every thing else and get this into the papers at once.

[Booker T. Washington]

TLd Con. 160 BTW Papers DLC.

[1] Though BTW does not mention Archibald H. Grimké here, his letter to Grimké of June 5, 1899 (below), suggests this as the probable date.

[2] This open letter, "Lynchings in the South," was sent to the Montgomery *Advertiser*, Birmingham *Age-Herald*, Jacksonville *Florida Times-Union*, Nashville *American*, New Orleans *Times-Democrat*, and probably other southern white newspapers. It is reproduced above, 1:149-54. A pamphlet reprint is in Con. 955, BTW Papers, DLC.

To Archibald Henry Grimké

Paris, June, 5th, 1899

Personal

Dear Mr. Grimké: Friends in Boston have been kind enough to send me a copy of the Transcript containing your recent strong and eloquent address delivered at the mass meeting held to protest against the practice of Lynching in the South. I feel sure that your words will do good and I thank you for them. I have asked my Sec. to send you a copy of the paper containing an article which I have written to the Southern white people upon this subject. I have kept silent, because I wanted to wait until I knew the white people of the South were in that frame of mind where they were willing to listen to what I had to say. I know that there are those who have found fault with me for my utterances or lack of such, but I do not believe that I have ever said any thing over my signature that you or any other friend of the race disagree with.[1] For me to attempt to contradict many of the absurd and foolish things, which are attributed to me through the Press, would be simply a waste of time and a piece of folly.

Please remember me very kindly to your brother,[2] and be kind enough to send him a copy of the paper which my Sec. will send you. Yours truly,

Booker T. Washington

TLSr Archibald H. Grimké Collection DHU. The letter contained minor corrections in BTW's hand and the signature was in Margaret Murray Washington's hand.

[1] For Grimké's response to BTW's letter on lynching see Grimké to BTW, July 8, 1899, below.
[2] Francis James Grimké.

From Albert Bushnell Hart

Cambridge, Mass. June 5, 1899

My dear Sir: Yours of the 12th relative to Professor Du Bois is at hand. Du Bois seems to me to occupy a very unusual situation.

Practically no member of his race in America has had so thorough and so well qualified opportunities for the highest education. There are no better advantages in the world than those of any first class American University, combined with foreign study, and with opportunities for investigation. It is worth a great deal for your cause to have such an example of a man of excellent abilities, thoroughly trained and at the same time modest and sensible. He is a standing refutation of some of the hardest things said about the negro race.

I write with renewed interest because of the very excellent appearance which Du Bois made here in Cambridge a few weeks ago when you were present. His address seemed to me just right; eloquent, witty and suggestive. I felt that the man had justified the expectations of his friends.

Now I do not feel sufficiently well acquainted with the conditions of the educational work in the South to say where Du Bois can render greatest service, but wherever that is he ought to be. Tuskegee of course fills a great arc in popular attention both North and South, and probably the same effort applied there will have a wider range than if put into a smaller and less famous institution. My natural interest would be to see him associated with you. I will write him in that sense.

I hope, Mr. Washington, that when you next come to Boston, you will do me the favor to let me know beforehand. I want to know more about your work; if I can help it on in any way, I want to do it. I shall feel honored to have the opportunity to make your better acquaintance. Sincerely yours,

Albert Bushnell Hart

TLS Con. 155 BTW Papers DLC.

From Warren Logan

Tuskegee, Ala., June 7, 1899

Dear Mr. Washington: I have received your letter of the 13th of May written on board the steamer and mailed at Vlissengen May 20th.

We were very glad indeed to receive your two cablegrams announcing your safe arrival on the other side of the Atlantic and expressing your congratulations and best wishes on commencement day.

The latter message I read with good effect at the commencement exercises just after Wesley Jefferson[1] had delivered his oration on the "Achievements of Cyrus W. Field." The cheering of the students, teachers and visitors at the conclusion of the reading attested the warm appreciation of your kind expressions of interest on the closing day of the Institute. The commencement exercises passed off very smoothly, and while there was the absence of the usual crowd, there was no lack of interest in the exercises which were of as high an order as any. The two addresses by Dr. Banton[2] and Mr. Kealing[3] were especially fine. We have not had a better commencement address than the one delivered by Mr. Kealing.

I presume Mr. Scott has sent you papers containing accounts of the commencement. Mr. Bedford was with us ten days and was especially helpful in many ways.

The trustees held a meeting on the day preceding commencement, the principal matter before them being the sale of the government lands. I had secured proxies from the non-resident trustees including Mr. Baldwin. The latter expressed some doubt as to the wisdom of selling the lands right now, and in deference to his opinion the trustees decided to adjourn until such time as Mr. Baldwin could be present and I was instructed to write him to come to Tuskegee at once and confer with the trustees upon this important matter. He telegraphed that if Mr. Campbell and the executive committee were unanimous for the sale that he would vote to confirm it. He afterwards telegraphed that he had seen Gen. Wheeler while in New York and that the Gen. was of the opinion that the lands were worth much more than what had been offered for them. On receipt of the last telegram a meeting of the trustees was held and it was decided to decline the offer of $125,000 for the lands made by the syndicate which Pinckard[4] represents.

I have information that the Montevallo school is willing to sell its interest in the lands for $125,000 but the syndicate will not buy unless we also agree to sell. Mr. Hare thinks that he can sell the lands for much more than the price we have been offered, but it is very hard to tell about this. Mr. Thompson[5] says that the two schools will not get more than 25,000 acres of coal land and that this is all of the coal land in the State that is worth developing. If we can be certain of getting twelve or fifteen thousand acres of coal land in the division I think there is but little doubt of our being able to realize at least $125,000 for it, and perhaps a great deal more. Mr. Hare cites an instance of a man in Georgia getting $80,000 for three thousand acres of coal land last month. Mr. Thompson has shown great activity in this whole matter: indeed, he seems to be the paid agent of Pinckard to purchase the land from the school. Of course I cannot say that this is true but indications point in that direction. Mr. Campbell has written Mr. Baldwin, and I believe Mr. Chas. Thompson who has been appointed trustee of the Montevallo school, has also written him.

I suppose you have heard that Reynolds has been deposed from the presidency of the Montevallo school and that Dr. Eager[6] has been elected in his place. Dr. Eager has not yet decided whether he will accept the presidency or not.

I enclose a note just received from Mr. Taylor. I have told him that I think he should notify you at once in regard to his intention not to return to Tuskegee next year. I am surprised that he did not let you know about it before you left for Europe; he must certainly have known about it in the spring.

We received and disbursed during the month of May nearly $50,000, but this sum was not sufficient to pay every thing that we owe.

I am hoping that the receipts for the summer months will be sufficient to keep us from getting into debt. I trust you are beginning to feel some benefit from your vacation. I am sure you did not enter upon it a day too soon.

Please remember [me] very kindly to Mrs. Washington and accept for yourself the very best wishes of us all. Very truly yours,

Warren Logan

TLS Con. 160 BTW Papers DLC.

1 Wesley Warren Jefferson of Florence, S.C., was the salutatorian of the Tuskegee class of 1899. BTW recommended Jefferson to Joseph Sturge as principal of the industrial school that Sturge had founded in Montserrat, B.W.I. Jefferson organized the school on a former sugar plantation in the summer of 1899, but he left after less than two years in ill health and disappointed at the extreme poverty and lack of opportunity that seemed to make West Indian advancement impossible. In 1904

he graduated from Howard University's dental school, and in 1910 he began a successful dental practice in Norfolk, Va.

2 Rev. W. C. Banton, pastor of St. Luke's A.M.E. Church in Eufaula, Ala.

3 Hightower T. Kealing (b. 1859) was editor of the *A.M.E. Church Review* from 1896 to 1912. Earlier he was an educator in Texas and president of Paul Quinn College, an A.M.E. Church school in Waco, Tex. In 1906 BTW sought to purchase the Chicago *Conservator*, a black weekly newspaper, and install Kealing as editor, but Kealing would not be free from his commitment to the *A.M.E. Church Review* until the denomination's quadrennial conference the following year, and by then the paper was no longer for sale. (Kealing to Scott, Dec. 29, 1906, Con. 335, Scott to Kealing, Feb. 7, 1906, Con. 351, BTW Papers, DLC.) After 1912 Kealing was president of Western University at Quindaro, Kan.

4 Possibly Lucius Pinckard of Atlanta.

5 William Watson Thompson.

6 George Boardman Eager (1847–1929) was born in Jefferson County, Miss., and educated at Mississippi College, receiving his A.M. in 1871. Eager entered the Baptist ministry the following year and served at churches in Virginia, Tennessee, and Alabama. While pastor of the First Baptist Church in Montgomery, he became a trustee from the state at large of the Alabama Girls' Industrial School at Montevallo. After consultation with his parishioners, Eager declined the presidency of the Montevallo school. In 1901 Eager was minister of a church in Chicago.

An Article in the New York *Age*

Paris, June 8 [1899]

ON THE PARIS BOULEVARDS

On a beautiful sunny day, combine the whirl of fashion and gayety of New York city, Boston and Chicago on a prominent avenue, and one then has some idea of what is to be seen here in Paris upon one of her popular boulevards. Fashion seems to sway everything here in this great city; for example, when I went into a shoe store a few days ago to purchase a pair of shoes, I could not find a pair sufficiently large to be comfortable. I was gently told that it is not the fashion to wear large shoes here.

One of the things I had in mind when I came to France was to visit the tomb of Toussaint L'Ouverture, but I have just learned from some Haytian gentlemen residing here that the grave of this general is in the northern part of France, and these same gentlemen inform me that his burial place is still minus a monument of any description. It seems that it has been in the minds of the Haytians for some time to remove the body to Hayti, but thus far it has been neglected. The Haytian government and people owe it to themselves, it seems to me, to see to it that the resting place of the great hero is given a proper memorial either here in France or on the island.

Speaking of the Haytians — there are a good many well educated and cultured Haytians in Paris. Numbers of both men and women are sent here each year for education and these take high rank in scholarship. It is greatly to be regretted, however, that some of these do not take advantage of the excellent training which is given here in the colleges of physical sciences, agriculture, mechanics and domestic sciences. They would then be in a position to return home and assist in developing the agricultural and mineral resources of their native land. Hayti will never be what it should until a large number of the natives receive that education which will fit them to develop agriculture, public roads, start manufactories, build bridges, railroads, and thus keep in the island the large amount of money which is now sent outside for productions which these people themselves can supply.

Although, in our effort to secure complete rest, we have tried as far as possible to escape attention, many Americans and Frenchmen as well have been very cordial and have shown us attention. The American ambassador, General Horace Porter,[1] and his wife have not been neglectful of us. Soon after our arrival in Paris, the ambassador and the first secretary of the legation called at our hotel. At Mrs. Porter's reception we were made to feel entirely at home. At a meeting of the American University Club, which is composed of college men of America, ex-President Harrison, Archbishop Ireland[2] and myself were the speakers. There is a beautiful church here called the American Chapel where the citizens of my country insisted that I occupy the pulpit last Sunday. In the audience were ex-President Harrison and his wife.

It was our privilege to breakfast with Auguste Laugel a few days ago, the French gentleman who showed himself such a friend to the Union and who was an especial friend of Lincoln and General Grant during our Civil War. He was one of the first to enter Richmond after its fall. Mr. Laugel is one of the commissioners of the Paris Exposition and is still deeply interested in all that concerns the colored race and America. His lovely wife, who is an American woman, is equally so. We have also dined at the home of Theodore

Tilton, the friend of the Garrisons, and the man who has always proven himself a friend to our race.

Mrs. Washington desires me to incorporate into this letter the following announcement to the National Association of Colored Women:

"The National Association of Colored Women will hold their convention in the city of Chicago the 13th, 14th, 15th, 16th and 17th of August. There will be reduced rates on all the roads. It is hoped that there will be a large delegation from all sections of the country. Any information with reference to the coming convention may be had from Mrs. M. C. Terrell,[3] president, 826 P street, N.W., Washington, D.C.; or from Mrs. L. A. Davis,[4] 5017 Armour avenue, Chicago; or from Mrs. Washington's secretary, Miss Daisy Walker,[5] Tuskegee, Ala."

In all the European countries which we have visited, we have compared the conduct of the rank and file of the people on the streets and other public places with that of our own people in the Southern States and have no hesitation in saying that in all that marks a lady or gentleman our people in the South do not suffer at all by comparison. Even at the camp meetings and other holiday gatherings in the South, the deportment of the mass of the colored people is quite up to the standard of that of the average European in the larger cities which we have thus far seen.

I should strongly advise our people against coming to Europe and especially to Paris with the hope of securing employment unless fortified by strong friends and a good supply of money. Within the last week, three Afro-American citizens have called to see me, and in each case I found them in practically a starving condition and my purse was the worse off by reason of their call. They were well-meaning, industrious men who had come here with the idea that life was easy and work sure, but notwithstanding the fact that they have walked the streets for days they still have no work. The fact that they do not speak the language nor understand the habits and customs of the people here makes their life just so much harder. With the assistance of other Americans, I have just secured passage for one of these men to the United States. His parting word to me was, "the United States is good enough for me in the future."

Booker T. Washington

New York *Age*, July 13, 1899, Clipping Con. 1031 BTW Papers DLC. The article also appeared in the Indianapolis *Freeman*, July 15, 1899, 1.

[1] Horace Porter (1837-1921) was aide-de-camp to General U. S. Grant during the Civil War and later was a railroad executive. Porter was U.S. ambassador to France from 1897 to 1905.

[2] John Ireland (1838-1918) became Roman Catholic archbishop of St. Paul, Minn., in 1888.

[3] Mary Eliza Church Terrell (1863-1954) was born in Memphis, the daughter of Robert R. Church, Sr. (1838-1912), "the Boss of Beale Street," who rose from slavery to become a powerful political leader and financier in Memphis. Robert R. Church's fortune, estimated at a million dollars, came from investments in real estate, saloons, and gambling houses in the black section of Memphis, especially along colorful Beale Street.

Reared by her mother, Louisa Ayers Church, after a separation from her father, Mary Church attended Oberlin College, graduating in 1884. She taught at Wilberforce for two years and earned an M.A. from Oberlin in 1888. In 1891 she married Robert Heberton Terrell (see above, 4:447), whom she met while teaching school in Washington, D.C., and the Terrells became prominent in Washington black society. She founded the National Association of Colored Women in 1896 and served as its first president. She was the first woman president of the Bethel Literary and Historical Association and the first woman member of the District of Columbia Board of Education, serving from 1895 to 1901 and from 1906 to 1911.

Though her husband secured a judgeship on the municipal court of the District of Columbia through BTW's influence and was an active supporter of the Tuskegean, Mary Church Terrell took a more independent course. This was particularly the case after President Roosevelt's dismissal of black troops following the Brownsville incident, when she petitioned Roosevelt to reinstate the soldiers while BTW acquiesced in Roosevelt's decision. In 1909 she became a charter member of the NAACP.

An active woman suffragist, Terrell spoke at several national suffrage meetings and attended the International Congress of Women at Berlin in 1904. During World War I she supervised the work of Negro women in the War Camp Community Service. In 1919 she represented the United States at the meeting of the Women's International League for Peace and Freedom in Zurich. During the Great Depression she was active in welfare work in southwest Washington, D.C. In 1949 she headed the coordinating Committee for Enforcement of the District of Columbia Anti-Discrimination Laws, and was the chief complaining witness in the Thompson Restaurant case. Success in this case opened public accommodations in the national capital on an integrated basis. She told her success story in *A Colored Woman in a White World* (1940).

[4] Elizabeth Lindsay Davis, of Peoria, Ill., taught school in Frederick, Md., until her marriage. She then returned to her home state, where she became an active clubwoman. In Mar. 1896 she organized the Phyllis Wheatley Women's Club and became its first president. The following year she was a founder and officer of the Woman's Civil League of Illinois. Mrs. Davis took great pride in her membership in the National Association of Colored Women, which she served in both national and state offices. In 1934, as national historian, she wrote *Lifting as They Climb, the History of the National Association of Colored Women*.

[5] Dayse D. Walker taught geography in 1898-99 and reading in the preparatory grades in 1899-1900 at Tuskegee Institute.

From Henry Sylvester Williams

London, W.C. 8.6.99 [June 8, 1899]

Dear Sir, I am authorised by the Officers & Committee of Our Association to bring to your notice the propose[d] Conference which you will notice on the enclosed circular. At this meeting, we are anxious of discussing the "Lynching Question" from the Afro American standpoint, & as you are the leader of an important association in the States, we would like your Association to send a representative over, if not, we shall be pleased to welcome you.

Will you kindly make this known as widely as is possible, & if persons who are desirous of coming will send on their names in advance, no doubt we shall be able to prepare them comfortable stopping places — which is of importance in London. Believe me, Yours truly

H. S. Williams

ALS Con. 164 BTW Papers DLC. Addressed to Tuskegee Institute on stationery of the African Association, of which Williams was secretary.

From Timothy Thomas Fortune

Greenville, Greene Co., N.Y., June 13, 1899

My dear Friend: I have your card and letter of the 1st June today, and I am glad to hear from you as always. I have been sick with a heavy cold on the chest and pains in the small of my back ever since May 11, and the doctor advised me to spend ten days here in the Catskill Mountains. It has done me lots of good and I wish that I could stay here at least a week longer, but shall have to go back to New York on Thursday next.

I am glad you liked the Leadership article in the Transcript. I sent you a copy of it in a long letter to the London address, which will account for your not hearing from me. I would have written oftener but have been too unwell to do so.

Gov. Johnston has a vile article in the Independent of last week.[1] A Chicago detective has reported on the Hose lynching and says the whites have lied about the whole thing.[2] He was employed by a Chicago committee headed by Mrs Ida Wells Barnett. The whole thing is vile, as far as the whites are concerned.

I have been doing some good editorial work for the Transcript, and am keeping it up.

Have explained about the Chicago meeting in the letter you will find in London.

Glad that Tanner[3] is doing well. I am 14 miles from a railroad and have seen but one daily newspaper in 8 days so that I donot know the news.

Will write again soon. I miss you very much. With kind regards for you and Mrs Washington, Yours truly

T Thomas Fortune

ALS   Con. 154   BTW Papers   DLC.

[1] Joseph F. Johnston, "Negro Suffrage in Alabama," *Independent*, 51 (June 8, 1899), 1535-37, supported white supremacy and disfranchisement. Johnston said that the lesson of Reconstruction was that blacks were unfit for self-government and were content with a benign white rule. Whites, Johnston stated, were willing to support black education even though it might cause blacks to become discontented or deprive the state of its supply of unskilled labor.

[2] Louis Le Vin, a private detective, reported at a meeting in Bethel A.M.E. Church that he had secured his information while posing as a seller of hog-cholera medicine. He said that the white man, Cranford, was killed after a quarrel over wages and not because of an attempt to assault his wife. When Cranford ran into his house and returned with a revolver aimed at Hose, the black man seized an axe and threw it at Cranford, killing him instantly. Le Vin said that Mrs. Cranford, who saw the whole thing, confirmed his account and denied that Hose had touched her. (Chicago *Inter Ocean*, June 5, 1899, 6.)

[3] Henry Ossawa Tanner.

Emmett Jay Scott to William Elisha King[1]

[Tuskegee, Ala.] June 15, 1899

My dear friend King: I do not know how much surprised you will be to receive this letter from me. First of all, I want to congratulate you upon the excellent newspaper you are publishing; my interest in everything Texan is just as acute as ever. It is not tossing bouquets at you to say that the Express is very well to the fore front of all the newspapers being published in the interest of the race.

I have wanted to write you for sometime upon another matter since I have been at Tuskegee but have always desisted because of the fact that you would likely suppose that I was urged to write you this with regard to the man with whom I am now connected in the capacity of private secretary. As one having been schooled under our mutual friend and leader, Norris Wright Cuney, it must be improbable for you to conclude that I could become identified with any man who was not manly in deliverance and honest in his intentions to be of real practical service for the race. You have most certainly misunderstood Booker T. Washington. He is one of the grandest men of the century. I speak this because I am right in the zone of his immediate influence and am in position to know that this man is laboring unselfishly and unwearyingly for the race. No man who knows the diplomat that is in him, who knows the efforts which he puts forth from time to time could by any possible means conclude that he was the creature which at various times you yourself have thought him to be. He needs no defense, even from his private secretary, but as an old friend I feel that I have the right to address this note to you and to call your attention to what has seemed to be on your part undeserved criticism. Whether speaking before cultured audiences in the North or before purely white organizations of the South he is always to be found making manly declarations. The one thing that has served to aggravate some of our thin-skinned race leaders is the fact that the man dares to speak the truth. He says, even as you have often said in your valuable sheet, that all black men are not angels nor all white men brutes and vice versa. I remember only a few weeks ago noticing in some of the newspapers references such as this: "Now that the Legislature of Alabama is about to disfranchise the Negroes in Booker T. Washington's own state, the time has come for him to display some of his influence with the Southern white people." Since the Legislature has adjourned and no constitutional convention is called, the critics immediately cease their babbling and refuse even to suppose that he could have had any influence in the bringing about of this result. He was a most material factor in this matter, and when the history of recent events in Alabama is written it will be found that he had a great deal to do with the failure to call together a constitutional convention as well as in the matter of having defeated the bill which had for its object the separation of the money paid by the black people and the white people of Alabama into two separate parts for their respective public schools.

I have written to you in all frankness and courtesy without any effort to influence you, but knowing you as I do know you, I am sure you will not be willing to have even Booker T. Washington from whom you have honestly differed, to suffer at your hands. Any man who has the respect of the country as this man has and who is received in the places where this man is received can[not] be without merit and deserving of the cordial assistance of the members of his own race in his efforts to bring about a more cordial understanding in the matter of this vexed race problem. The honors which have come to him thick and fast in the last four years even have not made him other than the modest man that he has always been, but on every one of these occasions he has deported himself in a way to bring forth glory to the race with which we are identified.

He does not believe, as so many people assume to explain for him, that industrial education is the panecea for all the ills that beset the black man; he does believe, and so do I and so do all men who are willing to understand the subject just as it is.[2] This is no assumption of superior wisdom on my part, but hinges on observations which have been mine to see in a large number of cases.

[Emmett J. Scott]

TLc Con. 160 BTW Papers DLC.

1 William Elisha King was born in Macon, Miss., about 1865, and taught school from 1881 to 1888, when he became business manager and editor of *Jacob's Friend* in Helena, Ark. The following year he co-founded *Fair Play*, a weekly newspaper, in Meridian, Miss. In 1893 King founded the Dallas *Express*, which he edited for many years. King was active in Texas Republican politics, serving as delegate and alternate to the 1900, 1912, and 1916 national Republican conventions. In 1906 he attended the "black-and-tan" or Reorganized Republican convention at Houston and seconded the convention's nominations for governor and lieutenant governor.

2 Scott failed here to complete his thought.

From Emmett Jay Scott

Tuskegee, Ala., June 23, 1899

Dear Mr. Washington: You will note that the Advertiser published your letter[1] in full. The Constitution, true to its old tricks, refused to print the letter in full but instead dates it from Birmingham, Ala., and garbles it so as to rob it of its real practical effect, for that reason I shall send out more especially the copies of the newspapers containing the letter in full as I think you are entitled to have your full position stated instead of as garbled by the Constitution. Yours truly,

E J Scott

The Age-Herald display is good.[2] The

TLS Con. 161 BTW Papers DLC. The postscript in Scott's hand was incomplete.

1 BTW's open letter, "Lynchings in the South." See above, 1:149-54.
2 The Birmingham *Age-Herald* on June 22, 1899, carried the letter on the second page, with a large headline: "BOOKER T. WASHINGTON WRITES OF RACE PROBLEM IN THE SOUTH."

From Timothy Thomas Fortune

Saratoga Springs, N.Y., June 23, 1899

My dear Friend: Your letters of the 9th and 13th were received in the same mail and I am glad to have them. I thank you for the two clippings. Rev. Charles Spencer Smith will always hang himself if he is given enough rope, and he is by no means "the only pebble on the beach" of the same size.[1] Well, yes, it was rather amusing to have Bishop Walters call me conservative, but the fact is that he had been going at such an unbridaled gate that I was compelled to call him down in a public address.

I think from Gov. Johnston's article in the Independent that the convention scheme in Alabama has only been defeated for the time being. As to the Louisiana matter we will talk it over when you return and I hold myself ready, as usual, to do what you think for the best. Perhaps by going to New Orleans and possibly Baton Rouge what to do best could be most readily ascertained.

You are very kind to suggest an outing for me on your return and I appreciate it; but my health got so bad and the heat and humidity of New York used me up so that the doctor advised me to give up the western trip and come here instead; so I took the bull by the horns and came here and shall remain here until you return in August. Already I begin to feel the good effects of the air and waters here. So send your letters here.

Yes; I rushed through the matter for the Chicago firm and Scott thinks it great stuff, but the firm wrote Scott that they are rushing a Dewey book and are unable to pass upon the manuscript for the present. I dare say they will reach you about July 20. They howled long and loud enough before they got it.

Yes, I am sorry we were unable to make the Chicago date as you wished. It would have suited me better for September or October for there are cooler places in August than Chicago.

As to the West Virginia trip it will be a delight to take it with you. As for the western trip it could be made to advantage and I would be glad if I could spend Jan., Feb. and March in California. We must talk it over when we meet. I am keeping Pledger up to the Atlanta reception. It ought to be made the most *notable* thing of the kind ever given in the south, and it can be made so, if Pledger is not left with[out] proper suggestion in the plan and scope of it.

As to my being President of the Council I will sound the waters and see how the matters stand. Most of the preachers will be against me.

I don't see how the President and I can "make up and be good friends." There is not an honest bone in him. He can't come to me and I would not go near him except upon invitation. I shall soon open the editorial battery upon him.

I am pleased to learn that you miss me, because we are in the same box on that score. The fact is that I feel like a fish out of the water with you so far away. I shall be glad when you return.

I have seen extracts from your address on the lynchings but not the text, which Mr. Scott forgot to send me. I have asked for the text as I want to see it. The Southern papers appear to have given it a show.

I am glad you and Mrs Washington are enjoying your trip. I am sure you will both have great benefit from it. Mrs Fortune and the childen are well, and in Brooklyn.

I am keeping up the Sun and Transcript work and am very much pleased with my editorial work on the Transcript. With my kind regards, your friend,

T Thomas Fortune

ALS Con. 154 BTW Papers DLC.

[1] Fortune probably refers here to Smith's recently published pamphlet, *The Race Question Reviewed* (1899). Smith endorsed industrial education but said: "I challenge the assertion of those who claim that the only solution of the so-called race problem lies in the direction of the industrial and mechanical training of the Negro." He urged a continued concern with politics and civil rights, and observed that study by blacks of scientific agriculture would do little good if they did not own the land they worked.

From Joseph Forney Johnston

[Montgomery, Ala.] June 28. 1899

Dear Sir   Complaint is made to me that an agent of the Tuskegee Normal School has taken from Cuba and is now conducting to your school five white boys. The complaint comes from Cuba and it is alleged that the parents of these lads did not know that your school was exclusively for the education of colored youths; it is intimated that this fact was intentionally suppressed. I am quite sure if the statements are true that you had no part in any concealment or misrepresentation. Section 3600 of the Code prohibits coeducation of the races.[1]

I am sure that I only need to call your attention to this matter in order that proper steps may be taken if the statements are true. Resp &c

Jos. F Johnston
Govr

ALS   Con. 156   BTW Papers   DLC.

[1] The Alabama state code provided: "Separate schools for the two races. In no case shall it be lawful to unite in one school children of the white and colored races." (*Code of Alabama, 1897*, 1:1010-11.)

From Joseph Forney Johnston

[Montgomery, Ala.] June 30th 1899

Dear Sir   I am obliged for yours which is entirely satisfactory. Some letters have been sent me from Cuba tending to show that the statements submitted were correct.

I paid out of my Contingent Fund $55 to the land office here & $25 to the office in Huntsville for Township Plats of the mineral lands for the use of the Commissioners in selecting the grants to Montevallo & Tuskegee upon the promise that this would be refunded. Kindly have check sent me for $40 one half. Yrs truly

> Jos. F Johnston
> Gov.

ALS   Con. 156   BTW Papers   DLC.

To the Editor of the Washington *Colored American*

Paris, France [June 1899]

Our race owes much to the family of the Right Reverend Benjamin T. Tanner. It is very seldom that the children of a prominent man make for themselves such a unique and valuable place in life as is true of Bishop Tanner's children.

A few years ago, Mrs. Hallie T. Dillon, now Mrs. Hallie T. Johnson, the oldest daughter of the Bishop, graduated from the Woman's Medical College of Philadelphia. After her graduation she came to the State of Alabama, and passed the State Medical Board after a severe examination, lasting ten days. She was not only the first colored woman who had done this, but she was the first woman of any race. After holding the position of resident physician of the Tuskegee Normal and Industrial Institute for a number of years, she became the wife of Rev. J. Q. Johnson, a successful minister now located in the city of Montgomery, Ala.

But I began this article with a view of writing especially about Henry O. Tanner, the eldest son of the family, who now resides in the city of Paris, and who has taken a high position here as an artist. Paris is today beyond question the headquarters of the world in art. Thousands of artists come here from all parts of the world, and many of them toil for years without their names ever becoming known to the public.

Mrs. Washington and I have seen much of Mr. Tanner and his work since we have been in Paris. We have not only seen him and his work, but have had an opportunity of hearing the opinion of others regarding him. Mr. Tanner is still a young man, being now a little over forty years of age, yet in the art world, and out of it as well, his accomplishments are well known. Until we visited his studio in the Latin quarter, where most of the artists reside, we did not get a full insight into the life of this brilliant young American artist. He has achieved his success by hard study and persistent work. He permits nothing to turn him aside from his life's ambition. Mr. Tanner is determined that he shall not be known as merely a successful Negro artist, but that his work shall stand upon its merit alone. Here in France no one judges a man by his color. The color of the face neither helps nor hinders. "A man's a man for a' that and a' that."

There are two results for which almost every artist in Paris, and in the world for that matter, strives. One is that he may produce a painting that shall be of such high merit as to be purchased by the French Government and placed on exhibition in the Luxembourg Palace; the other is that the painting shall be so valued that on the death of the artist it may be given a place in the palace known as "The Louvre," which is the most remarkable palace in the world for its vast extent and for the magnificence of its architecture, and for the priceless art treasures it contains. The first object Mr. Tanner, though young as he is, and with all the obstacles he has had to overcome, has accomplished and has done it grandly.

A few evenings ago, when I remarked to some of my American friends that I was going to the Luxembourg Palace to look at a painting of a young American colored man, they looked at me in astonishment, and remarked that I must be mistaken. It hardly seemed possible to get it through their heads that a Negro had produced a painting that the highest critics of art would place in this palace; but when I finally convinced them of the truth of my statement, they, too, were on their way to the palace and were glad to claim Mr. Tanner as a fellow-countryman.

In this connection I would further remark that only two or three Americans have thus far been successful in getting their paintings in this Luxembourg Palace. The subject of Mr. Tanner's painting which hangs in the palace is "The Raising of Lazarus." I think he considers this so far, his masterpiece; but I feel sure that this is only a beginning of his great work. Other paintings of his which have attracted attention both in France and America are "Daniel in the Lion's Den," "The Annunciation," "The Jews' Wailing Place," "Flight into Egypt," and "The Still Hunt."

Mr. Tanner works slowly and carefully, producing, as a rule, but one painting a year. In order to do the best work, he has spent two winters in the Holy Land, and it was there that his "Jews' Wailing Place" and "Flight into Egypt" were conceived. I feel quite sure that our American friends would be glad to read some remarks made by the press with regard to the work of this young man. Le Temps, the most conservative paper in the city of Paris, says of Mr. Tanner's "The Raising of Lazarus," "The artist is a young American, who has perhaps not shown a deep religious sentiment, but he has exhibited sufficiently the qualities of a rare artist — one whom you do not meet every day." La Fin du Jour says: " 'The Raising of Lazarus,' by Mr. Tanner, is one of the best renderings in the salon."

There is another side to the efforts of Mr. Tanner, to which he may not thank me for alluding. In his early struggles to get upon his feet, I fear the race has not given him that practical and substantial support which it might have done. An earnest effort was made in Philadelphia and elsewhere some time ago to get our people to contribute sufficient money to purchase "The Bagpipe Lesson," an early work of the artist, but with little or no practical success. Quite a number of excellent orations and speeches were made upon the subject, but an artist can not live on fine oratory and speech making. This first work of Mr. Tanner's was finally, I believe, purchased by some Philadelphia white people. Few of the race are able individually to purchase Mr. Tanner's original paintings, but hundreds are able to secure the photographs of these productions. Will they do it? This is the practical test in a large measure of our gratitude to and admiration for Mr. Tanner. These photographs can be had for a small sum, and they should adorn the homes of thousands of our people in America. Mr. Tanner's address is 51 Boulevard St. Jacques, Paris, France. A man who has done the work which Mr. Tanner has done, and is still doing, should be placed in a position where his mind will not be concerned about the matter of bread and butter. Will we help to do this or shall we leave it all to others to do?

Booker T. Washington

Washington *Colored American,* July 22, 1899, 2.

A News Item in the London *Times*

London, July 4, 1899

THE COLOURED RACE IN AMERICA

The Rev. Dr. and Mrs. Brooke Herford[1] gave a reception at Essex-hall, Essex-street, Strand, yesterday afternoon to meet Mr. Booker T. Washington, a coloured gentleman, who is the founder and principal of the Normal and Industrial Coloured School at Tuskegee, Alabama, and Mrs. Washington. After the reception, Mr. J. H. Choate,[2] the United States Ambassador, presided at a meeting at which Mr. Washington gave an address on the condition and prospects of the coloured race in America. Those present included Mr. James Bryce,[3] M.P., Sir E. Durning-Lawrence,[4] M.P., Mr. Hodgson Pratt,[5] Mr. Murray Macdonald, and Mr. W. Copeland Bowie.[6]

The chairman expressed the pleasure which he felt at having been asked to preside and to introduce to the meeting his friend Mr. Booker T. Washington. There were 10,000,000 coloured persons in the United States living side by side with some 60,000,000 of whites. The freedom of which the negroes had been deprived for more than 200 years had been restored to them, but the question was how best they could be enabled to take advantage of it. The blacks were an interesting race. Fidelity was their great characteristic. During the civil war, when the South was stripped of every man and almost every boy to sustain their cause in arms, the women and children were left in the sole care, he might say, of these slaves, and no instance of violence or outrage that he had been able to learn was ever reported. He thought it would be admitted, therefore, that on that occasion they amply manifested their loyalty and fidelity to their masters. The black people had done much for themselves. About one-tenth of the men had acquired some portion of land, and they had made a certain advance. Mr. Washington was a pupil of the late General Armstrong, who devoted many years of his life to the establishment and maintenance of the leading school at Hampton, Virginia. Mr. Washington had qualified himself to follow in Armstrong's path. He also had founded a school, or training college, at Tuskegee, Alabama, where the pupils were not only given a primary education, but were afforded the means of earning a livelihood. There were now 1,100 pupils in the school. About half the number of those who passed through it went out as teachers to spread the light and the knowledge they had acquired there among their own race, and the other half were put into a position to support themselves by manual trades. The Government of the United States thought well of the work. It gave the school a grant of 25,000 acres of land in Alabama only last year. The State of Alabama, in which it was placed, gave it an annual donation. In addition it derived something from the funds left by the great philanthropist, George Peabody, and from another fund founded by an American philanthropist. The remainder of the sum needed for carrying on the work — some £15,000 a year — was derived from voluntary contributions, which were stimulated by the appeals made by Mr. Washington, whom he regarded as the leader of his race in America. (Cheers.)

Mr. Washington in a brief and interesting speech described the condition and prospects of the coloured race in America. Immediately after receiving their freedom, he said, the negroes, for the most part, got into debt, and they had not been able to free themselves to the present day. In many places it was found that as many as three-fourths of the coloured people were in debt, living on mortgaged land, and in many cases under agreements to pay interest on their indebtedness ranging between 15 and 40 per cent. The work of improving their condition was far from hopeless, and he was far from being discouraged. If his people got no other good out of slavery they got the habit of work. But they did not know how to utilize the results of their labour; the greatest injury which slavery wrought upon them was to deprive them of executive power, of the sense of independence. They required education and training, and this was gradually being provided. Starting in 1881 in the little town of Tuskegee with one teacher and 30 students, they had progressed until in the present day they had built up an institution which had connected with it over 1,000 men and women. They had some 86 instructors, and in all that they did they tried to make a careful and honest study of the condition of the negroes and to advance their material and moral welfare. Industrial education was a vital power in helping to lift his people out of their present state. Twenty-six different industries were taught, and every student had to learn some trade or other in addition to the studies of the classroom. The coloured students came from upwards of 20 States and territories, and the labour which they performed had an economic value to the institution itself. There were 38 buildings upon the grounds of the college, including a chapel having seating capacity for 2,500 persons, built by the students themselves. The value of the entire property was about $300,000. Seeing that one-third of the population of the South was of the negro race, he held that no enterprise seeking the material, civil, or moral welfare of America could disregard this element of the population, and reach the highest good. (Cheers.)

Mr. Bryce, M.P., expressed his cordial agreement with what Mr. Washington had said as to the importance of basing the progress of the coloured people of the South upon industrial training. Having made two or three visits to the South he had got an impression of the extreme complexity and difficulty of the problem which Mr. Washington was so nobly striving to solve. It was no wonder that it should be difficult seeing that the whites had such a long start of the coloured people in civilization. He believed that the general sentiment of white people was one of friendliness and a desire to help the negroes. The exercise of political rights and the attainment to equal citizenship must depend upon the quality of the people who exercised those rights, and the best thing the coloured people could do, therefore, was to endeavour to attain material prosperity by making themselves capable of prosecuting these trades and occupations which they began to learn in the days of slavery, and which now, after waiting for 20 years, they had begun to see were necessary to their well-being. (Cheers.)

A vote of thanks was passed to Mr. Choate for his services in the chair on the motion of Sir E. Durning-Lawrence, M.P., seconded by Mr. Murray Macdonald.

London *Times*, July 4, 1899, 13.

1 Brooke Herford was a Unitarian minister in London whom BTW had once known during a period of residence in Boston.

2 Joseph Hodges Choate (1832-1917) was U.S. ambassador to Great Britain from 1899 to 1905.

3 James, Lord Bryce (1838-1922) was a British Victorian leader in many fields. Born in Belfast, he was educated at the University of Glasgow and at Trinity College, Oxford, where he graduated in 1862 with a double first class. He practiced law until 1870, when he became Regius Professor of Civil Law at Oxford, a chair he held until 1893. Bryce began his political career in 1885, when he was elected as a Liberal to Parliament from South Aberdeen. He served as undersecretary for foreign affairs under Gladstone in 1886 and as chief secretary for Ireland in the Campbell-Bannerman cabinet in 1905-6. In the 1890s, as chairman of the Royal Commission on Secondary Education, he participated in a major reorganization of English schools. A frequent traveler in the United States, he wrote in 1888 *The American Common-wealth*, which as a foreigner's study of American institutions is outranked only by Tocqueville's work. Bryce was ambassador to the United States from 1907 to 1913. In the successive editions of *The American Commonwealth*, Bryce endorsed BTW's leadership and philosophy.

4 Sir Edwin Durning-Lawrence (1837-1914), a Liberal-Unionist member of Parliament, included among his many philanthropic interests the support of polytechnic institutes which provided industrial training.

5 Hodgson Pratt (1824-1907), after a long career with the East India Company in Bengal, partly spent as an inspector of public instruction, returned to England and became actively engaged in the international peace movement. He was an advocate of craft and technical training and of higher education for adult workers.

6 William Copeland Bowie (1855-1936), a Unitarian minister, was a member of the London School Board and secretary of the British and Foreign Unitarian Association.

Henry Morton Stanley[1] to Mary French Sheldon[2]

Whitehall, S.W. [London] July 4th 1899

My dear Mrs. Sheldon   It is a very busy time with me just now. But if your friend Mr. Washington cannot wait until Saturday why not let him come to the House of Commons Lobby & we can find a seat to talk some afternoon say Friday.

Thursday I go down to Windsor. Tomorrow we close Early, or

perhaps he could call here about 6 P.M. to-morrow. I give you this choice of dates as I want to oblige you. Yours sincerely

Henry M. Stanley

ALS Con. 162 BTW Papers DLC.

1 Henry Morton Stanley (1841-1904), the African explorer, met with BTW in the House of Commons. BTW recalled: "I talked with him about Africa and its relation to the American Negro, and after my interview with him I became more convinced than ever that there was no hope of the American Negro's improving his condition by emigrating to Africa." (See above, 1:366.)

2 Mary French Sheldon (1847-1936) was born in Pittsburgh, Pa., a great-great-granddaughter of Isaac Newton. Her father was an engineer and her mother a spiritualist and faith healer. Though educated as a physician, Mrs. Sheldon never practiced medicine. She became a novelist, essayist, and translator. In 1892 she published an account of her travels in central Africa to study women and children in primitive societies. Mrs. Sheldon took up residence in London in the mid-1890s.

To Joseph Forney Johnston

Tuskegee, Ala., July 5, 1899

Dear Sir: In compliance with your request of June 30th, I beg to hand you herewith our treasurer's check for $40, same being amount paid out of your contingent fund for the use of the commissioners in selecting the land grant for Tuskegee.

Thanking you very cordially for your help, I am, Yours truly,

Booker T. Washington

P. S. Since writing you before our agent has returned from Cuba accompanied by five Cubans, four boys and one girl. There is not one in the party who under any circumstances could be mistaken for a white, and I am sure that a very great mistake has been made in advising you differently.

TLSr Governor's Letter File G59 A-Ar. Signed in E. J. Scott's hand.

From Francis Joseph Campbell[1]

Upper Norwood S.E. [London] July 5th 1899

Dear Sir: I was at the Banquet of the American Society[2] last evening and was much interested in the speeches. As we have at Norwood the most successful institution for the Blind in the world, which was founded in 1872, I wish to come and speak with you in regard to visiting us, to-morrow morning.[3] Will you be so good as to look at the accompanying pamphlets which I am sending herewith.

As reference was made by one or more of the speakers to the battle of Lexington and Concord, perhaps you may be interested to know that Colonel Faulkner fired the signal gun from the Faulkner house to rouse the men of Acton to march to the battle of Concord; that old farm has been in the Faulkner family since 1735; as my wife is a Faulkner I was interested to have this old place, and bought up the other shares, and it is now our American home.

I shall come between 10 and 11 to-morrow with the hope of finding you. I am, Dear Sir, Yours faithfully,

F. J. Campbell

P.S. I think it will interest you to know that I am a native of Tennessee, and lived there until 1856 when I was driven away, first because I taught coloured people to read, and next because I refused to vote for Buchanan; further, an anti-slavery paper was sent me from Boston, which was seized in the post office. In the first instance I was to be hanged, but was afterwards ordered to leave the place and never return.

TLSr Con. 151 BTW Papers DLC. On stationery of the Royal Normal College and Academy of Music for the Blind. Addressed to BTW at the Inns of Court Hotel.

1 Francis Joseph Campbell (1832-1914) was born in Franklin County, Tenn. Accidentally blinded in childhood, he attended the newly opened institution for the blind in Nashville and the normal school in Bridgewater, Mass. Franklin taught piano and music at the Wisconsin Institute for the Blind and later in Tennessee. He was hounded in his home state, however, for his abolitionist views, and became a professor of music at the Perkins Institute in South Boston, Mass. Believing that the blind should be self-sufficient, Campbell became an accomplished mountain climber

and was the first blind person to climb the Matterhorn. On a visit to England in 1871 he discovered there was no school there where the blind could learn self-supporting skills. The next year he founded the Royal Normal College and Academy of Music for the Blind. The school offered a curriculum in general education, science-teacher training, and piano tuning, and claimed that nine out of ten graduates secured jobs in music-related fields. Campbell was knighted in 1909 and retired as principal of the school in 1912.

2 The American Society in London, comprised principally of members of the diplomatic corps and businessmen, was founded to promote fellowship among Americans resident in England and also to promote Anglo-American amity.

3 Washington did visit the college and gave what Campbell described as a "very kind and sympathetic speech." (Campbell to BTW, July 20, 1899, Con. 151, BTW Papers, DLC.)

From William N. Armstrong

Honolulu, Hawaiian Islands. July 8th, 1899

My dear Mr. Booker; I would like to have your opinion, if you can spare the time to give it, on a matter of some importance.

The sugar planters of these Islands are greatly in need of laborers. They employ many Asiatics and Portuguese, but annexation to the U.S. will prevent them from contracting for laborers from foreign countries. I have been asked whether or not the colored man could be induced to settle here. The same question was asked in 1881, but my brother (Gen S.C.A.) and I discouraged it. One reason was, and it was quite sufficient at that time, the laborers were not treated properly by the plantation managers, and the wages were very low. But great changes have taken place. Wages with house accommodations, have risen to $18. and $20. per month, and I believe will rise to $25. Wages are promptly paid.

Several large plantations in the hands of "missionary" people old friends of the General's need several thousand more laborers, and they are introducing the just and excellent system of furnishing the land and water, and making advances without interest, and then of purchasing the cane from the laborer at market rates. The laborers are therefore paid for their brain work. On one plantation this plan works well, and the Chinese and Japanese laborers are making good incomes, some as high as $40. per month. This plan is possible only when irrigation is adopted, and the crop is assured.

On reflection, I am of the opinion that there is a remarkably good opening here for several thousand colored men with their families but I would not be a party to any scheme of immigration unless the immigrants were placed in the hands of reliable men, who would treat them well, men who have done much for the Hawaiians who are dying out and are so few in numbers that they cannot begin to supply the needs of the plantations.

But the question in my mind is, can a fairly good class of colored men be induced to emigrate? Can they not do well enough at home if they choose to? I believe that you might be able to give me some valuable suggestions in the matter. I would [be] glad if you would do so. If you should give any encouragement to a carefully prepared scheme of bringing out an experimental colony, I would call on you later on in the year when I shall be in the States.

I have long believed in irrigation by the small farmer. Until it is done all over the country, farming will be an uncertain business. A half acre of land with a small windmill supplying water from only a well makes a sure crop. Even pumping with mule power will do wonders. The prosperity of these Islands is fabulous. Cuba can raise 1 and ½ tons of sugar to the acre. Some of these plantations raise with irrigation, 12 tons to the acre. I can see one from my window which was a barren waste ten years ago, and over which there is now pumped over 60,000,000 of gallons of water every day.

I keep a general track of your good work. It seems to be absolutely on the right lines. There is here an institution with a magnificent endowment, which tries to give the native Hawaiians an industrial training but it is managed by men who do not grasp the subject, and little is done.

I hope you will find time to send me your thoughts on the subject I have mentioned. Sincerely yours

Wm N. Armstrong

TLS Con. 1 BTW Papers DLC.

From Archibald Henry Grimké

Washington, July 8/99

Dear Mr. Washington: I beg to acknowledge the receipt of your kind note from Paris regarding my Boston address on Southern outrages against the Negro,[1] to thank you for the same, and to say also that I have rec'd and read with deep & painful interest your letter to the Southern people on the subject of lynching.

You have spoken plainly & wisely, and your words ought to be heeded, & I trust that they will be heeded by the people to whom they are addressed. But candor compels me to add that of this I am not at all sanguine, for the whole body of the white people of that section, excepting possibly a righteous remnant of 5 per cent., seems to have gone mad on the subject of the Negro and his rights. Our duty is, however, none the less clear. We must do what in us lies, to arouse the Nation to the peril which threatens its institutions & civilization from this baleful source.

My brother[2] desires to be kindly remembered to you. Ever faithfully yours,

Archibald H. Grimké

ALS Con. 154 BTW Papers DLC.

[1] See F. J. Garrison to BTW, May 15, 1899, above.
[2] Francis James Grimké.

From William Edward Burghardt Du Bois

Atlanta, Ga., 12 July 1899

My Dear Sir: I have taken time to think over carefully your kind offer of May 12th. I assure you I appreciate the honor. For the coming year I shall as you suggest feel under obligations to remain at Atlanta University. I shall however consider your offer for the year 1900-01 and shall decide during the winter as to whether I think a change best for all interests. Meantime I should like to hear from you more definitely as to the work you would expect & the salary. You have as you know my best sympathy for the Tuskeegee work and whether or not I see my way clear to join you in it my interest will be the same & I shall be ready to help by word or deed.

I shall try during the summer & fall to think out a plan of work that I might accomplish at Tuskeegee & when I have I shall submit it to you. I trust you will write me freely & frankly as to any plans you may have, that we may understand each other thoroughly.

I hope you & Mrs. W. are enjoying your outing as I know you must be. My regards to you both. Very Sincerely,

W. E. B. Du Bois

ALS   Con. 152   BTW Papers   DLC.

From Timothy Thomas Fortune

Saratoga Springs, N.Y., July 14, 1899

My dear Mr. Washington: Your letter of the 4th inst was received and I am very glad to hear from you, as your previous letter was dated at Paris June 19 and I had begun to be a bit uneasy because of your silence. The American newspapers gave a fair account of the Essex Hall reception, but I am glad to have the news clipping and the reception card. I am glad that you are meeting with so much distinguished attention. Your Paris article in The Age this week is hot stuff. I have sent the Transcript a short editorial based on it. Indeed I have had several editorial references to you in the Transcript.

I am getting better. Beginning with this week I begin to feel like my old self and have consequently been working rather hard all the week. There is always so much to do.

Your lynch article has made a most favorable impression on our journalists and the references to you are uniformly general and generous.

The proposed mixed meeting in Atlanta is worth debating. The Constitution is doing its best to create bad feeling against me because of my Sun articles on lynching, but I donot care a rap about that. We have got the whole of them howling and squirming, as they can't answer the facts. There's where we want to keep them.

I shall be glad to see the Atlantic article.[1] Oh, yes; the English treat our people badly everywhere except in the Islands of Great Britain. And old Kruger[2] is what you style him — an old dog, a shade better perhaps than Cecil Rhodes.[3]

The Chicago people[4] wanted 32 pages but the subject could not be covered in less than 62. *They accepted 62 pages* and want to square up for the whole by paying for half or $96. Mr. Scott is demanding $186, the figures I gave him on their letter of advice and the work accepted, and we shall have to hold them even to a civil suit to that. I spent 30 days in Washington reading up on that matter and 10 in writing, making 40 days taken from other work.

Five dollars a day for such work — well I wouldn't take another job like it at that figure. I hope they will pay for the 15,000 words without a row, but they must pay.

I shall be here until you return, I think. Let me know in your next when you will reach New York.

Mrs Fortune and the children and join me in kind regards for you and Mrs Washington. Yours truly

T. Thomas Fortune

ALS Con. 154 BTW Papers DLC.

1 BTW, "The Case of the Negro," *Atlantic Monthly,* 84 (Nov. 1899), 577-87. The article contained a brief comparison of the denial of rights to Englishmen in the Transvaal to the plight of blacks in the South.

2 Stephanus Johannes Paulus Kruger (1825-1904), president of the South African Republic from 1883 to 1900.

3 Cecil John Rhodes (1853-1902) was the leading figure in the building of Britain's African empire in the late nineteenth century. His business ambitions and territorial expansionism led to the Jameson Raid in 1895 and ultimately to the Boer War in 1899. A provision of his will led to the establishment of the Rhodes scholarships at Oxford.

4 J. L. Nichols and Co.

To the Editor of the Indianapolis *Freeman*

London, England, July 15, 1899

Editor The Freeman, Indianapolis, Ind.: Nowhere can one get such a good idea of what is transpiring in all parts of the world as in London. England has out her "feelers" in every part of the globe.

The English colonial system brings each year hundreds of representatives of all races and colors from every part of the world to London. Among the many representatives one finds a large number of Negroes, some from Africa, some from British Guiana and others from the West Indian Islands, and not a few from America. Among those from the latter country who are doing much to give the race standing and respectability in England, are Mr. F. J. Loudin,[1] of the Fisk Jubilee Singers and Mr. D. E. Tobias.[2] The latter is making a thorough study of [the] English penal system, with the hope of fitting himself to be of great service in America, in the matter of prison reform. Few colored men from America are so highly respected as is true of Mr. Loudin.

In connection with the assembling of so many Negroes in London from different parts of the world, a very important movement has just been put upon foot. It is known as the Pan-African Conference.[3] Representatives from Africa, the West Indian Islands and other parts of the world, asked me to meet them a few days ago with a view to making a preliminary program for this conference and we had a most interesting meeting. It is surprising to see the strong intellectual mould which many of these Africans and West Indians possess. The object and character of the Pan-African Conference is best told in the words of the resolution which was adopted at the meeting referred to, viz:

"In view of circumstances and the wide-spread ignorance which is prevalent in England about the treatment of native races under European and American rule, the African Association, which consists of members of the race resident in England, and which has been in existence now for nearly two years, have resolved during the Paris Exhibition of 1900 (which many representatives of the race may be visiting) to hold a conference in London in the month of May of the said year in order to take steps to influence public opinion on existing proceedings and conditions affecting the welfare of the natives in the various parts of the world, viz: South Africa, West Africa, the West Indies and the United States."

The resolution is signed by Mr. H. Mason Joseph,[4] president and Mr. H. Sylvester Williams, as honorable secretary. The honorable secretary will be pleased to hear from representative natives who are desirous of attending at an early date. He may be addressed Common Room, Gray's Inn, London, W.C. This conference is to continue in session for three days. Among the subjects to be discussed, are first, "The conditions favoring the development of a high standard of African humanity"; second, "The cruelty of civilized Paganism of which our race is the victim"; third, "The industrial development of our people in the light of current history"; fourth, "Africa the Sphinx of history in the light of its unsolved problems"; fifth, "Europe's atonement for her blood guiltiness to Africa, is the loud cry of current history"; sixth, "Organized plunder versus human progress has made our race its battlefield."

I beg to advise as many of our people as can possibly do so, to attend this conference. In my opinion it is going to be one of the most effective and far reaching gatherings that has ever been held in connection with the development of the race.

It is pretty hard for one to get away from the many social engagements in London, which seem well nigh to overwhelm, but Mrs. Washington and I have had the privilege of seeing something of English country life. For one to appreciate thoroughly the strength, beauty, culture and generosity of these English people he should have the privilege of being the guests of the owners of various English country homes, where one gets up at nine o'clock in the morning, eats six times a day, and spends the rest of the day in driving. We have had the privilege of enjoying the kindness and hospitality of the daughters of John Bright and Richard Cobden, two of the greatest men that England has produced, and two of the best friends that our race ever had.

Some people in America think that some of us make too much ado over the matter of industrial training of the Negro. I wish some of the sceptics might come to Europe and see what the races who are years ahead of us are doing in this direction. I will not occupy space in outlining what is being done for men in the direction of industrial training, but will give an outline of what I have seen done for women as an example. Mrs. Washington and I have just visited the Agricultural College for women at Swanley, England,[5] where we found forty intelligent cultured women who are mostly graduates of high schools and colleges engaged in studying theoretical and practical agriculture and horticulture, dairying and poultry raising. We found them in the laboratory, studying agricultural chemistry, botany, zoology, and applied mathematics, and we also saw these same women in the garden planting vegetables,

trimming rose bushes, scattering manure, growing grapes, and raising fruit in the hot houses and in the field. Bearing upon this same
subject I give an outline of the discussion that took place a few
days ago in London during the International Council of Women.[6]
The general subject was "Farming in its various branches as an
occupation for women." This discussion embraced dairying, poultry farming, stock breeding, bee-keeping, silk culture, veterinary
surgery, horticulture, gardening as an employment for women, and
the training of women as gardeners. As another pointer for our
people I must mention two other instances: One of the leading
members of Parliament left his duties for three days to preside at a
meeting of the National Association of Poultry Raisers, which was
largely attended from all parts of the United Kingdom. In our own
country, the son of Mr. Cornelius Vanderbilt after graduating at
Yale College, took a post graduate course in Mechanical Engineering, and has just completed the building of a locomotive.[7] At the
last commencement of Yale he received his degree as a Mechanical
Engineer.

Do all of these things contain any lesson for all people?

Booker T. Washington

Indianapolis *Freeman*, Aug. 12, 1899, 1.

[1] Frederick J. Loudin (1840-1904) was the son of a prosperous black farmer in
Portage County, Ohio. Though qualified by training, Loudin was refused employment by white printers in Ohio, and after the Civil War went south in search of
work. Having an excellent bass voice, he joined the Fisk Jubilee Singers just prior
to their second tour of Great Britain in 1875 and remained with the group after it
was disbanded by Fisk University and reorganized as a joint-stock company. Imbued
with a mission to spread the knowledge of black music, Loudin organized a six-year
world tour of the group after becoming managing director in 1882. With his share
of the proceeds he formed a shoe-manufacturing company in Lorain, Ohio. Loudin
led the Jubilee Singers on another tour of the British Isles from 1900 to 1903. While
in London, he attended the Pan-African Conference and served on the executive
committee of the Pan-African Association, organized as a result of the meeting.

[2] D. E. Tobias was born in South Carolina about 1870 of illiterate former slaves.
Tobias favored adequate public school financing in the South and opposed the
convict-lease system and labor union discrimination against black workers.

[3] The Pan-African Conference, held July 23-25, 1900, in London, was attended by
more than thirty delegates, principally black professional men from England, the
United States, and the British West Indies. The conference was called to express
concern over Britain's maltreatment of her African subjects, especially in South
Africa and Rhodesia, and a petition expressing their grievances was sent to Queen
Victoria. The Pan-African Association that evolved from the conference was significant chiefly as the first attempt at Pan-Africanism. W. E. B. Du Bois, who at-

tended the 1900 conference and another similar one at London in 1911, revived the concept in calling the Pan-African Congress at Paris immediately after World War I.

4 H. Mason Joseph, a native of Antigua, B.W.I., collaborated with Henry Sylvester Williams in establishing the African Association in London and was its first president. The association tried to protect the rights and privileges of British subjects of African descent. Joseph was a delegate to the Pan-African Conference of 1900.

5 The Horticultural College at Swanley, Kent, was founded in 1889 as an institution for men only, but in 1892 it admitted women, being the first such school in England to do so. By 1903 the school enrolled women students only. Students, who generally came from the professional and merchant classes, were trained in practical and theoretical subjects and were most often employed as gardeners in private homes or as teachers of botany and nature study. In 1945 the Swanley Horticultural College for Women was incorporated into Wye College of the University of London.

6 The International Council of Women was founded by forty-nine delegates from seven countries in Washington, D.C., in 1888, to encourage women to work together in the struggle for their rights as well as to examine "the great questions now agitating the world." Among the American organizers were Susan B. Anthony, Frances Willard, Elizabeth Cady Stanton, and May Wright Sewall. Delegates from twenty-eight countries attended the London conference in 1899 to discuss arbitration of international disputes, women's employment rights, and subsidized maternity benefits.

7 Cornelius Vanderbilt III (1873-1942) worked as an apprentice engineer on the New York Central while getting his M.E. degree from Yale in 1899. During his lifetime Vanderbilt patented thirty devices that improved the operation of locomotives and freight cars.

From Henry Sylvester Williams

Dublin   17-7 99

Dear Mr Washington   I heard of you through our friend Mr Alfred Webb[1] and was delighted to know you were still in London doing good work. He gave me your lecture to read which appeared in the Montgomery Advertiser some time since. It was a masterpiece, and cannot but serve an able purpose. Our plans for the Pan African Conference is maturing gradually. Have had a very favourable reply from Mr Benito Sylvain;[2] & he has promised to be with us. Have you given the idea of the conference serious thought? We must open the eyes of our detractors to the advances made despite the critical & opposing periods of our career. The Conference to my mind will be the precentor to the 20th Century, and my only anxiety is that our folks will attend. I should like the various professions to be represented, and papers read and discussed on the various phases. What do you think? A kindly suggestion from you on the usual proceedure of such [a] Conference will be gratefully received. If any of our Coloured American Papers have taken up the matter may I thank you for the opportunity to read their references. Our Womanhood must be represented also. They deserve a prominent position in the Conference, & it must be given them.

Hoping to hear from you, I am   Yours truly

H Sylvester Williams

P S   Please do all you can to further and awaken interest in the Conference Cause.

ALS   Con. 164   BTW Papers   DLC.

[1] Probably Alfred John Webb (1834-1908), the son of Richard Davis Webb (1805-1872), a prominent Irish Quaker antislavery advocate. Alfred Webb followed his father's printing trade, but also wrote for several journals. An early supporter of Irish home rule, Webb was sent to Parliament from 1890 to 1895 as a member of the Irish Home Rule party. Webb served many liberal causes and was particularly interested in Indian constitutional reform. He presided over the Tenth Indian National Congress in Madras in 1894.

[2] Marie-Joseph Benoit Dartagnan Sylvain (Benito Sylvain) was born in Haiti in 1868 and educated in Paris, where he also founded a newspaper, *La Fraternité*, that defended Haitian interests in particular and those of the black race in general. In 1889 he was secretary of the Haitian legation in London, and in 1891 he represented Haiti at the Brussels antislavery conference. Apparently impressed by the victory of the Ethiopian emperor, Menelik II, over the Italians at Adowa in 1896, Sylvain visited Ethiopia and in 1897 became an aide-de-camp in the imperial household. At the Pan-African Conference in London in 1900, Sylvain, representing both Haiti and Ethiopia, denounced Britain's harsh colonial policies and demanded recognition of natives' rights. His book, *Du Sort des Indigenes dans les Colonies d'Exploitation* (1901), established Sylvain as a world leader in black affairs. In later years he traveled widely in Europe, the United States, and Canada, and made three more trips to Ethiopia. Sylvain was in communication with BTW after the Haitian returned from Ethiopia in 1897 and said that as a result of his association with the American he first thought of a Pan-African association, of which he claimed to be "the principal promoter." In 1910 Sylvain was appointed adjutant general in the Haitian navy and two years later he was elected deputy of the Haitian *Corps Législatif*. He died in Port-au-Prince in 1915.

From D. E. Tobias

Camden Town   London N.W. 17 July 1899

My dear Mr. Washington: Am now returning documents which you so kindly allowed me to take.

Have perused the same with the keenest attention and the deepest personal interest and I have very great pleasure in offering my personal thanks to you, for this most *cogent* appeal which you have so earnestly made on behalf of sheer human justice. After reading your very brave and most patriotic letter addressed to the Louisiana people, in 1898 with regards to the backward step which the whites of that State took, when they passed measures, disfranchising Afro-American citizens; and now that I have read your brave appeal to the white people of the whole South, to allow the law of their own making to take its course, and thus save the Southern States in particular and the *American nation* in general from the dreadful *sin* and *shame* that now rest upon them, I am bound to say, that to me, *you* are *not* only the leader of the *Afro-American race*, but, I think, I do you only half credit, when I say, that you are the leader of the entire Southern section of the Republic, in modern thought, action and most of all, common sense!

I am not slow to confess that *I* could not exercise $\frac{1}{100}$ part of the patience and wisdom with the Southern whites as you do & I certainly congratulate you upon the wonderful amount of common sense, which you are exercising in bringing the Southern whites to their right senses.

I firmly believe that you have presented your case in such a perfectly p[l]ain and straightforward manner that hundreds of Southern people, will see the *enormity* of lawlessness and its consequences upon the Country, in a way that they have never before seen it. No one who read your letter can but feel that you are speaking out of the fullness [of] your soul in a serious vein which the entire country will do well to consider.

That letter will surely do good if the South has not proceeded beyond all redemption. And I for one, do hope it has not.

May I now beg leave to deal with one or two points in your letter which are of more than peculiar personal interest to me in the studies I am endeavoring to make.

Under the heading of "There is too much Crime": The first is this: "The figures for a given period show that in the *United States*, 30 per cent of the crime committed is by the negroes." I do not know to what figures you refer, but the statement is, I think, absolutely true, with all due modifications of course. According to the United States Census Bulletin No. 199 returned at Washington

D.C. 1890 — and there has been no national census taken since then and will not be until 1900 — Afro-Americans numbered 7,470,040 which was about 13.51 per cent. of the total population of the United States and yet, they did contribute one third of all the convicts in the country, though only 8.8 per cent of the paupers and a very much smaller number of mutes and insanes was found among them. This is indeed very remarkable, because according to facts found in the study of social problems of the hour, the one thing that is invariably true, that every poor and defective race in any country, always furnishes proportionately more paupers than prisoners!

Why is this not the case in the United States with reference to the Coloured population? The answer is perfectly obvious! There is something radically wrong somewhere. What is it? and where is it? Let me again quote from the United States census Bulletin 1890 which shows that the average sentence of Penitentiary convicts in the United States was for a native white of native parentage 5 Years and 208 days, that of a coloured convict for the same crime 6 years and 183 days. You will observe that this was for the whole country. Again for all convicts serving sentences for less than life, the native whites, of native parentage, had 64.335 years to serve; and the native colored, 86.359 years. Thus coloured convicts have 22.024 years more to serve for the same crime than the whites! Now let us take t[w]o States; an Eastern State and a Southern State. Say Rhode Island and Mississippi, and what do we find? In Rhode Island, the average Penitentiary sentence is 2 years and 356 days: while in Mississippi the average penitentiary sentence is 12 years and 116 days. There is a little disparity to say the least! The reason is obvious enough. Rhode Island has no "co[n]vict Lease system": by means of which, prisoners are manufactured for the market and another reason, being that justice reigns and too; there are far more white convicts than coloured! I could furnish much more authority to show that the *Convict Lease System* so prevalent in the ex-slave States, is responsible for such a large number of coloured prisoners being found in the United States. Abolish this huge evil and the mischief will be *abated*.

I am not wholly prepared to accept even the figures from the United States Census as being entirely accurate on criminality among the coloured people in the *North* and *West*.

But as these statistics are national, I venture to think that we may accept them as the most authoritive and therefore most *reliable*. Statements as to the number of Afro Americans in the States vary. Some say there are 10,000,000, and others say 12,000,000. But I quote from the National estimate — I suppose we may call it as no one seems exactly sure about the definite number. As to the increase of crime particularly among coloured people in the Northern States, the census at Washington does not show that. It rather shows that the coloured population is far least criminal than other poor races in the large manufacturing cities. In fact, there is really no definite way by which one can tell as to whether crime is on the increase among coloured people in the Eastern States save making personal study of the case. This, I have done to some extent and am perfectly satisfied from information gained from prison wardens and other authorities, in some of the Eastern States, that the colored people could furnish a few more prisoners before they had their proportionate number according to the coloured population. At Concord Reformatory School, where I have visited and studied the conditions with special reference to coloured students, they have done remarkably well and that in most cases splendid records have been made. The same is true in Rhode Island and Maine.

As for *pauperism* among coloured people that is not known only in cases of illness and absolute inability to assist themselves. Then, in most cases, their coloured friends assist them rather than allow them [to] become an expense to the States and cities. I am stating facts gained from personal study of these questions. May I say that Mr. F. L. Hoffman, in his book,[1] issued Aug. 1896, "Race Traites and Tendencies of the Negro," does prove that the Negro is a criminal by nature! But this "Tractate" was written to show that freedom has been a curse rather than a blessing to the Coloured Race. We must therefore bear in mind and keep before us, who Mr. Hoffman is and what his purpose was in writing such a "Tractate." I am sorry to say that Yale College made much of this book and used it, I think as a standard work on the social problem of the Coloured Race and so did Brown University. I am sure of that for I was a student at the university when this book was published. To my surprise, coloured students were thorough believers in this man, whose object was to show their uselessness as freedmen compared to their father's worth as slaves. I protested against the book from first to last. But was absolutely without support from my coloured colleagues and fellow students. Please [do] not accept my statements about these most important matters. But rather look into them on your return home and I think you will find that I am right in the main. If not in all details. What I say in this note is not in any sense an attempt to contradict a single word of what you have said. But rather to point out a few facts which I happened to have and I venture to think they are useful bearing upon the work in which we both are heart and soul interested.

I shall hope to keep in full communication and touch with you and Mrs Washington and feel sure we shall be able to weaken "the Convict Lease System" to some extent through patience skill and tact, and of course by continuing to hammer at it. Am sorry that I cannot return to America now and attend that meeting which the women are to have in Chicago during August. But I have a certain line of study, I wish to pursue in this country for a short time yet before I return home to take up a definite line of work having a particular programme of propaganda I have in mind. In due time I shall lay the whole matter before you for advice and cooperation in any way you may be good enough to assist. I enclose cutting from D.C. leader which may interest you. Shall call tomorrow AM. With all best wishes to both you & Mrs. Washington I am, Most faithfully yours

D. E. Tobias

P.S. We must bear in mind and keep before us the fact that crime is increasing in the U.S.A. among all classes and races & I think the same is true the world over, not the coloured alone. That's my point! I send these today as you may need to send them away before tomorrow though I wish I might be allowed to keep your letter.

ALS Con. 163 BTW Papers DLC.

1 Frederick L. Hoffman's *Race Traits and Tendencies of the American Negro* (1896) was a publication of the American Economic Association. Hoffman was a statistician employed by the Prudential Insurance Co., which led the movement to establish discriminatory rates for blacks seeking life insurance. He sought to prove that the Negro race was doomed to extinction because of inherent moral and hereditary weaknesses, and that in the meanwhile the Negro was "a serious hindrance to the economic progress of the white race." Kelly Miller, *A Review of Hoffman's Race Traits and Tendencies of the American Negro* (1897), a publication of the American Negro Academy, answered Hoffman's hereditarian points with en-

vironmentalist arguments. Hoffman's belief in the decline of black population was based partly on the faulty census of 1890, but undoubtedly also on his desire for the fulfillment of his prophecy. The 1900 census put the claim to rest, as black population was shown to be increasing.

To the Editor of the Washington *Colored American*

London, England, July 20, 1899

Editor The Colored American. Outside of Africa there is no better place to study Africa than London, and, in some respects, London is better for a careful investigation than Africa itself. A large part of African interests center here by reason of the fact that Great Britain controls the most valuable part of the Dark Continent. I have always had the highest respect for those of our race, who in trying to find a solution for our southern problem, advised a return of the race, in a large measure, to Africa; and because of my respect for those who have thus advised, especially Bishop Turner, I have tried to make a careful, unbiased study of the question, during my sojourn in England, to see what opportunities present themselves in Africa for self-development and self-government.

I am free to say that I see no way out of our present condition in the South by returning to Africa. Aside from other almost insurmountable obstacles, there is no place in Africa for us to go where our condition would be improved. All Europe, especially England, France and Germany, have been running a mad race during the last twenty years, to see which could gobble up the greater part of Africa, and there is practically nothing left. Old King Cetewayo[1] put it pretty well when he said, "First come Missionary, then Rum, then come Traders, then come Army"; and Cecil Rhodes has expressed the prevailing sentiment more recently in these words, "I would rather have land than niggers," and Cecil Rhodes is directly responsible for the killing of thousands of black natives in South Africa, that he might secure their land. In a talk recently with Henry M. Stanley, the explorer, he tells me that he knows no place in Africa where we of the United States might go to advantage, but I want to be more specific. Let us see how Africa has been divided, and then decide whether there is a place left for

164

us. On the Mediterranean coast of Africa, Morocco is an independent state; Algeria is a French possession; Tunis is a French protectorate; Tripoli is a province of the Ottoman Empire; Egypt is a province of Turkey. On the Atlantic coast, Sahara is a French protectorate; Adrar is claimed by Spain; Senegambia is a French trading settlement; Gambia is a British crown colony; Sierra Leone is a British crown colony; Liberia is a republic of freed Negroes; Gold Coast and Ashanti are British colonies and British protectorates; Togoland is a German protectorate; Dahomey is a kingdom subject to a French influence; Slave Coast is a British colony and British protectorate; Niger Coast is a British protectorate; Cameroons are trading settlements protected by Germany; French Congo is a French protectorate; Congo Free State is an international African Association; Angola, Benguela is a Portuguese Protectorate, and the inland countries are controlled as follows:

The Niger States, Masina, etc. are under French protection. Land Gandu is under British protection, administered by the Royal Hausan Niger Company.

South Africa is controlled as follows: Demata and Namaqua Land are German protectorates; Cape Colony is a British colony, Basutoland is a crown colony, Bechuanaland is a British protectorate, Natal is a British colony, Zululand is a British protectorate, Orange Free State is independent; the South African Republic is independent, and the Zambesia is administered by the British South African Company. Lourenco Marques is a Portuguese possession.

East Africa has also been disposed of in the following manner: Mozambique is a Portuguese possession; British Central Africa is a British protectorate; German East Africa is in the German sphere of influence. Zanzibar is a sultanate, under British protection; British East Africa is a British protectorate; Somaliland is under British and Italian protection; Abyssinia is independent. East Soudan (including Nubia Kordofan, Dafur and Wadai) is in the British sphere of influence. It will be noted that when one of these European countries cannot get direct control over any section of Africa, it is in the "sphere of its influence," a very convenient term. If we are to go to Africa, and be under the control of another government, I would think we would prefer to take our chances in the "sphere of influence" of the United States. In many parts of the world, controlled by Great Britain and other European States, the weaker races are well treated, but this is not true in most cases in Africa. The following newspaper report of an address delivered here by Mr. H. S. Williams, secretary of the African Association, will tell its own story: Mr. Williams read a letter from a native of Buluwayo, Rhodesia, stating that the British people of that country deny the natives all rights. They are treated worse than the Uitlanders of the Transvaal, and their restrictions are worse than were the cruelties of slavery in the United States of America. Mr. Williams thinks the British nation is responsible to a great extent, and that it ought to put a check upon those who go out to represent it.

It is a well known fact that slavery still exists in Zanzibar, which is under the control of the British government, as well as in other portions of Africa, controlled by Great Britain. Be it said, however, to their credit, that the British Anti-Slave Society is making strenuous efforts to have slavery abolished, wherever the Union Jack floats.

Booker T. Washington

Washington *Colored American*, Aug. 19, 1899, 6.

1 King Cetewayo (Ketshewayo, Cetshwayo) (1826-83) became King of Zululand in 1872 after defeating his half-brother in battle. Cetewayo was captured by the British during the Zulu War of 1879 and imprisoned in Capetown for three years. In 1882 he was taken to England, where he met Queen Victoria and was treated as a celebrity. Restored as king early in 1883, Cetewayo died in battle that summer.

From Henry Sylvester Williams

London, W.C. [ca. July 1899]

Dear Mr Washington: So far it was decided that our conference[1] should cover three days — morning & evening "sessions." Papers will be read by primary & secondary persons — and discussion to follow. I am instructed to get the names of representative men who are capable to deal with the following headings upon which the conference will proceed —

    1. ["]The conditions favouring the development of a high standard of African Humanity."

2. ["]The crudity & cruelty of civilised paganism of which our race are the victim."
3. "The industrial emancipation of our people in the light of current history."

   "This is yours of course."
4. ["]Africa the sphinx of history in the light of its unsolved problems."
5. "Europe's attonement for her blood guiltiness to Africa" is the loud cry of current history.
6. "Organised plunder versus human progress has made our race its battlefield."

Of course there are other details which time will develop as the expected co-operation comes. This is but an outline, and from your practical and interested experience any suggestions coming from you will be gladly received.

Resolutions will of necessity follow the various items, and according to our rules, will be submitted to central governments.

Thanking you for your kindness, we shall expect from you fullest co-operation from our People across the "blue pond." With the very best regards, I am, Yours truly

H. S. Williams

P.S. I am leaving for York today by 3.30 PM, & will be in Scotland for a little time. Let me know all news at the above address.

ALS Con. 164 BTW Papers DLC. On stationery of the African Association.

1 The Pan-African Conference at London in 1900.

From Samuel Sidney McClure[1]

New York, August 2, 1899

My dear Mr. Washington: Thank you for sending us the article on President McKinley's visit to your institute. It is not an article that we can use, I am sorry to say. The news interest in the event which you make the principal point of the article, is, of course, entirely passed. It is not a thing, either, to which we attach very great importance.

There is a suggestion, however, in this article which seems to us of great value, and which, if you are willing to carry it out, we think can be developed into an article bound to attract attention and do good. The first four pages of your story are devoted to your personal struggles; they tell the story of the development of your resolution and outline the sound reasoning which you applied to yourself, and your conditions. I believe that if you should tell the story of your own personal development and of the way in which you have carried out your idea of an industrial institute, that you would do a piece of work which would open the eyes of many of the white race and be a stimulus to your own race. If you are willing to take the time to work out your story in much the style that you have done in the first four pages of this article, I feel confident that it would stand a very good chance of finding a place in *McClure's Magazine.* I do not say absolutely that it would, because it is our rule never to promise to publish anything until we have read it. I do feel, however, like urging you to undertake it, and I do this because I believe that it would do something more than give us a good magazine article; I believe it would illuminate the whole race question.

Will you not be good enough, my dear Mr. Washington, to let me know what you think about this matter? Very sincerely yours,

S. S. McClure

TLSr Con. 158 BTW Papers DLC.

1 Samuel Sidney McClure (1857-1949) was the publisher of *McClure's Magazine.* Born in County Antrim, Ireland, he was brought to the United States in 1866 and grew up in Indiana. Graduating from Knox College in 1882 after some experience as editor of his college newspaper, McClure became editor of *The Wheelman,* a Boston magazine devoted to the new vogue of cycling. In 1884 he established a syndicate, selling articles and stories of some of the leading writers of the day. In 1893 he founded *McClure's Magazine,* and when in 1903 it published articles by Lincoln Steffens on city bosses, Ida M. Tarbell on the Standard Oil monopoly, and Ray Stannard Baker on issues between capital and labor, the muckraking movement was born. *McClure's* remained for nearly a decade a leader in the journalism of exposure, even after some of its leading writers founded a rival journal, the *American Magazine,* in 1906. McClure lost control of his magazine in 1912, and from 1915 to 1917 he edited the New York *Evening Mail.* He regained control of *McClure's* in 1923 but sold it two years later.

McClure's chief contribution to discussion of race problems was an article by

Carl Schurz in 1904 critical of southern denial of Negro rights, and a rebuttal by Thomas Nelson Page, both of them moderate in tone and supported by much factual detail. The Committee of Twelve for the Advancement of the Negro Race reprinted Schurz's article as a pamphlet.

To Warren Logan

Grand Union Hotel. New York. Aug. 5, 1899

Dear Mr. Logan: We arrived in New York this morning after a safe & very pleasant trip across the Atlantic. I am very glad to have your letter, but sorry to note the great amount of sickness there has been at the school. My present feeling is that we should have a sanitary expert look into the matter of the typhoid fever. Another matter I wish you would give attention immediately is that of having Mr. Thompson[1] make a report weekly of the land selected, where located & the value as you yourself suggest. I should recommend that you deal *gently* with him until you get the matter out of his hands, as he can cause us much expense & trouble. I think it will be best to have the *Executive Committee* take the ini[ti]ative. We want to keep right behind him every week till the land is entirely selected which should be as soon as possible. I shall write you about other matters later. Yours very truly

Booker T. Washington

HLS Con. 16 BTW Papers ATT.

[1] William Watson Thompson.

Margaret James Murray Washington to Francis Jackson Garrison

New York City. Aug 7. 1899

Dear Mr. Garrison. I hope that I am not intruding upon you but I want to thank you for the interest you have shown in my husband's work and more especially for that which you have shown in him for I often feel that people overlook him altogether in their zeal for the school. You can understand my feelings in this matter I am sure.

This trip came not a day too soon. Mr W. was just ready I believe to fall. When we left the shore going over, he began to sleep and there was such an exhaustion about the sleep that I could scarcely control my feelings, for ten days he slept & even after we got to France he slept on; all of which goes to prove that he needed this God sent release just at this time. I can never make you & the others understand how my heart goes out to you each for this timely and thoughtful kindness.

We have had a restful pleasant and profitable journey. All board, both crossing & recrossing we were treated with the greatest courtesy and by many very cordially. Mr. W. spoke on the ships both of them and I am sure he made friends. If only he could get an endowment at this time of his life, how much longer he might live. The whole thing fills [me] with terror.

We saw English life and to me it is most beautiful. Mrs. Clark spoke frequently of you & Mrs. Garrison. We spent a few days at Bristol with Miss Estlein[1] & the Misses Priestmans.[2] How lovely they are. We both spoke there in the Town Hall. At Birmingham, we were with the the Sturges. We have succeeded in getting one of our young men to go to Montserrat to take charge of the school for Mr. Sturge.

In London, we met with a warm reception. We lunched with Mr & Mrs. Bryce, Mrs & Mr Unwin,[3] Mr & Mrs. McLaren, had tea with dear Mrs. Moon, Brooke Hereford, Mr. Stendhal and in every way feasted our souls in England's hospitality & beauty. Mr W. spoke at a meeting at which Mr Choate presided, also at one at which the Duke of West Minister presided. We were at Mr. Choate's reception, also Mr. Porter's in Paris. What a beautiful house Ambassador Porter has and how beautifully gay everything about their home is but there is a certain sort of substantiality about people in London, if they are Americans that you do not find in Paris even if they are Americans. We saw the dear old Queen and had tea in her banqueting Hall, we did this later by invitation of the Woman's Congress. It would tire you if I were to attempt to tell you all we did and saw & heard & *felt*.

But you will please accept my gratitude for this last act of yours.

I know of no way by which we can ever repay you except by re-doubled efforts for our people in whom your honored father had such an interest and for whom you too are working. Yours very respectfully,

Margaret J Washington

ALS   Francis J. Garrison Papers   NN-Sc.

1 Mary A. Estlin and her father had actively cooperated with the American abolitionists. In 1899 she was about eighty years old.

2 Neighbors and close friends of Mary A. Estlin, and also formerly active in the antislavery movement.

3 T. Fisher Unwin was a leading London book publisher. His wife was a daughter of Richard Cobden.

To Jabez Lamar Monroe Curry

[Grand Union Hotel, New York, Aug. 12, 1899]

My Dear Sir: Mrs. Washington and I have just returned from Europe after a very valuable and restful trip. We feel in much better condition than ever before. I was in Washington yesterday and called at the War Department in the interest of Maj. Curry. I was told he would at least retain his present position until hostilities in the Phillipines at least cease. As soon as the President returns to Washington I will go there to see him. My present plan is to have three or four of the most prominent colored men go with me to urge upon the President this recognition of your long and valuable service in behalf of Negro Education. I believe that such a plea will prove successful. I do not know your present address but presume this letter will reach you. Yours very truly,

Booker T. Washington

HLS   J. L. M. Curry Papers   NcD.

To Ednah Dow Littlehale Cheney

Grand Union Hotel, New York, Aug. 12, 1899

My dear Mrs. Cheney: Mrs. Washington and I reached America a few days ago after a very restful stay of three months abroad. Both of us feel in excellent condition for work. Mrs. Washington has gone to Chicago to attend the Womans National Convention[1] and from there she goes to Tuskegee. Many friends in Europe were very kind to us. In addition to the rest we made many valuable friends for our cause.

I am greatly disturbed over the continual reports of crime and lynching in the South. This is proving a very trying year for our race. I hope that a change for the better will come soon.

I am not sure that I shall be able to see you before I go South the latter part of this month.

We are most grateful to you and the other kind friends who made it possible for us to go abroad. We shall try to repay the kindness by more effective work for the cause which all of us have so much at heart. Yours truly

Booker T. Washington

ALS   Sophia Smith Collection   MNS

[1] About 150 women, representing forty-six Negro women's clubs, met at Chicago in late August. Several of the delegates were entertained at Hull House by Jane Addams and the young settlement workers associated with her. (*Outlook*, 62 [Aug. 26, 1899], 925.)

From Francis Jackson Garrison

Boston, August 13/99

Dear Mr. Washington: I have received your letter of credit, & see that you made a final draft of £30 on me, July 28, which has not yet been presented but which will probably turn up tomorrow. This makes a total of £155, or about $768.00. Adding to this the cost of

passage tickets in advance	198.50	
& the cash & gold given you	147.00	then
total cost of the trip amounts to	$1113.50	

This is somewhat more than Miss Mason figured in advance, it being her idea that the $800 subscribed would amply cover everything, but I know she was counting on your securing board in Paris at $8.00 or $10 a week (apiece), & I presume that the quarters to which Mr. Stanton sent you were more expensive than that. As to London, I don't know whether you went to Smith's Hotel in Southhampton Row or not, but the advertised rates of that are so low that I thought, with all the private hospitality you would receive, that you would find London less expensive than Paris. I ran over the matter hastily with you, the afternoon you were in Boston, & thought I had explained the facts clearly to you, but we were so hurried that it is not surprising if you did not fully absorb them. What I said, in effect, was that we had raised $800; that $300 of this had been expended for tickets & your preliminary expenses, leaving $500 for hotel & travelling expenses on the other side, an average of $8.00 a day. But I added that for convenience & to avoid any possible chance of your running short of funds, I had taken out a credit for a thousand dollars, & that you were authorized to draw all you needed, as we should hold ourselves responsible for the amount of your trip, whatever it was. Subsequently, Miss Mason, as I wrote you, told me that if you would only prolong your stay she would add $125 to her subscription, making it $200 all told. (She had given $75 towards the $800.) Later yet she wrote me that she would be responsible for the balance; so her individual contribution will be nearly $400.

I write thus frankly that you may know her generous part in the matter, & not, I am sure you will understand, in any criticism or complaint about the excess of the actual expenses over our too conservative estimate, for I do not for a moment question the prudence or economy with which you travelled, & I know how unexpected expenses occur in travelling. And from your remark that you had not drawn *all* the money on your letter of credit, I infer that you thought that represented money actually subscribed in advance, & that you felt a pride in not having needed the whole of it. If the trip had cost twice what it did, it would have been one of the best investments for Tuskegee ever made, & worth more than a $40000 building!

I am looking forward to seeing you next week & want much to talk over the Southern outlook with you. Lynching is horribly on the increase, & there are signs of a vicious reaction against negro education, but we must lose neither heart nor hope. The eternal forces are with us. Yours faithfully,

Francis J. Garrison

ALS Con. 154 BTW Papers DLC.

A Report to the Tuskegee Institute Finance Committee from Lewis Adams and Others

Tuskegee Inst. Aug 18 '99

To Finance Com. We your com. beg leave to make the following report:

On July 11 two of the Cuban boys appeared at Dr Kenniebrew's door and asked for Jas German,[1] who was at this time at Porter Hall. The Dr. decided that the boys meant to do violence to German. There upon the Dr borrowed a loaded pistol of Mr A Johnson and proceeded toward Porter Hall and upon meeting German in public road handed him the pistol, in presence of students, with instructions to defend himself. Upon these boys coming towards P. H. from the east side German met them near the Hall door and drew the pistol on them. The Cubans threw up their hands. At this time Mr Logan called to German not to shoot. The Cubans proved to be without weapons of any kind.[2]

Lewis Adams
J N Calloway
J. H. Washington

ALS Con. 149 BTW Papers DLC.

[1] James Drayton German of McClellanville, S.C., entered Tuskegee as a junior in the night school in 1897. He left about 1900 without graduating.

[2] For another version of the incident, see From Cuban Students at Tuskegee Institute, Sept. 8, 1899, below.

From Peter Jefferson Smith, Jr.

Palmer House, Chicago. Aug 19th 1899

My dear Mr Washington   You have probably seen by the morning papers a lot of newspaper rot about your being denounced by the Council this morning.[1] Well now there is not one word of truth in it. It happened in this way. Mrs Washington asked that her name be left off the program and when her request was presented to the Council it was made to appear as if she had expressed considerable indignation about it, this coupled with your absence from the meeting was like shaking the red flag in the bulls face so one or two of those crazy hot heads whose only mission on earth is to talk and *do* nothing, ranted round and blew off a lot of silly gas against you. No action was taken by the Council except to accept Mrs Washington's declination. Some crazy chump of a reporter anxious for sensation, rushes the rot you may have read into print. As soon as we saw it everything else was suspended and resolutions deprecating the action of the sensational reporter and heartily endorsing you and the great work you are doing were passed unanimously amid cheers and applause.

Prof Duboise, Henderson[2] of Indiana   Bishop Walters   Maj Buckner[3] and all those who could get a word in were loud in there endorsement. Dr Bently[4] was at the meeting and helped in every way that he could to disabuse the public's mind of any such thing. You will doubtless see the subsequent action of the Cou[n]cil in the later editions. I shall tell you more when I see you in Boston.

With best wishes for a successful meeting   I am faithfully yours

P. J. Smith Jr.

ALS   Con. 162   BTW Papers   DLC.

[1] On the third and final day of the Afro-American Council meeting at Chicago on Aug. 19, 1899, there was a stormy debate as the Rev. Reverdy C. Ransom of Chicago and B. T. Thornton of Indianapolis denounced BTW and his wife for not attending the meeting, even though they were in Chicago at the time. Bishop Alexander Walters, the president, said that BTW's relation to the people of both races in the North and South "made it impracticable for him to connect himself with the discussion of an organization which might be radical in its utterances to the destruction of his usefulness in connection with many causes." This assertion was supported by the council when it formally endorsed BTW and his "noble efforts." (Chicago *Tribune*, Aug. 20, 1899, 4.)

2 Rev. Thomas Wellington Henderson was born free in Greensboro, N.C., in 1845. His parents were proprietors of a bakery, where he worked as a clerk. Befriended by Quakers, he went to Oberlin, Ohio, at the age of fourteen, and attended Oberlin College. After the Civil War he was a Freedmen's Bureau agent in Missouri for a time and then moved to Kansas. Becoming an A.M.E. minister, he held several Kansas pastorates and edited the Leavenworth *Colored Radical.* During the black migration to Kansas in 1879 he helped to care for the migrants prior to their first crops. Entering politics, he almost gained the Republican nomination for lieutenant governor. He was elected chaplain of the Kansas House of Representatives and was twice elected to the Lawrence Board of Education. He was pastor of churches in St. Louis, Chicago, Indianapolis, and Boston.

3 John C. Buckner was a waiter and politician in Chicago, and organized in 1890 a black battalion of the Illinois militia, of which he was major. He served from 1894 to 1898 in the Illinois House of Representatives.

4 Charles Edwin Bentley of Chicago was one of the leading black radicals of the early twentieth century. Born in Cincinnati in 1859, he graduated from Gaines High School there and in 1887 graduated from the Chicago School of Dental Surgery. He further studied oral surgery at the Rush Medical College Dispensary from 1887 to 1890, and established a dental practice in Chicago, at the same time securing a professorship at Harvey Medical College. He was the founder and first president of the Odontographic Society of Chicago and a contributor to dental journals. As a black political activist, Dr. Bentley helped to organize in 1903 the Equal Opportunity League, a Chicago group protesting segregation in Chicago public schools. It was also the center of anti-BTW sentiment in the city. In 1905 he was one of two Chicagoans present at the founding meeting of the Niagara Movement. When the NAACP was formed, he was one of the founders, and he organized the Chicago branch in 1912.

From Theophile Tarence Allain

Chicago, Aug. 20th 1899

Dear Prof. Washington — Your little colored man with the *glasses,*[1] if he had *remained* in the *Committee* room on *resolutions* at all of *its sessions* — the *resolution* to *indorse you* that was *sent* to *our committee would have* been *carried* in the *first place* before the *fight* on the *Floor* — as Rev. Ransom,[2] in the Committee defeated me by *one vote* — and had *your man been there* the vote would have been *on our side* — and that would have kept Ransom, in the Committee Room — but, after defeating me and Henderson, and others of your friends in Committee — he (Ransom) left us in Committee and when many of our men were at dinner or in Committee made his speech against you. But — Henderson, called your friends at once on the Committee on Resolutions, reported a splendid endorsement for you and for "Tuskegee," and we gave Ransom "Hell" from the word go — and it will be a damn long time before another "Yankee" "Nigger" — will attempt Ransom's methods. Well — they defeated me and would not strike out Section 4 — but, I keep them under fire for 4 hours, and showed the World their cowardice, and their ignorance of practical methods and after they did not ask the President to say one word in his next December message — which

I am glad that I had the manhood, because I well knew what was coming, to say: (that the condition of things — are such that you must not come to the sessions of the Council.) And, now, as the Old Plantation Woman said: "Child, I told you so."

When the facts are considered that Lyons,[3] Cheatham,[4] Green,[5] Arnett[6] — and others who should have been there and who were afraid to face the music were not on hand — and it is a well known fact — that if I had not been there to show the "Radicals," that they had "Hell" to meet every inch — and, that too in a Eleven different Volumns, They would have gone much further than what they did.

As it is — they have very little to "brag about." As to Pinchback, and other, who intended to come here against McKinley — they did the sensible thing — for had they come, we would have busted the Assembly in a thousand parts.

As it is — there is not so much harm done as a general thing.

Well — now — for me personally, you are my friend — I am yours at any cost — any where — and at any time.

I am getting old, I will be 53 in on Oct 1st 1899 — and I want Mr. McKinley, to help my friend Senator Cullom[7] to secure for me when the Senate will organize anew in Dec. Asst. Doorkeeper — or Asst. Sergeant at Arms of the Senate and I want you to write to Mr. McKinley — and tell him that he has a letter from you in March 1897, recommending me for Fourth Auditor.

And — I have our "baby" boy Allen J. Allain, I will send him to you in Nov. or between then and Jan. 1st 1900 — he is a first class boy 17 years old — and I want you to take him — and see what there is in him — we will give and send to him his clothing and shoes — hats and all — but — for his schooling — room and board — you will charge up to me, and give me a chance to meet it. Best Wishes —

Theophile T. Allain

From and after Aug. 22 to Sept. 16th 1899 — to House Document
Room, Washington D.C.

ALS   Con. 161   BTW Papers   DLC.

1 Emmett Jay Scott.

2 Reverdy Cassius Ransom (1861–ca. 1946) was a leading clergyman of the A.M.E.
Church and an outspoken champion of black civil rights. Born in Flushing, Ohio,
he graduated from Wilberforce with a B.D. degree in 1886. An eloquent pulpit orator
and energetic worker, he quickly rose to pastorates in leading A.M.E. churches in
Pennsylvania and Ohio and in Boston and New York City. He was a member of the
Niagara Movement, the Constitutional League, and the NAACP.

As early as 1897 Ransom suggested that the socialists who put human rights above
property rights were closer than others to the spirit of Jesus and more likely to bring
about a solution to the race problem. Ransom saw Christianity in activist terms as a
religion of social reform and concern for the downtrodden. In 1900 he founded, with
R. R. Wright, Jr., the Institutional Church and Social Settlement in Chicago at a
time when the A.M.E. Church hierarchy was opposed to such activity, and the experiment lasted only four years. In 1912 Ransom was elected editor of the influential
A.M.E. Church Review, much to the chagrin of BTW and his conservative followers,
who did not like the thought of such a journal being in the hands of such an outspoken man as Ransom. Ransom's religious philosophy became more race-oriented
until he was preaching that blacks were the only true Christians. (Fullinwider, *Mind
and Mood of Black America*, 41-45.) About 1924 Ransom was raised to bishop. He
played a prominent role in the Democratic party during the New Deal years.

3 Judson Whitlocke Lyons.

4 Henry Plummer Cheatham (1857-1935) was a leading black politician of North
Carolina. A graduate of Shaw University, he served in the U.S. Congress as a Republican from 1889 to 1893. From 1897 to 1901 he was recorder of deeds of the
District of Columbia. A moderate in racial strategy, Cheatham defended BTW and
remarked in the 1898 Afro-American Council session that "hot-headed meetings in
the North are making it impossible for the Negroes of North Carolina to live peace-
ably in their Southern home." (Meier, *Negro Thought*, 172-73.)

5 John Paterson Green.

6 Benjamin William Arnett.

7 Shelby Moore Cullom (1829-1914) culminated a long career as a Republican
political leader by serving as U.S. senator from Illinois from 1883 until 1913. He was
chairman of the Senate committee that established the Interstate Commerce Commission.

An Interview in the New York *Times*

[Saratoga, N.Y., Aug. 20, 1899]

THE AFRO-AMERICAN QUARREL: BOOKER T. WASHINGTON
DEFINES HIS ATTITUDE FOR HIS CRITICS

Booker T. Washington of Tuskegee, Ala., said to-night, with regard to the reports sent out from Chicago as to the attack made

upon him by two members of the Afro-American Council at Chicago after Washington had left there to fill an engagement in Saratoga:

"When I left Chicago it was with the very happiest understanding with all of the leading spirits of the council, from President Walters down. We agreed as to the good that could be accomplished along the lines which I regard as for the best interests of the race. Some of my race think I ought to participate in political activity and discussion. Personally, I have not entertained this view, and I shall not do so. There are plenty of others to do it. I shall still continue in the future, as in the past, to devote myself to the moral, educational, and industrial development of the race. In this way I feel I can be of more service at this time than in any other. Whatever a few critics may say in public and in private as to my work and as to my course, I have the satisfaction of knowing I am sustained by the knowledge that I enjoy the confidence, the sympathy, and the respect of the most thoughtful and forceful members of the Afro-American race."

New York *Times*, Aug. 21, 1899, 7.

From Max Bennett Thrasher

Charlemont, Mass. Aug. 22nd, 1899

Dear Mr. Washington, Mr. Fortune thought I had better write to you at Boston, duplicating the letter we sent yesterday, for fear you might not get that. In view of what was contained in the letter you gave me at the station he thought best not to as he said, "rush into the Transcript," but to content himself with writing a strong editorial for the Age, which we wrote and sent. He said tell you not to worry any more about the matter, and that is my own advice. I was not able to get the New York papers this morning before I left Saratoga, and cannot get them here, but you will no doubt be able to get all those where you are. I enclose a few editorial opinions which I have collected since I got here. Almost every paper I have seen has said something, and all pointing the same way. I believe it will do you a great deal of good, in the end. Don't feel annoyed over it longer. It is only a mountain which is high enough to be seen above the hills. So long as you are so successful as you are you will have these attacks. You will soon get somewhat toughened to them. Not while they come fast and frequent is the time for you to be anxious, but when they cease to come, for that would mean that your position was not so high that you invited jealousy and detraction.

I will continue to watch all the papers I can see.

When you go by the news stand buy a copy of "The Woman's Home Companion," and read the article by Mrs. Washington about her Mothers' Meeting at Tuskegee.[1] I would send you a copy from here but the only one I could find in Saratoga this morning I have sent to her. I got the material from her last spring, and put it in her name because it would attract so much more attention that way. What they say about yourself, in the second paragraph was inserted in their office, I suppose for explanation. It does no harm, but is not worded just as I would have done.

I plan now to leave Westmoreland, unless I hear something from you to lead me to do otherwise, Monday afternoon, for New York, reach Washington Tuesday forenoon and go along as soon as I can from there. That ought to get me to Charleston in good season Wednesday. I shall go from here to Westmoreland, N.H. Friday, so as to get any letters you may write me there while you are in Boston. Please write me if there is anything you want me to be looking up in Charleston before you get here. Who has charge of the meeting, or whom shall I look up, to get information from? Am I to be entertained there by some one or shall I go to a hotel?

Now don't worry any more. I have been extremely anxious about you ever since you left me yesterday morning. Very sincerely yours,

M. B. Thrasher

TLS Con. 163 BTW Papers DLC.

1 Thrasher was not only a ghost-writer for BTW, but in this case performed the same service for Mrs. Washington as well. "The 'Mothers' Meeting' at Tuskegee," *Woman's Home Companion*, 26 (Sept. 1899), 21, described Mrs. Washington's efforts to teach black women in the Tuskegee area such subjects as sewing and hygiene.

From Scott C. Burrell[1]

Richmond, Va., Aug. 22, 1899

Dear Sir & Friend; In one of the daily papers of our city I read where there was an effort made to denounce you as a traitor, at the Afro-American Convention which was held in Chicago. I wish to say that there is one if no other in the person of myself who do not agree with such. A man who has done so much and who is still doing all that is in his power to lift up his people, as you have done, can never have such herald [hurled] at him without stirring up his friends. I am with you in all your moves especially knowing you as I do. First you have God with you, and second, Right. So you need not fear but press on in your good work. May God give you the strength to do so. I send you the clippings of two of the papers of our city, one is an editorial of the Richmond Leader. Yours in the work,

S. C. Burrell

TLS   Con. 150   BTW Papers   DLC.

1 Rev. Scott C. Burrell was from 1899 to 1907 and perhaps for a longer time general secretary of the Richmond Colored YMCA.

From Emmett Jay Scott

Tuskegee, Ala., August 23, 1899

Dear Mr Washington: The Ransom attack at the closing of the Afro-American Council was unwarranted, and failed completely of its purpose. It only served to give you another opportunity to emphasize your views and the object of your work as you did at Saratoga. Your reply was sent out by the Associated Press & will do good. Du Bois and others sustain you well in the Chicago Record.

It is well you never get disgusted at the smallness of some of these little hypocritical fellows. Your composure only shows them up in painful, envious contrast. You certainly have my sincere congratulations upon the way you met this silly attack. Yours Faithfully —

Emmett J. Scott

ALS Con. 161 BTW Papers DLC.

From Timothy Thomas Fortune

Saratoga, N.Y. Aug. 25–1899

Dear Mr. Washington, I have your telegram of even date. I will explain that after talking over the extent and scope of the work cut out for Bruce he very candidly stated his position and felt that the consideration I offered him was inadequate for the work and for the necessity he would be under in the future to defend, his position as an ally of ours; hence my telegram changing the figure, which I consider a reasonable compensation under the circumstances.[1] He has to day submitted to me the drafts of two of the proposed letters — and corrected them together. They are the ones for the Springfield Republican[2] and the New York Press.[3] We shall have the one for the colored papers ready tomorrow. As to the one to the Constitution[4] I am balancing in my mind the wisdom and the expediency of sending it any thing. It is a very ticklish force with which to deal.

The Independent[5] and the Outlook[6] current both have references to you in the Chicago matter but rather in your favor than otherwise. Both references appear to bear modification along the lines of my letter.

I am glad to say that I am feeling brighter to day and the swelling in my hand is less intense. Yours truly,

T. Thomas Fortune

HLSr Con. 154 BTW Papers DLC.

[1] This is one of the earliest examples of BTW's practice of paying black journalists to write material favorable to the Tuskegean's position. It is possible, however, that BTW paid John Edward Bruce for articles much earlier, for in 1896 he wrote to Bruce: "Use your pen as much as possible. You help all along the line." (Apr. 21, 1896, John Edward Bruce Papers, NN-Sc.) In this case in 1899, BTW paid Bruce $100

to write four statements defending BTW's policies against northern black critics at the National Afro-American Council convention in Chicago. (See Fortune to BTW, Aug. 28, 1899, and BTW to Fortune, Sept. 16 and 22, 1899, below.)

2 In a letter to the editor dated at Albany, N.Y., Sept. 8, 1899, Bruce pronounced "unwarranted and undeserved" the criticism of BTW at the Afro-American Council meeting. His critics had not improved on BTW's methods, said Bruce, who thoroughly endorsed industrial education rather than political means for solving the race problem. He continued: "In all of his public utterances bearing on politics, Mr. Washington has been at pains to plainly state it as his firm belief that it is not good for the white man or the black man that the political rights of the black man should be curtailed or abridged or denied in any greater degree than the political rights of white men are abridged or denied. The real friends of the negro will applaud Mr. Washington for his good sense and wise judgment in avoiding entangling political alliances, which would result only in bringing upon himself and the particular work in which he is engaged infinite confusion. An effort to combine industrial education and politics could not result otherwise." Bruce ended by praising those, including Du Bois and Bishop Henry M. Turner, who had defended BTW, by saying of BTW and his critics: "He has done something, and an appropriate answer to those who are continually carping about the distinguished educator, would be: 'Go thou and do likewise.'" (Springfield *Republican*, Sept. 11, 1899, 4.)

3 Possibly a letter to the editor, dated at Albany, N.Y., Sept. 7, 1899, in which Bruce urged that President McKinley use the statute for enforcement of the Fourteenth Amendment, of Apr. 20, 1871, to take federal action against lynchings that deny the civil rights of blacks. (New York *Press*, Sept. 10, 1899, 6.)

4 Nothing from Bruce's pen appeared in the Atlanta *Constitution* in this period.

5 An editorial in the *Independent*, 51 (Aug. 24, 1899), 2312, suggested that the hissing of BTW's name resulted partly from disappointment at not hearing him, but also from the fact that industrial education was less popular among blacks than among whites because "it comes too far short of what is needed for their intellectual and material development above the sphere of an inferior class that has no right to rule."

6 The *Outlook* did not mention BTW in its discussion of the Afro-American Council meeting. (*Outlook*, 63 [Aug. 26, 1899], 925.)

From Isaac Fisher

Stamford, N.Y., Catskill Mts., Aug. 25, '99

Dear Mr. Washington: We arrived here yesterday. Our engagement was at Churchill Hall, but we did nothing. One trifling young colored man defeated us here.

This gentleman (?) in question, went to the Hall and discovered that we would sing at 8 o'clock, p.m. Promptly at twenty minutes of 8 he appeared on the steps of the hotel — I was there — and to the accompaniment of his guitar began singing "Negro Minstrel" songs. Those songs are very popular with the young white people, but they bring no money. He injured us in that he drew the crowd to the steps, and further that many of the guest[s] who really wanted to hear us, became disgusted and went up stairs, thinking that he was one of our number; and so when we went to the music room, we could get but few to listen to us. We collected only $6.50.

I think I have never been so handicapped before as I am here. Every colored man is regarded as a beat, because of the great numbers of fakes who have been here and are yet here. Last night I filled my last engagement until next Tuesday, leaving me 4 nights to fill in or do nothing. I have made dates for three nights but do not expect to make expenses. Mr. Smith wrote me that if I did not hear from him when I arrived here I would have to do the best I could. I have heard nothing and hence the necessity for me to fill in those 4 nights. Considering the kind of colored people I am meeting here, what they sing and why they sing, I am not surprised when the proprietor of a hotel refuses me permission to sing in his hotel. The Presbyterian minister refused me after consulting with his advisers, because he was inclined to the idea that we were minstrels. I couldn't, with all the proofs to the contrary, convince him otherwise. He was afraid that if we sung the Plantation Songs we'd slip in a secular one anyhow.

My next engagement Tuesday is in the Adirondack Mts. I fear very much that I will not be able to get there. Have not been able to hear from Mr. Logan since the 9th inst., though I write him every week. If I can pay my board and lodging and get to Albany, N.Y., I'll be doing well. I have been to every hotel here trying to get an engagement so that we won't get stranded.

Do you wish me to write you every day after you reach Tuskegee? I didn't understand that clearly. I am spending a tremendous amount of money on the railroads. Sincerely yours,

Isaac Fisher
45 Greenwich St., Boston, Mass.

Please remember me kindly to Mrs. Washington, and tell her that it is often with pleasure that I bear witness to the statement that "Mrs. Washington is a lovely woman, and a power."

ALS   Con. 161   BTW Papers   DLC.

From Timothy Thomas Fortune

Saratoga N.Y. Aug. 28–'99

My dear Mr. Washington, It was my purpose to write you this letter to morrow when Mr. Taylor[1] will be here, but on receipt of your telegram to day with the directions of which I promptly complied, I decided it best to submit the Bruce matter to you to day.

I hand you herewith telegram and letters which explain themselves. In justification of the telegram I wish to make the following detailed explanation: Bruce came here on Thursday at 11 A.M. I made him a plain statement of what I wanted, that is that he write four separate statements to be manifolded in eleven separate letters, to be written in his own way giving the facts as they occurred at the morning and afternoon session of the Council on Saturday. I told him that I did not desire that he write any thing contrary to the facts or to his prejudices or preconceptions. He readily consented to do this, stating that he had a very warm spot for you. I told him that the whole job should be finished by Saturday, or it would be regarded as flat matter. He was to get off the New York and Springfield matter on Thursday and Friday respectively. He returned at 4 o'clock with the draft of a splendid article which I corrected and interpolated and directed him to recopy and send immediately to the Republican, after writing one in like vein, but shorter, for The New York Press. I gave him the money for which I sent you the memorandum.

He came back the next morning ten o'clock and abruptly stated that he had not sent the Springfield and New York letters the night before as he promised. I got angry at this and told him that the letters would be no good for those papers beyond Sunday. He said he didn't think that he was getting enough for the work and for committing himself to our view, I told him that was his affair and not mine and asked him what he wanted. He stated his price and I wired you for information. He came in soon after I received your telegram which I showed to him and told him to go ahead with the work, that I should hear from you by letter Saturday but that he would not probably get the balance of the money before Sept. 5th. He came around Saturday morning with the third letter for the Negro press which was better and stronger than the other two and which I told him to manifold and file out at once. When he found I had not heard from you on the 9 o'clock mail his face showed that he had lost faith in the situation. He announced that he had to go to Albany on the 12 o clock train — all right I said, as I had become tired and disgusted. To my surprise he showed up along with the mail carrier at 12:15 saying he had missed his train. He left on the 1 o'clock train with the understanding that the matter would go ahead. Sunday at 12 o'clock I got his first letter and decided that we could get along without the scamp. The sort of cur he really is, is disclosed in his last letter to [me]. We shall hear from him in many directions but we shall have more credit in the opposition than in the cooperation of a character so depraved. We have the situation firmly in hand and by wise generalship we shall not lose it. I quite agree with you in The Independent matter. I don't understand Dr. Ward.[2] I enclose Outlook letter. My hand is much better. With kind regards, Your friend

T. Thomas Fortune

HLSr   Con. 153   BTW Papers   DLC.

[1] Robert W. Taylor, northern financial agent of Tuskegee.
[2] William Hayes Ward.

From Theophile Tarence Allain

Washington, D.C., Aug 29th, 1899

My Dear Sir: Enclosed please find the Washington Post. The Editor is an old friend of mine and a Louisiana man.[1]

Rev. R. C. Ransom took it all back in an open letter to the Inter Ocean of Aug. 25th.[2]

I took that paper to the Editor, and he wrote what he thought best. I am so glad that I did so much to keep you away from the Afro-American Council — as I am of the opinion that as matters turned out, the *cause* that you are doing so much to advance — is benefited by the general publications in your behalf.

The President will be here about Sept. 12th — and as my friends in Illinois will present my name to the caucus of the Senate for an

$1800 place in Dec. I want a letter from you to him — and I know that the President is friendly to me. (Will return to Chicago after Sept. 16th.) Best Wishes —

Theophile T. Allain

ALS Con. 149 BTW Papers DLC.

1 The editor in 1899 was Beriah Wilkins (1846-1905), from Ohio. Allain probably meant an editorial writer and reporter, Richard Coxe Weightman (1845-1914), a Confederate veteran who reported for the New Orleans *Times* (later *Times-Democrat* and then *Picayune*) from 1872 to 1888. He worked for the Washington *Post* from 1888 to about 1909 or 1910.

2 In a letter to the editor in the Chicago *Inter Ocean*, Aug. 25, 1899, 6, Ransom said: "I arose at the urgent request of Mrs. Booker T. Washington to move that her name be stricken from the programme of the National Afro-American Council." He denied that he had called BTW "a traiter, or a trimmer, or a coward, as every one who was present when I spoke well knows." He said it was possible that those words might have been uttered from the audience. He insisted that he simply protested against BTW's refusal to attend the convention while claiming to be the leader and Moses of the race. Ransom wrote: "It may have been unwise for me to have referred to Mr. Washington at all; but I certainly did not do so with any intention either to misrepresent him or do him harm; but when to the fact that the evening before I made these remarks he sent for Bishop Walters, the president, and stood under the lamp post in front of my house, which is opposite the church, and talked for quite a while, was added the fact that he had previously sent for him to confer with him at his hotel, I felt that if he had any message to convey to the council, or desired to exercise any control over its deliberations, he should have come into our midst. We had met to deliberate upon our social, industrial, educational, financial, and civil conditions; we needed the help of our best and wisest minds." BTW received a similar criticism from Nathan F. Mossell. See BTW to Fortune, Sept. 22, 1899, below.

From Timothy Thomas Fortune

Saratoga, N.Y. Aug 29 '99

Dear Mr. Washington — I enclose you Bill Arp's talk in the Atlanta Constitution of last Sunday.[1] Please return it to me at once as I need it. The dirty old sinner goes after you and Mrs. Washington with a sharp stick.

They don't put handles to Negro Women's names in the Constitution, which you ought to write to Clark Howell protesting against referring to your wife as that woman.

I enclose you a letter from Dancy. The poor fellow is your friend and I am sorry for him. I enclose also a letter from the Albany black-guard[2] and direct your attention to the brave insolence of the last paragraph. May God have mercy on his dirty Soul.

I have not answered his letter and shall not do so until I hear from you to-morrow, when I shall enclose the balance on the agreement with a courteous note simply saying that we feel under obligations to fulfill my end of the understanding and you bet the black-guard will never return the cheque.

My hand is much better and I feel full of fight. I hope you [have] a pleasant trip and experience in West Virginia.

Pledger wants to know your movements and I have sent them to him to-day. Yours truly

T. Thomas Fortune

HLSr Con. 153 BTW Papers DLC.

[1] Bill Arp (Charles Henry Smith), racist columnist for the Atlanta *Constitution*, wrote: ". . . it is impossible to keep up with the lies and slanders that are circulated by northern politicians and southern negro editors and educators. It is all a scheme to get money from the northern dupes." Arp cited Mrs. Washington, who had attacked the convict-lease system and pleaded that black women prisoners should not be locked up at night with male prisoners. Arp contended that this was never done in the state of Georgia and that BTW and his wife should be held accountable for such "malignant slanders." (Atlanta *Constitution*, Aug. 27, 1899, 19.) Other southern newspapers picked up Arp's column, prompting D. W. McIver of the Montgomery *Advertiser* to write BTW that he had always supported BTW but that his faith had been shaken by Mrs. Washington's charge, since he did not believe that male and female prisoners were ever locked up together in any southern state. (Sept. 5, 1899, Con. 158, BTW Papers, DLC.)

[2] John Edward Bruce.

An Address at Burlew Opera House, Charleston, W.Va.[1]

Charleston, W.Va. [Aug. 31, 1899]

My Friends. It was in 1872 that I left this county a poor unknown ignorant boy in search of an education. You cannot realize with what surprise and gratification I received, while in Europe, an invitation a few weeks ago signed by the leading colored men in this state, the Governor, the Mayor and members of the City Council of Charleston and many prominent officials and citizens, asking me to return to Charleston and Kanawha county, for the purpose of permitting the people in the county and state where I was reared, to express at a public reception their appreciation for what I have tried to do for my race and country. To say that I am profoundly grateful and surprised at the honor which you do me, but feebly expresses my feeling on this occasion. While I am gratified because of your attention, I confess that I am almost oppressed by a consciousness of the feeling that I am unworthy of the attention and the kind words which you literally pile upon me. I have tried simply to do my duty as an American citizen as best I could. Sometimes perhaps I have succeeded; sometimes I have failed, but in either case I have tried to follow honestly the teachings of my heart and head.

Since I left here as a boy, it has been my privilege to receive very many honors both in America and Europe, but nothing that I have seen, nothing with which I have been brought into contact has made my love for you any less intense. Neither the great capitals of Europe, nor the great cities of America, nor the Black Belt of Alabama have in any degree lessened my love for these rivers, these mountains and valleys, and the coal mines and salt furnaces where I used to work. It was in this county that I first had the privilege of attending a public school. It was in this county that I first learned to read. It was in the midst of these beautiful valleys and mountains that I first got the inspiration which gave me the determination to attempt to do something to improve the condition of the millions of my race in the far South. How well I have succeeded I prefer that others would state.

Not far from here in the family of a noble white woman, whom most of you know, I received a training in the matter of thoroughness, cleanliness, promptness and honesty, which, I confess to you, in a large measure enables me to do the work for which I am given credit. As I look over my life, I feel that the training which I received in the family of Mrs. Viola Ruffner was the most valuable part of my education. [Waving of handerchiefs and applause.]

Starting in 1881, at the little town of Tuskegee, Alabama, in the midst of the "Black Belt" of the South in a little shanty with one teacher and thirty students, with absolutely no property, an institution has grown that now has over a thousand students, coming from twenty-three states, Porto Rico, Cuba, Africa, and other foreign countries. In all of our departments there are eighty-six instructors, and if I add the families of our instructors, we have a standing population upon our school grounds of about twelve hundred persons. Students are not only taught in academic and religious branches, but they receive instruction in twenty-six different industries. When I began this institution there was only one building on the grounds; today there are thirty-eight buildings, counting large and small, and all of these buildings except four have been almost wholly erected by laboring students. Plans for the buildings are drawn upon our school grounds, and the students do the work of building, from the making of the bricks to the putting in of the electric fixtures. The institution owns twenty-three hundred acres of land, seven hundred of which are cultivated by the labor of the students. On the farm we have nearly four hundred head of live stock, including horses, mules, cows, etc. We have sent out nearly four hundred graduates, who are employed as teachers, mechanics, farmers, housekeepers and dressmakers in almost every state of the Union, and the work of these graduates is gradually changing for the betterment of the condition of the South. [Applause.]

In all this work I have sought not alone to benefit my own race, but by lifting up the black man at the same time to assist the white man in removing the burdens that have come to him as a result of American slavery. To me "a man is but a man for a' that and a' that." The two races are to live in this country together, and he is an enemy to both who tries to array one race against the other. In proportion as the Negro grows intelligent, industrious and good at heart, in the same proportion will the white man be helped. In proportion as the white man permits himself to oppress the Negro, in the same degree is the white man degraded, and his progress retarded. In proportion as the white man becomes intelligent and prosperous, in the same degree does he learn to accord to the Negro the rights that belong to men. [Applause.]

The years that we are now passing through are serious and trying ones so far as the question of the white and black races are concerned. I may not be able to advise that which will bring complete remedies for all our ills, but I believe that there never was a time when the Negro needed to give more attention to the matter of making himself intelligent, industrious, law abiding, and to the cultivation of high moral habits. I acknowledge that my heart is greatly and constantly troubled by the large number of Negro boys and men who stand in idleness about the streets of our cities and towns. My friends, I confess to you that since I left here nearly thirty years ago, I do not believe that I have spent a single day in complete idleness. The Negro is too poor to be idle. He is too far behind to let others get ahead of him in learning useful occupations. He is too weak to fail to secure that strength and respect which comes to any one through the ownership of property and the conduct of business. I do not find too much fault; the Negro in proportion to his opportunities has made unparalleled progress, but I want the progress in the future to be far greater than in the past.

The man who is able to do something as well or better than any one else is the individual who is honored and respected regardless of his race or color. [Applause.]

In connection with the efforts of the Negro himself to improve and to obey the law, it is most important at the present time that those in authority see to it that the law is enforced in the interest of black man and white man alike. Any deviation from this course will bring ruin to both races and to our country. The official who breaks a law when a Negro is concerned, will ere long, break it when a white man is concerned. We cannot have one code of justice for a white man and another for the black man without both races being made to suffer. I want to implore my race not to get discouraged during this trying time. Perhaps we needed these trying days to prod us on to greater effort and more conscientious duty. Without sorrow there is no joy; without trial there is no triumph; without the storm there is no strong oak.

Almost the whole problem of the Negro in the South rests itself upon the fact as to whether the Negro can make himself of indispensable service to his neighbor and the community, that no one can fill his place in the body politic. There is at present no other safe course for the black man to pursue. If the Negro in the South has a friend in his white neighbor and a still larger number of friends in his own community, he has a protection and a guarantee of his rights that will be more potent and more lasting than any our Federal Congress or any outside power can confer. [Loud applause.]

The Negro in the South has it within his power, if he properly utilizes the forces in hand, to make of himself such a valuable factor in the life of the South that he will not in any large degree seek privileges, but they will be conferred upon him. To bring this about, the Negro must begin at the bottom and lay a sure foundation, and not be lured by any temptation into trying to rise on a false foundation. While the Negro is laying the foundation, he will need help, sympathy and justice from the law. Progress by any other method will be but temporary and superficial, and the latter end of it will be worse than the beginning. American slavery was a great curse to both races, and I would be the last to apologize for it; but in the Providence of God, I believe that slavery laid the foundation for the solution of the problem that is now before us in the South. During slavery, the Negro was taught every trade, every industry that constitutes the foundation for a living. Now, if on this foundation, laid in rather a crude way it is true, but a foundation nevertheless, we can gradually grow and improve, the future for us is bright.

The man who learns to do something better than any one else, has learned to do a common thing in an uncommon manner, is the man who has a power and influence that no adverse surroundings can take from him. It is better to show a man how to make a place for himself than to put him in one that some one else has made for him. The black man who can make himself so conspicuous as a successful farmer, a large tax payer, a wise helper of his fellowmen, as to be placed into a position of trust and honor, whether the position be political or otherwise, by natural selection, is a hundred fold more secure in that position than one placed there by mere outside force or pressure. [Prolonged applause.]

Washington *Colored American*, Sept. 9, 1899, 5.

1 For BTW's account of his Charleston reception, see above, 1:155-57 and 368-70. The Washington *Colored American* described BTW's homecoming as "a Red-Letter Event in West Virginia's History." Governor G. W. Atkinson introduced BTW in a ten-minute speech that praised the Tuskegean for having "the correct conception of what is termed 'the Negro problem in the South.'" He said BTW was "easily the foremost man of his race on this continent." The audience of about 2,000 greeted BTW with thunderous applause. "When Booker T. Washington faced the audience,"

the *Colored American* reported, "a scene was presented at once thrilling and dramatic. Men and women rose as a single individual, and participated in a tumultuous wave of applause, the fair sex fluttering dainty handkerchiefs in Chautauqua salute. No hero returning from a victorious campaign could have been more royally received." BTW spoke for two hours. (Washington *Colored American*, Sept. 9, 1899, 1, 5.)

BTW was accompanied on his visit to Charleston by his daughter Portia and two newspapermen, Max Bennett Thrasher and Richard W. Thompson. Though white dignitaries were the principal sponsors of BTW's visit, he stayed at the house of Rev. D. W. Shaw, a black clergyman, and met with his friends, Byrd Prillerman, Phil Waters, and Dr. Henry F. Gamble. The black people of Charleston entertained him after his speech at a banquet at the City Club, which had previously not admitted blacks. On the following day he visited his sister Amanda and other old friends in Malden.

From Timothy Thomas Fortune

Saratoga, N.Y., Aug 31. [1899]

Dear Friend: Please find my letter to Bruce, with express receipts for the $80 sent to him. I can't imagine a more depraved character than he is, *but his capacity for mischief is very great.* I think the $100 will cork him up, as he hardly lets go a dollar when he gets hold of it.

Yes, I think it material and urgently important that you and Bishop Walters get to gether as soon as possible.

Smith got here last night and he and Taylor go to Boston to day. We have had some talk about the situation.

Of course you hold on to all the Bruce correspondence and receipts. We may need them.

I can use my right hand a bit but it is painful work.

The Constitution of the 28 August has a good editorial on your African letter in The Age.[1]

I hand you a memorandum of my requirements to square up here. Please send a certified check or draft on New York as long distance checks are taken here *only for collection.* I shall go to New York soon after I hear from you. Yours truly

T. Thomas Fortune

ALS Con. 154 BTW Papers DLC.

[1] The New York *Age* also carried BTW's letter from London. (See To the Editor of the Washington *Colored American*, July 20, 1899, above.) An Atlanta *Constitution*

editorial supported BTW's arguments against emigration to Africa. Ironically, it used BTW to score a point against Fortune, saying: "Quite recently, a very intelligent negro — T. Thomas Fortune — declared in point that a negro who had the respect of the southern whites, or who conducted himself toward them politely, is a sneak and spy, with a streak of villainy running through his nature. What is to be done with people who entertain such ideas? There is but one remedy, and that is to be found in the application of Booker Washington's plan of education to the whole race. He has succeeded thus far because he is on the right lines. . . ." (Atlanta *Constitution*, Aug. 31, 1899, 4.)

From Reverdy Cassius Ransom

Chicago, Ill. August 31st, 1899

My dear Mr. Washington: I appreciate more than I shall be able to express, your most earnest letter, almost every line of which breathed with the spirit of profound interest for the welfare of your people and mine. I am most happy to take this opportunity of expressing to you personally what I have said from my platform and through the press. That I did not, nor have not at any time, referred to you in tones of disrespect, nor did I seek in what was said either to misrepresent you or do you harm.

I very much regret that I referred to you at all if such reference has in any way embarrassed you or done you harm. I think I can, in a measure, appreciate your position before the American people as a whole, and before your race. I felt however, that we should have had the benefit of your presence, but it may be doubtless true that reasons which influenced your judgement to remain away were the wisest and the best. Some of your friends and admirers, with that disposition which is largely common to human nature, who like to stand in the shadow of a great or famous man and thus attract a little passing attention to themselves, in their over-zealous championship are probably responsible for much of the misrepresentation that has gone forth.

I regard your career as one of the most fruitful and remarkable of any man of our race, and your work as the most fundamental and helpful of any that is being done for the great mass of our people who, if they rise at all, must do so through habits of industry, frugality, character and thrift.

If in my small way, I can ever at any time be of service to you in any line of work which you are doing for the help of our people and mankind, I am yours to command. With confidence in the sincerity of your purposes I am, with high regard, Very sincerely yours.

R. C. Ransom

TLS Con. 160 BTW Papers DLC.

From Timothy Thomas Fortune

Saratoga, N.Y., Sept. 5 [1899]

Dear Friend: I have your telegram of even date concerning the whereabouts of Bruce. I will send him a note at Albany. I sent a note to Rev. J. H. Anderson[1] at Binghampton yesterday, asking if the letter for Bruce sent to his post office had been delivered to him. I should hear from him tomorrow morning.

I heard Mr. Baldwin's paper at the American Social Science Association this morning and the *low tone of disparagement of the race developed by the discussion surprised* me.[2] I answered some of the mis[s]tatements of fact and conclusion. It is a pity that the friends *we have [have] to give away so much in discussion to gain so little*. I give away nothing.

My hand is very stiff and painful today, but the doctor says it is doing very well, and he ought to know. He began on the other ailment today, and found it in satisfactory condition. I hope for the best. Yours truly

T. Thomas Fortune

ALS Con. 154 BTW Papers DLC.

[1] James Harvey Anderson, born in Maryland in 1848, was a minister of the A.M.E. Church at Binghamton, N.Y. He was a regular columnist on the *Star of Zion* for thirty years and was its editor from 1916 to 1920.

[2] In his speech before the American Social Science Association in Saratoga, N.Y., William H. Baldwin, Jr., attempted to win the support of the white South by conceding many racial views commonly held by whites. Using the analogy of a child who lacks self-control, Baldwin described the newly freed slave as too eager for the superficial and ornamental of life. He saw a decline in the quality of black life after emancipation as the Negro artisan gradually disappeared and the Negro politician took his place. Critical of higher education for blacks, Baldwin said the northern white teachers who went south after the Civil War made the mistake of assuming that

blacks should be educated in the same way as whites. "Instead of educating the negro in the lines which were open to him," Baldwin said, "he was educated out of his natural environment and the opportunities which lay immediately about him." Baldwin praised the work of Samuel Chapman Armstrong at Hampton and added that BTW was carrying out Armstrong's work and was "the Moses; Tuskegee, his creation, his life, and the hope of the race." Probably the parts of the speech that upset Fortune most were Baldwin's capsule pronouncements on several controversial subjects. Baldwin said: "Social recognition of the negro by the white is a simple impossibility, and is entirely dismissed from the minds of the white and by the intelligent negroes. There is no need of social recognition." He accused those who advocated social equality of being "sentimental theorists." On the issue of civil rights Baldwin urged that blacks and whites alike should be disfranchised if they were not qualified to vote. He attacked lynching as an evil but went on to say: "Lynching, however, indicates progress. No progress is made without friction."

In the discussion that followed the address Fortune gained the floor and said: "I am thoroughly convinced that it is impossible to pin down the Afro-American people entirely to industrial education or to higher education, for the simple reason that they are just like any other race." Fortune praised BTW as "the greatest man we have to-day," then went on to say that "I have always considered, in the main, that the Tuskegee idea was correct; but the principle is wrong that a man should first learn to work and then develop his head." Baldwin rejoined that he was all for higher education for some blacks but that his address referred to the "great black mass of poor, poverty-stricken negroes who are at the bottom." (*Journal of Social Science,* 37 [Dec. 1899], 52-68.)

To Josephine Beall Wilson Bruce

[Tuskegee, Ala.] Sept. 6, 1899

My dear Mrs. Bruce: Please excuse me for my long delay in answering your letter of August 25th; I did not reach home until early this week and have scarcely had a minute to write since coming home. Mrs. Washington, however, tells me that she wrote you several days ago. I have just sent you a telegram saying that we expect you next week.

Anticipating newspaper announcements in regard to your coming here I have prepared a short reference to the matter which I have sent out to some of the leading white and colored papers. I have placed it in a form which I feel quite sure will not be objectionable to you. Had the matter been left for the newspapers to get hold of the best way they could to make their own announcements I fear the announcements would not have been so satisfactory.

Suppose for the present we place the salary at $80 per month and board,[1] board to include all expenses except traveling. If later on I can see my way clear to make it a larger fig. . . .

[Booker T. Washington]

TLpf Con. 282A BTW Papers DLC.

[1] She had asked for a salary of $90 per month, a larger amount than BTW's original offer. (Bruce to BTW, Aug. 25, 1899, Con. 150, BTW Papers, DLC.)

From Timothy Thomas Fortune

Saratoga, N.Y., Sept 7, 1899

My dear Friend: Here is a card from Rev. Anderson, to whose care the Bruce letter was sent. Evidently the rogue did not go near Binghampton, but simply said he was going *as a bluff* to make me hurry up the payment of the additional $80.00, although I had told him the payment would hardly be made before Sept. 4. I wrote to him at Albany yesterday about the matter, as I had not heard from Mr. Anderson and I ought to have a line from him tomorrow, unless he has gone to Jersey City to see Bishop Walters.

Bishop Walters and I had two talks here about Bruce, when I made him understand that *Bruce was a good man to use but a bad man to trust*; I was therefore surprised to see in the public prints that Bruce had been made *financial secretary* of the Council and allowed to name C. W. Anderson as a member of the executive committee with me for New York.

Bishop Walters wants me to stand for chairman of the Executive committee, but I am disposed to get out of the thing entirely, but will await your advice and be governed largely by it.

Rev. Ransom has made a statement in the Chicago Inter Ocean, which I rather like and may reproduce in The Age, concerning his attitude at the morning session of the Council towards you.

Your telegram of yesterday about the money was received. I will get it Friday or Saturday and shall square up and leave for New York Monday or Tuesday. I may stop a day or two in the Caatskills on the way down, but I shall be in New York on Thursday sure.

My general health is better and my hand is less stiff and painful.

I hope the Boston affair to you in October may not be a boomerang. We can't afford any more breaks at this time.

The more I study Mr. Baldwin's address the more I dislike certain parts of it. I would like to blue pencil these parts. They are bound to hurt the race and Tuskegee. Yours truly

T. Thomas Fortune

P.S. Read Bill Arp's article in last Sunday's Constitution on W. H. Council and his rot.[1]

ALS Con. 154 BTW Papers DLC.

1 Bill Arp praised a speech William H. Councill gave in Kansas which urged northerners to leave the South alone. Arp wrote: "That negro's head and heart are both right. He is a brave man and dares to speak the truth." (Atlanta *Constitution*, Sept. 3, 1899, 19.)

From Emmett Jay Scott

[Tuskegee, Ala.] Sept. 8, 1899

Dear Mr. Washington: I wish to thank *you* very sincerely for the testimony as to the value of my services to *you* & the school. I have all along felt that you should not, out of your own pocket pay any part of my salary and I am glad that you are arranging it differently. I need not tell you that I shall continue to render as faithful and conscientious service as I can. Again thanking you, I am, Yours very truly —

Emmett J. Scott

ALS Con. 161 BTW Papers DLC.

From Edward Elder Cooper

Washington, D.C., Sept. 8, '99

My dear Friend Washington: Your favor of the 6th inst. is to hand and noted. I must thank you for your friendship and your generous disposition towards me. The $5.00 you spoke of was really not in the contract. I made Mr. Scott the proposition of $25.00 or $30.00 and so sent the bill for $30.00. So you see I must thank you for the extra $5.00 as that was not really part of the contract. The other I received, for which I am grateful.

Mr. Thompson came back delighted with his trip and has given you a 5 column write-up, which you will see in The Colored American this week. He also got a very nice article in The Post. It always pleases me when we can work this way together and I hope you will not forget to call on me or those whom I control for any assistance I may be able to render you. For some reason or other John E. Bruce has become of late, unfriendly to you and has written some very bitter letters which I have and which I will not publish. I have written to him that while we are friends (Bruce and Cooper) Washington and Cooper are also friends and that he must ring off, so to speak, in his talk on you. I shall control him.

Of course when you come through the city you will make it a point to inform me so that I may see you and say some things in person that time will not permit in this letter. Yours very truly,

E. E. Cooper

TLS Con. 151 BTW Papers DLC.

From Cuban Students at Tuskegee Institute

Tuskegee, Ala., Sept. 8, 1899

Sir: Concerning the disturbance on the campus this summer; I will endeavor to give you in detail as near as I can remember, a straight unbiased account.

One Sunday evening we were throwing ball, Mr Palmer came up to us and asked us to stop. We did so, But shortly afterwards I was looking over a paper and saw where "Base-Ball" was being played on Sunday. I called the attention of the other boys to the matter, and we concluded that it must not have been any harm.

So we went out and began playing the second time.

When we finished playing we went to Supper very shortly afterwards, and there was nothing but corn bread and syrup, we did not want it so we came out, not only us but nearly all the students, came out without any supper.

We went down to the well to get some water. While there, Mrs Kenniebrew came out where we were and scolded us, and remarked to some of the boys that worked in the Kitchen, to go and get Mr Logan.

Dr Kenniebrew[1] also came out and tried to make us go on the other side of the campus, and told the kitchen boys if we did not do so to beat us.

Directly after the conversation with Dr Kenniebrew Mr Logan came up and told us very kind to go on the other side we did so. On Monday morning we went to breakfast, there was nothing but bacon and cold biscuits warmed over. So we decided to go down to the farm and hunt something to eat. There we found something nice to eat and was very kindly treated.

Not knowing where we were there was search made for us.

We were down to the farm about four hours altogether, before we returned.

The next day we went to work all except John Gomez.

In the afternoon while we were in the class-room Mr Penny excused Gomez from class so Mr J. M. Greene could get him and put him in jail.

The new boys that had just come looked out of the window, and saw Mr Greene after Gomez, they did not know what he was intending to do; but for fear that he meant to beat him, they all rushed out and jumped on Mr Green.

During the Scuffle, German jumped on Sixto[2] and bruised him up very bad. Shortly after we went down to Supper, and Dr Kenniebrew, German and the boys that worked in the kitchen, came up behind us as we were going and remarked that we had a pistol in the crowd. Dr Kenniebrew then gave German his pistol and told him to "Kill that black Cuban."

In the meantime Mr Logan came up then German slipped the pistol to Dr Kenniebrew. Dr. K. put the pistol in his pocket and went to his room.

Mr Jackson then taken Antonio Soto[3] to Dr. Johnston, and the other boys went to Dr Kenniebrew. Sixto was laid up in bed two or three days. Gomez and myself were locked up in the "Guard House."

The night after the disturbance Mr Palmer turned Gomez and I out at 8: o-clock, and I went to Sixto's room to see how he was, there I found Mr Jackson,[4] Mr Scott and Mr Hunt,[5] with a large watermelon, he asked me if I wanted some I told him no Sir I thank you.

It made us very angry to see that Mr Jackson acted as he did in the matter. We started to write the N.Y. Herald about how the Cubans were treated at Tuskegee, but when we reflected and thought of the harm it would do the school, we refrained from doing so; especially on your account, because you are responsible for us and we do not want to put you to any trouble.

We believed also, that if you knew just how we were treated you would, you would give us satisfaction, and punish the guilty parties.

This, and only this, is why we have not gotten satisfaction.

The following morning after Gomez and I came out of the "Guard house" Some of the students said to us that Dr Kenniebrew said he was going to Kill Gomez and I.

And every-where we went around on the grounds the kitchen boys and some other students would pick at us and annoy us, and said that they had orders from Dr Kenniebrew to do so, So that we would be made to do something then he could get a chance to hurt us.

Of course I got scared and went down town and bought me a pistol in order to be ready when the fun came, and prepared to do my duty in protecting myself.

The pistol mentioned above is the one Mr Jackson took away from me.

When Mr Jackson went to Cuba he told our parents we would be treated all right up here, then when he came back and that little disturbance came up, he cried out to the students "Why dont you come back and take the whole crowd, meaning the Cuban boys." That is all as near as I can remember about the fuss. Now Mr Washington I would like to mention a few other things aside from that, which is this.

Our food has not been so good this summer; and we earnestly hope it will be better this winter.

Then why is it Mr Washington, when we ask for clothes or any thing we need, we are asked so many questions and sometime doesn't get it.

We dont get the half of what we ask for.

Since the Cuban girl has been here to this school she has not gotten a thing she asked for except 1 pr shoes, is that right?

The following is a list of the articles she asked for that she needed. Two dresses, three pair stockings one trunk half a dozen handkerchiefs 1 corset 3 shirt waist 1 comb 1 hair brush 1 tooth brush 3 Under shirts 3 pair pantalettes 1 pair shoes I cant remember what else at present.

She told me this in Spanish and I wrote it to Mrs Kenniebrew in english. She only has gotten one pair of shoes.

When our mothers write and ask us how are we getting along we do not tell them exactly how we are treated because we do not want them to become confused and worried.

We would like to know Mr Who is to pay our expenses to and from home when we go to see our parents?

You will greatly favor us if you will answer this letter as early as possible to the satisfaction of Your ob't servants

Alfredo Perez[6]	Pedro Salina
Sixto Rodriguez	Guillermo Fernandez[8]
Carlos Rivera[7]	Delfin Valdes[9]
Antonio Soto	Julian Valdes[10]

HLS Con. 152 BTW Papers DLC.

1 For BTW's reaction to Kenniebrew's role in the episode, see BTW to Kenniebrew, Sept. 29, 1899, below.

2 Sixto Rodriguez of Havana attended Tuskegee from 1898 to 1901.

3 Antonio Maria Soto of Havana attended Tuskegee from 1899 to 1902.

4 Thomas J. Jackson was a teacher of mathematics in 1897-98 and agent of the Tuskegee Negro Conference from 1898 to 1901. In 1900-1901 he was also employed by the Negro Department of the Charleston Exposition.

5 Nathan Hunt, born in Springboro, Ohio, was reared in Ohio and received a college education with the aid of some Quaker benefactors. He joined the Tuskegee Institute staff in 1895 as BTW's private secretary and stenographer, often accompanying BTW on his fund-raising tours. Even after the arrival of Emmett Jay Scott in 1898, Hunt remained one of BTW's close aides as traveling secretary and stenographer. The many letters he transcribed, and often signed with a representation of BTW's signature, are identified by the letter *H* usually found near the bottom left margin. After BTW's death Hunt became secretary to his successor, Robert R.

Moton. He accompanied Moton to Europe during World War I, and remained at Tuskegee until his death in 1932.

6 Alfredo Perez of Havana attended Tuskegee from 1899 to 1900.

7 Carlos Rivera of Havana attended Tuskegee from 1899 to 1900.

8 Guillermo Antonio Fernandez of Havana attended Tuskegee from 1899 to 1902.

9 Luis Delfin Valdes of Havana attended Tuskegee from 1899 to 1908.

10 Julian Valdes of Havana attended Tuskegee from 1898 to 1906.

To Timothy Thomas Fortune

Tuskegee, Ala., Sept. 11, 1899

My dear Mr. Fortune: I have received your kind letter of Sept. 7th in regard to matters connected with the National Council. I hardly know what to say about the matter at present; my judgment is we had better let things stand as they are until you and I can have a conference regarding matters. I understand from private sources that Bruce Grit has sent out some dirty stuff to some newspapers which the papers have refused to print. If Bishop Walters means to tie up to that kind of an individual I think we should have an understanding before we go further.[1] I hope you will not at least refuse to be chairman of the Executive Committee before I have seen you. I think you can hold the matter off for a while.

I suppose you have seen something of the industrial convention to be called in Huntsville on the 10th of October. It is going to be a very important affair, having white representatives from all portions of the South. Many of the governors are to be in attendance. I have been invited to speak there and considering the importance of the occasion did not feel that I could afford to miss it and have therefore broken several other engagements.[2] The only thing I dislike about it is being associated with that fellow Council who is in every way an undesirable individual.[3]

I note what you say about the Boston affair. I think I shall rather hold that off for awhile, at least until matters get clear.

I am sorry that you are so disturbed by Mr. Baldwin's address; I should like to see it and wish you would send me a copy of it. He is a person that will bear educating and I think if you will write him frankly about the portions of the address with which you disagree I think he will appreciate it.

Bruce Grit I am sure will make a fine financial secretary in his own interest.

I have just been going over the editorials which are very large in number, written concerning the outbreak against me in the Council. The editorials are so strong in condemnation of the Council that I question whether or not that body has not been very seriously injured.

I think nothing I have written in recent years has so wide a quotation as the African letter published in the Age. You will notice the last issue of Harper's Weekly has an article on the subject and refers to the Age.[4]

I am very glad to see the letter from Essie Jean.

I hope at sometime you can find an opportunity to write out the address which you gave here on "Heroes and Hero Worship." It is by far the best thing that has ever come from you in my opinion. I have sent for the Transcript of the 6th in order to read Sanborn's[5] and Wilcox's[6] letters. Yours truly,

Booker T. Washington

The enclosed clipping represents the consensus of opinion as exhibited by the editorials so far as the white papers are concerned. What the general trend of the editorials of the Negro press is you know better than I do but on the whole it seems to me it has been favorable. The enclosed clipping from the Burlington, Vt., Free Press, I think has been stereotyped.

TLS   Con. 161   BTW Papers   DLC.

1 On Sept. 14, 1899, Fortune wrote BTW: "Bishop Walters is a weak brother. We shall have to confer before we can determine where we are. I shall not budge in the Council matter until I have seen you." (Con. 154, BTW Papers, DLC.)

2 For BTW's address at Huntsville, on Oct. 12, 1899, see above, 1:157-62. BTW considered this one of his important speeches, and it was reprinted at Tuskegee in pamphlet form in 1899 and 1902. (Pamphlet, Con. 961, BTW Papers, DLC.) It also appeared in E. Davidson Washington, ed., *Selected Speeches of BTW*, 78-86.

Another who spoke at Huntsville was William Hooper Councill, who said that there was plenty of opportunity for blacks in the South. "I do not ask for the negro the supreme right to rule," said Councill, "but the God-given privilege to do an honest day's labor. The man who counts me out at the ballot box may defeat the evil schemes of selfish politicians. But the man who counts me out of an equal and fair chance to earn a dollar robs me of my birthright, sends the wolf to my door and digs a grave for my wife and children." He also asked of the white South: "Protect us and we will build as our fathers did for you."

Former governor William Alexander MacCorkle of West Virginia made the best speech of the day, as BTW viewed it. MacCorkle said that three solutions to the race problem were generally discussed: colonization, diffusion, and amalgamation. He dismissed all three and said the solution was industrial education and a restrictive but fair franchise. MacCorkle blended a conservative southern view of the horrors of Reconstruction, when an "alien race" dominated politics, with a rather liberal appeal for voting rights. He assumed, however, that any franchise restriction based on property or education would disfranchise far more blacks than whites but that this would be necessary for ultimate advancement. "The only plan upon which the Negro can work out his destiny," MacCorkle said, "is along the lines of a separate race entity." (MacCorkle, *Some Southern Questions*, 47-110.) BTW thought MacCorkle's speech was an especially bold utterance for a white southern Democrat. (See BTW to Henry Floyd Gamble, Oct. 14, 1899, below.)

3 Fortune had written to BTW: "Councill makes me tired and so you harnessed with him in print makes me ugly." (Sept. 8, 1899, Con. 154, BTW Papers, DLC.)

4 A *Harper's* feature, "This Busy World," by E. S. Martin, stated: "Booker T. Washington has no opinion of Africa as a refuge for American negroes. Writing from London to the New York *Age*, he points out that Europeans have now got control of almost the whole African continent." The article cited cases of racial violence in America but concluded that more blacks were doing well in America than in Africa, where news of racial outrages was not reported as fully as it was in the American press. (*Harper's Weekly*, 43 [Sept. 9, 1899], 900.)

5 Franklin Benjamin Sanborn (1831-1917), an intimate of John Brown, was an editor and author of books on Brown, Thoreau, Emerson, and others. He was a founder, with William Torrey Harris, of the Concord School of Philosophy. In his speech before the American Social Sciences Association in Saratoga, N.Y., in Sept. 1900, Sanborn said that the color feud in the South was a disgrace to civilization. He also spoke on the topics of immigration and the accumulation of wealth in America and expressed the belief that these two factors were leading to greater social inequity in America. (Boston *Transcript*, Sept. 6, 1899, 6, 13.)

6 Walter Francis Willcox (see above, 3:408) spoke at the same convention and said that crime among black youths was on the increase because they no longer had the kind of family training that was partly provided by slave masters. Other factors contributing to black crime, according to Willcox, were a lack of job opportunities and a growing fanatical reaction to lynchings in the South. (Boston *Transcript*, Sept. 6, 1899, 6, 13.) For BTW's reaction to Willcox's remarks at Saratoga, see BTW to Willcox, Sept. 16, 1899, below.

To Walter Francis Willcox

Tuskegee, Ala., Sept. 16, 1899

My dear Professor Willcox: I want to thank you very sincerely for the very valuable paper which you read at Saratoga. While the facts brought out in it may appear disagreeable to many at first, in the end I am sure that it will do our whole cause lasting good. There is no question in my mind but idleness, lack of permanent productive employment is at the bottom of a great deal of crime among the race. Yours truly,

Booker T. Washington

Please send me if printed a full copy of your address.

B. T. W.

TLS   Con. 6   Walter F. Willcox Papers   DLC.   The postscript is in BTW's hand.

To Timothy Thomas Fortune

Tuskegee, Ala., Sept. 16, 1899

Dear Mr. Fortune: Mr. Proctor[1] and Mr. Pledger are working up the Atlanta affair alright and I go there on the 25th. It now promises to be a successful occasion. A similar affair is in preparation for Montgomery to take place on the 27th. The present plan in Atlanta is that both Governor Candler and Clark Howell are to be present and speak on the same occasion. This puts a rather dangerous phase on the situation. Nobody knows what they may say. If I can go through this ordeal and escape unhurt I think I shall consider myself proof against all kinds of dangers. Proctor, however, writes that it may be that both of them will be called away on account of the Dewey reception[2] in New York about that time, but both of them have consented to be present and speak.

I have just written a letter to Huntsville urging the importance of inviting at least a half dozen colored men to be present at the Industrial Convention. The more I think of it the more I think that I shall be compromised by Council and I do not want to go there and be identified with Council as representing the sentiment of all of the colored people. We ought to have at least a half dozen good strong colored men in the meeting. Yours very truly,

Booker T. Washington

TLS   Con. 161   BTW Papers   DLC.

1 Henry Hugh Proctor (1868-1933) was pastor of the First Congregational Church in Atlanta from 1894 to 1920. Born in Tennessee, from 1885 to 1891 he attended

Fisk University, where he was a friend and classmate of BTW's wife and also of W. E. B. Du Bois. He received a B.D. from Yale Divinity School in 1894 with a thesis entitled "The Theology of the Songs of the Southern Slave." Proctor wrote that he believed that slave songs were based on "a real theological system" and that they represented "the true American music." Proctor first met BTW in 1895 when the Tuskegean delivered the Atlanta Compromise address. He later recalled, "I sat beside his wife as he leaped into fame." He was an active promoter of BTW's speaking engagements in Georgia, and BTW often stayed at his home when in Atlanta. Proctor found BTW helpful in raising money for his church. "I found his name a key North and South," he remembered. In 1906 Proctor was instrumental in relieving tensions after the Atlanta Riot and was one of a handful of black and white citizens who were credited with restoring order in the city. In 1919 he toured France for the YMCA, speaking to black troops. Writing in 1925, Proctor compared BTW with Du Bois: "They are the right and left wings of a great movement. Just as a bird must have both wings for successful flight, so must any movement have the radical and conservative wings." He saw no conflict in his warm personal relations with both men. (Proctor, *Between Black and White*, 45, 100-101.)

2 The celebration of the return from Pacific duty of Adm. George Dewey (1837-1917), hero of the battle of Manila Bay.

To Timothy Thomas Fortune

Tuskegee, Ala., Sept. 16, 1899

Dear Mr. Fortune: I beg to hand you herewith Bruce-Grit's letter. I have read same and confess that I was greatly surprised to receive it and in the same mail a copy of the Springfield Republican containing one of his letters. He is, as you suggest, a queer individual. Yours very truly,

Booker T. Washington

TLS Con. 154 BTW Papers DLC.

From Timothy Thomas Fortune

Brooklyn, N.Y., Saturday, Sept. 16, 1899

My dear Friend: I have just read the enclosed article in the Evening Post,[1] and it has left a bad taste in my mouth. I send it to you because of the importance of it and for fear that it might otherwise escape you.

Your success and popularity are predicated almost entirely upon your undeviating optimism in the possibilities of your race. This writer says you came back from Europe "more discouraged than ever in your life about your own race." Where did he get that? *You can't afford to get discouraged,* and if you should *avowal of it so that* it will *get in the public prints will do no more*[2] *than anything else to discourage the friends of your work and to lessen the financial support of your work.* You know all this as well as I do, but this Post article is a storm signal, written by an enemy who may be masquerading as your friend.

Others may get discouraged, but you can't without inviting disaster.

Then, the Post writer knocks the props from under you by placing you in an attitude of doubt upon the *vital question* of the race's moral reliability. "I don't know" is used by him as a negative reply. You can't have any doubts on the subject; and if you have, if you donot keep them to yourself you give the whole case away. But my idea is that the Post writer has drawn upon his imagination in both the points he makes or that he has violated your confidence in the way he has used the points or in using them at all. His whole article and the calling of the conference are made to hinge upon alleged pessimism of yours.

My hand pains me very much tonight, as I have been using it, and was compelled to do so, incessantly the past two days. Your friend

T. Thomas Fortune

ALS Con. 153 BTW Papers DLC.

[1] The unsigned item in the New York *Evening Post,* Sept. 16, 1899, 21, said that philanthropists were becoming skeptical of contributions to black education in the South. Many contributors, the article stated, were worried about the racial violence in the South while others believed that the black population was increasing faster than financial aid, thus wiping out any real gains. According to the article even BTW upon his return from Europe expressed discouragement over race progress in America.

[2] Fortune obviously meant to say "will do more."

To Timothy Thomas Fortune

Tuskegee, Alabama. Sept 18, 1899

My dear Mr. Fortune: I thank you for calling my attention to the Post article of last Saturday. This article was inspired and I think written by the American Missionary Association Secretaries who have always been jealous of Tuskegee and ready to do anything to break my influence.

The whole article is based upon a falsehood. When I had the conference with the A.M.A. people I was careful to have Mr. Scott present so that he could witness what was said. The funds of the A.M.A. have been dropping off lately and they want to place me in the same bag with themselves.

The meeting of all the Secs. for Nov. 1 was suggested and urged by me. I hope some good will come from it.

When I speak in Atlanta next Monday night I shall take occasion to say something to off set the "Post" article. If the associated press does not use it, I will deny it in the Post over my signiture. I hope that you will watch the influence of the Post article.

I am glad that your arm is better and that your general health is improving.

I hear that Dunbar is in a bad fix and has gone to Colorado. Yours Sincerely

Booker T. Washington

ALS   Con. 153   BTW Papers   DLC.

From Charles Satchell Morris

Lovedale Institute, South Africa [Sept. 19, 1899]

My Dear Mr Washington — I am now at the Tuskeege of South Africa a great school of some 550 students from nearly all tribes of South of the Zambesie. I have a little wooden box about two by 4 inches presented to me to give to you. I will take it all around Africa and then bring it home to you. I am in splendid health and spirits. I have ridden out here some forty miles on my wheel over some pretty tough mountain roads.

This is a great country with superb openings for men with brains & trained hands. I have travelled over the most of the Southern part of the country. Now I go to the Zambesie region. At this writing the war clouds are gathering thick and fast and it looks as if the Briton & the Boer would close in on each other in a life & death struggle for the mastery of all this great region. I am very glad to know of your pleasant voyage & your safe return. Give my kindest regards to your wife & all friends. Yours with warm appreciation,

Charles S. Morris

ACS Con. 158 BTW Papers DLC. Postmarked Sept. 19, 1899.

To Timothy Thomas Fortune

Tuskegee, Ala., Sept. 22, 1899

My dear Mr. Fortune: Dr. Mossell's letter is interesting from several points of view.[1] I think Mossell is inspired or led on largely by his wife. Enclosed, however, I send you a clipping which shows exactly what I said at the Philadelphia meeting. In reading this you must bear in mind that I had just reached Philadelphia the next day after the Palmetto burning[2] occurred and there was intense excitement in Philadelphia the night I was to speak. I did not feel that I could enter upon a detailed discussion of the lynching with safety or with any degree of profit so I said substantially what the enclosed clipping reports me as saying but not what Mossell said I stated. I should think a man in Dr. Mossell's position would be careful to get possession of facts before making a statement. Our total income last year, for example, was $104,000; of this amount we got $4,500 from the State of Alabama. This latter figure is our regular appropriation and not $8,000 as the doctor states it. Any one can see at a glance that we could lose this state appropriation and not be seriously inconvenienced. Knowing that I had not discussed the question of lynching in my Philadelphia address I took the first occasion, as you can testify, to speak out plainly on the sub-

ject in my lynching article as you know. I am sure you will be glad
to see the enclosed letter from Mr. Clement. His stockholders are
giving him some trouble I think, that is what he has reference to.

I shall send you a check within a day or two to cover Bruce Grit's
deficit.[3]

I thank you for Mr. Baugh's[4] letter. I shall endeavor to see him
soon. I am debating somewhat between him and Thompson in
Washington. Thompson, I think, is the stronger man and more
preferable if he is all right otherwise.

I think the Atlanta affair is going to be quite a success. Yours
truly,

Booker T. Washington

TLS Con. 161 BTW Papers DLC.

[1] Nathan F. Mossell, a black physician of Philadelphia, criticized BTW for re-
fusing to make public statements on controversial race matters. He said BTW was
reluctant to speak out because he was afraid it would hurt his educational work.
"This awful condition of affairs," Mossell wrote, "causes Mr. Washington to appear
before his audiences to a great disadvantage. In fact, when he is not thoughtful
enough to make this frank admission in the beginning of his addresses, he is made
to appear at times as an apologist, a trimmer, and a traitor to his race." Mossell also
attacked BTW's use of anecdotes in his speeches, since "they don't always illustrate
the highest aspirations and emotions of our people, but, like most men who are
collecting money for similar work, they appear at times to magnify the degradations
of the people whom they seek to elevate. . . ." Mossell said it was possible to understand BTW's actions as a southern educator, but he questioned whether such conduct could be tolerated from a man often called the Moses of his race. (*The Independent*, 51 [Sept. 28, 1899], 2638-39.)

[2] The lynching of Sam Hose. See p. 91 above.

[3] Bruce's receipt, dated at Albany, Sept. 9, 1899, acknowledged "For writing four
letters for the Press in re Booker T Washington $100.00," and claimed a balance of
$12.13 for travel expenses. (Con. 154, BTW Papers, DLC.)

[4] Possibly William Edward Baugh, a black man from Alabama who later taught
at Howard University.

To Francis Jackson Garrison

Tuskegee, Ala., Sept. 23, 1899

My dear Mr. Garrison: I thank you for your letter of September
18th. I am glad you appreciate so keenly the situation in which
I am placed in reference to these receptions. I have refused to go
to several places where I have been invited lately largely on the

ground which your letter suggests.[1] The idea of the reception at Charleston, W.Va., as is true of the one at Atlanta, was started by the colored people but the white people were invited to take a part. I am especially fearful that Gov. Candler will attempt in some way to compromise me by what he will say in Atlanta. In my address I intend to give him full credit for all that he has done to stop lynching in Georgia, but at the same time I shall hew to the course which I have mapped out and which you understand so well. I think as you do, that Gov. Candler is very glad to deliver the address of welcome in connection with this Atlanta reception for the reason that he wants to blot out as fast as possible the record which he suffered the State of Georgia to make during the Sam Hose and other outrages.

My misery, however, will not be over after I have been at Atlanta. I see the Huntsville Convention has invited W. H. Council to deliver an address on the same day that I speak. You may not know it, but Council for a number of years has had the reputation of simply toadying to the Southern white people and I very much fear that my position will be compromised by being associated with him as a speaker. I shall count myself proof against all kinds of dangers if I can come out of both of these meetings unhurt.

I thank you for the clipping from the News and Courier.[2] I shall get hold of Pamphlet No. 6 published by the American Negro Academy and read it carefully.[3] Yours truly,

Booker T. Washington

TLS   Francis J. Garrison Papers   NN-Sc.

[1] Garrison, referring to BTW's receptions with Gov. George W. Atkinson of West Virginia and Gov. Allen D. Candler of Georgia, wrote BTW that Candler's purpose was to "strengthen his position in fighting lynching." He then added: "Possibly also some of these Southern officials in showing you honor may have an ulterior motive of giving the impression that you approve, or do not mind, the steady disfranchisement by State after State of the colored voters." (Sept. 18, 1899, Con. 154, BTW Papers, DLC.)

[2] In his letter to BTW on Sept. 18, 1899 (Con. 154, BTW Papers, DLC), Garrison enclosed an editorial from the Charleston *News and Courier* entitled "The 'Black-Code' Vindicated." The editorial stated that racial hostility in America was the result of misrule in the South during Reconstruction. The black codes in the South in 1865-66, the editorial maintained, offered a reasonable solution to the relations between the races, but Radical Republicans and black politicians had overturned them. "If the black codes had been allowed to work," the editorial concluded, "instead of evoking such unmeasured censure and undeserved abuse, [they] would have been

applauded as the offspring of wisdom and the product of enlightened statesmanship." (Charleston *News and Courier*, Sept. 12, 1899, 4.)

3 John L. Love, *The Disfranchisement of the Negro* (1899), concluded that the disfranchisement movement was the first step in an attempt by the South to limit the freedom of blacks and eventually reinstate the black codes.

From Timothy Thomas Fortune

New York, Sept 23. [1899]

My dear Mr. Washington: I have your letter of the 18th instant and am glad to have the inspiration of the Post article. I did not care a rap about the article but the light it placed you in with the quotations, which I could not see how you could have fathered for publication. The A.M.A. must be in a tight place if they can resort to such disreputable tactics. I am glad you will say something at Atlanta to offset the publication, and I hope the Associated Press will use it. I will watch the influence of the Post article, but the damage of it will be done with those who sustain our educational work and are never heard of in the public prints. The writer of the article was gunning for just that sort of effect.

I too understand that Dunbar is in a bad way and has gone to Colorado Springs. When I last saw him he declared that he would not go near Colorado, so I judge from his going that he is in worse shape than when I saw him last. Then I did not think he would live six months. If he pulls through the winter I shall be surprised.

I had a talk with Durham[1] Thursday. He had evidently been talking with R. G. Ogden,[2] from the tenor of his remarks. Of course Ogden likes you very well when you donot get in the way of Hampton. We will talk the matter over when we meet.

I hope the Atlanta affair will come off to the general advantage and that nothing will transpire of an unpleasant character.

Remember me kindly to Pledger. Yours truly,

T. Thomas Fortune

My health continues to improve.

ALS Con. 153 BTW Papers DLC.

1 John Stephens Durham.
2 Robert Curtis Ogden.

To Timothy Thomas Fortune

Tuskegee, Ala., Sept. 24, 1899

My dear Mr. Fortune: There is a matter about which I have been intending to speak to you for some time but I have delayed it hoping to see you when I could talk it over more fully and with more satisfaction. I think I mentioned to you sometime ago that a firm in Boston was very anxious to have me put my various addresses and magazine articles in book form. This I have decided to do very largely for the reason that I need the money that I think will come from such a publication and also for the reason that I feel that the firm which has made me rather a generous offer is a good one and one that will pay me to get connected with. Before giving the manuscript to the publishers I wanted you to have an opportunity of going over it. Mr. Scott and I have just had a lengthy conversation on this point and after looking over the manuscript rather carefully we find that there is very little of it that you have not already seen, but I am very anxious that you go over the proof of the book. It was the original plan for either Mr. Scott or myself to go to New York and take the manuscript so that you could go over it with one of us but it seems impossible for either of us to leave at the present time but you will arrange it so that you can go over the proof with one of us. The manuscript I think has been reasonably well arranged and I think is going to present a pretty respectable appearance in book form.

One thing which the publishers and I have not agreed upon is the title; they are inclined to call it "The Future of The Negro." I have had a little fear that that will be misleading and seem like biting off a little more than one can chew. Mr. Scott gave the manuscript a very careful reading yesterday and is inclined to the view that "The Future of The Negro" will be a proper title. I send you a copy of a letter just received from the publishers on this point. I shall, however, leave the whole matter of the title undecided until you have had an opportunity to go through the manuscript.

While of course I want to get some financial returns from the book, I am determined to do nothing that will in any way sacrifice the good of our cause or my reputation for the mere matter of dollars and cents.

The publishers have had a wide-awake and experienced book man here for the last three or four weeks working helping me prepare the manuscript.

I shall speak in Chicago October 3d before the Baptist Social Union. Yours truly,

Booker T. Washington

TLS Con. 160 BTW Papers DLC.

An Address in Atlanta

[Atlanta, Ga., Sept. 25, 1899]

[The Race Problem in Light of European Travel]

I thank Governor Candler most heartily for his words of welcome and encouragement; and I am also deeply gratified and grateful for the generous remarks expressed by Colonel Pledger, who speaks for the colored citizens of Atlanta, as well as to the other gentlemen who have so kindly added their voices of welcome upon this occasion.[1]

The presence of the governor of the state of Georgia, the state commissioner of education as well as other distinguished citizens of the white race, who join this large and representative negro audience on this occasion, is added proof that the noblest members of the Anglo-Saxon race in the south have a deep and abiding interest in the progress of the negro.

It is fitting that I should take advantage of this occasion to thank your governor in the name of the negro race and all good people throughout the country for the manly and courageous manner in which he is having the law for the protection of human life enforced in this state. By his recent actions, as well as his words, Governor Candler has served notice that hereafter Georgia will be a state where no man can be too humble or too black as to place him outside the protection of the law of your state, and that no man with his consent shall receive punishment without legal conviction. In this blessed work of re-enthroning the law of blotting out crime, your governor should have, as I believe he will have, the active aid and sympathy of every black and white man in the state. With the

215

cleanest and strongest members of both races standing shoulder to shoulder in favor of blotting out crime and enforcing the law there can be no doubt as to the future prosperity and happiness of each race.

I heard a few days ago that it has been reported that I came back from Europe discouraged and disheartened as to the condition and prospects of my race in this country. So far from this being true I have never felt more hopeful about the future of the race than I feel at present. If other evidence were needed the mere presence of your chief executive and other officials tonight is proof that the south desires the elevation and not the degradation of the negro; that the south desires to encourage him and not oppress him.

I have unwavering faith in the providence of God. Who knows but that events within the last year have been God's way of teaching the race that it must make friends in every manly way with people among whom it lives and upon whom in a large measure it depends for daily subsistence?

Our problem is not to be solved by looking to congress or to the north alone, but by the reputation that each individual creates for himself in his own community and county.

So long as the negro is permitted unmolested to secure education, property, employment and is given the protection of the law I shall have great faith in our being able to work out our own destiny. The south has been guilty of a great many crimes, but I believe that it has rarely if ever been guilty of murdering men simply because they sought honest employment. There is little difference between the slavery that compels a man to work without pay and that which forces him to refrain from working for pay.

Over and over again while in Europe I had constantly impressed upon me the advantage which the negro has in the south in the opportunity to enter successful business as compared with poor people in Europe.

If you ask me for the source and foundation for my encouragement over the prospects of the race, I would point you to the negro who is engaged in business in the south. In all parts of the south I have met the negro carpenter, truck gardener, the contractor, the butcher, the merchant — they speak hopefully and encouragingly. Everywhere they tell me that in business in the south there is practically no color line and that in some cases one-half of their business is with their white neighbors. The two races are to live in this country together, and he is an enemy to both who tries to array one race against the other. In proportion as the negro grows intelligent, industrious and good at heart, in the same proportion will the white man be helped. In proportion as the white man permits himself to oppress the negro, in the same degree is the white man degraded, and his progress retarded. In proportion as the white man becomes intelligent and prosperous, in the same degree does he learn to accord to the negro the rights that belong to man.

The years that we are now passing through are serious and trying ones so far as the question of the white and black races are concerned. I may not be able to advise that which will bring a complete remedy for all our ills, but I believe that there never was a time when the negro needed to give more attention to the matter of making himself intelligent, industrious, law-abiding, and to the cultivation of high moral habits. I confess that my heart is greatly and constantly troubled by the large number of negro boys and men who stand in idleness about the streets of our cities and towns. My friends, I confess to you that since thirty years ago, I do not believe that I have spent a single day in complete idleness. The negro is too poor to be idle. He is too far behind to let others get ahead of him in learning useful occupations. He is too weak to fail to secure that strength and respect which comes to any one through the ownership of property and the conduct of business. I do not find too much fault; the negro, in proportion to his opportunities, has made unparalleled progress, but I want the progress in the future to be far greater than in the past.

The man who is able to do something as well or better than anyone else is the individual who is honored and respected regardless of his race or color.

In connection with the efforts of the negro himself to improve and obey the law, it is most important at the present time that those in authority see to it that the law is enforced in the interests of black man and white man alike. Any deviation from this course will bring ruin to both races and to our country. The official who breaks the law when a negro is concerned will ere long break it when a white man is concerned. We cannot have one code of justice for a white man and another for the black man without both races being made to suffer. I want to implore my race not to get discouraged during this trying time. Perhaps we needed these trying days to prod us on to greater efforts and more conscientious duty. Without sorrow there is no joy, without trial there is no triumph, without the storm there is no strong oak.

Almost the whole problem of the negro in the south rests itself upon the fact as to whether the negro can make of himself such a valuable factor in the life of the south that he will not in any large degree seek privileges, but they will be conferred upon him. To bring this about the negro must begin at the bottom and lay a sure foundation and not be lured by any temptation into trying to raise on a false foundation. While the negro is laying this foundation he will need help, sympathy and justice from the law. Progress by any other method will be but temporary and superficial and the latter end will be worse than the beginning. American slavery was a great curse to both races, and I would be the last to apologize for it, but in the providence of God I believe that slavery laid the foundation for the solution of the problem that is now before us in the south. During slavery the negro was taught every trade, every industry that constitutes the foundation for a living. Now, if on this foundation, laid in rather a crude way, it is true, but a foundation nevertheless, we can gradually grow and improve, the future for us is bright.

The man who has learned to do something better than any one else has learned to do a common thing in an uncommon manner, is the man who has a power and influence that no adverse surroundings can take from him. It is better to show a man how to make a place for himself than to put him in one that some one else has made for him. The black man who can make himself so conspicuous as a successful farmer, a large taxpayer, a wise helper of his fellowman as to be placed into a position of trust and honor, whether the position be political or otherwise, by natural selection is a hundred fold more secure in that position than one placed there by mere outside force or pressure.

Some people in America think that some of us make too much ado over the matter of industrial training for the negro. I wish some of the skeptics might go to Europe and see what races who are years ahead of us are doing in this direction. I will not occupy time in outlining what is being done for men in the direction of industrial training, but will give an outline of what I have seen being done for women; as an example, I visited the Agricultural college for women at Swanley, England, where we found forty intelligent, cultured women, who are mostly graduates of high schools and colleges, engaged in studying theoretical and practical agriculture, horticulture, dairying and poultry raising. I found them in the laboratory studying agricultural chemistry, botany, zoology and applied mathematics, and I also saw these women in the garden planting vegetables, trimming rose bushes, scattering manure, growing grapes and raising fruit in the hot houses and in the field. Bearing upon this same subject I give an outline of a discussion that I heard during the meeting of the International Council of Women. The general subject was "Farming in Its Various Branches as an Occupation for Women." The discussion embraced dairying, poultry farming, stock-breeding, bee-keeping, silk culture, agriculture, horticulture, veterinary surgery, gardening as an employment for women, the training of women as gardeners.

As another pointer for our people, I mention two other instances: One of the leading members of parliament left his duties for three days to preside at a meeting of the National Association of Poultry Raisers, which was largely attended, all parts of the United Kingdom being represented. In our country the son of Cornelius Vanderbilt, after graduating at Yale college, took a post graduate course in mechanical engineering, and has just completed the building of a locomotive. At the last commencement of Yale he received his degree as a mechanical engineer. Do all these things contain any lesson for our people?

Atlanta *Constitution*, Sept. 26, 1899, 7.

1 Allen Daniel Candler welcomed BTW on behalf of the state of Georgia and remarked that he was astonished at the progress blacks had made since emancipation. He blamed black problems on the "dirty politician." He urged blacks to follow the lead of BTW and said: "Your work will aid me in putting down the mob in the South." William A. Pledger welcomed BTW on behalf of the black citizens of Georgia and spoke briefly and somewhat pessimistically on the need for civil rights, referring to discrimination on railroad cars. Also on the speakers' platform, which was decorated with a large American flag draped around a picture of BTW, were Gustavus R. Glenn, state school superintendent, J. M. Henderson, president of Morris Brown College, and Henry Hugh Proctor, pastor of the black First Congregational Church in Atlanta, where the reception was held. (Augusta *Chronicle*, Sept. 26, 1899, Clipping, Con. 1931, BTW Papers, DLC.)

John Temple Graves, well known for his outspoken anti-Negro views, was among those in the audience. He later praised the entire affair and complimented the black speakers including BTW, Pledger, and Henderson. He concluded his remarks, however, by raising the standard racist question: in spite of the fine presentations, who among the whites would invite any of the black speakers home to dinner or who would vote for them for high public office. (Springfield *Republican*, Oct. 2, 1899, Clipping, Con. 1031, BTW Papers, DLC.)

The atmosphere of the reception, however, was generally cordial, despite the presence of whites like Graves and some of BTW's black critics, including Bishop Henry M. Turner. After BTW's speech Turner arose in the back of the hall and said: "While I do not agree with Mr. Washington's views on the race problem, I move that the audience thank him by a rising vote for his grand speech." Another black bishop, Wesley J. Gaines, stood and said: "I second the motion; but will add that I do agree with Mr. Washington's views of the race problem." This exchange provoked laughter in the hall, as the audience rose to applaud BTW. (Atlanta *Journal*, Sept. 26, 1899, 3.)

From Timothy Thomas Fortune

New York, Sept 25, 1899

My dear Mr. Washington: I have your letter of the 22nd inst. You may be right in the reason of Dr. Mossell's antagonize, as I am sure the lady does not like you, but the doctor himself has a mule's propensity to kick in all directions. But when he comes my way I can manage things from my point of view. He is much like Ida Wells Barnett, who has just written me a sassy letter complaining about the cutting out of her disparaging reference to you in her Chicago letter. Peterson[1] however did the cutting. She is a sort of bull in a China Shop like Mossell.

I have read the Clement letter with a great deal of interest. It would be a *serious* loss to us if he should loose his grip on the policy of The Transcript and his letter indicates that that is not an improbability.

I note what Councill says. I am anxious about the outcome of the Huntsville conference and am praying that no fat should get in the fire tomorrow night.

All right about the Bruce Grit check.

As between Baugh and Thompson you are the better judge. Baugh is [a] very sober and studious and *close mouthed* person.

I would go to Saratoga on Thursday and see the doctor *and escape the Dewey racket* if I could afford it.

I submitted my collection of verse to F Tennyson Neely[2] this morning, but more than half expect to have it "Returned with thanks." That is the character of my luck.

My health is fair and spirits high. Yours truly

T. Thomas Fortune

ALS Con. 154 BTW Papers DLC.

1 Jerome Bowers Peterson.

2 Frank Tennyson Neely was a New York publisher and the author of several illustrated books, including *Panorama of Our New Possessions* (1898), which celebrated the acquisition of new territory as a result of the Spanish-American War. He went out of business about 1900.

To Timothy Thomas Fortune

Tuskegee, Ala., Sept. 27, 1899

Dear Mr. Fortune: I meant to have written you immediately after the meeting in Atlanta but yesterday I was tremendously busy all day and today I am suffering with an intense headache besides having had to spend a great deal of time with Mr. Horace White,[1] editor of the Evening Post, who is giving us a visit. The meeting on the whole was a great success I think. I have sent you a marked copy of the Constitution referring to it. You must not become discouraged over the portion of Gov. Candler's address which is reported in the Constitution. He spoke for at least thirty minutes and the small portion of his address which is in the Constitution is really the only objectionable part of what he said. I was greatly surprised and gratified over the liberal manner in which he expressed himself. He went so far as to say that there were many Negroes in the United States who understood the science of government and were as capable of administering government as a great many white people. He said many other things equally as strong and liberal but of course the Constitution left them out. The house was packed. Mr. Pledger made a good speech. I was greatly surprised, however, to see him go over to the side of John Temple Graves as he did. Graves was in the audience.

When my head is in better condition I shall try to write you more about the whole matter.

I go to Montgomery tonight for a similar reception there. Yours truly,

Booker T. Washington

Dictated.

TLSr   Con. 161   BTW Papers   DLC.

[1] Horace White (1834-1916) was editor-in-chief of the New York *Evening Post* from 1899 to 1903.

To John Huston Finley[1]

Tuskegee, Alabama. Sept. 28, 1899

My dear Mr. Finley: Your very kind note was received while in Atlanta night before last. I send you some extracts from my speech rather hastily prepared. I do not use manuscript in speaking neither do I commit to memory as a rule hence it is very difficult for me to furnish accurate accounts of my addresses.

I look forward with pleasure to going to Galesburg and my only regret is that I shall not find you there. I have followed you and your work with much interest. It is my present plan to be in New York either in October or November and I shall take pleasure in calling to see you.

I hope that the matter which I sent reached you in time. Yours Sincerely

Booker T. Washington

ALS   John H. Finley Papers   NN.

[1] John Huston Finley (1863-1940) was an educator and later a newspaperman. He was president of Knox College in Galesburg, Ill., from 1892 to 1899, and then was a professor at Princeton from 1900 to 1903. He was president of the College of the City of New York from 1903 to 1913, and then served for eight years as New York state commissioner of education. From 1921 to 1937 Finley was associate editor of the New York *Times* and then served one year as editor-in-chief.

From Timothy Thomas Fortune

New York, Sept 28, 1899

My dear Mr. Washington: Your letter of the 24th instant was received. You had spoken to me about the publication of your speeches, talks and magazine articles by a Boston firm, the anticipated publication of which was announced in the Transcript when I was at Saratoga. I am glad that you have got the collection in satisfactory shape and shall be ready to go over the manuscript or proof with you or Mr. Scott when you are ready. Of course in such matters it is better to go over the manuscript than the proof, but this is not always possible. The Title is of much importance. I do not like the term Negro because it is inaccurate — means too much in one way and not enough in another. "The Afro-American's Future" would be far better, provided you dealt *only* with the future phase of the subject. But we can determine that later.

As far as the Monograph[1] is concerned I find that there is no such thing as a history of the public school system in the United States. That will necessitate a great deal of delving in many side quarters for the historical data. All these technical works require lots of special search and study.

The current Independent reproduces Dr. Mossell's *City and State* article and endorses it as being "the exact case in reference to Mr. Booker T. Washington's position on race questions."[2] So there you are. If Dr. Ward can weaken your position he is bound to do it. He has been telling a party in private conservation [conversation] that your advice to the race to abstain from political activity is injuring the Republican party and the McKinley administration.

And that leads me to say R. R. Wright has just had a very long talk with me along the line of letting up on the Administration. He has been in the East the past four weeks, I think, guaging the sentiment of the race towards the Administration. He did not appear to be happy over the prospect. He wants you and me and him to reach an understanding between us as to the Administration, and he desires me to ask you to fix a date when he can meet you at Tuskegee or Montgomery between Oct 1 and 15. I wish you would give him an appointment, and if the three of us can reach an understanding that will work for the general good I should regard it as a substantial gain.[3] With kind regards, Yours truly

T. Thos. Fortune

ALS Con. 153 BTW Papers DLC.

[1] Fortune ghosted a monograph for BTW on "Education of the Negro," which was part of the series *Monographs on Education in the United States,* under the editorship of Nicholas Murray Butler of Columbia University. The series was part of the New York state exhibit at the Paris Exposition of 1900.

[2] See BTW to Fortune, Sept. 22, 1899, above.

[3] Richard R. Wright, Sr., later wrote to President McKinley that BTW and Fortune "have both shown their good faith" in the Republican party. On Oct. 23, 1899, Wright had overheard a conversation at the Southern Hotel in Washington, D.C., between Fortune and Representative John R. McLean, who was trying to convince Fortune to make some speeches in Ohio against the Republican administration. According to Wright, Fortune refused and told McLean that despite his disagreement with some aspects of McKinley's policy on racial matters that he was still a Republican and his feud "was in the nature of a family quarrel. . . ." (Wright to McKinley, Oct. 24, 1899, McKinley Papers, DLC.)

To Alonzo Homer Kenniebrew

Tuskegee, Ala., Sept. 29, 1899

Dear Dr. Kenniebrew: I have already spoken with you briefly about some matters that took place during the summer. Some time ago a committee was appointed to investigate the truthfulness of several matters in relation to yourself. This committee has now made a full report to the Finance Committee. There are several matters brought in this report that more or less effect both you and the school among them improper language and unwarranted charging to students, all of which is against the policy of the school, but as you have already been made aware of them and I feel sure will profit by the discussion of them I am inclined to believe that there is but one matter that is so serious in its nature as to warrant further action. I regret exceedingly the necessity for the further consideration because I recognize that the peculiar nature and professional eminence of a physician places him in a position that should not be made common by too frequent connection with matters outside of his profession. The matter that I refer to is your conduct in relation to the Cuban students. I have heard your own statement as well as that of the committee together with an unasked for statement from the Cuban students. After taking plenty of time to get all the facts and weigh all the information both the Finance Committee and myself are convinced that you made a serious error in taking the action that you did in relation to the Cuban students. Neither the committee nor myself can see any justification for it and think that you not only erred in judgement but did that which was calculated to injure yourself professionally. In this connection you will perhaps recall a serious breach of order and decorum committed by you in the spring. I sent you a copy of the report of another committee which at that time very frankly and plainly condemned your action and recommended that radical steps be taken about your conduct. The mere sending of that report to you I hoped would serve to prevent future mistakes of the kind.

By reason of your connection with the trouble in the spring and then during the summer both the committee and myself feel that we can not do less than to let you know how severely we condemn such conduct and how much it hurts the whole institution and we hope that in future you will exercise such self control as to make such mistakes impossible. The committee also decides that justice to the Cuban students demands that they be informed by the Principal that this institution does not countenance such actions on the part of its teachers.

This I hope closes the whole matter and will leave you free for a good years work.

[Booker T. Washington]

ALd Con. 703 BTW Papers DLC.

From Alonzo Homer Kenniebrew

Tuskegee, Ala., 9-30 1899

Prof. Washington   Sometime ago I prepared a batch of this medicine for you and it did quite a deal of good in preventing those congestive headaches and also tones the system. I have just been able to get one of its ingredients from New York — and I hope you will take this before meals. It does not taste so well but you will get use to it. Let me know when it is out. Yours for health

A. H. Kenniebrew

ALS   Con. 156   BTW Papers   DLC.

From Thomas Junius Calloway

Washington, D.C., October 4, 1899

My dear Sir: I am compiling arguments to present to the management of the United States Exhibit at the Paris Exposition to persuade the managers to provide for a Negro Exhibit in connection with the United States Exhibit at that exhibition during the next year.[1] The principal argument I hope to use is that the leading members of our race desire it. For securing a statement from you I address you in this letter.

While I deplore as deeply as any other member of my race the matter of drawing the color line at any time where it is not already drawn by the other race, there are times, and this is one, when we owe it to ourselves to go before the world as Negroes. Every one who knows about public opinion in Europe will tell you that the Europeans think us a mass of rapists, ready to attack every white woman exposed, and a drug in civilized society. This notion has come to them through the horrible libels that have gone abroad whenever a Negro is lynched, and by the constant reference to us by the press in discouraging remarks. The social and political economists of the Old World put down the erroneous accounts of such cases as that of Sam Hose as truth, and, not hearing the actual facts, reach conclusions which do us wrong.

How shall we answer these slanders? Our newspapers they do not subscribe for, if we publish books they do not buy them, if we lecture they do not attend.

To the Paris Exposition, however, thousands upon thousands of them will go and a well selected and prepared exhibit, representing the Negro's development in his churches, his schools, his homes, his farms, his stores, his professions and pursuits in general will attract attention as did the exhibits at Atlanta and Nashville Expositions, and do a great and lasting good in convincing thinking people of the possibilities of the Negro.

Not only will foreigners be impressed, but hundreds of white Americans will be far more convinced by what they see there than what they see, or can see, every day in this country, but fail to give us credit for. Hundreds of Southern white people were amazed at the evidences of culture and progress they saw in the Negro Exhibits in Nashville and Atlanta, and yet you know that if they would only visit the churches and the homes of our best families in those cities alone they would see an exhibit, far more pronounced, of the culture of the race. But this they will not do and we must prove our cause in other ways.

Please write me your views (on your official letter-head) and I trust you can do so immediately, as the earlier the plan is laid before our Commission the better. Very truly yours,

Thos. J. Calloway

TLS Con. 160 BTW Papers DLC.

1 Calloway was successful in lobbying for the Negro exhibit. He wrote BTW on Jan. 25, 1900, "Our bill for $15000.00 has now passed both houses of Congress and I suppose will be signed by the President within 24 hours. Public sentiment was so unanimous in its favor that the only questions asked me have been 'Is it enough?' " (Con. 168, BTW Papers, DLC.)

From George Leonard Chaney

Leominster, Mass. Oct. 9, 1899

Dear Washington. I am very sorry that I cannot attend the special meeting of the Tuskegee Trustees next week. I could not possibly be away from home at that time. If possible, I shall try to visit Tuskegee sometime this winter and will do anything I can to counsel or assist you then. Let me hear the meat of the meeting, if you can, without too much trouble.

I more than ever believe in your way of solving the political problem, by flanking prejudice with intelligence, character and wealth. I remember discussing the question with Grady, when he wrote his article in Plain Black and White.[1] His plea was that the governing privilege belonged to the white man because he was superior in intelligence and wealth. I pointed out to him the logical necessity of accepting black rule on that theory, if intelligence and wealth should be on that side. He saw the point but would not admit the possibility. You and your co-workers are going to demonstrate that possibility. It is an inspiring undertaking. I believe you will accomplish it. Yours as ever

G. L. Chaney

ALS Con. 151 BTW Papers DLC.

[1] Henry W. Grady wrote "In Plain Black and White" for *Century Magazine*, 29 (Apr. 1885), 909-17, a reply to an earlier *Century* article by George W. Cable, "The Freedmen's Case In Equity," 29 (Jan. 1885), 409-18. Cable had argued that the greatest social problem facing America was the race problem, and that the way to solve this problem was through the abolition of race prejudice left over from slave days and through equal treatment under law. Grady in reply called Cable "sentimental rather than practical." Grady pronounced the South adamant against "social intermingling of the races," and said that both blacks and whites had a race instinct that would keep them apart. He thought white domination the proper order of southern society because it was based on character, intelligence, and property.

To William H. Breed[1]

[Tuskegee, Ala., ca. Oct. 9, 1899][2]

My Dear Sir: I am very sorry not to be able to be present at the meeting of the Baptist Social Union, as I had planned. An engagement of very great importance in another direction seems to make it my duty to respond to it, while yet cherishing the hope that at another time in the near future I shall have the opportunity of meeting with the Union & its friends.

At Huntsville, Alabama, at the Southern Industrial Convention, which convenes there this week & where I shall speak, I hope to be of some humble service in the promotion of a correct understanding of the relations that should exist in the South between the two races. There is no white man of the South whose heart is more wrapped up in its every interest, & loves it more dearly than I do. The South can have no sorrow that I do not share. She can have no prosperity in which I do not rejoice. She can commit no error that

I do not deplore. She can take no step forward that I do not approve. The Negro though different in race, in color, in history, can & will teach the world that although thus differing it is possible for us to dwell side by side, in love, in peace, in mutual prosperity. We can, & we will, be one in a larger degree than ever in sympathy, purpose, forbearance & mutual helpfulness. No man can seek the elevation of another race without himself being elevated; no man can plan the degradation of another race without being himself degraded.

The Negro is fitting himself by education, by the acquiring of property, by the cultivation of the friendship & good will of his neighbor, white & black, for all the duties of an enlightened citizenship. He needs, & will need for some time to come, the hearty sympathy & help of all sections of our country. These thoughts crowd themselves upon me as I write, and I hope to present them as best I can to this great assembly of representatives of the best brain, wealth, power & influence of the South. I am quite sure that yourself, & the Baptist Social Union, are in sympathy with these sentiments. Again thanking you for the very kind invitation extended asking me to address your meeting — & regretting my inability to be present, I am, with very great respect, Sir, Yours very truly,

[Booker T. Washington]

HLd Con. 150 BTW Papers DLC. This draft is in Emmett J. Scott's hand.

1 William H. Breed was president of the Baptist Social Union of Boston.

2 The dating of this letter is suggested by BTW's reference to the Southern Industrial Convention in Huntsville, Ala., "which convenes there this week." BTW had apparently notified Breed earlier that he would not be able to speak in Boston on Oct. 11, 1899. (See Breed to Francis J. Garrison, Sept. 12, 1899, Con. 150, BTW Papers, DLC.) This appears to be a follow-up letter giving reasons for the cancellation, possibly for public reading before the Baptist Social Union.

From Robert Lloyd Smith

Columbus, Colorado Co., Texas, Oct 12, 189[9]

Dear Friend, Bishop Grant[1] leaves us this PM after delivering an inspiring address to a very large audience yesterday and another last night and reviewing the parade & display (agricultural) to day. We have much success. We have captured the whites especially the white women of this town by our magnificent exhibition which is the *best* ever given by the race in the state. The lecture of the bishop against emigration to Africa was superb. He will stop over in Atlanta as he goes through and hit Bishop Turners African emigration scheme a whack. He will kill it wherever he speaks. Call or invite him to Tuskegee. I would like to have in detail the plans especially the time I am to go North with you. Have arranged to run my school while gone. The people are crazy to see you. Prof Carver never came much to my disappointment. Cordially,

R L Smith

Newspapers will be sent.

ALS Con. 162 BTW Papers DLC.

1 Abram L. Grant (1848-1911), a bishop of the A.M.E. Church, was born in slavery in Lake City, Fla. He worked his way through Cookman Institute by clerking in a Jacksonville, Fla., grocery store. In the 1870s he served briefly as inspector of customs in Jacksonville and as a county commissioner in Duval County. In 1878 he moved to Texas, where he became vice-president of Paul Quinn College at Waco. Grant was elected bishop in 1888 and served in the South and West until 1900, when he was transferred to the Midwest. From 1904 to 1911 he was bishop for Missouri, Kansas, Colorado, and California, residing in Kansas City, Kan. He was a founder of Payne Theological Seminary in 1891, and also was a trustee of Wilberforce University. Grant had an amicable relationship with BTW and generally supported the Tuskegean's approach to race problems. In 1908 he campaigned for the Republicans at BTW's request. (Meier, *Negro Thought*, 218-19.)

A Petition to the President of the United States

[New York City, Oct. 13, 1899]

William McKinley, President of the United States: The undersigned representatives of American public and private life most respectfully petition you to offer the friendly services of the United States in mediation between Great Britain and the republics of the Transvaal and the Orange Free State.

Articles 1, 2 and 3 of the plan adopted by the Peace Congress make such offers the right of any friendly power, "even during the course of hostilities."

We respectfully submit that it is not only the right and duty of this nation, but also its high privilege, to strive to prevent the wiping out of two of our sister republics, the desolation of thousands of English and South African homes, the slaughter of thousands of civilized men and the drenching of South Africa with blood and tears.

———————

This petition has been indorsed by the President of the South African Republic, the President of the Orange Free State, the Premier of the British Cape Colony. It has been signed by the following array of representatives of American character, distinction and influence:

George F. Edmunds, Patrick A. Collins, Frederic R. Coudert, John Sherman, Adlai E. Stevenson, John B. Henderson, Charles F. Manderson, John J. Ingalls, J. Sterling Morton, Major-Gen. O. O. Howard, John P. Altgeld, Carl Schurz, Horace Boies, Gen. John McClernan, Rev. Dr. Cyrus Hamlin, Augustus Van Wyck, James S. Clarkson, John W. Briedenthal, William B. Hornblower, Gen. Simon B. Buckner, J. Q. A. Brackett, Chester Holcombe, Ernest H. Crosby, T. Estrada Palma, William V. Allen, Clifton R. Breckinridge.

Archbishops Ireland of St. Paul, Kain of St. Louis, Christie of Portland, Ore., and sixteen Bishops of the Roman Catholic Church.

Bishops Potter of New York, Dudley of Kentucky, Whittle of Virginia, Hare of South Dakota and fourteen other Bishops of the Protestant Episcopal Church.

Presidents Jordan of Leland Stanford University, Harper of the University of Chicago, Thwing of the Western Reserve University, Faunce of Brown University, Butler, of Colby University, Maine, Booker T. Washington of Tuskegee Institute, Alabama, Lloyd of the Polytechnic College, Texas, and eighty-two other Presidents of colleges and universities in every section.

Judges Wallace of New York, Jackson of West Virginia, Jenkins of Wisconsin, Caldwell of Arkansas, Morrow of California and ten other Judges of United States Courts.

Chief-Justices Peters of Maine, Gaines of Texas, Cartwright of

Illinois, Hazelrigg of Kentucky, Blodgett of New Hampshire, Doster of Kansas, Bartch of Utah, and thirty-four Justices of the Supreme Courts of States in all parts of the Union, and twenty Judges of New York courts.

Senators Sewell of New Jersey, Gallinger of New Hampshire, Burrows of Michigan, Mason of Illinois, Pettigrew of South Dakota, Perkins of California, Cockrell of Missouri, McLaurin of South Carolina; Representative Grosvenor of Ohio, and fifty-five other Senators and Representatives in Congress.

Gov. Tyler of Virginia, Lieut.-Gov. Woodruff of New York, Speaker Mason of the Ohio House of Representatives, President Bolte of the Missouri Senate, Speaker Dare of the Minnesota House of Representatives, Speaker McCool of the Mississippi House of Representatives, Lieut.-Gov. Browning of Texas, and forty other Governors, Lieutenant-Governors and presiding officers of State Legislatures.

Mayors Britten of New Orleans, Phelan of San Francisco, Harrison of Chicago, Preston of Hartford, Malster of Baltimore, and eight other Mayors of important cities.

Editors L. Clarke Davis of the Philadelphia Ledger, Ottendorfer of the New Yorker Staats-Zeitung, Norton of the Portland (Me.) Express, McLean of the Cincinnati Enquirer, Howell of the Atlanta Constitution, Rosewater of the Omaha Bee, De Young of the San Francisco Chronicle, and twelve other editors of influential newspapers.

Rev. Father Malone, Dr. Robert Collyer, Dwight L. Moody, Dr. Edward Everett Hale, John Burroughs, George W. Cable and forty-two other clergymen and authors.

Prof. Alexander Graham Bell, Andrew H. Green, Frank Moss, Theodore W. Myers, Henry Clews, Robert Treat Paine and sixty-five other men conspicuous in commerce and the professions.

New York *World*, Oct. 13, 1899, 8.

From Timothy Thomas Fortune

Washington, D.C., Oct 13, 1899

Dear Mr Washington: It is now 2 p.m. and I have no telegram about the proceedure in the matter of the proof of your book.[1] I donot know how far you want me to use the blue pencil on the proof, or whether you want me to hold the proof or return it to the publishers with my corrections.

I read the first 19 galleys of matter this morning and had to use the blue pencil very freely. Your propensity to cut sentences short and to leave out qualifying clauses in subordinate sentences can not be tolerated in a book. Clearness of thought and lucidity of diction in a book are indispensable.[2]

Then I worry over your unconscious habit of apologising for the shortcomings of white men, as in the Reconstruction deviltry, and I have qualified it where I could; otherwise you would have a tornado at your heels. I hold the 19 proofs until I hear from you.

I will try to read the 20 galleys that came today by in the morning. I wish you were here.

Referring to your letter of the 11th — I have read some of "Minervy Ann"[3] and will read the whole when issued in book form. The only way we can meet this sort of thing is to go into fiction and do it, and I shall go in and do my share if possible. My "After War Times"[4] will be an eye opener.

You have got to checkmate Turner, Councill, Graves, et. al. or they will queer the situation.

Pledger sends his kind regards. Your friend.

T. Thomas Fortune

ALS Con. 154 BTW Papers DLC.

1 *The Future of the American Negro.*

2 Fortune wrote to Emmett J. Scott the next day: "I have 40 galleys from the Boston house and more to follow on the Wizard's book. *I am appalled at the literary execution of the work.* It would ruin us to go as it stands. My reading of 20 galleys makes it look like a cyclone had struck it. The printers will howl murder." (Oct. 14, 1899, Con. 154, BTW Papers, DLC.)

3 Joel Chandler Harris, *The Chronicles of Aunt Minervy Ann* (1899), was the fictional reminiscences of a black cook in Georgia and her husband Hamp. Typical of the writings of Harris and others of the period, the story was told in dialect, and all characters were stereotyped. Minervy Ann was cast as a black mammy and her

husband was a comic Negro who wore fancy clothes, including a stovepipe hat, and served in the Georgia legislature during Reconstruction.

4 This may have been an article Fortune was working on at the time. More than twenty years later he used "After War Times" as the title for a series of reminiscences of his Florida boyhood that he wrote for the Norfolk *Journal and Guide*. (Thornbrough, *Fortune*, 356.)

To Henry Floyd Gamble[1]

Tuskegee, Ala., Oct. 14, 1899

Dear Dr. Gamble: I have just returned from the industrial convention at Huntsville where Gov. MacCorkle[2] presided and where he made an address. He made the strongest, wisest and most effective address on the matter of giving justice to the Negro that I have ever heard from the lips of any Southern white man, perhaps with the exception of Dr. Curry. He carried the convention with him from start to finish. He told the Southern white people plainly that the time had come when they must treat the Negro with absolute justice, especially at the ballot box; that they must cease cheating him and give the black man the same chance that the white man has. What he has said has done a world of good in this part of the South and has changed public sentiment in favor of the Negro as few other things have done. He took the position on the floor of the convention that if the ignorant Negro was to be disfranchised the ignorant white man should also be disfranchised, and that there should be no loophole in the law which would give one an opportunity for voting and the same opportunity be withheld from the other. Yours truly,

[Booker T. Washington]

TLc Con. 151 BTW Papers DLC.

1 Henry Floyd Gamble (1862-1932), a black physician, was a graduate of Lincoln University (1888) and Yale Medical School (1891). He practiced medicine in Charleston, W.Va., for forty years. He was president of the National Medical Association from 1911 to 1912.

2 William Alexander MacCorkle (1857-1930) was a longtime resident of Kanawha County and the governor of West Virginia. Born in Rockbridge County, Va., he spent much of his youth in Missouri. After his father's death in the Confederate Army, he returned with his mother to Virginia, where he worked for a time in a store. He taught school in West Virginia for a year, then returned to Virginia to attend the

law school at Washington and Lee University, where he received his degree in 1879. Moving to Charleston, W.Va., he taught school during the day and practiced law at night. An active Democrat, he became county prosecutor from 1880 to 1889, city solicitor of Charleston, and governor from 1893 to 1897. A racial moderate, Governor MacCorkle sought to curb the power in the state of outside corporations, lumber and coal barons, and speculators. During his last two years as governor, he was handicapped by a Republican majority in the legislature. At a commercial convention in Huntsville, Ala., in 1899, and at the Montgomery Race Conference in 1900, he spoke against disfranchisement of blacks as such but in favor of property and educational qualifications. Continuing an active interest in public affairs, he was a state senator for a year in 1910 and led the state Liberty Loan campaign during World War I. He was a bank president in Charleston and a real estate developer. (MacCorkle, *Recollections of Fifty Years.*)

From William Henry Baldwin, Jr.

N.Y. [City] October 17, 1899

Dear Mr. Washington: I have your letters of October 11, 12, & 14 this morning, and am very much interested in all you have to say. I shall hope to hear promptly from you with respect to the meeting on the 16th at the Governor's office.

I am glad that you are not going to open the Trades Building until December, as I fancy it will be in better condition at that time to be showed to the Trustees.

I shall expect to meet you here about November first, when I would like to talk over with you various matters connected with the number of students to be received by Tuskegee each year, the qualifications for admission, and a secondary school system in connection with your school.

I think that a meeting in New York and in Brooklyn would be a good thing. I don't know whether Governor Roosevelt is the man. I think it would be better, perhaps, to have Mr. Cleveland, but I shall be in a position to find out exactly from Governor Roosevelt with how much earnestness he would take hold of the subject.

I am more than interested in the Huntsville meeting. Governor MacCorkle's position was of the highest importance. It seems to me that it is the first fearless, honest statement by a representative southern white man. I refer particularly to the reference to suffrage. I have written him a personal letter of thanks.

Don't you think after all that it was far better for me not to appear at that meeting? As long as it did go just right by and with the aid of southern people only, it means much more than to have been helped along or directed by any northerner.

I note your reference to Mr. Council. I want to know all about it, but would suggest that you be very guarded to whom you speak on that matter.

I am glad that you will use Mr. Dodge's gift of $1,000. for the shoemaking shop, and glad you wrote Mr. Dodge.

The newspaper editorials which you enclosed are very interesting, and I will keep them until you come and turn them over to you at that time. I remain, Yours very truly,

W H Baldwin Jr

TLS   Con. 792   BTW Papers   DLC.

From William Henry Baldwin, Jr.

N.Y. [City] Oct 17, 1899

Dear Washington: I just want to write a line to tell you that my mind and my heart are constantly on you and your work. The daylight has come.

I only wish I could give time to the work, but I cannot do more now, or I would be criticised by my associates. My time is not my own yet.

Do keep well.

Plan to stay at my house in November if you wish to. I have several important plans to talk over, in reference to the number of students, and the secondary school system. Sincerely yours

W H Baldwin Jr

ALS   Con. 149   BTW Papers   DLC.

From Edward Elder Cooper

Washington, D.C., Oct. 17, '99

My dear Mr. Washington: Your note of the 14th inst., also a very well written article by Mr. Chas. Alexander, were both received this morning. I shall dove-tail the two letters together in a proper way and have them appear in the current issue of The Colored American.[1] I think you show most excellent judgment and foresight by giving credit and recognition and honor to those who deserve it. The race needs more such men as Ex-Gov. MacCorkle of W.Va.

We are looking for you up this way and the town is agog as to when and where you will speak.

With best wishes, I am, Yours very truly,

E. E. Cooper

TLS   Con. 151   BTW Papers   DLC.

[1] Charles Alexander, "Prime Factor in the South," Washington *Colored American*, Oct. 21, 1899, 4. The article contained the text of BTW's remarks at the Southern Industrial Convention in Huntsville, Ala., and a summary of William A. MacCorkle's speech cautioning the southern states against the disfranchisement of black voters.

From Francis Jackson Garrison

Boston, Oct. 17, 1899

Dear Mr. Washington: I have been more or less absent from my office, of late, taking my vacation in disjointed fragments, and more especially devoting the time to dismantling my old home in Roxbury, and disposing in one way or another of my household effects. Consequently I have been too delinquent in replying to your letter about the meeting at Atlanta, and thanking you for that and the newspaper report of your excellent speech, and now I have to thank you also for your most gratifying letter of the 13th inst, which I find awaiting me on my return to business this morning. I am surprised and deeply gratified by the brave stand taken by ex-Governor McCorkle at the Huntsville Convention, and think that you did a fine thing in persuading him to stay over another day and clinch the matter by securing the passage of the resolution in favor of equal laws, and equal administration of them, for white and black. Remembering what Mr. Page said in his remarks at Cambridge last spring, I cannot help hoping that there are some white southerners who are realizing more and more the disastrous effects upon their own race of the iniquitous disfranchising methods and enactments at the South, and who, stimulated by a man of the courage and frankness of Gov. McCorkle, may yet develop a public sentiment that will withstand the spread of this disfranchising epidemic, and in time secure fairer laws and juster enforcement of them. To this end I know that you are working to the full extent of your powers and possibilities, and I know also that it is a work which requires consummate tact and rare wisdom, but of the ultimate success of truth and right there can be no question, however long or thorny the path. With abiding faith and regard, Sincerely yours,

Francis J. Garrison

P.S. I shall be glad to see the McCorkle resolutions.

TLS Con. 154 BTW Papers DLC. Postscript in Garrison's hand.

From James Lewis[1]

New Orleans, La., October 19, 1899

Esteemed Professor: Yours of the 17th inst. in reply to mine of the 14th has been received, and I assure you that I was pleased with your address, both at Atlanta, Ga. and Huntsville, Ala. The work of the best thinkers of our Race at this time for peace and harmony between the Races in the South is hard, because anything out of the old political rut is unpopular with the would-be leaders of our Race, and tends to stop a proper adjustment between the better classes of both Races, who have a common interest.

I am a Republican, and don't believe that grand old party that has done so much for my Race requires a continued sacrifice of life, home, and all that is dear to the colored men of the South at this time.

I am pleased to learn that you contemplate visiting our City on or about the 10th November. If so, Mrs. Lewis joins me in extending to you the hospitality of our home, #2415 Canal St., opposite The Straight University.

With kind regards to you and yours, I am very truly,

James Lewis

TLS Con. 157 BTW Papers DLC.

1 James Lewis (1832-1914), son of a white father and a mulatto mother, was born in Mississippi and grew up in Bayou Sara, La. During the Civil War, he left his post as steward on a Confederate ship when Gen. Benjamin F. Butler called on blacks to join the Union forces in New Orleans. In Sept. 1862 Lewis raised the first regiment of black troops to serve in the U.S. Army. After the war Lewis was a traveling agent in the educational department of the Freedmen's Bureau. When the bureau closed he was appointed customs inspector, the first black to hold a civil office in the federal government in Louisiana. Lewis entered the metropolitan police force in 1869 and the following year was appointed colonel in the state militia and administrator of police. President Hayes appointed Lewis naval officer of the port of New Orleans, and in 1884 he became the superintendent of the federal bonded warehouse and surveyor general of Louisiana in the Interior Department land office in New Orleans. Lewis's political preferment derived from his leadership in the state Republican party and his lifetime association with the Masonic order. He served as surveyor general in the McKinley, Roosevelt, and Taft administrations. Lewis and Walter Cohen were BTW's political allies after BTW became active politically as an adviser to Theodore Roosevelt. They led the black-and-tan faction in its continuous struggle with the lily-white faction in the Louisiana Republican party.

From George Wesley Atkinson

Charleston, West Virginia. October 20, 1899

Confidential

My Dear Friend: The more I think of the scheme of yours, Governor MacCorkle's and others, to establish an educational qualification as a basis of suffrage in the South, the more I am opposed to it. You know I told you out at the Normal School at Huntsville the other day, that I was opposed to it in every shape and form. It seems to me that the result of the scheme will be the disfranchisement of at least three-fourths of the colored voters of the South, while the ignorant white people will be allowed to vote on just as they have been doing in the past. I have very little confidence in the pledges of Southern Democrats to treat the colored voters properly, therefore, I look with disfavor upon the scheme suggested by yourself, Governor MacCorkle and others at [the] Huntsville Convention. I am satisfied it is only a trap, which will result in the practical disfranchisement of the colored voters of the South.

You will remember, in our brief conversation while we were walking over the grounds of the Colored Normal School near Huntsville, you asked me to see to it that when the resolution came forward in the Convention that it must apply to ignorant white people as well as ignorant colored people. This I watched carefully, and was ready to speak upon it if it had not been in proper shape. I said to two or three gentlemen who were sitting on the platform when it came in, that I felt it to be my honest duty to oppose it openly, but, inasmuch as I had made an unpopular speech for Southern people, because I told them of their shortcomings, I said nothing, and thought best to only cast my vote against it, which I did. It is not my purpose, in this letter, to discuss the merits of this case. I simply call your attention to what seems to me to be a serious matter, endangering the rights of the colored voters of the South. You are extremely popular with the Democratic element of the South, simply because, I believe, they think they can use you to accomplish a purpose they could not accomplish unless they had your aid. The world is going forward, not backward. It took a revolution to enfranchise the colored people of this Country, and it seems to me that nothing short of a revolution should disfranchise them, and, yet, I am not a revolutionist. If I were in your place, I would go extremely slow in this matter. I heard yesterday that one of the leading colored men of Charleston was circulating a paper, getting the colored people to endorse it, thanking Governor Mac-Corkle for the splendid stand he took at Huntsville for the advancement of the colored race. While I am a warm friend of Governor MacCorkle's, and believe that he is far in advance of his party, and is very much fairer towards the colored people than ninety-nine out of every hundred of his party, yet, I do not believe it is a proper thing for colored people to undertake to endorse him or you or any one else in a movement to disfranchise the legal and legitimate voters of the South.

This letter is absolutely private, and must not be published. You have known me long enough to know that I am not a schemer nor a trickster; that I stood by the colored people in this State when it took nerve and courage to advocate their cause; that I was perhaps the only white man in all this portion of the State of West Virginia who openly advocated the adoption of the 13th, 14th and 15th amendments of the Constitution of the United States, which made men out of the colored people who were formerly slaves. I believe in progression — not retrogression. Cordially and truly yours,

G. W. Atkinson

TLS   Con. 1   BTW Papers   DLC.

From Henry Floyd Gamble

Charleston W Va   Oct 23 '99

Dear Sir: Yours of the 14th was very gladly received. When you were here last month I made a statement of my opinion of Gov MacCorkle, and I was very anxious to know what impression he made on you at the convention. I am glad you were pleased.

It was quite a pleasure to carry out your request and it was indeed a very pleasant task. You will see from the clipping enclosed a part of what was done.[1] The governor had nothing but praise for you. I suppose he kept me an hour talking about the masterly way you filled the occasion at the Convention. I learned by accident that Gov Atkinson is still quite chafed because Gov McCorkle was so liberally praised for his speech and so very little was said about his (Gov A's); this I got through confidence man. I have seen extracts from your speech; Governor McCorkle gave me a copy of his. I would like ever so much to have your speech and Prof Counsels if at any time they should be printed or put in any form obtainable.

Please accept my profoundest thanks for what you are so nobly doing for our people. I have the honor to remain   Your most obedient servant

H. F. Gamble

P.S. Your letter being marked "private" I thought it wise to keep you, all mention of you and your request in the back ground excep[t] in our talk with Gov Mc   Especially since I learned of Gov A's feeling.

ALS   Con. 154   BTW Papers   DLC.

1 No clipping was found with the letter.

From Isaac Fisher

Athol, Mass., Oct. 23, 1899

Dear Mr. Washington: In my last letter, I told you that we had begun work again, and that our Sunday collections were $42.76.

The collections for the remainder of the week, just ended, were as follows:

Monday, Oct. 16th, didn't sing in a church, but had the Southampton, Mass. town hall — $17.45; Tuesday — 17th, Leeds, Mass., Leeds Chapel, $8; Wednesday — 18th, Congregational Church, Hatfield, Mass., $21; Thursday — 19th, Unitarian Church, Deerfield, Mass., $13 and $2 more pledged. I was not able to make a date for Friday night. Last night, I filled the first of Mr. Smith's[1] dates in the Unitarian Church at this place. Received $8.75.

The quartette is singing very well, nobody denies that, and I am holding them to the old "Plantation Songs," as you told me to do when you saw me at Saratoga. But I have a question to ask with reference to the quartette, and I ask it with all seriousness. I note that quite a number of the people are disappointed when the young men do not accompany their singing with the shouting and mourning so largely characteristic of the Negro religious meetings, South. We are told to our faces often that though our quartette is one of the best that has ever been heard up here, they would like us better if we would "play the Nigger — their own words — more."

A lady said last week, and one said last night, "You are the most gentlemenly set of colored young men I have ever met — just as nice as you can be, but you look and act so cultured and refined that we don't dare ask you to play the ignorant Darkey, as some do who come up here."

Now when the young men are stopping with friends, I give them liberty to oblige those friends in their homes by singing what they please to ask for, but in the churches, there are some songs and actions which I bar out. But we give a varied entertainment, my constant care being to keep the party above the level of Negro Minstrels.

I want to serve Tuskegee as best I can, and so I feel constrained to ask if it is your desire that the quartette shall "ape" the ignorant characteristics of our people. Personally I am opposed to the continual holding up of our faults for the pleasure of anybody. I feel that persons who cannot be touched by the beauty of our dear old songs as our quartette sings them would not be touched by our catering to their conception of what the Negro ought to be; but I don't mean to let my personal feelings stand in the way of the school's good. What are your wishes with reference to this? I have learned to love the South since I have been up here. Write me at 45 Greenwich St., Boston. Sincerely yours,

Isaac Fisher

ALS Con. 172 BTW Papers DLC. Docketed in Emmett J. Scott's hand: "Carry on work as now. Be sure that circulars [are distributed?]."

1 Presumably Peter J. Smith, Jr.

To Warren Logan

[Tuskegee, Ala.] Oct. 24, 1899

Mr. Logan: I note that quite a large proportion of the Dizer Fund is uninvested. I wish you would make a special effort to see that the Dizer Fund is kept invested in the way that Mr. Dizer meant it should be. You will have to be constantly on the lookout to find new borrowers. I think our experience teaches that we should not lend money very far outside of Macon County. I am very anxious to convince Mr. Dizer that we have the ability to handle this money successfully, and unless he sees that we are getting a good income from it he will not be encouraged to increase the fund. It is his intention to increase it eventually to $10,000 but he will not do so unless what he has already given is kept invested. In some way you will have to arrange to keep the matter constantly before the people in and about Tuskegee.

Booker T. Washington

TLS Con. 16 BTW Papers ATT.

To William McKinley

Tuskegee, Ala., Oct. 24, 1899

Dear Sir: Referring to the conversation which I had with you a few days ago in regard to a separate educational exhibit representing the progress of the Negro race at the Paris Exposition, I beg to say that Mr. Howard J. Rogers,[1] representing Mr. Peck,[2] who has charge of the educational and sociological exhibit, agrees to a separate Negro exhibit. As we are very anxious to secure a creditable exhibit I hope you can see your way clear to direct Mr. Peck to provide the means for the salary and other expenses of a competent person to prepare and install this exhibit.

I am convinced that the best person to have charge of this exhibit is Mr. Thomas J. Calloway, who was formerly one of our teachers at Tuskegee and who has had large experience in this kind of work, and I hope you can see your way clear to bring about his appointment.

As the time is very short it will be a great advantage if you can see your way clear to have this matter taken up at once. Yours truly,

Booker T. Washington

TLSr Copy BTW Folder ViHaI.

1 Howard J. Rogers, director of education and social economy of the exposition, wrote Calloway: "It seems to me that the plan as outlined by you can not fail to correct many misapprehensions which now exist and to give a very complete and valuable view of the status of the Negro in this Country." (Oct. 23, 1899, Con. 151, BTW Papers, DLC.)

2 Ferdinand W. Peck was assistant commissioner general of the U.S. Commission to the Paris Exposition.

To William Edward Burghardt Du Bois

[Tuskegee, Ala.] Oct. 26, 1899

Dear Sir: I have delayed writing you a little longer than I intended to do, but this has been an exceedingly busy fall with me.

I write to renew the proposition that you connect yourself permanently with this institution. What I wish you to do is to make your home here and to conduct sociological studies that will prove helpful to our people, especially in the gulf states, including both the country districts, smaller towns and cities. I am especially anxious that some systematic and painstaking work be done with the country districts in the Black Belt. Our printing office will be wholly at your service and you could use it in a way that would scatter your writings all through the country.

I should like, if possible, for you to teach at least one class in our institution, this would result in keeping the students in close touch with the line of work which you would be pursuing.

All the work of course would be done in your own name and over your own signature. I should like, of course, for the name of the institution to be in some way attached to whatever publications you should make. I repeat that it would be the policy of the school to leave you free to use your time as you decide would be most desirable.

I would have made you this offer several years ago but I did not feel it would be doing you justice to ask you to come here and tie your hands with routine work. For this work we can pay you a salary of fourteen hundred dollars ($1400.) per year and furnish you a comfortable and convenient house. If any portion of this proposition is not satisfactory to you I shall be glad to make any reasonable changes in it.

I had a letter a few days ago from Prof. Hart asking whether or not we had come to any definite decision. Yours truly,

[Booker T. Washington]

TLp   Con. 282A   BTW Papers   DLC.

245

From Timothy Thomas Fortune

Washington, D.C., Oct 26, 1899

Dear Mr. Washington: Your two letters of the 24th were received and particularly appreciate the autograph concerning the Neely business. My heart is set on getting the book on the market, as well as other matter in hand for which the poems will pave the way, and I can't afford to lose the $200. Neely writes me that he has reorganized and that the new corporation will go ahead. I hope so. I can't well gave [give] way to discouragement, but the hard luck that chases me often makes me blue and hesitant.

As to your book, I have to say I was satisfied with it after I had corrected the first proof. I went at it just as would have done with the manuscript, consequently the 41 book pages I read yesterday were very smooth. I had few changes to make. I sent the matter back last night, and shall do so as fast as the mat[ter] reaches me, unless I find something that you should pass upon. In the form we have corrected it I am sure you will have a creditable book, especially from the literary point, about which I was mostly concerned in the revision. You have ideas to burn, but your style of expression is more oratorical than literary, and in the written word the oratorical must be used most sparingly. I am glad I have a chance to go over book critically in the proof, and while I appreciate what you say on that point I am sure that you know that friendship alone dictated the interest I took in the work and shall take until it appears in print. I want the book to be a success with readers and critics and I now believe it will be in substance and manner of treatment.

I work for The Age today.

You will have the copy of the Monograph on schedule time if my wrist holds out. It is doing fairly well. Mailed a first installment to you last night. Your friend

T. Thomas Fortune

ALS   Con. 154   BTW Papers   DLC.

From LeGrand Powers[1]

Washington, D.C., October 27, 1899

My dear Sir: I have been unable to keep my promise to forward to you copies of letters sent to the editors of Africo-American newspapers until to-day.

You will find them under another cover.

Some Africo-American editors have taken hold of the matter in good temper and with good effect, but many have made no reply either by letter or through their newspapers. Some have not answered the letters from this office but have used the Census matter enclosed to them or published editorials of their own construction. The latter have been very good indeed; more effective perhaps than anything that could have been prepared by any officer of the Government.

We have discussed the matter in the office since your visit to us, and have become much impressed with the good you yourself can do by your writings and speakings in behalf of the coming Census. Many either take no newspapers or do not readily read and write. We think that great good can come from asking those who do read and write and who do have opportunities for becoming informed concerning the Census to discuss its requirements with those who do not.

The long and short of it is that each person will be required to tell the enumerator the acreage, quantity and value of all of his crops and the quantity and value of all of his farm products, and June 1, next, the number and value of all of his live stock, bees' swarms and fowls.

We also think that if the entire colored race can be imbued with the idea that they can only give themselves a favorable standing in the Census reports by the side of the white men by giving full information on these points, it will be a powerful stimulant in stirring them all to their best efforts.

Of course you need no suggestions of this kind. This letter is merely to keep my promise to send certain matters to you and to say emphatically that we fully appreciate and cordially thank you for any efforts you may put forth to aid in a more perfect and satisfactory census of the colored people. Sincerely yours,

> L. G. Powers
> Chief Statistician
> In Charge of Agriculture

TLS Con. 159 BTW Papers DLC. Written on stationery of the Census Office, Department of the Interior.

1 LeGrand Powers, originally of New York, was one of five chief statisticians for the U.S. Census of 1900. He had solicited BTW's advice ten days earlier, when he wrote: "We desire to know what prejudices there may be to overcome; the best methods of attempting to overcome them and the best means of reaching practically all of the colored race with such information as will let them know precisely what information they must furnish to the Census enumerators." (Oct. 17, 1899, Con. 159, BTW Papers, DLC.) BTW sent Powers his suggestions on Oct. 24, 1899, but no copy of that letter has been located. BTW did, however, encourage blacks to cooperate with the census takers. (See To the Editor of the Washington *Colored American*, ca. May 4, 1900, below.)

From Sallie Agee Poe

Handley W Va   Oct 27 1899

My dear Cousin Booker   I will write to you to ask you to please send me some money as I am in need of cloths   the weather is getting cold and mother are both in need and if you and your wife can please send me something right away as soon as you get this and I will be so thankful to you   I am going away the third of next month and need some money to get me some things before I go we are all well now as usual

Now if you will do me this kindness I will be under everlasting obligations to you   with love to you I am as ever you[r] Cousin

> Sallie Poe

ALS Con. 163 BTW Papers DLC.

To Timothy Thomas Fortune

Tuskegee, Ala., Oct. 28, 1899

Dear Mr. Fortune: I beg to hand you herewith a short article from the pen of Bruce-Grit, which I am advised will appear in Howard's American Magazine for November.[1] He seems to be piling it on lately. Please have the kindness to have it returned after you have noted.[2] Yours very truly,

Booker T. Washington

TLS Con. 154 BTW Papers DLC.

[1] BTW had received galley proofs of Bruce's article, "The Wizard of Tuskegee." Bruce stated that the consensus of white America regarding the race question was that "Tuskegee is one of the great agencies which the Almighty is using to solve the problem in the South, and that Booker Washington is the instrument He is employing to give the right direction to the solution of this problem." Bruce referred to BTW as "the most conspicuous character in the Negro race," and praised his honesty and loyalty to the cause of black advancement. (Galley proof, Con. 150, BTW Papers, DLC.)

No doubt BTW was doubly pleased when he saw the article in print, for it was preceded by a photograph of William McKinley and his tribute to BTW, which was taken from the President's speech at Tuskegee the year before. Also appearing as an illustration to Bruce's article was a letter from department-store millionaire John Wanamaker addressed to the publishers of Howard's, which stated: "I regard the work of Prof. Booker T. Washington at Tuskegee as the largest contribution that any one man has yet made since the War for the elevation of the race to which he belongs." In addition the magazine ran a brief autobiographical sketch by BTW which stressed his rise from humble origins to head of a large institution. (Howard's American Magazine, 4 [Nov. 1899], 3-8.)

[2] Fortune thought Bruce's article was "a very fair one" and that Bruce "seems to have developed a genuine admiration for you." He added: "You get some queer fish in your net." (Fortune to BTW, Nov. 1, 1899, Con. 154, BTW Papers, DLC.)

From George Wesley Atkinson

Charleston. [W. Va.] October 28, 1899

My Dear Friend: I own receipt of your letter of the 25th inst., in which you review, with a great deal of carefulness, the suggestions I made to you in my letter of last week. I agree with you that the colored voters of the South are at this time practically disfranchised, but they are robbed of their rights by the white people of the South, by their dictum, and not by authority of law. I am aware of the fact that one or two Southern States have, by acts of their Legislatures, disfranchised what they class the ignorant colored people within the limits of their States. Such disfranchisement, however, is in violation of the amendments of the Constitution of the United States relative to the colored people of our Country. What I sought to impress upon your mind was the fact simply that no colored man and no white man who is really friendly to the colored people should give his support to any movement which looks to the disfranchisement of either colored or white people. As I understand the situation, the world is moving forward and not backward. The colored people have been enfranchised by the authority of the American Congress, and to disfranchise them, therefore, in my judgment, is nothing short of a revolutionary movement. As I said in my former letter, it took a revolution to enfranchise the colored people, and nothing short of a revolution should disfranchise them. Upon this proposition I stand firmly and unequivocally. I will never give my consent, as an American citizen who believes in the rights of all of our people under the law, to any movement for the disfranchisement of anybody, white or black.

I am aware of the fact that the position you have taken, along with a number of other prominent colored men of the South, backed by a large element of white people, provides an educational qualification as a basis of suffrage. I will not even go this far; but, if the Southern authorities would see to it, honestly and fairly, that ignorant white people should not be allowed to vote, it might be some excuse for disfranchising ignorant colored people. Having been a close observer of the Southern situation for many years past, I am free to say to you that I have no sort of confidence in any pledges made by Southern white people along the lines which you are working. You will find in the end that if your ideas are carried out, practically all of the negroes of the South will not be allowed to vote, and practically all of the white people of the South will be allowed to vote. You seem to have very much more faith in the white people of the South than I have, and, yet, I am a Southern man, bred and born, as you know. I never believed in human slavery, and never will. I have given the best efforts of my life to elevate all mankind, white as well as black. I believe in lifting men up rather than pulling them down, and I recognize a man — a real man — whether he is white or black. You seem to think that if your proposition were carried out, that at least the intelligent portion of the colored people of the South will be allowed to vote their honest sentiments, and have their votes counted the way they intended them to go, without any interference whatever. I am sorry to say that I do not agree with you upon this idea.

I am sure Governor MacCorkle meant every word he said in his speech at the Huntsville Convention. He himself is far in advance of his Democratic white brethren in the South. If the matter were left to him, his and your proposition for an educational qualification as a basis of the right to vote, would be honestly and fairly carried out. But he is in a hopeless minority in his party in the Southern States. I agree with him that the time has come when there should be a fair count of the votes cast at elections in the South, but he and I and you may agree that such should be done, and, yet, the same old role will be performed that has been carried on in the South since the negro was enfranchised. I have for many years past held that the South should be relieved of a large portion of its representation in Congress, for the reason that the negroes, who make up a very material portion of the votes of the Southern States, are not counted in elections. I could give you statistics covering this point which, doubtless, would amaze you. There are many Districts in the South represented by members of Congress where not one-tenth of the votes cast to elect such Congressmen were counted. Either all of the votes should be counted, or the representation of the Southern States should be cut down to a proper and honest basis. But how is this going to be done? This is a momentous problem, and one which you and I cannot solve. All we can do, and all we ought to do, is to stand for our rights as American citizens, against all comers. If Southern election officers decide that colored men should not be allowed to vote, or refuse to count the result properly, or cast out the colored vote entirely, as is often done, we cannot help it. All we can do is to stand up as honorable men and protest. This I have been doing, as you know, for almost a generation, and I shall continue to do so as long as I am in public

life. I repeat again that I will never give my consent to the disfranchisement of anybody in this alleged free country of ours. Cordially and truly yours,

G. W. Atkinson

TLS   Con. 1   BTW Papers   DLC.

An Outline for a Speech

[Tuskegee, Ala.] Oct 28. 1899

Talk to teachers on European Trip
Cost of Trip.
Sea voyage.
Holland & Belgium.
Antwerp   *use of dogs*
   through Holland
(a) Canals & boats —
(b) women & children.
(c) smoking and wind mills.
(d) Agriculture & Dairying
Holliday in Rotterdam.
Brussells. Waterloo.

———

Paris —
 (a) art
 (b) Gayity —
 (c) morality
 (d) Beggars.
 (e) Tips.
 (f) Americans } Club, &
  Cheating. } Church.
  Excitement.
   Food.
  Black men in Paris.
  Tanner.

England —
  Greatness of London.
  Home life.
  Social Functions:
  Law & order — Cabs
  Parliament — No *humor.*
  Conservitism.
  No soda fountains. No ice.
  Electric cars.
  thoroughness — College.
  Great technical schools.
  Swanley.
  women's Congress.
  Royal family & Poor —
  Seeing the Queen.
  Negro & Africa

AM   Con. 164   BTW Papers   DLC.

From George Washington Henderson

New Orleans, La., Oct. 30 1899

My dear Mr. Washington: I fear I am too late in offering you the hospitality of our home, though not too late to assure of a cordial welcome should it be possible for you to come even for a little while. I understand that the President[1] invited you to the university, but that you had already been assigned to Col. Jas. Lewis's.

Would it be possible to take tea with Mrs. Henderson and myself before going to the lecture? We could discuss the subject of common interest between us, and afterward perhaps meet a few gentlemen in conference on the same subject. Of course I refer to the Louisiana Election law. I take this course because I wish to ask the politicians, into whose hands I suspect you have fallen, though just now under a disguise, and who discredit and generally disgrace whatever they touch. You are probably no stranger to politicians, but the Louisiana species forms a class by itself. A large meeting was called in Sept. ostensibly to consider the general subject of progress, but was perverted into a political move, which was the real motive from the first, and resulted in such a disgraceful scene that the large hall in which it was held has been closed to our people, so that a church had to be obtained for your lecture. I make these statements that you may understand my wish to keep the movement to test the constitutionality of the La. Election Law out of their hands, for in any case, they will do nothing unless they can see a chance to subserve their personal interests.

An individual here or there may be useful, if detached from the rest.

Moreover, not one of them I fear comprehends the real character of the question.

All friends will be glad to welcome you to the city. The University will be especially pleased to greet you. Very truly Yours —

Geo. W. Henderson

P.S. Please observe my new address.

ALS Con. 155 BTW Papers DLC.

[1] Oscar Atwood (1842-1909) was president of Straight University from 1890 to 1906.

From Oswald Garrison Villard[1]

New York City. Nov. 2, 1899

Dear Mr. Washington: I enjoyed your recent article in the "Atlantic Monthly" so much, and also your contribution in the "Southern Workman," reprinted from the New Orleans *Times-Democrat*, that I am moved to ask whether you could not send me a contribution for the supplement of the *Evening Post*.[2] I give you absolutely the choice of your subject, and shall pay you our highest rate. That is not very high in comparison with magazine rates, but it is the best we can offer, and we can, of course, assure you a circle of readers unequalled in the North, as you know. At any rate let me take this opportunity to add my small word of encouragement in your great work. A letter from a white woman in Marietta, Ga., lying before me says, "Would that the South had a thousand Booker Washingtons." Echoing that sentiment, I am   Very sincerely yours,

Oswald Garrison Villard

TLS   Con. 162   BTW Papers   DLC.

1 Oswald Garrison Villard (1872-1949), editor of the New York *Evening Post*, was a grandson of the abolitionist William Lloyd Garrison. Educated at Harvard, where he received a B.A. in 1893 and an M.A. in 1896, Villard at first planned a career as a teacher of American history but soon turned to journalism as his father, the railroad baron Henry Villard, groomed him to take over the *Evening Post*. He inherited ownership of the *Evening Post* in 1900, and turned it into one of the best-known liberal papers in America. The supplement of the *Evening Post* eventually became *The Nation*, one of the leading journals of liberal opinion, under Villard's editorship from 1918 to 1932.

Villard inherited not only the family newspaper, but also the reform causes which his family had championed. Throughout his life he took great pride in being the grandson of the Great Liberator, and his interest in black advancement began with his support of black education in the late 1890s. Villard, his uncles Francis Jackson Garrison and Wendell Phillips Garrison, and his mother Fanny Garrison Villard were all donors to Tuskegee Institute. They also gave money, however, to Atlanta University and other schools for higher education of blacks. In 1905, with the death of BTW's closest white associate William H. Baldwin, Jr., Villard filled the vacuum and became BTW's link with the northern philanthropists. As head of the Baldwin Memorial Fund, Villard raised several hundred thousand dollars for Tuskegee before 1908. BTW often sent Villard items for his paper that were too controversial to appear over his own signature on such topics as lynching, peonage, and discrimination in the South.

Villard became disillusioned with BTW's conservative approach and his refusal to become publicly outraged at racial injustice, and by 1908 their relationship had cooled somewhat, although Villard still consulted BTW on educational matters and favorably reported the Tuskegean's work in the *Evening Post*. In 1909 Villard was the author of "The Call," which led to the founding of the NAACP. He served as its first disbursing treasurer and was on the board of directors for many years.

Villard's interest in reform spanned most of the liberal causes of his generation, including woman suffrage, civil liberties, pacifism, and anti-imperialism. He wrote a number of books on the American press and on international affairs and wrote a biography of John Brown which was the standard work on Brown for many years. (See Villard, *Fighting Years;* Wreszin, *Oswald Garrison Villard, Pacifist at War;* Humes, *Oswald Garrison Villard, Liberal of the 1920s.*)

2 BTW had T. Thomas Fortune ghost an article for the New York *Evening Post*. (See Fortune to BTW, Feb. 10, 1900, below.) The article, "Lifting Up the Negro," contained an account of how Tuskegee students were an example of self-help as they acquired an education and then went out to teach others in the "grand army of industrialism that will help build up the material fortunes of the race, and make our beloved Southland 'blossom as a garden of the Lord.' " (New York *Evening Post*, Mar. 10, 1900, 13.)

From William E. Benson

Kowaliga, Ala., Nov. 2, 1899

Dear Sir: I regret very much the long delay in replying to your letter which you wrote me just before you sailed for Europe, but I did
not wish to mar the pleasure of your journey with my own affairs
by replying immediately; so I thought I would await your return.
I had hoped to talk with you long before this, but I have been very
busy until now, and have not had the opportunity to write you any
details. However, you state in your letter, before me, that you do
not wish to do us any harm "by your word or by your silence," and
ask us to outline the work which we have in hand in Kowaliga.

We are simply trying to build up just such a school as you have
so often encouraged and instructed our people to work for, to
educate the people in an isolated and a very needy community to
an intelligent, industrious and self-relying people; with Christian
motives and principles. It is one of the enterprises in the way of
self-help and self-development, for which we have so often heard
you plead, and we are sure it deserves your sympathy. You once
wrote that our efforts were praiseworthy. We have not changed our
plans or purposes since, and our aim is to develop these praiseworthy efforts into praiseworthy results for the good of our people.
We ought, I think, to be confident of your good word and help in
such a work.

I shall hope to have a talk with you sometime this winter and I
think when you once understand me, thoroughly, you will be convinced of my good intentions. Very Truly.

Wm. E. Benson

ALS Con. 280 BTW Papers DLC.

To Timothy Thomas Fortune

Tuskegee, Ala., Nov. 7, 1899

Personal

My dear Mr. Fortune: There is another exasperating condition of
things in Georgia. Certain parties are making a desperate effort

through the state legislature to pass a disfranchising bill.[1] I am almost disgusted with the colored people in Georgia. I have been corresponding with leading people in the state but cannot stir up a single colored man to take the lead in trying to head off this movement. I cannot see that they are doing a thing through the press.[2] I am tempted to put a strong article in the Atlanta Constitution. I am writing it now but do not know whether I will publish it.[3] It is a question how far I can go and how far I ought to go in fighting these measures in other states when the colored people themselves sit down and will do nothing to help themselves.[4] They will not even answer my letters. Yours truly,

Booker T. Washington

TLS   Con. 1   BTW Papers   DLC.

[1] A bill introduced in the Georgia legislature by Thomas William Hardwick provided that no person be allowed to vote unless he could read, write, and interpret any paragraph of the state constitution. The bill contained a grandfather clause that exempted from the educational qualification all persons who could vote as of Jan. 1, 1867, and all of their descendants. The bill failed to pass by a wide margin. Most of the white newspapers were opposed to it, and white Democratic representatives from predominantly black counties feared they would lose to the Populists if blacks were disfranchised. Disfranchisement did occur in Georgia in 1908, when it was accomplished through a constitutional amendment.

[2] At the same time that BTW was complaining about the inactivity of Georgia blacks, a number of leading black citizens were preparing a petition to the legislature. Dated Nov. 8, 1899, the petition stated that blacks were in general agreement with the need for election reform in Georgia but that they were opposed to the understanding clause and the grandfather clause. The petition stated that "any law which proposes discrimination against 850,000 souls, and which openly clears the way for dishonesty in popular elections, is contrary to the genius of our Christian civilization and a menace to free democratic institutions." The petition was signed by twenty-four men, including Henry Hugh Proctor, William A. Pledger, William H. Crogman, W. E. B. Du Bois, C. C. Wimbish, Henry A. Rucker, and John Hope. (Atlanta *Constitution*, Nov. 10, 1899, 7.)

[3] See An Interview in the Atlanta *Constitution*, Nov. 10, 1899, below.

[4] Fortune advised BTW that his protest against disfranchisement should be general rather than specific, so that he would not be open to the charge of meddling in the affairs of others. Fortune hoped that blacks in Georgia would lead in the battle against disfranchisement in that state. (Fortune to BTW, Nov. 10, 1899, Con. 153, BTW Papers, DLC.)

From Edgar Dean Crumpacker

Valparaiso, Ind., Nov. 7, 1899

My dear Sir: I have been greatly interested in your work for the practical education and upbuilding of the colored race in the southern states. Your race is undergoing the experience that seems to be necessary according to natural laws of social development. I was a member of the Committee on Elections and the Committee on Census in the last congress and will probably be a member of the Committee on Census in the present congress, and in the investigation of election cases I became somewhat acquainted with the degree to which colored men were admitted to political rights under the administration of laws in the South. I was profoundly impressed with the fact that the provision of the federal constitution calculated to bestow suffrage upon the negro was a practical nullity. In a number of the states an educational qualification is so established and so administered as to deny to fully ninety per cent of the negroes any participation in political privileges. In my investigation of the subject, I arrived at the conclusion that a fair educational qualification, honestly administered, would promote the permanent interests of your people but I know of no state that has such a qualification in which it is honestly administered. The object in conferring the right of suffrage upon the colored man was to give him importance as a political factor and thus give him means of recognition and self-protection. The whole scheme has been a dismal failure. It will be the duty of the Committee on Census in the next congress to prepare a bill for the apportionment of representatives under the 12th census. The 14th constitutional amendment makes it the imperative duty of congress to base representation upon population, but where any state disfranchises its male inhabitants over twenty-one years of age who are citizens of the United States, the representation of such state shall be reduced in the proportion that the number of disfranchised inhabitants bears to the total number of male inhabitants over twenty-one years of age. If this amendment were enforced it would deprive a number of southern states of a large share of influence in the federal government. I am inclined to believe that it ought to be done, and I will, in all probability, intoduce a bill at the beginning of congress requiring the Director of the Census to supply such information as may be necessary to intelligently enforce that constitutional provision. It is doubtless true that legislation cannot infuse character into people nor qualify them for responsibilities which their history and training have given them no adequate power to discharge. It occurs to me that the solution of the race problem in the South must come by the long and tedious process of evolution. In order, however, for that process to work efficiently many local prejudices and artificial barriers should be removed. There is no doubt that the prejudice against the colored race in the South is so intense that if they were well qualified to intelligently perform all of the duties of citizenship, unjust discriminations would still be made against them, both socially and politically. If an honest educational qualification should be established and justly administered, whenever a man, white or colored, should secure the qualifications for suffrage, it would enhance his appreciation of the right and increase his self-respect. If, however, a race is unjustly discriminated against, there will be no inducement to make the necessary preparation and the tendency will be to relapse into a condition of hopelessness. If the 14th amendment should be enforced and states deprived of a large share of their representation in the federal congress and in the electoral college, they would be interested in securing the vote of every person who was fairly qualified to discharge that function. It would set in motion a counteracting force and between an educational law and a bill reducing representation, the proper equilibrium might be accomplished and all men, white and colored, be given full political rights as soon as they were fairly qualified to discharge them. I submit these views to you and would be glad to have your opinion respecting the question. You have given the question the most intelligent consideration, in all its aspects, of any man whom I know in the country. Your views would be of much value to me. I would be under additional obligations to you if you would send me a copy of the last report of your Institute. Very truly yours,

E. D. Crumpacker

TLS Con. 151 BTW Papers DLC.

To Timothy Thomas Fortune

Tuskegee, Ala., Nov. 10, 1899

Dear Mr. Fortune: I have just returned from Atlanta where I put in a hard day's work in connection with other colored men there, trying to defeat the bill before the Georgia Legislature for the disfranchisement of the colored people and I think we will accomplish some good. I think the Constitution is going to be on our side. I can tell better, however, when I see its editorial which will appear today or next day. At any rate a whole broadside against the disfranchising measure will appear in tomorrow morning's Constitution. They readily gave us all the space we wanted. I telegraphed Wright[1] to come from Savannah and he came. If we do not win we have certainly shown them that we were not cowards sleeping over our rights. I have the feeling that the bill is not going to pass but I may be disappointed. If it passes I do not think it will pass in its present form. As it now stands it has both an "understanding" clause and a "grandfather" clause.

I plan to pass through New York on the 15th; I do not know whether I shall have time to see you. I shall try to telegraph you.

Booker T. Washington

Dictated.

TLSr Con. 1 BTW Papers DLC.

[1] Richard R. Wright, Sr.

An Interview in the Atlanta *Constitution*

Atlanta, Ga., November 10 1899

WASHINGTON URGES EQUAL TREATMENT
Danger to the South in Unjust Race Discrimination
GIVES DETAILED OPINION
Thinks Law Would Injure White People in the End
AN ELOQUENT PLEA FOR FAIRNESS
The Great Negro Leader Discusses Election Law
Tendencies, Wherein Danger, as He Sees It, Lies

Professor Booker T. Washington, the head of the famous industrial school for colored youths at Tuskegee, and probably the
foremost man of his race today, gave his views on the question of
franchise restriction to a representative of The Constitution yesterday. Professor Washington spent the day in the city, having
come here on business.

When asked for an expression on the Hardwick bill, he said that
he did not care to discuss that or any other specific measure, but on
the subject of an educational qualification restricting the ballot to
the intelligence of the country, he had very decided views.

"I dread the idea of seeming to intrude my views too often upon
the public," said Professor Washington, "but I feel that I can speak
very frankly upon this subject, because I am speaking to the south
and the southern people. It has been my experience that when our
southern people are convinced that one speaks from the heart and
tries to speak that which he feels is for the permanent good of both
races, he is always accorded a respectful hearing. No possible influence could tempt me to say that which I thought would tend
merely to stir up strife or to induce my own people to return to the
old-time method of political agitation rather than give their time,
as most of them are now doing, to the more fundamental principles
of citizenship, education, industry and prosperity.

DECISION LEFT TO THE SOUTH

"The question of the rights and elevation of the negro is now
left almost wholly to the south, as it has been long pleaded should

be done," added Professor Washington. "The south has over and over said to the north and her representatives have repeated it in congress, that if the north and the federal government would 'hands off,' the south would deal justly and fairly with the negro. The prayer of the south has been almost wholly answered. The world is watching the south as it has never done before.

"Not only have the north and the federal congress practically agreed to leave the matter of the negro's citizenship in the hands of the south, but many conservative and intelligent negroes in recent years have advised the negro to cast his lot more closely with the southern white man and to cease a continued senseless opposition to his interests. This policy has gained ground to such an extent that the white man controls practically every state and every county and township in the south.

VARIOUS ELECTION LAWS

"There is a feeling of friendship and mutual confidence growing between the two races that is most encouraging. But in the midst of this condition of things one is surprised and almost astounded at the measures being introduced and passed by the various law-making bodies of the southern states. What is the object of these election laws? Since there is white domination throughout the south, there can be but one object in the passing of these laws — to disfranchise the negro. At the present time the south has a great opportunity as well as responsibility. Will she shirk this opportunity, or will she look matters in the face and grapple with it bravely, taking the negro by the hand and seeking to lift him up to the point where he will be prepared for citizenship?

"None of the laws passed by any southern state, or that are now pending, will do this. These new laws will simply change the form of the present bad election system and widen the breach between the two races, when we might, by doing right, cement the friendship between them.

DANGEROUS ALL AROUND

"To pass an election law with an 'understanding' clause simply means that some individual will be tempted to perjure his soul and degrade his whole life by deciding in too many cases that the negro does not 'understand' the constitution and that a white man, even though he be an ignorant white foreigner with but recently acquired citizenship, does 'understand' it.

"In a recent article President Hadley,[1] of Yale University, covers the whole truth when he says: 'We cannot make a law which shall allow the right exercise of a discretionary power and prohibit its wrong use.' The 'understanding' clause may serve to keep negroes from voting, but the time will come when it will also be used to keep white men from voting if any number of them disagree with the election officer who holds the discretionary power.

"While discussing this matter, it would be unfair to the white people of the south and to my race if I were not perfectly frank. What interpretation does the outside world and the negro put upon these 'understanding' clauses? Either that they are meant to leave a loophole so that the ignorant white man can vote or to prevent the educated negro from voting. If this interpretation is correct in either case the law is unjust. It is unjust to the white man because it takes away from him incentive to prepare himself to become an intelligent voter. It is unjust to the negro because it makes him feel that no matter how well he prepares himself in education for voting he will be refused a vote through the operation of the 'understanding' clause.

IN A FALSE POSITION

"And what is worse this treatment will keep alive in the negro's breast the feeling that he is being wrongfully treated by the southern white man and therefore he ought to vote against him, whereas with just treatment the years will not be many before a large portion of the colored people will be willing to vote with the southern white people.

"Then again I believe that such laws put our southern white people in a false position.

"I cannot think that there is any large number of white people in the south who are so ignorant or so poor that they cannot get education and property enough that will enable them to stand the test by the side of the negro in these respects. I do not believe that these white people want it continually advertised to the world that some special law must be passed by which they will seem to be given an unfair advantage over the negro by reason of their ignorance or poverty.

"It is unfair to blame the negro for not preparing himself for citizenship by acquiring intelligence and then when he does get education and property, to pass a law that can be so operated as to prevent him from being a citizen even though he may be a large taxpayer. The southern white people have reached the point where they can afford to be just and generous; where there will be nothing to hide and nothing to explain. It is an easy matter, requiring little thought, generosity or statesmanship, to push a weak man down when he is struggling to get up. Any one can do that. Greatness, generosity, statesmanship are shown in stimulating, encouraging every individual in the body politic to make of himself the most useful, intelligent and patriotic citizen possible. Take from the negro all incentive to make himself and [his] children useful property-holding citizens and can any one blame him for becoming a beast capable of committing any crime?

REPRESSION WILL FAIL

"I have the greatest sympathy with the south in its efforts to find a way out of present difficulties, but I do not want to see the south tie itself to a body of death. No form of repression will help matters. Spain tried that for 400 years and was the loser. There is one, and but one, way out of our present difficulties and that is the right way. All else but right will fail. We must face the fact that the tendency of the world is forward, and not backward. That all civilized countries are growing in the direction of giving liberty to their citizens, not withholding it. Slavery ceased because it was opposed to the progress of both races and so all forms of repression will fail — must fail — in the long run. Whenever a change is thought necessary to be made in the fundamental law of the states, as Governor Candler says in his recent message:

" 'The man who is virtuous and intelligent, however poor or humble; or of whatever race or color, may be safely intrusted with the ballot.'

"And as the recent industrial convention at Huntsville, Ala., composed of the best brains of the white south puts it:

" 'To move the race problem from the domain of politics, where it has so long and seriously vexed the industrial progress of the south, we recommend to the several states of the south the adoption

of an intelligent standard of citizenship THAT WILL EQUALLY APPLY
TO BLACK AND WHITE ALIKE.'

"We must depend upon the mental, industrial and moral elevation of all the people to bring relief. The history of the world proves
that there is no other safe cure. We may find a way to stop the
negro from selling his vote, but what about the conscience of the
man who buys his vote? We must go to the bottom of the evil.

SHOULD BE EQUALITY OF TREATMENT

"Our southern states cannot afford to have suspicion of evil intention resting upon them. It not only will hurt them morally, but
financially.

"In conclusion let me add that the southern states owe it to
themselves not to pass unfair election laws because it is against
the constitution of the United States and each state is under a
solemn obligation that every citizen, regardless of color, shall be
given the full protection of the laws. No state can make a law
that can be so interpreted to mean one thing when applied to a
black man and another thing when applied to a white man, without disregarding the constitution of the United States. In the second
place, unfair election laws in the long run, I repeat, will injure
the white man more than the negro, such laws will not only disfranchise the negro, but the white man as well.

"The history of the country shows that in those states where the
election laws are most just, there you will find the most wealth, the
most intelligence and the smallest percentage of crime. The best
element of white people in the south are not in favor of oppressing
the negro, they want to help him up, but they are sometimes mistaken as to the best method of doing this.

"While I have spoken very plainly, I do not believe that any one
will misinterpret my motives. I am not in politics, per se, nor do I
intend to be, neither would I encourage my people to become mere
politicians, but the question I have been discussing strikes at the
very fundamental principles of citizenship."

Atlanta *Constitution*, Nov. 10, 1899, 7. Reprinted as a pamphlet at the Tuskegee Institute Steam Press in 1902.

1 Arthur Twining Hadley (1856-1930), an economist, was president of Yale University from 1899 to 1921.

To Timothy Thomas Fortune

Tuskegee, Ala., Nov. 13, 1899

My dear Mr. Fortune: You will see by the marked copy of the Constitution which I send you how nearly our minds run together. I thought it best to put what I wanted to say in the form of an interview instead of a letter. You will also notice that I have carried out your idea of not making my interview specific but it rather bears upon the general subject of disfranchisement. The colored people in Atlanta are now thoroughly awake and are working hard.

Neither the Journal nor the Constitution has so far taken a position in favor of the constitutional amendment. The Journal has had two editorials indirectly against it. The Constitution has not taken a position yet. Clark Howell has promised me to fight it and I have the hope that he will do so when the test comes. At any rate I do not think after what he said to me that he can afford to favor the bill.[1] Yours truly,

Booker T. Washington

TLS   Con. 160   BTW Papers   DLC.

[1] Shortly after the defeat of the Hardwick bill to disfranchise blacks in Georgia the Atlanta *Constitution* declared: "In some directions, the bill would have done good. It would have stimulated the negroes in the direction of securing an education; but its overwhelming defeat showed that the Georgia representatives believed that its basis was an injustice; and when injustice shows its head in Georgia, its existence is but momentary." The editorial stated that all that was needed now to insure racial harmony was for black Georgians "to take to heart the wise advice of Booker Washington and profit by it." (Atlanta *Constitution*, Dec. 4, 1899, 4.)

From Francis Jackson Garrison

Boston. Nov. 18, 1899

Dear Mr. Washington: I have received and read with the most unalloyed satisfaction and delight your admirable statement in the Atlanta Constitution of Nov. 10th with respect to the Hardwick Bill and similar disfranchising measures urged in the South, and I do not see how it would have been possible for you to have stated the case more temperately, forcibly, and convincingly than you have done. Especially effective is your use of Gov. Candler's message and the resolution of the Huntsville Convention. Knowing as I do that the latter was due to your earnest and tactful efforts, I can see the wise and shrewd manner in which you are proceeding, and the firm path which you are treading. The latest tribute to you by the Mayor of New Orleans[1] is another evidence of the hold which you have obtained upon the better men of the South, and the manner in which you are testing their sincerity, by holding them to their professions & by putting them on their honor, cannot fail to be effective. If the rising tide of injustice is stayed and further reactionary measures are prevented, it will be due to your wisdom and statesmanship more than to anything else.

I received a letter yesterday from my friend Mrs. Mawson, of Newcastle, expressing the great pleasure which it gave her to meet you in London, and her deep regret that you and Mrs. Washington were unable to visit her at Newcastle. She spoke of having received a recent paper from you, and I doubt not that you are keeping in touch with many English friends whom you met by sending them copies of the Southern Newsletter and other papers, from time to time. With kindest regards to Mrs. Washington, believe me, Faithfully yours,

F. J. Garrison

P.S. If you still have a spare copy of the Constitution of the 10th, I wish you would send a marked copy to Walter H. Page, Hotel Margaret, 97 Columbia Heights, Brooklyn, N.Y. I should be very glad to have a dozen copies of the paper, and will gladly send the price of them if you can spare them. My brother William is delighted with your statement.

The protest of the colored citizens of Georgia against the Hardwick Bill is altogether admirable.

TLS Con. 154 BTW Papers DLC.

1 Walter C. Flower, a New Orleans attorney and cotton planter, was mayor from 1896 to 1900.

From James B. Washington

Tuskegee, Ala., Nov 20– 99

My Dear Brother: We are about [to] introduce a new feature in the social and Athletic side of Tuskegee, and I must write you for your support, both financially and morally. On the 15th of December we are to engage Atlanta University on our grounds in a game of foot ball, and of course we need co-operation from you. If you wont be back by that time, I am sure we would like a word from you. If you can find time to dictate an encouraging letter to the team and school to be read in the Chapel, it will greatly spur the boys on to victory, or at least a trial to that end. We are also raising their R.R. fare by private subscription and any amount you will give will be highly appreciated. It is going to take a mighty effort to raise $75.00, but we must do it. The teachers are greatly enthused and students also. We hope by charging for seats, and what students and teachers give with assistance from the white citizens in town who are very anxious to see the game, to raise this amount. It will also require some favors from the Council also. Will you kindly drop a line or two to that body for us. It seems that we should be shown some consideration, when we take into consideration the faithfulness of the work-students to work and work so incessantly. We are never able to make a decent showing from the fact the boys are never able to get off but I really believe with a word from you to the Council, they are willing to deviate from the policy of the school on such an important event as this. Am sorry to worry you with these matters, which perhaps in your mind are trivial, but all look to you for redress. I hope to impress those Atlanta folks as to how to be received and treated, a point which all who have visited there will say, they are weak on. We are aiming to make their trip here, one of pleasure, also profitable, in fact it is intended to make the day a gala one. Mr. Wood[1] and Mr. Jackson[2] are working with might to make all go off nicely. I am, Your brother,

J. B. Washington

Mr. Hunt[3] — You may send your one hundred down to the athletic fund also.

J. B.

ALS Con. 164 BTW Papers DLC.

1 Charles Winter Wood was born in Nashville in 1870 and moved in 1882 to Chicago, where he became a bootblack. Wood developed an interest in the theater at an early age and often amazed his customers with his recitations from Shakespeare. A sign in the window of his basement shoeshine parlor read: "The Charles Winter Wood Shakespearean Bootblacking Establishment." Through the aid of a wealthy benefactor Wood studied theater and elocution at Beloit College. Later he received a B.D. from the University of Chicago's divinity school and an M.A. from Columbia University. Wood traveled for a while with several black theater groups in the Midwest and West before joining the Tuskegee faculty in 1898. He taught grammar and elocution at Tuskegee and also served as a northern agent. In 1904 he became librarian of the Carnegie Library at Tuskegee, a position he held for many years after BTW's death. Wood introduced Shakespeare and other classics to the Tuskegee students and faculty and became over the years one of the outstanding members of the faculty who toured widely as a spokesman and fund raiser for the school. (Kansas City *Star*, May 4, 1900, Clipping, Con. 1032, BTW Papers, DLC.)

2 Thomas J. Jackson.

3 Nathan Hunt.

From Timothy Thomas Fortune

New York, Nov 20 1899

Dear Mr Washington: I have your letter of the 18th, with Congressman Crumpacker's letter enclosed.

1. Reduction of Southern representation in Congress and the electoral college in conformance with the 14th amendment is inevitable, as the North and West will not put up with the injustice of it; but you can afford to be cautious in dealing with the matter (*a*) because you have to reckon with the white South and (*b*) with the race in all the States.

2. Reduction will benefit the voters of the North and West and cripple the white South. *Will it help us?* It would in the long run if it should be the means of forcing the white South to deal justly. Will it do that? I am afraid not.

3. Past Congresses have about decided by acquiescence in Supreme Court decisions that the States can do about as they please in dealing with the suffrage question, *so long as a given law applies to black and white alike.*

4. The only thing that Crumpacker's committee can do is to apportion representation between the States on the basis of the last

census returns as prescribed by the constitution as *modified by the 14th amendment*, and you can afford to commit yourself that far, guardedly, without getting in hot water.

5. The constitutions of Mississippi, South Carolina and Louisiana are unjust and immoral and the Supreme Court has refused, in the case of Mississippi to so declare them; Congress should find a way to remedy the matter. To sanction by reduction of apportionment the injustice and immorality would be National compounding of the rascality. Yours truly

T. Thomas Fortune

ALS Con. 153 BTW Papers DLC.

To Warren Logan

Grand Union Hotel, New York. Nov. 23, 1899

Dear Mr. Logan: The more I think of it the more I am inclined to believe that when we do dispose of our school lands it will be best to put them up at auction, at any rate give the public a chance to bid on them and see if they cannot be disposed of in this way.

I call your attention to the enclosed bill of fare for the students. It seems to me that they are having too much fat meat; you will notice that they had bacon and gravy for two meals. Yours truly,

Booker T. Washington

TLS Con. 16 BTW Papers ATT.

To Warren Logan

Grand Union Hotel, New York. Nov. 23, 1899

Dear Mr. Logan: I understand that the Atlanta football team is to come to Tuskegee on the 15th of December; if this is true, I think it wise for the Council or yourself to make some contribution from the school to help entertain the visiting team properly. I also hope the Council will be as liberal as possible in arranging for the students to attend the game, but every precaution should be taken to keep the boys and girls separate. Yours truly,

Booker T. Washington

TLS Con. 16 BTW Papers ATT.

To Francis Jackson Garrison

Grand Union Hotel, New York. Nov. 24, 1899

My dear Mr. Garrison: Your letter of November 18th has been received. You do not know how much encouragement and strength it gives me. I thank you sincerely for it. I have strong hope, based upon recent information, that the Hardwick bill will fail before the Georgia Legislature. I shall send you a marked copy of the Atlanta Constitution either today or tomorrow and shall also send one to Mr. Page. I hope to see you a few minutes when I come to Boston next week.

You will be interested I am sure to see the enclosed letter which please return to me.

As soon as I get additional copies of the Atlanta Constitution I will send them to you. Yours truly,

Booker T. Washington

TLS James Weldon Johnson Collection CtY.

From Edgar Dean Crumpacker

Valparaiso, Ind., Nov. 24, 1899

My dear Sir: Your kind letter of the 18th inst. is at hand and its contents have been read with deep interest. I will observe your injunction of privacy respecting our correspondence upon this subject and hope I may have an opportunity at an early day of discussing with you personally the situation. Very truly yours,

E. D. Crumpacker

TLS Con. 151 BTW Papers DLC.

From Francis Jackson Garrison

Boston, Nov. 25, 1899

Dear Mr. Washington: Thanks for your letter of yesterday with enclosure, which last I at once return, and hope that you will be able to accept the invitation to Nashville. You are wise in improving every opportunity of this sort that will count, and you have a keen discrimination as to what will or will not be worth the subtraction of your time and strength from your manifold other duties, for such purposes. I am much encouraged by what you write about the probability of failure of the Hardwick Bill. It is of course a great point to have Gov. Candler and the *Constitution* opposed to it.

You will be grieved to learn of the death of our dear and honored friend Rev. Samuel May, of Leicester, who passed away yesterday in his 90th year. His interest in you and Tuskegee has always been strong. He was practically the last survivor of the anti-slavery leaders, and I shall miss him inexpressibly. His funeral will take place on Monday at one P.M., at Rev. Chas. G. Ames's Church here in Boston, and I could wish that your Boston appointments might bring you here in time to attend it. I know how fully mortgaged your days are, and I fear it may not be possible for you to do so. As the representative of your race* in the United States to-day, your presence at the funeral would be a fitting and significant tribute, and one that would be marked and appreciated not only by his family and friends, but by the country at large. Yours very truly,

Francis J. Garrison

*Excuse this phrase, which I do not like, & to which you have the right to retort, as Fredk Douglass did, "Which race?" You are fast becoming the representative of both races to a greater degree than any other man.

I enclose a notice of your book from to-day's *Advertiser*.[1]

TLS Con. 154 BTW Papers DLC.

[1] The Boston *Advertiser*, Nov. 25, 1899, 4, praised *The Future of the American Negro* and described it as a handy reference to BTW's philosophy.

To Francis Jackson Garrison

Grand Union Hotel, New York. Nov. 29, 1899

My dear Mr. Garrison: By this mail I send you six additional copies of the Atlanta Constitution. You have already, I presume, noted in this morning's paper that the Hardwick bill was overwhelmingly defeated in the Georgia legislature. It only received three votes and only one speech was made in favor of it and that by Mr. Hardwick himself. You will also note that one member said in his speech that it was no worse for the Negro to sell his vote than for the white man to buy it. I feel quite sure that this action of the Georgia legislature means the turning point in the South. I have just telegraphed the leading colored people in Atlanta to take some action that will let the people of Georgia know their gratitude in this matter. The policy of putting these people absolutely upon their honor is going to bear fruit I think.

I am very sorry indeed that it was an impossibility for me to be present at the funeral of our dear departed friend, Mr. May. I sent a telegram to Mr. Ames regretting my absence. He was a good, great and helpful friend, and the loss of such workers as he places a great responsibility upon those of us who are left behind.

I hope to see you a few minutes Friday or Saturday. Yours truly,

Booker T. Washington

TLS   Francis J. Garrison Papers   NN-Sc.

From Emmett Jay Scott

Tuskegee, Ala., Nov. 29–1899

Dear Mr. Washington: No receipts today. We have had no Atlanta, or Eastern mail due to a wreck between here & Atlanta I hear. Well, the Hardwicke Bill was "skotched" unmercifully! I am sure your interview did much to help on the killing. You can accept congratulations! Faithfully,

Emmett J. Scott

ALS   Con. 161   BTW Papers   DLC.

From Timothy Thomas Fortune

Thompson Cottage. Saratoga, N.Y., Nov. 29, 1899

My dear Mr. Washington: I was delighted to get the telegram this morning. The defeat of the Hardwick bill is the only substantial victory we have had in the South in a long time and I am sure the result is due in large part to your work and influence. More strength to your arm.

I am working like a steam engine the past two days. An article for the Transcript yesterday and one for the Sun today.

I want to begin on the Evening Post article tomorrow or Friday, but although I have a letter from Scott dated the 25th he does not say a word about the data on successful students of Tuskegee.

My health is fair, my appetite is good, *and I don't want to see New York and wish I never should again.* Yours truly

T. Thomas Fortune

ALS   Con. 154   BTW Papers   DLC.

Edgar Webber to Emmett Jay Scott

[Tuskegee, Ala., ca. November 1899][1]

Mr. Scott: The memorandum which I last handed Mr. Washington covers the whole of his life. It is precisely like the one he already had with the addition of references concerning his European trip and other events since his trip to Europe ending with Huntsville Speech. Chronologically Mr. Washington has brought his narative almost down to the time of his Atlanta speech and it is concerning the events which lead up to that event that he ought now to write. It has been difficult to get him to write chronologically, but he needs to cover the ground from the point I name above, down to the present. The references he will need begin in scrapbook No. 2, and go on through book 5. It has been so hard to get him to go right through with the matter. He always prefers to write about something that has just happ[en]ed. Truly

Webber

ALS Con. 164 BTW Papers DLC.

1 The dating is suggested by Webber's reference to BTW's Huntsville speech of Oct. 12, 1899.

An Interview by Frank George Carpenter[1]
in the Memphis *Commercial Appeal*

Washington, D.C., Dec. 2, 1899

PROMISE OF THE FUTURE

WHAT COMING YEARS OFFER THE SOUTHERN NEGRO

HIS MATERIAL CHANGES

B. T. WASHINGTON SENSIBLY DISCUSSES THE OUTLOOK

MANY PROBLEMS INVOLVED

HE DECLARES THE SOUTHERN WHITES TO BE THE NEGRO'S MOST CONSIDERATE FRIENDS AND DENIES THAT ANY BUT THE SOCIAL LINES ARE DRAWN AGAINST HIM

I had a long chat this afternoon with Prof. Booker T. Washington of Tuskegee, Ala. Prof. Washington is today the leading colored man of the United States. As an orator he has taken the place that Frederick Douglass held for so many years, and at the same time he is doing more in a practical way to solve the problems of the future of the negro than any man who has yet appeared. Born a slave, raised in a log cabin, getting his first education at night school by toiling in the mines of West Virginia, walking hundreds of miles from the mountains to the sea in order that he might enter the school at Hampton, he is now, at the age of 40, at the head of one of the great educational institutions of this country. He has established and built up an industrial school at Tuskegee in which there are now more than one thousand students, coming from twenty-three States and territories and also from Jamaica, Cuba,

Porto Rico, Africa and England. Beginning to teach in a shanty his institute has now forty-two buildings, the most of which have been put up by the students themselves. Its property is valued at $300,000, and the school farms comprise more than 2,000 acres of land.

In the school colored students over fourteen are given a practical, industrial education. They have thorough mental and religious training, but at the same time are taught such trades and professions as will make them self-supporting. The students pay a large part of their expenses in labor. Last year they made more than one million bricks, more than three hundred thousand garments were washed in the college laundries, and seventy cows were milked daily in the dairy division. The students are being taught all sorts of trades, such as farming, blacksmithing, masonry, carpentering and carriage making. There are departments of cooking, dairying and drawing, plastering, plumbing and painting, shoemaking, stock raising, tailoring and tinning, and in fact, all sorts of trades which will make men self-supporting. The school has done wonders for the race in Alabama. Branch colleges have been established, and in the future there will probably be similar institutes throughout the South.

PORTO RICO AND PHILIPPINE VIEWS

My conversation with Booker T. Washington began with the discussion of the improvement of the natives of Porto Rico and the Philippines. I asked him whether institutes like this would not do much to make these people good American citizens. He replied: "I doubt whether any other method can be adopted which will so soon accomplish the desired results. There is only one solution of the race problem, and that is to show the people how they can support themselves, to educate their hands, as well as their heads; to give them mental and religious culture, and at the same time industrial training. We must teach them first how to make a living, make them independent and show them that labor is both manly and profitable."

"Have you had any experience with the Cubans and Porto Ricans, Prof. Washington?" I asked.

"Yes, we have a number of them in our school. They do fairly well, and I can not see why they should not be educated into being good American citizens, though such a training must necessarily be a matter of time. We have one Porto Rican who was quite savage when he first came to Tuskegee. He carried a knife with him, and he had a way of becoming very angry, raging about and flourishing his knife. He attempted to vent his rage upon one of our boys whereupon the young American took the knife from him and gave him a good thrashing. From that time on the Porto Rican changed his methods. He learned to control himself, and is now one of the quietest boys in the school."

ENCOURAGING CHANGE PERCEPTIBLE

"How about your work in the South, Mr. Washington? Can you see any material change in the condition of the negro as a result of it?"

"There is a considerable change in Alabama," was the reply. "We can see the change in the character of the applications for admission to the school. At first many of those who sent their children were anxious to have them taught books, and expressly said that they did not want them to be taught to work. They had the idea that they should be educated only for medicine, the law or the ministry. This is all changed. The students now enter with the idea of learning to work, and the boy lost caste who refused to work. We have already educated about three thousand students, and these are now scattered all over the South."

"How about the negroes generally? Are they growing better?"

"I think so," said Mr. Washington. "They have learned that the road to advancement is along the line of industrial and personal success and not wholly along the lines of political working. They see that their future depends upon themselves. They are striving to better their conditions, and many of them are doing so. I believe this race problem will work itself out just in proportion as the black man, by reason of his skill, intelligence and character, can show himself the equal of the white man, or can produce what the white man wants. As our people accumulate property, you will find that they will be respected. The negro who has $50,000 to lend will not want for friends and customers among his white neighbors. The black man that spends $10,000 a year in freight charges can secure first-class accommodations in a railroad car, or the company will put on a Pullman palace car for him. It is the same with other things; when our people have elevated themselves along industrial and educational lines they will have improved the best. Southern white people do not want to keep the negro down.

"It will be the same in all fields," continued Booker T. Washington. "When the black man, by reason of his knowledge of chemistry of the soil and improved methods of agriculture, can produce forty bushels of corn on any acre of land, while his white brother produces only twenty bushels, the white man will come to the black man to learn, and they will be good friends. An instance of this kind recently happened in Alabama not far from me. A black man I know produced a crop of 261 bushels of sweet potatoes from a single acre of land. This was twice as much as any man in that community had produced, and every one of the dozen white men who came to see how it was done was ready to take off his hat to that black man.

"I don't think the people of the North quite appreciate the situation of the colored man in the South in such respects. The whites there are perfectly willing to do business with the blacks. They will patronize a colored grocer just as quickly as they will a white grocer. The man who has the best store and keeps the best goods gets the trade. It is the same with the colored mechanic and with the colored businessman."

ONLY SOCIAL DIFFERENCES

"The differences, I suppose, are entirely social?"

"Yes, almost altogether so," said Mr. Washington. "The two races are in this respect apart."

"Will they continue so; or do you think the conditions will ever be such that the races will join? Will the blacks be swallowed up in the whites?"

"I think the two races will continue to be distinct as races," was the reply. "They do not mix in an immoral manner so much as they did during the days of slavery, though in matters of business, education and things that tend to improve the general character of both races there is more union at the present time in the South than has ever existed. I say this, notwithstanding the fact that I am aware of the many outrages which have been perpetrated against our people in some portions of the South during the last two or three years. The negroes are increasing rapidly. I think the last census showed that the negroes were increasing more rapidly in proportion to their number than the whites. Of course it is to be considered that the negro does not have any accession to his numbers by reason of immigration, while the white race does."

Said I, "Might there not come such a time when they would equal us in number?"

"I have some doubt as to that. The mortality of the blacks in the cities at the present time is very great, although we have a higher birth rate than the whites. We are, I believe, equally healthy in the country districts. As the negro gets education the death rate decreases."

"Do you think the day will come when the black man will be the equal of the white man in all respects throughout the United States?"

"That is a big question, and time will have to answer it in a large measure. I see no reason, however, why the negro should not strive to be the equal of the white man in all that is best in our American life. As soon as he shows himself to possess the same qualities that the white man possesses he will be given many opportunities that are now denied him."

"Do you think, Mr. Washington, that the black child is naturally endowed with intellectual faculties equal to the white child?"

"I do," replied the negro educator. "I am speaking, of course, of the average child of both races."

"But, professor, do you not think there is a limit to the possibilities of the colored man in the United States? Do you think the time might ever come, that any circumstance might ever arise, by which a black man might become president of the United States?"

"I should hope so," was the reply; "but this is another very big question."

NEGRO'S UNFORTUNATE ENVIRONMENT

"How about the moral standing of the black man? Is he born with a conscience equal to that of the white?"

"There is no doubt in my mind as to that matter," replied Booker T. Washington. "The colored man is naturally religious. Our consciences are somewhat a matter of education and our moral condition is largely influenced by our surroundings. What state of morality or practical Christianity could you expect where as many as six, eight or even ten cook, eat, sleep, get sick and die in one room? It is often charged that a black man has rather loose ideas of property rights as regards the white man. But take a look at former conditions. While we were in slavery our people reasoned thus: 'My body belongs to my master, and taking master's chickens to feed master's body is not stealing.' Indeed, one old colored man who was discovered in such a theft by his master, said:

" 'Now, massa, it's true you's got a few less chickens, but, massa, don't you see, you's got a good deal more nigger.'

"Some of our people reason that the wealth of the whites came from the work of the blacks, and therefore this property equitably belongs to them. Of course the better educated of our people have no such ideas, but you can see how among the ignorant such thoughts might affect their ideas of mine and yours."

Freedmen North and South

At this point I asked Mr. Washington whether he thought the negro had justice in the South. He replied: "Not always, but I consider that matters are growing better in this direction. While he does not always get justice in the South, it is to be borne in mind that in many cases in the North he does not get justice; especially is this true in regard to securing employment. The negro has a far better opportunity in the South to earn a living than he has in the North. The trades unions are not there to bar him out of employment in the same degree that is true of the North. While there are many things that are not yet as they should be, it is an encouraging sign to note that many of the most intelligent and prominent Southern white people are beginning to take hold with a view of improving the negro's condition."

Mr. Washington then went on to speak of lynchings, which have been so common during the last few years. Said he: "The entire people of the South have felt keenly the injury that has been done to it by reason of these lynchings, and I feel that there is now a general effort being put forth to blot out lynchings. This is especially true in the State of Georgia, which has had more lynchings recently than any other State. Governor Candler deserves a great deal of credit for his recent efforts in stopping lynchings and in his public expressions of condemnation. Many of the best white people feel that these lynchings are not only hurting us in the eyes of the world, but in our moral and material growth. A short time ago I spoke plainly through the Southern white papers on this subject, and I was surprised to note the friendly manner in which the Southern press commented editorially upon what I had to say.

"I have been gathering some figures upon the subject of lynchings," Mr. Washington continued. "Within six years almost as many people were lynched in the Southern States as the number of soldiers who lost their lives in the Spanish-American war in Cuba. The number was nearly nine hundred. In 1892, 241 persons were lynched. Last year 171 were killed in this way. The people of the United States have the idea that lynching is resorted to only for crimes against women and that they are confined to negroes. Of those lynched last year twenty-three were whites and two were Indians, and only one-fifth of the whole were for crimes of that nature. Sixty-one of the lynchings were for murder, thirteen for being suspected of murder and six for theft. During one week last spring thirteen negroes in one of the Southern States were accused of murder or house burning and lynched. They were killed without being allowed to go before a court, so that their innocence or guilt could be tested. Within the past six years a half dozen colored women have been lynched, and lynching is now being resorted to in some cases by black people as well as whites. But I am glad to state that during the last few months we have had very few lynchings, and there is a strong public sentiment growing in the South against this crime, and I believe within a few years, through the aid of the best negroes and the best white people, it will be blotted out."

"What effect does lynching have upon crime?"

"I doubt whether it materially restrains it. There is no evidence that it does. It certainly hurts the neighborhood in which the lynching is done. It drives the negroes to other sections of the country. Many of them leave the farming districts, where they are really needed, and move into the cities. I think the remedy for crime lies in education and the enforcement of the law. If the laws are not sufficient to properly punish the crime they should be changed. But punishment should be by law and not by individuals. The history of the world shows that where the laws are most enforced there is the least crime, and also that where the people take the law into their hands there is the most crime.

Education the Great Need

"Crime also decreases with the education of the people. We need more schools in the South. Eighty-five per cent of the colored people of the Gulf States are on the plantation and in small towns, where a majority of them are in ignorance. Many of them, I am sorry to say, are still in debt and mortgage their crops for food, paying or attempting to pay interest rates that are outrageous. In most cases on these plantations the colored people live in one-room cabins on rented land, and their schools rarely last more than four months. I wonder if you have any idea of the amount of money that is spent in the education of our people in some of the Southern States? The average per colored scholar in some of the counties of the South is not more than 83 cents annually, while each child in Massachusetts has spent upon him annually between $18 and $20. The Massachusetts child has all the surroundings of libraries and of an advanced civilization. The colored child is in the backwoods so far as many of the modern facilities are concerned. Alabama has recently extended its school system by appropriation of more money, and Georgia has done the same thing. I think that both the government and the church should give more attention to the education of the negro. The negroes must be educated in head, hand and heart before they can become equal to the best class of American citizens.

"On the whole I am most hopeful in regard to our race in the South. I do not think we have any reason to despair. We must not spend our time in complaining, but in hard work and an earnest effort to bring about friendly relations between the black man and the white man."

Memphis *Commercial Appeal*, Dec. 17, 1899, 15. This copyrighted interview appeared in several newspapers.

1 Frank George Carpenter (1855-1924) was a prominent American journalist and world traveler.

From Grover Cleveland

Princeton N.J. Dec. 3d 1899

My dear Mr Washington: My inability to attend the meeting[1] to-morrow evening, in the interest of Tuskegee Institute, is a very great disappointment to me.[2] If my participation could have in the slightest degree aided the cause you represent, or in the least encouraged you, in your noble efforts, I should have felt that my highest duty was in close company with my greatest personal gratification.

It has frequently occurred to me that in the present condition of our free negro population in the South, and the incidents often surrounding them we cannot absolutely calculate that the future of our nation will be always free from dangers and convulsions, perhaps not less lamentable than those which resulted from the enslaved negroes, less than forty years ago. Then the cause of trouble was the injustice of the enslavement of four millions; but now we have to deal with eight millions, who though free, and invested with all the rights of citizenship, still constitute, on the body politic, a mass largely affected with ignorance, slothfulness, and a resulting lack of appreciation of the obligations of that citizenship.

I am so certain that these conditions cannot be neglected, and so convinced that the mission marked out by the Tuskegee Institute presents the best hope of their amelioration, and that every consideration makes immediate action important, whether based upon Christian benevolence, a love of country or selfish material interests — that I am profoundly impressed with the necessity of such prompt aid to your efforts as will best insure their success.

I cannot believe that your appeal to the good people of our country will be unsuccessful. Such disinterested devotion as you have exhibited and the results already accomplished by your unselfish work, ought to be sufficient guarantee of the far reaching and beneficent results that must follow such a manifestation of Christian charity and good citizenship as would be apparent in a cordial and effective support of your endeavor.

I need not say how gratified I am to be able to indicate to you that such support is forthcoming. It will be seen by the letters which I enclose that already an offer has been made, through me, by a benevolent lady in a Western City, to contribute twenty five Thousand dollars ($25000.) toward the Endowment Fund, upon condition that other subscriptions to this Fund, aggregate the amount required. With so good a beginning I cannot believe it possible that there will be a failure in securing the endowment which Tuskegee so much needs. Yours very truly,

Grover Cleveland

HLS Con. 151 BTW Papers DLC.

[1] On Dec. 4, 1899, BTW held a meeting for the benefit of the Tuskegee endowment fund at the Madison Square Garden Concert Hall in New York City. Among those on the platform were Morris K. Jesup, William E. Dodge, Charles H. Parkhurst, Hamilton W. Mabie, William Dean Howells, J. P. Morgan, William H. Baldwin, Jr., and Lyman Abbott. Carl Schurz presided at the affair and read Cleveland's letter to the audience. Among others in attendance were Mr. and Mrs. John D. Rockefeller, Mr. and Mrs. Collis P. Huntington, and Seth Low. (New York *Times*, Dec. 5, 1899, 8; Boston *Transcript*, Dec. 5, 1899, 9.)

BTW's speech was typical of many of his utterances on industrial education and is, therefore, not reproduced here. He said that there was a consensus North and South that blacks should receive an industrial education, and he restated his belief that blacks would advance by laying a foundation based on property, intelligence, and thrift. (Con. 955, BTW Papers, DLC.) While this was not BTW's first appeal to the wealthy of New York, it was symbolic of the fact that he was turning more often to the capitalists of New York for support rather than relying, as earlier, on the abolitionist-oriented philanthropy of Boston and other parts of New England.

[2] Cleveland had wired BTW earlier from Princeton, N.J.: "I am laid up with severe attack of rheumatism. Will try hard to attend meeting. But it may be impossible." (Nov. 29, 1899, Con. 540, BTW Papers, DLC.) Three days later Cleveland wired BTW again: "I can neither stand nor walk on my feet. . . ." (Dec. 2, 1899, Con. 540, BTW Papers, DLC.)

From Henry Wysham Lanier[1]

New York   December 5, 1899

Dear Mr. Washington: We have ordered the two copies of "McClure's" to be sent to the Reading Room, and hope that they will meet your needs.

In regard to the financial end of the proposed book— our idea would be that we would endeavor to secure advantageous serialization for as much of it as possible, either in "McClure's Magazine" or elsewhere, turning over to you the entire proceeds of anything made in this way. If it proved feasible to use twenty or thirty thousand words in magazines, the direct return to you would, of course, be quite large. As for the book— our plan would be to push it as much as lies in our power, with the idea of giving it a really wide circulation, and to pay you an increasing royalty: 10% on the first 2,500, 12½% on the second, and 15% on all copies thereafter. Of course, unless we believed that we really had a chance to make it thoroughly successful and to handle it satisfactorily both to you and ourselves, we would not want to go into it at all; but we do really feel that there is a chance to make it a popular, as well as an extremely interesting and valuable book.

I hope sincerely that you will want to go ahead with it, and that you will want to let us see what we can do with it. We are managing to work out some new ideas in the line of publishing and pushing books, and we should be extremely gratified to try to apply them to this story of your own life and work.

Hoping that we may hear from you, or have a call from you at your convenience, and that you will tell us with entire frankness just what you feel about the matter, I remain, Sincerely yours,

Henry Wysham Lanier

TLS   Con. 160   BTW Papers   DLC.

[1] Henry Wysham Lanier (1873-1958), son of the poet Sidney Lanier, was employed by Doubleday and McClure Co. in 1899, and from 1900 to 1912 was secretary of Doubleday, Page and Co. He founded and published the *Golden Book Magazine* from 1925 to 1930.

To Emmett Jay Scott

Grand Union Hotel, New York. Dec. 6, 1899

Dear Mr. Scott: I wish you would get the enclosed into as many of the colored newspapers as you can.

Our meeting here Monday night was a great success so far as numbers and enthusiasm were concerned. Several people told me that we have the very creme of New York present including such men as Mr. Huntington,[1] Mr. Wm. E. Dodge, Mr. Morris K. Jesup and many others. The hall was packed, I do not think there was a vacant seat in the room and many people stood up. The only disappointment was in Mr. Cleveland not being present. He sent a telegram saying he was not able to walk or stand on his feet owing to rheumatism. His heart was very much in the meeting as you will see by the enclosed letter. Please give this letter to Mrs. Washington after you have read it. The conditional subscription of $25,000 was secured through him. We hope for good results from the meeting.

I shall arrange the matter of your vacation when I come.

Please send Mr. Chandler[2] what information you can, or tell him where he can get it. Yours truly,

Booker T. Washington

TLS Con. 160 BTW Papers DLC.

[1] Mr. and Mrs. Collis P. Huntington donated $50,000 to the Tuskegee endowment fund. Scott wrote to BTW: "Your telegram to Mrs. Washington announcing the gift of $50,000 by Mr. and Mrs. Huntington came while we were at evening prayers and was read to the students amid much hand clapping and rejoicing. Mr. Penney proposed the singing of the Doxology and prayers, both of which were had."

[2] Albert M. Chandler, a Harvard student, had written to BTW for information he needed for a debate on Negro suffrage. (Dec. 2, 1899, Con. 151, BTW Papers, DLC.)

From Wesley Warren Jefferson

Montserrat, B.W.I. 12-6, 1899

Dear Principal: I am in Montserrat and have been for some little time, after what I consider a very long and tiresome journey. I would have written you before now, but owing to the fact that the communicating system of this Island is in very poor condition, I have been prevented from so doing.

Will say to begin with, I do not like the place.[1] Candidly speaking it is, just as Mr. Fortune said, the poorest place on earth. The Island has a population of not less than 9,000 Negroes 8900 of which are in a condition of slavery. There is a good deal of starvation going on in the Island. Many have not clothes with which to cover their bodies. They are willing to work but actually there is nothing to do. The whole Island is nothing but mountains. Women get 4 & 5 pence a day, and out of this they must feed and clothe themselves. Just think 8 & 10 cts. per day in our money. The men get a shilling per day 24 cts. in our money. This problem is more intricate than the American problem.

I know if you had only known where you were sending me, and under what disadvantages I would have to work you would not have sent me. The schools are all managed by Gov'ment Inspectors, and they are very good. Will say they are much better than the average American public school. Education is compulsory in all of the Island. The studies taught in this school are as follows: Reading, writing, Arithmetic, Geography, History, Gram'r, Science & Book-keeping. We also have in this school what are known as Gov'ment Pupil Teachers, who teach and are to be trained by the School Master in the following subjects: Arithmetic, Grammar, Algebra, School Methods; Ancient & Modern History; Latin Geography Physical; Tropical Agriculture; Physiology Book-keeping and Domestic Economy, so you see I have work to do. There is quite a contrast between our ideas along educational lines. Every thing is different. In school they deal altogether with £1 S 1 & d 1 in Arithmetic. This you know requires study on my part.

I will have to be examined just as soon as the Inspector of Schools comes. He is expected on tomorrow. I understand the examination will be in the above subjects named for Pupil Teachers. I am going to give the whole thing, at the lowest calculation, a trial. I have been going on for a few weeks with the school work and every thing has been very successful. I have been studying Latin, Tropical, Agriculture, School Methods, Physical Geography; Domestic Economy and all that sort of thing that we don't bother with, trying to get in readiness for the examination.

The Quebec Steam Ship company was to have been responsible for my passage to Montserrat, but allow me to inform you that it was not all the way although that was the impression I labored under, until we had traveled for a week, when I was told to go ashore at night and this was about 100 miles from Montserrat. Through the kindness of an Irish gentleman from the old Dominion, I reached Montserrat safely. He gave me $3.00. I relate this to show just the experiences I have gone through. When I reached Montserrat I found no school building in which to teach nor house in which to live, but now we have a nice stone structure (School-building) and a 2 room framed house in which to live. I had to stay at a Boarding house in the town, where I had to pay 6 shillings for board and lodging per day, without 1 cent and before I had made 1 cent. Six shillings in our money would be $1.44 cts.

The letter the Quebec Steam Ship Company wrote me while in Washington, was a disappointment and I stayed in New York 4 day[s] waiting to sail. There I spent all the money I had, out for board & lodging. Kind regards to students teachers and family. Awaiting a reply, I am very truly yours,

Wesley W. Jefferson

P.S. The prejudice is just as great here as it is in America. The people are fairly intelligent but very very poor.

ALS   Con. 176   BTW Papers   DLC.

1 After more than seven months at Montserrat Jefferson was still depressed about the poverty of the people he encountered. "People are leaving the Island in large numbers," he wrote, "because of being unable to get work. Hunger is causing many to steal who have never been known to steal before." The trouble, according to Jefferson, was that "the white man has the monopoly of every thing in the Island, and no money is being spent, so the poor Negro must suffer." He told BTW that he had complete faith in BTW's emphasis on industrial education but found that it did not seem applicable to the West Indies since whites would not hire blacks to work. (Jefferson to BTW, July 10, 1900, Con. 176, BTW Papers, DLC.)

From Lyman Abbott

New York   December 9, 1899

My dear Mr. Washington: I have just been reading your volume, and it has renewed and increased my admiration for your work. It is easily within bounds to say that no one in America has thrown so much light or exerted so beneficent an influence upon what we call the negro problem, as you have done. I doubt whether all other influences combined since the close of the Reconstruction period have been as efficient and beneficent as yours.

I hope at an early day to give to our readers what seem to me to be substantial principles which you inculcate, founding that statement upon this volume.

Meanwhile I am minded to write this letter to you, asking of you a service which if I do not misjudge, will be of great use to the cause which you have at heart. This is that you write for us an autobiography or autobiographical reminiscences of about fifteen to twenty thousand words in length. We should probably publish it in three or four parts. My thought is that in such reminiscences you could show our readers by incidents in your own life and career what are the trials, difficulties and obstacles thrown in the way of the progress of your race and how those obstacles may be met and surmounted. Writing as you would necessarily do in an anecdotal and reminiscent mood, your articles would be read by a great many who are not greatly interested in the problem as a problem, and whose interest would be awakened by such a story as you could tell, while at the same time such incidents would necessarily illustrate the principles for which you contend and the solution which you propose to the problem which confronts us.

I know that you are a busy man, and that you may naturally begrudge the time for such an undertaking; but I also am sure that you will appreciate the advantage of enlarging the constituency to which appeal can be made for interest in this problem, and I hope you will see as I do that in no better way could that constituency be enlarged than by such a story of your life.

If the general idea of such a biography strikes you favorably, I should like to have a personal conference with you about length, scope and price (which we should expect to make satisfactory to you) when you next come to New York. Yours sincerely,

Lyman Abbott

TLS   Con. 160   BTW Papers   DLC.

From Clifford H. Plummer

Boston, December 12, 1899

My dear sir: Yours of the 7th inst., expressing gratitude to the citizens of Boston, received.

Indeed, if you never knew it before, it may now go without saying that the citizens of Boston and vicinity congratulate themselves in having such a man as you identified with our race. In speaking this way I can readily say that I speak whereof I know, as I have never allowed my professional position to draw me away from the masses of the people, but have always remained in touch with them. Their wrongs I have always been among the first to try to right, and their complaints of such wrongs have seldom been made to any other young man for the last few years before they have been made to me. I do not say this with egotism, but I speak it as a matter of fact, and when I have told you in the past of the people's attitude towards you, I have spoken what I know; and I think while you were in Boston you had evidence of the fact.

I believe, sir, that our people, the rank and file the country over, endorse both you and your movement. Opposition, of course, is from a few ambitious, would-be leaders in our race ranks, and all they need is occasionally a man to rise up and serve notice on them with all the force he can that their position will not be tolerated, and that their plans and their motives are known. I think, however, that the matter has been pretty thoroughly demonstrated in Boston, for ever since the Reception here, all I have heard on all sides, from both white and colored, is the highest commendation of you, the cause you represent, and the action of the citizens in behalf of you and your cause in Boston.

The thing that pained me most was that the opposition you had in Boston was from men, and a few women, who themselves came to Boston only a few years ago, and many of them were educated here through public charity, and they now dare to assume the dictates of Boston people! From my early childhood I have been in Massachusetts, though like yourself I was born in Virginia, where all of my parents were. My mother and father were Massachusetts citizens at the time of my birth, but my grandmother resided in Virginia, and it was there that my mother went when these occasions occurred which many fathers glory in. There were four such occasions in my family, but my heart beats for the cause of my people, and my highest desire is for their welfare, first, last and always, and my respect and appreciation for those who are concerned in the upbuilding of my race have no bounds.

Let me assure you, sir, the doors of Boston among your race are always open for you and any of your friends who represent the principles that you represent, and let me give you the liberty, whenever any of your friends are journeying this way, to say they will always find a warm welcome from me, and I shall endeavor to see that there will be no obstacle in their way in regard to respect that shall be paid to them while they here sojourn.

Believe me to be, with best wishes and sincerest regard   Yours very respectfully,

Clifford H. Plummer

TLS   Con. 181   BTW Papers   DLC.

From Frederick Taylor Gates

New York. December 15th., 1899

Dear Sir: Toward the debt of the Tuskegee Normal and Industrial Institute, contracted for the current expenses of last year, understood to be about twelve thousand dollars ($12,000.00), Mr. Rockefeller will contribute five thousand dollars ($5,000.00).

Toward the current expenses of the Institute for the fiscal year ending May 31st., 1900, Mr. Rockefeller will contribute five thousand dollars ($5,000.00).

Kindly indicate to whom you desire these funds to be sent? Yours very truly,

F. T. Gates

TLSr   Con. 154   BTW Papers   DLC.

From Amanda Ferguson Johnston

Malden W Va   Dec. 18. 99

My Dear Brother   I was more than glad to Hear from yu & tu get the Contents   Brother I am keeping resturant & Doing verry well   I need A showcase   Albert Promised to Send me five which it will Cost   Brother as I Hafter use so much grocers if Can raise enoug by friday ill go tu town & get Coffee sugar Lard meat flour   I make good money on Oysters   I get them from C. H Person[1] Baltimore M.D. I did not know where yu were up north   Albert told

me yu were ther But did [not] say where. I thank yu So much for
that Book   I dont Sleep much   I read when I Shut up at night
the works Have Bin running for three weaks & will Contunia
for the winter So they Say   I seene where C.p. Hunting[ton] give
to School   am glad. Hop yu a Happy Xmass   Love to all. I am
trying to get a Start to Save Some money   Ben Has a team & Paying on it   Halls Coal to Charleston   from yur Only Sister

A Johnston

ALS   Con. 156   BTW Papers   DLC.

¹ C. H. Pearson Packing Co., a black-owned firm.

From Henry Hugh Proctor

[Atlanta, Ga.] Dec. 22, 99

My dear Mr. Washington: I have just received your telegram requesting exact copy of the Bill.¹ No copy has yet been printed. I
can, however, give you the substance of it.

It does not provide for separate "cars," only separate "compart-
ments." Any passenger failing to comply is to be ejected by train-
men who are under penalty of a misdemeanor.

Then it makes this proviso:

"Provided, That nothing in this act shall be construed to compel
sleeping-car companies or railroads operating sleeping cars to carry
persons of color in sleeping or parlor cars." An exception is made
to servants in company with their employers.

This would indicate that the intention was to shut the Negro
out entirely.

You will be interested to know of the history of this bill. On its
back are the following entries:

Senate

Read, First,   November 9, 1898
  "   Second,   "   11   "
  "   Third,   "   21   "
Passed Ayes 23, Nays 0

House

Read, First,		November 26,	1898
"	Second	Dec. 8	1898
"	Third	Dec 15	1899

Passed Ayes 88, Nays 0.

Note the last reading, over a year from the second. We supposed it dead. It was put through at the last moment under cover.

We are organizing to fight it to the last ditch. Sincerely Yours,

H. H. Proctor

ALS   Con. 181   BTW Papers   DLC.

[1] See *Acts and Resolutions of the General Assembly of . . . Georgia, 1899*, pt. I, title 8, pp. 66-67.

To Warren Logan

[Tuskegee, Ala.] December 23, 1899

Mr. Logan: Some time within the next week I wish very much that you would let me have a list of plantation songs, both new and old which the choir and students might be taught to sing well.

B. T. W.

TLI   Con. 16   BTW Papers   ATT.

From Robert Lloyd Smith

Oakland, Texas, Dec 26 1899

My dear Mr Washington   I am very proud of your last letter and I sincerely hope that the endowment will reach $250000 during 1900.

I am almost made over by my trip. I can see so much further into things now. Indeed it was absolutely necessary for me to get the course in education I got with you at the North. We are planning big things in Texas. Our land 100 acres will probably be bought sometime this year. Our committee meets on Sat to devise ways and means. We *will come through all right* if you'll come down and give us one of your common sense talks. You cannot do a better thing for the race than a trip here next fall and I[']m almost sure under good management it will *pay* equally as well as an ordinary trip North. One great thing it will do. It will put our society upon a firmer basis than ever and will enable me possibly to pay for the ground and one building. The success of the fair this year has only laid the foundation for the greatest gatherings of Negroes for *educational purposes from the platform* that the country has ever seen.

I want an exhibit from Tuskegee. We will pay the expenses. This exhibit alone will give us the growth necessary to show that the fair and society are growing. Track already laid nearly to the building. A minimum of handling. I have a corps of teachers who have *volunteered*. Will complete it with agriculturist as soon as I can see any money in sight. Please write me assuring me that unless Providence intervenes you will be with us & Tuskegee will exhibit mechanical work. Texas gave me an extensive ad on account of Northern trip. Another move in this direction and you'll do for me what Howells did for Dunbar. Cordially

R L Smith

ALS   Con. 162   BTW Papers   DLC.

From Timothy Thomas Fortune

Washington, D.C., Dec 30, 1899

My dear Mr Washington: I have your letter and telegram of the 26th and letter of the 27th. I dismiss the matter of our conversation as a mistake in the effort to better my condition which it is not good to remember.

I note what you say of the check and wired Peterson to day to send it here, special delivery, as I need it.

I have done what I could to keep the council's[1] Ex. Com. in the middle of the road, and succeeded. These things usually go as I want them to when I am on hand. The local council at New Orleans will institute a test case in the matter of the suffrage clause of the Constitution and wants the sympathy and support of the National Council to help them. We gave it.

They were all dead set for the Crumpacker bill and reduction of southern representation, *but it is a false step and will involve us in trouble in the future.*

I have made Chase promise to let you alone.

I have the situation in hand. Yours respectfully

T Thomas Fortune

ALS Con. 154 BTW Papers DLC.

1 The National Afro-American Council.

From Timothy Thomas Fortune

Washington, D.C., Dec 31, 1899

Dear Mr. Washington: Perry Heath[1] sent a man to New York December 25 to see if I would take charge of an headquarters here as the Afro-American end of his literary bureau of the National Committee. I wasn't satisfied with the power of the person to talk terms and so I told him I would rather see Mr Heath when he returns from the West next week, that is, after New Year's. Yesterday Bishop Walters called on the President and [in] the course of the conversation the President told him that he had advised Mr Heath to give me that end of the work. We shall see what comes of the scheme.[2]

At the banquet last night for the Negro Academy and Council people remaining in the city Prof. Grisham[3] of Kansas City jumped upon your industrial theories with both feet and made things mighty warm for a season. I followed him and did what I could to break the force of his position and to show the wisdom and advantage of your position and that there was plenty of room for the widest development of both industrial and higher education. Bishop Walters followed in the same line, and while the brethren were not all of them convinced, as far as argument went, the honors were even and the subject was dropped. The position of the Virginia Superintendent of Education has riled the brethren of the Negro Academy a heap.[4]

Mrs. Fortune went to Jacksonville on Thursday. I could secure a ticket over the Southern one way from Washington to Jacksonville. It cost $79.50 to piece out the ticket and secure the sleeper. She will remain 4 weeks.

I shall return to New York this afternoon.

Hoping you and yours [have] a Happy New Year. Yours truly,

T Thomas Fortune

ALS Con. 154 BTW Papers DLC.

[1] Perry Sanford Heath (1857-1927) was a newspaperman who became active in Republican national politics as a campaign manager and promoter. During the McKinley campaign of 1896, he revolutionized the publishing role of the Republican national committee by distributing tons of Republican propaganda and by organizing hundreds of writers to keep Republican issues before the public.

[2] Fortune wrote BTW a few weeks later: ". . . I find by a letter from Perry S. Heath today that we have been barking up the wrong tree. No Bureau of that kind is contemplated at this time, although the President has suggested the wisdom of establishing such a Bureau." (Jan. 22, 1900, Con. 172, BTW Papers, DLC.)

[3] Presumably G. N. Grisham, who was principal of the Lincoln High School in Kansas City, Mo.

[4] The report of Superintendent Joseph W. Southall contained a brief section on the education of Negroes which concluded that blacks were not making progress because they were given a smattering of book learning when what they needed was moral and industrial education. The superintendent cited BTW, J. L. M. Curry, and Hollis B. Frissell as being the real authorities on black education. The report obviously infuriated members of the National Negro Academy, who were dedicated to higher education. (*Biennial Report of the Superintendent of Public Instruction of . . . Virginia* [1899], xxxiv-xxxvii.)

From Walter Hines Page

Cambridge, Mass   31 Dec. 1899

Dear Mr Washington: I have just read your article in the Jan'y *Century*.[1] The story of William Edwards & how he changed the whole character of Mr. S. & the story of the colored woman whose flower-garden changed her white neighbor— these are the things, I tell you, that strike home in print just as they do in life; & these are the things that will make a most interesting book. When you come to write your autobiography string along the narrative of your own life just as many human stories of this kind as you can. A whole life is *summed* up in every one of them.

I hope that you will get released from the technical prohibition in your contract & can go about the book at an early time.

I do not know whether you have heard that Mr. Doubleday & I have formed a partnership, along with several others, for carrying on & developing the book-publishing business with which he has been so successful.

I hope that the Endowment Fund keeps growing.

My regards to Mrs. Washington and all good wishes for the New Year. Sincerely yours

Walter H. Page

ALS   Con. 31   BTW Papers   ATT.

[1] BTW, "Signs of Progress among the Negroes," *Century Magazine*, 59 (Jan. 1900), 472-78. The article contained the story of William Junior Edwards, an 1893 Tuskegee graduate, who so impressed a white planter, R. O. Simpson, that he donated land for a school for blacks and Edwards became its principal. BTW often used an anecdote about a black woman whose flower garden was so beautiful that a passing white woman was forced to stop and admire it. Eventually she entered the black woman's yard to discuss the cultivation of flowers. Finally, with race prejudice allayed by this mutual interest, she entered the black woman's home.

The Future of the American Negro

1899

Booker T. Washington's *The Future of the American Negro* (Boston, 1899) brought together in a single volume a number of his public addresses after the Atlanta Exposition address and articles in *The Independent, Atlantic Monthly, Appleton's Popular Science Monthly*, and other periodicals. Though the style is uneven and there are some repetitions, it was the closest Washington ever came to an inclusive and systematic statement of his social philosophy and racial strategy.

Washington stressed by repetition the economic means to black advancement and the philosophy of self-help, mutual aid, and education. He pronounced Reconstruction a failure because of its political approach, its wrong kind of education for blacks, and its encouragement to the freedmen to begin at the top instead of at the bottom. He stressed the mutual interdependence of whites and blacks in their common southern homeland. While he urged blacks to make themselves useful to whites as a means of gaining the full civil and political rights currently denied them, in occasional bursts of frankness he admonished those whites who practiced discrimination, exploitation, and violent repression against blacks.

When Washington asked his close adviser T. Thomas Fortune to edit and proof the galleys, Fortune took the opportunity to lecture Washington on both his writing style and his conservative outlook. "Clearness of thought and lucidity of diction in a book are indispensable," he wrote of Washington's convoluted sentences. He also chided Washington for his "unconscious habit of apologising for the shortcomings of white men." Conceding that the scissors-and-paste preparation of the manuscript had given him "a great deal of uneasiness," Washington thanked Fortune for his modification of the offending passages. (Fortune to BTW, Oct. 13, 1899, above; BTW to Fortune, Oct. 27, 1899, Con. 160, BTW Papers, DLC.)

The reviewers were kinder than Fortune when the book appeared in late 1899. Lyman Abbott in the *Outlook* lauded Washington for his perception and courage and suggested that every northern teacher in a southern black school should read the book. (*Outlook*, 64 [Jan. 6, 1900], 14-17.) Abbott wrote Washington that the volume renewed and increased his admiration for Washington's work, saying: "I doubt whether all other influences combined since the close of the Reconstruction period have been as efficient and beneficent as yours." He urged Washington to express his ideas in an autobiographical work that "would be read by a great many who are not greatly interested in the problem as a problem." (Dec. 9, 1899, above.)

Other critics were equally complimentary. Walter Hines Page praised the book as "intensely practical," not a speculative treatise but a guide to solving the nation's number one problem. (*Book Buyer*, 20 [Mar. 1900], 144-45.) The reviewer in the *Southern Workman*, George S. Dickerman, went so far as to compare it with *Uncle Tom's Cabin*, not as a story but as a guide to the race problem, "a calm setting forth of facts and conclusions by one whose life has been a steady training in the mastery of his subject." (*Southern Workman*, 28 [Dec. 1899], 504-6.) The black novelist Charles W. Chesnutt, a personal friend of Washington despite ideological differences, praised the book as a practical guide to the present problems and immediate future of the Negro. He noted, however, that Washington had "almost nothing to say about caste prejudice, the admixture of the races, or the remote future of the negro." Chesnutt felt that Washington was "doing his part" by smoothing over asperities and appealing to the dormant love of justice among whites, but that the race problem could not be solved until the whole country was ready to treat blacks with equal and exact justice. (*The Critic*, 36 [Feb. 1900], 160-63.)

THE FUTURE OF
THE AMERICAN NEGRO

Booker T. Washington

Boston
Small, Maynard & Company
1899

To

REV. H. B. FRISSELL, D.D.,

Principal of the
Hampton Normal and Agricultural Institute,
Hampton, Virginia,
My friend and the successor of
General S. C. Armstrong,
This volume is
Dedicated.

The Future of the American Negro

PREFACE

In giving this volume to the public, I deem it fair to say that I have yielded to the oft-repeated requests that I put in some more definite and permanent form the ideas regarding the Negro and his future which I have expressed many times on the public platform and through the public press and magazines.

I make grateful acknowledgment to the "Atlantic Monthly" and "Appleton's Popular Science Monthly" for their kindness in granting permission for the use of some part of articles which I have at various times contributed to their columns.

Booker T. Washington

Tuskegee Normal and Industrial Institute
Tuskegee, Ala., October 1, 1899

The Future of the American Negro

CHAPTER I

In this volume I shall not attempt to give the origin and history of the Negro race either in Africa or in America. My attempt is to deal only with conditions that now exist and bear a relation to the Negro in America and that are likely to exist in the future. In discussing the Negro, it is always to be borne in mind that, unlike all the other inhabitants of America, he came here without his own consent; in fact, was compelled to leave his own country and become a part of another through physical force. It should also be borne in mind, in our efforts to change and improve the present condition of the Negro, that we are dealing with a race which had little necessity to labour in its native country. After being brought to America, the Negroes were forced to labour for about 250 years under circumstances which were calculated not to inspire them with love and respect for labour. This constitutes a part of the reason why I insist that it is necessary to emphasise the matter of industrial education as a means of giving the black man the foundation of a civilisation upon which he will grow and prosper. When I speak of industrial education, however, I wish it always understood that I mean, as did General Armstrong, the founder of the Hampton Institute, for thorough academic and religious training to go side by side with industrial training. Mere training of the hand without the culture of brain and heart would mean little.

The first slaves were brought into this country by the Dutch in 1619, and were landed at Jamestown, Virginia. The first cargo consisted of fourteen. The census taken in 1890 shows that these fourteen slaves had increased to 7,638,360. About 6,353,341 of this number were residing in the Southern States, and 1,283,029 were scattered throughout the Northern and Western States. I think I am pretty safe in predicting that the census to be taken in 1900 will show that there are not far from ten millions of people of African descent in the United States. The great majority of these, of course, reside in the Southern States. The problem is how to make these millions of Negroes self-supporting, intelligent, economical and valuable citizens, as well as how to bring about proper relations between them and the white citizens among whom they live. This is the question upon which I shall try to throw some light in the chapters which follow.

When the Negroes were first brought to America, they were owned by white people in all sections of this country, as is well known, — in the New England, the Middle, and in the Southern States. It was soon found, however, that slave labour was not remunerative in the Northern States, and for that reason by far the greater proportion of the slaves were held in the Southern States, where their labour in raising cotton, rice, and sugar-cane was more productive. The growth of the slave population in America was constant and rapid. Beginning, as I have stated, with fourteen, in 1619, the number increased at such a rate that the total number of Negroes in America in 1800 was 1,001,463. This number increased by 1860 to 3,950,000. A few people predicted that freedom would result disastrously to the Negro, as far as numerical increase was concerned; but so far the census figures have failed to bear out this prediction. On the other hand, the census of 1880 shows that the Negro population had increased from 3,950,000 in 1860 to 7,638,260 twenty-five years after the war. It is my opinion that the rate of increase in the future will be still greater than it has been from the close of the war of the Rebellion up to the present time, for the reason that the very sudden changes which took place in the life of the Negro, because of having his freedom, plunged him into many excesses that were detrimental to his physical well-being. Of course, freedom found him unprepared in clothing, in shelter and in knowledge of how to care for his body. During slavery the slave mother had little control of her own children, and did not therefore have the practice and experience of rearing children in a suitable manner. Now that the Negro is being taught in thousands of schools how to take care of his body, and in thousands of homes mothers are learning how to control their children, I believe that the rate of increase, as I have stated, will be still greater than it has been in the past. In too many cases the Negro had the idea that freedom meant merely license to do as he pleased, to work or not to work; but this erroneous idea is more and more disappearing, by reason of the education in the right direction which the Negro is constantly receiving.

During the four years that the Civil War lasted, the greater proportion of the Negroes remained in the South, and worked faithfully for the support of their masters' families, who, as a general rule, were away in the war. The self-control which the Negro exhibited during the war marks, it seems to me, one of the most important chapters in the history of the race. Notwithstanding he knew that his master was away from home, fighting a battle which, if successful, would result in his continued enslavement, yet he worked faithfully for the support of the master's family. If the Negro had yielded to the temptation and suggestion to use the torch or dagger in an attempt to destroy his master's property and family, the result would have been that the war would have been ended quickly; for the master would have returned from the battlefield to protect and defend his property and family. But the Negro to the last was faithful to the trust that had been thrust upon him, and during the four years of war in which the male members of the family were absent from their homes there is not a single instance recorded where he in any way attempted to outrage the family of the master or in any way to injure his property.

Not only is this true, but all through the years of preparation for the war and during the war itself the Negro showed himself to be an uncompromising friend to the Union. In fact, of all the charges brought against him, there is scarcely a single instance where one has been charged with being a traitor to his country. This has been true whether he has been in a state of slavery or in a state of freedom.

From 1865 to 1876 constituted what perhaps may be termed the days of Reconstruction. This was the period when the Southern States which had withdrawn from the Union were making an effort to reinstate themselves and to establish a permanent system of State government. At the close of the war both the Southern white man and the Negro found themselves in the midst of poverty. The ex-master returned from the war to find his slave property gone, his farms and other industries in a state of collapse, and the whole industrial or economic system upon which he had depended for years entirely disorganised. As we review calmly and dispassionately the period of reconstruction, we must use a great deal of sympathy and generosity. The weak point, to my mind, in the reconstruction era was that no strong force was brought to bear in the direction of preparing the Negro to become an intelligent, reliable citizen and voter. The main effort seems to have been in the direction of controlling his vote for the time being, regardless of future interests. I hardly believe that any race of people with similar preparation and similar surroundings would have acted more wisely or very differently from the way the Negro acted during the period of reconstruction.

Without experience, without preparation, and in most cases without ordinary intelligence, he was encouraged to leave the field and shop and enter politics. That under such circumstances he should have made mistakes is very natural. I do not believe that the Negro was so much at fault for entering so largely into politics, and for the mistakes that were made in too many cases, as were the unscrupulous white leaders who got the Negro's confidence and controlled his vote to further their own ends, regardless, in many cases, of the permanent welfare of the Negro. I have always considered it unfortunate that the Southern white man did not make more of an effort during the period of reconstruction to get the confidence and sympathy of the Negro, and thus have been able to keep him in close touch and sympathy in politics. It was also unfortunate that the Negro was so completely alienated from the Southern white man in all political matters. I think it would have been better for all concerned if, immediately after the close of the war, an educational and property qualification for the exercise of the franchise had been prescribed that would have applied fairly and squarely to both races; and, also, if, in educating the Negro, greater stress had been put upon training him along the lines of industry for which his services were in the greatest demand in the South. In a word, too much stress was placed upon the mere matter of voting and holding political office rather than upon the preparation for the highest citizenship. In saying what I have, I do not mean to convey the impression that the whole period of reconstruction was barren of fruitful results. While it is not a very encouraging chapter in the history of our country, I believe that this period did serve to point out many weak points in our effort to elevate the Negro, and that we are now taking advantage of the mistakes that were made. The period of reconstruction served at least to show the world that with proper preparation and with a sufficient foundation the Negro possesses the elements out of which men of the highest character and usefulness can be developed. I might name several characters who were brought before the world by reason of the reconstruction period. I give one as an example of others: Hon. Blanche K. Bruce, who had been a slave, but who held many honourable positions in the State of Mississippi, including an election to the United States Senate, where he served a full term; later he was twice appointed Register of the United States Treasury. In all these positions Mr. Bruce gave the greatest satisfaction, and not a single whisper of dishonesty or incompetency has ever been heard against him. During the period of his public life he was brought into active and daily contact with Northern and Southern white people, all of whom speak of him in the highest measure of respect and confidence.

What the Negro wants and what the country wants to do is to take advantage of all the lessons that were taught during the days of reconstruction, and apply these lessons bravely, honestly, in laying the foundation upon which the Negro can stand in the future and make himself a useful, honourable, and desirable citizen, whether he has his residence in the North, the South, or the West.

CHAPTER II

In order that the reader may understand me and why I lay so much stress upon the importance of pushing the doctrine of industrial education for the Negro, it is necessary, first of all, to review the condition of affairs at the present time in the Southern States. For years I have had something of an opportunity to study the Negro at first-hand; and I feel that I know him pretty well, — him and his needs, his failures and his successes, his desires and the likelihood of their fulfilment. I have studied him and his relations with his white neighbours, and striven to find how these relations may be made more conducive to the general peace and welfare both of the South and of the country at large.

In the Southern part of the United States there are twenty-two millions of people who are bound to the fifty millions of the North by ties which neither can tear asunder if they would. The most intelligent in a New York community has his intelligence darkened by the ignorance of a fellow-citizen in the Mississippi bottoms. The most wealthy in New York City would be more wealthy but for the poverty of a fellow-being in the Carolina rice swamps. The most moral and religious men in Massachusetts have their religion and morality modified by the degradation of the man in the South whose religion is a mere matter of form or of emotionalism. The vote of the man in Maine that is cast for the highest and purest form of government is largely neutralised by the vote of the man in Louisiana whose ballot is stolen or cast in ignorance. Therefore, when the South is ignorant, the North is ignorant; when the South is poor, the North is poor; when the South commits crime, the nation commits crime. For the citizens of the North there is no escape; they must help raise the character of the civilisation in the South, or theirs will be lowered. No member of the white race in any part of the country can harm the weakest or meanest member of the black race without the proudest and bluest blood of the nation being degraded.

It seems to me that there never was a time in the history of the country when those interested in education should the more earnestly consider to what extent the mere acquiring of the ability to read and write, the mere acquisition of a knowledge of literature and science, makes men producers, lovers of labour, independent, honest, unselfish, and, above all, good. Call education by what name you please, if it fails to bring about these results among the masses, it falls short of its highest end. The science, the art, the literature, that fails to reach down and bring the humblest up to the enjoyment of the fullest blessings of our government, is weak, no matter how costly the buildings or apparatus used or how modern the methods of instruction employed. The study of arithmetic that does not result in making men conscientious in receiving and counting the ballots of their fellow-men is faulty. The study of art that does not result in making the strong less willing to oppress the weak means little. How I wish that from the most cultured and highly endowed university in the great North to the humblest log cabin school-house in Alabama, we could burn, as it were, into the hearts and heads of all that usefulness, that service to our brother, is the supreme end of education. Putting the thought more directly as it applies to conditions in the South, can you make the intelligence of the North affect the South in the same ratio that the ignorance of the South affects the North? Let us take a not improbable case: A great national case is to be decided, one that involves peace or war, the honour or dishonour of our nation, — yea, the very existence of the government. The North and West are divided. There are five million votes to be cast in the South; and, of this number, one-half are ignorant. Not only are one-half the voters ignorant; but, because of the ignorant votes they cast, corruption and dishonesty in a dozen forms have crept into the exercise of the political franchise to such an extent that the conscience of the intelligent class is seared in its attempts to defeat the will of the ignorant voters. Here, then, you have on the one hand an ignorant vote, on the other an intelligent vote minus a conscience. The time may not be far off when to this kind of jury we shall have to look for the votes which shall decide in a large measure the destiny of our democratic institutions.

When a great national calamity stares us in the face, we are, I fear, too much given to depending on a short "campaign of education" to do on the hustings what should have been accomplished in the school.

With this idea in view, let us examine with more care the condition of civilisation in the South, and the work to be done there before all classes will be fit for the high duties of citizenship. In reference to the Negro race, I am confronted with some embarrassment at the outset, because of the various and conflicting opinions as to what is to be its final place in our economic and political life.

Within the last thirty years — and, I might add, within the last three months, — it has been proven by eminent authority that the Negro is increasing in numbers so fast that it is only a question of a few years before he will far outnumber the white race in the South, and it has also been proven that the Negro is fast dying out, and it is only a question of a few years before he will have completely disappeared. It has also been proven that education helps the Negro and that education hurts him, that he is fast leaving the South and taking up his residence in the North and West, and that his tendency is to drift toward the low lands of the Mississippi bottoms. It has been proven that education unfits the Negro for work and that education makes him more valuable as a labourer, that he is our greatest criminal and that he is our most law-abiding citizen. In the midst of these conflicting opinions, it is hard to hit upon the truth.

But, also, in the midst of this confusion, there are a few things of which I am certain, — things which furnish a basis for thought and action. I know that whether the Negroes are increasing or decreasing, whether they are growing better or worse, whether they are valuable or valueless, that a few years ago some fourteen of them were brought into this country, and that now those fourteen are nearly ten millions. I know that, whether in slavery or freedom, they have always been loyal to the Stars and Stripes, that no school-house has been opened for them that has not been filled, that the 2,000,000 ballots that they have the right to cast are as potent for weal or woe as an equal number cast by the wisest and most influential men in America. I know that wherever Negro life touches the life of the nation it helps or it hinders, that wherever the life of the white race touches the black it makes it stronger or weaker. Further, I know that almost every other race that has tried to look the white man in the face has disappeared. I know, despite all the conflicting opinions, and with a full knowledge of all the Negroes' weaknesses, that only a few centuries ago they went into slavery in this country pagans, that they came out Christians; they went into slavery as so much property, they came out American citizens; they went into slavery without a language, they came out speaking the proud Anglo-Saxon tongue; they went into slavery with the chains clanking about their wrists, they came out with the American ballot in their hands.

I submit it to the candid and sober judgment of all men, if a race that is capable of such a test, such a transformation, is not worth saving and making a part, in reality as well as in name, of our democratic government. That the Negro may be fitted for the fullest enjoyment of the privileges and responsibilities of our citizenship, it is important that the nation be honest and candid with him, whether honesty and candour for the time being pleases or displeases him. It is with an ignorant race as it is with a child: it craves at first the superficial, the ornamental signs of progress rather than the reality. The ignorant race is tempted to jump, at one bound, to the position that it has required years of hard struggle for others to reach.

It seems to me that, as a general thing, the temptation in the past in educational and missionary work has been to do for the new people that which was done a thousand years ago, or that which is being done for a people a thousand miles away, without making a careful study of the needs and conditions of the people whom it is designed to help. The temptation is to run all people through a certain educational mould, regardless of the condition of the subject or the end to be accomplished. This has been the case too often in the South in the past, I am sure. Men have tried to use, with these simple people just freed from slavery and with no past, no inherited traditions of learning, the same methods of education which they have used in New England, with all its inherited traditions and desires. The Negro is behind the white man because he has not had the same chance, and not from any inherent difference in his nature and desires. What the race accomplishes in these first fifty years of freedom will at the end of these years, in a large measure, constitute its past. It is, indeed, a responsibility that rests upon this nation, — the foundation laying for a people of its past, present, and future at one and the same time.

One of the weakest points in connection with the present development of the race is that so many get the idea that the mere filling of the head with a knowledge of mathematics, the sciences, and literature, means success in life. Let it be understood, in every corner of the South, among the Negro youth at least, that knowledge will benefit little except as it is harnessed, except as its power is pointed in a direction that will bear upon the present needs and condition of the race. There is in the heads of the Negro youth of the South enough general and floating knowledge of chemistry, of botany, of zoölogy, of geology, of mechanics, of electricity, of mathematics, to reconstruct and develop a large part of the agricultural, mechanical, and domestic life of the race. But how much of it is brought to a focus along lines of practical work? In cities of the South like Atlanta, how many coloured mechanical engineers are there? or how many machinists? how many civil engineers? how many architects? how many house decorators? In the whole State of Georgia, where eighty per cent. of the coloured people depend upon agriculture, how many men are there who are well grounded in the principles and practices of scientific farming? or dairy work? or fruit culture? or floriculture?

For example, not very long ago I had a conversation with a young coloured man who is a graduate of one of the prominent universities of this country. The father of this man is comparatively ignorant, but by hard work and the exercise of common sense he has become the owner of two thousand acres of land. He owns more than a score of horses, cows, and mules and swine in large numbers, and is considered a prosperous farmer. In college the son of this farmer has studied chemistry, botany, zoölogy, surveying, and political economy. In my conversation I asked this young man how many acres his father cultivated in cotton and how many in corn. With a far-off gaze up into the heavens he answered that he did not know. When I asked him the classification of the soils on his father's farm, he did not know. He did not know how many horses or cows his father owned nor of what breeds they were, and seemed surprised that he should be asked such questions. It never seemed to have entered his mind that on his father's farm was the place to make his chemistry, his mathematics, and his literature penetrate and reflect itself in every acre of land, every bushel of corn, every cow, and every pig.

Let me give other examples of this mistaken sort of education. When a mere boy, I saw a young coloured man, who had spent several years in school, sitting in a common cabin in the South, studying a French grammar. I noted the poverty, the untidiness, the want of system and thrift, that existed about the cabin, notwithstanding his knowledge of French and other academic studies.

Again, not long ago I saw a coloured minister preparing his Sunday sermon just as the New England minister prepares his sermon. But this coloured minister was in a broken-down, leaky, rented log cabin, with weeds in the yard, surrounded by evidences of poverty, filth, and want of thrift. This minister had spent some time in school studying theology. How much better it would have been to have had this minister taught the dignity of labour, taught theoretical and practical farming in connection with his theology, so that he could have added to his meagre salary, and set an example for his people in the matter of living in a decent house, and having a knowledge of correct farming! In a word, this minister should have been taught that his condition, and that of his people, was not that of a New England community; and he should have been so trained as to meet the actual needs and conditions of the coloured people in this community, so that a foundation might be laid that would, in the future, make a community like New England communities.

Since the Civil War, no one object has been more misunderstood than that of the object and value of industrial education for the Negro. To begin with, it must be borne in mind that the condition that existed in the South immediately after the war, and that now exists, is a peculiar one, without a parallel in history. This being true, it seems to me that the wise and honest thing to do is to make a study of the actual condition and environment of the Negro, and do that which is best for him, regardless of whether the same thing has been done for another race in exactly the same way. There are those among the white race and those among the black race who assert, with a good deal of earnestness, that there is no difference between the white man and the black man in this country. This sounds very pleasant and tickles the fancy; but, when the test of hard, cold logic is applied to it, it must be acknowledged that there is a difference, — not an inherent one, not a racial one, but a difference growing out of unequal opportunities in the past.

If I may be permitted to criticise the educational work that has been done in the South, I would say that the weak point has been in the failure to recognise this difference.

Negro education, immediately after the war in most cases, was begun too nearly at the point where New England education had ended. Let me illustrate. One of the saddest sights I ever saw was the placing of a three hundred dollar rosewood piano in a country school in the South that was located in the midst of the "Black Belt." Am I arguing against the teaching of instrumental music to the Negroes in that community? Not at all; only I should have deferred those music lessons about twenty-five years. There are numbers of such pianos in thousands of New England homes. But behind the piano in the New England home there are one hundred years of toil, sacrifice, and economy; there is the small manufacturing industry, started several years ago by hand power, now grown into a great business; there is ownership in land, a comfortable home, free from debt, and a bank account. In this "Black Belt" community where this piano went, four-fifths of the people owned no land, many lived in rented one-room cabins, many were in debt for food supplies, many mortgaged their crops for the food on which to live, and not one had a bank account. In this case, how much wiser it would have been to have taught the girls in this community sewing, intelligent and economical cooking, house-keeping, something of dairying and horticulture? The boys should have been taught something of farming in connection with their common-school education, instead of awakening in them a desire for a musical instrument which resulted in their parents going into debt for a third-rate piano or organ before a home was purchased. Industrial lessons would have awakened, in this community, a de-sire for homes, and would have given the people the ability to free themselves from industrial slavery to the extent that most of them would have soon purchased homes. After the home and the neces-saries of life were supplied could come the piano. One piano lesson in a home of one's own is worth twenty in a rented log cabin.

All that I have just written, and the various examples illustrat-ing it, show the present helpless condition of my people in the South, — how fearfully they lack the primary training for good living and good citizenship, how much they stand in need of a solid foundation on which to build their future success. I believe, as I have many times said in my various addresses in the North and in the South, that the main reason for the existence of this curious state of affairs is the lack of practical training in the ways of life.

There is, too, a great lack of money with which to carry on the educational work in the South. I was in a county in a Southern State not long ago where there are some thirty thousand coloured people and about seven thousand whites. In this county not a sin-gle public school for Negroes had been open that year longer than three months, not a single coloured teacher had been paid more than $15 per month for his teaching. Not one of these schools was taught in a building that was worthy of the name of school-house. In this county the State or public authorities do not own a single dollar's worth of school property, — not a school-house, a blackboard, or a piece of crayon. Each coloured child had had spent on him that year for his education about fifty cents, while each child in New York or Massachusetts had had spent on him that year for education not far from $20. And yet each citizen of this county is expected to share the burdens and privileges of our democratic form of government just as intelligently and conscientiously as the citizens of New York or Boston. A vote in this county means as much to the nation as a vote in the city of Boston. Crime in this county is as truly an arrow aimed at the heart of the government as a crime committed in the streets of Boston.

A single school-house built this year in a town near Boston to shelter about three hundred pupils cost more for building alone than is spent yearly for the education, including buildings, apparatus, teachers, for the whole coloured school population of Alabama. The Commissioner of Education for the State of Georgia not long ago reported to the State legislature that in that State there were two hundred thousand children that had entered no school the year past and one hundred thousand more who were at school but a few days, making practically three hundred thousand children between six and eighteen years of age that are growing up in ignorance in one Southern State alone. The same report stated that outside of the cities and towns, while the average number of school-houses in a county was sixty, all of these sixty school-houses were worth in lump less than $2,000, and the report further added that many of the school-houses in Georgia were not fit for horse stables. I am glad to say, however, that vast improvement over this condition is being made in Georgia under the inspired leadership of State Commissioner Glenn,[1] and in Alabama under the no less zealous leadership of Commissioner Abercrombie.[2]

These illustrations, so far as they concern the Gulf States, are not exceptional cases; nor are they overdrawn.

Until there is industrial independence, it is hardly possible to have good living and a pure ballot in the country districts. In these States it is safe to say that not more than one black man in twenty owns the land he cultivates. Where so large a proportion of a people are dependent, live in other people's houses, eat other people's food, and wear clothes they have not paid for, it is pretty hard to expect them to live fairly and vote honestly.

I have thus far referred mainly to the Negro race. But there is another side. The longer I live and the more I study the question,

[1] Gustavus Richard Glenn (1848-1939).
[2] John William Abercrombie (1866–1940).

the more I am convinced that it is not so much a problem as to what the white man will do with the Negro as what the Negro will do with the white man and his civilisation. In considering this side of the subject, I thank God that I have grown to the point where I can sympathise with a white man as much as I can sympathise with a black man. I have grown to the point where I can sympathise with a Southern white man as much as I can sympathise with a Northern white man.

As bearing upon the future of our civilisation, I ask of the North what of their white brethren in the South, — those who have suffered and are still suffering the consequences of American slavery, for which both North and South were responsible? Those of the great and prosperous North still owe to their less fortunate brethren of the Caucasian race in the South, not less than to themselves, a serious and uncompleted duty. What was the task the North asked the South to perform? Returning to their destitute homes after years of war to face blasted hopes, devastation, a shattered industrial system, they asked them to add to their own burdens that of preparing in education, politics, and economics, in a few short years, for citizenship, four millions of former slaves. That the South, staggering under the burden, made blunders, and that in a measure there has been disappointment, no one need be surprised. The educators, the statesmen, the philanthropists, have imperfectly comprehended their duty toward the millions of poor whites in the South who were buffeted for two hundred years between slavery and freedom, between civilisation and degradation, who were disregarded by both master and slave. It needs no prophet to tell the character of our future civilisation when the poor white boy in the country districts of the South receives one dollar's worth of education and the boy of the same class in the North twenty dollars' worth, when one never enters a reading-room or library and the other has reading-rooms and libraries in every ward and town, when one hears lectures and sermons once in two months and the other can hear a lecture or a sermon every day in the year.

The time has come, it seems to me, when in this matter we should rise above party or race or sectionalism into the region of duty of man to man, of citizen to citizen, of Christian to Christian; and if the Negro, who has been oppressed and denied his rights in a Christian land, can help the whites of the North and South to rise, can be the inspiration of their rising, into this atmosphere of generous Christian brotherhood and self-forgetfulness, he will see in it a recompense for all that he has suffered in the past.

CHAPTER III

In the heart of the Black Belt of the South in *ante-bellum* days there was a large estate, with palatial mansions, surrounded by a beautiful grove, in which grew flowers and shrubbery of every description. Magnificent specimens of animal life grazed in the fields, and in grain and all manner of plant growth this estate was a model. In a word, it was the highest type of the product of slave labor.

Then came the long years of war, then freedom, then the trying years of reconstruction. The master returned from the war to find the faithful slaves who had been the bulwark of this household in possession of their freedom. Then there began that social and industrial revolution in the South which it is hard for any who was not really a part of it to appreciate or understand. Gradually, day by day, this ex-master began to realise, with a feeling almost indescribable, to what an extent he and his family had grown to be dependent upon the activity and faithfulness of his slaves; began to appreciate to what an extent slavery had sapped his sinews of strength and independence, how his dependence upon slave labour had deprived him and his offspring of the benefit of technical and industrial training, and, worst of all, had unconsciously led him to see in labour drudgery and degradation instead of beauty, dignity, and civilising power. At first there was a halt in this man's life. He cursed the North and he cursed the Negro. Then there was despair, almost utter hopelessness, over his weak and childlike condition. The temptation was to forget all in drink, and to this temptation there was a gradual yielding. With the loss of physical vigour came the loss of mental grasp and pride in surroundings. There was the falling off of a piece of plaster from the walls of the house which was not replaced, then another and still another. Gradually, the window-panes began to disappear, then the door-knobs. Touches of paint and whitewash, which once helped to give life, were no more to be seen. The hinges disappeared from the gate, then a board from the fence, then others in quick succession. Weeds and

319

unmown grass covered the once well-kept lawn. Sometimes there were servants for domestic duties, and sometimes there were none. In the absence of servants the unsatisfactory condition of the food told that it was being prepared by hands unschooled to such duties. As the years passed by, debts accumulated in every direction. The education of the children was neglected. Lower and lower sank the industrial, financial, and spiritual condition of the household. For the first time the awful truth of Scripture, "Whatsoever a man soweth, that shall he also reap," seemed to dawn upon him with a reality that it is hard for mortal to appreciate. Within a few months the whole mistake of slavery seemed to have concentrated itself upon this household. And this was one of many.

We have seen how the ending of slavery and the beginning of freedom produced not only a shock, but a standstill, and in many cases a collapse, that lasted several years in the life of many white men. If the sudden change thus affected the white man, should this not teach us that we should have more sympathy than has been shown in many cases with the Negro in connection with his new and changed life? That they made many mistakes, plunged into excesses, undertook responsibilities for which they were not fitted, in many cases took liberty to mean license, is not to be wondered at. It is my opinion that the next forty years are going to show by many per cent. a higher degree of progress in the life of the Negro along all lines than has been shown during the first thirty years of his life. Certainly, the first thirty years of the Negro's life was one of experiment; and consequently, under such conditions, he was not able to settle down to real, earnest, hard common sense efforts to better his condition. While this was true in a great many cases, on the other hand a large proportion of the race, even from the first, saw what was needed for their new life, and began to settle down to lead an industrious, frugal existence, and to educate their children and in every way prepare themselves for the responsibilities of American citizenship.

The wonder is that the Negro has made as few mistakes as he has, when we consider all the surrounding circumstances. Columns of figures have been gleaned from the census reports within the last quarter of a century to show the great amount of crime committed by the Negro in excess of that committed by other races. No one will deny the fact that the proportion of crime by the present generation of Negroes is seriously large, but I believe that any other race with the Negro's history and present environment would have shown about the same criminal record.

Another consideration which we must always bear in mind in considering the Negro is that he had practically no home life in slavery; that is, the mother and father did not have the responsibility, and consequently the experience, of training their own children. The matter of child training was left to the master and mistress. Consequently, it has only been within the last thirty years that the Negro parents have had the actual responsibility and experience of training their own children. That they have made some mistakes in thus training them is not to be wondered at. Many families scattered over all parts of the United States have not yet been able to bring themselves together. When the Negro parents shall have had thirty or forty additional years in which to found homes and get experience in the training of their children, I believe that we will find that the amount of crime will be considerably less than it is now shown to be.

In too large a measure the Negro race began its development at the wrong end, simply because neither white nor black understood the case; and no wonder, for there had never been such a case in the history of the world.

To show where this primary mistake has led in its evil results, I wish to produce some examples showing plainly how prone we have been to make our education formal, superficial, instead of making it meet the needs of conditions.

In order to emphasise the matter more fully, I repeat, at least eighty per cent. of the coloured people in the South are found in the rural districts, and they are dependent on agriculture in some form for their support. Notwithstanding that we have practically a whole race dependent upon agriculture, and notwithstanding that thirty years have passed since our freedom, aside from what has been done at Hampton and Tuskegee and one or two other institutions, but very little has been attempted by State or philanthropy in the way of educating the race in this one industry upon which its very existence depends. Boys have been taken from the farms and educated in law, theology, Hebrew and Greek, — educated in everything else except the very subject that they should know most about. I question whether among all the educated coloured people in the United States you can find six, if we except those from the institutions named, who have received anything like a thorough training in agriculture. It would have seemed that, since self-support, industrial independence, is the first condition for lifting up any race, that education in theoretical and practical agriculture, horticulture, dairying, and stock-raising, should have occupied the first place in our system.

Some time ago, when we decided to make tailoring a part of our training at the Tuskegee Institute, I was amazed to find that it was almost impossible to find in the whole country an educated coloured man who could teach the making of clothing. We could find them by the score who could teach astronomy, theology, grammar, or Latin, but almost none who could instruct in the making of clothing, something that has to be used by every one of us every day in the year. How often has my heart been made to sink as I have gone through the South and into the homes of people, and found women who could converse intelligently on Grecian history, who had studied geometry, could analyse the most complex sentences, and yet could not analyse the poorly cooked and still more poorly served corn bread and fat meat that they and their families were eating three times a day! It is little trouble to find girls who can locate Pekin or the Desert of Sahara on an artificial globe, but seldom can you find one who can locate on an actual dinner table the proper place for the carving knife and fork or the meat and vegetables.

A short time ago, in one of the Southern cities, a coloured man died who had received training as a skilled mechanic during the days of slavery. Later by his skill and industry he built up a great business as a house contractor and builder. In this same city there are 35,000 coloured people, among them young men who have been well educated in the languages and in literature; but not a single one could be found who had been so trained in mechanical and architectural drawing that he could carry on the business which this ex-slave had built up, and so it was soon scattered to the wind. Aside from the work done in the institutions that I have mentioned, you can find almost no coloured men who have been trained in the principles of architecture, notwithstanding the fact that a vast majority of our race are without homes. Here, then, are the three prime conditions for growth, for civilisation, — food, clothing, shelter; and yet we have been the slaves of forms and customs to such an extent that we have failed in a large measure to look matters squarely in the face and meet actual needs.

It may well be asked by one who has not carefully considered the matter: "What has become of all those skilled farm-hands that used to be on the old plantations? Where are those wonderful cooks we hear about, where those exquisitely trained house servants, those cabinet makers, and the jacks-of-all-trades that were the pride of the South?" This is easily answered, — they are mostly dead. The survivors are too old to work. "But did they not train their children?" is the natural question. Alas! the answer is "no." Their skill was so commonplace to them, and to their former masters, that neither thought of it as being a hard-earned or desirable accomplishment: it was natural, like breathing. Their children would have it as a matter of course. What their children needed was education. So they went out into the world, the ambitious ones, and got education, and forgot the necessity of the ordinary training to live.

God for two hundred and fifty years, in my opinion, prepared the way for the redemption of the Negro through industrial development. First, he made the Southern white man do business with the Negro for two hundred and fifty years in a way that no one else has done business with him. If a Southern white man wanted a house or a bridge built, he consulted a Negro mechanic about the plan and about the actual building of the house or bridge. If he wanted a suit of clothes or a pair of shoes made, it was to the Negro tailor or shoemaker that he talked. Secondly, every large slave plantation in the South was, in a limited sense, an industrial school. On these plantations there were scores of young coloured men and women who were constantly being trained, not alone as common farmers, but as carpenters, blacksmiths, wheelwrights, plasterers, brick masons, engineers, bridge-builders, cooks, dressmakers, housekeepers, etc. I would be the last to apologise for the curse of slavery; but I am simply stating facts. This training was crude and was given for selfish purposes, and did not answer the highest ends, because there was the absence of brain training in connection with that of the hand. Nevertheless, this business contact with the Southern white man, and the industrial training received on these plantations, put the Negro at the close of the war into possession of all the common and skilled labour in the South. For nearly twenty years after the war, except in one or two cases, the value of the industrial training given by the Negroes' former masters on the plantations and elsewhere was overlooked. Negro men and women were educated in literature, mathematics, and the sciences, with no thought of what had taken place on these plantations for two and a half centuries. After twenty years, those who were trained as mechanics, etc., during slavery began to disappear by death; and gradually we awoke to the fact that we had no one to take their places. We had scores of young men learned in Greek, but few in carpentry or mechanical or architectural drawing. We had trained many in Latin, but almost none as engineers, bridge-builders, and machinists. Numbers were taken from the farm and educated, but were educated in everything else except agriculture. Hence they had no sympathy with farm life, and did not return to it.

This last that I have been saying is practically a repetition of what I have said in the preceding paragraph; but, to emphasise it, — and this point is one of the most important I wish to impress on the reader, — it is well to repeat, to say the same thing twice. Oh, if only more who had the shaping of the education of the Negro could have, thirty years ago, realised, and made others realise, where the forgetting of the years of manual training and the sudden acquiring of education were going to lead the Negro race, what a saving it would have been! How much less my race would have had to answer for, as well as the white!

But it is too late to cry over what might have been. It is time to make up, as soon as possible, for this mistake, — time for both races to acknowledge it, and go forth on the course that, it seems to me, all must now see to be the right one, — industrial education.

As an example of what a well-trained and educated Negro may now do, and how ready to acknowledge him a Southern white man may be, let me return once more to the plantation I spoke of in the first part of this chapter. As the years went by, the night seemed to grow darker, so that all seemed hopeless and lost. At this point relief and strength came from an unexpected source. This Southern white man's idea of Negro education had been that it merely meant a parrot-like absorption of Anglo-Saxon civilisation, with a special tendency to imitate the weaker elements of the white man's character; that it meant merely the high hat, kid gloves, a showy walking cane, patent leather shoes, and all the rest of it. To this ex-master it seemed impossible that the education of the Negro could produce any other results. And so, last of all, did he expect help or encouragement from an educated black man; but it was just from this source that help came. Soon after the process of decay began in this white man's estate, the education of a certain black man began, and began on a logical, sensible basis. It was an education that would fit him to see and appreciate the physical and moral conditions that existed in his own family and neighbourhood, and, in the present generation, would fit him to apply himself to their relief. By chance this educated Negro strayed into the employ of this white man. His employer soon learned that this Negro not only had a knowledge of science, mathematics, and literature in his head, but in his hands as well. This black man applied his knowledge of agricultural chemistry to the redemption of the soil; and soon the washes and gulleys began to disappear, and the waste places began to bloom. New and improved machinery in a few months began to rob labour of its toil and drudgery. The animals were given systematic and kindly attention. Fences were repaired and rebuilt. Whitewash and paint were made to do duty. Everywhere order slowly began to replace confusion; hope, despair; and profits, losses. As he observed, day by day, new life and strength being imparted to every department of his property, this white son of the South began revising his own creed regarding the wisdom of educating Negroes.

Hitherto his creed regarding the value of an educated Negro had been rather a plain and simple one, and read: "The only end that could be accomplished by educating a black man was to enable him to talk properly to a mule; and the Negro's education did great injustice to the mule, since the language tended to confuse him and make him balky."

We need not continue the story, except to add that to-day the grasp of the hand of this ex-slaveholder, and the listening to his hearty words of gratitude and commendation for the education of the Negro, are enough to compensate those who have given and those who have worked and sacrificed for the elevation of my people through all of these years. If we are patient, wise, unselfish, and courageous, such examples will multiply as the years go by.

Before closing this chapter, — which, I think, has clearly shown that there is at present a very distinct lack of industrial training in the South among the Negroes, — I wish to say a few words in regard to certain objections, or rather misunderstandings, which have from time to time arisen in regard to the matter.

Many have had the thought that industrial training was meant to make the Negro work, much as he worked during the days of slavery. This is far from my idea of it. If this training has any value for the Negro, as it has for the white man, it consists in teaching the Negro how rather not to work, but how to make the forces of nature — air, water, horse-power, steam, and electric power — work for him, how to lift labour up out of toil and drudgery into that which is dignified and beautiful. The Negro in the South works, and he works hard; but his lack of skill, coupled with ignorance, causes him too often to do his work in the most costly and shiftless manner, and this has kept him near the bottom of the ladder in the business world. I repeat that industrial education teaches the Negro how not to drudge in his work. Let him who doubts this contrast the Negro in the South toiling through a field of oats with an old-fashioned reaper with the white man on a modern farm in the West, sitting upon a modern "harvester," behind two spirited horses, with an umbrella over him, using a machine that cuts and binds the oats at the same time, — doing four times as much work as the black man with one half the labour. Let us give the black man so much skill and brains that he can cut oats like the white man, then he can compete with him. The Negro works in cotton, and has no trouble so long as his labour is confined to the lower forms of work, — the planting, the picking, and the ginning; but, when the Negro attempts to follow the bale of cotton up through the higher stages, through the mill where it is made into the finer fabrics, where the larger profit appears, he is told that he is not wanted.

The Negro can work in wood and iron; and no one objects so long as he confines his work to the felling of trees and sawing of boards, to the digging of iron ore and making of pig iron. But, when the Negro attempts to follow this tree into the factory where it is made into desks and chairs and railway coaches, or when he attempts to follow the pig iron into the factory where it is made into knife-blades and watch-springs, the Negro's trouble begins. And what is the objection? Simply that the Negro lacks the skill, coupled with brains, necessary to compete with the white man, or that, when white men refuse to work with coloured men, enough skilled and educated coloured men cannot be found able to super-intend and man every part of any one large industry; and hence, for these reasons, they are constantly being barred out. The Negro must become, in a larger measure, an intelligent producer as well as a consumer. There should be a more vital and practical connec-tion between the Negro's educated brain and his opportunity of earning his daily living.

A very weak argument often used against pushing industrial training for the Negro is that the Southern white man favours it, and, therefore, it is not best for the Negro. Although I was born a slave, I am thankful that I am able so far to rid myself of prej-udice as to be able to accept a good thing, whether it comes from a black man or a white man, a Southern man or a Northern man. Industrial education will not only help the Negro directly in the matter of industrial development, but also in bringing about more satisfactory relations between him and the Southern white man. For the sake of the Negro and the Southern white man there are many things in the relation of the two races that must soon be changed. We cannot depend wholly upon abuse or condemnation of the Southern white man to bring about these changes. Each race must be educated to see matters in a broad, high, generous, Chris-tian spirit: we must bring the two races together, not estrange them. The Negro must live for all time by the side of the Southern white man. The man is unwise who does not cultivate in every manly way the friendship and good will of his next-door neighbour, whether he be black or white. I repeat that industrial training will help cement the friendship of the two races. The history of the world proves that trade, commerce, is the forerunner of peace and civilisation as between races and nations. The Jew, who was once in about the same position that the Negro is to-day, has now rec-ognition, because he has entwined himself about America in a busi-ness and industrial sense. Say or think what we will, it is the tangible or visible element that is going to tell largely during the next twenty years in the solution of the race problem.

CHAPTER IV

One of the main problems as regards the education of the Negro is how to have him use his education to the best advantage after he has secured it. In saying this, I do not want to be understood as implying that the problem of simple ignorance among the masses has been settled in the South; for this is far from true. The amount of ignorance still prevailing among the Negroes, especially in the rural districts, is very large and serious. But I repeat, we must go farther if we would secure the best results and most gratifying returns in public good for the money spent than merely to put academic education in the Negro's head with the idea that this will settle everything.

In his present condition it is important, in seeking after what he terms the ideal, that the Negro should not neglect to prepare himself to take advantage of the opportunities that are right about his door. If he lets these opportunities slip, I fear they will never be his again. In saying this, I mean always that the Negro should have the most thorough mental and religious training; for without it no race can succeed. Because of his past history and environment and present condition it is important that he be carefully guided for years to come in the proper use of his education. Much valuable time has been lost and money spent in vain, because too many have not been educated with the idea of fitting them to do well the things which they could get to do. Because of the lack of proper direction of the Negro's education, some good friends of his, North and South, have not taken that interest in it that they otherwise would have taken. In too many cases where merely literary education alone has been given the Negro youth, it has resulted in an exaggerated estimate of his importance in the world, and an increase of wants which his education has not fitted him to supply.

But, in discussing this subject, one is often met with the question, Should not the Negro be encouraged to prepare himself for any station in life that any other race fills? I would say, Yes; but the surest way for the Negro to reach the highest positions is to prepare himself to fill well at the present time the basic occupations. This will give him a foundation upon which to stand while securing what is called the more exalted positions. The Negro has the right to study law; but success will come to the race sooner if it produces intelligent, thrifty farmers, mechanics, and housekeepers to support the lawyers. The want of proper direction of the use of the Negro's education results in tempting too many to live mainly by their wits, without producing anything that is of real value to the world. Let me quote examples of this.

Hayti, Santo Domingo, and Liberia, although among the richest countries in natural resources in the world, are discouraging examples of what must happen to any people who lack industrial or technical training. It is said that in Liberia there are no wagons, wheelbarrows, or public roads, showing very plainly that there is a painful absence of public spirit and thrift. What is true of Liberia is also true in a measure of the republics of Hayti and Santo Domingo. The people have not yet learned the lesson of turning their education toward the cultivation of the soil and the making of the simplest implements for agricultural and other forms of labour.

Much would have been done toward laying a sound foundation for general prosperity if some attention had been spent in this direction. General education itself has no bearing on the subject at issue, because, while there is no well-established public school system in either of these countries, yet large numbers of men of both Hayti and Santo Domingo have been educated in France for generations. This is especially true of Hayti. The education has been altogether in the direction of *belles lettres*, however, and practically little in the direction of industrial and scientific education.

It is a matter of common knowledge that Hayti has to send abroad even to secure engineers for her men-of-war, for plans for her bridges and other work requiring technical knowledge and skill. I should very much regret to see any such condition obtain in any large measure as regards the coloured people in the South, and yet this will be our fate if industrial education is much longer neglected. We have spent much time in the South in educating men and women in letters alone, too, and must now turn our attention more than ever toward educating them so as to supply their wants and needs. It is more lamentable to see educated people unable to support themselves than to see uneducated people in the same condition. Ambition all along this line must be stimulated.

If educated men and women of the race will see and acknowledge the necessity of practical industrial training and go to work with a zeal and determination, their example will be followed by others, who are now without ambition of any kind.

The race cannot hope to come into its own until the young coloured men and women make up their minds to assist in the general development along these lines. The elder men and women trained in the hard school of slavery, and who so long possessed all of the labour, skilled and unskilled, of the South, are dying out; their places must be filled by their children, or we shall lose our hold upon these occupations. Leaders in these occupations are needed now more than ever.

It is not enough that the idea be inculcated that coloured people should get book learning; along with it they should be taught that book education and industrial development must go hand in hand. No race which fails to do this can ever hope to succeed. Phillips Brooks gave expression to the sentiment: "One generation gathers the material, and the next generation builds the palaces." As I understand it, he wished to inculcate the idea that one generation lays the foundation for succeeding generations. The rough affairs of life very largely fall to the earlier generation, while the next one has the privilege of dealing with the higher and more aesthetic things of life. This is true of all generations, of all peoples; and, unless the foundation is deeply laid, it is impossible for the succeeding one to have a career in any way approaching success. As regards the coloured men of the South, as regards the coloured men of the United States, this is the generation which, in a large measure, must gather the material with which to lay the foundation for future success.

Some time ago it was my misfortune to see a Negro sixty-five years old living in poverty and filth. I was disgusted, and said to him, "If you are worthy of your freedom, you would surely have changed your condition during the thirty years of freedom which you have enjoyed." He answered: "I do want to change. I want to do something for my wife and children; but I do not know how, — I do not know what to do." I looked into his lean and haggard face, and realised more deeply than ever before the absolute need of captains of industry among the great masses of the coloured people.

It is possible for a race or an individual to have mental development and yet be so handicapped by custom, prejudice, and lack of employment as to dwarf and discourage the whole life. This is the condition that prevails among the race in many of the large cities of the North; and it is to prevent this same condition in the South that I plead with all the earnestness of my heart. Mental development alone will not give us what we want, but mental development tied to hand and heart training will be the salvation of the Negro.

In many respects the next twenty years are going to be the most serious in the history of the race. Within this period it will be largely decided whether the Negro will be able to retain the hold which he now has upon the industries of the South or whether his place will be filled by white people from a distance. The only way he can prevent the industrial occupations slipping from him in all parts of the South, as they have already in certain parts, is for all educators, ministers, and friends of the race to unite in pushing forward in a whole-souled manner the industrial or business development of the Negro, whether in school or out of school. Four times as many young men and women of the race should be receiving industrial training. Just now the Negro is in a position to feel and appreciate the need of this in a way that no one else can. No one can fully appreciate what I am saying who has not walked the streets of a Northern city day after day seeking employment, only to find every door closed against him on account of his colour, except in menial service. It is to prevent the same thing taking place in the South that I plead. We may argue that mental development will take care of all this. Mental development is a good thing. Gold is also a good thing, but gold is worthless without an opportunity to make itself touch the world of trade. Education increases greatly an individual's wants. It is cruel in many cases to increase the wants of the black youth by mental development alone without, at the same time, increasing his ability to supply these increased wants in occupations in which he can find employment.

The place made vacant by the death of the old coloured man who was trained as a carpenter during slavery, and who since the war had been the leading contractor and builder in the Southern town, had to be filled. No young coloured carpenter capable of filling his place could be found. The result was that his place was filled by a white mechanic from the North, or from Europe, or from elsewhere. What is true of carpentry and house-building in this case is true, in a degree, in every skilled occupation; and it is becoming true of common labour. I do not mean to say that all of the skilled labour has been taken out of the Negro's hands; but I do mean to say that in no part of the South is he so strong in the matter of skilled labour as he was twenty years ago, except possibly in the country districts and the smaller towns. In the more northern of the Southern cities, such as Richmond and Baltimore, the change is most apparent; and it is being felt in every Southern city. Wherever the Negro has lost ground industrially in the South, it is not because there is prejudice against him as a skilled labourer on the part of the native Southern white man; the Southern white man generally prefers to do business with the Negro mechanic rather than with a white one, because he is accustomed to do business with the Negro in this respect. There is almost no prejudice against the Negro in the South in matters of business, so far as the native whites are concerned; and here is the entering wedge for the solution of the race problem. But too often, where the white mechanic or factory operative from the North gets a hold, the trades-union soon follows, and the Negro is crowded to the wall.

But what is the remedy for this condition? First, it is most important that the Negro and his white friends honestly face the facts as they are; otherwise the time will not be very far distant when the Negro of the South will be crowded to the ragged edge of industrial life as he is in the North. There is still time to repair the damage and to reclaim what we have lost.

I stated in the beginning that industrial education for the Negro has been misunderstood. This has been chiefly because some have gotten the idea that industrial development was opposed to the Negro's higher mental development. This has little or nothing to do with the subject under discussion; we should no longer permit such an idea to aid in depriving the Negro of the legacy in the form of skilled labour that was purchased by his forefathers at the price of two hundred and fifty years of slavery. I would say to the black boy what I would say to the white boy, Get all the mental development that your time and pocket-book will allow of, — the more, the better; but the time has come when a larger proportion — not all, for we need professional men and women — of the educated coloured men and women should give themselves to industrial or business life. The professional class will be helped in so far as the rank and file have an industrial foundation, so that they can pay

332

for professional service. Whether they receive the training of the hand while pursuing their academic training or after their academic training is finished, or whether they will get their literary training in an industrial school or college, are questions which each individual must decide for himself. No matter how or where educated, the educated men and women must come to the rescue of the race in the effort to get and hold its industrial footing. I would not have the standard of mental development lowered one whit; for, with the Negro, as with all races, mental strength is the basis of all progress. But I would have a large measure of this mental strength reach the Negroes' actual needs through the medium of the hand. Just now the need is not so much for the common carpenters, brick masons, farmers, and laundry women as for industrial leaders who, in addition to their practical knowledge, can draw plans, make estimates, take contracts; those who understand the latest methods of truck-gardening and the science underlying practical agriculture; those who understand machinery to the extent that they can operate steam and electric laundries, so that our women can hold on to the laundry work in the South, that is so fast drifting into the hands of others in the large cities and towns.

Having tried to show in previous chapters to what a condition the lack of practical training has brought matters in the South, and by the examples in this chapter where this state of things may go if allowed to run its course, I wish now to show what practical training, even in its infancy among us, has already accomplished.

I noticed, when I first went to Tuskegee to start the Tuskegee Normal and Industrial Institute, that some of the white people about there rather looked doubtfully at me; and I thought I could get their influence by telling them how much algebra and history and science and all those things I had in my head, but they treated me about the same as they did before. They didn't seem to care about the algebra, history, and science that were in my head only. Those people never even began to have confidence in me until we commenced to build a large three-story brick building, and then another and another, until now we have forty buildings which have been erected largely by the labour of our students; and to-day we have the respect and confidence of all the white people in that section.

There is an unmistakable influence that comes over a white man when he sees a black man living in a two-story brick house that has been paid for. I need not stop to explain. It is the tangible evidence of prosperity. You know Thomas doubted the Saviour after he had risen from the dead; and the Lord said to Thomas, "Reach hither thy finger, and behold my hands; and reach hither thy hand, and thrust it into my side." The tangible evidence convinced Thomas.

We began, soon after going to Tuskegee, the manufacture of bricks. We also started a wheelwright establishment and the manufacture of good wagons and buggies; and the white people came to our institution for that kind of work. We also put in a printing plant, and did job printing for the white people as well as for the blacks.

By having something that these people wanted, we came into contact with them, and our interest became interlinked with their interest, until to-day we have no warmer friends anywhere in the country than we have among the white people of Tuskegee. We have found by experience that the best way to get on well with people is to have something that they want, and that is why we emphasise this Christian Industrial Education.

Not long ago I heard a conversation among three white men something like this. Two of them were berating the Negro, saying the Negro was shiftless and lazy, and all that sort of thing. The third man listened to their remarks for some time in silence, and then he said: "I don't know what your experience has been; but there is a 'nigger' down our way who owns a good house and lot with about fifty acres of ground. His house is well furnished, and he has got some splendid horses and cattle. He is intelligent and has a bank account. I don't know how the 'niggers' are in your community, but Tobe Jones is a gentleman. Once, when I was hard up, I went to Tobe Jones and borrowed fifty dollars; and he hasn't asked me for it yet. I don't know what kind of 'niggers' you have down your way, but Tobe Jones is a gentleman."

Now what we want to do is to multiply and place in every community these Tobe Joneses; and, just in so far as we can place them throughout the South this race question will disappear.

Suppose there was a black man who had business for the railroads to the amount of ten thousand dollars a year. Do you suppose that, when that black man takes his family aboard the train, they are going to put him into a Jim Crow car and run the risk of losing that ten thousand dollars a year? No, they will put on a Pullman palace car for him.

Some time ago a certain coloured man was passing through the streets of one of the little Southern towns, and he chanced to meet two white men on the street. It happened that this coloured man owns two or three houses and lots, has a good education and a comfortable bank account. One of the white men turned to the other, and said: "By Gosh! It is all I can do to keep from calling that 'nigger' Mister." That's the point we want to get to.

Nothing else so soon brings about right relations between the two races in the South as the commercial progress of the Negro. Friction between the races will pass away as the black man, by reason of his skill, intelligence, and character, can produce something that the white man wants or respects in the commercial world. This is another reason why at Tuskegee we push industrial training. We find that as every year we put into a Southern community coloured men who can start a brickyard, a saw-mill, a tin-shop, or a printing-office, — men who produce something that makes the white man partly dependent upon the Negro instead of all the dependence being on the other side, — a change for the better takes place in the relations of the races. It is through the dairy farm, the truck-garden, the trades, the commercial life, largely, that the Negro is to find his way to respect and confidence.

What is the permanent value of the Hampton and Tuskegee system of training to the South, in a broader sense? In connection with this, it is well to bear in mind that slavery unconsciously taught the white man that labour with the hands was something fit for the Negro only, and something for the white man to come into contact with just as little as possible. It is true that there was a large class of poor white people who laboured with the hands, but they did it because they were not able to secure Negroes to work for them; and these poor whites were constantly trying to imitate the slaveholding class in escaping labour, as they, too, regarded it as anything but elevating. But the Negro, in turn, looked down upon the poor whites with a certain contempt because they had to work. The Negro, it is to be borne in mind, worked under constant protest, because he felt that his labour was being unjustly requited; and he spent almost as much effort in planning how to escape work

as in learning how to work. Labour with him was a badge of degradation. The white man was held up before him as the highest
type of civilisation, but the Negro noted that this highest type of
civilisation himself did little labour with the hand. Hence he
argued that, the less work he did, the more nearly he would be
like the white man. Then, in addition to these influences, the slave
system discouraged labour-saving machinery. To use labour-saving
machinery, intelligence was required; and intelligence and slavery
were not on friendly terms. Hence the Negro always associated
labour with toil, drudgery, something to be escaped. When the
Negro first became free, his idea of education was that it was something that would soon put him in the same position as regards work
that his recent master had occupied. Out of these conditions grew
the habit of putting off till to-morrow and the day after the duty
that should be done promptly to-day. The leaky house was not repaired while the sun shone, for then the rain did not come through
While the rain was falling, no one cared to expose himself to stop
the rain. The plough, on the same principle, was left where the last
furrow was run, to rot and rust in the field during the winter. There
was no need to repair the wooden chimney that was exposed to the
fire, because water could be thrown on it when it was on fire. There
was no need to trouble about the payment of a debt to-day, because
it could be paid as well next week or next year. Besides these conditions, the whole South at the close of the war was without proper
food, clothing, and shelter, — was in need of habits of thrift and
economy and of something laid up for a rainy day.

To me it seemed perfectly plain that here was a condition of
things that could not be met by the ordinary process of education.
At Tuskegee we became convinced that the thing to do was to
make a careful, systematic study of the condition and needs of the
South, especially the Black Belt, and to bend our efforts in the
direction of meeting these needs, whether we were following a
well-beaten track or were hewing out a new path to meet conditions probably without a parallel in the world. After eighteen years
of experience and observation, what is the result? Gradually, but
surely, we find that all through the South the disposition to look
upon labour as a disgrace is on the wane; and the parents who themselves sought to escape work are so anxious to give their children
training in intelligent labour that every institution which gives

training in the handicrafts is crowded, and many (among them Tuskegee) have to refuse admission to hundreds of applicants. The influence of Hampton and Tuskegee is shown again by the fact that almost every little school at the remotest cross-road is anxious to be known as an industrial school, or, as some of the coloured people call it, an "industrous" school.

The social lines that were once sharply drawn between those who laboured with the hands and those who did not are disappearing. Those who formerly sought to escape labour, now when they see that brains and skill rob labour of the toil and drudgery once associated with it, instead of trying to avoid it, are willing to pay to be taught how to engage in it. The South is beginning to see labour raised up, dignified and beautified, and in this sees its salvation. In proportion as the love of labour grows, the large idle class, which has long been one of the curses of the South, disappears. As people become absorbed in their own affairs, they have less time to attend to everybody's else business.

The South is still an undeveloped and unsettled country, and for the next half-century and more the greater part of the energy of the masses will be needed to develop its material resources. Any force that brings the rank and file of the people to have a greater love of industry is therefore especially valuable. This result industrial education is surely bringing about. It stimulates production and increases trade, — trade between the races; and in this new and engrossing relation both forget the past. The white man respects the vote of a coloured man who does ten thousand dollars' worth of business; and, the more business the coloured man has, the more careful he is how he votes.

Immediately after the war there was a large class of Southern people who feared that the opening of the free schools to the freedmen and the poor whites — the education of the head alone — would result merely in increasing the class who sought to escape labour, and that the South would soon be overrun by the idle and vicious. But, as the results of industrial combined with academic training begin to show themselves in hundreds of communities that have been lifted up, these former prejudices against education are being removed. Many of those who a few years ago opposed Negro education are now among its warmest advocates.

This industrial training, emphasising, as it does, the idea of

337

economic production, is gradually bringing the South to the point where it is feeding itself. After the war, what profit the South made out of the cotton crop it spent outside of the South to purchase food supplies, — meat, bread, canned vegetables, and the like, — but the improved methods of agriculture are fast changing this custom. With the newer methods of labour, which teach promptness and system and emphasise the worth of the beautiful, the moral value of the well-painted house, the fence with every paling and nail in its place, is bringing to bear upon the South an influence that is making it a new country in industry, education, and religion.

It seems to me I cannot do better than to close this chapter on the needs of the Southern Negro by quoting from a talk given to the students at Tuskegee:[3] —

"I want to be a little more specific in showing you what you have to do and how you must do it.

"One trouble with us is — and the same is true of any young people, no matter of what race or condition — we have too many stepping-stones. We step all the time, from one thing to another. You find a young man who is learning to make bricks; and, if you ask him what he intends to do after learning the trade, in too many cases he will answer, 'Oh, I am simply working at this trade as a stepping-stone to something higher.' You see a young man working at the brick-mason's trade, and he will be apt to say the same thing. And young women learning to be milliners and dressmakers will tell you the same. All are stepping to something higher. And so we always go on, stepping somewhere, never getting hold of anything thoroughly. Now we must stop this stepping business, having so many stepping-stones. Instead, we have got to take hold of these important industries, and stick to them until we master them thoroughly. There is no nation so thorough in their education as the Germans. Why? Simply because the German takes hold of a thing, and sticks to it until he masters it. Into it he puts brains and thought from morning to night. He reads all the best books and journals bearing on that particular study, and he feels that nobody else knows so much about it as he does.

"Take any of the industries I have mentioned, that of brick-making, for example. Any one working at that trade should determine to learn all there is to be known about making bricks; read

---

[3] See above, 4:480–84.

all the papers and journals bearing upon the trade; learn not only to make common hand-bricks, but pressed bricks, fire-bricks, — in short, the finest and best bricks there are to be made. And, when you have learned all you can by reading and talking with other people, you should travel from one city to another, and learn how the best bricks are made. And then, when you go into business for yourself, you will make a reputation for being the best brick-maker in the community; and in this way you will put yourself on your feet, and become a helpful and useful citizen. When a young man does this, goes out into one of these Southern cities and makes a reputation for himself, that person wins a reputation that is going to give him a standing and position. And, when the children of that successful brick-maker come along, they will be able to take a higher position in life. The grandchildren will be able to take a still higher position. And it will be traced back to that grandfather who, by his great success as a brick-maker, laid a foundation that was of the right kind.

"What I have said about these two trades can be applied with equal force to the trades followed by women. Take the matter of millinery. There is no good reason why there should not be, in each principal city in the South, at least three or four competent coloured women in charge of millinery establishments. But what is the trouble?

"Instead of making the most of our opportunities in this industry, the temptation, in too many cases, is to be music-teachers, teachers of elocution, or something else that few of the race at present have any money to pay for, or the opportunity to earn money to pay for, simply because there is no foundation. But, when more coloured people succeed in the more fundamental occupations, they will then be able to make better provision for their children in what are termed the higher walks of life.

"And, now, what I have said about these important industries is especially true of the important industry of agriculture. We are living in a country where, if we are going to succeed at all, we are going to do so largely by what we raise out of the soil. The people in those backward countries I have told you about have failed to give attention to the cultivation of the soil, to the invention and use of improved agricultural implements and machinery. Without this no people can succeed. No race which fails to put brains into agriculture can succeed; and, if you want to realize the truth of this statement, go with me into the back districts of some of our Southern States, and you will find many people in poverty, and yet they are surrounded by a rich country.

"A race, like an individual, has got to have a reputation. Such a reputation goes a long way toward helping a race or an individual; and, when we have succeeded in getting such a reputation, we shall find that a great many of the discouraging features of our life will melt away.

"Reputation is what people think we are, and a great deal depends on that. When a race gets a reputation along certain lines, a great many things which now seem complex, difficult to attain, and are most discouraging, will disappear.

"When you say that an engine is a Corliss engine, people understand that that engine is a perfect piece of mechanical work, — perfect as far as human skill and ingenuity can make it perfect. You say a car is a Pullman car. That is all; but what does it mean? It means that the builder of that car got a reputation at the outset for thorough, perfect work, for turning out everything in first-class shape. And so with a race. You cannot keep back very long a race that has the reputation for doing perfect work in everything that it undertakes. And then we have got to get a reputation for economy. Nobody cares to associate with an individual in business or otherwise who has a reputation for being a trifling spendthrift, who spends his money for things that he can very easily get along without, who spends his money for clothing, gewgaws, superficialities, and other things, when he has not got the necessaries of life. We want to give the race a reputation for being frugal and saving in everything. Then we want to get a reputation for being industrious. Now, remember these three things: Get a reputation for being skilled. It will not do for a few here and there to have it: the race must have the reputation. Get a reputation for being so skilful, so industrious, that you will not leave a job until it is as nearly perfect as any one can make it. And then we want to make a reputation for the race for being honest, — honest at all times and under all circumstances. A few individuals here and there have it, a few communities have it; but the race as a mass must get it.

"You recall that story of Abraham Lincoln, how, when he was

postmaster at a small village, he had left on his hands $1.50 which the government did not call for. Carefully wrapping up this money in a handkerchief, he kept it for ten years. Finally, one day, the government agent called for this amount; and it was promptly handed over to him by Abraham Lincoln, who told him that during all those ten years he had never touched a cent of that money. He made it a principle of his life never to use other people's money. That trait of his character helped him along to the Presidency. The race wants to get a reputation for being strictly honest in all its dealings and transactions, — honest in handling money, honest in all its dealings with its fellow-men.

"And then we want to get a reputation for being thoughtful. This I want to emphasise more than anything else. We want to get a reputation for doing things without being told to do them every time. If you have work to do, think about it so constantly, investigate and read about it so thoroughly, that you will always be finding ways and means of improving that work. The average person going to work becomes a regular machine, never giving the matter of improving the methods of his work a thought. He is never at his work before the appointed time, and is sure to stop the minute the hour is up. The world is looking for the person who is thoughtful, who will say at the close of work hours: 'Is there not something else I can do for you? Can I not stay a little later, and help you?'

"Moreover, it is with a race as it is with an individual: it must respect itself if it would win the respect of others. There must be a certain amount of unity about a race, there must be a great amount of pride about a race, there must be a great deal of faith on the part of a race in itself. An individual cannot succeed unless he has about him a certain amount of pride, — enough pride to make him aspire to the highest and best things in life. An individual cannot succeed unless that individual has a great amount of faith in himself.

"A person who goes at an undertaking with the feeling that he cannot succeed is likely to fail. On the other hand, the individual who goes at an undertaking, feeling that he can succeed, is the individual who in nine cases out of ten does succeed. But, whenever you find an individual that is ashamed of his race, trying to get away from his race, apologising for being a member of his race, then you find a weak individual. Where you find a race that is ashamed of itself, that is apologising for itself, there you will find a weak, vacillating race. Let us no longer have to apologise for our race in these or other matters. Let us think seriously and work seriously: then, as a race, we shall be thought of seriously, and, therefore, seriously respected."

CHAPTER V

In this chapter I wish to show how, at Tuskegee, we are trying to work out the plan of industrial training, and trust I shall be pardoned the seeming egotism if I preface the sketch with a few words, by way of example, as to the expansion of my own life and how I came to undertake the work at Tuskegee.

My earliest recollection is of a small one-room log hut on a slave plantation in Virginia. After the close of the war, while working in the coal mines of West Virginia for the support of my mother, I heard, in some accidental way, of the Hampton Institute. When I learned that it was an institution where a black boy could study, could have a chance to work for his board, and at the same time be taught how to work and to realise the dignity of labor, I resolved to go there. Bidding my mother good-by, I started out one morning to find my way to Hampton, although I was almost penniless and had no definite idea as to where Hampton was. By walking, begging rides, and paying for a portion of the journey on the steam-cars, I finally succeeded in reaching the city of Richmond, Virginia. I was without money or friends. I slept on a sidewalk; and by working on a vessel the next day I earned money enough to continue my way to the institute, where I arrived with a capital of fifty cents. At Hampton I found the opportunity — in the way of buildings, teachers, and industries provided by the generous — to get training in the class-room and by practical touch with industrial life, — to learn thrift, economy, and push. I was surrounded by an atmosphere of business, Christian influence, and spirit of self-help, that seemed to have awakened every faculty in me, and caused me for the first time to realise what it meant to be a man instead of a piece of property.

While there, I resolved, when I had finished the course of training, I would go into the Far South, into the Black Belt of the South, and give my life to providing the same kind of opportunity for self-reliance, self-awakening, that I had found provided for me at Hampton.

My work began at Tuskegee, Alabama, in 1881, in a small shanty church, with one teacher and thirty students, without a dollar's worth of property. The spirit of work and of industrial thrift, with aid from the State and generosity from the North, have enabled us to develop an institution which now has about one thousand students, gathered from twenty-three States, and eighty-eight instructors. Counting students, instructors, and their families, we have a resident population upon the school grounds of about twelve hundred persons.

The institution owns two thousand three hundred acres of land, seven hundred of which are cultivated by student labor. There are six hundred head of live-stock, including horses, mules, cows, hogs, and sheep. There are over forty vehicles that have been made, and are now used, by the school. Training is given in twenty-six industries. There is work in wood, in iron, in leather, in tin; and all forms of domestic economy are engaged in. Students are taught mechanical and architectural drawing, receive training as agriculturists, dairymen, masons, carpenters, contractors, builders, as machinists, electricians, printers, dressmakers, and milliners, and in other directions.

The value of the property is $300,000. There are forty-two buildings, counting large and small, all of which, with the exception of four, have been erected by the labour of the students.

Since this work started, there has been collected and spent for its founding and support $800,000. The annual expense is now not far from $75,000. In a humble, simple manner the effort has been to place a great object-lesson in the heart of the South for the elevation of the coloured people, where there should be, in a high sense, that union of head, heart, and hand which has been the foundation of the greatness of all races since the world began.

What is the object of all this outlay? It must be first borne in mind that we have in the South a peculiar and unprecedented state of things. The cardinal needs among the eight million coloured people in the South, most of whom are to be found on the plantations, may be stated as food, clothing, shelter, education, proper habits, and a settlement of race relations. These millions of coloured people of the South cannot be reached directly by any missionary agent; but they can be reached by sending out among them strong, selected young men and women, with the proper training of head, hand, and heart, who will live among them and show them how to lift themselves up.

The problem that the Tuskegee Institute keeps before itself constantly is how to prepare these leaders. From the outset, in connection with religious and academic training, it has emphasised industrial, or hand, training as a means of finding the way out of present conditions. First, we have found the industrial teaching useful in giving the student a chance to work out a portion of his expenses while in school. Second, the school furnishes labour that has an economic value and at the same time gives the student a chance to acquire knowledge and skill while performing the labour. Most of all, we find the industrial system valuable in teaching economy, thrift, and the dignity of labour and in giving moral backbone to students. The fact that a student goes into the world conscious of his power to build a house or a wagon or to make a set of harness gives him a certain confidence and moral independence that he would not possess without such training.

A more detailed example of our methods at Tuskegee may be of interest. For example, we cultivate by student labour seven hundred acres of land. The object is not only to cultivate the land in a way to make it pay our boarding department, but at the same time to teach the students, in addition to the practical work, something of the chemistry of the soil, the best methods of drainage, dairying, cultivation of fruit, the care of live-stock and tools, and scores of other lessons needed by people whose main dependence is on agriculture.

Friends some time ago provided means for the erection of a large new chapel at Tuskegee. Our students made the bricks for this chapel. A large part of the timber was sawed by the students at our saw-mill, the plans were drawn by our teacher of architectural and mechanical drawing, and students did the brick-masonry, the plastering, the painting, the carpentry work, the tinning, the slating, and made most of the furniture. Practically, the whole chapel was built and furnished by student labour. Now the school has this building for permanent use, and the students have a knowledge of the trades employed in its construction.

While the young men do the kinds of work I have mentioned, young women to a large extent make, mend, and launder the clothing of the young men. They also receive instruction in dairying, horticulture, and other valuable industries.

One of the objections sometimes urged against industrial education for the Negro is that it aims merely to teach him to work on the same plan that he worked on when in slavery. This is far from being the object at Tuskegee. At the head of each of the twenty-six industrial divisions we have an intelligent and competent instructor, just as we have in our history classes, so that the student is taught not only practical brick-masonry, for example, but also the underlying principles of that industry, the mathematics and the mechanical and architectural drawing. Or he is taught how to become master of the forces of nature, so that, instead of cultivating corn in the old way, he can use a corn cultivator that lays off the furrows, drops the corn into them, and covers it; and in this way he can do more work than three men by the old process of corn planting, while at the same time much of the toil is eliminated and labour is dignified. In a word, the constant aim is to show the student how to put brains into every process of labour, how to bring his knowledge of mathematics and the sciences in farming, carpentry, forging, foundry work, how to dispense as soon as possible with the old form of *ante-bellum* labour. In the erection of the chapel referred to, instead of letting the money which was given to us go into outside hands, we made it accomplish three objects: first, it provided the chapel; second, it gave the students a chance to get a practical knowledge of the trades connected with the building; and, third, it enabled them to earn something toward the payment of their board while receiving academic and industrial training.

Having been fortified at Tuskegee by education of mind, skill of hand, Christian character, ideas of thrift, economy, and push, and a spirit of independence, the student is sent out to become a centre of influence and light in showing the masses of our people in the Black Belt of the South how to lift themselves up. Can this be done? I give but one or two examples. Ten years ago a young coloured man came to the institute from one of the large plantation districts. He studied in the class-room a portion of the time, and received practical and theoretical training on the farm the remainder of the time. Having finished his course at Tuskegee, he returned to his plantation home, which was in a county where the coloured people outnumbered the whites six to one, as is true of many of the counties in the Black Belt of the South. He found the Negroes in debt. Ever since the war they had been mortgaging their crops for the food on which to live while the crops were growing. The majority of them were living from hand-to-mouth on rented land, in small one-room log cabins, and attempting to pay a rate of interest on their advances that ranged from fifteen to forty per cent. per annum. The school had been taught in a wreck of a log cabin, with no apparatus, and had never been in session longer than three months out of twelve. He found the people, as many as eight or ten persons, of all ages and conditions and of both sexes, huddled together and living in one-room cabins year after year, and with a minister whose only aim was to work upon the emotions. One can imagine something of the moral and religious state of the community.

But the remedy! In spite of the evil the Negro got the habit of work from slavery. The rank and file of the race, especially those on the Southern plantations, work hard; but the trouble is that what they earn gets away from them in high rents, crop mortgages, whiskey, snuff, cheap jewelry, and the like. The young man just referred to had been trained at Tuskegee, as most of our graduates are, to meet just this condition of things. He took the three month's public school as a nucleus for his work. Then he organized the older people into a club, or conference, that held meetings every week. In these meetings he taught the people, in a plain, simple manner, how to save their money, how to farm in a better way, how to sacrifice, — to live on bread and potatoes, if necessary, till they could get out of debt, and begin the buying of lands.

Soon a large proportion of the people were in a condition to make contracts for the buying of homes (land is very cheap in the South) and to live without mortgaging their crops. Not only this; under the guidance and leadership of this teacher, the first year that he was among them they learned how and built, by contributions in money and labour, a neat, comfortable school-house that replaced the wreck of a log cabin formerly used. The following year the weekly meetings were continued, and two months were added to the original three months of school. The next year two more months were added. The improvement has gone on until these people have every year an eight months' school.

I wish my readers could have the chance that I have had of going into this community. I wish they could look into the faces of the people, and see them beaming with hope and delight. I wish they could see the two or three room cottages that have taken the place of the usual one-room cabin, see the well-cultivated farms and the religious life of the people that now means something more than the name. The teacher has a good cottage and well-kept farm that serve as models. In a word, a complete revolution has been wrought in the industrial, educational, and religious life of this whole community by reason of the fact that they have had this leader, this guide and object-lesson, to show them how to take the money and effort that had hitherto been scattered to the wind in mortgages and high rents, in whiskey and gewgaws, and how to concentrate it in the direction of their own uplifting. One community on its feet presents an object-lesson for the adjoining communities, and soon improvements show themselves in other places.

Another student, who received academic and industrial training at Tuskegee, established himself, three years ago, as a blacksmith and wheelwright in a community; and, in addition to the influence of his successful business enterprise, he is fast making the same kind of changes in the life of the people about him that I have just recounted. It would be easy for me to fill many pages describing the influence of the Tuskegee graduates in every part of the South. We keep it constantly in the minds of our students and graduates that the industrial or material condition of the masses of our people must be improved, as well as the intellectual, before there can be any permanent change in their moral and religious life. We find it a pretty hard thing to make a good Christian of a hungry man. No matter how much our people "get happy" and "shout" in church, if they go home at night from church hungry, they are tempted to find something to eat before morning. This is a principle of human nature, and is not confined alone to the Negro. The Negro has within him immense power for self-uplifting, but for years it will be necessary to guide him and stimulate his energies.

The recognition of this power led us to organise, five years ago,[4] what is known as the Tuskegee Negro Conference, — a gathering that meets every February, and is composed of about eight hundred representatives, coloured men and women, from all sections of the Black Belt. They come in ox-carts, mule-carts, buggies, on mule-back and horseback, on foot, by railroad. Some travel all night in order to be present. The matters considered at the conference are those that the coloured people have it in their own power to control, — such as the evils of the mortgage system, the one-room cabin, buying on credit, the importance of owning a home and of putting money in the bank, how to build school-houses and prolong the school term, and to improve their moral and religious condition. As a single example of the results, one delegate reported that since the conference was started, seven years ago, eleven people in his neighbourhood had bought homes, fourteen had gotten out of debt, and a number had stopped mortgaging their crops. Moreover, a school-house had been built by the people themselves, and the school term had been extended from three to six months; and, with a look of triumph, he exclaimed, "We's done libin' in de ashes."

Besides this Negro Conference for the masses of the people, we now have a gathering at the same time known as the Tuskegee Workers' Conference, composed of the officers and instructors of the leading coloured schools in the South. After listening to the story of the conditions and needs from the people themselves, the Workers' Conference finds much food for thought and discussion. Let me repeat, from its beginning, this institution has kept in mind the giving of thorough mental and religious training, along with such industrial training as would enable the student to appreciate the dignity of labour and become self-supporting and valuable as a producing factor, keeping in mind the occupations open in the South to the average man of the race.

This institution has now reached the point where it can begin to judge of the value of its work as seen in its graduates. Some years ago we noted the fact, for example, that there was quite a movement in many parts of the South to organise and start dairies. Soon after this, we opened a dairy school where a number of young men could receive training in the best and most scientific methods of

4 Actually seven years earlier, in 1892.

dairying. At present we have calls, mainly from Southern white men, for twice as many dairymen as we are able to supply. The reports indicate that our young men are giving the highest satisfaction, and are fast changing and improving the dairy product in the communities where they labour. I have used the dairy industry simply as an example. What I have said of this industry is true in a larger or less degree of the others.

I cannot but believe, and my daily observation and experience confirm me in it, that, as we continue placing men and women of intelligence, religion, modesty, conscience, and skill in every community in the South, who will prove by actual results their value to the community, this will constitute the solution for many of the present political and sociological difficulties. It is with this larger and more comprehensive view of improving present conditions and laying the foundation wisely that the Tuskegee Normal and Industrial Institute is training men and women as teachers and industrial leaders.

Over four hundred students have finished the course of training at this institution, and are now scattered throughout the South, doing good work. A recent investigation shows that about 3,000 students who have taken only a partial course are doing commendable work. One young man, who was able to remain in school but two years, has been teaching in one community for ten years. During this time he has built a new school-house, extended the school term from three to seven months, and has bought a nice farm upon which he has erected a neat cottage. The example of this young man has inspired many of the coloured people in this community to follow his example in some degree; and this is one of many such examples.

Wherever our graduates and ex-students go, they teach by precept and example the necessary lesson of thrift, economy, and property-getting, and friendship between the races.

CHAPTER VI

It has become apparent that the effort to put the rank and file of the coloured people into a position to exercise the right of franchise has not been the success that was expected in those portions of our country where the Negro is found in large numbers. Either the Negro was not prepared for any such wholesale exercise of the ballot as our recent amendments to the Constitution contemplated or the American people were not prepared to assist and encourage him to use the ballot. In either case the result has been the same.

On an important occasion in the life of the Master, when it fell to him to pronounce judgment on two courses of action, these memorable words fell from his lips: "And Mary hath chosen the better part." This was the supreme test in the case of an individual. It is the highest test in the case of a race or a nation. Let us apply this test to the American Negro.

In the life of our Republic, when he has had the opportunity to choose, has it been the better or worse part? When in the childhood of this nation the Negro was asked to submit to slavery or choose death and extinction, as did the aborigines, he chose the better part, that which perpetuated the race.

When, in 1776, the Negro was asked to decide between British oppression and American independence, we find him choosing the better part; and Crispus Attucks, a Negro, was the first to shed his blood on State Street, Boston, that the white American might enjoy liberty forever, though his race remained in slavery. When, in 1814, at New Orleans, the test of patriotism came again, we find the Negro choosing the better part, General Andrew Jackson himself testifying that no heart was more loyal and no arm was more strong and useful in defence of righteousness.

When the long and memorable struggle came between union and separation, when he knew that victory meant freedom, and defeat his continued enslavement, although enlisting by the thousands, as opportunity presented itself, to fight in honourable combat for the cause of the Union and liberty, yet, when the suggestion and the temptation came to burn the home and massacre wife and children during the absence of the master in battle, and thus insure his liberty, we find him choosing the better part, and for four long years protecting and supporting the helpless, defenceless ones intrusted to his care.

When, during our war with Spain, the safety and honour of the Republic were threatened by a foreign foe, when the wail and anguish of the oppressed from a distant isle reached our ears, we find the Negro forgetting his own wrongs, forgetting the laws and customs that discriminate against him in his own country, and again choosing the better part. And, if any one would know how he acquitted himself in the field at Santiago, let him apply for answer to Shafter and Roosevelt and Wheeler. Let them tell how the Negro faced death and laid down his life in defence of honour and humanity. When the full story of the heroic conduct of the Negro in the Spanish-American War has been heard from the lips of Northern soldier and Southern soldier, from ex-abolitionist and ex-master, then shall the country decide whether a race that is thus willing to die for its country should not be given the highest opportunity to live for its country.

In the midst of all the complaints of suffering in the camp and field during the Spanish-American War, suffering from fever and hunger, where is the official or citizen that has heard a word of complaint from the lips of a black soldier? The only request that came from the Negro soldier was that he might be permitted to replace the white soldier when heat and malaria began to decimate the ranks of the white regiments, and to occupy at the same time the post of greater danger.

But, when all this is said, it remains true that the efforts on the part of his friends and the part of himself to share actively in the control of State and local government in America have not been a success in all sections. What are the causes of this partial failure, and what lessons has it taught that we may use in regard to the future treatment of the Negro in America?

In my mind there is no doubt but that we made a mistake at the beginning of our freedom of putting the emphasis on the wrong end. Politics and the holding of office were too largely emphasised, almost to the exclusion of every other interest.

I believe the past and present teach but one lesson, — to the Negro's friends and to the Negro himself, — that there is but one way out, that there is but one hope of solution; and that is for the Negro in every part of America to resolve from henceforth that he will throw aside every non-essential and cling only to essential, — that his pillar of fire by night and pillar of cloud by day shall be property, economy, education, and Christian character. To us just now these are the wheat, all else the chaff. The individual or race that owns the property, pays the taxes, possesses the intelligence and substantial character, is the one which is going to exercise the greatest control in government, whether he lives in the North or whether he lives in the South.

I have often been asked the cause of and the cure for the riots that have taken place recently in North Carolina and South Carolina.* I am not at all sure that what I shall say will answer these questions in a satisfactory way, nor shall I attempt to narrow my expressions to a mere recital of what has taken place in these two States. I prefer to discuss the problem in a broader manner.

In the first place, in politics I am a Republican, but have always refrained from activity in party politics, and expect to pursue this policy in the future. So in this connection I shall refrain, as I always have done, from entering upon any discussion of mere party politics. What I shall say of politics will bear upon the race problem and the civilisation of the South in the larger sense. In no case would I permit my political relations to stand in the way of my speaking and acting in the manner that I believe would be for the permanent interest of my race and the whole South.

In 1873 the Negro in the South had reached the point of greatest activity and influence in public life, so far as the mere holding of elective office was concerned. From that date those who have kept up with the history of the South have noticed that the Negro has steadily lost in the number of elective offices held. In saying this, I do not mean that the Negro has gone backward in the real and more fundamental things of life. On the contrary, he has gone forward faster than has been true of any other race in history, under anything like similar circumstances.

If we can answer the question as to why the Negro has lost ground in the matter of holding elective office in the South, perhaps we shall find that our reply will prove to be our answer also as to the cause of the recent riots in North Carolina and South Carolina. Before beginning a discussion of the question I have asked, I wish to say that this change in the political influence of the Negro has continued from year to year, notwithstanding the fact that for a long time he was protected, politically, by force of federal arms and the most rigid federal laws, and still more effectively, perhaps, by the voice and influence in the halls of legislation of such advocates of the rights of the Negro race as Thaddeus Stevens, Charles Sumner, Benjamin F. Butler, James M. Ashley, Oliver P. Morton,

* November, 1898.

Carl Schurz, and Roscoe Conkling, and on the stump and through the public press by those great and powerful Negroes, Frederick Douglass, John M. Langston, Blanche K. Bruce, John R. Lynch, P. B. S. Pinchback, Robert Browne Elliott, T. Thomas Fortune, and many others; but the Negro has continued for twenty years to have fewer representatives in the State and national legislatures. The reduction has continued until now it is at the point where, with few exceptions, he is without representatives in the law-making bodies of the State and of the nation.

Now let us find, if we can, a cause for this. The Negro is fond of saying that his present condition is due to the fact that the State and federal courts have not sustained the laws passed for the protection of the rights of his people; but I think we shall have to go deeper than this, because I believe that all agree that court decisions, as a rule, represent the public opinion of the community or nation creating and sustaining the court.

At the beginning of his freedom it was unfortunate that those of the white race who won the political confidence of the Negro were not, with few exceptions, men of such high character as would lead them to assist him in laying a firm foundation for his development. Their main purpose appears to have been, for selfish ends in too many instances, merely to control his vote. The history of the reconstruction era will show that this was unfortunate for all the parties in interest.

It would have been better, from any point of view, if the native Southern white man had taken the Negro, at the beginning of his freedom, into his political confidence, and exercised an influence and control over him before his political affections were alienated.

The average Southern white man has an idea to-day that, if the Negro were permitted to get any political power, all the mistakes of the reconstruction period would be repeated. He forgets or ignores the fact that thirty years of acquiring education and property and character have produced a higher type of black man than existed thirty years ago.

But, to be more specific, for all practical purposes, there are two political parties in the South, — a black man's party and a white man's party. In saying this, I do not mean that all white men are Democrats; for there are some white men in the South of the highest character who are Republicans, and there are a few Negroes in

353

the South of the highest character who are Democrats. It is the general understanding that all white men are Democrats or the equivalent, and that all black men are Republicans. So long as the colour line is the dividing line in politics, so long will there be trouble.

The white man feels that he owns most of the property, furnishes the Negro most of his employment, thinks he pays most of the taxes, and has had years of experience in government. There is no mistaking the fact that the feeling which has heretofore governed the Negro — that, to be manly and stand by his race, he must oppose the Southern white man with his vote — has had much to do with intensifying the opposition of the Southern white man to him.

The Southern white man says that it is unreasonable for the Negro to come to him, in a large measure, for his clothes, board, shelter, and education, and for his politics to go to men a thousand miles away. He very properly argues that, when the Negro votes, he should try to consult the interests of his employer, just as the Pennsylvania employee tries to vote for the interests of his employer. Further, that much of the education which has been given the Negro has been defective, in not preparing him to love labour and to earn his living at some special industry, and has, in too many cases, resulted in tempting him to live by his wits as a political creature or by trusting to his "influence" as a political time-server.

Then, there is no mistaking the fact, that much opposition to the Negro in politics is due to the circumstance that the Southern white man has not become accustomed to seeing the Negro exercise political power either as a voter or as an office-holder. Again, we want to bear it in mind that the South has not yet reached the point where there is that strict regard for the enforcement of the law against either black or white men that there is in many of our Northern and Western States. This laxity in the enforcement of the laws in general, and especially of criminal laws, makes such outbreaks as those in North Carolina and South Carolina of easy occurrence.

Then there is one other consideration which must not be overlooked. It is the common opinion of almost every black man and almost every white man that nearly everybody who has had anything to do with the making of laws bearing upon the protection of the Negro's vote has proceeded on the theory that all the black men for all time will vote the Republican ticket and that all the white men in the South will vote the Democratic ticket. In a word, all seem to have taken it for granted that the two races are always going to oppose each other in their voting.

In all the foregoing statements I have not attempted to define my own views or position, but simply to describe conditions as I have observed them, that might throw light upon the cause of our political troubles. As to my own position, I do not favour the Negro's giving up anything which is fundamental and which has been guaranteed to him by the Constitution of the United States. It is not best for him to relinquish any of his rights; nor would his doing so be best for the Southern white man. Every law placed in the Constitution of the United States was placed there to encourage and stimulate the highest citizenship. If the Negro is not stimulated and encouraged by just State and national laws to become the highest type of citizen, the result will be worse for the Southern white man than for the Negro. Take the State of South Carolina, for example, where nearly two-thirds of the population are Negroes. Unless these Negroes are encouraged by just election laws to become tax-payers and intelligent producers, the white people of South Carolina will have an eternal millstone about their necks.

In an open letter to the State Constitutional Convention of Louisiana,[5] I wrote: "I am no politician. On the other hand, I have always advised my race to give attention to acquiring property, intelligence, and character, as the necessary bases of good citizenship, rather than to mere political agitation. But the question upon which I write is out of the region of ordinary politics. It affects the civilisation of two races, not for to-day alone, but for a very long time to come.

"Since the war, no State has had such an opportunity to settle, for all time, the race question, so far as it concerns politics, as is now given to Louisiana. Will your convention set an example to the world in this respect? Will Louisiana take such high and just grounds in respect to the Negro that no one can doubt that the South is as good a friend to him as he possesses elsewhere? In all this, gentlemen of the convention, I am not pleading for the Negro alone, but for the morals, the higher life, of the white man as well.

"The Negro agrees with you that it is necessary to the salvation of the South that restrictions be put upon the ballot. I know that

5 See above, 4:381-84.

you have two serious problems before you; ignorant and corrupt government, on the one hand; and, on the other, a way to restrict the ballot so that control will be in the hands of the intelligent, without regard to race. With the sincerest sympathy with you in your efforts to find a good way out of the difficulty, I want to suggest that no State in the South can make a law that will provide an opportunity or temptation for an ignorant white man to vote, and withhold the opportunity or temptation from an ignorant coloured man, without injuring both men. No State can make a law that can thus be executed without dwarfing, for all time, the morals of the white man in the South. Any law controlling the ballot that is not absolutely just and fair to both races will work more permanent injury to the whites than to the blacks.

"The Negro does not object to an educational and property test, but let the law be so clear that no one clothed with State authority will be tempted to perjure and degrade himself by putting one interpretation upon it for the white man and another for the black man. Study the history of the South, and you will find that, where there has been the most dishonesty in the matter of voting, there you will find to-day the lowest moral condition of both races. First, there was the temptation to act wrongly with the Negro's ballot. From this it was an easy step to act dishonestly with the white man's ballot, to the carrying of concealed weapons, to the murder of a Negro, and then to the murder of a white man, and then to lynching. I entreat you not to pass a law that will prove an eternal millstone about the necks of your children. No man can have respect for the government and officers of the law when he knows, deep down in his heart, that the exercise of the franchise is tainted with fraud.

"The road that the South has been compelled to travel during the last thirty years has been strewn with thorns and thistles. It has been as one groping through the long darkness into the light. The time is not far distant when the world will begin to appreciate the real character of the burden that was imposed upon the South in giving the franchise to four millions of ignorant and impoverished ex-slaves. No people was ever before given such a problem to solve. History has blazed no path through the wilderness that could be followed. For thirty years we have wandered in the wilderness. We are now beginning to get out. But there is only one road out; and all makeshifts, expedients, profit and loss calculations, but lead into swamps, quicksands, quagmires, and jungles. There is a highway that will lead both races out into the pure, beautiful sunshine, where there will be nothing to hide and nothing to explain, where both races can grow strong and true and useful in every fibre of their being. I believe that your convention will find this highway, that it will enact a fundamental law that will be absolutely just and fair to white and black alike.

"I beg of you, further, that in the degree that you close the ballot-box against the ignorant you will open the school-house. More than one-half of the population of your State are Negroes. No State can long prosper when a large part of its citizenship is in ignorance and poverty, and has no interest in the government. I beg of you that you do not treat us as an alien people. We are not aliens. You know us. You know that we have cleared your forests, tilled your fields, nursed your children, and protected your families. There is an attachment between us that few understand. While I do not presume to be able to advise you, yet it is in my heart to say that, if your convention would do something that would prevent for all time strained relations between the two races, and would permanently settle the matter of political relations in one Southern State at least, let the very best educational opportunities be provided for both races; and add to this an election law that shall be incapable of unjust discrimination, at the same time providing that, in proportion as the ignorant secure education, property, and character, they will be given the right of citizenship. Any other course will take from one-half your citizens interest in the State, and hope and ambition to become intelligent producers and tax-payers, and useful and virtuous citizens. Any other course will tie the white citizens of Louisiana to a body of death.

"The Negroes are not unmindful of the fact that the poverty of the State prevents it from doing all that it desires for public education; yet I believe that you will agree with me that ignorance is more costly to the State than education, that it will cost Louisiana more not to educate the Negroes than it will to educate them. In connection with a generous provision for public schools, I believe that nothing will so help my own people in your State as provision at some institution for the highest academic and normal training, in connection with thorough training in agriculture, mechanics, and domestic economy. First-class training in agriculture, horticulture, dairying, stock-raising, the mechanical arts, and domestic economy, would make us intelligent producers, and not only help us to contribute our honest share as tax-payers, but would result in retaining much money in the State that now goes outside for that which can be as well produced at home. An institution which will give this training of the hand, along with the highest mental culture, would soon convince our people that their salvation is largely in the ownership of property and in industrial and business development, rather than in mere political agitation.

"The highest test of the civilisation of any race is in its willingness to extend a helping hand to the less fortunate. A race, like an individual, lifts itself up by lifting others up. Surely, no people ever had a greater chance to exhibit the highest Christian fortitude and magnanimity than is now presented to the people of Louisiana. It requires little wisdom or statesmanship to repress, to crush out, to retard the hopes and aspirations of a people; but the highest and most profound statesmanship is shown in guiding and stimulating a people, so that every fibre in the body and soul shall be made to contribute in the highest degree to the usefulness and ability of the State. It is along this line that I pray God the thoughts and activities of your convention may be guided."

As to such outbreaks as have recently occurred in North Carolina and South Carolina, the remedy will not be reached by the Southern white man merely depriving the Negro of his rights and privileges. This method is but superficial, irritating, and must, in the nature of things, be short-lived. The statesman, to cure an evil, resorts to enlightenment, to stimulation; the politician, to repression. I have just remarked that I favour the giving up of nothing that is guaranteed to us by the Constitution of the United States, or that is fundamental to our citizenship. While I hold to these views as strongly as any one, I differ with some as to the method of securing the permanent and peaceful enjoyment of all the privileges guaranteed to us by our fundamental law.

In finding a remedy, we must recognise the world-wide fact that the Negro must be led to see and feel that he must make every effort possible, in every way possible, to secure the friendship, the confidence, the co-operation of his white neighbour in the South. To

358

do this, it is not necessary for the Negro to become a truckler or a trimmer. The Southern white man has no respect for a Negro who does not act from principle. In some way the Southern white man must be led to see that it is to his interest to turn his attention more and more to the making of laws that will, in the truest sense, elevate the Negro. At the present moment, in many cases, when one attempts to get the Negro to co-operate with the Southern white man, he asks the question, "Can the people who force me to ride in a Jim Crow car, and pay first-class fare, be my best friends?" In answering such questions, the Southern white man, as well as the Negro, has a duty to perform. In the exercise of his political rights I should advise the Negro to be temperate and modest, and more and more to do his own thinking.

I believe the permanent cure for our present evils will come through a property and educational test for voting that shall apply honestly and fairly to both races. This will cut off the large mass of ignorant voters of both races that is now proving so demoralising a factor in the politics of the Southern States.

But, most of all, it will come through industrial development of the Negro. Industrial education makes an intelligent producer of the Negro, who becomes of immediate value to the community rather than one who yields to the temptation to live merely by politics or other parasitical employments. It will make him soon become a property-holder; and, when a citizen becomes a holder of property, he becomes a conservative and thoughtful voter. He will more carefully consider the measures and individuals to be voted for. In proportion as he increases his property interests, he becomes important as a tax-payer.

There is little trouble between the Negro and the white man in matters of education; and, when it comes to his business development, the black man has implicit faith in the advice of the Southern white man. When he gets into trouble in the courts, which requires a bond to be given, in nine cases out of ten, he goes to a Southern white man for advice and assistance. Every one who has lived in the South knows that, in many of the church troubles among the coloured people, the ministers and other church officers apply to the nearest white minister for assistance and instruction. When by reason of mutual concession we reach the point where we shall consult the Southern white man about our politics as we now consult him about our business, legal and religious matters, there will be a change for the better in the situation.

The object-lesson of a thousand Negroes in every county in the South who own neat and comfortable homes, possessing skill, industry, and thrift, with money in the bank, and are large tax-payers co-operating with the white men in the South in every manly way for the development of their own communities and counties, will go a long way, in a few years, toward changing the present status of the Negro as a citizen, as well as the attitude of the whites toward the blacks.

As the Negro grows in industrial and business directions, he will divide in his politics on economic issues, just as the white man in other parts of the country now divides his vote. As the South grows in business prosperity it will divide its vote on economic issues, just as other sections of the country divide their vote. When we can enact laws that result in honestly cutting off the large ignorant and non-tax-paying vote, and when we can bring both races to the point where they will co-operate with each other in politics, as they do now in matters of business, religion, and education, the problem will be in a large measure solved, and political outbreaks will cease.

CHAPTER VII

One of the great questions which Christian education must face in the South is the proper adjustment of the new relations of the two races. It is a question which must be faced calmly, quietly, dispassionately; and the time has now come to rise above party, above race, above colour, above sectionalism, into the region of duty of man to man, of American to American, of Christian to Christian.

I remember not long ago, when about five hundred coloured people sailed from the port of Savannah bound for Liberia, that the news was flashed all over the country, "The Negro has made up his mind to return to his own country," and that, "in this was the solution of the race problem in the South." But these short-sighted people forgot the fact that before breakfast that morning about five hundred more Negro children were born in the South alone.

And then, once in a while, somebody is so bold as to predict that the Negro will be absorbed by the white race. Let us look at this phase of the question for a moment. It is a fact that, if a person is known to have one per cent. of African blood in his veins, he ceases to be a white man. The ninety-nine per cent. of Caucasian blood does not weigh by the side of the one per cent. of African blood. The white blood counts for nothing. The person is a Negro every time. So it will be a very difficult task for the white man to absorb the Negro.

Somebody else conceived the idea of colonising the coloured people, of getting territory where nobody lived, putting the coloured people there, and letting them be a nation all by themselves. There are two objections to that. First, you would have to build one wall to keep the coloured people in, and another wall to keep the white people out. If you were to build ten walls around Africa to-day you could not keep the white people out, especially as long as there was a hope of finding gold there.

I have always had the highest respect for those of our race who, in trying to find a solution for our Southern problem, advised a return of the race to Africa, and because of my respect for those who have thus advised, especially Bishop Henry M. Turner, I have tried to make a careful and unbiassed study of the question, during a recent sojourn in Europe, to see what opportunities presented themselves in Africa for self-development and self-government.

I am free to say that I see no way out of the Negro's present condition in the South by returning to Africa. Aside from other insurmountable obstacles, there is no place in Africa for him to go where his condition would be improved. All Europe — especially England, France, and Germany — has been running a mad race for the last twenty years, to see which could gobble up the greater part of Africa; and there is practically nothing left. Old King Cetewayo put it pretty well when he said, "First come missionary, then come rum, then come traders, then come army"; and Cecil Rhodes has expressed the prevailing sentiment more recently in these words, "I would rather have land than 'niggers.'" And Cecil Rhodes is directly responsible for the killing of thousands of black natives in South Africa, that he might secure their land.

In a talk with Henry M. Stanley, the explorer, he told me that he knew no place in Africa where the Negroes of the United States might go to advantage; but I want to be more specific. Let us see how Africa has been divided, and then decide whether there is a place left for us. On the Mediterranean coast of Africa, Morocco is an independent State, Algeria is a French possession, Tunis is a French protectorate, Tripoli is a province of the Ottoman Empire, Egypt is a province of Turkey. On the Atlantic coast, Sahara is a French protectorate, Adrar is claimed by Spain, Senegambia is a French trading settlement, Gambia is a British crown colony, Sierra Leone is a British crown colony. Liberia is a republic of freed Negroes, Gold Coast and Ashanti are British colonies and British protectorates, Togoland is a German protectorate, Dahomey is a kingdom subject to French influence, Slave Coast is a British colony and British protectorate, Niger Coast is a British protectorate, the Cameroons are trading settlements protected by Germany, French Congo is a French protectorate, Congo Free State is an international African Association, Angola and Benguela are Portuguese protectorates, and the inland countries are controlled as follows: The Niger States, Masina, etc., are under French protection; Land Gandu is under British protection, administered by the Royal Hausan Niger Company.

South Africa is controlled as follows: Damara and Namaqua Land are German protectorates, Cape Colony is a British colony, Basutoland is a Crown colony, Bechuanaland is a British protectorate, Natal is a British colony, Zululand is a British protectorate, Orange Free State is independent, the South African Republic is independent, and the Zambesi is administered by the British South African Company. Lourenco Marques is a Portuguese possession.

East Africa has also been disposed of in the following manner: Mozambique is a Portuguese possession, British Central Africa is a British protectorate, German East Africa is in the German sphere of influence, Zanzibar is a sultanate under British protection, British East Africa is a British protectorate, Somaliland is under British and Italian protection, Abyssinia is independent. East Soudan (including Nubia, Kordofan, Darfur, and Wadai) is in the British sphere of influence. It will be noted that, when one of these European countries cannot get direct control over any section of Africa, it at once gives it out to the world that the country wanted is in the "sphere of its influence," — a very convenient term. If we are to go to Africa, and be under the control of another government, I think we should prefer to take our chances in the "sphere of influence" of the United States.

All this shows pretty conclusively that a return to Africa for the Negro is out of the question, even provided that a majority of the Negroes wished to go back, which they do not. The adjustment of the relations of the two races must take place here; and it is taking place slowly, but surely. As the Negro is educated to make homes and to respect himself, the white man will in turn respect him.

It has been urged that the Negro has inherent in him certain traits of character that will prevent his ever reaching the standard of civilisation set by the whites, and taking his place among them as an equal. It may be some time before the Negro race as a whole can stand comparison with the white in all respects, — it would be most remarkable, considering the past, if it were not so; but the idea that his objectionable traits and weaknesses are fundamental, I think, is a mistake. For, although there are elements of weakness about the Negro race, there are also many evidences of strength.

It is an encouraging sign, however, when an individual grows to the point where he can hold himself up for personal analysis and study. It is equally encouraging for a race to be able to study itself, — to measure its weakness and strength. It is not helpful to a race to be continually praised and have its weakness overlooked, neither is it the most helpful thing to have its faults alone continually dwelt upon. What is needed is downright, straightforward honesty in both directions; and this is not always to be obtained.

There is little question that one of the Negroes' weak points is physical. Especially is this true regarding those who live in the large cities, North and South. But in almost every case this physical weakness can be traced to ignorant violation of the laws of health or to vicious habits. The Negro, who during slavery lived on the large plantations in the South, surrounded by restraints, at the close of the war came to the cities, and in many cases found the freedom and temptations of the city too much for him. The transition was too sudden.

When we consider what it meant to have four millions of people slaves to-day and freemen to-morrow, the wonder is that the race has not suffered more physically than it has. I do not believe that statistics can be so marshalled as to prove that the Negro as a race is physically or numerically on the decline. On the other hand, the Negro as a race is increasing in numbers by a larger percentage than is true of the French nation. While the death-rate is large in the cities, the birth-rate is also large; and it is to be borne in mind that eighty-five per cent. of these people in the Gulf States are in the country districts and smaller towns, and there the increase is along healthy and normal lines. As the Negro becomes educated, the high death-rate in the cities will disappear. For proof of this, I have only to mention that a few years ago no coloured man could get insurance in the large first-class insurance companies. Now there are few of these companies which do not seek the insurance of educated coloured men. In the North and South the physical intoxication that was the result of sudden freedom is giving way to an encouraging, sobering process; and, as this continues, the high death-rate will disappear, even in the large cities.

Another element of weakness which shows itself in the present stage of the civilisation of the Negro is his lack of ability to form a purpose and stick to it through a series of years, if need be, — years that involve discouragement as well as encouragement, — till the end shall be reached. Of course there are brilliant exceptions to this rule; but there is no question that here is an element of weakness, and the same, I think, would be true of any race with the Negro's history.

Few of the resolutions which are made in conventions, etc., are remembered and put into practice six months after the warmth and enthusiasm of the debating hall have disappeared. This, I know, is an element of the white man's weakness, but it is the Negro I am discussing, not the white man. Individually, the Negro is strong. Collectively, he is weak. This is not to be wondered at. The ability to succeed in organised bodies is one of the highest points in civilisation. There are scores of coloured men who can succeed in any line of business as individuals, or will discuss any subject in a most intelligent manner, yet who, when they attempt to act in an organised body, are utter failures.

But the weakness of the Negro which is most frequently held up to the public gaze is that of his moral character. No one who wants to be honest and at the same time benefit the race will deny that here is where the strengthening is to be done. It has become universally accepted that the family is the foundation, the bulwark, of any race. It should be remembered, sorrowfully withal, that it was the constant tendency of slavery to destroy the family life. All through two hundred and fifty years of slavery, one of the chief objects was to increase the number of slaves; and to this end almost all thought of morality was lost sight of, so that the Negro has had only about thirty years in which to develop a family life; while the Anglo-Saxon race, with which he is constantly being compared, has had thousands of years of training in home life. The Negro felt all through the years of bondage that he was being forcibly and unjustly deprived of the fruits of his labour. Hence he felt that anything he could get from the white man in return for this labour justly belonged to him. Since this was true, we must be patient in trying to teach him a different code of morals.

From the nature of things, all through slavery it was life in the future world that was emphasised in religious teaching rather than life in this world. In his religious meetings in *ante-bellum* days the Negro was prevented from discussing many points of practical religion which related to this world; and the white minister, who was his spiritual guide, found it more convenient to talk about heaven than earth, so very naturally that to-day in his religious meeting it is the Negro's feelings which are worked upon mostly, and it is description of the glories of heaven that occupy most of the time of his sermon.

Having touched upon some of the weak points of the Negro, what are his strong characteristics? The Negro in America is different from most people for whom missionary effort is made, in that he works. He is not ashamed or afraid of work. When hard, constant work is required, ask any Southern white man, and he will tell you that in this the Negro has no superior. He is not given to strikes or to lockouts. He not only works himself, but he is unwilling to prevent other people from working.

Of the forty buildings of various kinds and sizes on the grounds of the Tuskegee Normal and Industrial Institute, in Alabama, as I have stated before, almost all of them are the results of the labour performed by the students while securing their academic education. One day the student is in his history class. The next day the same student, equally happy, with his trowel and in overalls, is working on a brick wall.

While at present the Negro may lack that tenacious mental grasp which enables one to pursue a scientific or mathematical investigation through a series of years, he has that delicate, mental feeling which enables him to succeed in oratory, music, etc.

While I have spoken of the Negro's moral weakness, I hope it will be kept in mind that in his original state his is an honest race. It was slavery that corrupted him in this respect. But in morals he also has his strong points.

Few have ever found the Negro guilty of betraying a trust. There are almost no instances in which the Negro betrayed either a Federal or a Confederate soldier who confided in him. There are few instances where the Negro has been entrusted with valuables when he has not been faithful. This country has never had a more loyal citizen. He has never proven himself a rebel. Should the Southern States, which so long held him in slavery, be invaded by a foreign foe, the Negro would be among the first to come to the rescue.

Perhaps the most encouraging thing in connection with the lifting up of the Negro in this country is the fact that he knows that he is down and wants to get up, he knows that he is ignorant and wants to get light. He fills every school-house and every church which is opened for him. He is willing to follow leaders, when he is once convinced that the leaders have his best interest at heart.

Under the constant influence of the Christian education which began thirty-five years ago, his religion is every year becoming less emotional and more rational and practical, though I, for one, hope that he will always retain in a large degree the emotional element in religion.

During the two hundred and fifty years that the Negro spent in slavery he had little cause or incentive to accumulate money or property. Thirty-five years ago this was something which he had to begin to learn. While the great bulk of the race is still without money and property, yet the signs of thrift are evident on every hand. Especially is this noticeable in the large number of neat little homes which are owned by these people on the outer edges of the towns and cities in the South.

I wish to give an example of the sort of thing the Negro has to contend with, however, in his efforts to lift himself up.

Not long ago a mother, a black mother, who lived in one of our Northern States, had heard it whispered around in her community for years that the Negro was lazy, shiftless, and would not work. So, when her only boy grew to sufficient size, at considerable expense and great self-sacrifice, she had her boy thoroughly taught the machinist's trade. A job was secured in a neighbouring shop. With dinner bucket in hand and spurred on by the prayers of the now happy-hearted mother, the boy entered the shop to begin his first day's work. What happened? Every one of the twenty white men threw down his tools, and deliberately walked out, swearing that he would not give a black man an opportunity to earn an honest living. Another shop was tried with the same result, and still another, the result ever the same. To-day this once promising, ambitious black man is a wreck, — a confirmed drunkard, — with no hope, no ambition. I ask, Who blasted the life of this young man? On whose hands does his life-blood rest? The present system of education, or rather want of education, is responsible.

Public schools and colleges should turn out men who will throw open the doors of industry, so that all men, everywhere, regardless of colour, shall have the same opportunity to earn a dollar that they now have to spend it. I know of a good many kinds of cowardice and prejudice, but I know none equal to this. I know not which is the worst, — the slaveholder who perforce compelled his slave to work without compensation or the man who, by force and strikes, compels his neighbour to refrain from working for compensation.

The Negro will be on a different footing in this country when it becomes common to associate the possession of wealth with a black skin. It is not within the province of human nature that the man who is intelligent and virtuous, and owns and cultivates the best farm in his county, is the largest tax-payer, shall very long be denied proper respect and consideration. Those who would help the Negro most effectually during the next fifty years can do so by assisting in his development along scientific and industrial lines in connection with the broadest mental and religious culture.

From the results of the war with Spain let us learn this, that God has been teaching the Spanish nation a terrible lesson. What is it? Simply this, that no nation can disregard the interest of any portion of its members without that nation becoming weak and corrupt. The penalty may be long delayed. God has been teaching Spain that for every one of her subjects that she has left in ignorance, poverty, and crime the price must be paid; and, if it has not been paid with the very heart of the nation, it must be paid with the proudest and bluest blood of her sons and with treasure that is beyond computation. From this spectacle I pray God that America will learn a lesson in respect to the ten million Negroes in this country.

The Negroes in the United States are, in most of the elements of civilisation, weak. Providence has placed them here not without a purpose. One object, in my opinion, is that the stronger race may imbibe a lesson from the weaker in patience, forbearance, and childlike yet supreme trust in the God of the Universe. This race has been placed here that the white man might have a great opportunity of lifting himself by lifting it up.

Out from the Negro colleges and industrial schools in the South there are going forth each year thousands of young men and women into dark and secluded corners, into lonely log school-houses, amidst poverty and ignorance; and though, when they go forth, no drums beat, no banners fly, no friends cheer, yet they are fighting the battles of this country just as truly and bravely as those who go forth to do battle against a foreign enemy.

If they are encouraged and properly supported in their work of educating the masses in the industries, in economy, and in morals, as well as mentally, they will, before many years, get the race upon such an intellectual, industrial, and financial footing that it will be able to enjoy without much trouble all the rights inherent in American citizenship.

Now, if we wish to bring the race to a point where it should be, where it will be strong, and grow and prosper, we have got to, in every way possible, encourage it. We can do this in no better way than by cultivating that amount of faith in the race which will make us patronise its own enterprises wherever those enterprises are worth patronising. I do not believe much in the advice that is often given that we should patronise the enterprises of our race without regard to the worth of those enterprises. I believe that the best way to bring the race to the point where it will compare with other races is to let it understand that, whenever it enters into any line of business, it will be patronised just in proportion as it makes that business as successful, as useful, as is true of any business enterprise conducted by any other race. The race that would grow strong and powerful must have the element of hero-worship in it that will, in the largest degree, make it honour its great men, the men who have succeeded in that race. I think we should be ashamed of the coloured man or woman who would not venerate the name of Frederick Douglass. No race that would not look upon such a man with honour and respect and pride could ever hope to enjoy the respect of any other race. I speak of this, not that I want my people to regard themselves in a narrow, bigoted sense, because there is nothing so hurtful to an individual or to a race as to get into the habit of feeling that there is no good except in its own race, but because I wish that it may have reasonable pride in all that is honourable in its history. Whenever you hear a coloured man say that he hates the people of the other race, there, in most instances, you will find a weak, narrow-minded coloured man. And, whenever you find a white man who expresses the same sentiment toward the people of other races, there, too, in almost every case, you will find a narrow-minded, prejudiced white man.

That person is the broadest, strongest, and most useful who sees something to love and admire in all races, no matter what their colour.

If the Negro race wishes to grow strong, it must learn to respect itself, not to be ashamed. It must learn that it will only grow in proportion as its members have confidence in it, in proportion as they believe that it is a coming race.

We have reached a period when educated Negroes should give more attention to the history of their race; should devote more time to finding out the true history of the race, and in collecting in some museum the relics that mark its progress. It is true of all races of culture and refinement and civilisation that they have gathered in some place the relics which mark the progress of their civilisation, which show how they lived from period to period. We should have so much pride that we would spend more time in looking into the history of the race, more effort and money in perpetuating in some durable form its achievements, so that from year to year, instead of looking back with regret, we can point to our children the rough path through which we grew strong and great.

We have a very bright and striking example in the history of the Jews in this and other countries. There is, perhaps, no race that has suffered so much, not so much in America as in some of the countries in Europe. But these people have clung together. They have had a certain amount of unity, pride, and love of race; and, as the years go on, they will be more and more influential in this country, — a country where they were once despised, and looked upon with scorn and derision. It is largely because the Jewish race has had faith in itself. Unless the Negro learns more and more to imitate the Jew in these matters, to have faith in himself, he cannot expect to have any high degree of success.

I wish to speak upon another subject which largely concerns the welfare of both races, especially in the South, — lynching. It is an unpleasant subject; but I feel that I should be omitting some part of my duty to both races did I not say something on the subject.

For a number of years the South has appealed to the North and to federal authorities, through the public press, from the public platform, and most eloquently through the late Henry W. Grady, to leave the whole matter of the rights and protection of the Negro to the South, declaring that it would see to it that the Negro would be made secure in his citizenship. During the last half-dozen years the whole country, from the President down, has been inclined more than ever to pursue this policy, leaving the whole matter of the destiny of the Negro to the Negro himself and to the Southern white people, among whom the great bulk of Negroes live.

By the present policy of non-interference on the part of the North and the federal government the South is given a sacred trust. How will she execute this trust? The world is waiting and watching to see. The question must be answered largely by the protection it gives to the life of the Negro and the provisions that are made for his development in the organic laws of the State. I fear that but few people in the South realise to what an extent the habit of lynching, or the taking of life without due process of law, has taken hold of us, and is hurting us, not only in the eyes of the world, but in our own moral and material growth.

Lynching was instituted some years ago with the idea of punishing and checking criminal assaults upon women. Let us examine the facts, and see where it has already led us and is likely further to carry us, if we do not rid ourselves of the evil. Many good people in the South, and also out of the South, have gotten the idea that lynching is resorted to for one crime only. I have the facts from an authoritative source. During last year one hundred and twenty-seven persons were lynched in the United States. Of this number, one hundred and eighteen were executed in the South and nine in the North and West. Of the total number lynched, one hundred and two were Negroes, twenty-three were whites, and two Indians. Now, let every one interested in the South, his country, and the cause of humanity, note this fact, — that only twenty-four of the entire number were charged in any way with the crime of rape; that is, twenty-four out of one hundred and twenty-seven cases of lynching. Sixty-one of the remaining cases were for murder, thirteen for being suspected of murder, six for theft, etc. During one week last spring, when I kept a careful record, thirteen Negroes were lynched in three of our Southern States; and not one was even charged with rape. All of these thirteen were accused of murder or house-burning; but in neither case were the men allowed to go before a court, so that their innocence or guilt might be proven.

When we get to the point where four-fifths of the people lynched in our country in one year are for some crime other than rape, we can no longer plead and explain that we lynch for one crime alone.

Let us take another year, that of 1892, for example, when 241 persons were lynched in the whole United States. Of this number 36 were lynched in Northern and Western States, and 205 in our Southern States; 160 were Negroes, 5 of these being women. The facts show that, out of the 241 lynched, only 57 were even charged with rape or attempted rape, leaving in this year alone 184 persons who were lynched for other causes than that of rape.

If it were necessary, I could produce figures for other years. Within a period of six years about 900 persons have been lynched in our Southern States. This is but a few hundred short of the total number of soldiers who lost their lives in Cuba during the Spanish-American War. If we would realise still more fully how far this unfortunate evil is leading us on, note the classes of crime during a few months for which the local papers and the Associated Press say that lynching has been inflicted. They include "murder," "rioting," "incendiarism," "robbery," "larcency," "self-defence," "insulting women," "alleged stock-poisoning," "malpractice," "alleged barn-burning," "suspected robbery," "race prejuduce," "attempted murder," "horse-stealing," "mistaken identity," etc.

The evil has so grown that we are now at the point where not only blacks are lynched in the South, but white men as well. Not only this, but within the last six years at least a half-dozen coloured women have been lynched. And there are a few cases where Negroes have lynched members of their own race. What is to be the end of all this? Furthermore, every lynching drives hundreds of Negroes out of the farming districts of the South, where they make the best living and where their services are of greatest value to the country, into the already overcrowded cities.

I know that some argue that the crime of lynching Negroes is not confined to the South. This is true; and no one can excuse such a crime as the shooting of innocent black men in Illinois, who were guilty of nothing, except seeking labour. But my words just now are to the South, where my home is and a part of which I am. Let other sections act as they will; I want to see our beautiful Southland free from this terrible evil of lynching. Lynching does not stop crime. In the vicinity in the South where a coloured man was alleged recently to have committed the most terrible crime ever charged against a member of my race, but a few weeks previously five coloured men had been lynched for supposed incendiarism. If lynching was a cure for crime, surely the lynching of those five would have prevented another Negro from committing a most heinous crime a few weeks later.

We might as well face the facts bravely and wisely. Since the beginning of the world crime has been committed in all civilised and uncivilised countries, and a certain percentage of it will always be committed both in the North and in the South; but I believe that the crime of rape can be stopped. In proportion to the numbers and intelligence of the population of the South, there exists little more crime than in several other sections of the country; but, because of the lynching evil, we are constantly advertising ourselves to the world as a lawless people. We cannot disregard the teachings of the civilised world for eighteen hundred years, that the only way to punish crime is by law. When we leave this anchorage chaos begins.

I am not pleading for the Negro alone. Lynching injures, hardens, and blunts the moral sensibilities of the young and tender manhood of the South. Never shall I forget the remark by a little nine-year-old white boy, with blue eyes and flaxen hair. The little fellow said to his mother, after he had returned from a lynching: "I have seen a man hanged; now I wish I could see one burned." Rather than hear such a remark from one of my little boys, I would prefer to see him in his grave. This is not all. Every community guilty of lynching says in so many words to the governor, to the legislature, to the sheriff, to the jury, and to the judge: "We have no faith in you and no respect for you. We have no respect for the law which we helped to make."

In the South, at the present time, there is less excuse for not permitting the law to take its course where a Negro is to be tried than anywhere else in the world; for, almost without exception, the governors, the sheriffs, the judges, the juries, and the lawyers are all white men, and they can be trusted, as a rule, to do their duty. Otherwise, it is needless to tax the people to support these officers. If our present laws are not sufficient properly to punish crime, let the laws be changed; but that the punishment may be by lawfully constituted authorities is the plea I make. The history of the world proves that where the law is most strictly enforced there is the least crime: where people take the administration of the law into their own hands there is the most crime.

But there is still another side. The white man in the South has not only a serious duty and responsibility, but the Negro has a duty and responsibility in this matter. In speaking of my own people, I want to be equally frank; but I speak with the greatest kindness. There is too much crime among them. The figures for a given period show that in the United States thirty per cent. of the crime committed is by Negroes, while we constitute only about twelve per cent. of the entire population. This proportion holds good not only in the South, but also in Northern States and cities.

No race that is so largely ignorant and so recently out of slavery could, perhaps, show a better record, but we must face these plain facts. He is most kind to the Negro who tells him of his faults as well as of his virtues. A large percentage of the crime among us grows out of the idleness of our young men and women. It is for this reason that I have tried to insist upon some industry being taught in connection with their course of literary training. It is vitally important now that every parent, every teacher and minister of the gospel, should teach with unusual emphasis morality and obedience to the law. At the fireside, in the school-room, in the Sunday-school, from the pulpit, and in the Negro press, there should be such a sentiment created regarding the committing of crime against women that no such crime could be charged against any member of the race. Let it be understood, for all time, that no one guilty of rape can find sympathy or shelter with us, and that none will be more active than we in bringing to justice, through the proper authorities, those guilty of crime. Let the criminal and vicious element of the race have, at all times, our most severe condemnation. Let a strict line be drawn between the virtuous and the criminal. I condemn, with all the indignation of my soul, any beast in human form guilty of assaulting a woman. I am sure I voice the sentiment of the thoughtful of my race in this condemnation.

We should not, as a race, become discouraged. We are making progress. No race has ever gotten upon its feet without discouragements and struggles.

I should be a great hypocrite and a coward if I did not add that which my daily experience has taught me to be true; namely, that the Negro has among many of the Southern whites as good friends as he has anywhere in the world. These friends have not forsaken us. They will not do so. Neither will our friends in the North. If we make ourselves intelligent, industrious, economical, and virtuous, of value to the community in which we live, we can and will work out our salvation right here in the South. In every community, by means of organised effort, we should seek, in a manly and honourable way, the confidence, the co-operation, the sympathy, of the best white people in the South and in our respective communities. With the best white people and the best black people standing together, in favour of law and order and justice, I believe that the safety and happiness of both races will be made secure.

We are one in this country. The question of the highest citizenship and the complete education of all concerns nearly ten millions of my people and sixty millions of the white race. When one race is strong, the other is strong; when one is weak, the other is weak. There is no power that can separate our destiny. Unjust laws and customs which exist in many places injure the white man and inconvenience the Negro. No race can wrong another race, simply because it has the power to do so, without being permanently injured in its own morals. The Negro can endure the temporary inconvenience, but the injury to the white man is permanent. It is for the white man to save himself from this degradation that I plead. If a white man steals a Negro's ballot, it is the white man who is permanently injured. Physical death comes to the one Negro lynched in a county; but death of the morals — death of the soul — comes to those responsible for the lynching.

Those who fought and died on the battlefield for the freedom of the slaves performed their duty heroically and well, but a duty remains to those left. The mere fiat of law cannot make an ignorant voter an intelligent voter, cannot make a dependent man an independent man, cannot make one citizen respect another. These results will come to the Negro, as to all races, by beginning at the bottom and gradually working up to the highest possibilities of his nature.

In the economy of God there is but one standard by which an individual can succeed: there is but one for a race. This country expects that every race shall measure itself by the American standard. During the next half-century, and more, the Negro must continue passing through the severe American crucible. He is to be tested in his patience, his forbearance, his perseverance, his power to endure wrong, — to withstand temptations, to economise, to acquire and use skill, — his ability to compete, to succeed in commerce, to disregard the superficial for the real, the appearance for the substance, to be great and yet small, learned and yet simple, high and yet the servant of all. This, — this is the passport to all that is best in the life of our Republic; and the Negro must possess it or be barred out.

In working out his own destiny, while the main burden of activity must be with the Negro, he will need in the years to come, as he has needed in the past, the help, the encouragement, the guidance, that the strong can give the weak. Thus helped, those of both races in the South will soon throw off the shackles of racial and sectional prejudice, and rise above the clouds of ignorance, narrowness, and selfishness into the atmosphere, that pure sunshine, where it will be the highest ambition to serve man, our brother, regardless of race or previous condition.

CHAPTER VIII

Before ending this volume, I have deemed it wise and fitting to sum up in the following chapter all that I have attempted to say in the previous chapters, and to speak at the same time a little more definitely about the Negro's future and his relation to the white race.

All attempts to settle the question of the Negro in the South by his removal from this country have so far failed, and I think that they are likely to fail. The next census will probably show that we have about ten millions of Negroes in the United States. About eight millions of these are in the Southern States. We have almost a nation within a nation. The Negro population within the United States lacks but two millions of being as large as the whole population of Mexico. It is nearly twice as large as the population of the Dominion of Canada. It is equal to the combined population of Switzerland, Greece, Honduras, Nicaragua, Cuba, Uruguay, Santo Domingo, Paraguay, and Costa Rica. When we consider, in connection with these facts, that the race has doubled itself since its freedom, and is still increasing, it hardly seems possible for any one to consider seriously any scheme of emigration from America as a method of solution of our vexed race problem. At most, even if the government were to provide the means, but a few hundred thousand could be transported each year. The yearly increase in population would more than overbalance the number transplanted. Even if it did not, the time required to get rid of the Negro by this method would perhaps be fifty or seventy-five years. The idea is chimerical.

Some have advised that the Negro leave the South and take up his residence in the Northern States. I question whether this would leave him any better off than he is in the South, when all things are considered. It has been my privilege to study the condition of our people in nearly every part of America; and I say, without hesitation, that, with some exceptional cases, the Negro is at his best in the Southern States. While he enjoys certain privileges in the North that he does not have in the South, when it comes to the matter of securing property, enjoying business opportunities and employment, the South presents a far better opportunity than the North. Few coloured men from the South are as yet able to stand up against the severe and increasing competition that exists in the North, to say nothing of the unfriendly influence of labour organisations, which in some way prevents black men in the North, as a rule, from securing employment in skilled labour occupations.

Another point of great danger for the coloured man who goes

North is in the matter of morals, owing to the numerous temptations by which he finds himself surrounded. He has more ways in which he can spend money than in the South, but fewer avenues of employment are open to him. The fact that at the North the Negro is confined to almost one line of employment often tends to discourage and demoralise the strongest who go from the South, and to make them an easy prey to temptation. A few years ago I made an examination into the condition of a settlement of Negroes who left the South and went to Kansas about twenty years ago, when there was a good deal of excitement in the South concerning emigration to the West. This settlement, I found, was much below the standard of that of a similar number of our people in the South. The only conclusion, therefore, it seems to me, which any one can reach, is that the Negroes, as a mass, are to remain in the Southern States. As a race, they do not want to leave the South, and the Southern white people do not want them to leave. We must therefore find some basis of settlement that will be constitutional, just, manly, that will be fair to both races in the South and to the whole country. This cannot be done in a day, a year, or any short period of time. We can, it seems to me, with the present light, decide upon a reasonably safe method of solving the problem, and turn our strength and effort in that direction. In doing this, I would not have the Negro deprived of any privilege guaranteed to him by the Constitution of the United States. It is not best for the Negro that he relinquish any of his constitutional rights. It is not best for the Southern white man that he should.

In order that we may, without loss of time or effort, concentrate our forces in a wise direction, I suggest what seems to me and many others the wisest policy to be pursued. I have reached these conclusions by reason of my own observations and experience, after eighteen years of direct contact with the leading and influential coloured and white men in most parts of our country. But I wish first to mention some elements of danger in the present situation, which all who desire the permanent welfare of both races in the South should carefully consider.

First. — There is danger that a certain class of impatient extremists among the Negroes, who have little knowledge of the actual conditions in the South, may do the entire race injury by attempting to advise their brethren in the South to resort to armed resistance or the use of the torch, in order to secure justice. All intelligent and well-considered discussion of any important question or condemnation of any wrong, both in the North and the South, from the public platform and through the press, is to be commended and encouraged; but ill-considered, incendiary utterances from black men in the North will tend to add to the burdens of our people in the South rather than relieve them.

Second. — Another danger in the South, which should be guarded against, is that the whole white South, including the wide, conservative, law-abiding element, may find itself represented before the bar of public opinion by the mob, or lawless element, which gives expression to its feelings and tendency in a manner that advertises the South throughout the world. Too often those who have no sympathy with such disregard of law are either silent or fail to speak in a sufficiently emphatic manner to offset, in any large degree, the unfortunate reputation which the lawless have too often made for many portions of the South.

Third. — No race or people ever got upon its feet without severe and constant struggle, often in the face of the greatest discouragement. While passing through the present trying period of its history, there is danger that a large and valuable element of the Negro race may become discouraged in the effort to better its condition. Every possible influence should be exerted to prevent this.

Fourth. — There is a possibility that harm may be done to the South and to the Negro by exaggerated newspaper articles which are written near the scene or in the midst of specially aggravating occurrences. Often these reports are written by newspaper men, who give the impression that there is a race conflict throughout the South, and that all Southern white people are opposed to the Negro's progress, overlooking the fact that, while in some sections there is trouble, in most parts of the South there is, nevertheless, a very large measure of peace, good will, and mutual helpfulness. In this same relation much can be done to retard the progress of the Negro by a certain class of Southern white people, who, in the midst of excitement, speak or write in a manner that gives the impression that all Negroes are lawless, untrustworthy, and shiftless. As an example, a Southern writer said not long ago, in a communication to the New York *Independent:* "Even in small towns the husband cannot venture to leave his wife alone for an hour at night. At no time, in no place, is the white woman safe from insults and assaults of these creatures." These statements, I presume, represented the feelings and the conditions that existed at the time they were written in one community or county in the South. But thousands of Southern white men and women would be ready to testify that this is not the condition throughout the South, nor throughout any one State.

Fifth. — Under the next head I would mention that, owing to the lack of school opportunities for the Negro in the rural districts of the South, there is danger that ignorance and idleness may increase to the extent of giving the Negro race a reputation for crime, and that immorality may eat its way into the moral fibre of the race, so as to retard its progress for many years. In judging the Negro in this regard, we must not be too harsh. We must remember that it has only been within the last thirty-four years that the black father and mother have had the responsibility, and consequently the experience, of training their own children. That they have not reached perfection in one generation, with the obstacles that the parents have been compelled to overcome, is not to be wondered at.

Sixth. — As a final source of danger to be guarded against, I would mention my fear that some of the white people of the South may be led to feel that the way to settle the race problem is to repress the aspirations of the Negro by legislation of a kind that confers certain legal or political privileges upon an ignorant and poor white man and withholds the same privileges from a black man in the same condition. Such legislation injures and retards the progress of both races. It is an injustice to the poor white man, because it takes from him incentive to secure education and property as prerequisites for voting. He feels that, because he is a white man, regardless of his possessions, a way will be found for him to vote. I would label all such measures, "Laws to keep the poor white man in ignorance and poverty."

As the Talladega *News Reporter*, a Democratic newspaper of Alabama, recently said: "But it is a weak cry when the white man asks odds on intelligence over the Negro. When nature has already so handicapped the African in the race for knowledge, the cry of the boasted Anglo-Saxon for still further odds seems babyish. What wonder that the world looks on in surprise, if not disgust. It cannot help but say, if our contention be true that the Negro is an inferior

379

race, that the odds ought to be on the other side, if any are to be given. And why not? No, the thing to do — the only thing that will stand the test of time — is to do right, exactly right, let come what will. And that right thing, as it seems to me, is to place a fair educational qualification before every citizen, — one that is self-testing, and not dependent on the wishes of weak men, letting all who pass the test stand in the proud ranks of American voters, whose votes shall be counted as cast, and whose sovereign will shall be maintained as law by all the powers that be. Nothing short of this will do. Every exemption, on whatsoever ground, is an outrage that can only rob some legitimate voter of his rights."

Such laws as have been made — as an example, in Mississippi — with the "understanding" clause hold out a temptation for the election officer to perjure and degrade himself by too often deciding that the ignorant white man does understand the Constitution when it is read to him and that the ignorant black man does not. By such a law the State not only commits a wrong against its black citizens; it injures the morals of its white citizens by conferring such a power upon any white man who may happen to be a judge of elections.

Such laws are hurtful, again, because they keep alive in the heart of the black man the feeling that the white man means to oppress him. The only safe way out is to set a high standard as a test of citizenship, and require blacks and whites alike to come up to it. When this is done, both will have a higher respect for the election laws and those who make them. I do not believe that, with his centuries of advantage over the Negro in the opportunity to acquire property and education as prerequisites for voting, the average white man in the South desires that any special law be passed to give him advantage over the Negro, who has had only a little more than thirty years in which to prepare himself for citizenship. In this relation another point of danger is that the Negro has been made to feel that it is his duty to oppose continually the Southern white man in politics, even in matters where no principle is involved, and that he is only loyal to his own race and acting in a manly way when he is opposing him. Such a policy has proved most hurtful to both races. Where it is a matter of principle, where a question of right or wrong is involved, I would advise the Negro to stand by principle at all hazards. A Southern white man has no respect for or confidence in a Negro who acts merely for policy's sake; but there are many cases — and the number is growing — where the Negro has nothing to gain and much to lose by opposing the Southern white man in many matters that relate to government.

Under these six heads I believe I have stated some of the main points which all high-minded white men and black men, North and South, will agree need our most earnest and thoughtful consideration, if we would hasten, and not hinder, the progress of our country.

As to the policy that should be pursued in a larger sense, — on this subject I claim to possess no superior wisdom or unusual insight. I may be wrong; I may be in some degree right.

In the future, more than in the past, we want to impress upon the Negro the importance of identifying himself more closely with the interests of the South, — the importance of making himself part of the South and at home in it. Heretofore, for reasons which were natural and for which no one is especially to blame, the coloured people have been too much like a foreign nation residing in the midst of another nation. If William Lloyd Garrison, Wendell Phillips, and George L. Stearns were alive to-day, I feel sure that each one of them would advise the Negroes to identify their interests as far as possible with those of the Southern white man, always with the understanding that this should be done where no question of right and wrong is involved. In no other way, it seems to me, can we get a foundation for peace and progress. He who advises against this policy will advise the Negro to do that which no people in history who have succeeded have done. The white man, North or South, who advises the Negro against it advises him to do that which he himself has not done. The bed-rock upon which every individual rests his chances of success in life is securing the friendship, the confidence, the respect, of his next-door neighbour of the little community in which he lives. Almost the whole problem of the Negro in the South rests itself upon the fact as to whether the Negro can make himself of such indispensable service to his neighbour and the community that no one can fill his place better in the body politic. There is at present no other safe course for the black man to pursue. If the Negro in the South has a friend in his white neighbour and a still larger number of friends in his community, he has a protection and a guarantee of his rights that will.

be more potent and more lasting than any our Federal Congress or any outside power can confer.

In a recent editorial the London *Times*, in discussing affairs in the Transvaal, South Africa, where Englishmen have been denied certain privileges by the Boers, says: "England is too sagacious not to prefer a gradual reform from within, even should it be less rapid than most of us might wish, to the most sweeping redress of grievances imposed from without. Our object is to obtain fair play for the outlanders, but the best way to do it is to enable them to help themselves." This policy, I think, is equally safe when applied to conditions in the South. The foreigner who comes to America, as soon as possible, identifies himself in business, education, politics, and sympathy with the community in which he settles. As I have said, we have a conspicuous example of this in the case of the Jews. Also, the Negro in Cuba has practically settled the race question there, because he has made himself a part of Cuba in thought and action.

What I have tried to indicate cannot be accomplished by any sudden revolution of methods, but it does seem that the tendency more and more should be in this direction. If a practical example is wanted in the direction that I favour, I will mention one. The North sends thousands of dollars into the South each year, for the education of the Negro. The teachers in most of the academic schools of the South are supported by the North, or Northern men and women of the highest Christian culture and most unselfish devotion. The Negro owes them a debt of gratitude which can never be paid. The various missionary societies in the North have done a work which, in a large degree, has been the salvation of the South; and the result will appear in future generations more than in this. We have now reached the point in the South where, I believe, great good could be accomplished by changing the attitude of the white people toward the Negro and of the Negro toward the whites, if a few white teachers of high character would take an active interest in the work of these high schools. Can this be done? Yes. The medical school connected with Shaw University at Raleigh, North Carolina, has from the first had as instructors and professors, almost exclusively, Southern white doctors, who reside in Raleigh; and they have given the highest satisfaction. This gives the people of Raleigh the feeling that this is their school, and not something located in, but not a part of, the South. In Augusta, Georgia, the Paine Institute, one of the best colleges for our people, is officered and taught almost wholly by Southern white men and women. The Presbyterian Theological School at Tuscaloosa, Alabama, has all Southern white men as instructors. Some time ago, at the Calhoun School in Alabama, one of the leading white men in the county was given an important position in the school. Since then the feeling of the white people in the county has greatly changed toward the school.

We must admit the stern fact that at present the Negro, through no choice of his own, is living among another race which is far ahead of him in education, property, experience, and favourable condition; further, that the Negro's present condition makes him dependent upon the white people for most of the things necessary to sustain life, as well as for his common school education. In all history, those who have possessed the property and intelligence have exercised the greatest control in government, regardless of colour, race, or geographical location. This being the case, how can the black man in the South improve his present condition? And does the Southern white man want him to improve it?

The Negro in the South has it within his power, if he properly utilises the forces at hand, to make of himself such a valuable factor in the life of the South that he will not have to seek privileges, they will be freely conferred upon him. To bring this about, the Negro must begin at the bottom and lay a sure foundation, and not be lured by any temptation into trying to rise on a false foundation. While the Negro is laying this foundation he will need help, sympathy, and simple justice. Progress by any other method will be but temporary and superficial, and the latter end of it will be worse than the beginning. American slavery was a great curse to both races, and I would be the last to apologise for it; but, in the presence of God, I believe that slavery laid the foundation for the solution of the problem that is now before us in the South. During slavery the Negro was taught every trade, every industry, that constitutes the foundation for making a living. Now, if on this foundation — laid in rather a crude way, it is true, but a foundation, nevertheless — we can gradually build and improve, the future for us is bright. Let me be more specific. Agriculture is, or has been, the basic industry of nearly every race or nation that has succeeded.

The Negro got a knowledge of this during slavery. Hence, in a large measure, he is in possession of this industry in the South to-day. The Negro can buy land in the South, as a rule, wherever the white man can buy it, and at very low prices. Now, since the bulk of our people already have a foundation in agriculture, they are at their best when living in the country, engaged in agricultural pursuits. Plainly, then, the best thing, the logical thing, is to turn the larger part of our strength in a direction that will make the Negro among the most skilled agricultural people in the world. The man who has learned to do something better than any one else, has learned to do a common thing in an uncommon manner, is the man who has a power and influence that no adverse circumstances can take from him. The Negro who can make himself so conspicuous as a successful farmer, a large tax-payer, a wise helper of his fellow-men, as to be placed in a position of trust and honour, whether the position be political or otherwise, by natural selection, is a hundred-fold more secure in that position than one placed there by mere outside force or pressure. I know a Negro, Hon. Isaiah T. Montgomery, in Mississippi, who is mayor of a town. It is true that this town, at present, is composed almost wholly of Negroes. Mr. Montgomery is mayor of this town because his genius, thrift, and foresight have created the town; and he is held and supported in his office by a charter, granted by the State of Mississippi, and by the vote and public sentiment of the community in which he lives.

Let us help the Negro by every means possible to acquire such an education in farming, dairying, stock-raising, horticulture, etc., as will enable him to become a model in these respects and place him near the top in these industries, and the race problem would in a large part be settled, or at least stripped of many of its most perplexing elements. This policy would also tend to keep the Negro in the country and smaller towns, where he succeeds best, and stop the influx into the large cities, where he does not succeed so well. The race, like the individual, that produces something of superior worth that has a common human interest, makes a permanent place for itself, and is bound to be recognised.

At a county fair in the South not long ago I saw a Negro awarded the first prize by a jury of white men, over white competitors, for the production of the best specimen of Indian corn. Every white man at this fair seemed to be pleased and proud of the achievement of this Negro, because it was apparent that he had done something that would add to the wealth and comfort of the people of both races in that county. At the Tuskegee Normal and Industrial Institute in Alabama we have a department devoted to training men in the science of agriculture; but what we are doing is small when compared with what should be done at Tuskegee and at other educational centres. In a material sense the South is still an undeveloped country. While race prejudice is strongly exhibited in many directions, in the matter of business, of commercial and industrial development, there is very little obstacle in the Negro's way. A Negro who produces or has for sale something that the community wants finds customers among white people as well as black people. A Negro can borrow money at the bank with equal security as readily as a white man can. A bank in Birmingham, Alabama, that has now existed ten years, is officered and controlled wholly by Negroes. This bank has white borrowers and white depositors. A graduate of the Tuskegee Institute keeps a well-appointed grocery store in Tuskegee, and he tells me that he sells about as many goods to the one race as to the other. What I have said of the opening that awaits the Negro in the direction of agriculture is almost equally true of mechanics, manufacturing, and all the domestic arts. The field is before him and right about him. Will he occupy it? Will he "cast down his bucket where he is"? Will his friends North and South encourage him and prepare him to occupy it? Every city in the South, for example, would give support to a first-class architect or house-builder or contractor of our race. The architect and contractor would not only receive support, but, through his example, numbers of young coloured men would learn such trades as carpentry, brick-masonry, plastering, painting, etc., and the race would be put into a position to hold on to many of the industries which it is now in danger of losing, because in too many cases brains, skill, and dignity are not imparted to the common occupations of life that are about his very door. Any individual or race that does not fit itself to occupy in the best manner the field or service that is right about it will sooner or later be asked to move on, and let some one else occupy it.

But it is asked, Would you confine the Negro to agriculture, mechanics, and domestic arts, etc.? Not at all; but along the lines that I have mentioned is where the stress should be laid just now and for many years to come. We will need and must have many teachers and ministers, some doctors and lawyers and statesmen; but these professional men will have a constituency or a foundation from which to draw support just in proportion as the race prospers along the economic lines that I have mentioned. During the first fifty or one hundred years of the life of any people are not the economic occupations always given the greater attention? This is not only the historic, but, I think, the common-sense view. If this generation will lay the material foundation, it will be the quickest and surest way for the succeeding generation to succeed in the cultivation of the fine arts, and to surround itself even with some of the luxuries of life, if desired. What the race now most needs, in my opinion, is a whole army of men and women well trained to lead and at the same time infuse themselves into agriculture, mechanics, domestic employment, and business. As to the mental training that these educated leaders should be equipped with, I should say, Give them all the mental training and culture that the circumstances of individuals will allow, — the more, the better. No race can permanently succeed until its mind is awakened and strengthened by the ripest thought. But I would constantly have it kept in the thoughts of those who are educated in books that a large proportion of those who are educated should be so trained in hand that they can bring this mental strength and knowledge to bear upon the physical conditions in the South which I have tried to emphasise.

Frederick Douglass, of sainted memory, once in addressing his race, used these words: "We are to prove that we can better our own condition. One way to do this is to accumulate property. This may sound to you like a new gospel. You have been accustomed to hear that money is the root of all evil, etc. On the other hand, property — money, if you please — will purchase for us the only condition by which any people can rise to the dignity of genuine manhood; for without property there can be no leisure, without leisure there can be no thought, without thought there can be no invention, without invention there can be no progress."

The Negro should be taught that material development is not an end, but simply a means to an end. As Professor W. E. B. DuBois puts it, "The idea should not be simply to make men carpenters, but to make carpenters men." The Negro has a highly religious temperament; but what he needs more and more is to be convinced of the importance of weaving his religion and morality into the practical affairs of daily life. Equally as much does he need to be taught to put so much intelligence into his labour that he will see dignity and beauty in the occupation, and love it for its own sake. The Negro needs to be taught that more of the religion that manifests itself in his happiness in the prayer-meeting should be made practical in the performance of his daily task. The man who owns a home and is in the possession of the elements by which he is sure of making a daily living has a great aid to a moral and religious life. What bearing will all this have upon the Negro's place in the South as a citizen and in the enjoyment of the privileges which our government confers?

To state in detail just what place the black man will occupy in the South as a citizen, when he has developed in the direction named, is beyond the wisdom of any one. Much will depend upon the sense of justice which can be kept alive in the breast of the American people. Almost as much will depend upon the good sense of the Negro himself. That question, I confess, does not give me the most concern just now. The important and pressing question is, Will the Negro with his own help and that of his friends take advantage of the opportunities that now surround him? When he has done this, I believe that, speaking of his future in general terms, he will be treated with justice, will be given the protection of the law, and will be given the recognition in a large measure which his usefulness and ability warrant. If, fifty years ago, any one had predicted that the Negro would have received the recognition and honour which individuals have already received, he would have been laughed at as an idle dreamer. Time, patience, and constant achievement are great factors in the rise of a race.

I do not believe that the world ever takes a race seriously, in its desire to enter into the control of the government of a nation in any large degree, until a large number of individuals, members of that race, have demonstrated, beyond question, their ability to control and develop individual business enterprises. When a number of Negroes rise to the point where they own and operate the most successful farms, are among the largest tax-payers in their county, are moral and intelligent, I do not believe that in many portions of the South such men need long be denied the right of saying by their votes how they prefer their property to be taxed and in choosing those who are to make and administer the laws.

In a certain town in the South, recently, I was on the street in company with the most prominent Negro in the town. While we were together, the mayor of the town sought out the black man, and said, "Next week we are going to vote on the question of issuing bonds to secure water-works for this town; you must be sure to vote on the day of election." The mayor did not suggest whether he must vote "yes" or "no"; he knew from the very fact that this Negro man owned nearly a block of the most valuable property in the town that he would cast a safe, wise vote on this important proposition. This white man knew that, because of this Negro's property interests in the city, he would cast his vote in the way he thought would benefit every white and black citizen in the town, and not be controlled by influences a thousand miles away. But a short time ago I read letters from nearly every prominent white man in Birmingham, Alabama, asking that the Rev. W. R. Pettiford, a Negro, be appointed to a certain important federal office. What is the explanation of this? Mr. Pettiford for nine years has been the president of the Negro bank in Birmingham to which I have alluded. During these nine years these white citizens have had the opportunity of seeing that Mr. Pettiford could manage successfully a private business, and that he had proven himself a conservative, thoughtful citizen; and they were willing to trust him in a public office. Such individual examples will have to be multiplied until they become the rule rather than the exception. While we are multiplying these examples, the Negro must keep a strong and courageous heart. He cannot improve his condition by any short-cut course or by artificial methods. Above all, he must not be deluded into the temptation of believing that his condition can be permanently improved by a mere battledore and shuttlecock of words or by any process of mere mental gymnastics or oratory alone. What is desired, along with a logical defence of his cause, are deeds, results, — multiplied results, — in the direction of building himself up, so as to leave no doubt in the minds of any one of his ability to succeed.

An important question often asked is, Does the white man in the South want the Negro to improve his present condition? I say, "Yes." From the Montgomery (Alabama) *Daily Advertiser* I clip the following in reference to the closing of a coloured school in a town in Alabama: —

"Eufaula, May 25, 1899.

"The closing exercises of the city coloured public school were held at St. Luke's A. M. E. Church last night, and were witnessed by a large gathering, including many white. The recitations by the pupils were excellent, and the music was also an interesting feature. Rev. R. T. Pollard[6] delivered the address, which was quite an able one; and the certificates were presented by Professor T. L. McCoy, white, of the Sanford Street School. The success of the exercises reflects great credit on Professor S. M. Murphy, the principal, who enjoys a deservedly good reputation as a capable and efficient educator."

I quote this report, not because it is the exception, but because such marks of interest in the education of the Negro on the part of the Southern white people can be seen almost every day in the local papers. Why should white people, by their presence, words, and many other things, encourage the black man to get education, if they do not desire him to improve his condition?

The Paine Institute in Augusta, Georgia, an excellent institution, to which I have already referred, is supported almost wholly by the Southern white Methodist church. The Southern white Presbyterians support a theological school at Tuscaloosa, Alabama, for Negroes. For a number of years the Southern white Baptists have contributed toward Negro education. Other denominations have done the same. If these people do not want the Negro educated to a high standard, there is no reason why they should act the hypocrite in these matters.

As barbarous as some of the lynchings in the South have been, Southern white men here and there, as well as newspapers, have spoken out strongly against lynching. I quote from the address of the Rev. Mr. Vance,[7] of Nashville, Tennessee, delivered before the National Sunday School Union in Atlanta, not long since, as an example: —

"And yet, as I stand here to-night, a Southerner speaking for my

6 Robert Thomas Pollard of Selma, Ala., was born in slavery in Gainesville, Ala., in 1860. A graduate of Selma University in 1886, he became a Baptist clergyman and later returned to Selma University, where he served twenty-one years as its president.

7 James J. Vance, a minister of the Methodist Episcopal Church.

section, and addressing an audience from all sections, there is one foul blot upon the fair fame of the South, at the bare mention of which the heart turns sick and the cheek is crimsoned with shame. I want to lift my voice to-night in loud and long and indignant protest against the awful horror of mob violence, which the other day reached the climax of its madness and infamy in a deed as black and brutal and barbarous as can be found in the annals of human crime.

"I have a right to speak on the subject, and I propose to be heard. The time has come for every lover of the South to set the might of an angered and resolute manhood against the shame and peril of the lynch demon. These people, whose fiendish glee taunts their victim as his flesh crackles in the flames, do not represent the South. I have not a syllable of apology for the sickening crime they meant to avenge. But it is high time we were learning that lawlessness is no remedy for crime. For one, I dare to believe that the people of my section are able to cope with crime, however treacherous and defiant, through their courts of justice; and I plead for the masterful sway of a righteous and exalted public sentiment that shall class lynch law in the category with crime."

It is a notable and praiseworthy fact that no Negro educated in any of our larger institutions of learning in the South has been charged with any of the recent crimes connected with assaults upon females.

If we go on making progress in the directions that I have tried to indicate, more and more the South will be drawn to one course. As I have already said, it is not for the best interests of the white race of the South that the Negro be deprived of any privilege guaranteed him by the Constitution of the United States. This would put upon the South a burden under which no government could stand and prosper. Every article in our federal Constitution was placed there with a view of stimulating and encouraging the highest type of citizenship. To permanently tax the Negro without giving him the right to vote as fast as he qualifies himself in education and property for voting would work the alienation of the affections of the Negro from the States in which he lives, and would be the reversal of the fundamental principles of government for which our States have stood. In other ways than this the injury would be as great to the white man as to the Negro. Taxation without the hope of becoming a voter would take away from one-third the citizens of the Gulf States their interest in government and their stimulant to become tax-payers or to secure education, and thus be able and willing to bear their share of the cost of education and government, which now weighs so heavily upon the white tax-payers of the South. The more the Negro is stimulated and encouraged, the sooner will he be able to bear a larger share of the burdens of the South. We have recently had before us an example, in the case of Spain, of a government that left a large portion of its citizens in ignorance, and neglected their highest interests.

As I have said elsewhere, there is no escape through law of man or God from the inevitable: —

> "The laws of changeless justice bind
>   Oppressor with opprest;
> And, close as sin and suffering joined,
>   We march to fate abreast."

"Nearly sixteen millions of hands will aid you in pulling the load upward or they will pull against you the load downward. We shall constitute one-third and more of the ignorance and crime of the South or one-third its intelligence and progress. We shall contribute one-third to the business and industrial prosperity of the South or we shall prove a veritable body of death, stagnating, depressing, retarding, every effort to advance the body politic."

My own feeling is that the South will gradually reach the point where it will see the wisdom and the justice of enacting an educational or property qualification, or both, for voting, that shall be made to apply honestly to both races. The industrial development of the Negro in connection with education and Christian character will help to hasten this end. When this is done, we shall have a foundation, in my opinion, upon which to build a government that is honest and that will be in a high degree satisfactory to both races.

I do not suffer myself to take too optimistic a view of the conditions in the South. The problem is a large and serious one, and will require the patient help, sympathy, and advice of our most patriotic citizens, North and South, for years to come. But I believe that, if the principles which I have tried to indicate are followed, a solution of the question will come. So long as the Negro is permitted to get education, acquire property, and secure employ-

391

ment, and is treated with respect in the business or commercial world, — as is now true in the greater part of the South, — I shall have the greatest faith in his working out his own destiny in our Southern States. The education and preparing for citizenship of nearly eight millions of people is a tremendous task, and every lover of humanity should count it a privilege to help in the solution of a great problem for which our whole country is responsible.

Extracts from an Address in Birmingham

Birmingham, Alabama, January 1, 1900

I wish to congratulate you among other things upon the excellent and far reaching work that has been done in Birmingham and vicinity through the wide and helpful influence of the Alabama Penny Savings Bank. Few organizations of any description in this country among our people have helped us more, not only in cultivating the habit of saving, but in bringing to us the confidence and respect of the white race. We must make up our minds that in order to be respected we must cultivate habits of economy, thrift and industry. No people who spend all that they make, can ever attain to any high degree of success. No matter how much education they may receive, they will not be respected so long as they are without bank accounts and without homes. There is no question but that one of the weak points of the race is that we lack in too large a degree the saving habit. We are too much inclined to spend all that we earn at the end of the week or yield too often to the temptation when we get a few dollars ahead to cease work until all of that is spent. I most earnestly advise you to save money, not so much for money's sake, but because a bank account represents foresight, self-denial, thrift and economy.

The people who save money, who make themselves intelligent, and live moral lives, are the ones who are going to control the destinies of the country. Our children should be taught from their youth to save money. There is no more useful lesson that can be taught in our schools, than the habit of saving pennies and nickels. Every school, so far as possible, should have its savings bank department. In this same connection it is most important that we bear in mind that we can never attain any high degree of success until we own our homes and until we cease to live in rented cabins in dirty, filthy alleys. Many of us throw away enough money every two or three years, to buy a respectable home. Whenever a man owns a home, he begins to respect himself, begins to take pride in keeping that home clean and attractive and in making himself and family happy and comfortable. The home is the foundation upon which our civilization is based. If it is weak, all else will be uncertain and unsatisfactory.

I believe that the habit of saving has a great deal to do with one's moral and even religious character. While we have a great number of colored ministers in the South whose lives are in every way all that could be expected, on the other hand we must acknowledge that still a very large number of our colored ministers are morally unfit for their work. We can gain nothing by attempting to smother or overlook this unwholesome truth. Improvment is going on from year to year in the character of the ministers, but such improvement will only continue in proportion as the minister is made to feel that the weight of public sentiment is in the right direction. There are far too many ministers and others who have received a little education, who are travelling from one end of the country to the other, trying to live by their wits and by every scheme known to man, except by hard and earnest and honest work. At one time they are in politics, at another time they are preaching, at another time they are organizing some cheap and uncertain society for the purpose of extorting money from people by unholy means. We must give our ministers and teachers to understand that they cannot remain in our pulpits or cannot remain as our teachers, unless they live correct lives. What seems the hardest course to pursue, is often the easiest in the long run. When a minister acts wrong, it is a great deal better to hold him up as an example before the world, instead of trying to shield his sins by transferring him from one district to another. When once the minister understands that the people are going to tolerate no immorality, no weakness on their part, we will have an improved pulpit. Many of these so-called ministers are led into evil ways because they are trying to live without work. They have church organizations that are too weak to support them and instead of going to work, they attempt to live by scheming and thereby bring disgrace upon the whole race. I repeat that in Birmingham, Montgomery and throughout Alabama, there are as upright ministers as can be found among any race, and I am glad to note a tendency among the bishops and other church officials to be more strict in the standard required of the ministers, but, notwithstanding all of this I repeat that we ourselves must make great progress before the ministry will be brought to that point where it will have the confidence and respect of the people to the extent that it should have.

TM   Con. 955   BTW Papers   DLC.

To Timothy Thomas Fortune

Tuskegee, Ala., Jan. 2, 1900

Dear Mr. Fortune: Enclosed I send an article which I thought you might be able to get into the Transcript in the form of an editorial.[1] Do not use my name in connection with it to anybody. If you can get Mr. Clement to print it as coming from you I think it will do good. I can scatter the papers pretty well in the South. Yours very truly,

Booker T. Washington

TLS Con. 172 BTW Papers DLC.

[1] See An Item from the Boston *Transcript*, Jan. 6, 1900, below.

To Timothy Thomas Fortune

Tuskegee, Ala., Jan. 3, 1900

Dear Mr. Fortune: I am very glad to have your last letter written from Washington. The more I think of it the more I am inclined to favor the Heath scheme and I want to do whatever I can to help it forward. I have written to-day to Prof. Wright regarding it. If you will keep me informed I shall be very glad to assist in the matter.

I cannot understand some of our people. Prof. Grisham in Kansas City has been making and is making a desperate effort to secure money from the City to establish an Industrial School in connection with his work. How a man can favor a thing and oppose it at the same time is past my understanding.

I saw the Associated Press dispatch to which you refer in reference to the Virginia Superintendent's report, but I have not seen the report in full and I cannot glean from the dispatch whether he favors my views or opposes them.

I am very glad to know that Mrs. Fortune has gone to Jacksonville; if she could come by here on her return North Mrs. Washington would be very glad indeed to have her do so. We have the opening of our Trades' Building next week and shall be very busy with it. After next week I shall go West on a lecturing tour, going as far as Denver and Omaha.

I am very glad to know that matters went off in such a satisfactory manner in connection with the Executive Committee of the National Council. As yet the Pullman car people have taken no step in regard to preventing Negroes from riding in their cars. I went to Atlanta a few nights ago mainly to test them and nothing was said. Proctor rode between Atlanta and Macon the same day without any trouble. Yours very truly,

Booker T. Washington

TLS Con. 172 BTW Papers DLC.

From Richard W. Thompson

Washington, D.C., Jan. 3, 1900

Dear Mr. Washington: Your very kind letter of December 29 was handed to me this morning by Mr. Cooper. As usual, I was glad to hear from you. I must here congratulate you upon the splendid progress you are making toward Tuskegee's $500,000 endowment fund. I heartily appreciate the friendly sentiments expressed with reference to myself, and am deeply grateful for your timely assistance. I cannot refrain from saying that of all the public men I know today, I look upon you as my warmest and staunchest friend. It shall be my aim to prove worthy of the confidence you have reposed in me.

Ere you receive this you will have doubtless learned through Gov. Merriam[1] that I am on the Census Roll at $600 per annum, and credited to your quota. As I have taken no examination this is not at all bad, and Mr. Langley[2] assures me that I can be examined after a little bit, and when thus qualified, promotion to $900 will follow. They seem to think a great deal of you in this Bureau. I have been assigned to the Division of Manufactures, under E. W. Parker,[3] special expert agent, who is also Director of the Geological Survey. He asked that I be sent to him, when he learned that you were my sponsor, remarking that "any young man whom Booker Washington indorses, is certain to be all right." We have very pleasant quarters in the old Post Office building, 7th and F streets. The apartments are newly fitted up and are bright and cheerful. The heads are gentlemen of the best caliber and I think we can get along agreeably.

While $50 per month is not a fortune, it is a living. My wife also has a place at the Government Printing Office, worth about $40 per mo. By observing your advice "to stick close to Merriam" and attending to business he will do better for me after we "get warm" in the office. I shall continue with Cooper, writing the editorials and special features, and I expect shortly to take hold of several good papers and write general letters. In this way I can help my friends and not lose my own identity. Any suggestions looking to means by which I can further your work, will be welcomed at any time. Thanking you for many favors past and present, not forgetting the fine engraving just sent, I am   Ever your friend,

R. W. Thompson

Address in future, "Geological Survey"
I return herewith the Merriam letter. It is quite encouraging. Will keep you advised of conditions as they come.

T

ALS   Con. 185   BTW Papers   DLC.

1 William Rush Merriam (1849-1931) was a former governor of Minnesota (1889-93) and director of the twelfth U.S. Census (1899-1903).

2 John W. Langley, born in Kentucky, was appointment clerk for the twelfth U.S. Census.

3 Edward W. Parker, born in Maryland, was a statistician for the U.S. Geological Survey.

From John Robert E. Lee[1]

[Tuskegee, Ala.] Jan. 3– 1900

Dear Mr. Washington, I am puzzled to know what the last assignment of work means. Yesterday, I had handed to me an assignment of six (6) classes each day and two (2) at night: making eight (8) recitations to be heard each day; besides, I am required to look up the mathematics — study the best methods and advise with the teachers of mathematics — and am held responsible that all the work in mathematics be done well. Leaving out the question of directing the mathematics, I cannot see how any teacher with *extraordinary* ability can prepare and teach *well* 8 classes a day. I can "keep" 8 classes a day but no man can *teach them* well. It has been truly said by a great educator that "a *good teacher* can teach 3 or 4 classes each day; a poor teacher can teach 5 or 6 classes each day and a *humbug* and *intellectual wrecker* can teach 7 or 8 or even any number of classes each day."

Mr. Washington, I have given the work of *teaching* the most earnest study for more than ten years and I am convinced that every institution in the land that professes to do really first-class work, has found it necessary to have each teacher make special preparation for every class he or she is to teach. *The lower* the *class the more careful the preparation.*

Our school work here will be the object of adverse criticism as long as this course is taken. I am here to give my heart's interest for the best good of Tuskegee. I am here for *all* I am *able to do.* If I did not feel most heartily interested in it I would not say a word, I would go on and "keep" my pupils.

The teacher *must,* if he teaches correctly, study other text books besides the one in hand — he *must study other methods than his own* — consult the journals of education and be fresh for good class work.

Mr. Washington, Tuskegee's reputation and possibilities call for a different class of work from that which a teacher is able to do with such a daily assignment.

If any of the visitors of next week are *teachers* and are studying the work of teaching I shall be very sorry to have them know about this particular feature of our work. They will know, *without examination* that the work *must be poorly done* — if a teacher is attempting 8 classes each day.

I regard teaching as sacred a work as the ministry and should be as *conscientiously* done as *true ministerial work.*

I do not want you to feel that I am seeking leisure. I *have none* — want none — have never had any. *Work* is all I know.

I put in every moment of today endeavoring to be able to teach the next and tomorrow's classes better. I *came here* to *work* — to do the *best work* not the *poorest* and to *help* the *institution*. Every moment is spent in that effort. I am in hearty sympathy with all the work — the Industrial as well as the literary.

These words are prompted out of a heart full of interest for our best good.

When I have a moment I get hold of the teachers journals or go into the other classes to suggest and help the work.

Under the present arrangement when am I to look over papers handed in by my pupils? Converse with my mathematical teachers? Visit the classes? How can I be held responsible for the class of work which is done in mathematics?

Surely you will take up this matter and relieve me and others, if any, who are thus confronted or hampered.[2]

There are country schools which are run on the method of one teacher having 8, 10 and 12 classes a day — the result of which we see in the utter ignorance and stupidity of many of our pupils here today — but no institution which stands for what Tuskegee does can afford to adopt this course of dwarfing teachers and *half-teaching* pupils. I am yours to serve in advancing Tuskegee,

J. R. E. Lee

ALS Con. 272 BTW Papers DLC.

[1] John Robert E. Lee (1864-1944) was born and reared in Texas and was a graduate of Bishop College at Marshall, Tex. He taught mathematics at Tuskegee from 1899 to 1904 when he joined the staff of Benedict College at Columbia, S.C. From 1904 to 1909 he also was president of the National Association of Teachers in Colored Schools. In 1906 he returned to Tuskegee Institute as director of the academic department, a position he held until 1915. During his tenure at Tuskegee, Lee was a promoter of the Alabama State Teachers' Association and the NNBL. Lee moved to Kansas City, Mo., and from 1915 to 1921 was principal of Lincoln High School. He was active in black social life in Kansas City as an organizer and promoter of clubs and charitable work. From 1921 to 1924 he was extension secretary for the National Urban League assigned the task of fund-raising among blacks. From 1924 to 1944 he was president of Florida A & M College at Tallahassee, where he administered a reorganization of the school and brought in new funds from such agencies as the General Education Board, the Rosenwald Fund, and the Carnegie Foundation that resulted in an expansion of campus facilities. (See Neyland and Riley, *History of Florida A & M University*.)

[2] Leonora Love Chapman Kenniebrew also complained to BTW about her work assignment. She wrote: "May I presume to criticise the action of the Council in deciding that teachers must work all day and at night?" She believed that many teachers would do inferior work in the classroom not because of a lack of ability but from overwork. (Jan. 8, 1900, Con. 177, BTW Papers, DLC.)

399

From William Denison McCrackan[1]

New York   Jan. 4th 1900

Mr. Booker T. Washington, dear sir — I am in receipt of a letter from you setting forth the needs of Tuskegee Normal and Industrial Institute. Allow me to tell you how much I admire the noble spirit which animates your enterprise and to wish you a successful New Year. Mr. Edwin D. Mead[2] and others of my friends have repeatedly called my attention to your work, so that I am more or less familiar with it.

I regret that I have no funds available from which I could send you a contribution, but, if I may, I should like to send you a thought in regard to this whole question of education.

Unfortunately it can never become a fundamental cure for the persistance of poverty in the midst of advancing wealth. What you are doing is noble work, fine work. It is saving individuals but do not allow yourself to believe that you can save your race thereby. Chattel slavery is now abolished, but industrial slavery remains for both black and white, and education cannot abolish that.

Poverty and suffering among the masses are not due to lack of education, but to land monopoly, to the locking up of natural opportunities. Wealth can only be produced by the access of labor to land in its various forms, such as building sites, agricultural lands, forests, mines etc.

Education can avail the individual only in so far as it makes him superior to his fellows, but if you succeed in raising the educational standard of your whole race, wages will not rise, because wages do not depend upon the real earnings of labor, but upon what is left to labor after rent is taken out. In other words the more intelligently your race works, the harder they strain, the higher will their rents rise.

I cannot attempt to do justice to this thought in a short letter and therefore, I send you a book under another cover.

With the best of good wishes I remain yours truly

W. D. McCrackan

ALS   Con. 158   BTW Papers   DLC.

[1] William Denison McCrackan of New York was born in Germany in 1864. He

was the author of several books on Switzerland and was president of the Manhattan Single-Tax Club.

2 Edwin Doak Mead (1849-1937) was a prominent Boston reformer and editor of the *New England Magazine*. He was opposed to the Spanish-American War, and was a staunch anti-imperialist. Mead was active in the American Peace Society, and in 1910 was a founder of the World Peace Foundation.

From Walter Hines Page

New York   January 5th, 1900

Dear Mr Washington: I acknowledge your letter of Dec. 28th which reached me a little belated on account of an absence of a few days from New York, and a copy of Dr Abbott's letter which you enclosed.[1]

The Doubleday & McClure Co, Book Publishers, have, as I presume you know, become independent of the S.S. McClure Co which owns the McClure Magazine; and I have become a partner in the Doubleday & McClure Company which in a little while, as soon as the legal formalities can be complied with, will become Doubleday, Page & Company.

I am not sure whether you knew of this change or not, but of course this makes no change with reference to your book about which we talked and to which we look forward with an increasing interest. I do heartily hope that you will very soon get the technical permission of the western publishers to go ahead with the narrative. I am made the more eager about it by reading "The Future of the American Negro" as well as by such a circumstance, of course, as Dr Abbott's letter.

I do not know whether we have ever talked definitely of publishing terms to you, but if we have not, when you get back to New York we will enter into a definite bargain about the book rights on terms which I have no hesitancy in assuring you now will be satisfactory to you. Nor have I any doubt about the success of the book. In my eyes, and in yours, the principal element of success is, of course, the effect it will have on public opinion and its influence in furthering the good cause. But incidentally I think it stands a very good chance, too, of reaching a very considerable financial success. All this we will go over and bring to a definite bargain when you come again, or sooner, if you wish.

Now concerning the serial rights. Since we have nothing directly to do with McClure's Magazine but are of course upon the friendliest possible terms with Mr McClure, Mr Phillips[2] and Mr Finley, I shall set about at once getting a definite proposition for you from them about the serial publication, and I will write to you as soon as I can. Unfortunately both Mr McClure and Mr Phillips are in Europe, but if Mr Finley can make a definite bargain, I will have him do so tomorrow when I will see him (by the way we have moved to 34 Union Square East). I know that the McClure people want at least a part of the narrative, and I think there will be no difficulty in my getting from them for you a definite proposition; but in case they do not, of course the thing to do is to accept Dr Abbott's proposition, for he has in some respects just as good a channel as McClure's Magazine although the "Outlook" does not reach as many people as McClure's. I shall attend to all this matter for you with great pleasure, and whatever arrangements we can help you to make for serial publication I shall make with great pleasure as a means of furthering a good work, we of course to have the book when the book is ready.

Busy as I am I do not think that I could be tempted to write a book review for anybody or about any book except about "The Future of the Negro," but when "The Book Buyer" asked me the other day to write something about it, I could not resist; so that in addition to seven days' labor a week with my own business I am trying to find an eighth day in some week to do this.[3] With kind regards, Very heartily yours,

Walter H. Page

TLS Con. 181 BTW Papers DLC.

[1] Presumably the letter of Dec. 9, 1899, above.

[2] John Sanborn Phillips (1861-1949), an editor and publisher, was a partner of S. S. McClure beginning in 1882. From 1893 to 1906 Phillips was manager and treasurer of *McClure's Magazine*. He was editor of the *American Magazine* from 1906 to 1915, and advisory editor from 1915 to 1938.

[3] Page's review praised the book and its author. "No other man," he wrote, "has worked out so completely, or so thoroughly tested, a plan for the building-up of the Negro population in the South as Mr. Washington." Page described the book as "intensely practical," and said, "There is not a phase of the whole complex problem

that he does not take up in this little book. . . ." He was critical, however, of the "literary crudities" and some organizational problems that blemished the book. (*Book Buyer*, 20 [Mar. 1900], 144-45.)

James B. Washington to the Tuskegee Institute Finance Committee

Tuskegee, Ala., Jany., 5th '00

To Finance Committee: Last May I was informed that my salary was to be raised $3.00, but I find it hasn't been done, according to notification. For 5 or 6 years I have been allowed $47. per month and an additional $2.00 was given me for services in the band, making $49. for services. I am now informed that you intended me to have $1. more. If, after working 6 years my services are not worth more than a $1. raise, I prefer it to remain as it was at first. I should not for a moment, ask for such a raise, after such long service for low wages. I dont make this assertion because I dont need the dollar, but because I feel that I either deserve more of a raise than that or nothing. Hoping if that is the case you will please rectify it as soon as possible. I understand my salary was to be 50. and the $2.00 was to stand as it has always done. I received the increase in my salary beginning June 1 and throughout the Summer, when there was no band and am confident that you didn't mean to cut off the am't received in the band. The $3.00 raise should not interfere with what I have already been receiving. Resp.

J. B. Washington

ALS   Con. 186   BTW Papers   DLC.

An Item in the Boston *Transcript*[1]

Boston, January 6, 1900

A PITIABLE SPECTACLE IN GEORGIA

A very pitiable spectacle took place a few days ago in Georgia, one that perhaps could have taken place nowhere in the civilized

world but in the United States. The occurrence is mainly important in showing how much is necessary to be done for our country
before we can boast that we are a highly civilized and really Christian people. The senior bishop in a great arm of the Christian
Church, while in the performance of his duties in Savannah, was
stricken with paralysis as the result of over-work. Bishop Henry M.
Turner, who has travelled in nearly all the foreign countries, has
been entertained by British royalty, breakfasted with Gladstone,
been the guest of the queen of Spain, preached in scores of white
pulpits in the South, and is greatly esteemed for his moral worth
and usefulness. When stricken by disease and asked to be permitted to ride in a sleeping-car from Savannah to Atlanta, was refused, because he was born a Negro. The fellow-Christians in
Georgia of this great bishop, those who pray every Sabbath that the
Lord may turn the heathen from their ways to the ways of the
Christians, the Christian officials of the Georgia road told the sick
man that, notwithstanding he was almost helpless, the high state of
Christian civilization existing in Georgia would not permit the
road to allow him to have a berth in the sleeping-car.

It was a pitiable spectacle, not that Bishop Turner, who was
thus treated, is to be pitied so much as the white men who perpetrated the heartless act. It seems strange that in this enlightened
day any white men could be found in America whose hearts can
be so hardened to natural impulses, to kindness, who are so far
without sympathy, sense of justice, to say nothing of manhood, as
to thus treat a fellow-man. But the old institution that placed one
class of men beneath the others brutalized everything it touched,
and we are still having manifestations of its influence. For our part
we would rather be in Bishop Turner's place a thousand times
over than in the place of those who degraded themselves by trying
to degrade a Christian gentleman. Through it all Bishop Turner
was great, truly great. Without a murmur, without a complaint,
this man suffered himself to be carried in his feebleness into the
filthy "Jim Crow" car, fully conscious of the fact that no human
being could degrade his soul. He was sustained by the fact that
even in the poorly ventilated, tobacco-scented car he could be
great in soul, in purpose, could pray for those who would despite-
fully use him.

This brutal act of the Georgia Railroad was perpetrated before the new separate sleeping-car law of Georgia had become operative. If other Southern States should adopt similar legislation, in conjunction with the prevailing separate car laws of those States, it will make it extremely difficult and annoying for self-respecting Afro-Americans to travel below the Potomac River.

Boston *Transcript*, Jan. 6, 1900, 16.

1 BTW drafted this unsigned editorial except for the last sentence, which was added by T. Thomas Fortune. (See BTW to Fortune, Jan. 9, 1900, below.) BTW often sent information or editorial matter to the Boston *Transcript* or the New York *Evening Post* that was bolder than his conservative public utterances. On Jan. 8, 1900, after seeing the editorial in print, Fortune wrote to BTW: "There are more ways to kill a cat than one." (Con. 172, BTW Papers, DLC.)

To Timothy Thomas Fortune

Tuskegee, Ala., Jan. 9, 1900

Dear Mr. Fortune: I see the Bishop Turner editorial appeared in the Transcript of January 6th and shows up well. I am sorry that you added the last sentence; it will I fear serve as a pointer to Southern legislatures and to the Pullman car people themselves as to the method that can be pursued in excluding our people from sleeping cars altogether.

We have the dedication of our new building tomorrow and I wish that you could be here. Yours truly,

Booker T. Washington

TLS   Con. 172   BTW Papers   DLC.

From Edgar Gardner Murphy[1]

Montgomery, Alabama. January 9, 1900

My Dear Dr. Washington: I venture to write you briefly this morning in order to call your attention to the enclosed clipping from The Montgomery Advertiser of this date.[2] May I ask you to be kind enough to give the clipping a full and interested reading? We believe that Southern sentiment, if given such expression as we propose, will demonstrate to the world that the two races are now trying in the South to be fair to each other, and we hope that our conference will have a deep educational influence, not only upon the negroes and the whites at the South, but upon the public mind at large. On your next trip through Montgomery, will you not stop with us a few hours for a personal conference with certain members of the Executive Committee? We believe that you can give us suggestions which will be of large and serious use both to ourselves and to our common cause. We shall also be glad, in case you can give us your interest and co-operation to furnish you with further copies of this clipping, in order that you may send them to any whom you may wish to interest. If such a conference can secure the national interest which it deserves, and if visitors can be brought to Montgomery from the various quarters of our country, the movement should be of great benefit not only to the South in general, but to our State School, and to Tuskegee in particular. You will see, I am sure, why we have taken such pains to guard ourselves from misapprehension by certain classes of our Southern whites. We must first secure the interest, confidence and co-operation of the white people of the South, or the conference will be unrepresentative and valueless. But you will also find among us, I am sure, the fullest appreciation of all the nobler aspirations and the marvellous progress of your own race. As Major Screws, the Editor of the Advertiser, pointed out in his address at our meeting, it is impossible for us to deal with this question as though the interests of the whites and the blacks were in conflict. That standpoint has been forever abandoned by the thinking men of the North and South. We realize that the welfare of each race is involved in the welfare of the other; that whatever is a difficulty for one, is a difficulty for both; and that the true removal of difficulties must open the way of development for all the classes of our population.

Asking your interest and co-operation, and awaiting your reply as to an interview in Montgomery, I am   Cordially and Faithfully yours,

Edgar Gardner Murphy

TLS Con. 179 BTW Papers DLC.

1 Edgar Gardner Murphy (1869-1913) was a Protestant Episcopal clergyman in Montgomery and one of the organizers of A Southern Society for the Consideration

of Race Problems in Relation to the Welfare of the South, which held the Montgomery Race Conference in May 1900. Born in Fort Smith, Ark., Murphy attended school in San Antonio, Tex., the University of the South, Sewanee, Tenn., and the General Theological Seminary in New York City. Active in Montgomery civic affairs, beginning with his pastorate at St. John's Church in 1898, he helped found an Episcopal church for blacks, was instrumental in establishing the YMCA and YWCA in the city, and was a founder of the Carnegie Library in Montgomery. In 1903 Murphy resigned from the ministry to devote more time to the cause of child labor reform and the Southern Education Movement.

In the South Murphy was a racial liberal who had publicly condemned lynching in 1893, but his paternalism toward blacks, his fear of publicly offending more racist individuals, and his strong sectional bias greatly limited his ability to be a champion of blacks. He hoped that the Montgomery Race Conference would lead to a new dialogue on the race question, but with blacks excluded from participation and many speakers advocating repeal of the Fifteenth Amendment, the conference was clearly in the hands of conservative whites and reflected the white supremacy movement more than it did a spirit of progressivism. The Southern Society planned to have a series of conferences on race but after the first meeting no more followed. Murphy found no city willing to be host to a second conference, and some members of the Southern Society feared that any further conferences might bring forth more extreme opinions that would only polarize thought on the subject. (Bailey, *Edgar Gardner Murphy*, 52.) Murphy turned to another cause, child labor, and became the first chairman of the Alabama Child Labor Committee in 1901. He was a founder of the National Child Labor Committee in 1904 but resigned in 1907 when he broke with Albert J. Beveridge and others who sponsored a national child labor bill. Murphy opposed federal child labor legislation and firmly believed that it was a matter for the states to decide. His opposition to the bill was largely responsible for its defeat.

From 1903 to 1908 Murphy served as the first executive secretary of the Southern Education Board. He promoted the concept of universal education and believed that education was the key to the solution of the race problem. Murphy, like other southern progressives, was afraid to antagonize white supremacists by radical measures, and hoped instead to win them over by reason, tact, and good will. His plight represented the paradox of progressivism in the South. By supporting the concept of universal education, he hoped black education would somehow also prosper. By 1907, however, Murphy lamented: "Passionate and rapidly developing enthusiasm for white education is bearing sharply and adversely upon the opportunities of the negro." (Harlan, *Separate and Unequal*, 254.)

Murphy wrote *Problems of the Present South* (1904), an exploration of educational conditions in the South, and *The Basis of Ascendancy* (1909), a discussion of the race problem. Murphy was in poor health most of his life, and his worsening physical condition led to his retirement in 1908. He spent his last years in New York. From the roof of his apartment he studied the heavens and wrote *A Beginner's Star Book* (1912) under the pseudonym of Kelvin McKready.

2 No enclosure was found with the letter. Presumably the clipping was an announcement of the forthcoming Montgomery Race Conference.

From Max Bennett Thrasher

New York, Jan. 9th, 1900

Dear Mr. Washington: The copy containing the reference to Mr. Carnegie came this morning — pages 214 to 219 — in season to go in with the other in next week's chapter. That made a good long chapter, over 4,000 words, and a very interesting one.

When I went down with it I happened to meet Mr. Lawrence Abbott[1] and Mr. R. D. Townsend[2] together in the latter's office. In the course of the conversation which followed Mr. Abbott began to speak of things that he wished you would touch upon — merely expressing his own personal interest, just as any one might in a chance talk. When he found that I was making notes of what he was saying, with the intention of sending his suggestions to you, he was much distressed for fear you would think that he had been criticising, but I told him I knew you would not, and that you would be glad of the suggestions. He said that he wished you would talk about yourself more, not, as he was careful to explain, that he was not intensely interested in Tuskegee, but that he was more interested in you. He felt that the personal element in such a life as yours was tremendously interesting and valuable.

He dwelt at some length upon the possibilities in your English trip; said emphasize little details. He would like to know what steamer you crossed on, if you had ever been before, if you were sea sick, your impressions of the ocean, and of the voyage, if you went about the steamer (engine room, etc.) if you got acquainted with the captain, steward, etc. Whom you met on board, how you were treated, etc. Then your impressions of Europe very fully, people you met, etc. He spoke particularly of what you thought of the treatment by masters and mistresses there of their servants — whether you thought England was more or less democratic than this country. He said give them a long chapter all about that — one chapter that should be all of it "away from Tuskegee." He said "for instance we know what Hawthorne, Holmes, Lowell, Howells thought of England. Let us know what Booker Washington thinks of it."

He spoke also of your tours through the west. The impressions you receive, characteristics of different cities and sections, people you meet. (He spoke particularly of Pres. Cleveland, there.) He also said that for himself he did wish that you felt that you could touch more on politics.

He spoke particularly of your reading; if you found time to read, and if so what books most interest you, and your opinions of them. I spoke there of your omnivorous reading of newspapers, especially on the train, when you buy and run through the local papers of every town of any size in which the train stops. He thought that was very interesting, and wished you would touch on it.

He wanted to know what your diversions are. I told him you didn't have any, and had said so once in this series of articles. He wanted to know "for instance, does he play billiards?" and that made me laugh.

He said that the fact that Miss Tarbell's[3] life of Lincoln was so interesting was because she had given us so much of the personal life of the man.

The only thing that worried or interested Mr. Townsend at all was to know if he was going to have the next two chapters by Jan. 15th. I assured him solemnly on my word of honor that he should, and that I would be on hand on the morning of the 16th to read the proof, this being the only chance there would be to see it, he said.

I have dashed these notes off very hastily, as I wanted to get them started to you at once. Very truly yours,

M. B. Thrasher

TLS Con. 212 BTW Papers DLC.

1 Lawrence Fraser Abbott (1859-1933) was publisher of the *Outlook* from 1891 to 1922. He was the son of the editor-in-chief, Lyman Abbott.

2 Robert Donaldson Townsend (b. 1854) became managing editor of the *Outlook* in 1897.

3 Ida Minerva Tarbell (1857-1944), a muckraking journalist, was an editor of *McClure's Magazine* from 1894 to 1906 and then an editor of the *American Magazine* from 1906 to 1915. Probably her best-known work was *The History of the Standard Oil Company* (1904). She wrote several books on Lincoln including *The Life of Abraham Lincoln* (1900).

A Petition from Tuskegee Faculty Members

[Tuskegee, Ala.] Jan. 9, 1900

Principal Booker T. Washington: We, the undersigned, while desiring to burden you as little as possible with matters of this nature, nevertheless feeling that an unjust infringement is being made on our rights as teachers, ask that affairs be readjusted and more satisfactory regulations made.

In the first place it is to our minds wholly unfair to compel us to pay for our board and then whenever one minute behind a certain hour be locked out of the dining room.

In the second place, it is extremely humiliating to have a student stand guard and oftentimes insolently slam the door in our faces; then afterwards openly boast as to how he admits or excludes those who are supposed to be his superiors but who in reality are his subordinates.

Thirdly, it sometimes happens that the bells are so disarranged that it is absolutely impossible for those who have no watches to tell when the proper hour for breakfast arrives. In such cases no allowance is made and the door is closed as usual. This applies especially to breakfast.

Finally, we feel that the meal hours can be so arranged as to make it unnecessary to resort to a "lockout policy" and that teachers can be and should be placed on their honor or their willingness to be governed by a sense of right to the extent that they be allowed to come to their meals without having compulsory or prohibitory regulations inflicted on them.

Thomas J. Jackson	M[itchell] D. Garner
L[avisa] M. Crum	I[da] A. Morgan
Wm. Chas. Morris	Rosa Mason
Susie B. Thomas	L[aura] E. Mabry
Nathan Hunt	W[illiam] A. Richardson
Edgar Webber	M[oses] B. Lacy
S[herman] W. Grisham	W[illiam] V. Chambliss
F[rederick] C. Johnson	C[harles] L. Diggs
D[anella] E. Foote	S[usan] D. Cooper
E[mma] T. Nesbitt	John J. Wheeler
[Edna] A. Spears	Alice C. Pinyon

E[lizabeth] W. Morse
M[abel] L. Keith
C[arrie] Leo. Spies
E[liza] S. Adams
Bessie Roane
Dayse D. Walker
W[allace] A. Rayfield
Lizzie Baytop
B[utler] H. Peterson

H[enry] E. Cooper
Wm Gregory
B[ernard A.] Nesbitt
Chas. H. Evans
S May Smith
G[eorge] W. Owens
J. W. R. McDonald
C[ampbell] A. Gilmore

TLS   Con. 182   BTW Papers   DLC.

To Emily Howland

Tuskegee, Ala., Jan. 12, 1900

My dear Miss Howland: I thank you very much for your good letter and for your generous check, both are most encouraging and helpful, I assure you.

I am glad that you have my book and hope that you will find time to read it. I have been surprised at the many good things that have been written and said about it. And also surprised at the large number of copies which have been sold. I feel that it is accomplishing good; not only in the North, but what is more important in the South. I believe that day light is beginning to break in the South at a rapid rate. A meeting was held in Montgomery a few days ago composed of the leading citizens of that place. A Conference was organized whose object is to be to bring about a better relation between the two races. The two leading spirits[1] in the Council were here this week and they seem to be thoroughly in earnest and I think are going to accomplish good. A large Conference is to be held in May at which time they want me to speak.

I hope in the future to do more writing than I have been doing in the past. Several book publishing firms are offering me some excellent opportunities to get my thoughts before the public. I have already sent a copy of my book to Mrs. Moore,[2] whom Mrs. Washington and I enjoyed seeing very much.

In regard to the Endowment Fund; as I wrote, we have been

411

making an effort to increase that fund this year. At the present time we have in hand, or in sight, $151,000. We hope to secure at least 200,000 before the end of this school year. I do not remember that you *promised* anything to this fund, but of course we shall be glad of any contribution you may see your way clear to make to it.

Our Conference occurs February 21-22, and if you can be here at that time I shall be very glad. Yours very truly,

Booker T. Washington

TLS   Emily Howland Papers   NN-Sc.

1 Edgar Gardner Murphy and George Boardman Eager.
2 Rebecca Moore of London, England.

From John Fletcher Lacey

Washington, D.C. January 12 1900

My dear Mr. Washington: Your letter is at hand. In view of the scandal connected with the Montevallo School lands my advice would be to hold your lands for endowment purposes and not re-open the question in Congress. Coal land is about the best thing that any one can buy for a *long time* investment. It will constantly and steadily appreciate. *Lease* it or parts of it if you can on royalty. Yours Truly

John F. Lacey

ALS Con. 177 BTW Papers DLC. On stationery of the U.S. House of Representatives.

From Edgar Gardner Murphy

Montgomery, Alabama. January 13, 1900

My Dear Mr. Washington: Dr. Eager has informed me of a suggestion made to him by your private secretary in regard to the association of your name with certain other speakers of your race. He has probably also told you that our mistake was due to our ignorance of the situation, and I send you this word to give you further assurance that our revised statement as to the programme will be carefully guarded in this respect. There is to be another meeting of the committee this afternoon at 5 o'clock at Judge Gaston's[1] office, and our general statement of our plans will then be modified in this and one or two other points. We shall increase the committee of twenty-five to a committee of fifty, and perhaps eventually to a committee of one hundred. Let us have any suggestions which may occur to you, and even if we cannot adopt them in all respects, you may depend upon us to give them a cordial and generous hearing. If you think it would be wiser for you to correspond directly with myself or with Dr. Eager, rather than in an official way with the committee as a whole, you may write to either of us, and we will present your suggestions with due mention of their source. In the near future, I hope it will be possible for you to meet the committee personally in Montgomery.

I am enclosing to you one of the proofs of our original presentation of our project. Kindly give it a careful and critical reading, and make such suggestions in relation to this statement as may occur to you, and return the same to me at the earliest possible hour. Even if we cannot include these notes of yours in our next edition of the statement, there will be a further edition in which we will probably be glad to include them. I will send you a number of copies of each of these editions of our statement, and we shall be glad to have you call the attention of your friends in all parts of the country to our movement. Be most careful not to give the public the impression that this conference is to be solely and only an anti-lynching movement. There are a few people who have already taken that view of it. Nothing could be more unfortunate for the success of our undertaking than the prejudices in the South which will be aroused by such a conception of our effort. I am sure that the congress here upon the general problem will demonstrate the fact that there are very few thinking and responsible men in the South who advocate lynch methods as a public policy. At the same time, we must demonstrate to all classes of our Southern people that the congress is to be absolutely fair. It must frankly represent Southern thought as it actually exists. I believe profoundly in the educational influence of a free arena, of the clash of ideas, and of those oppositions of opinion which always force a prejudice, no

413

matter how deeply seated, to fall back upon those weapons of reason and of thought which (if the prejudice be wrong) can always be turned against it. But we wish for many reasons not to make this subject in any aspect of it the dominating theme of our conference. Such a perversion of the conference would be unjust to both the negro and the white man. We wish to deal with the subject in its broadest sense. We shall open probably with a discussion of the relation of the negro to the franchise, and we shall pass on to a discussion of other subjects which may bear upon the industrial, the religious and the educational phases of the general problem.

Besides sending us, therefore, your *suggestions* as to the enclosed statement, will you not send to me definite *titles* under any of the above heads which you think can be made *subjects* of fruitful debate? I do not care how long you make this list, for we shall select those that are best suited to our uses, leaving the others to another year. In the third place, will you send me a list of the names, with addresses, of the men in the North (and especially in the *South*) whom you may think best qualified to discuss these questions in the spirit of justice and wisdom?

I noticed after my brief address the other day, that there were stenographers at the front who had been taking notes. I have had several requests for copies of what I tried to say, but I spoke so entirely without preparation, I cannot remember even the outline of what I said. I should be glad, therefore, if there are any notes in existence, to have a copy in order that I may give the little speech more effective form, and may send copies to those who have asked for it. I do not care especially to polish it because I think the touch of immediateness is one of the essential factors of such an utterance, but it is not unlikely that there were positive errors in diction which should be removed.

Thanking you for your many courtesies during our brief stay at Tuskegee, and asking the blessing of God upon your work for the South, I am very Sincerely,

Edgar Gardner Murphy

TLS Con. 179 BTW Papers DLC.

1 John Brown Gaston (b. 1834) was a prominent Montgomery physician who was mayor of Montgomery in the 1880s and became judge of the probate court in 1895.

From Robert Curtis Ogden

New York, Jan. 15th, 1900

Dear Mr. Washington: I look backward to the experiences of last week at Tuskegee with intense interest, and, although I am not particularly optimistic, I yet have hope that the Montgomery people may start a movement that will result in great good, primarily for the South, secondarily for the whole country. I sympathise with you very deeply in the burden of care that you are carrying, and I am delighted at the measure of success that must bring you inspiration and encouragement.

If in any small way I can be of service to you, please command me. You know my other interests are exacting. Yours very truly,

Robert C Ogden

TLS Con. 180 BTW Papers DLC.

To Leonard Wood[1]

Tuskegee, Ala., 1-16-1900

Dear Sir: Immediately after the close of the Spanish American war I began an effort looking towards securing a number of bright young colored men and women from Cuba in order that they might be trained in academic and industrial branches at this Institution with a view of returning to Cuba and helping the people along the line of industrial education.

We have at the present time nine bright, promising young men from Cuba and Porto Rica. I have found people in the North who pay for their board and tuition. The Government has so far very kindly given us free transportation for these students.

If you think well of the idea, I will be very glad to have you send us two or three more young men or women of the Negro race. They should be between 15 and 20 years of age.

If I can be of any service in this direction, please be kind enough to use me. Very truly,

[Booker T. Washington]

TL Copy Con. 187 BTW Papers DLC.

1 Leonard Wood (1860-1927), physician and army officer, was the organizer and leader of the Rough Riders. He was military governor of Cuba from 1899 to 1902 and U.S. Army chief of staff from 1910 to 1914. In 1916 and again in 1920 he was a candidate for the Republican presidential nomination.

To the Editor of the St. Paul *Pioneer Press*

Duluth, Minn. Jan 16 1900

Dear Sir: In the editorial of your paper of this date you seem to be under the impression that I am connected officially or otherwise with the Insurance company recently started in Chicago by certain Colored people.[1] I am not in any way either actively, officially or financially connected with this enterprise. Some days ago I delivered an address under its auspices in the same spirit that I have spoken for my own race on other occasions. I wish for this organization the highest degree of success but I do not intend to enter into any enterprise, business or otherwise, that would in the least draw my attention or strength aside from the work which I am trying to do for the uplifting of my people through the medium of The Tuskegee Normal and Industrial Institute in Alabama.

While I stand ready to encourage all legitimate business enterprise among our people I make it a rule to enter nothing that would prevent me from giving my undivided attention to the work that I have in hand. Respectfully

Booker T Washington

Dictated

HLSr Copy Con. 186 BTW Papers DLC. Written on stationery of the Spalding Hotel.

1 The St. Paul *Pioneer Press*, Jan. 16, 1900, 4, reported that BTW was instrumental in founding a new black-owned insurance company in Chicago. The *Pioneer Press* did not mention the company by name, but it was the United Brotherhood Fraternal Insurance Co., which was founded by two Duluth men, Alexander Miles and Mason H. Seely. Two of BTW's closest associates in Chicago, S. Laing Williams and Daniel Hale Williams, were on the "imperial council" of the company.

Daniel Hale Williams had written BTW earlier urging him to support the company, which Williams described as "the most comprehensive and promising business proposition that colored men have ever entered into in this country and one that will do a vast amount of good." (Williams to BTW, Nov. 24, 1899, Con. 187, BTW Papers, DLC.) BTW was not directly involved in the company, but he did endorse its creation and spoke at the opening meeting in the Bethel A.M.E. Church in Chicago on Jan. 14, 1900. (Chicago *Inter Ocean*, Jan. 14, 1900, 36.) The company failed in late 1900 when an officer absconded with its funds. (Spear, *Black Chicago*, 116.)

From Walter Hines Page

New York   January 19th, 1900

My dear Mr Washington: Mr McClure and Mr Phillips are both in Europe. The principal responsibility in editing "McClure's Magazine" in the meantime falls to Miss Tarbell, who really wrote to you the first correspondence that the magazine had with reference to your autobiography. I have had a long talk with Miss Tarbell about using parts of your autobiography in the magazine, and I explained to her fully and frankly the situation, telling her that you wished to give Dr Abbott a definite answer and that you greatly preferred McClure's to the "Outlook," all conditions being equal. She told me that she could make no definite promise to use any matter in the magazine that had not first been read by her; this is the uniform policy of McClure's. They accept nothing unconditionally before reading it; but she felt sure that they would be able to use certainly one article, probably two, but she doubted whether they would be able to use more. For this one or these two articles taken out of the most interesting parts of the book, they would be willing to pay $250.00 to $300.00 apiece, if they could use them.

My own judgment is that there would be little doubt about their using one article. I do doubt whether they would care to use more than one. But as to the probability in this matter I, of course, can only guess, and they will not commit themselves in advance.

On the other hand, I interpret Dr Abbott's letter to mean that he would run a serial covering some months, using from six to ten or perhaps a dozen chapters. The "Outlook" reaches fewer people than McClure's, and pays less per article, but I am not sure that the circulation of the "Outlook" is any less favorable for this purpose than the circulation of McClure's. It goes to a somewhat more serious-minded class of readers, and people read it in a more serious

417

frame of mind than they read the magazine. My own guess would be that the moral effect of the articles in the "Outlook" would be quite as great as in McClure's. Since the "Outlook" will, as I understand it, use a good deal more matter than McClure's, the total payment that you would get for this serial use of the matter would also be greater than from the "Outlook."[1]

My advice to you, therefore, would be to write to McClure's Magazine, saying frankly that if they do not see their way to publish at least as many as four articles, and unless they can definitely promise to do so, you would prefer to place the articles elsewhere. I do not know whether you are under any definite obligation to McClure's Magazine or not, but if you are, it seems to me that an obligation is a thing that has two sides to it and that if they do not make you any definite promise, you would be at liberty to go elsewhere.

I send you this candid and frank advice confidentially of course. I should not like for either of these periodicals to know that I had written you any preference in the matter, because I am, of course, on the most cordial possible terms with them both; but what I am driving at is to give you the best information I can to enable you to make up your mind most advantageously.

My advice, then, to sum up, would be to accept Dr. Abbott's proposition, if you are at liberty to do so, and to tell him when you do accept it that arrangements have already been made for the publication of the book.

While we are writing upon the subject, let me say, by the way, that it seems to us that a fair rate for the book publication would be a 10% royalty on the first 2500 copies, 12½% on the second 2500 and 15% on all copies sold thereafter. Does this strike you favorably?

I hope that you will quickly get release from your technical obligation to the people in Chicago and that you can begin to turn out your copy for serial use early enough to permit us to bring out the book next Fall. Be sure and let me know as soon as you get to New York again. Very heartily yours,

Walter H. Page

TLS Con. 182 BTW Papers DLC.

1 Page obviously meant to write "McClure's."

From William Henry Baldwin, Jr.

Brooklyn Heights. 1/19/1900

Dear Washington   I shall expect to hear from your office later just what you recommend for dairy barn, dairy house, etc. with plans showing style of finish etc.

Bear in mind that we must be able to say how much the barn costs *per animal* — so that it will be a proper object lesson for the South — it must be built on true economic theories. Yours truly

W H Baldwin Jr

ALS Con. 792 BTW Papers DLC.

From Susan Brownell Anthony

N.Y. [City] Jan. 23. 1900

My Dear Friend: I received yours of the 16th. Certainly whenever I go to Atlanta again, it is my intention to visit Tuskegee. I am, however, hoping that my time of going will be postponed to next Autumn, when the legislatures of several of the Southern States will be in session. I think then would be a much better time for us to be in the South, and to speak perchance before every one of the legislatures, and thus send at least a representative from every district in the state, home to his constituents with a little idea of what this woman's rights movement means.

It is one of my dreams to visit Tuskegee, and to see you and Mrs. Washington and Mrs. Logan, and all of the good men and women engaged in the splendid work of that institute. Wishing you the best of success, I am, Very sincerely yours,

Susan B. Anthony

TLS Con. 166 BTW Papers DLC. Written on stationery of the National American Woman Suffrage Association. Addressed to BTW in St. Paul, Minn.

From Andrew Carnegie

New York   23rd January 1900

Dear Mr Washington, My secretary tells me you called today in regard to payment of the twenty thousand dollars I promised for a Library for Tuskegee, and I have instructed my cashier, Mr R. A. Franks,[1] Carnegie Building, Pittsburgh, to honor the drafts of Tuskegee Institute authorities to the extent of $20,000, in sums as needed from time to time to pay for the building. Very truly yours,

Andrew Carnegie

TLS   Con. 170   BTW Papers   DLC.

[1] Robert A. Franks was Andrew Carnegie's business secretary and treasurer for many years. He was in charge of disbursing much of the Carnegie fortune.

From William Henry Baldwin, Jr.

N.Y. [City] January 24, 1900

Personal

Dear Mr. Washington: I cannot get any answer from the Pullman people.[1] I have written them twice and have not received reply. Therefore do not wait for me. Would it not be well when test is made of this question to have a light mulatto of good appearance, but unquestionably colored, make the test.

I don't believe that the Pullman Company will attempt to exclude the colored man from the car, but that the interpretation of the Bill will be to exclude them from the same section as the white person. I should suppose that the best place to make the test is at the Pullman ticket office in Atlanta. I wish you would let me know the developments in the case. I do hope it can be tested by someone other than yourself. Yours very truly,

W H Baldwin Jr

TLS   Con. 792   BTW Papers   DLC.

[1] BTW had asked Baldwin to intercede with Robert Todd Lincoln, son of the Great Emancipator and president of the Pullman Car Company, over the issue of

southern Jim Crow practices in Pullman cars. BTW engaged in behind-the-scenes efforts over the next six years to fight this issue. (See Harlan, "Secret Life of BTW," 399-401; Meier, *Negro Thought*, 113-14; and Crofts, "The Warner-Foraker Amendment," 341-58.)

From Joseph Eugene Ransdell[1]

Washington, D.C., Jan. 24th, 1900

Dear sir: As you are doubtless aware the Crumpacker bill, now pending in the House, aims at reducing the number of Representatives in Congress from the southern states which have passed laws to restrict the suffrage among negroes. I am one of the Representatives from Louisiana which is one of the states principally aimed at. In my opinion the passage of the Crumpacker law would be very injurious to the South, and of course to the negroes who form such a large part of the population of the South. The suffrage is undoubtedly very much restricted among them, but in Louisiana I am satisfied that they are more prosperous and more contented than when they were constantly stirred up [by] designing politicians. Under the Louisiana election laws (and I believe those of the other southern states which attempt to restrict suffrage are substantially the same) every one with a fair smattering of education is permitted to vote. It seems to me that the true policy is for the races in the South to live together in as much harmony and peace as possible, and work out their own destiny unimpeded by laws which are bound to bring about friction and bad feeling. If this law goes into effect and southern representation in Congress is very materially reduced, it will leave practically without representation a large class of people who most need it, for, as you know, the negroes as a race are like children and need a quieting and protecting hand.

If I construe your public utterances correctly, you would be opposed to any such measure as that of Mr. Crumpacker. I understand that you think that suffrage should be restricted among all ignorant people until they are sufficiently educated to appreciate its benefits, but I do not understand that you would favor absolute depreciation of representation in the halls of Congress while these ignorant people are being prepared to exercise the highest rights of citizenship.

I will be very glad to hear from you on this subject and to have a clear statement of your opinion as to this Crumpacker bill and others of a similar character. Hoping to hear from you soon, I am with much respect, Yours truly,

Jos. E. Ransdell

TLS Con. 182 BTW Papers DLC. Docketed: "They are apparently scared! I told him you are away. He is anxious to drag *you* into that controversy now going on in Congress. You will doubtless wish to answer at your convenience. EJ Scott 1/26."

1 Joseph Eugene Ransdell (1858-1954) of Louisiana was a cotton planter who was in the U.S. House of Representatives from 1899 to 1913 and in the Senate from 1913 to 1931.

From William Henry Baldwin, Jr.

N.Y. [City] January 26, 1900

Dear Mr. Washington: I have to notify you that since my return to New York I have received a check for $2,500. from a lady in Brooklyn, and a check for $3,000. from a gentleman who does not wish to have his name used publicly, and therefore I shall not give it. This gives a fund of $5,500. to be expended in such manner as I think best, and I want your best advice. I do not want it turned over to the general fund, but I want it to do certain specific things which have not been done for lack of funds, so that I can point to those particular things and say to the donors just what improvements have been made.

I don't want this announced in the local papers. Keep the matter quiet. Since I left Tuskegee I have received several letters from various white schools and colored schools in the South and they put me in a more or less embarrassing position. Of course I am equally interested in white education, but unfortunately I have no funds to give to that cause, and I do not like to be explaining constantly why I cannot do it.

I shall wait to hear from you and shall be guided by your advice. Now is the time for you to round out your work. Get the plant in good operating condition. Stop expending until you get a sure income sufficient to pay the way and keep off of the rocks which we were approaching last year. Let us get into a business like condition and then fight to stay there.

I would like very much to talk with you further about that Marshall farm. On mature thought I do not feel that we should continue that farm unless it at least pays its way. It ought to make money, it seems to me, in view of the fact that they receive credit for everything that they produce, but I do not believe that it can be made to produce any net result with the head farmer a non-resident. I should think that anyone connected with your Institution should devote his whole time to it, and have no other business or farming interest.

Since I left Tuskegee so many things come into my mind! I shall hope that your business will call you East again sometime soon. With very kind regards, I am   Yours very truly,

W H Baldwin Jr

TLS   Con. 792   BTW Papers   DLC.

An Article in the Denver *Post*

[Denver, Colo., Jan. 28, 1900]

Booker T. Washington's Stay
in Denver

Booker T. Washington is a quiet, unassuming man, whose comings and goings are noted by the press,[1] and cultured people delight to do him honor. He is a colored man, an Afro-American, president of the Tuskegee (Alabama) college, a prominent educator of his race, and probably the most notable colored man of the present day. Before he came to Denver it was arranged that he should stop at the Brown Palace hotel,[2] and it was announced that he would be at the hotel during his stay in Denver. It was at his request before he came to Denver, quarters be secured for him at some hotel and not at a private house. Manager Tabor[3] of the Brown, when approached by C. L. Stonaker[4] of the lecture course, said there would be no objection to housing Mr. Washington, as he was a distinguished man, whose color was a secondary consideration. It was understood that Mr. Washington was to be treated as any other guest, and that no restrictions were to be put upon him.

"He is in the class of Frederick Douglass, and above popular prejudice," said Mr. Tabor.

Nevertheless, Mr. Washington was requested, and did take all his meals in his room. To a friend he said it was the first time in his public career that he had been thus discriminated against.

"It is nothing to me," he said. "The hotel management was very polite about it and treated me otherwise in the most considerate manner. It is the principle."

When asked to make a statement for publication, however, he said it was not a matter he wished to discuss.

"It is better not discussed, in fact," said he, in his quiet dignified manner. Though betraying no feeling it was evident that he felt keenly his treatment, and thought the discussion would only be disadvantageous to the principles for which he has been struggling. The idea of all his teaching is to elevate the colored race, socially and financially. It is furthermore his idea that the colored man shall have a fixed, though it may be unobtrusive social status, that he always goes to hotels when traveling and not to private houses.

His own personality is unapproachable [unreproachable?], and he is attempting to show the people wherever he travels what the future colored man may be, and thus eradicate prejudice against his race. He has been, in a large measure, successful. He has never before been refused all the privileges of any hotel or railroad at which he had been received.

Mr. Washington was tendered a reception by his friend and former pupil, Joseph D. D. Rivers,[5] proprietor of the Colorado Statesman, yesterday noon. The reception was held in the parlors of Mr. Rivers' home at 225 West Eleventh avenue, and while the number of guests present was small, the affair was elaborate, and no pains were spared to make the entertainment enjoyable to the fullest extent. The assemblage was probably as notable a collection of colored people as ever sat down at one time, and spoke well of the achievements of the race in the last thirty years.

At the head of the table sat the guest of honor, Booker T. Washington, who believes the colored race has at its hand the means of its own uplifting.

To the left of Mr. Washington sat Paul Laurence Dunbar, the colored author and poet, a young man, and yet one who has already given to English literature some matchless lyrics. On the other hand sat Dr. P. E. Spratlen,[6] a well known physician and politician. Attorney J. H. Stewart[7] and Attorney E. H. Hackley[8] sat side by side. S. H. Hobson,[9] city editor of the Colorado Statesman, was also a guest. W. D. Phillips,[10] proprietor of the Arapahoe cafe, and the Rev. Oscar J. W. Sweet[11] completed the circle of distinguished colored men.

The possibility thirty years ago of such an assemblage of colored men, filling such positions and filling them well could not have been dreamed of.

The conversation at the banquet, which comprised several courses, was exceedingly interesting, sparkling with bright sayings and apropos quotations from the best English literature, showing a degree of reading and observation not often met with.

Among the topics that were informally brought up and discussed during the dinner was the kindly feeling the best classes of Southern people have for the colored people and the deep interest they take in their welfare. It was agreed without a dissenting voice that Southern people were the most friendly to colored people, understood their nature and affections better and were more willing to assist them than any class of people.

Following the banquet the guests adjourned to the smoking room, where they chatted over their wine and cigars until the party was broken up by the enforced departure of Mr. Washington for Colorado Springs, where he lectured last evening.

Mr. Rivers was a pupil of Professor Washington during the years 1879 to 1881 at the Hampton Normal and Agricultural institute, Virginia. Professor Washington left that institution in 1881, going to Tuskegee, Ala., as president of the normal school there.

The following year Mr. Rivers graduated and later came to Colorado.

It was pleasing to see the interest Mr. Washington took in his former pupil's welfare, and the pride he manifested in his success. "Well," said Mr. Rivers, "I'm doing my best to follow out your ideas."

The banquet was something to be remembered as a future appetizer, the table gleaming with fine linen, sparkling with cut glass, and burdened with flowers. The parlors were handsomely decorated with palms, potted plants and cut flowers.

This evening Mr. Washington will address the congregation at Shorter's chapel, Twenty-third and Washington streets, of which Rev. O. J. W. Scott is pastor. Later he leaves for Omaha.

Denver *Post,* Jan. 28, 1900, Clipping Con. 1032 BTW Papers DLC.

1 An unidentified clipping from a Denver newspaper contained the following account of BTW's physical appearance:

"A pair of large, comfortably shod feet bore Booker T. Washington to the door of room 307 at the Brown Palace hotel this morning.

"The early caller had glanced at the feet in the distance and for some reason his gaze was fascinated by them, and remained on them as they moved toward him. They seemed so characteristic of the man who built up the Normal and Industrial institute at Tuskegee, Ala., and has been for years the leading light of the negro race in America. They were not ill-shapen, these feet, but they had such a luxurious spread in the soft, square-toed shoes that encased them, and the observer found them quite in keeping with the sturdy legs, the rolling gait, the thick-set figure and complacent face that belonged to Mr. Washington's fuller personality."

The article mentioned that BTW would speak on the future of the American Negro and then added:

"The color of Mr. Washington is an indescribable shade of yellow brown, his features are heavy and African, and yet there is some huge but definite chiseling about his thick lips that is peculiar. A deep vertical groove runs down his upper lip, and the edges of its fellow below are clear cut. The nose is large and somewhat flat, but it has shape, and there is plastic force in the set of the nostrils. His hair is woolly, but it too has individuality, for it stands where it is put, and that without the process of string training used in the old slavery days.

"There is great intelligence in the gaze of Mr. Washington, and he has far more variety of expression in his face than is usually found in the negro countenance. For the rest he is dignified and serious and deliberate."

The reporter said that when he asked BTW how much white blood he had in his veins, BTW replied: "I am just one-eighth white, I believe." The reporter then asked: "And you do not, as some do, attribute your unusual intelligence to that fact, eh?" "Why no," BTW replied, "I might be entirely white and still not exhibit any unusual mental qualities, might I not?" (Clipping, [ca. Jan. 28, 1900], Con. 1032, BTW Papers, DLC.)

2 The H. C. Brown Hotel, or the Brown Palace Hotel, was the most exclusive and lavish hotel in Denver and was billed as the finest hotel between Chicago and San Francisco. It was built in 1892 in an Italian Renaissance style and was decorated with Louis XIV and Louis XVI antiques.

3 Nathaniel Maxcy Tabor, a member of the Denver Chamber of Commerce.

4 Clarence L. Stonaker, who helped arrange BTW's trip to Denver, was secretary of the Colorado State Board of Charities and Correction.

5 Joseph D. D. Rivers, born in Virginia in 1856 or 1858, was an 1882 graduate of Hampton Institute. He moved to Denver in 1885, where he studied law and ran a real estate business before assuming the proprietorship of the weekly *Colorado States-*

man. He was active in black affairs in Denver as a member of the executive board of the Denver Colored Civic Association.

6 Paul Edward Spratlin was born in Alabama in 1861 and graduated from Atlanta University in 1881. He taught school in the South from 1881 to 1889 before moving to Denver, where he received a medical degree in 1892 from the Denver Medical College of the University of Denver. From 1895 to 1899 he was Denver's chief medical inspector. He was active in many institutions in the black community of Denver, including the Douglass Undertaking Co., the Lincoln-Douglass Consumptive Sanitarium, the A.M.E. Church, and the Y.M.C.A.

7 Joseph H. Stuart, a black Denver attorney.

8 Edwin H. Hackley, born in Michigan in 1859, was a black lawyer who clerked in the Arapahoe County recorder's office for twelve years before 1900, when he became a clerk in the city auditor's office in Denver.

9 Samuel H. Hobson, born in Tennessee in 1871.

10 Wharton D. Phillips, who entertained BTW and fifty guests, including Colorado's governor Charles Spalding Thomas, at his restaurant after BTW's speech.

11 Oscar Jefferson Waldo Scott, not Sweet, was born in Ohio in 1867 and graduated from Ohio Wesleyan University in 1895. He received a B.D. degree from Drew Theological Seminary in Madison, N.J., in 1897, and a D.D. from Wilberforce in 1902. He was a minister of the A.M.E. Church in Denver at Shorter's Chapel from 1897 to 1902. From 1902 to 1905 he was stationed in Kansas City, Mo., and from 1905 to 1909 he was a minister in Washington, D.C. Later he served as chaplain with the 25th Infantry from 1907 to 1917 and then with the 10th Cavalry from 1917 to 1922. He taught theology at Howard University for several years before his death in 1927 or 1928.

From William Henry Baldwin, Jr.

Brooklyn Heights. Jan 28, 1900

Dear Washington, Glad to get your letter from Omaha. I do not believe that the Western people have yet reached a point of giving largely to educational institutions outside of their local surrounding country, but it is well to have them understand the question, and there may be another surprise in store for you, similar to the old lady[1] in Ohio, who gave the $25,000.

There are several letters from me at Tuskegee, and I won't burden you with more — I have had a long letter from Rev. Murphy. He is coming to Phila to speak — possibly to New York. He was apparently impressed with the paper I sent him on the "present problem" — the one I gave at Saratoga. He says he feels that I am "one of us." They will want a meeting in Montgomery in May. I think I better send them a contribution of $100. toward it, and let

427

them think it is to them instead of Tuskegee. It is certainly a legitimate part of *your* work! Tuskegee has started them all going. If the Montgomery Conference is well handled, it will certainly help the whole cause very considerably.

I want to get hold of some good friends somewhere to help out on the house matter. I think it will be well for you to say (and have others also) that the Trustees insisted on having a suitable house for the many Northern friends who visit Tuskegee! Nothing is too good for you — but it might seem too good for the cause, and those 2 x 4 Trustees who criticise should be encouraged!

I hope Mrs Washington is well, and that all goes prosperously at the School.

Mrs Baldwin sends her regards to you and your family. Faithfully yours

W. H. Baldwin Jr

ALS   Con. 792   BTW Papers   DLC.

1 Possibly Catherine M. Tuttle of Columbus, Ohio, who donated $15,000 to Tuskegee in 1907. (See Tuttle to BTW, Mar. 29, 1907, Con. 728, BTW Papers, DLC.)

To Francis Jackson Garrison

Tuskegee, Ala., Feb. 3, 1900

My dear Mr. Garrison: I do not know whether you have seen anything in regard to a movement mentioned in the enclosed pamphlet, if not I am sure that this little pamphlet will interest you. This movement was started by three ministers, the Episcopalian,[1] Presbyterian[2] and Baptist[3] ministers, in Montgomery. I sat up till near midnight last night in Montgomery with these three gentlemen. They are thoroughly in earnest and mean to do something to better the condition of our race. They are not only in earnest but they have the courage of their convictions, but they are going to be prudent. They are very anxious to get hold of the element in the South that has always opposed everything tending towards the elevation of the Negro. If the first conference is not managed on very conservative lines they will not get hold of the very element that now gives the greatest trouble. To have this movement start in Montgomery, Alabama, which is perhaps one of the most conservative towns in the South and formerly the headquarters of the Confederate government, means a great deal. These three gentlemen have already enlisted a hundred leading business men in Montgomery in this movement. We read together many of the letters received from these business men and almost everyone who was asked to join the movement heartily responded in the affirmative. The most discouraging letter that I read came from a Methodist minister. You must not expect too much from this first conference. In order not to get itself in bad odor with the fire eating element of the South the Conference is going to give the anti-Negro element the opportunity to state their case at the first conference. Of course there will be speakers to represent the pro-Negro element, and these gentlemen are determined that the conference itself be kept always in the hands of the pro-Negro element. Almost nothing in the last dozen years has served to give me so much hope and encouragement as this movement. The three ministers to whom I have referred have the most earnest and satisfactory convictions regarding the elevation of our people and are determined to devote a great part of their time and strength in the future to this end. At the same time, in order that they may accomplish the most good they want to be sure to so conduct themselves in a way to keep their hold on their congregations which are by far the most aristocratic and influential in Montgomery.

I plan to be in Boston about the middle of the month and hope to talk this matter over with you. Yours truly,

Booker T. Washington

TLS   Francis J. Garrison Papers   NN-Sc.

1 Edgar Gardner Murphy.

2 Neal L. Anderson, pastor of the Central Presbyterian Church, was also an associate of Murphy and George B. Eager in child labor reform in Alabama.

3 George Boardman Eager.

To Edgar Gardner Murphy

Tuskegee, Ala., 2-3-1900

Dear Mr. Murphy: What do you think of the idea of securing Hon. Chauncey M. Depew to make one of the principal addresses at the opening meeting of the Conference? I think that some such national character as that would serve a good purpose. Mr. Depew has sensible views of the race question and would not say anything that would injure the meeting.

Rev. H. H. Proctor, pastor of the 1st Congregational Church, Atlanta, Ga, is a colored man of a great deal of wisdom and discretion, who might very properly be invited to attend the Conference. Bishop Wm. J. Gaines[1] of Atlanta, Ga. and Bishop Henry M. Turner of Atlanta I think might be invited. Very truly,

[Booker T. Washington]

TL Copy   Con. 182   BTW Papers   DLC.

1 Wesley John Gaines (1840-1912) was born a slave on the plantation of the Robert Toombs family in Wilkes County, Ga. He became a bishop in the A.M.E. Church in 1888. During his pastorate in Atlanta from 1881 to 1884, he built the Bethel A.M.E. Church, known locally as Big Bethel, at the time the largest black church in the South. Gaines was a conservative on racial matters and generally followed BTW's gradualist philosophy of economic progress and self-help as the best hope for racial advancement. (Meier, *Negro Thought*, 218-19.)

To Hollis Burke Frissell

Tuskegee, Ala., Feb. 5, 1900

My dear Dr. Frissell: I have recently returned from Montgomery where I met the members of the executive committee that have charge of the conference which is to be held in Montgomery in May. I very much hope that you will decide to attend this conference. I do not believe that any movement that has ever been started in the South is so pregnant of good as this one. Of course the whole effort of the convention at first especially is going to be very conservative, but I think the very conservatism of the people who have it in charge constitute[s] its greatest hopefulness. After further discussion and consideration it has been decided wise not to place any colored man on the public programme in May though colored people will attend private conferences. You, I think, will be the only person invited to speak on the public platform that is directly connected with any Negro school and I think this makes it all the more important that you be present. Yours truly,

Booker T. Washington

TLS   BTW Folder   ViHaI.

From Arthur Ulysses Craig[1]

Tuskegee 2-5-00

Mr B. T. Washington: It will cost $6,700.00 to ins[t]all electric lights in all the buildings and light the grounds. The above does not include a duplicate dynamo. Yours very truly

Arthur U. Craig

ALS   Con. 168   BTW Papers   DLC.

[1] Arthur Ulysses Craig (1871-1959) was born in Weston, Mo., and attended high school in Atchison, Kan. In 1895 he graduated from the University of Kansas school of electrical engineering, probably the first black graduate in that field. He taught at Tuskegee from 1896 to 1901, introducing electrical engineering into the curriculum. Under his direction students installed much of the electrical lighting on campus, maintained the school's power plant, and installed and operated the campus telephone system. Craig also designed the lighting for the Tuskegee Institute chapel and planned the lighting system for the town of Tuskegee, which was supplied from the school power plant.

After leaving Tuskegee, Craig taught high school in Washington, D.C., for seventeen years and was active in organizing playgrounds in the District of Columbia. From 1904 to 1906 he was principal of the Armstrong Manual Training Night School. While in Washington he also operated a small poultry farm and dairy. Later he moved to New York, where he held a variety of positions including mechanic, draftsman, heating engineer, teacher, and editor of a Harlem newspaper. His first wife, Luella Cassandra Gladys Moore, whom he married in 1896, was a teacher at Tuskegee Institute. In 1932 he married Althea M. Rochon (1879-1970), a graduate of Straight University, who had worked in the auditor's office at Tuskegee from 1911 to 1918.

From Edgar Gardner Murphy

Montgomery, Ala., Feb. 7, 1900

Dear Mr. Washington: I have your kind letters, and I thank you for the enclosures and suggestions. For the first year, it would perhaps be unwise to ask an address from a man so thoroughly associated with the Republican party as Mr. Depew. He is personally a man of eminent tactfulness, and would make no mistake, but he is known through the rural districts of the South chiefly as a Republican, and while it may be possible for us to request such a speech from him next year, or the year after, I think that for the first conference it would be better to ask men who are not in politics at all, or who represent the Democratic party of the North. The names of colored men I will file, and I have no doubt that they will all be accepted by the Committee as appropriate representatives in the private conference at that time.

With reference to the Industrial Convention at Chattanooga, I may say that I had noticed the conflict of date through telegrams in the Montgomery Advertiser, but after careful consideration, we have decided to make no change in our present plans. There are so many reasons for this determination, that it would hardly be worth while for me to try to cover them in a letter. I am glad to see that you are disposed to use your influence in our direction, and I earnestly trust that Gov. MacCorkle will be present. I understand that he is a man who will do full justice to the case of the negro in relation to the suffrage, and I wish, therefore, to urge his name for a place upon our program in the discussion of this subject. I have no right, however, as yet to speak for the whole committee, but I rather think that the suggestion will go through. Just as soon as it is decided, I shall write to Gov. MacCorkle. I send you to-day another lot of copies of our prospectus.

My wife[1] and her mother, Mrs. King, who is on a visit here from Concord, Mass., would like to come up to Tuskegee, but I wish them to come when you are there. Will you kindly inform me when it will be best for them to do so? I have an umbrella in the Rectory that is without an owner. Did you leave yours here on the evening of your visit? With kind regards, I am very sincerely,

Edgar Gardner Murphy

TLS Con. 179 BTW Papers DLC.

1 Maud King Murphy (1865-1957), of Concord, Mass., married Edgar G. Murphy in 1891.

From James Bryce

[London, England] Feb. 7th 1900

Dear Mr. Washington I thank you cordially for the copy of your book which has just reached me. I shall read it with the greatest interest, and am sure I shall learn much from it. That which I heard from you here in England leads me to believe that I shall also — so far as I can venture to express an opinion — find myself in accord with your views. Social moral and intellectual progress are the first things — it seems to me — for your people to aim at: the rest will come in the train of these. And industrial training seems one of the best roads to social & moral progress.

With most earnest wishes for the success of the work of your Institute, I am Very faithfully yours

James Bryce

ALS Con. 167 BTW Papers DLC. Reprinted in the Washington *Colored American*, Mar. 10, 1900, 11.

From Francis Jackson Garrison

Boston, Feb. 8, 1900

Dear Mr. Washington: I have your letter of the 3d inst., and the enclosed pamphlet, which is very interesting. I trust that the movement may assume the importance and have the favorable result which you anticipate. I confess that I feel pretty sceptical of much practical good coming from a movement begun in such a timid and hesitating manner, and shall not be greatly surprised if the "fire-eating element" which the Conference is so afraid of getting in bad odor with, shall prove more aggressive and dominant. That the three clergymen who are engineering the movement wish so to

433

conduct themselves as to keep their hold on their congregations is altogether characteristic, for the instances are very few where a clergyman who has a comfortable berth and a rich congregation will preach or say anything that will offend his employers. That is what destroys the moral power of the clergy in our country to-day, as it did forty years ago, and they need never be looked to for leadership in any great moral or social reform. I shall be glad to see you in Boston this month. Yours very truly,

Francis J. Garrison

P.S. I have just received a letter from Mrs. Clark of Street, expressing the great pleasure you & Mrs. Washington gave her & her family by your visit.

TLS   Con. 173   BTW Papers   DLC.

From Alonzo Homer Kenniebrew

Tuskegee, Ala., 2–9 1900

Dear Prof Washington   In thus writing you, I mean to call attention to a few things which might be worthy of some consideration only.

As to my work, it is plesant as I have learned to make it so. Yet there are ways by which it could be made more plesant as the health of the school would be improved.

It seems that the girls should have regular monthly lectures in *hygiene* and laws of health as the young men have. The *experience* of last year bears me out in this and *that* of this year *shows* the want of hygienic lectures. We are *having* more sickness among the girls from small preventable causes than is true of the boys, our hospital records will show it. Our hygienic talks are so arranged as to give information & advise in preventing the diseases peculiar to each month and season before they come. The effects are evident. So far not a single case of Pneumonia among the boys this term and we have had three among girls &c. (Against none of last year.)

It seems that the academic work would be improved if the teaching *body* had a little more *respect* for their head teacher,[1] as I know it, they have a *very* little *respect* for him. May be, if he was little more reasonable & considerate it would help matters. To ill[ustrate] — Whenever one is sick — lady or gentleman teacher I report it to *head teacher* who as a rule declares the said party is not sick but playing [o]ff — as students do. This all the teachers know. Another — having no con[si]deration for one's individual adaptability as to subjects to teach. Every teacher cannot teach — arithmetic — or history.

It may be that they don't say it to you — but there is a certain amount of resentment and disgust on part of teachers to accept criticisms, from the council, of their teaching, because the council as a whole is not composed of people who do that kind of work, hence the feeling is that the council members as such are not the ones to criticise and suggest. But a Special Committee of the best teachers of each department to visit & criticise and suggest would do by far more good.

I wish to bring to your attention again the manner of ordering drugs. As a rule the orders are late being passed upon by the finance committee as they are either sent back or away to be valued, and too often quite a lapse of time as high as 5 weeks have passed and a larger bill is probably made in the city for less than half of the drugs. We order only just what we *want* or *need* and there is no *making out* without them and it is a useless waste of time and money to delay orders.

The matter of killing and cutting up meats *needs much improvement* and I see no way to do it — only by getting a regular butcher. Too often meat is killed which is not wholesome and is dangerous. The cutting is very badly done & good meat is often spoiled by so doing. To illustrate first assertion. Three weeks ago — meat was killed one afternoon and it was spoiled (decomposed & smelling badly) by next morning. Mr Mabry[2] called my attention to it and I took quite a large fleshy piece and carefully examined it and found that the cow *was dangerously ill* when she was killed.

Another serious error existing among students. The girls I find are allowed to wear their *corsets* every *day* — and take *gymnastics*. Gymnastics are to develope & strengthen the body. Corsets weaken & prevent developement — and when used by people persuing such training they produce serious results. Already several girls have suffered severely and had quite a doctors bill — and have become

435

more or less maimed from such practice. *One or the other* must be stopped for sake of the girls' health. The corset waists — like the girls wore last year will blight the evil.

I am under the impression that I am at head of department of physiology or that it comes under health division. Yet I have never been informed by *head teacher* as to who — what or anything — but have only received a little slip of paper telling me to meet a class at 11.20 Science Hall — that was two days (2-2 1900) after the class had first met for physiology.

I don't know a thing about the night classes nor who is teaching them yet I hear such exists. The *head teacher accepted* my plan of *work* with Mrs Kenniebrew to assist me — very heartily. Yours for health

A. H. Kenniebrew

ALS Con. 177 BTW Papers DLC.

[1] James Dickens McCall.

[2] Henry Grant Maberry, a Tuskegee graduate in 1896, was commissary of the boarding department at Tuskegee Institute from 1896 to 1898 and in charge of the boarding department from 1899 to 1904.

From Jesse Lawson

Washington, D.C., February 9th 1900

My Dear Sir: Your very kind favor of the 5th instant was duly received by me, and I sincer[e]ly thank you for the generous offer contained therein.[1] I shall regard the matter as being strictly confidential and shall not mention your name in connection therewith.

We cannot begin action until we have, at least, $2000 in hand, and promise of three thousand dollars on demand from reliable sources.

We are doing all in our power to get things in such shape that we may be able to institute proceedings at a very early date. Of course, we must secure the best available legal talent and influential men in the community where the action will be commenced, and good lawyers, you know, always demand payment of retainer fees in advance.

We are terribly in earnest about this matter, and we want to begin action in such a manner as to insure success. Yours truly,

Jesse Lawson

HLS   Con. 178   BTW Papers   DLC.

1 BTW had received a circular letter from the Afro-American Council dated Jan. 30, 1900. The letter was an appeal for funds for the purpose of testing in the courts the disfranchisement provisions of the Louisiana Constitution. Signed by Lawson and John H. Hannon, chairman of the council's finance committee, the letter declared: "It is not the part of freemen to tamely submit to outrage against their rights, and our fitness for citizenship will be estimated by our unity of purpose to resist, by every means possible, encroachments on our rights, and by our willingness to make individual sacrifices for the protection of the same." Emmett J. Scott docketed BTW's copy: "Mark letter personal. If get suit started will be responsible for $100. in courts of La." (Con. 174, BTW Papers, DLC.)

From Joseph Eugene Ransdell

Washington, D.C., Feby. 10th, 1900

Dear sir: Your letter of the 6th to hand, also your article in the Atlantic Monthly and interview published in the Atlanta Constitution.[1] I have read both of them with a great deal of interest. Will be glad to have a conference with you when you come to Washington. The Crumpacker bill directs the Census Bureau to make a careful compilation of all the election and registration laws in the country, and statistics as to the number of persons of voting age and the number who vote in the different parts of the country. Its object is to reduce the representation in Congress from those states which restrict suffrage, and it is unquestionably aimed at the southern states which have passed suffrage regulations. In my judgment, if the object of this bill is carried out it will to a great extent disturb the pleasant relations existing between the races in the South which are so well described by you in the Atlantic Monthly article. I do not believe such legislation will do any good and it may do very much harm. In my judgment the best thing to do is to let the people of the South, white and black, work out their own salvation with as little interference as possible. Even in the days of slavery, representation in Congress was given, in part at least, to the negroes and it would seem very strange to cut it off now. I have no idea that the bill will become a law but deem its agitation at this time ill advised. Very truly yours,

Jos. E. Ransdell

TLS Con. 182 BTW Papers DLC.

1 BTW, "The Case of the Negro," *Atlantic Monthly*, 84 [Nov. 1899], 577-87; see An Interview in the Atlanta *Constitution*, Nov. 10, 1899, above.

From Rosa Mason

[Tuskegee, Ala.] Feb. 10–1900

Mr. Washington, In answer to your note of Feb. 3rd, in regard to the work of the teachers of the Academic Department, I will say, that in my mind, in the first place there have been too many changes. The teachers do not in many cases get acquainted with the class before it is taken away.

In the second place teachers have too many different subjects. No teacher, unless he is very extraordinary, can do justice to the number of subjects that some of us are called upon to teach.

In the third place we have to teach too many periods during the day. There is not sufficient time for preparation.

I will give you some of my own experience in this matter. I haven't a single class, except a Bible class on Monday, that I had at the beginning of the term.

At present I give each day 12 lessons. Subjects taught: Reading, Arithmetic, Geography, Nature Study, Language, Spelling and Bible.

Now, while I know a little about all of these subjects I am *not* prepared to *teach* all of them as they should be taught.

Then too, Mr. Washington you seem to overlook the fact that the teachers, and especially the ladies, do not have all of their work in the class-room. There are other duties which they must perform.

I also think that a teacher should have some time to give students with whom she comes in contact, some individual attention. Our students need it very much.

Now, I come to a personal matter, but it affects me very seriously. There is a piano in Senior Home in the room next to mine, upon which the girls practice.

I am so unfortunate as to be very sensitive to noise, and when I come home in the afternoon all tired out, and then have to prepare another set of lessons for night, I find the constant banging on the piano positively painful. Sometimes I have to leave the room.

I wish you would, if possible, have the piano put somewhere else. Very truly yours,

Rosa Mason

ALS Con. 179 BTW Papers DLC.

From Timothy Thomas Fortune

Brooklyn, NY., Saturday Evening [Feb. 10, 1900][1]

Dear Mr Washington: I omitted to enclose Mr Villard's letter to you concerning the article he asked you for and which I sent to you early in the week. You should have Mr. Villard's letter in submitting the article to him.

I enclose a Dunbar story which appeared in the Evening Post today. The story has thoroughly exasperated me. If noble effort in our men is to be habitually dereded in fiction and all asperation is to be jeered at as Dunbar invariably does then it would be better for the race if it had no shining light in literature.

Fortunately we are able to turn from Dunbar to Chesnutt,[2] from pure niggerism from the white man's point of view hashed up by a black man, to the genuine negro presented by a literary artist who has full sympathy with the low tendencies and the high asperations of the race. I am reading "the Wife of His Youth" now. Yours truly

T Thomas Fortune

ALS Con. 172 BTW Papers DLC.

1 The dating is suggested by the Paul Laurence Dunbar story, "Silas Jackson," mentioned in the letter, which appeared in the New York *Evening Post* on Feb. 10,

1900, 15. The melodramatic story was about a farm boy who went to the big city and was corrupted by the evil he found there. His salvation came when he returned to his family and true friends on the farm.

2 Charles Waddell Chesnutt (1858-1932) was born in Cleveland, Ohio, and spent his first eight years there before his family moved to North Carolina, where his father ran a store in Fayetteville. From 1879 to 1881 Chesnutt was principal of the State Colored Normal School in Fayetteville. Disliking the proscription of southern society, Chesnutt returned to the North, where he hoped for a freer opportunity to develop his talents as a writer. It was not until twenty years later that he achieved his goal of being a full-time writer. In the meantime he worked as a reporter in New York City, and returned to Cleveland in 1883 to become a clerk in the legal office of the Nickel Plate Railroad Co. Chesnutt studied law and passed the Ohio bar examination in 1887. He earned modest wealth operating a legal stenographic service in Cleveland for many years.

His first rejection slip as a writer came in 1882, and his first story was published in 1885. Chesnutt did not bill himself as a black writer, and his first story in the *Atlantic Monthly* in 1887 was accepted without knowing his race. On the other hand, Chesnutt did not try to hide his racial identity, although he was light-skinned enough to pass for white if he so desired. In 1899, however, with the publication of *The Conjure Woman*, Chesnutt became well known as a black author. Walter Hines Page helped Chesnutt achieve prominence and promoted his work just as he helped promote BTW's *Up From Slavery*. In 1899 Chesnutt also published *The Wife of His Youth and Other Stories* and *Frederick Douglass*. Through his writings he hoped to break down racial barriers. He maintained that he was writing as much for whites as for blacks, since white prejudice was at the heart of the race problem. Reflecting the demands of the marketplace, his earlier stories were typical of the American humor and romanticism acceptable by the popular family magazines of the turn of the century. As Chesnutt matured as a writer, however, his humor became more subtle and satirical. Many of his themes were drawn from black life in the Cape Fear area of North Carolina and were set in the Reconstruction period. His characters at first glance often seemed to be standard literary stereotypes such as the contented slave or the comic Negro, but Chesnutt usually added a dimension of subtlety to their roles that broke the simple stereotype. His themes stressed the humanity and high aspiration of blacks, the mistreatment of minority groups, and the fallibility of human nature.

Chesnutt was not as widely known among his contemporaries as Paul Laurence Dunbar. According to Sylvia L. Render, Chesnutt was in many ways advanced for his time. While Dunbar glorified an idealized past, Chesnutt was exposing the hypocrisy of American race relations. After the three works published in 1899 Chesnutt wrote *The House behind the Cedars* (1900), *The Marrow of Tradition* (1901), and *The Colonel's Dream* (1905). He also contributed to magazines such as the *Atlantic Monthly* and *Century Magazine*. But after only a brief period of success from 1899 to 1901 Chesnutt found that his dream of sustaining himself as a writer had faded, and he reopened his legal stenographic office in 1901. (Render, *The Short Fiction of Charles W. Chesnutt*, 3-56.)

Chesnutt's racial philosophy often put him at odds with BTW, even though the two men maintained a cordial personal relationship. Chesnutt championed full equality for blacks and blamed whites for failing to live up to their democratic ideals. BTW, on the other hand, was reluctant to attack openly the faults of white society. Chesnutt's persuasion was much closer to that of BTW's chief critics W. E. B. Du

Bois and William Monroe Trotter. In 1908 Chesnutt spoke before a Niagara Movement meeting and became an active member of the NAACP in 1910. He refused, however, to enter into the camp of either BTW or the radicals and remained somewhat detached from black politics and independent in judgment. (Meier, *Negro Thought*, 234-44.)

From Edgar Gardner Murphy

Montgomery, Ala., Feb. 17, 1900

Dear Mr. Washington: We had our meeting of the Program Committee last evening, and if those accept whom we shall invite, the Conference will be all that I could expect or desire. I am sure that you will be glad to know that among those upon whom we have definitely decided for addresses, are Dr. Frissell, Dr. Curry and Walter H. Page.[1] I write you now in order to make further inquiry with regard to Gov. MacCorkle. The committee are prepared to invite him, and indeed they will probably ask him for a speech, no matter what the particular subject to which he is assigned. The question before us, however, is as to the line which he will take and the measure of ability which you consider him to possess. On the morning of May 9th, at 10 o'clock, there will be a discussion of the franchise in the South. Addresses will probably be made by Governor Longino[2] of Mississippi, and by Col. Waddell,[3] Mayor of Wilmington, N.C. Both of these men may be expected to present in the most forcible way the arguments for the disfranchisement of our negro population. Now, we are going to give some one who is in favor of making the suffrage-limitation applicable to both races alike, the privilege of closing the debate (so far as set speeches are concerned). While he will speak after the two gentlemen whom I have named, yet that large advantage should be exercised by a man of the very best capacities. I may say confidentially that I regard you as best able to select a man to present some one for your side of the case. We know that Gov. MacCorkle is a strong platform speaker, and it is possible that he will also present a thorough and logical discussion of the subject. But we are so anxious to place upon our platform the very strongest man in the South that we can secure, that if there is anyone else besides Gov.

MacCorkle whom you think would take that position more forcibly and more persuasively before a Southern audience, send me his name at once, and we will transfer Gov. MacCorkle to some other part of the program. I am sure you see what our purpose is. We wish the very strongest advocate of equal justice to the negro and the white man who can be found.

One of the members of the committee has also suggested in regard to this debate that it would be to the advantage of your side of this question if a strong speaker could be found who is living himself under conditions which present the problems in their acutest form. There are many men in the South with whom the words, "a West Virginian" would not go very far, for the reason that race conditions there do not place the Negro at the enormous numerical advantage which he finds in certain sections of the South. On the other hand, we want a man, no matter what his section, who will deal with the case upon its merits, with the greatest intelligence and force. *If you are prepared to tell us that Gov. Mac-Corkle is this man, I shall at once write and invite him to come to us for that purpose.* We shall allow him one hour if he needs it. Kindly reply at the earliest possible moment. Cordially and Sincerely,

Edgar Gardner Murphy

TLS Con. 182 BTW Papers DLC.

1 Page later declined to participate in the Montgomery Race Conference when he discovered that William Bourke Cockran, representing the North, was to speak on the same program for the purpose of advocating the repeal of the Fifteenth Amendment. Page wrote Murphy that it would be fatal to the conference to have any addresses advocating repeal. He added that it had been a "grave mistake" when the Fifteenth Amendment had been adopted, "but I should consider it a much graver mistake to repeal it now, even if it were possible to repeal it." (Apr. 5, 1900, Walter Hines Page Papers, MH.) Murphy wired Page again urging his participation and stating that Page was being unfair to him, the committee, and the cause of the Negro, and that "Washington earnestly advises acceptance." (Apr. 16, 1900, Walter Hines Page Papers, MH.) Page replied: "You have put me in company that my friends think unjust to me & unfortunate for Conference. I decline with great regret." (Apr. 17, 1900, Walter Hines Page Papers, MH.)

2 Andrew Houston Longino (1855-1942) was a U.S. district attorney before serving as governor of Mississippi from 1900 to 1904. He was elected on a platform of economy in government, and his most notable achievement was the construction of a new state capitol that was paid for in cash without incurring new state debts. He was an unsuccessful candidate for governor in 1919.

3 Alfred Moore Waddell (1834-1912), a lawyer and formerly an editor and congressman, was the leader of the bloody Wilmington Riot in 1898. During the white

supremacy fever that preceded the elections that year, Waddell inflamed white Wilmingtonians by declaring race conditions intolerable in a city where "nigger lawyers are sassing white men in our courts; nigger root doctors are crowding white physicians out of business." (Edmonds, *The Negro and Fusion Politics in North Carolina,* 164.) During the riot town officials were driven from office and Waddell was elected mayor in a virtual coup d'etat. He served as mayor until 1904.

From William Edward Burghardt Du Bois

Atlanta, Ga., Feb 17 1900

Confidential.

My Dear Mr. Washington: I have taken a rather unreasonable amount of time to consider your kind offer to come to Tuskeegee, and I have not yet fully decided. I want however to lay some considerations before you & then when I come to the Conference as I now think I shall, we can talk further. Since your offer was made I have had two other chances — tho' not formal offers: one to stand for a professorship in Howard University and the other to enter the race for the position of Superintendant of the Washington colored schools. Then of course there are the claims of the work here.

Now the question that really puzzles me in these cases is the one as to where I would really be most useful. Howard I cut from the list without hesitation — I'm sure I shouldn't get on well there for it's a poorly conducted establishment. On the other hand I really question as to how much I am really needed at Tuskeegee. I think to be sure I could be of use there but after all would it not be a rather ornamental use than a fundamental necessity? Would not my department be regarded by the public as a sort of superfluous addition not quite in consonance with the fundamental Tuskeegee idea? On the other hand there is no doubt that I am needed at Atlanta and that in the future as much closer cooperation between Tuskeegee Atlanta & Hampton is possible in the future than in the past. Well this is the line along which I had been thinking some months, when there came letters urging me to seek the position of superintendent of the Washington D.C. schools. It seems that Mr. Cook[1] who has held the position over 20 years has some thoughts of resigning. Now the question comes Is not this the most useful place of the three & could I not serve both your cause & the general cause of the Negro at the National capital better than elsewhere? I wish you'd think this matter over seriously & give me your best advice. Boiled down the questions are: 1st Am I really needed at Tuskeegee. 2nd Considering the assured success of the Tuskeegee institute already are there not weaker places where pioneer work is necessary. 3rd Is not the Washington position — provided always I could get it — such a place?

Of course if I should apply for the W. place your indorsement would go further probably than anyone's else. Could you conscientiously give it?

I write you thus frankly & hope you will consider the matter from my point of view & give me the results of your wisdom. Very Sincerely

W. E. B. Du Bois

ALS Con. 170 BTW Papers DLC.

1 George Frederick Thompson Cook (1835-1912) was superintendent of the black schools of the District of Columbia almost continuously from 1868 to 1900. He was one of a small number of blacks who held membership in the Washington Board of Trade, the leading business organization of the city. The Cook family was among the most prominent black families in Washington. John F. Cook, George F. T. Cook's father, was a longtime educator in the city before the Civil War and a founder of the Fifteenth Street Presbyterian Church.

From Timothy Thomas Fortune

Washington, D.C., Feb 20, 1900

Dear Mr. Washington: I have read Congressman Randell's letters with interest. You and I have gone over the Crumpacker bill thoroughly, and I have explained my views to you thoroughly. There has nothing occurred to cause me to change them.

I am very sure that it will be bad *for us* to have the United States recognize the right of any State to disfranchise a part of its citizenship for failure to live up to the requirements of the 14th and 15th amendments. The Crumpacker bill will do that.

I am still of the opinion that it would be bad policy for you to get mixed up in the controversy. I understand that the party leaders have decided to let the measure go over until after the presidential election. Yours truly

T. Thomas Fortune

ALS Con. 172 BTW Papers DLC.

William Henry Baldwin, Jr., to Henry C. Davis[1]

[New York City] February 21, 1900

Dear Mr. Davis: I have your letter and note what you say about the higher education of the negro. I raise no question whatever about the higher education of some negroes, but you and I are dealing with the question broadly in the South. Let me warn you that from a personal knowledge of the point of view of the negroes in Boston that their leadership is the last one to follow. The influence of some negroes who have been highly educated at Harvard College, is purely an attempt on their part to be white people. I say this deliberately. I know it from their own people. Now you and I know that that point of view is destructive when dealing with the mass of the negroes in the South. If the negro in Boston can put himself on the plane of the white man, let him do it. He is welcome to it. But he is a false teacher if he tries to apply those principles to the education of the negro in the South. Yours very truly,

W. H. Baldwin Jr.

TLSr Con. 792 BTW Papers DLC. Marked "Copy to Mr. Washington."

1 Henry C. Davis, grandson of Lucretia Mott, was a Philadelphia wool merchant and capitalist. Davis was an abolitionist and Quaker who believed that education was the means of salvation for black Americans. He was a trustee of Tuskegee Institute from 1899 until his death in Jan. 1901 at the age of sixty-two.

From John Elmer Milholland[1]

London, Feb. 23rd/1900

Personal

My Dear Sir, Our commonalty of interests in the Negro Race is sufficient justification, I hope, for this letter to you.

Some weeks ago I received a request from the Editor of Howard's Magazine for an article based on my experience over here.

I have become somewhat weary of the average contribution on this subject of the Negro's future. The treatment has become conventional, where it is not pessimistic. I have thrown together a few thoughts that present matters, I hope, in a little more comprehensive way, and, consequently, more hopeful. Just as Toryism is rapidly reaching its limit here in England, so the wave of Negro oppression is nearing the ebb at home.

I send you the article to transmit to Howard's Magazine if you think best. I don't know anything about the publication, but the single copy I saw impressed me favorably; that is to say I think it represents a serious effort to build up a publication that might be of value in the general work of securing fair play for our fellow citizens of African descent.

But I have made some mistakes in my co-operative efforts with your people in the past; mistakes which I would like to avoid repetition of in the future; mistakes based upon a lack of knowledge and undue confidence; so I want you to feel free to use the article wherever you please. Let it appear anonymously.

I have been over here in Europe for several months, but I shall sail for New York within a short time, so perhaps you had better reply to my office in the Tribune Building, New York.

I saw in a stray copy of "The Tribune" that your efforts to raise a large fund for your Institute had met with a considerable success. How did it come out? Did you get your money?

I would like to know from you what are the best newspapers and magazines at present that are conducted primarily in the interests of the Negro. Outside of Fortune and his "Age" I know of very few worthy of any consideration whatever. Sincerely yours,

Jno. E. Milholland

P.S. A friend of yours here, Mrs. Fisher-Unwin, was dining at my house this week. She is one of the charter members of this Internation Club, which may interest you. Perhaps I shall have the pleasure of seeing you in New York soon.

J. E. M.

TLS Con. 182 BTW Papers DLC. The postscript is in Milholland's hand.

1 John Elmer Milholland (1860-1925) was a writer, businessman, and reformer. He was educated in England and Ireland as a youth and later attended New York University. He was a reporter and editorial writer for the New York *Tribune* for twelve years. Milholland became a wealthy businessman as the result of his development of the underground system of delivering mail in New York City. He was president of the Batcheller Pneumatic Tube Co. and director of the American Pneumatic Tube Service Co. In 1904 he organized a foreign syndicate which controlled tube delivery of mail in Europe.

Milholland was an active member of the Republican State Club of New York beginning in 1892. He championed numerous causes including prison reform, pacifism, woman suffrage, federal aid to education, and election reform. His daughter, Inez Milholland Boissevain, was known as the American Joan of Arc for her role in the women's rights movement. John E. Milholland promoted the cause of civil rights as president of the Constitutional League of the United States beginning in 1903. He believed that the best way for blacks to secure civil rights was through test cases, a philosophy that was used later in the work of the NAACP. He was a founder of the NAACP in 1909 and served as its first treasurer. He proposed that the Constitutional League merge with the National Negro Committee for the purpose of engaging in legal work to advance black rights, but the merger never occurred.

Milholland, like other white liberals such as Oswald Garrison Villard, supported BTW in the 1890s but became disillusioned with his conservative leadership. In 1905, at a meeting of the NNBL where Milholland was to speak, BTW drew him aside and asked him not to discuss disfranchisement in his speech. This alienated Milholland, who turned toward activists such as W. E. B. Du Bois and William Monroe Trotter who shared his sense of outrage concerning racial injustice. (Fox, *Guardian of Boston*, 123.)

From Charles Waddell Chesnutt

Cleveland, O., February 24, 1900

My dear Mr. Washington, I am in receipt of your favor acknowledging my reviews of your book. It was very kind of you to write, for so many good things are said of you that they are no novelty. I am glad to add my weak voice to the chorus.

I also have your letter requesting copies of my books for the Tuskegee library. I have ordered "The Conjure Woman" and "The Wife of His Youth" sent to you, and will see that you get the other — the "Life of Frederick Douglass." A visit to Tuskegee at some time in the future is one of the pleasures I look forward [to]. I have met a number of gentlemen who have been there, and they all agree upon the wonderful results accomplished by your labors. Sincerely yours,

Chas. W. Chesnutt

ALS Con. 168 BTW Papers DLC.

An Item in the Washington *Colored American*

Indianapolis, Ind. [Feb. 24, 1900]

RACE PREJUDICE IN INDIANA

With much regret I mention a fact detrimental to the principles and reflecting no credit upon the reputation of our state. It was the refusal of the Hotel Doxey, the leading hotel at Anderson, this State, to entertain Booker T. Washington who was engaged as principal speaker at the Indiana League of Republican Clubs, held in that city February 12th. The landlord promptly informed the committee that no colored person would be accommodated at that house. But the remaining hotels as well as the homes of many private individuals were proffered the committee for the use of the distinguished visitor. The incident is much deplored by the committee in charge, and Hotel Doxey comes in for much unpleasant notoriety, made more emphatic by the attitude of the mayor of the city, Mr. Dunlap,[1] who when consulted as to his pleasure about riding with Mr. Washington, replied without a moment's hesitation, "I shall be glad to do so, if Mr. Washington doesn't object," which attitude stands out in commendable contradistinction to that of the Hotel Doxey management.

Washington *Colored American*, Feb. 24, 1900, 6.

[1] Morey M. Dunlap, a lawyer, was mayor of Anderson from 1894 to 1902.

448

From Albert Enoch Pillsbury[1]

Boston   25 Feb 1900

My dear Sir: I have the *Atlantic* which you were good enough to send me, but I had read the article as the closing chapter of your book: indeed I quoted it at the meeting referred to in our correspondence.

I fully appreciate, and I well understand that you do, the impatience, not to say indignation, of the more ambitious colored men at the suggestion that they are fit for nothing but to be hewers of wood and drawers of water, and if I were one of them it is quite possible that I should be crying aloud for the impossible and unattainable, as some of them are. I deeply regret, too, that the public sentiment of the country does not demand, nor indeed permit, the enforcement of the Constitution throughout the Southern States, for black men equally with white: and I still hope that the nefarious attempts to defraud your race of its political rights under forms of law will be defeated in the Supreme Court. I feel that if I were a colored man I would never lay down my arms until this battle had been fought and won. At the same time I am compelled, however reluctantly, to accept your view of this question, and to believe that the black man must, as a practical matter, work his way to political equality through industrial elevation and the influence which the possession of property and of skilled labor will command. In short, I believe with you, and sympathise with those who refuse to accept this conclusion.

I need not say that I shall be very happy to see you whenever you find it convenient to call, tho' I should not think of making any demand upon the time of a man engaged in so important a work as yours. I am with great respect   Yours very truly

A. E. Pillsbury

ALS Con. 181 BTW Papers DLC.

1 Albert Enoch Pillsbury (1849-1930) was a Boston lawyer who served as attorney general of Massachusetts from 1891 to 1894. Beginning in 1896 he lectured on constitutional law at Boston University Law School. Pillsbury was an active member of the Boston Committee to Advance the Cause of the Negro, which in 1911 became a branch of the NAACP. It was Pillsbury who drafted the bylaws of the NAACP. He continued to play an active role in NAACP affairs for many years. In 1913 he re-

signed his membership in the American Bar Association when that organization rejected the membership of William H. Lewis, a black assistant U.S. attorney and supporter of BTW. While Lewis and two other black attorneys were eventually accepted as a compromise measure, it was clear to Pillsbury that the bar association was drawing the color line.

From William Edward Burghardt Du Bois

Atlanta, Ga., Feb 26 190[0]

My Dear Mr Washington: On reaching here yesterday I found several urgent letters asking me to apply for the Washington position before it was too late. I thought therefore that application would do no harm even if on later personal investigation I found the place not to my liking. Therefore I wired you asking for your endorsement. I do not of course want you to do anything which would compromise you or make you appear to be "in politics" but if without prejudice to your position & the school's you could endorse me I shall appreciate it. I repeat that I have not definitely decided to accept the Washington place nor am I certain of not coming to Tuskegee. My present leaning however is toward Washington for I seem to see there a chance for a great work. However I shall go there next month & investigate. I want to thank you again for your hospitality during my very pleasant stay at Tuskegee. Yours &c

W. E. B. Du Bois

ALS   Con. 170   BTW Papers   DLC.

To Francis Jackson Garrison

Tuskegee, Ala., Feb. 27, 1900

Dear Mr. Garrison: A number of responsible colored men are now making a systematic effort to have the Louisiana Election Law tested before the United States Supreme Court. It is difficult to get all the cash necessary to pay competent lawyers, and I have thought that perhaps you might like to help us find persons in Boston who would consider it a pleasure to contribute towards this object.[1] I prefer that my name not be used in connection with the matter. Yours truly,

Booker T. Washington

TLS   Francis J. Garrison Papers   NN-Sc.

1 Garrison replied that he would call the matter to the attention of some Bostonians and asked BTW for more details about the strategy of the case and the names of the lawyers involved, which he felt he needed to know before soliciting contributions. (Mar. 2, 1900, Con. 173, BTW Papers, DLC.)

From Richard Price Hallowell

Boston, March 2, 1900

Dear Mr. Washington: Your favor of the 27th ult. received. I shall be glad to help along an effort to have the Louisiana Election Law tested before the United States Supreme Court, and for that purpose I hand you herewith my check to your order for $20. Money spent for such purposes is too often expended injudiciously, but as this is to go through your hands I have no hesitation on that account.

You suggest that I shall find persons here "who would consider it a pleasure to contribute towards this object." Unfortunately at present there seems to be a profound indifference in regard to the political rights of the Southern colored people, and I question whether any appeal of mine, made simply on my own responsibility, would avail. You, however, have the ear of what is called the conservative as well as that of the more radical friends of your race, and applications from you would undoubtedly be favorably received.[1] If you have not time to give the matter your personal attention, I will take it off your hands and acting as your agent will make application to any and every one in Boston whose name you will send to me. This proposition I know is contrary to your wish that your "name shall not be used in connection with the matter," but without it I would prefer to limit my connection to my own contribution. Very truly yours,

R. P. Hallowell

TLS   Con. 199   BTW Papers   DLC.

1 Hallowell continued to urge BTW to endorse publicly the fight against the Louisiana Constitution, but BTW preferred to remain behind the scenes. (See Hallowell to BTW, Oct. 10, 1900, and a statement written for Richard Price Hallowell, ca. Oct. 10, 1900, below.)

From John Wesley Ross[1]

Washington   March 6, 1900

Dear Sir: Knowing your intelligent interest in the cause of education, I take the liberty of addressing you with regard to a possible vacancy at the end of the current school year in the position of Superintendent of Colored Schools in the District of Columbia.

The present incumbent, Mr. Cook, is a man whom everybody respects for his personal qualities; but the entire Board of School Trustees has recommended a change. There are many ambitious applicants in the District; but, in view of the division in the ranks of the people here and the many cases of those who are prominent having relatives in the schools as teachers, it would seem to be advisable to find if possible some one thoroughly educated, of first class executive ability and of incorruptible integrity who would be available.

If you will kindly give me your views on this important matter, I assure you that they will receive due consideration by the Board of Commissioners, and that no publicity will be given to the same without your consent. Some names which have been suggested are: W. S. Scarborough, of Wilberforce; W. E. B. DuBois, of Atlanta; and Prof. Brown, of Hampton. Very truly yours,

John W. Ross
Commissioner

TLS Con. 182 BTW Papers DLC. Written on stationery of the Commissioners of the District of Columbia.

1 John Wesley Ross (1841-1902) was postmaster of Washington, D.C., from 1888 to 1890 and commissioner of education for the District of Columbia from 1890 to 1900.

From Henry C. Davis

Phila   7th Mar. 1900

My dear Mr. Washington   After talking with Dr. Murphy, I am satisfied that it would be unwise for you to come over to the dinner I give him on Friday evening.[1] It would be sure to get into the newspapers and be reported at the South & would give his opponents a handle to attack him, which none of us want. Both he & I regret this, but he feels that you will appreciate it & I shall not be surprised if your reply to my invitation is that your judgement is that you had better not be there. Yours very truly

Henry C. Davis

ALS Con. 170 BTW Papers DLC.

[1] Davis had written BTW on March 5, 1900, about the Murphy dinner at the Union League. He said: "I shall be glad to have you come over." (Con. 170, BTW Papers, DLC.)

From Lyman Abbott

New York   March 9, 1900

My dear Mr. Washington: Thank you for your letter of February 27th. My impression was derived, not from the article in the "Atlantic," but from conversation with you, in which probably you spoke of employing some Southern white people, and I derived from it the impression that you employed some Southern white teachers.[1]

I have written to Mr. Adams in explanation.

I shall hope to see you when you next come to New York, and confer with you on the subject of the biographical reminiscences we are very desirous to secure from you, and the publication of which we are sure will do good to the cause you have at heart. Yours, sincerely,

Lyman Abbott

TLSr Con. 166 BTW Papers DLC.

1 BTW had a strict rule that no whites could be employed as regular full-time resident faculty. Several whites were employed as northern agents, but these persons were not on campus. Alice J. Kaine, a white home economics expert, worked on campus several months each year from 1894 to 1896, and BTW employed Max Bennett Thrasher as a ghost-writer and public relations man from 1895 to 1903. Thrasher, however, seldom remained on campus for any length of time. Other whites who were employed off campus were Robert Charles Bedford, a northern agent, Daniel Cranford Smith, an accountant, and Robert E. Park, a ghost-writer. BTW wanted Tuskegee Institute to be a model of black self-help, and he did not want the school's success attributed to whites.

From Hollis Burke Frissell

Hampton, Va. March 10, 1900

My dear Mr. Washington: Accept my thanks for your letter of the 20th ult. in regard to the Fort Valley School, which has awaited my return from the north. I am glad to know about it and will take the liberty of forwarding it to Mr. Dickerman,[1] as I want him to have all the information about these schools that he can get, so as to make some sort of a report to the Capon Springs Conference.

I attended a dinner for Dr. Murphy held in Philadelphia last evening, and feel that a good start has been made towards interesting our northern friends in his work; the impression which he made seemed an excellent one.

Two matters have come up during this northern trip which I will speak frankly about to you, as I always do. One of them is in regard to Benson. The interest in Benson is very strong, especially in Springfield. I saw Mr. Brooks,[2] who as you know, has gone on the board of trustees; also one of the editors of the Springfield Republican, both of whom seemed somewhat troubled about your position. I am wondering whether it is not best for us to take up Benson's school, and set it right, for the man seems to have created a favorable feeling, and if he is working along agricultural and industrial lines, is it not best for us to try and set him right rather than to oppose him? I could see that your position was misunderstood, and though I did my best to explain it, I felt that my explanation was not quite satisfactory to his friends.

The other point I wished to speak of was in connection with your relation to the Unitarian Church. I have always stoutly denied that you were a Unitarian. The Presbyterian clergyman in Newark told me that Dr. Weaver[3] reported that a lady in Pittsburg intended to make a large gift to Tuskegee, but when she questioned you, you were unwilling to deny that you were a Unitarian, and her gift was withdrawn. Dr. Weaver is stating that you are a Unitarian, and backs it by the statement of Dr. J. K. Cowan,[4] of the Presbyterian Board. Now I am not at all sure whether it is worth while to take up this matter, but I thought that you ought to know just how it stands.

If you think it is worth while for us to try to straighten things out at Kowaliga, perhaps I can get a day or two when I go to the Montgomery Conference in May.

I have promised Mr. Davis to speak at the Philadelphia meetings on the 19th and 22nd of this month. Sincerely yours,

H. B. Frissell

TLS Con. 172 BTW Papers DLC.

1 George Sherwood Dickerman (1843-1937), a Congregational minister of New Haven, Conn., was field superintendent of the American Missionary Association from 1893 to 1895. He was general field agent of the Conference for Education in the South from 1899 to 1901, general field agent of the Southern Education Board from 1902 to 1905, associate secretary of the Southern Education Board from 1905 to 1910, and general field agent of the John F. Slater Fund from 1907 to 1910. Dickerman's reports of the educational needs of whites and blacks in the South were instrumental in launching and sustaining the Southern Education Movement.

2 John Graham Brooks (1846-1938) was a lecturer and labor expert whose interests encompassed many reform movements of the Progressive Era such as child labor, anti-imperialism, consumer protection, and southern education. In 1910 Brooks wrote *An American Citizen*, a biography of William H. Baldwin, Jr. (Mooney, *John Graham Brooks*.)

3 Possibly Edward Ebenezer Weaver (1864-1931), a Presbyterian clergyman in Baltimore from 1899 to 1901.

4 Possibly Edward Payson Cowan (1840-1918), who was corresponding secretary of the Board of Missions for Freedmen from 1893 to 1918.

From Richard Price Hallowell

Boston, March 10, 1900

Dear Mr. Washington: Under date of Nov. 11, 1896, you gave me a strong endorsement of the Kowaliga Academic & Industrial Institute, Mr. C. J. Calloway, principal, Mr. Wm. E. Benson, treasurer. You have never withdrawn this endorsement and on the strength of it I have made moderate contributions to the support of this institute. Mr. Benson is now in Boston, and from him I learn that you are no longer a trustee and that you have withdrawn your approval both of him and the School. Mrs. Barrows, one of the trustees, advises me that she has seen you recently and has questioned you in regard to this matter, but for some reason you were not very definite in stating the cause of the change in your estimate of the Institution and the young man who once had your confidence. Mrs. Barrows has just returned from Kowaliga and expresses herself quite strongly in her approval of both Mr. Benson and the school. Mr. Benson has made a very favorable impression upon the people of Boston who are interested in the education of the Southern colored people, but your change of attitude, very naturally and very properly, throws a cloud upon him and his work. He has shown me some of your letters to him and has talked over the matter with me quite freely, but I have failed to draw from him any satisfactory explanation. If he is unworthy of support, the sooner he is discredited here the better for all concerned. If he is not, there is no one who would be quicker than you will be to remove so far as is in your power all cause of distrust. Will you kindly tell me just what it is that prompted you to withdraw & now prompts you to withhold your endorsement? Very truly yours

Richard P. Hallowell

TLS   Con. 199   BTW Papers   DLC.

To Emmett Jay Scott

Grand Union Hotel, New York, Mar. 11, 1900

Dear Mr. Scott: In addition to sending the Advertiser regularly also please send the Tuskegee News when I am away.

I meant to have written you about the conference which I held in Washington last Sunday. It was attended by Congressman White, Mr. Fortune, Mr. Cooper, Mr. Chase, Mr. Murray, Mr. Lawson and several others. We put on foot some plans which I think are going to result in good regarding the Louisiana election law. One interesting part of the meeting was that Chase complained that the trouble with present conditions was that the situation needed a conservative leader and that I ought to have the place occupied by Bishop Walters.

I have just written Dr. Grant to postpone the Chicago meetings. This makes considerable change in my plans. I found that I could not get out of presiding at the meeting on April 3d and will have to do so. After the meeting on April 3d I want to have time enough to reach the nearest engagement in either Mississippi or Arkansas, and I wish you would ask Mr. Palmer to arrange for us to spend just as little time in holding the four meetings as possible. After the four meetings are over I want to go back to Tuskegee if possible and spend as much time as I can there before going to Cleveland. Please work this whole matter out and let me have a new schedule. You can get the check cashed and give Mr. Palmer what he needs and keep the other until I get there. Tell Mr. Palmer to keep an account of his expenses.

Please dispose of as many of the lithographs of the school grounds as you can in the South.

All the letters that I have received relate to Berkshire pigs. I presume that you wrote about the Jersey bull and an Ayrshire bull also.

Please have the school pay this Education bill. It is not a personal matter; I do not remember subscribing for it personally and I never read it. It always goes to the reading room.

What about the voucher for the $250?

I hope you will see that the catalogue is hurried up. It should be gotten out before school closes. In making up the catalogue instead of using the word "Psychology" please use "mind study."

Please get the name and address of the colored lady with whom I was corresponding regarding coming to Tuskegee last year. She is now in Straight University.

I want to sign the letters that go to the graduates. Yours truly,

Booker T. Washington

No Advertisers received yet.

Please remind Mrs. Washington to get Mrs. Bruce's cut and send it to me as soon as possible.

B.T.W.

TLS   Con. 186   BTW Papers   DLC.

To Francis Jackson Garrison

Grand Union Hotel, New York, Mar. 11, 1900

My dear Mr. Garrison: Replying briefly to your kind letter of recent date regarding the Louisiana Election Law I would say that I had a conference with friends in Washington as I came through a few days ago, and as near as we can get at the matter now it will require $2,000 to take the case up through the Supreme Court. The present plan is to get lawyers in Louisiana to take the case through the state courts, and then if it becomes necessary to take it to the Supreme Court the committee has decided to secure the services of Hon. George Edmunds.

This will be my address for the next week. Yours truly,

Booker T. Washington

TLS   Francis J. Garrison Papers   NN-Sc.

To William Edward Burghardt Du Bois

Grand Union Hotel, New York. Mar. 11, 1900

Dear Dr. Du Bois: Please consider the contents of this letter strictly private. If you have not done so, I think it not best for you to use the letter of recommendation which I have sent you. I have just received a letter[1] direct from one of the Commissioners in the District asking me to recommend some one for the vacancy there and I have recommended you as strongly as I could. Under the circumstances it would make your case stronger for you not to present the letter which I have given you for the reason that it would tend to put you in the position of seeking the position. It is pretty well settled, judging by the Commissioner's letter, that some one outside of the District is going to be appointed.

This will be my address for the next week. Yours truly,

Booker T. Washington

TLS   W. E. B. Du Bois Papers   MU.

1 See John Wesley Ross to BTW, Mar. 6, 1900, above.

From John Wesley Ross

Washington. March 12, 1900

My dear Sir: Your courteous response to my letter to you of March 6 was duly received; and I assure you that I appreciate the kindly interest you have taken in the matter.

I will see that your wishes with regard to not allowing your name to be made public is observed; and will take pleasure, also, in bringing your views to the attention of my associate Commissioners. Again thanking you, I am, Very truly yours,

John W. Ross

TLS   Con. 182   BTW Papers   DLC.

From Timothy Thomas Fortune

Washington, D.C., March 12, 7 P.M. [1900]

Dear Mr. Washington: I have some interesting inside information as the result of the day's developments: Commissioner Ross, who will dispose of the Superintendency is a Democrat. W. H. Councill has the backing of the Alabama and other Democrats for the position. Ross, I understand, favors you and will tender you the position. If you decline Councill will stand the next best show, unless proof is forthcoming that he is morally unfit. *We can't have Councill.* Terrell[1] stands next in line, then Hugh M. Browne. Now, I don't know how you feel about the matter as it relates to you personally, and make no expression thereon, as you have your own work, but if you should be offered the job and should think of taking it *Terrell will give you the full benefit of his abilities* and *experience in the work.* But we must defeat the Councill movement. Let me hear from you fully so that I can direct my fight against Councill intelligently and effectively. Of course I am with you.

Saw Chase today and he is on the inside [of] these things. But the crank is going to rebegin the war on Cooper.

I hand you Richards'[2] letter. Give the answer.

I am awfully tired.

Good night. Yours truly

T. Thomas Fortune

ALS   Con. 172   BTW Papers   DLC.

[1] Fortune had written BTW earlier the same day: *"I am very anxious for Terrell to win because he is the best man in the situation and because he is your and my good and active friend."* (Mar. 12, 1900, Con. 172, BTW Papers, DLC.)

[2] William Henry Richards was born of free parents in Tennessee in 1856. He received a law degree from Howard University Law School in 1881. In 1890 he became a lecturer in law at Howard, and he was president of the Howard University Alumni Association from 1889 to 1908. He also served two terms as president of the Bethel Literary and Historical Association. Richard's letter apparently referred to arrangements for BTW to speak before Bethel Literary on May 22.

To Timothy Thomas Fortune

Grand Union Hotel, New York. March 14, 1900

My dear Mr. Fortune: I have your letter of recent date regarding the superintendent of the public schools there. I don't believe that you are on the right scent yet. I have some other information tho I thank you for writing me so fully. It would be a disgrace to get that man from Alabama[1] into so important a position and it must be defeated. I find that I can be in Washington on the 23d of the month. Suppose you communicate with Wright at once and see if he can be there on that day. When I see you I will go over fully with you the situation in regard to the public school matter there.

I have gone pretty fully through the article for the International Magazine and find that you seem to have misunderstood the subject. The subject which you have discussed you have discussed well, but you will find that the subject which I promised to write about was "The Economic Relation of the Negro to American Progress" while you simply have the relation of the Negro to American life or something of that kind. I shall be able, however, in revising the matter to use a good portion of your matter but not all of it.

I have heard nothing from the Nichols people and presume they are going ahead with the publication without re-submitting it to you altho I told them to submit it to you again.

I have been very busy during the last few days, having to go to Boston among other things. Yours truly,

Booker T. Washington

Will send you some money this week.

B.T.W.

TLS Con. 172 BTW Papers DLC. The postscript is in BTW's hand.

[1] William Hooper Councill.

From Richard W. Thompson

Washington, D.C., Mar. 14, 1900

Confidential

Dear Mr. Washington: Luck is rather against my seeing you of late when you pass through Washington. I was called home to Indianapolis Feb. 27, to bury my mother. This was the day you wrote me, and I received it at office when I reported Monday morning the 12th. I feel grateful for your kindly consideration, and shall try to deserve the favors you repeatedly show me. I had occasion to say

461

something in your interest last week at a largely attended meeting of the Propagandist Club at Indianapolis, and the house concurring with my refutation of the principal speaker's arguments against your educational theory, we succeeded in forcing him to acknowledge that the Washington idea was growing so popular that he felt obliged to take an opposite view in order to bring out a full and interesting discussion. The leaders of thought in the city were present — Knox,[1] Bagby,[2] Lewis,[3] Manning,[4] Baughman,[5] Furniss,[6] Lott,[7] et al. Indianapolis is solid for you.

Owing to demands on my time and inadequate compensation (to be frank), I have relinquished the "managing editorship" of The Colored American, and am planning to write news letters, special articles, etc. on my own hook. Several papers have arranged to give me right of way on general matters, with power to make special arrangements for special productions. This gives far more latitude than I have been able to get lately on The Colored American. I may start a feature with it, however, under some fanciful title. I hope to be able to serve my friends, and any suggestion from those who have stood by me, will receive prompt and "prayerful" attention.

Anent the Louisiana case, some of us have our doubts about the Parlange test reaching the marrow of the situation. It is well to understand the issue thoroughly, before going into battle on it. As soon as I can learn particulars, I shall let you know the status of things hereabouts.

I have not received the birds-eye picture noted in your letter. I should like to get it, and frame it for my home study, which I am gradually fitting up, with features of interest to the race.

As to the school superintendency, I am inclined to believe that the most *popular* appointment would be a man long identified with District interests — Terrell, for instance. He is young, full of originality, ambitious, clean, thoroughly educated and a "good mixer." If a squabble arises and the plum goes outside, Du Bois, of Atlanta would be the most *acceptable* man in the country — acceptable from a *scholarly* standpoint. Du Bois would command respect because of his attainments, but not popularity. It looks to people here that the fight is between Terrell and Du Bois against a minor field, and for reasons which cannot be given here, with the rank and file, the victory of either would be an "even break."

Personally, I would prefer Terrell, as against Du Bois, and the young men in the schools and departments stand with him. But, like all progressive spirits, he has bitter enemies, and he must also shoulder the enemies of his wife. These would favor Du Bois — or any outsider. Your name is mentioned, and it is conceded that you could have it by a nod of assent, and everybody of moment would be satisfied and the town would feel honored. The feeling is that you probably could not afford to locate here, but some say the acceptance of this post would enable you to happily combine the industrial and the higher education, with the result of silencing in three months all of the croakers who have been trying to corner you for the last four years. This is the situation candidly stated. A "tip" from you would put some ginger into the fight, and give it a national coloring. Suppose you are asked if you would accept the superintendency, would it not be a good idea to give me half-a-column interview to use as I see fit? *If you think so*, send to me at Census Office. I have undertaken the Washington correspondence of The Freeman, The World, Baltimore Afro-American Ledger, and Atlanta Age, and can, of course, put it in The American. More anon. Your friend,

R. W. Thompson

P.S. I am getting along nicely at office. While I am on only $50, they are giving me light clerical work, and state that by the middle of April, I am to be examined, and promoted, probably to $900. It is hinted by the authorities that I shall *pass*.

T.

ALS Con. 185 BTW Papers DLC.

1 George L. Knox, born in slavery in Tennessee, migrated to Indianapolis during the Civil War and became a successful barber. In the 1880s his shop in the Bates House, a leading hotel, was among the finest in the city and employed about fifteen persons. Knox purchased the Indianapolis *Freeman*, which he published until 1926. Although he never held office, Knox was influential in Republican politics in Indiana. In 1904 he planned to run for Congress, but BTW persuaded him not to enter the race because he might hurt Roosevelt's chances in Indiana. This experience, plus the Republican handling of the Brownsville affair two years later, soured Knox on the Republicans, and he urged blacks to vote independently. (Thornbrough, *The Negro in Indiana*, 360–61; Meier, *Negro Thought*, 186.)

2 The Bagby family was prominent in black life in Indianapolis. Four members of the family attended Oberlin College and three of these settled in Indianapolis. The fourth, Edwin Bagby, moved to Terre Haute, where he was a school principal. Robert Bruce Bagby, Benjamin D. Bagby, and James D. Bagby were all school principals

in Indianapolis. They also started the first successful black newspaper in Indiana-polis, *The Leader*, which they published from 1879 to 1885. Robert B. Bagby was the first black member of the Indianapolis City Council. (Thornbrough, *The Negro in Indiana*, 334, 384.)

3 Possibly Anderson Lewis, a successful blacksmith and carriage maker in the firm of O'Brien and Lewis.

4 Alexander E. Manning (1856-1925) was born in slavery in Virginia, moving to Indianapolis in 1882. A leading black Democrat, he was editor and publisher of the Indianapolis *World* for thirty-two years and was also the official courier of the Democratic national committee for thirty years.

5 Possibly Leonard Baughman, a black carpenter who was born in Kentucky in 1825.

6 Sumner Alexander Furniss (1874-1953) was a prominent Indianapolis physician, the founder and president of Lincoln Hospital, the first hospital for blacks in that city. He was a lifetime member of the NNBL. William H. Furniss, his father, was also well known among Indianapolis blacks. Originally from Massachusetts, William H. Furniss had been assistant secretary of state of Mississippi during Reconstruction and briefly headed Alcorn A & M College before moving in 1890 to Indianapolis, where he worked as a postal clerk.

7 James H. Lott was a lawyer in Indianapolis beginning in 1895. Earlier, from 1887 to 1890, he was an attorney for the Wabash Railroad in Illinois.

From William Edward Burghardt Du Bois

Atlanta, Ga., Mch 16 1900

My Dear Mr Washington: I called on Mr. Hardwick yesterday. He was pleasant but cautious. He admitted that conductors of the S.R. had been given orders as to sleeping cars, but said this did not apply to inter-state travel. He *thought* a journey from here to Washington would be considered inter-state & that sleepers could be taken. He asked me to state my case in writing & he would lay it before the legal department of the R.R. & give me an early reply. I sent the enclosed letter to him today.[1] Yours &c

W. E. B. Du Bois

ALS Con. 170 BTW Papers DLC.

1 On the evening of Feb. 19, 1900, Du Bois boarded a train in Atlanta for a journey to Savannah and was denied a berth because of his race. Du Bois argued with the Pullman conductor, the train conductor, the flagman, and the car porter, but to no avail. Even though there were plenty of berths available, Du Bois was forced to sit up all night. He later complained to S. H. Hardwick, an agent of the Southern Railway in Atlanta, insisting that the railroad make its policy regarding black travelers clear and hinting at further action on his part. (Mar. 15, 1900, Con. 170, BTW Papers, DLC.)

From Timothy Thomas Fortune

Washington, D.C. March 16, 1900

My dear Mr. Washington: Your telegram of the 15 came yesterday and the letter of the 14th came this morning, and of course I am glad to hear from you. I may be on the wrong scent in the school matter but what I have told you *came from the inside* and was the condition of affairs at that time.

Now we have another development. Chase came in here a moment ago, with D. B. Macrary,[1] cashier of the bank. They came from Commissioner Ross. They want Terrell, as does Cooper, and all the District people want *a District man appointed*. Chase, Cooper, Terrell, Pledger and I are pulling together for Terrell. Ross gave Chase to understand that if you could be brought around to Terrell he would be in a position to appoint and expressed a desire to have a talk with you and me about it. Now, would it not be the best thing for you to do to come here on the 23rd instant, since you have your foot in it, and talk over the situation with Chase, Pledger and me? I think so.

I am sorry I got the International article pitched in the wrong key. I donot often do that.

I have given up the Nichols people, and I am afraid we shall have a lot of typographical and other errors in the book.

My health is good. Yours truly

T. Thomas Fortune

Expect to hear from Wright tomorrow.

ALS Con. 172 BTW Papers DLC.

1 Douglass B. McCary, born in Mississippi in 1865, graduated from Howard University Law School in 1897 and received a master of laws from Howard the following year. He was the cashier of the Capital Savings Bank, the first black-operated bank in the District of Columbia. The bank began operations in 1888 and failed in 1904. Among its officers were a number of BTW's associates in Washington. These included John R. Lynch, who was the bank's president, Whitefield McKinlay, Robert H. Terrell, W. S. Montgomery, Wyatt Archer, and J. A. Johnson, who were all directors. McCary left the bank in 1902 but remained in Washington until about 1904 as a patent attorney and insurance salesman.

From William A. Pledger

Washington, D.C. March-16-00

Dear Washington: I am sorry that you endorsed Dubois for the Supt Negro schools here. He is not of your people. Your friends almost to a man are against him.[1] We want Terrell and you. I hope [you] can find a way to so modify your endorsement that you will not be actively against him. It might be that you could [see] commissioner Ross and go over the case. I know you make no mistake in considering the matter. We fight to make you and you must sometimes listen to us. Come over as soon as you can. I shall be here for several days. Your fr[ien]d

W A Pledger

ALS Con. 181 BTW Papers DLC.

[1] A few days later the prominent black physician John R. Francis, who ran a private sanitarium on Pennsylvania Avenue in Washington, D.C., wrote BTW that Du Bois was the best man for the job and urged BTW to support him. Francis told BTW: *"You can land him."* (Mar. 22, 1900, Con. 172, BTW Papers, DLC.)

To Timothy Thomas Fortune

Grand Union Hotel, New York. March 18, 1900

My dear Mr. Fortune: Please forgive me for my long delay. I now plan to be there on the 23d and we will go over the whole situation, tho I think it by far the best for me to confine my interview with you and Col. Pledger. I do not want to get mixed up in local affairs there. When I explain to you what I have done I think you will see pretty clearly as I do. If I had had any idea that the matter was going to assume so great importance I should have consulted you before making any move then we could have all been working in the same direction. That is the best thing to do and I shall see to it hereafter.

I have a check for $20 for you from the Evening Post people and shall get it into your hands soon.

I suppose you have heard from Prof. Wright by this time. I hope he will be there on the 23d.

I spent an evening last week with your friend Mr. J. E. Milholland. He is a fine fellow and is going to prove helpful to Tuskegee. He thinks a lot of you and you should stick close to him. Yours truly,

Booker T. Washington

TLS   Con. 172   BTW Papers   DLC.

From William Henry Baldwin, Jr.

N.Y. [City] March 19, 1900

Dear Mr. Washington: I have just had a full talk with the President of one of the Southern Lines, (not Mr. Spencer,[1] who is ill at home and cannot be seen) on the subject of the Pullman Bill which was recently passed in Georgia.

I can say for your information that it is the private disposition and intention of the railroad companies to ignore this Bill as far as possible. The railroads have talked it over thoroughly and hope that no question will be raised by the colored people. It is to their interest as railroads not to have such a Bill passed, and they have prevented it in South Carolina and in North Carolina this year. They have talked it over thoroughly with the people in Georgia who passed the Bill and found what position would be taken by the Georgia people if a test case is made. They will interpret the Law to mean that a separate compartment shall be provided for colored people, which shall not be used by white people thereafter. They will aim to put this whole question on to the Pullman Company, and try to avoid it as railroad companies. They feel that if the colored people should raise an issue it would cause nothing but bitterness, and no one would suffer except the colored people. It is even suggested that if it were demanded, and colored people should, by any process of law, secure a berth, and word was sent ahead to some station, it might result in serious conflict. I was impressed with the feeling that if a test case is not made it will soon become a dead letter, but that if it is tested the railroads will be forced to make a fight as well as the Pullman Company. I cannot help advising then even if it may trouble some colored people for

467

the present, that it would be far wiser to let the matter drift a little longer. In such cases as that of Mr. Du Bois,[2] or a possible interference with you, if suffered in silence, it would help as much as anything to bring about a liberal interpretation of the Law.

Let us talk further about it on your return to New York. Yours very truly,

W H Baldwin, Jr.

TLS Con. 792 BTW Papers DLC. Addressed to BTW in care of Henry C. Davis in Philadelphia.

[1] Samuel Spencer (1847-1906) was president and director of the Southern Railway and several other railroads.

[2] See Du Bois to BTW, Mar. 16, 1900, above.

From Joseph Hamilton Tucker[1]

Saint Nicholas Luzon, P.I. March 19th 1900

Sir: I have been in the Phillipine Islands or to be more explicit I have been on the Island of Luzon as a member of H Co. 24th Infantry, since August 11th 1899. Would have written you before but as I felt that to do justice to the Fillipinos I had better wait until I had seen more of him & his mode of living.

I have been in 4 fights since our arrival here and marched from Manila to Aparri (across Luzon) a distance of about 350 miles and I have come in contact with every tribe of Fillipinos on this Island and there is no question in my mind but what the Negro and the Fillipino are closer together than any 2 distinct races on the globe. I have talked with many of the brained men over here and they are all unanimous in their opinion that the Negro of America has an opportunity now that he can ill afford to throw aside, they refer to missionaries, both as teachers and Preachers. The white missionary will never succeed on this Island as the natives have learned to hate everything white. The tales they tell of outrages committed by the spaniard and to an extent by the white American Volunteers are enough to justify them in their persistent fight to be left alone. It is a fact that we have taken many towns without firing a shot and remained there for weeks at a time and never have any trouble. When a white company or regiment would relieve us we would not be gone more than 2 or 3 days until the Insurrectos would be firing on their out Post and keeping them in hot water continously all the time. In fact many of the members of the 24th Infantry have married into the best Fillipino families, and are doing real nicely.

The Fillipino is a slave to the Catholic Church and what ever a Priest tells him be it right or Wrong is believed without a question. But I must say about the worst class of men I ever saw in a Pulpit are the Catholic Priest in the Phillipine Islands. They drink and gambol and are regular attendants at the Sunday chicken fights. They have no schools in the smaller towns and thousands of young men & women are growing up ignorant of the fact that there is any other church than the catholic. Not one in ten wear hat or shoe and the women & children do all the work while the men drink, gambol and fight chickens.

Sir if there was ever an opportunity for the young educated negro to make his mark it is here in the Phillipines. The Fillipino have not the least idea of anything modern either in trades or Agricultural. The[y] set out rice by hand and pound it out in wooden troughs with long clubs, the women doing all the work while the men sit around & pow-wow. Send about 100 young & educated negro teachers, Preachers and tradesman and it would be hard to foretell the good that would be accomplished.

Give my regards to Dr. A. L. Gaines when you see him again and tell [him] I hope he will succeed in his fight for the editorship of the 'Christian Recorder.'

This is the Hot Dry season here at Present and there is much sickness among the Troops and as the fighting is about over the boys are begining to grow home sick. Just as long as there was only fighting to be done everyone was desireous of remaining and seeing the thing out, but now that it is all practically over and as the 24th Infantry have rendered such excellent service over here the boys feel they should at least be allowed to come home to do garrison duty and not be held over here through another rainy season.

All the boys were highly pleased with your Chicago Insurance speech as published in the Conservator. This is a town of about 7 thousand inhabitants and is 28 miles from Dagupan and the only rail-road on the Island, as it runs from Dagupan to Manila, so you see all of our supplies are transported 28 miles by bull-trains and during the rainy season the duty will be something frightful.

There is a large and costly Catholic church here surrounded by hundreds of lowly bamboo houses the homes of the Fillipino. All his earnings have gone to the church & Priest. No school of any kind, but there is fully 3 thousand children of school age within 2 miles of this great church edifice. The Priest at this place will tell you unblushingly that they know enough to be good Catholics and that is all that is required. It would be almost useless to send white missionares here and for that reason the Negro churches in America should get together and make one long strong pull together and put the young educated negro men & women who are now "slinging hash" and washing "Miss Jane's" clothing to work educating the young Fillipino and thereby give them an opportunity to make a mark for themselves and Prove to their many friends that they have not hoped in vain.

When you have an opportunity as I know your time is very valuable, I would be Pleased to hear from [you] and if my letters are of any interest to you I will be Pleased to write you from time to time.

Sir I have the honor to be   Yours Respectfully

Joseph H. Tucker
Private   Co. H,
24th Infantry

ALS   Con. 185   BTW Papers   DLC.

1 Joseph Hamilton Tucker, of Athens, Ga., had a stormy military career. He enlisted in the 9th Cavalry in 1892 as a regimental printer stationed in Wyoming, but he never received the extra pay to which a printer was entitled. After a series of minor offenses he was dishonorably discharged in 1894. In 1898 he enlisted at a fort in Nebraska and served until 1902, when he was again dishonorably discharged. He apparently roamed in the far West for several years, operated a saloon in San Francisco, and also lived in Seattle, Wash., for a time. In Jan. 1909 he enlisted in the army again under the alias of William Watson and then deserted the next day. He appeared in St. Louis several months later, when he was arrested on a forgery charge. He forfeited bail and moved to Indianapolis, where in 1910 the army apprehended him for desertion. Tucker was sentenced to three years in Fort Leavenworth Penitentiary. In 1911 Senator Albert J. Beveridge sought clemency for Tucker on grounds that his wife and infant needed his support. Several months later thirty black citizens of Indianapolis also petitioned for clemency for Tucker but to no avail. Finally in June 1912, after President Taft had asked for a review of the case, Tucker was released and returned to Indianapolis. (RG94, File 38307-1892, DNA.)

From William Henry Baldwin, Jr.

N.Y. [City] March 21, 1900

Dear Mr. Washington: I had a meeting with Mr. Bourke Cockran[1] this noon. He wants to meet you. When you return we will lunch together at the Lawyers' Club in a private room. He has many good ideas, and some that I am very anxious for you to talk with him about. He will advocate repealing the amendment to the Constitution, and I am very anxious for you to be prepared to talk with him on that point.

I saw Mr. Jesup this noon, and had a long talk with him about the subject matter of my letter to Dr. Curry. He is heartily in accord; more so than I had any idea of. I am very anxious to have you see me before their meeting of Apr. 4. Please let me know when you expect to return. Yours truly,

W H Baldwin Jr

TLS Con. 792 BTW Papers DLC.

1 William Bourke Cockran (1854-1923) was a colorful Irish-born New York lawyer and congressman. Active in Tammany Hall politics in the 1880s, he shifted party allegiance several times. He broke with the Democrats over the silver issue, campaigning for McKinley in 1896 and supporting Roosevelt in 1912. He was a Democratic congressman in the late 1880s and early 1890s and again from 1904 to 1909. In 1920 he worked for the nomination of Alfred E. Smith for president.

Cockran, representing the North, attended the Montgomery Race Conference in May 1900 and spoke on behalf of repeal of the Fifteenth Amendment. (See Fortune to BTW, May 10, 1900, below.) A few days later Cockran donated $500 to Tuskegee to be used as a rotating loan fund to help blacks purchase land. John E. Milholland, who defended the Fifteenth Amendment, matched Cockran's contribution.

From Robert Heberton Terrell

Washington, D.C. Mar. 25, 1900

My dear Mr. Washington, Strange as it may seem a proposition to change the whole school system here had been favorably reported to the U.S. Senate at the time we were talking over our dinner Friday night. Stranger still the very copy of the Evening Star which you had contained an account of the contemplated change.[1]

471

I send you a clipping from the Post which explains itself.[2] The bill as here outlined will be passed in its main features. I am satisfied that the dual superintendency is a thing of the past now. This new bill legislates that out of existence. It provides for one Superintendent (and we know he will be white) and gives him the power to name an assistant Superintendent — who, I am sure, will also be white, unless we can procure some modifications in the bill that will provide for two assistants and stipulate that one be colored and in charge of colored schools.[3] If this happens, I am a candidate for the place of assistant and if it is not inconsistent with the attitude you have already taken I should be very glad to have you support me. The appointing power is taken entirely out of power of Commissioners for District of Columbia and given to Superintendent, who himself will be appointed by a new Board of Education to be appointed by the President of United States. This Board will consist of five members. Of this number we cannot expect to get more than one. We have a Board of Eleven now, four of whom are colored. If we succeed in any event of getting such a concession that the Assistant be colored I shall stand for the position and I think that if I can get your support it will be a great help to me.

I have always maintained that the Office of Colored Superintendent would not stand in a storm. It is an anomaly. I am sorry it is gone for we cannot tell where its loss will lead to. Think this matter over. I hope you thoroughly understand my position. I am not asking that you take any action not in keeping with what is proper in light of what you have already done. With best wishes, I am, yours truly,

R. H. Terrell

ALS Con. 181 BTW Papers DLC.

1 Washington *Star*, Mar. 23, 1900, 10.

2 Washington *Post*, Mar. 24, 1900, 3.

3 The reorganization of the administration of the District of Columbia schools, part of the District appropriation bill, became effective in July 1900. Black citizens of Washington protested the abolition of the black superintendency and argued for the appointment of two superintendents, one to be placed in charge of the black schools. (Washington *Post*, Apr. 7, 1900, 9; Washington *Colored American*, Apr. 7, 1900, 1, 9.) As finally approved, the bill called for one superintendent and two assistant superintendents, one of whom was to be black. (Washington *Post*, May 12, 1900, 4.) The first black assistant superintendent was W. S. Montgomery, a Dartmouth graduate. James Bundy and Mrs. John R. Francis were the two black appointees to the

seven-member school board. (Washington *Bee*, June 30, 1900, 4; July 11, 1900, 5.) Robert H. Terrell remained a high school principal in Washington until BTW secured a judgeship for him on the municipal court of the District of Columbia in 1902.

From Richard W. Thompson

Washington, D.C., Mar. 27, 1900

Dear Mr. Washington: I had a very cordial interview with Commissioner Ross last evening. He went over the school question very carefully, explaining the effect of the proposed change in the method of governing the schools. You are doubtless familiar with this new phase, as it came out in the Star the day you were here. I send clipping from Post, however, as a recapitulation.

Mr. Ross received the proposition to tender you the appointment of superintendent with the utmost graciousness, but, of course, was doubtful as to your acceptance in view of large responsibilities at Tuskegee. I had no information as to what you would do, but argued for the moral effect the tender would have upon the country and the race, pointing out the satisfaction we all felt in the educational work you were doing, and that an attempt to secure your services would be an earnest to the citizens of the District that no pains were being spared to get the very best man available. To be offered the headship of the greatest school system in the world, controlled by colored people, was a distinction which no man would not entertain with pleasure, and I felt sure that such a tender would be regarded by you as a high compliment and as an expression of confidence that would be appreciated. I spoke as the president of the most largely attended debating Lyceum of Washington, and as the agent of that body, instructed by it to do what I could to bring order out of the existing chaos. Mr. Ross agreed to give the matter his most favorable consideration. He had heard you mentioned before, but had felt you could not afford to accept — had been told so by your friends. He recognized, however, the value of the phase I placed upon the subject, and wanted to do all he could for you and at the same time serve the schools. He placed great stress upon his respect for your judgment.

473

He will make no nomination until this new law is settled, as the power may all go from the commissioners. He thinks the colored people should speak out if they are opposed to the abolishment of the colored superintendency, and speak before it is too late. He had always contended for opportunities for the Negro to show his capacity for self-government, and did not wish to see them lose control of the schools.

After some investigation I have decided to make the school situation the subject for discussion next Sunday at the Second Baptist Lyceum. It is to be understood that it is to be in no sense an "indignation meeting," but a calm inquiry for the purpose of educating our people on a current public question and to make an expression that shall be typical of the best local thought. Not being able to find a Washington man to lead off, who is not prejudiced by local conditions, etc., I have invited a well-informed outsider to make principal address — the Hon. John P. Green, of Ohio. The Afro-American Council will probably go into the matter Monday night. It is thought if the bill is to pass, provision may be made for *two* assistant superintendents one of whom shall be colored. The papers will doubtless contain reports, and I shall see that you get copies. Terrell is well satisfied with your attitude toward him.

At your request I drop you a "reminder" of certain financial courtesies which you were kind enough to offer at our last meeting. Thanking you in advance for all that you may see your way clear to do for me, and with sincere gratitude for many past favors, I am Very truly yours,

R. W. Thompson

P.S. Picture of Tuskegee arrived all right. It is a beauty. Am having it nicely framed. Thanks.

Cooper has made no "arrangements" with me — presumably upon the theory that "the mountain cannot go to Mahomet."

R. W. T.

ALS   Con. 185   BTW Papers   DLC.

From Edgar Gardner Murphy

Montgomery, Ala., March 28, 1900

Dear Mr. Washington: I need hardly tell you that I entirely understood the spirit of your letter, and that I trust that you will always write to me with the same frankness. There is nothing to be gained through a policy of silence between men who honestly disagree, and there is much that may result from frank conference and discussion.

Let me say in the first place, that the Southern Society has no "objective" whatever but the education of the public mind which must result from full discussion. It has, therefore, no policy in reference to the XVth. Amendment, and our approaching Conference cannot and will not reveal any such policy. For myself, let me say that I have not advocated the "repeal" of the XVth. Amendment, and that I have distinctly said that I would not have the *potential* citizenship of the Negro destroyed. I do advocate such a "modification" of the Amendment as will make the definite terms of the franchise a local issue in each state of the Union. In taking this position, however, I have exhausted the possibilities of language to free myself from either the responsibility or the presumption of speaking as "a representative authority." You heard, my dear Mr. Washington, only a part of my address, and you heard that part only once. When the address is printed and circulated, there will be no doubt whatever as to my attitude. Let me call your particular attention to the following sentence: "There have been those who have advocated the re-consideration of the XVth. Amendment in order to destroy forever the political opportunity of the Negro. I advocate its re-consideration as the only practicable means of opening to the Negro the ultimate possibilities of political privilege."

I am surprised that you should have associated my position with the policy of the Society or its Conference. We took you most frankly and fully into our confidence in relation to the discussion upon the franchise, and we gave you the name of every man who is to make a set speech. We told you precisely the line each man would probably take, and we allowed you yourself to select as the closing speaker the strongest man whom you could recommend as an advocate of a franchise test that should be equally and justly applicable to both races. As stated to you, Mayor Waddell of Wilmington, will argue for the North Carolina solution of the franchise problem, and a man from Louisiana or Mississippi will argue for either the Louisiana or the Mississippi solution of that problem, and then Gov. MacCorkle will have the privilege of closing the debate in refutation of such provisions. I submit that nothing could have been fairer either to the Negro race or to you as its chief representative in Alabama.

I have no expectation that any of these gentlemen will take my position with reference to the XVth. Amendment. I have no more knowledge of their views than you could have, and I suspect that the opinion of the average man in public affairs in the South will be decidedly adverse to my proposal. I have talked to scores of them personally, and they feel that the attitude of the North in relation to the XVth. Amendment is precisely what they wish. The North has decided to allow the XVth. Amendment to stand, which decision guarantees to the South a full representation in Congress for every Negro of voting age. And the North has also decided not to interfere in the internal affairs of the Southern States, so that each Southern State can count the Negro out in the election, and can count him in for representation. This is the view of the "practical" men at the South. They are entirely satisfied with things as they are, and a proposal to modify the XVth. Amendment in any way which would reduce by even one per cent. the representation of the South in Congress, will meet with opposition.

So far as the Southern Society is concerned, I must say, however, that it welcomes the frankest and the fullest discussion on the part of its members. It believes, as I think the men of all races and of all sections should believe, that the difficulties of our situation have not been dissipated by a policy of silence. If there is an idea, it is better for every one concerned that it should be expressed than that it should be repressed. Believing as I do in the right and wisdom and justice of my contention, I have claimed simply the privilege of a member of the Southern Society to advocate that contention with all the force at my command. I should say again, in passing, that my acceptance of invitations at the North was based upon no claim to officially represent either the Southern Society or the Conference. I agreed to make those addresses before I became the Secretary of our Executive Committee, and I have distinctly repudiated over and over again, both in Philadelphia and in New York, any assumption of a right to speak for others.

On going to the North, however, I went with no understanding either explicit or implicit that I was to suppress any of my convictions with relation to our difficult problem. I have not asked aid or interest in behalf of the Southern Society from any man in the North or South upon the assumption that I was not to be free and that all the members of the Society are not to be free to express whatever might seem to the Southern man to be the truth of the situation. If absolute freedom in the expression of opinion is to lose us the support and the confidence of any element of our population, either North or South, then, the members of the Southern Society must, in my judgment, be prepared, however reluctantly, to pay the price. So far as I have known the men of the North, I find that while they may not agree with me upon this aspect of the subject, they feel that my mind is working on it upon unselfish and rational methods, and they are cordially willing to trust the *ultimate* results of all such effort. We have talked over our differences frankly, and we have *agreed* in reference to certain things that *we must disagree*, but that this disagreement should not prevent hearty co-operation along those lines of interest and conviction upon which we stand together. As to yourself, I see how your identification, directly or indirectly, explicitly or implicitly, with such a proposal as I make, may be a matter of great embarrassment to yourself. The bitter and relentless attacks that were made upon me in Philadelphia in the public press by certain members of the Negro race made me feel very keenly that in the North they are not ready for what I am trying to do, and that your identification in any way with my proposal would be a grave mistake. I think that there are also white men who might misunderstand you. Let me say, therefore, in conclusion, that there are two things of which you might make *public note*, wherever and whenever you care to do so. First, that *in relation to the whole problem of the XVth. Amendment, I have never claimed to represent a policy of the Southern Society or to represent any mind but my own.* Secondly, that *with reference to that subject, you frankly disagree with me, although you agree with other portions of my address and understand the motives which have prompted my conclusions.*

477

You need never fear that any ground of difference between you and myself, or any expression of difference, will be taken by me as a ground for the slightest feeling or resentment. I have absolute faith in ideas, and I have absolute faith in that general philosophy of civilization which is expressed in the maxim, "Nothing is ever settled until it is settled right." Two frightful blunders have been made in relation to the Negro race — the blunder of slavery, and the blunder of the franchise. The Southern man does not hesitate to admit the first, and to admit it publicly as well as privately. I have never talked to a Northern man who did not admit the second privately, but I know of very few who would admit it publicly. This to me is evidence of the fact that the XVth. Amendment does not represent to-day the intellectual conscience of the nation. So long as this is true, I must advocate such a modification of the Amendment as shall place it in line with the public conscience. I cannot suppress my arguments, and I would not if I could. But I cordially invite criticism and correction, and I welcome a debate which, with the injection of the problem of the Filipino, I believe to be inevitable. I admire you and I believe in you absolutely, and I trust that in the future, whether we agree or not, we shall be united in sympathetic co-operation for the welfare of the poor and dependent of both races. Faithfully and Cordially yours,

Edgar Gardner Murphy

Please pardon the unworthy appearance of this letter. My stenographer is to blame, and I have not time to rewrite it myself — and I must send it to you at once. E.G.M.

TLS Con. 1 BTW Papers DLC. Postscript in Murphy's hand.

From Henry C. Davis

Philadelphia, 31st. March, 1900

My dear Mr. Washington: Dr. Murphy sends me a copy of his letter to you of 28th. inst. which I have carefully noted.[1] He very clearly speaks solely for himself and I do not see reasonable grounds for the withdrawal of any of us and that it is wiser to await further developments. The aspect of the question, to which you and I object to is certain to be discussed at Montgomery and they are also certain to find out that no settlement can be made on those lines and resort to others, which are possible of accomplishment. I do not think that it is wise for us to be the first to say "we won't play marbles." A great point has been gained through the disposition of intelligent Southern men to discuss this question, which can only be finally settled with their co-operation and we must give them the chance and the time to find out their mistakes, which are largely based on old prejudices and to correct them.

We must accord to Mr. Murphy the same freedom to express his opinions as we claim for ourselves and when he writes that "nothing is ever settled until it is settled right" and lives up to it, which I believe is his intention, he must eventually come round to our way of thinking, if given enough time.

As for the time being you are one of the "Kitchen Cabinet" I do not see that your reputation or position is involved before the public and I hope that you will very carefully consider it before you publicly oppose the movement.

So far as the desired results are concerned I think that the XV Amendment is a failure and was solely a political move for party purposes and without any real sympathy for the cause of the Negro and I am surprised that, even as politicians, they did not see that the franchise, which re-construction gave to the Negro, could not be maintained by them, except through force and the public sentiment of the whole Country would not uphold force. I do not write this from the basis of what I think is right, but with the conditions we have before us and the deep race prejudice I appreciate that I know exists. To accomplish what we are after I feel that the education of the so called intelligent whites is as much of a factor and [as?] the education of the Negro and the trouble is that the former do not want to be educated but the reverse is the case with the Negro.

I am daily surprised at the number of intelligent men, who do not know of your existence, or of Tuskegee. The world are too busy with their own affairs and wholly ignore their duties as citizens.

I have been too busy and not had the strength to follow up my subscriptions since you were here, but I have added a little to my list and shall have more time next week. Yours very truly,

Henry C Davis

TLS Con. 170 BTW Papers DLC.

[1] Davis wrote Edgar Gardner Murphy a few days later stressing the need for an end to sectional feelings regarding Negro suffrage and urging that both northerners and southerners needed to be properly educated on racial matters before any solution to racial strife would result. "I have always felt," Davis said, "that the 'franchise' to the Negro was a monumental blunder of the Republican party, that but few who were responsible for it cared one particle for the rights of the Negro and that it was a political move to try to retain political power for party purposes." He told Murphy that he was honestly seeking "common grounds to stand on and if we fail in so doing let us still be friends." (Apr. 2, 1900, Con. 170, BTW Papers, DLC.)

From William Edward Burghardt Du Bois

Atlanta, Ga., April 10 1900

My Dear Mr. Washington: I am sorry to say that I have been unable to lay my hands upon the data mentioned and consequently could not forward it. I am sorry.

I think I ought not keep you any longer in uncertainty as to my coming to Tuskegee. I have given the matter long and earnest thought and have finally decided not to accept your very generous offer. I see many opportunities for usefulness and work at Tuskegee, but I have been unable to persuade myself that the opportunities there are enough larger than those here at Atlanta University to justify my changing at present. The only opening that would attract me now would be one that brought me nearer the centres of culture & learning and thus gave me larger literary activity. I thank you very much for the offer and for other kindnesses and I need not assure [you] that you will always have in your work my sympathy & cooperation. Very Sincerely,

W. E. B. Du Bois

ALS Con. 170 BTW Papers DLC.

From William Henry Baldwin, Jr.

N.Y. [City] April 15th., 1900

Dear Mr. Washington: I send you copy of a letter I have written Mr. N. F. Thompson.[1] I have also written Mr. Willcox.[2]

I am very sorry that I cannot be at Pittsburgh. It is a physical impossibility.

I have talked again with Mr. Jesup, and he is very anxious to have a meeting at his house between Dr. Frissel, you, and myself. He wants us to dine with him. When can you arrange it? He wants to start, at the expense of the Slater Fund, a national crusade, and to have meetings throughout the country under the auspices of the Slater Board.

I am glad that the Seaboard Air Line is not discriminating on account of color. Get everybody you can to ride over their Road, and make no fuss about it, as the white people might cause them trouble.

Mr. Spencer has not been able to talk any business yet. There is no use in attempting to settle matters with the Southern Railway until he can be seen.

I return Secretary Wilson's letter. I hope it will keep Carver at his work.[3]

I note your suggestions about my Saratoga address, and am very much obliged for them. Sincerely Yours,

W H Baldwin Jr

TLS Con. 792 BTW Papers DLC.

[1] Newcomb Frierson Thompson (b. 1844) entered the real estate and insurance business in Birmingham in 1885 and was secretary of the Birmingham Commercial Club from 1893 to 1895. Later he was associated with northern capitalists investing in land and business in the Huntsville area. He edited the *Citizens Alliance Bulletin*, the organ of the Citizens Alliance of Birmingham.

[2] William G. Willcox (1859-1923), a wealthy New York lawyer and insurance broker, was a trustee of Tuskegee for many years beginning in 1907, and also served on the school's committee on investment of the endowment fund.

[3] Carver wrote BTW that "unless my health improves greatly between this & the close of school I will be compelled to seek a new field of labor." He also complained that the correspondence in his agricultural work was "too much for any one person to do." (Mar. 1, 1900, Con. 168, BTW Papers, DLC.)

William Henry Baldwin, Jr.,
to Newcomb Frierson Thompson

[New York City] April 15th., 1900

My Dear Sir: I have your letter of 10th, containing a program of the Southern Industrial Convention, to be held in Chattanooga, from May 15th to 18th.

I am very much disturbed because I cannot leave New York City during the month of May, as I am attending very important meetings, every day, connected with the Tunnel and Subway work in New York City. I have been obliged to forego any trip from the City this spring.

I have great regard for the work which Gov. McCorkle and you represent, and I do hope that you have a very successful meeting.

The negro properly educated in industrial lines will make the future of the South assured. I cannot help feeling that labor unionism will grow and increase not only in the North but in the South, and that nothing can stop it. It is in the nature of things. If you try to stop it, you would give it the chance to become the stronger. There is a clash between the present labor unions and the negroes in labor trades, but I take it that there can be no labor interference with the negro as a farmer.

The union of white labor, well organized, will raise the wages beyond a reasonable point, and then the battle will be fought, and the negro will be put in at a less wage, and the labor union will either have to come down in wages, or negro labor will be employed. The last analysis is the employment of the negro in the various arts and trades of the South, but this will not be a clearly defined issue until your competition in the markets of the world will force you to compete with cheap labor in other countries. It is a vast and difficult subject, and such conventions and conferences as you are holding will help materially to bring out a clearer understanding of the difficulties and show the true way to proceed. I believe, as a last analysis, the strength of the South in its competition with other producing nations will lie in the labor of the now despised negro, and that he is destined to continue to wait for that time. Yours very truly,

WHBJr

TLI Copy Con. 792 BTW Papers DLC. Marked: "For Mr. Booker T. Washington."

From John Uri Lloyd[1]

Cincinnati, O. April 16th 1900

My Dear Professor Washington, I have read with deep interest, once over, your book "Future of the American Negro." Next I shall study it carefully and write you in some detail concerning a few points.

Let me now congratulate you on the use of the word *Negro* instead of the word or term "Colored Citizen" which in my opinion is an *affectation* born in semi-ridicule. Only in a few places in your book did I observe the word *Colored* and in my opinion these should be excised in your succeeding editions. Teach the negro people that no *odium* attaches itself to the one word they have heired as a birthright. Teach them that there are many African tribes many colored peoples (Chinese Indians, etc.) but that only one people, black people with crisped hair, are entitled to the term *Negro*. Teach them that to avoid this name is to deny their parentage, that to contaminate the blood is to debase their children. Teach these things my dear Mr Washington and you will uplift your people by leading them to honor their ancestors and bring no dishonor on their children.

But there are many things before you, many obstructions, many apparently insurmountable obsticles. You will have many heartaches by reason of the acts of your own people and I beg you to be patient. But, enough of this, possibly I may have the chance to talk matters over with you yet. Possibly too it may interest you to know that I am President of the Medical College which so far as I know was the first to matriculate and graduate a negro — west of the mountains. It may interest you to know that this act 15 or more years ago raised a commotion in our class which I met personally, I being the only democrat in our faculty. And, it may interest you to be told that the *Southern* students listened to my arguments and made no trouble whatever.

I will add that in my opinion the Negro must look for his real friend to the white man of the South. There should be *no* antagonism. Their interests are mutual. They are *not* antagonists. The success and elevation of the one uplifts the other. The man who arrays them against each other is not a friend of either nor yet is he a patriotic American. To transport the negroes to Africa would bankrupt the South. Let the negro work physically, intellectually, morally, teach him that this is his duty to his family, his race and his country. Be patient with him, very. Hastily Yours

John Uri Lloyd

ALS Con. 177 BTW Papers DLC.

1 John Uri Lloyd (1849-1936) was a chemist who became a partner in the Cincinnati pharmaceutical corporation of H. M. Merrel & Co. He published widely in the field of medicine, and in 1887 was elected president of the American Pharmaceutical Association. Later he was professor of chemistry and chairman of the board of trustees of the Eclectical Medical Institution in Cincinnati. He also founded the Lloyd Library and Museum in Cincinnati, which specialized in books and displays in the fields of botany, pharmacy, chemistry, and allied sciences. In 1900 his romantic novel, *Stringtown on the Pike, a Tale of Northern Kentucky*, was serialized in *The Bookman*. (See Lloyd to BTW, May 21, 1900, below.) The novel's principal character was a black man called "Old Cupe," and the serialized version printed "Negro" with a lower case *n* and frequently included such terms as "darkey" and "nigger." Although Lloyd assured BTW that the book version would capitalize the word "Negro," it was the same as the serialized version.

Timothy Thomas Fortune to Emmett Jay Scott

Washington, April 16. [1900]

My dear Scott: Your letter of the 13th was received, and I was glad as usual to hear from you.

Thanks for the Herald clipping.[1] It is of much value.

And thanks for your congratulations. Things are in fair shape, but I shall count *nothing* until the job is landed. I understand the headquarters are to be in Chicago, but I may be able to have my end of it at New York.

I am glad you spoke of the drink business if it was on your mind. *And you can give me no advice that would not be good advice.* Of late I have not drunk more than usual, and I have been tapering off steadily since I have been here. I hope to get the whole matter down to a basis satisfactory before I leave here, which will be Thursday or Friday next, for New York.

My health is good and I am working hard.

With much love for you and yours, Yours truly

Fortune

ALS   Con. 172   BTW Papers   DLC.

1 Probably the account of a Carnegie Hall meeting of the Ethical Culture Society at which Felix Adler, William H. Baldwin, Jr., and two Tuskegee representatives, Isaac Fisher and Robert W. Taylor, spoke on the virtues of industrial education. (New York *Herald*, Apr. 9, 1900, 12.)

From Margaret James Murray Washington

Tuskegee, Ala., April 17–1900

Mr. Washington: I have read your communication with reference to the work in the Laundry, and I wish to say that I keep up with the Laundry work each week, and there never has been a time this year when the work has been more than one or two days behind. We have fifty girls — forty two girls in night school, and ten girls in the day school — who work in the Laundry; and each week the work has been done up as I have said, to within two or three days — which I consider a great improvement over that of any previous year, and which is probably all that can be done in a Laundry so large as ours. I have taken special pains to keep in touch with Miss Mabry, who has charge of the Laundry, and together we have decided what things were best to leave undone, in case all of the clothes could not be gotten out on Saturday afternoons. There has never been a time this year when the students have ever failed to get clean clothes for three weeks, of this I am positive; so this makes Mr. J. H. Washington's statement untrue.

I do not think that the condition of the Laundry has anything to do with Miss Mabry's wishing to give up the work. I have the opinion that Miss Mabry feels that there is lack of satisfaction every week, or every little while, in connection with the Laundry work, and that the work is looked into and criticised. I have already

485

spoken with Miss Mabry, and tried to make her see that every department must of necessity be looked into and criticisms made. I wish to say further as I have said to you, that taking all things into consideration I think that Miss Mabry does the work at the Laundry quite well. Yours truly,

Mrs Washington

TLS Con. 182 BTW Papers DLC.

From Emmett Jay Scott

Tuskegee, Ala., Apr. 17, 190[0]

Dear Mr. Washington: I am sending you today under separate cover the Montgomery Advertiser. You will notice several items marked, among them a decision of the state Supreme Court of Alabama in reference to the matter of Negroes sitting in the rear or assigned seats in street cars. Also pronouncement of Morgan's[1] campaign manager as to the matter of a constitutional convention, and the decision of the United States Supreme court with reference to the matter of a Negro convicted of crime in Texas but who made an appeal to the Supreme Court on the ground that black men were excluded from the jury which tried him.[2] This case was handled by Mr. Wilford H. Smith[3] who you recommended to the Counsel General of the Liberian Government as Liberian Counsel at Galveston last year. He is a splendid man and has much tenacity in fighting his way in the courts. There is no bluster about him at all but he is a quiet worker who has had at least three decisions from the state Supreme Court of Texas in his favor and now this case of the U.S. Supreme Court which he argued last summer before it.

I feel that there is much work to be done in Alabama in view of the statement of Morgan's campaign manager and this decision as regards the matter of assigning places for Negroes in street cars.

I trust your meeting last evening was in every way a success. I see no reference to it in the associated press and so I can have no opinion. Yours truly,

Emmett J. Scott

TLS Con. 182 BTW Papers DLC.

1 John Tyler Morgan.

2 In Seth Carter *v.* Texas, decided Apr. 16, 1900, the U.S. Supreme Court over-turned the Texas courts and declared that Carter, a black man accused of first-degree murder, had been denied the right to challenge the selection of the grand jury that indicted him. He also had been denied the right of equal protection since blacks had been systematically excluded from the jury selection process. (*U.S. Reports* 177, 422.)

3 Wilford H. Smith (b. 1863), who became BTW's personal lawyer and behind-the-scenes legal negotiator, was an old friend of Emmett J. Scott. He was born in Mississippi, and practiced law for a time in Galveston, Tex. In 1901 Smith moved to New York City, where he established his law practice. Though his stationery an-nounced "Damage Suits a Speciality," Smith also dealt in real estate, and in 1902 tried to sell BTW some land opposite Grant's Tomb. It was as BTW's legal confidant, however, that Smith was most involved in the Tuskegean's affairs. Using code names in their correspondence, Scott and Smith secretly arranged a variety of legal actions affecting the civil rights of blacks. Smith also worked secretly to help preserve BTW's power from attacks by his critics. He acted several times on behalf of BTW to gain control of William Monroe Trotter's Boston *Guardian.* While Trotter was in jail after the Boston Riot, Smith secretly tried to force the paper into bankruptcy and to buy some of its stock. He also advised BTW on the libel actions the Tuskegean persuaded others to file against the *Guardian.* Smith was the attorney for the Afro-American Realty Co. from its founding in 1904 until he resigned two years later, complaining of disastrous mismanagement. He was also active in the National Negro Business League and the Afro-American Council and was a member of the Committee for Improving the Industrial Conditions of Negroes in New York, a forerunner of the National Urban League. Later Smith became a trusted associate of Marcus Garvey and served as attorney for Garvey's ill-fated steamship company, the Black Star Line. (Fox, *Guardian of Boston,* 49-69; Harlan, "Secret Life of BTW.")

From Henry Hugh Proctor

Atlanta, Ga. April 18, 1900

My dear Mr. Washington: I have your "personal" letter of the 7th instant regarding the street-car matter. We are keeping it before the public, and it is having effect. The roads are beginning to em-ploy boy-conductors, showing the necessity of cutting down ex-pense as a result of the boy-cott. It is reported that the roads sustained a loss of $1100.00 in one week as a result of the boy cott. There is talk in the air that the Road will sue the city for damages on acct of the passage of the law.

If you will send me a letter to Mr. Smith[1] perhaps he will give me a pass when I come down for the anniversary sermon.

With best wishes for the work and for your personal welfare, I am   Sincerely yours,

H. H. Proctor

ALS   Con. 181   BTW Papers   DLC.

1 George C. Smith.

From Edgar Gardner Murphy

Montgomery, Ala., April 19, 1900

Dear Mr. Washington: I send you herewith the mailing list of the Southern Society complete up to about ten days ago. The names, however, which you will find on these lists do not represent all, of course, who will be present. They are simply the names of our members. I should also say that it is not absolutely complete to date, for the reason that as the work progresses, numbers of acceptances to membership in the Society are coming in with almost every mail. I will try to have these written up for you, however, and mail them to you at a later date.

Mr. Page has definitely declined to be present, and his place will be taken by Dr. Paul B. Barringer,[1] Chairman of the Faculty of the University of Virginia. Dr. Barringer is one of the strongest men of the South, and his relation to that great university strengthens our program very much more than the name of Mr. Page. He, however, is not nearly so sympathetic in his attitude toward your race, and I fear, therefore, that it is the cause of the Negro, rather than the success of the Southern Society, which will suffer by Mr. Page's withdrawal. As I took pains to explain to you, nothing could be more unfortunate in connection with such a movement than for the friends of the Negro to withdraw from it. We have given them an abundant opportunity, and that is surely all that they can ask. If they refuse this opportunity, there is nothing for us to do but to turn to those for membership in the Society and for speeches at our Conference who are less sympathetic in their attitude, and who are less appreciative of the Negro as a factor in the life of the South. I hope that you will not fail to write immediately to such

488

men as Dr. Curry, Dr. Frissell, Mr. Baldwin, Mr. Ogden and others, and to urge this point upon them. I feel most concerned about it because I feel sure that Mr. Page would not have taken this attitude unless pressure had been brought to bear upon him from several different directions at the East. For the sake of the Negro, we must realize just now that the danger in connection with this movement in the South lies not in the intolerance of the South for Northern opinion, but in the intolerance of the North for certain opinions of the South. With kindest regards, I am very Cordially yours,

Edgar Gardner Murphy

TLS Con. 182 BTW Papers DLC.

1 Paul Brandon Barringer (1857-1941) was chairman of the faculty of the University of Virginia from 1896 to 1903 and president of Virginia Polytechnic Institute from 1907 to 1913. He wrote *The American Negro; His Past and Future* (1900). Barringer was extremely pessimistic about the future of blacks in America. In his address at the Montgomery Race Conference he predicted extinction for the race, which he claimed was only surviving on the stamina left over from the days of slavery. He thought it was a waste of time to educate blacks, even in industrial training. In his speech Barringer cited so many misleading statistics that the chairman of the conference, Hilary A. Herbert, was forced to challenge his assumption. (Bailey, *Edgar Gardner Murphy*, 47.) J. L. M. Curry complained to BTW that Barringer's speech before the Southern Education Association meeting in Dec. 1900 was "a revised and more objectionable edition of his Montgomery speech. . . ." Curry described it as "pessimistic and mischievous." (Curry to BTW, Dec. 31, 1900, Con. 169, BTW Papers, DLC.)

William Henry Baldwin, Jr., to Clark Howell

[New York City] April 21st., 1900

Dear Mr. Howell: I thank you exceedingly for your letter of 19th. No matter what rumor may say from time to time about remarks made by me on the Southern question, you may rest assured that I have never yet been taken to task by any Southerner, whose opinion either you or I cared about, for my opinions on this general question.

It seems to me perfectly ridiculous to discuss the question of repealing the XV Amendment. I have always said that it was from many points of view an absolute mistake in the beginning; but for political and other reasons it is ridiculous to talk about repealing it. Yours very truly,

W H Baldwin Jr

TLS Copy Con. 792 BTW Papers DLC. Marked: "For Mr. Booker T. Washington."

To Francis Jackson Garrison

Tuskegee, Ala., Apr. 30, 1900

My dear Mr. Garrison: Your kind letter of April 27th is just received. We are looking for the Clarks tonight, and you do not know how delighted we are at the prospect of having them with us for several days. I was at Hampton during the two days of commencement last week and the Clarks were there. Everyone was delighted to see them and gave them much attention. One of the speakers referred to the fact that a daughter of John Bright was in the audience.

The great Conference in Montgomery takes place within a few days. I do not think any one is brave enough to forecast the result of the meeting. I hope it will accomplish some good but I confess my faith has been somewhat shaken in it recently. I am very sorry to add that Mr. Walter H. Page has refused to address the Conference though he had promised to do so. He says he cannot afford to speak on the same platform on the same night with Bourke Cockran.

I am just in receipt of a letter from Mrs. Unwin. Mrs. Washington and I feel ourselves constantly indebted to you for the opportunity of meeting so many good people abroad. Mrs. Unwin wants us to be her guests the next time we visit London. Yours truly,

Booker T. Washington

TLS   Francis J. Garrison Papers   NN-Sc.

From Henry C. Davis

Philadelphia 30th. April, 1900

My dear Mr. Washington: Under another cover I send you a copy of the "Public Ledger" with a marked article on the franchise of the colored man and wish that it took a more advanced position.[1] The weakness of our side is our conservatism, we need not be too aggressive, but there are certain rights that should not be wholly ignored.

The time to stop a leak is when it is discovered and not when it assumes the magnitude of a torrent. Little encroachments, continually added to, finally require a revolution to set right. I have not much faith in the sense of justice on the part of the North for the Negro as a factor in the matter and think more can be accomplished by appealing to the selfish instincts of humanity, but I do not wish to be understood as ignoring the justice and right on our side, but it should be kept before the people that these inroads will eventually end in the total disenfranchisement of the colored man and without the equivalent decrease in representation and such conditions can only eventually end in revolution. It is a repetition of the old Anti-Slavery struggle, had the pleadings of the despised Abolitionists been heeded there would have been no Civil War. May the Nation be saved from a repetition of that experience.

Some of our Northern newspapers have had good editorials on Governor Candler's late speech, which I suppose you have seen.

I have been interested in the newspaper accounts of the proceedings at Hampton and greatly regretted my inability to get there. Dr. Dickerman writes me that a Committee was appointed to take up the question of investigating Colored Schools, but I fear that it will practically result about the same as the Capon Springs Conference, composed of very able men, but too busy with other matters to get the necessary work done.

Mr. Greene[2] sends me figures for a Cotton Mill, to cost $110,000. This is more than my other figures, but I shall have to defer work on it until next Fall. Yours very truly.

Henry C. Davis

TLS Con. 170 BTW Papers DLC.

1 The Philadelphia *Public Ledger*, Apr. 30, 1900, 6, contained an account of a

conference of editors held in New Orleans. Most southern editors, according to the article, were opposed to Negro suffrage.

[2] Possibly Charles W. Greene, farm manager and teacher of agriculture at Tuskegee Institute.

To John Uri Lloyd

Tuskegee, Ala. [April 1900]

My dear Sir: Your letter of April 16th is called to my attention upon my return to Tuskegee. I am very glad that you have found my book, "The Future of the American Negro" of some interest. I believe with you that no odium attaches to the name "Negro," but I very much wish that authors could see their way clear to spell it with a capital N since it is a race name the same as Filipino, Chinese, Indian, etc.

[Booker T. Washington]

TL Copy   Con. 177   BTW Papers   DLC.

To Francis Jackson Garrison

Tuskegee, Ala., May 2, 1900

Dear Mr. Garrison: We had a most delightful visit yesterday from the Clarks. Our only regret is that they could not remain with us except during a day and night. We had planned to have them with us at least three days but they thought they must hurry on. They went from here to Charleston. I gave them letters of introduction to several friends there. We had the whole school assemble in the afternoon and sing some plantation songs to them. Both Mr. and Mrs. Clark spoke most feelingly and helpfully to the school. We shall always remember their visit with the greatest satisfaction. I am most grateful to you for the privilege of becoming acquainted with such excellent people. Yours truly,

Booker T. Washington

TLS   Francis J. Garrison Papers   NN-Sc.

From Edgar Gardner Murphy

Montgomery, Ala., May 3, 1900

Dear Mr. Washington: Mrs. Murphy and Mrs. King very much enjoyed their day in Tuskegee, and they came back full of enthusiasm about the work of your noble institution.

I quite agree with you that it is a misfortune to the cause of the Negro that Mr. Page should have withdrawn. The Committee, however, cannot admit the right of any individual speaker to canvass and pass upon the intellectual ideas or the moral character of every man invited to speak at the Conference. If the gentleman[1] to whom he objected could speak in Faneuil Hall, Boston, under the auspices of the loveliest people in New England, as he did during the past six weeks, the Committee of the Montgomery Conference could hardly be faulted for inviting him to speak here. Even if Mr. Page's charges against this gentleman are all true, I do not think that we could admit the principle for which he stands. In connection with all gatherings of this kind, the Committee must look at the situation in the broad, and must do its best under all the given practical conditions which obtain. At the great Conference on Trusts in Chicago, at the same Conference on Trusts in New York City, at the Monetary Conference in Indianapolis, and in connection with other large meetings of a national or semi-national character, the makers of programs have not attempted to square all their speakers by the Ten Commandments, before inviting them to speak. This would involve us in the moral indorsement of every man we might ask, and as we cannot go into the private life of individuals, we should soon make ourselves ridiculous. We certainly knew nothing of Mr. Page's personal objections when the program was made, and even if we had been so informed, I do not think we could have admitted for a moment the principle for which he stands. His withdrawal has resulted just as I predicted it would result. The only cause which has really lost by it has been the very cause which Mr. Page particularly represents. He is not a Southern man in any real sense of the word, and he is out of sympathy with the normal tendencies of Southern thought. Personally, he is a man full of charm, and he commands my sincere esteem, but it was in a measure a relief to the Committee when he withdrew, because

493

after having selected him, we found that there was more criticism of this single appointment than of any other appointment which we made. Dr. Frissell is well known as a Northern man, but his appointment has been accepted with universal approval.

I do not regret that Dr. Barringer is to speak, for the reason that his contribution to the subject is one of very real value. His chief contentions are receiving the endorsement of some of the very best authorities in this country, as you will note by the editorial in the Medical Record of New York of last week. *I do not mean to imply that I fully agree with all that Dr. Barringer says.* He labors under two difficulties. In the first place, he has no intimate knowledge of such an institution as Tuskegee, where the colored man is doing admirable work under the direction of other men of his own race. In the second place, Dr. Barringer spoke in his Charleston address with a certain *anti-Negro animus. Animus* is always unfortunate, and no matter how soundly his conclusions may be based in the facts of the case, those conclusions will always lack something in *truth* and persuasiveness if they seem to carry within them the spirit of bias. This having been said, however, I feel that the *essential* contentions presented by Dr. Barringer are sound, and if they are stripped of the *tone* in which they are presented, there is nothing in them to which the Negro need object. I am glad, therefore, that he is to speak, *but* I do sincerely regret that *Mr. Page's place* should have fallen to his lot. We paid Mr. Page the very great courtesy of giving him a place from which no one could attack him. Such a position was accorded to only two other men, Mr. Herbert,[2] our presiding officer, and Mr. Bourke Cockran. Mr. Page would have wielded in such a position a very great advantage in the presentation of his ideas. Few things could have indicated more clearly the particular spirit of the Executive Committee of the Conference. Mr. Page, however, having withdrawn, Dr. Barringer was the strongest available man and he thus unfortunately falls heir to a position in which he will meet no *direct* criticism. There was nothing else for us to do, and if the last evening should betray a bias somewhat unfavorable to the Negro, I wish you and your friends to understand that it was not the fault of the Committee. All of the above, of course, I have written in a personal way, and not for publication. I have no objection to your speaking of these facts privately and personally to your acquaintances, but I do not wish them to gain the authority of print. With *kindest regards,* I am very Cordially yours,

Edgar Gardner Murphy

TLS Con. 182 BTW Papers DLC.

1 William Bourke Cockran.

2 Hilary Abner Herbert. See above, 2:243. Herbert's background made him a likely president for the Southern Society. The son of slave-holding parents, he came to abhor the institution of slavery after the Civil War. Yet he remained a southern apologist. In his book, *The Abolition Crusade and Its Consequences* (1912), Herbert stated that he opposed repeal of the Fifteenth Amendment because he believed that most blacks were not interested in voting and those who did vote would have little or no effect on American politics.

From Francis Jackson Garrison

Boston, May 4, 1900

Dear Mr. Washington: I have your letter of the 30th ult., and note your reference to the Montgomery Conference. If the rumors or prophecies which are coming to us concerning the probable trend of the Conference are at all correct, it is going to be distinctly disastrous to the cause of equal rights. I suspect that Mr. Page's refusal to speak on the same platform with Bourke Cockran may be because the latter is an anti-imperialist, and Mr. Page himself is an expansionist, but the papers of last evening and this morning intimate that Cockran is going to Montgomery to advocate the repeal of the 15th amendment, and the Transcript two or three nights ago had an editorial also saying that there were symptoms of a positive movement toward that retrogressive undertaking. I do not for a moment believe that such a repeal amendment could be ratified by 3/4 of the States, even if it should go through Congress, but the fact that it is seriously discussed is certainly a very disquieting symptom, and if the Montgomery Conference kindles such a firebrand, it would be far better that it had never been called. The doors having been thrown open to them, the advocates of a "white man's government" are evidently going to pour in and capture the

Conference. Our war with the Filipinos has distinctly lowered the tone, and weakened the power and disposition, of the Republicans to make a proper stand against such a movement, and you may be sure that if William McKinley felt that his re-election depended upon the repeal of the 15th amendment, he would do everything in his power to accelerate such an act and "save his bacon." Happily, his dictatorship, which is so absolute over the Philippines, is not yet supreme in his own country. Yours very truly,

F. J. Garrison

TLS Con. 173 BTW Papers DLC.

To the Editor of the Washington *Colored American*

[Tuskegee, Ala., ca. May 4, 1900]

Editor Colored American — Through your paper I wish to call the attention of our race as far as possible to the fact that the Census Bureau is planning to make a special effort during the taking of the census in June to find out the exact amount of property of every description that is owned by the Negro race. This means a great deal to us as a people and we will be very largely judged by the world by the result. It is of the utmost importance that each individual member of the race in every part of the country begin at once to make a careful list of the amount and value of the property that he owns so as to be ready to give it at once to the census taker. It is also important that as far as possible ministers and teachers call the attention of the people to this matter as far in advance as may be thought best. Yours truly,

Booker T. Washington

Washington *Colored American*, May 5, 1900, 7. This also appeared in the *Southern Workman*, 29 (June 1900), 380.

To Timothy Thomas Fortune

Tuskegee, Ala., May 5, 1900

My dear Mr. Fortune: I have just sent you a telegram reading as follows: "Send me at once all suggestions you can for my Washington address." I am sorry to trouble you in this matter but I want to say the very best things in my Washington address. Sometime ago you made several suggestions to me for this address. At the time they struck me as being very vital and important suggestions but most of them I find have slipped out of my head.

We shall have to be prepared for some very radical and I think unwise things in connection with the race Conference at Montgomery. I hope, however, that some good may come from the move. On the whole, I think it best for me to be on the ground at least for a part of the time.

I am very glad indeed to hear that your health continues so good. As I said in my last letter, you looked better than I had seen you for a long while.

I was very glad indeed to see the letter which you wrote Mr. Scott a few days ago. I am very glad you have made this choice. I am also very glad to hear that you are doing so much literary work. I have not heard anything from Marshall[1] regarding the article for the Herald. I do not understand the cause. I presume, however, he shall run it out before long, otherwise I shall have an answer from him I think.

I thank you very much for calling my attention to what Mr. Howells said of me in the Atlantic Monthly.[2] I had not seen this before tho I had laid aside the magazine intending to read what he said about Chesnutt but I did not know before your letter came that he had referred to me. Yours truly,

Booker T. Washington

TLS Con. 172 BTW Papers DLC.

[1] Edward Davis Marshall.

[2] In a glowing review of Charles W. Chesnutt's works, William Dean Howells said: "With Mr. Booker Washington the first American orator of our time, fresh upon the time of Frederick Douglass; with Mr. Dunbar among the truest of our poets; with Mr. Tanner, a black American, among the only three Americans from whom the French government ever bought a picture, Mr. Chesnutt may well be willing to own his color." (*Atlantic Monthly*, 85 [May 1900], 699-701.)

From Timothy Thomas Fortune

Brooklyn, N.Y., May 5, 1900

Dear Mr. Washington: Your telegram of even date reached the office at 5 o'clock this afternoon and Mr. Chase brought it over to the house. I hardly know how to comply with your request, as the subject is necessarily a large and *ticklish* one. For you, Washington is literally "the enemy's country," as Bryan once characterized New England and the Middle States. However, I will make the following suggestions:

1. State strongly and forcibly the industrial condition of the race and the high tension of competition which makes industrial education for the masses an absolute necessity.

2. Define your position emphatically but clearly and fully on higher education for the few, along the lines laid down in the Evening Post article to supply the demands of the pulpit, the learned professions, literature, and commerce, and to vindicate the intellectuality of the race.

3. Eschew politics entirely, but make a strong plea to the young men of the race who have had the advantages of a liberal education — graduates of the law and medicine and theology — to go out among the people in the South and be their leaders in the broadest sense, because what the masses need most are educated men of the race to show them by precept and example how to make the most of their opportunities. I should make this appeal without referring in the remotest way to the thousands of our men who are going to seed in the departments at Washington on $100 a month. The plea may fall upon some good soil.

4. I would urge that the educated men of the race engage more in general business pursuits in our own country and stand ready, by making the necessary preparation, to take some advantage of the commercial and other opportunities which are opening to the youth of the country in the enlargement of our National domain and the incorporation into our citizenship of a large alien population which must be educated in the ways of the Republic.

6.[1] Despite the hardships which confront the race on every hand we are making substantial progress in all directions, and must overcome them in the end, if we "trust in God and keep our powder dry." And we shall succeed not by relying upon others but upon ourselves. We should show ourselves worthy of the splendid opportunities we enjoy over our slave parents by making the most of them, and thus justify the faith of our friends, who do not all live in the North nor yet in the South, but all over the Republic — and confuse our enemies. "And God helps those who help themselves."

My editorial article in the Transcript of Apr 30 on "The Fifteenth Amendment" is being widely quoted and discussed.[2]

I am very well. Your friend,

T. Thomas Fortune

ALS Con. 961 BTW Papers DLC.

[1] Should be 5.

[2] An unsigned editorial, "The Fifteenth Amendment," apparently the one by Fortune, appeared in the Boston *Transcript*, May 1, 1900, 8. The editorial described the coming Montgomery Race Conference as really a movement of southern whites to gain public support for the repeal of the Fifteenth Amendment. Southern whites, the editorial continued, had asked to be left free to solve the race problem and had failed. Repeal of the Fifteenth Amendment would undo the work, valor, and sacrifice of 200,000 black soldiers who had helped crush slavery and preserve the Union.

From Paul Brandon Barringer

Charlottesville, Va. May 5, 1900

Dear Sir: Your kind invitation to stop over with you at Tuskegee, just to hand and I regret that the necessarily hurried trip to Montgomery cannot be made more pleasant by the acceptance of your invitation, but I find it impossible.

You are doubtless aware that, as regards your people, I am a pessimist, but this does not prevent my profound admiration for those of you who are standing bravely against the current. I wish all of your people could understand that in dealing with racial matters I speak of the *race* and not of individuals. The very generic tendencies which you have to combat makes the assumption of the position of worth and prominence among men the more to be appreciated. I am of the South, for the South, and primarily for the white people of the South—my own people—but as a native of that section of which your people form so essential a part, I can take interest and pride in all that they do to rise above the condition in which their brother man, regardless of motive, has placed them.

Again thanking you for your invitation, I remain, Yours respectfully,

P. B. Barringer

TLS   Con. 166   BTW Papers   DLC.

An Item in the *Tuskegee Student*

Tuskegee, Ala., May 5, 1900

Tonight at the new residence of Principal and Mrs. Washington, a rendition of Shakespeare's immortal tragedy Othello, will be given for the benefit of the Cemetery Fund of the institution. Preprations have been in progress for six weeks, and a treat is most likely in store for those who attend. The costumes to be worn are beautiful creations and will win much praise. Mrs. Warren Logan will read a critique upon "The Tragedy, Othello." The cast of characters is as follows: "Othello," Mr. Charles W. Wood; "Iago," Mr. Emmett J. Scott; "Cassio," Mr. Charles A. Warren;[1] "Montano" and "Lodivico," Mr. Charles Alexander; "Gratiano," Mr. Matthew T. Driver; "Desdemona," Miss Sarah L. Hunt;[2] and "Emilia," Mrs. H. E. Thomas. The curtain will rise promptly at 8 o'clock. This is the first pretentious effort to give private theatricals at Tuskegee.

Tuskegee Student, 12 (May 5, 1900), 2.

[1] Charles A. Warren taught horticulture at Tuskegee Institute from 1899 to 1901.
[2] Sarah L. Hunt, born in Sparta, Ga., in 1868, was the sister of Adella Hunt Logan, wife of Tuskegee's treasurer Warren Logan. She graduated from Tuskegee in 1888 and taught school in Georgia and Florida until 1894, when she returned to Tuskegee and taught in the academic department for many years. The 1900 census reported her as a member of the Warren Logan household.

A Sunday Evening Talk

Tuskegee, Ala., May 6, 1900

It seems rather appropriate during the closing days of school to re-emphasize, if possible, that for which this institution stands. We want every student to get what we have in our egotism, perhaps, called the "Tuskegee spirit"; that is, get hold of the spirit of the institution, get hold of that for which it stands, and then spread that spirit just as far and just as wide as possible, and plant it just as deeply as it is possible to plant it.

Now, we have each year a class to graduate; a class that does not expect to return to the institution in the capacity of regular students; and a large number of students who go out to spend their vacation: some to return at the close of vacation and some, for various reasons, not to return. Whether you go out as graduates, whether you go out to return or not to return, it is important that all of you get hold of the "Tuskegee spirit": the spirit of giving yourself in order that you may help lift up others no matter in how small a degree it may be, see that you are assisting some one else.

Now, after a number of years of experience, the institution feels that it has reached the point where with some degree of authority, it can give advice as to the best way you can spend your life. In the first place, as to your location, as to the place you shall work! I very much hope that the larger portion of the students who go out from Tuskegee will choose for their place of work the country districts, rather than the larger cities. In the first place, you will find that the larger places are supplied; the larger cities are much better supplied with helpers, and leaders than is true of the smaller towns and especially country districts. They are better supplied with churches, schools, with every thing that tends to uplift people; and they are at the same time much better supplied with those agencies which tend to pull people down. Notwithstanding all this, the greater portion by far of those who need help are in the country districts. I think a census report will show that 80 per cent. of our own people are to be found in the country districts, and smaller towns, and I advise you to go into the country districts, into the smaller towns, rather than into the larger cities.

Then, as to the manner of work! You have got to make up your mind in the first place, as I said in the beginning, that you are going to sacrifice, you have got to make up your mind that you are going to give your life in an unselfish way, in order that you may help some one. Go with a spirit that will not make you become discouraged when you have opposition, when you have obstacles to overcome, you have got to go with the spirit that you are going to succeed in that or this undertaking.

As to the kind of work you shall do! I don't attempt to give you specific advice, but I should say in a general way, that you can accomplish more good, and, perhaps, this will hold good for fifty or sixty years to come in the South; I believe you can accomplish more good by taking a country school as a nucleus for your work. Take a three-months school and gradually impress the people of that community, getting them to add one month to three months and then another month until they get to the point where they will have a school of five, six, seven or eight months; and then get them to the point where they will see the importance of building a decent school house — getting out of the one-room log cabin school house; where they will see the importance of having apparatus for the school house.

There are two things you must keep your mind on: 1. The building of a proper school house, 2. The arousing in the people at the same time of a spirit that will make them support you in your efforts. In order to do this, you must go to the community with the idea of staying there, —plant yourself with the community, and by economical living, year by year, manage to buy yourself a nice and comfortable home, and you will find the longer you stay there the more the people will get into your confidence, the more they will respect and love you, and you will find that the matter of salary will take care of itself. I find that many of our graduates have done excellent work by having at the same time a farm in connection with their school. I have in mind a man who did not graduate at Tuskegee. He has been teaching school down in Henry County, I think, for seven or eight years. He has lengthened his school to eight months, has a nice cottage with four rooms and a beautiful farm of forty acres. He is carrying out the true "Tuskegee idea."

There will be some of you who, by reason of industry, can spend your life to advantage by devoting your life to farming rather than to some other industry. I mention farming because I believe that's the great foundation upon which we have got to build for the future. I find at Hampton in their course of study that they are laying extra stress upon the subject of agriculture. I believe we are coming to the point where we are going to be recognized for our worth, in the proportion that we secure an agricultural foundation. There we find the greatest opportunities; there we find throughout the South we can give ourselves in a free, open way to getting hold of property, building houses, in a way we cannot do in any other one industry. No matter what you do, no matter where you go, remember you want to go with the "Tuskegee spirit."

He has the "Tuskegee spirit" who is found in the Sunday school on Sunday mornings, is the one who is found in the church, is the one who is always ready to give himself to the uplifting of people regardless of whether he is getting paid for each hour's service he performs, or not. I want the boys to go out and do as Mr. N. E. Henry[1] is doing; I want the girls to go out and do as Miss Lizzie E. Wright[2] is doing. I want you to go out into the country districts and build up schools. I would not advise you to be too ambitious. Be willing to begin with a small salary and gradually work your way up. I have in mind a young man who began teaching for five dollars per month; another who began teaching in the open air under a tree in Montgomery County, I believe, it was.

Then, too, I want you to go in a spirit of liberality toward the white people, with whom you may come in contact — that is an important matter. When I say this, I don't mean that you shall go lowering your dignity — lowering your manhood. Go in a manly way, go in a straightforward and honorable way; and then you will show the white people that you are not of a belittling race, that prejudice that so many people possess cannot come among you and those with whom you work. If you can extend a helping hand to a white person, feel just as happy in helping a white person as in helping a black person. In the sight of God there is no color line, and we want to have that spirit that will make us forget this color line. We want to be larger, broader than the white people who would oppress us on account of our color. No one ever loses anything by being a gentleman or a lady — no person ever lost anything by being broad. Remember if we are broad, if we are kind and useful, if we are moral; if we go out and practice all these things, no matter what people say about us, they cannot pull us down. But on the other hand, if we are without the spirit of usefulness, if we are without morality, without liberality, economy, without property, without all of these qualities which go to make a nation great and strong, no matter what we say about ourselves or what others may say about us, we are losing ground. Nobody can give us these qualities by merely talking, by merely praising us until we possess them, and nobody can take them from us by cursing us. We may be inconvenienced in our efforts to rise, but we can never be kept from rising!

Tuskegee Student, 12 (May 19, 1900) , 1, 2-3.

[1] Nelson Edward Henry, originally of Selma, Ala., graduated from Tuskegee Institute in 1893. Imbued with the "Tuskegee spirit," Henry settled down to farm and teach in southern Montgomery County, Ala., at the small town of Ramer. His letters describing his school often appeared in the pages of the *Tuskegee Student,* and BTW considered him a model graduate who had carried Tuskegee's ideals to the hinterlands. In 1900 the Ramer Colored Industrial School had 125 pupils, and Henry also conducted a monthly Negro conference patterned after BTW's annual conference. The *Tuskegee Student* (13 [Nov. 3, 1900], 3) reported in 1900, "There is not a more thoroughly unselfish teacher in all the South than Mr. Henry."

Henry's efforts to build a miniature Tuskegee at Ramer failed two years later, however, because of a racial incident. In 1902 BTW invited the nationally known woman photographer Frances Benjamin Johnston to do a series of photographs of Tuskegee and its people. Photographing of Henry's school as an example of the spread of the Tuskegee idea was among her assignments. An attractive thirty-six-year-old white woman, Johnston, accompanied by George Washington Carver, was met by Henry on arrival at Ramer. They proceeded by wagon toward Henry's house. A number of white townspeople who had gathered to watch Henry's actions with his visitor apparently decided that he had violated the unwritten law of association with a white woman. One of the young men drew a pistol and fired three shots at Henry, who was forced to flee. George Washington Carver later recounted that he did not think he would live through that night, but he helped Johnston to escape to a nearby town. White reaction to Henry's alleged transgression of social conventions kept him from returning to the town, and he escaped to Montgomery to avoid the mobs that roamed the streets of Ramer. The other teacher at the Ramer school also fled, and the school collapsed. (Carver to BTW, Nov. 28, 1902, Con. 261, BTW Papers, DLC.) Frances Johnston threatened to have her friend President Theodore Roosevelt intervene in the Ramer incident, and she visited the governor of Alabama to seek aid for the beleaguered Henry. The storm passed, however, and Henry quietly moved to Conecuh County, where he established another school in the town of China. In 1912 his school had four teachers and ninety-six pupils.

[2] Elizabeth Evaline Wright. See above, 3:71.

To Timothy Thomas Fortune

Tuskegee, Ala., May, 8, 1900

Dear Mr. Fortune: I have forgotten whether or not I have sent you the money for the Burrell[1] clipping. If I have not sent it let me know and I will forward it at once.

I have been expecting the upheaval in regard to the Long Island Railway. Mr. Baldwin had mentioned the matter to me. Mr. Baldwin, however, I think will come out on top. It will not hurt our cause for him to get his hands into the Pennsylvania Railroad.

I do not understand about Marshall.[2] If I do not hear from him soon I will write him a letter. In fact I have just determined to send him a letter by this mail. Yours truly,

Booker T. Washington

TLS Con. 172 BTW Papers DLC.

[1] Frank A. Burrelle was president of Burrelle's Press Clipping Bureau in New York City.

[2] Edward Davis Marshall.

From Timothy Thomas Fortune

New York, May 9, 1900

My dear Mr. Washington: Your letter of the 5th instant was received. I hope the outline of the Washington address I sent you last Saturday night will cover the case. I think you will do well to prepare the Washington address in advance and let us to go over it together. The educated friends of the race hereabouts are claiming that you are largely responsible for the concerted onslaught on higher education which is now in full swing in all directions, all the opponents of it using you as a club. I know otherwise, and doing what I can to stem the tide in the Age, the Sun and the Transcript. But you have got to come out squarely on the subject as against Barringer, Charles Dudley Warner[1] and Hilery A. Herbert[2] (yesterday's speech), and the Washington occasion will furnish the time and place. The matter is a vital one to you and the race.

As I anticipated, and judging from Herbert's address yesterday, the Montgomery conference will do us more harm than good. My editorial in the Age last week and the Sun Sunday and the Transcript yesterday, the 8th, on "The College Bred Negro," is the correct view. We can't trust white men North or South to shape thought for us, we must do it ourselves. That is a dead open and shut.

My health is all right and I am sticking to the Scott letter decision. I take a glass when I want to but I have stopped lushing and shall not begin again. I shall boss myself in that as in other things concerning myself. I know that I have injured myself in this matter and I regret it.

I am having something nearly every day in the editorial or special columns of the Transcript. I handed the Sun a two column smasher of Charles Dudley Warner's Washington rot today and I hope it will go.[3] I am flat financially and I am tired of it and shall keep my head and fire in the matter right along until things are as they should be.

I hope soon to have some returns from the Page matter. As Marshall has not returned the article he will use it. If you don't hear from the Page matter by the 13th send me some money on account, if you can, and I will go to Washington on the 18th and wait for you.

I enclose a letter just received from the Nichols people. They are a queer kettle of fish. Yours truly

T. Thomas Fortune

Tell me about the Montgomery conference in your next.

ALS   Con. 172   BTW Papers   DLC.

1 Charles Dudley Warner (1829-1900) was an outstanding essayist and editor. He was associate editor of the Hartford *Courant* from 1867 to 1900 and contributing editor of *Harper's Magazine* from 1884 to 1898. In his last years he was vice-president of the National Prison Association from 1898 to 1900 and president of the American Social Science Association from 1899 to 1900.

2 Herbert's position at the Montgomery Race Conference was less extreme than that of men like John Temple Graves, who urged deportation of blacks, or Paul Brandon Barringer, who believed blacks were doomed to extinction. While considering deportation an impossibility, Herbert nonetheless felt that Negro suffrage was a blunder. He also believed that millions of dollors had been wasted on Negro education, but he advocated a system of industrial education similar to that at Tuskegee. (New York *Sun*, May 10, 1900, 6.)

3 In a speech before the American Social Science Association on May 7, Warner stated that higher education for blacks in the South was a failure and that industrial education was the best way to educate the race. Fortune's article defended higher education in the South and accused Warner of being an outsider who had not studied the problem at first hand. Fortune praised the work of Hampton and Tuskegee but argued that Afro-Americans needed both industrial and higher education. (New York *Sun*, May 13, 1900, 6.)

From Timothy Thomas Fortune

New York, May 10, 1900

My dear Mr. Washington: I hand you an advertisement which appeared in the *Evening Journal* yesterday which will make you jump.

Hurrah for McCorkle! His speech yesterday is the only break in the dead level of flapdoodle which has characterized the past two days' meetings of the conference. The reference John Temple Graves made to you was highly indecent, far fetched and insulting.[1] Waddell's harangue will do us good.[2] The Northern newspapers are beginning to give the whole shooting match sheol. Now for Burke Cockran's wail.[3] Truth to say we [have] the rascals on the jump. And they will show what I prognosticated that they have failed to solve the race problem and have nothing to offer up their sleeve to get them out of the hole except to take away from us all that we got out of the war and have gained since; and the country at large is not going to accept that. From this point of view we shall be gainers by the conference.

Gaskins and Gaines say they will furnish me a bang up dinner for 12, in the afternoon of May 22, for $20 exclusive of wine and segars. Thirty dollars would cover the outlay.

I am glad to have the Page letter, but so far you have not expressed an opinion of "Sowing and Reaping."

My health is good and I am in fair working and fighting trim. Yours truly

T. Thomas Fortune

ALS Con. 172 BTW Papers DLC.

1 While most speakers were able to praise BTW, even while they discussed the disfranchisement of black voters, John Temple Graves of Georgia asked the delegates

"what man of you . . . would install this great and blameless negro in your guest chamber tonight? If he were unmarried, what man of you would receive with equanimity his addresses to your daughter or your ward? What man of you would vote for this proven statesman for Governor of Alabama?" Not one delegate answered Graves's challenge. (Harlan, *BTW*, 295.)

2 Alfred Moore Waddell, mayor of Wilmington, N.C., stated that the unrestricted ballot for blacks was a menace to society and that any education other than industrial would be a menace to the Negro. He urged repeal or modification of the Fifteenth Amendment to allow each state to determine its own voting laws. He said that blacks did not need political power but only the help and sympathy of whites. (New York *Sun,* May 10, 1900, 5.)

3 Cockran's speech combined sentimentalism and expressions of affection for blacks with a demand for repeal of the Fifteenth Amendment. After the speech BTW came down from the Jim Crow gallery to shake Cockran's hand. It is not clear whether he did so because he was moved by the speech or simply because he wanted to give some recognition to this northern politician and friend of William H. Baldwin, Jr., one of Tuskegee's trustees. (Harlan, *BTW*, 295.)

From William H. Venable[1]

Atlanta   May 11 1900

Dear Sir, You may perhaps remember me, as chai[r]man of the committee on colored exhibit Exposition year. I have been so very much interested in the progress of the colored race for years. We undertook to teach them to make granite blocks at our quarries at Stone Mountain and succeeded. We are having so much trouble with the stone cutters who come here from the east — that we have made up our minds to attempt to teach the negroes to cut stone. If we can do this it will be a new field and a better one than most any other & we can be independent of the labor organizations. We have been informed that there are many 1st class stone cutters amongst the colored in Va. & N.C. Our plan will be to take apprentices abt 16 to 18 years old to board clothe & house, and in a few years we can have any kind of stone work done by home folks. When we break away from these unions we will be condemned by every labor organization in the U.S. As you will know they will not admit a negro into the stone cutters union any where in the east — as for that matter they will not admit them in any organization. So you will appreciate the gravity of our position and its consequences if we take this step. In addition to this we want to erect on our property at Stone Mt. Ga. (we have 4000 acres) a large cotton factory & run it entirely by colored labor. To do this however we will have to seek the aid of people of the east Fall River or Boston to buy the equipment. We believe we could in few years have a happy, prosperus and progressive villege of your race at Stone Mt. & demonstrate your theory that they are capable of achiving success & independance in any kind of industrial pursuits. We want therefore to enlist your good offices 1st In giving us your candid opinion as to whether you think the plan is feasable for (securing good talent for stone cutters — boys with some good idea of angles, squares & figures &c). 2d In securing the necessary aid in the East to establish the cotton factory (we putting up lands, buildings &c) & others contributing machinery. 3d What you will be willing to spend some of your valuable time for, in the east to raise enough to buy the machin[er]y &c. This letter is in confidence — as the labor unions here would give us trouble in our present contracts if they knew we contemplated such a step. Let me hear from you. Very Truly

Wm H. Venable

ALS Con. 186 BTW Papers DLC.

1 William H. Venable of Atlanta was listed in the 1900 census as a white forty-seven-year-old granite contractor.

From W. F. Crockett[1]

Montgomery Ala. May 11th, 1900

My dear sir: I came down town early this morning, hoping to see you before you left the city, as I desired to extend to you my sincere thanks and congratulations for the noble work done, and assistance given by reason of your presence in the gallery among your people at a time when their dearest interests were being violently assailed. Indeed it was a great help in those trying moments for one to feel that you were not only there by your sympathies, but really there in person, not on the platform but side by side with those to whom you have given the best hours of your life. I have heard not a few express themselves, as having been stimulated by your presence in those moments when all hope seemed to have been buried beneath popular sentiment.

You were to them what the presence of a general is to his men in a great struggle for victory, when defeat seems imminent. There was no place where you could have been more eloquent, and powerful than where you were. Side by side with your own people. The lesson you have taught me in this one act will go with me through life. It is the great lesson that comes to us from the life and teaching of the Master, the one of all that is the most difficult to emulate. A life that can silently bear such great hardships as you must have borne during the past three days will some day be claimed as the heritage of the ages.

Wishing for you sufficient length of days to see the highest and best results of your work, I remain   Yours truly,

W. F. Crockett

TLS   Con. 168   BTW Papers   DLC.

1 W. F. Crockett was a black lawyer who was born in Virginia in 1859. In about 1903 he moved to Hawaii, where he was district attorney on the island of Maui.

From Timothy Thomas Fortune

New York, May 11, 1900

My dear Mr. Washington: I have your three favors of the 8th, under one enclosure, and am glad to have them.

The Transcript of yesterday declares that the Montgomery conference has been a failure, as I thought it would be. The Northern newspapers for the most part smash the "shoot" in the jaw, declaring that the 15th amendment will not be repealed, that Negro education has not been a failure, that deportation, expatriation and all the rest of it is "an iridescent dream,["] and that the Southern white man cannot hope to solve the race question by himself: he must solve it in conjunction with the black man. So there we are, and we shall be large gainers by the conference because it has shown the country the Southern white man's hand, which is not our hand by a jug full. We have the rascals now on the defensive; let us keep them there.

The Transcript yesterday editorially knocks the bottom out of John Temple Graves and I have an editorial in the same issue on "A Prophet of Unrest" in which I rip Bishop Turner up the back with a dagger out of your book, "The Future of the American Negro." Do you get the Transcript every day? You should. It is the best newspaper friend we have in the country.

O, yes, I am in splendid mental and physical condition, never better, and am working like a beaver, and the work is being published by those to whom I send it. I feel very grateful and hopeful and if my health holds out and the nerves donot go back on me I shall be in better shape soon. My eyes are giving me trouble and I shall have to go to Philadelphia soon to see my doctor about them — when I return from Washington, the 23rd, perhaps.

I am glad Scott thinks well of "Sowing and Reaping." He is a capable judge. I hope the publishers will confirm his opinion of the work. I note what you say of my oft repeated suggestions concerning the Sunday Talks.

I am gratified that the suggestions I sent you last Saturday concerning the Washington address will be helpful and that you will use them. You will have to jump to speak in Washington the 22d and in Columbus the 23rd. The babies are mighty close together.

Yes, you sent the $5.00 for Burrelle in the checks you sent me at Washington for $30. If Marshall did not intend to use your article he would have returned it. I think he has been holding it for an opportune time to print it. But it will do no harm to shake him up as you have done.

I am glad you think Mr Baldwin will come out on top in the railroad mix up. He is a strong man but he must be held in check. Perhaps he will now think better of my view of Murphy and the Montgomery program.

I will think over the Paris Juror matter and I may find a way out. I have no faith in Peck, and he has no faith in Calloway and I dare say is hedging on the matter because Calloway is urging it.

Hope to see you soon. Yours truly

T. Thomas Fortune

ALS Con. 172 BTW Papers DLC.

To the Editor of the Washington *Colored American*

Tuskegee, Alabama. [May 12, 1900]

Tuskegee, Ala., Special — Much interest is now being centered upon the "Southern Conference" just held in Montgomery, Alabama, May 8th-10th, to consider the interests of the two races in the South. While I have no connection with this Conference, there are one or two things that I think our people ought to know regarding it. In the first place, I think it fair to presume that some things are going to be said that we will not like and some things are going to be said that we will like. We must not be disappointed if the first meeting is not all that we had hoped for.

The most valuable point I think in connection with this Conference is, that it is going to help bring about that which the Negro has so long asked for, and the South so much needed — and that is free speech. The promoters of this Conference have been careful to see that provision is made that all sides of the race question may be heard, but as I understand it the discussion is to be confined at the first Conference at least to white men only.

It means a great gain when in the heart of the South we can have a Conference of any kind where white men are invited to speak out plainly their views in regard to the Negro. It would not be a Conference of free speech if the discussions were confined to those whom we consider already favorable to the highest interests of the Negro. There could be little gain to our cause if the meeting brought together only those who are already favorably disposed to the highest interest of the Negro. Let us not be alarmed if some of the speakers favor taking away from the Negro some of the rights which he possesses. If individuals have this feeling in their hearts it is better to give expression to it than to repress it. Our cause is just and we can stand the light of open free discussion.

As a Conference, I am assured that the organization is not going to commit itself by any resolutions or otherwise, to any of the much discussed plans for the solution of the race problem. It is simply going to serve as a medium through which white men, North and South can come together for an open, free and frank discussion. In looking over the program I see that the Executive Committee has tried to be fair to the assignment of speakers. The Negro's side will not suffer while such true and tried friends [of] our cause as Dr. H. B. Frissell, Dr. J. L. M. Curry, Walter H. Page and ex Gov. MacCorkle are there. If Hon. Bourke Cockran of New York, for example, [is] there to advocate, as he is likely to do, the repeal of the 15th Amendment as a solution ex Gov. MacCorkle will be there to advocate that the Negro be treated with absolute justice at the ballot box, through an educational test and property test for the voting that shall apply equally to both races.

Some of our race papers have misunderstood the motive of the Rev. Edgar Gardner Murphy, of Montgomery, one of the chief organizers of this Conference. Mr. Murphy has expressed personal views regarding the 15th Amendment, with which I do not and cannot agree, but in no sense will Mr. Murphy attempt to make the Conference stand for his personal views. No black man in the South who has had the opportunity to really know Mr. Murphy at his home in the South can doubt that while he may advocate a means of solving the problem, with which we are not in accord, at the same time he is a sincere friend of the Negro, as well as of the white man.

So let us prepare our minds as a race to hear an open, frank discussion and if anything in connection with the organization of the first Conference is not as we would have it, let us remember that it is a beginning and may in the providence of God in the future bring us great help as a race.

Booker T. Washington

Washington *Colored American*, May 12, 1900, 6.

Edgar Gardner Murphy to
William Henry Baldwin, Jr.

Montgomery, Ala., May 12, 1900

My Dear Mr. Baldwin: The Conference is over, and its success has exceeded the most sanguine expectations of any of us. There was a very fair report of Mr. Herbert's speech in the Times, and I presume you saw the expression of his conviction that the individual states will have to work out their problem of the suffrage in subordination to the XIVth. and XVth. Amendments. As Mr. Herbert was on the following day unanimously elected the President of the Southern Society, we have thus borne further testimony to the fact that the Society itself does not desire to stand committed to the proposition of repeal.

On the franchise debate of the following morning, we allowed Gov. MacCorkle of West Virginia to close the discussion in behalf of a suffrage test applicable to both races. Gov. MacCorkle also had this position of great vantage for his protest against any repeal or modification of the XVth. Amendment, and you will see from his printed speech that he dealt explicitly with my own proposal. Incidents of this kind will indicate how careful we have been to adjust the balance of debate with frankness and fairness. It would, however, have been as impossible for us to have prevented certain of our speakers from referring to the XVth. Amendment and from advocating its modification or repeal, as for us to have attempted to dam the Mississippi River. The minds of the speakers constantly went back to the thought that it stands for a great coercive injustice, and that so long as it occupies the position of *law* upon our federal statutes, it will *imply* at least the *possibility of military enforcement*. It operates, therefore, in my judgment, to intensely increase the feeling of our people against the Negro. At the same time, the South is not likely as a whole to ask for the repeal of the XVth. Amendment. The average politician at the South cannot bring himself to forego that increased representation in the electoral college and in Congress which the Amendment assures to this section of our country. I think a practical proposal for the repeal of the Amendment will come ultimately from the North. The North will at last see that it is ineffective, that it does not permit the Negro to vote, and the North, I believe, will unite in the advocacy of its repeal in order that the equilibrium of political influence may be adjusted in Congress in relation to the actual voting population of the country. What will then be the effect of the repeal of the Amendment? It will be the restoration of civic rights to the Negroes of the South. Every Southern State, in order to secure its former representation in Congress and in the electoral college, will hasten to enfranchise the blacks, just as rapidly as the conditions of social and political security will permit. This, however, is merely my own personal opinion, and for the reasons given above, I am quite sure that the South will not pursue to any practical conclusions the project of modification or repeal. I sincerely wish it would do so, because such a policy would be sustained with the force of conscience and with the principles of a sound political philosophy. Under the present operation of the XVth. Amendment (which secures no Negro the right to vote), the South has a larger representation in Congress and in the electoral college, in proportion to its voting population, than any other section of our country. This is a condition which involves injustice both to the Negro and to the North.

The net result of the Conference is hopefulness, courage and justice. Our own local press has frankly recognized the fact that the general trend of discussion was distinctly favorable to the better tendencies of Negro progress. The discussion on education was triumphantly hopeful. There was a great audience, and there was a most marked appreciation of Dr. Frissell's paper. He spoke with clear and commanding voice, and with a tactfulness and force that made his address not only interesting, but convincing. Dr. Curry closed the discussion with a speech that Washington and many others of his friends declare to be the greatest that he has ever made. It captured the enthusiasm of the great assembly, and held them to the close. That one evening would have justified all our efforts if the Conference had given us nothing more.

The religious discussion on the next morning was also interesting and inspiring. There was not a harsh note throughout. Among the volunteer speakers was Mr. Herbert Welsh,[1] of the Indian Rights Association, and Prof. W. F. Willcox, Chief Statistician of the Census Office at Washington. The discussion on lynching forced the fact to the front that the Committee had canvassed the South for some man to take the affirmative of the question, "Is Lynching Advisable," and we had been unable to secure a single response. Both the papers were strong and helpful, and I look for much good from their circulation. The evening session of the last day brought the Conference to a close, and the spectacle was something long to be remembered. Every part of the great Auditorium was packed with people, and it is the common testimony that Montgomery in all its history had never known such an audience before. There was not only an enormous crowd, but it was a crowd composed of the best thought and life of the state and the South. Dr. Barringer's address was valuable in certain of its statistics, but it was odious in spirit. His voice, I am not sorry to say, was too ineffective to give his words any extended influence. All of our thoughtful people, including even the representatives of the press, regarded the speech with distinct disfavor. I had read his Charleston address, and while I thought his animus unfortunate, I regarded his chief generalization as of real importance to the discussion of the subject, but this Montgomery paper was without largeness of mind or of heart. We regretted that Mr. Page's withdrawal should have made it necessary for us to give him Mr. Page's place, and I awaited the result with some apprehension. As things turned out, however, nothing could have been more fortunate. The paper wrought its own cure, and so far from his being exempt in that particular, Mr. Cockran, in his great oration of that evening, and Mr. Herbert, in his farewell address, paid their respects to him so thoroughly, that there was very little left of his philosophy of pessimism. No man was ever more thoroughly *smashed*, and how much better that this result should have been attained not in Boston, New York or Philadelphia, but right here in the South where the people might have been supposed to be in sympathy with some of his gloomy notions. He was overwhelmed not only by the arguments of those who followed him, but by the tumult of applause that greeted the refutation of his theories.

I have dwelt, however, with too great length upon this paper, because the surpassing power and beauty of Mr. Cockran's speech has almost made us forget what Dr. Barringer said. Mr. Cockran began at nine o'clock, and spoke for almost two hours. Many of the newspaper men who have frequently heard him have declared that it was by all means the greatest speech that he has ever made. No printed report can do justice to that combination of unfailing sagacity and of overwhelming earnestness which secured to him the consciousness and the appreciation of every element of his audience. There can be no doubt that the general effect of his speech will be an inspiration to all the friends of order and justice. In point of intellectual sincerity, of moral enthusiasm, of philosophic weight, as well as in diction, it is the greatest speech that I have ever heard. I do not know what Washington thinks of it, but I know that all of the intelligent *Negroes* in Montgomery regard it as one of the wisest and most effective presentations of their cause which could possibly have been conceived. There was not from the beginning to the end one repressive or oppressive note. It was full of large-heartedness and grasp and insight. It regarded the modification of the XVth. Amendment, just as I have regarded it, from the standpoint of the Negro's welfare. It was a superb contention for what was a self-evident truth to the Southern man, that the XVth. Amendment has been the chief ground for the denial to the Negro of every right which it was intended to secure, and that to cling to it is to emphasize the old saying about the letter which killeth and the spirit which maketh alive. This speech, however, went far beyond this immediate contention. It assumed that the industrial problem lies at the heart of the whole situation. That if the Negro will take hold of the problem of life, not first from the political end, but from the industrial end, the great forces of experience will at length accord him the privileges of civic power. The closing third of the speech dealt with the thought of the identity of interest which obtains between the two classes of our population, and when Mr. Cockran, criticizing Dr. Barringer, closed a tremendous sentence with the assertion that as he looked out upon the glorious world of this sunny Southern country, he regarded it as a garden not to mark where a race had been buried, but where a race had been saved, the overwhelming applause was so earnest and so sustained, that there could be no doubt as to the feeling of his hearers. Showing the economic necessity of the Negro to the white man and of each race to the other, he closed by indicating the relation between the mutual helpfulness of these races to the broader necessities and to the ultimate triumph of civilization.

I send you to-day a stenographic report of the address. Our facilities, however, in that direction are not very great at the South, and the report does not do justice to the speech. It will give you, however, a suggestion, at least, of the line of Mr. Cockran's thought. On the whole, I may say that we have made a beginning that has exceeded my largest hopes. We have commanded, by our policy of inclusion and representation, the confidence of all classes of our people. While there were some things said that some of us regret, the general trend of expression was distinctly wise and statesman-like. In conclusion, I cannot tell you how affectionately grateful I am for your personal confidence and aid. With sincere regards to you all, I am Cordially and Faithfully,

Edgar Gardner Murphy

TLS   Con. 1   BTW Papers   DLC.

1 Herbert Welsh (1851-1941), an author and editor, was corresponding secretary of the Indian Rights Association for more than thirty years and president for eleven years. He was an advocate of universal peace through arbitration and was an opponent of U.S. acquisition of the Philippines.

A Sunday Evening Talk

Tuskegee, Ala., May 13, 1900

I hope that each one of you as you go out for the summer, whether you go out with the view of returning here to finish your course of study, or whether you go out as graduates of the institution, I want each of you to remember that you are going to go backward or you are going to go forward. It will be impossible for you to stand still. You will either go upward or you will go downward, and as you go upward, you will take others up with you, or as you go downward, you will take others with you.

A great many people, as they go out into the world and fail to make progress, feel that they are not going backward. But this is not so; you either grow or decay. You will find that the surroundings into which you enter will either pull you downward, or you will be so strong that you will pull yourself up and pull other people up as you go up yourself. It is impossible for you to stand still.

One of the saddest sights is to see a young man or a young woman, who has received such advantages as you receive here, going backward year by year, not taking advantage of the opportunities by which they are surrounded. I have seen young men who have finished their studies here, not many I am glad to say, who are ashamed to face their teachers, who are really ashamed to visit the institution, because they feel deep down in their hearts that they have not followed the instruction of their teachers, they have not carried out the purpose of the institution, and they are failures; they are ashamed to meet and look their teachers in the face. They are ashamed to return here from year to year, as many of you do, to get the inspiration of the institution.

As I sat for three days in the convention, which met in Montgomery during the past week, it seemed to me the center of criticism, so far as there was criticism of our race, centered around the point of the moral weakness of the race. Now, we want to be sure that these charges that are brought against us have no foundation. That is one of the most essential things that we want to be sure about as a race. If we will live in a way that such criticism will have no foundation, it cannot have any lasting effect. But if it has foundation, if it is grounded upon facts and figures, no matter what we say, no matter how we try to shield ourselves, we will fail. In the first place, I feel very sure that the weakness of our race is in the large cities and towns. I am sure that we serve ourselves best, we serve our race best, when we keep away from the large cities, unless we have good cause to go to the city to do work that no one else is doing, unless we are sure we can do better work, unless we are sure that more lasting and effective work can be done than it is possible for us to do in some country district.

The more I study this question the more I am sure we are at our weakest in the large cities. And I should say that the bulk of our influence should be in keeping the race from the cities; keeping it on the farms, in the smaller towns, where the advantages are much more in its favor, where the opportunities are much more encouraging than they are in the larger cities. We find when we look at this problem carefully that a great deal of the moral weakness of the race centers in the fact that, in the large cities, there is a large idle class; that too large a proportion of us in our cities like Montgomery, Philadelphia, Washington and New York are in constant want, and wherever you go you should let your action tell against that kind of thing. Let your action tell against idleness; let it tell against our people coming into these large cities and being idle. Too large a proportion of our men, as you will see in such cities as Washington, Atlanta, New Orleans, are idle people and making a dishonest living. A large number of these men get their living by women working and feeding them. As soon as women cease to do that kind of thing, you will find that a larger proportion of these men will go to work and make a living. These are women working over the wash tub, the ironing table, the cooking-stove in order that they may feed some worthless creature, who would be better dead than alive. Remember, as you go out into these large cities, that you want to have the courage to throw the weight of your influence against that kind of life. In many cases, you will find that idleness leads to immorality, it leads to sin; and following in the wake of idleness in the large cities is physical weakness. You go in[to] Mobile, Atlanta, Washington and other places, and you will find that our people are dying about twice as fast as the white people are dying, and a very large proportion of the same people live in shanties, flats and sheds, as it were. Now, unless you who are educated in such institutions as this and have the moral strength to stand up against these kinds of things, the race will go on and on from one degree of worthlessness to another degree of worthlessness, and the end cannot help but be near.

In the first place, you want to be industrious. That is the safeguard against many of the weaknesses to which [I] have referred. We want to go out from here, feeling that it is a sin, a disgrace for an individual to be idle a single day.

And then, you want to go out with the idea that you are going to get hold of property; that you are going to have a bank account; that you are not going to live in poverty and shame. It is said that we are a poverty-stricken race, that we do not own property, that we do not have a bank account. There are cases where our people go out and spend in a very short time all the money that they have been a year or more earning. They are inclined to yield to the temptation of spending their money upon fine shoes, upon showy socks and neckties, upon high hats and upon many other things that they could do without. You want to set yourself against that kind of thing.

Get a bank account, get hold of some property, and then all things will come in due season. There are many young men who will spend two or three dollars in taking a buggy ride when perhaps that same young man is not getting more than three or four dollars a week. And you, young women, ought to be plain enough to say to such young men that you do not think they are able to spend two and three dollars for a buggy ride for you. I know it takes a great deal of bravery; I know that it takes a great deal of frankness to do that kind of thing. But we have got to come to it. Our graduates have got to come to the point where their influence and every action will be against worthlessness, where their influence will be in favor of industry, will be in favor of right living. A young man or young woman is not living honestly when he or she spends four-fifths of their salary in useless practices, when they should be investing that money in building a home, or in the bank.

And then, more and more we want to get hold of the reputation of keeping our word in all business affairs. In too many cases, we find our people's word in business cannot be depended upon — people have no confidence in what we say. You find that such people have no standing, as it were, in the business world. One of the things which made considerable discussion in the conference was the charge that we have no credit; that no one would attempt to sell us goods on credit. On the afternoon of the conference, two of these men were taken to Mr. J. W. Adams' store where this young man is doing a splendid business. Go ask what is his financial standing, go ask what is his standing in the business world. We went up stairs. Here was a beautiful outlay of hats to be sold. They had been made ready for sale by the young woman in charge of this department, a graduate from this institution. She showed them the work she had done — not what she was hoping to do, but what she had actually done.

A few days ago, when I was in the town of Tuskegee, I was talking with Mr. Campbell,[1] the President of the Macon County Bank, concerning some of the charges that were brought against the race. Mr. Campbell said he had implicit confidence in the race. He said: "Mr. Washington, my faith in your race is not based upon what I have read, nor upon what I have heard; my faith is based upon my actual experience with it." He said: "I loaned a black man $1200 sometime ago, and the only security the black man could give for the $1200 was one poor old mule." Said he: "And Mr. Washington, that man paid the last dollar of that $1200 — he paid the last dollar of that loan. People may talk to me a hundred years about the dishonesty of the Negro race, but I will have faith in them, because I have tried them."

This is the kind of object lesson we want to present to the people, and until we can have in every part of this country such examples as these men, talk will not amount to a great deal.

Now, we are about at the close of this year, and I want to see you go out from the institution with a new determination; that in your life, such is going to be your purpose; that you are going to be an example for others, and if we can thus place this influence in every part of the South, there will be no use for us to despair concerning the future of our people.

Tuskegee Student, 13 (June 2, 1900), 3-4.

1 George Washington Campbell.

To Timothy Thomas Fortune

Tuskegee, Ala., May 14, 1900

My dear Mr. Fortune: I am very glad to have had your various letters lately and have read them with care. I thank you also for the various clippings which you have sent me.

I am also glad to know that you are in good health and that you are sticking to your resolution which I think is most wise and needful. You will not regret it in the long run.

I thank you also for the suggestions which you have sent me for my Washington address. My present thought is to write the whole thing out carefully and stick pretty closely to my manuscript. In the present disturbed condition of things I do not see how I can escape referring to the franchise. There is so much discussion of this matter that it would seem to be a direct act of cowardice on my part to omit any discussion of it.

I am very glad that you are doing such excellent work for the Transcript. I seem to have missed the editorial, however, on the Race Conference in Montgomery. I get the Transcript every day. I saw the editorial on the John Temple Graves matter. Graves wants to have a conference with me. He says he is in the act of changing his views on the race question.

I do not think we had better have the dinner in Washington as I will not have time for that before going to Columbus. It will be a mistake for me to attempt to attend a dinner before I speak and I fear there will not be time enough for it afterward. Perhaps we had better defer the dinner until some other time.

Barringer pitched into industrial education in Montgomery. He did not refer to higher education but tried to smash industrial education. John Temple Graves did the same thing. Yours truly,

Booker T. Washington

TLS   Con. 172   BTW Papers   DLC.

From William Alexander MacCorkle

Charleston, W.Va. May 14, 1900

Dear Prof: I regretted not seeing you while in Alabama. I told Mr. Thrasher to tell you to come and see me.

I was very sorry that my speech was not the success I would [have] liked for it to have been. I was quite ill, however, and did not do myself justice. I did not so much care, however, as the Associated Press had my speech. It has been most favorably commented on all over the United States. A large number of Southern people told me that it was the right basis, but it seems that none of them had the strength to stand up and say what was right. I did not think it took any particular amount of courage to do so, although every human being in the sound of my voice seemed to be opposed to my idea. It seems to me that the determination seems to be to disfranchise the Negro. This is a crying wrong and I hope such will not be the case. There is nothing to do, however, but to stand up and give them a hard fight for what is right and just. I regret this, but it seems that it cannot be helped at this time. Believe me, Very sincerely yours,

W. A. MacCorkle

TLS   Con. 179   BTW Papers   DLC.

To Warren Easton[1]

[Tuskegee, Ala.] May 15, 1900

Dear Sir: I hope you will forgive me for being so tardy in answering your letter regarding the remodeling of your course of study in the colored schools and the placing of manual training into some of them.[2] I have delayed answering your letter for the reason that I hoped before now to have gotten time to have written something to be printed on this subject but I have not found the opportunity and so I must write you. I cannot put my hands on any printed matter that covers your case for the reason that at this institution we deal with students who are 14 years and more of age and our work is more in the direction of industrial training than manual training. I think if you will correspond with Mr. Gibson,[3] Supt. of Public Schools in Columbus, Ga., he may give you considerable information as he has gone further than any Southern city I know of in introducing manual training in both white and colored schools in that city. My own feeling is very strong that in the case of our own people that the children need some simple form of industrial training rather than manual training. In the case of the more wealthy white people of course industrial training is not so necessary. I feel that the primary need of our people is first that the children be taught habits of industry, the dignity of labor and some occupation by which the individual is sure of earning a living. Of course manual training I think is a good preparation for the industrial training, but I feel that manual training alone will not answer the needs of our people. The ideal plan in my mind would be this, to find out what each individual child is most likely to find to do in his immediate neighborhood and give the child training in the thing that he would be most likely to do at his home. This plan I find being followed very generally in the large polytechnic schools in England, when I was there last summer, but of course I understand that there would be difficulties in your carrying out this idea. I feel, however, that in a public school like those in New Orleans that all of the girls ought to be taught sewing in all its forms, and the larger girls something of cooking and laundering. The boys should receive training in some form of wood and iron work.

I am sorry that my letter must be so unsatisfactory. I hope next year to find some time when I can give the subject of manual training or industrial training for our people in the public schools some thorough study and after I have done so I hope to put my views in print. Yours truly,

[Booker T. Washington]

TL Copy   Con. 171   BTW Papers   DLC.

1 Warren Easton, born in Louisiana in 1854, was superintendent of New Orleans public schools from 1888 to 1910.

2 In 1900 the New Orleans school board limited black education in the city to the primary grades. After the fourth grade male students received manual training, and females were taught "domestic economy." The school board argued that 90 percent of the 9,000 black students in the New Orleans schools were in the primary grades and most of them dropped out of school before entering the "grammar" grades 5 through 8. The board maintained that more black students would be able to attend the primary grades under the new system because of a better use of the funds allocated for black education. (New Orleans *Picayune*, Aug. 18, 1900, 7.) New Orleans newspapers claimed that the school board was following BTW's philosophy of industrial education, but the Tuskegean believed that his position had been misunderstood. (See To the Editor of the New Orleans *Times-Democrat*, Aug. 29, 1900, and BTW to David A. Graham, Sept. 24, 1900, below.)

3 Carleton Bartlett Gibson.

From Charles Waddell Chesnutt

Cleveland, O. May 16, 1900

My dear Mr. Washington, I thank you for your kind words *apropos* of Mr. Howells's *Atlantic* article. I trust I may be able to write up to the standard he is good enough to set for me.

I appreciate your cordial invitation to visit Tuskegee some time in the future, and it is possible that I may avail myself of the privilege sometime during next Fall or Winter, as I hope to make a Southern trip within a year.

I have read various newspaper reports of the Montgomery Conference, which I hope may be as fruitful of good results as you anticipated. It has seemed to me that the thing most desired was the repeal of the Fifteenth Amendment. Cochran's argument that the amendment should go because it had been "lynched" by the States, is scarcely more than to say that because Negroes, forsooth, had been lynched in the South, it were better to withdraw from them the protection of the Courts, and leave them to the tender goodwill of their neighbors, who would treat them well because they didn't have to! I should like very much to know where to write for a complete report of the proceedings, which I understand are to be published; the newspaper reports have been only fragmentary.

I feel just a little ashamed that your visit here was not productive of larger immediate results, but I trust it may prove seed sown upon good ground. One thing is true about this city — it has apparently little enthusiasm for outside people — for the Negro in the abstract —but it gives those within its borders comparatively good opportunities to rise in the world. With best wishes, Sincerely yours,

Chas. W. Chesnutt

ALS Con. 168 BTW Papers DLC.

From William Edward Burghardt Du Bois

Atlanta, Ga., May 16 1900

My Dear Mr Washington: I shall try & get the list of business men[1] to you in a week or two. I have been very busy. Yours,

W. E. B. Du Bois

ALS Con. 170 BTW Papers DLC.

[1] While it was BTW who developed the National Negro Business League, the idea grew out of the work of Du Bois and others at Atlanta University during the Atlanta Conference of 1899 on the subject of "The Negro in Business." Du Bois was a member of the committee that drafted a call for the creation of local, state, and national associations of black businessmen. Later that year Du Bois became the director of the Afro-American Council's Negro business bureau with the responsibility of organizing local business leagues. Du Bois accepted this post with the stipulation that postage money was to be supplied by the council. Several months later, however, BTW's friend T. Thomas Fortune killed the appropriation of postage funds and Du Bois was unable to carry out his plans. Later BTW asked Du Bois for his list of names, which became part of the base on which BTW built his organization. (Harlan, *BTW*, 266-68; Harlan, "BTW and the NNBL.")

At the Afro-American Council convention held in Indianapolis in Aug. 1900, just a week after BTW had launched the NNBL, Du Bois was not re-elected as director of the Negro business bureau. Emmett J. Scott succeeded Du Bois in the position, thus assuring BTW's control of activities related to black businessmen in both the NNBL and the Afro-American Council. (Fredrick L. McGhee to Scott, Mar. 25, 1902, Con. 234, BTW Papers, DLC.)

From Edward Elder Cooper

Washington, D.C., May 16th, 1900

My dear Mr. Washington: Your letter of the 14th inst. is to hand and noted. You need not apologize at any time for any delay in answering my letters, for I know that you are always on the "go" and when you are not you are head-over-heels in work. I would not be a good friend, nor a sensible friend if I didn't understand these things.

I note what you say concerning the Montgomery Conference. I am not discouraged. The day is dawning and the sun goes higher up into the heavens. I can see your fine Italian hand all through the work and I believe the thinking men of the race see it as well.

I shall reserve the front page and as much space in The Colored American as you want for your address, to be delivered in this city next week. It might not be a bad idea at this time for me to run the full page cut of you, the salient points of your address and give you an editorial. The eyes of the country are more centered on you now than ever, and the particular good point in your favor now is that the venal white press is favorable to you. Yours very truly,

E. E. Cooper

TLS   Con. 168   BTW Papers   DLC.

An Address at the Metropolitan A.M.E. Church[1]

Washington, D.C. May 22, 1900

When a great ship at sea is being tossed during anxious days and nights by wind and wave, and its very life seems threatened by the elements of nature, then is the time for all on board, and especially those charged with the duty of managing the vessel, to keep a cool head, a clear conscience and a steady hand. In the midst of such danger and excitement it becomes doubly important that every insignificant and selfish consideration be lost sight of, that every fiber of energy of each individual on board the endangered vessel be bent in one direction — that of bringing the imperiled craft into a harbor of safety.

If ever a race needed supreme faith, calmness, unity and invincible determination those qualities are needed by the black race in America at the present time when it is passing through a season of trial and testing such as has seldom fallen to the lot of any race in the history of the world. But beyond and above all we must not lose hope or courage. In the midst of the storm let us be guided by the compass.

The ocean track through which our vessel is to pass was carefully and safely charted in Holy Writ more than eighteen hundred years ago. Let us examine it. The chart:

"In much patience, in affliction, in necessity, in distresses, in stripes, in imprisonments, in tumults, in labors, in watchings, in fastings; by pureness, by knowledge, by long suffering, by kindness, by the Holy Ghost, by love unfeigned, by the word of truth, by the power of God, by the armor of righteousness on the right hand and on the left, by honor and dishonor, by evil report and good report; as deceivers and yet true, as unknown and yet well known, as dying and behold we live, as chastened and not killed, as sorrowful, yet always rejoicing; as poor, yet making many rich; as having nothing and yet possessing all things."

It is in the storm that the vessel is tested and not in the calm.

In our case, the world should be constantly reminded that the problems that have grown out of our presence as a race in this country are not of our seeking or making. White Americans should always bear in mind that their duty toward the American negro is a unique one. Yea, more than that, it is a sacred obligation. The black man was not only brought to this country without his consent, but in the face of his most earnest protest. Every cry, every wail, every moan of anguish of the broken-hearted, heathen mother, as she saw her child forced aboard the slave ship; every suicide and every groan and every pleading in the middle passage that marked the journey of the negro from the shores of Africa to the shores of America was an earnest plea to the white man not to desecrate the soil of America by engrafting upon it the serious problems which are today demanding solution.

But the voice of right then, as I fear it is today in some quarters, was smothered by the voice of selfishness; the voice of the statesman was throttled, then, as now, in too many cases, by the voice of the short-sighted demagogue, and we went on sowing the wind, and now we reap the whirlwind. "Be not deceived, God is not mocked." Whatsoever a nation or a community sows, that it shall also reap.

But all this belongs to history. Our duty is with the present.

No one who looks deeply, calmly, conscientiously, into the present thought and activity can overlook the fact that we are now passing through a stage of race development which is serious at every step and demands as never before our deepest thought, ripest investigation and most unselfish assistance.

Political history in our case points to no path blazed through the forests, which is an absolute guide in the task before us. Ours is a task which demands and which should have the earnest assistance of the wisest statesmen, investigators and philanthropists of both races, in all sections of the country.

To be permanent in its influence and operation, every scheme for the settlement of the difficulties that beset us should have the indorsement of the white man at the south, the white man at the north and that of the negro himself. Our duty is to face the present and not to wail over the past. In the midst of the present seeming doubt, uncertainty and timidity on the part of many one or two things seem clear. We shall not settle our present problem by time spent in useless debate as to whether the white man north or the white man south was responsible for the introduction of American slavery.

No settlement will be permanent and satisfactory that does not command the confidence and the respect of the southern white man, the northern white man and the negro himself. Further, I am convinced that nothing can be gained, but much lost to the cause of the negro by time spent in the mere badinage of words of blame and censure between the white man north and the white man south. In the same spirit, I would add that the negro cannot make stronger his cause by aimless railings against the southern white man, neither can the southern white man assist much in the solution of the difficulty which is so vital to him, by mere condemnation of the negro.

Both the teachings of history and the warnings of the present emphasize that the question of the negro will not be settled, will not remove itself from across the pathway of our progress, till it is settled in absolute, unimpeachable justice to all parties concerned — justice to the north, who freed the negro; justice to the southern white man, in whose midst the negro resides, and justice to the negro himself.

The foundation of citizenship, it seems to me, rests upon the intrinsic worth of each individual or group of individuals. No law can push the individual forward when he is worthless, no law can hold him back when he is worthy. The worthy may be inconvenienced, but never defeated.

No praise on the part of ourselves or friends can help us if we are meritless. No abuse from any quarter can permanently injure us if we possess intrinsic worth.

In all the history of government I do not believe that in any large degree any race has been permitted to share in the control of government till a large number of the individual members of that race have demonstrated beyond question their ability to succeed in controlling successfully their own individual business affairs.

My own belief is that the time will come when the negro in this country will secure all the recognition which his merits entitle him to as a man and as a citizen, but such recognition will come through no process of artificial forcing, but through the natural law of evolution. In a word, we have got to pay the price for everything that we get, the price that every civilized race or nation has paid for its position, that of beginning gradually, naturally, at the bottom and working up toward the highest civilization. What I am most anxious about is that the negro shall be himself, not a second or third-rate imitation of someone else.

As Thomas Carlyle puts it:

"An original man; not a second hand, borrowing or begging man. Let us stand on our own basis, at any rate! On such shoes as we ourselves can get. On frost and mud, if you will, but honestly on that; on the reality and substance which nature gives us, not on the semblance, on the thing she has given another than us!"

If we are poor, let us be poor and not attempt in our poverty to imitate the rich and thus hold ourselves up to the ridicule of the world.

There is no more sad sight in christendom than to see a young colored man who is minus a bank account, minus a foot of real estate, minus a home for himself or parents, minus the saving habit, spending all he earns, and too often, more than he earns, in the mere vain attempt to deceive the world by superficial show. But the world has a way of not being deceived, and in the long run rates every individual and every race at its true worth.

For a number of years I have tried to advocate the advantages of industrial training for the negro, because it starts the race off on a real, sure foundation, and not upon a false and deceptive one.

Last year, when in England, I observed in Birmingham, London and elsewhere, in the large polytechnic schools, that thousands of men and women were being trained in the trades that cover work in the earth, in metal, wood, tin, leather, cloth, food preparation and whatnot.

When I asked why do you give this man or this woman training in this or that industry, the answer came that when these students come to us we ask in each case what are the prevailing occupations of the people in the community where the student lives. In a word, it is found out what the student can find to do in his immediate community, not what he ought to find to do, not what the instructors might desire him to do, but what the economic and other conditions prevailing in his neighborhood will actually permit him to do.

With this knowledge obtained the student was trained, for example, in leather because at his home that was the prevailing industry; that was the occupation at which he could find immediate and profitable employment. The same logical and common sense principle should be applied to our own race. For example, the great bulk of our people live directly or indirectly by work in the soil. This gives us a tremendous advantage in the way of a foundation.

From the beginning of time agriculture has constituted the main foundation upon which all races have grown useful and strong.

In the present condition of our race it is a grave error to take a negro boy from a farming community and educate him in about everything in heaven and earth, educate him into sympathy with everything that has no bearing upon the life of the community to which he should return, and out of sympathy with most that concerns agricultural life. The result of this process is that in too many cases the boy thus trained fails to return to his father's farm, but takes up his abode in the city and falls, in too many cases, into the temptation of trying to live by his wits, without honest, productive employment. And, my friends, if there is one thing at the present time that should give us more serious concern than another, it is the large idle class of our people that linger about the sidewalks, bar rooms and dens of sin and misery of our large cities.

Every influential man and woman should make it a part of his duty to reach the individuals of this class and either see that they find employment in the cities or are scattered to the four winds of the earth in agricultural communities where they can make an honorable living and where their services are needed.

If it be suggested that the white boy is not always thus dealt with, my answer is: My friends, the white man is three thousand years ahead of us, and this fact we might as well face now as well as later, and that at one stage of his development, either in Europe or America, he has gone through every stage of development that I now advocate for our race. No race can be lifted till its mind is awakened and strengthened. By the side of industrial training should always go mental and moral training. But the mere pushing of abstract knowledge into the head means little. We want more than the mere performance of mental gymnastics. Our knowledge must be harnessed to the things of real life.

Again, it is asked, would you limit or circumscribe the mental development of the negro boy? Emphatically I answer with a hundred "Noes." I would encourage the negro to secure all the mental strength, all the mental culture, whether gleaned from science, mathematics, history, language or literature, that his pocket book and circumstances will enable him to pay for, but I repeat with all the emphasis of my soul that the negro's education should be so directed and controlled for years to come that the greatest proportion of the mental strength of the masses will be brought to bear upon the every-day practical affairs of life, upon something that is needed to be done and something that they are permitted to do in the community where they reside.

When it comes to the professional class which our race needs and must have I would say, give them that training which will best fit them to perform in the most successful manner the service which the race demands. But would you confine the negro to industrial life, to agriculture, for example? No. But I would teach the race that here the foundation must be laid, and that the very best service which any one can render to what is called the higher education is to teach the present generation to provide a material or industrial foundation.

On this industrial foundation will grow habits of thrift, the love of work, economy, ownership in property, a bank account. Out of it in future generations will grow classical education, professional education, positions of public responsibility. Out of it will grow moral and religious strength. Out of it will grow that wealth which brings leisure and with it opportunity for the enjoyment of literature and the fine arts. In the words of the late Frederick Douglass, which I quote, "Every blow of the sledge hammer, wielded by a sable arm, is a powerful blow in support of our cause. Every colored mechanic is, by virtue of his circumstance, an elevator of his race. Every house built by black men is a strong tower against the allied hosts of prejudice. It is impossible for us to attach too much importance to this aspect of the subject. Without industrial development there can be no wealth; without wealth there can be no leisure; without leisure, no opportunity for thoughtful reflection and the cultivation of the higher arts."

I would set no limitations on the attainments of the negro in arts, letters or statesmanship, but, my friends, the surest and speediest way to reach these ends is by laying the foundation in the little things of life that are immediately at our door. The man who has never learned how to make money to pay his own debts is not the one to be intrusted with the duty of making laws to pay the national debt.

I have read recently an account of a young colored man in the District of Columbia who graduated from college and then from a school of technology, and then what? He did not go about seeking for a position which other brains and other hands had created, but used his knowledge of the sciences and mathematics in creating a bootblack establishment, where he manufactures his own blacking and polish. Starting with one chair, he now has a dozen; starting with one place of business, he now has several. What matters it to this man whether republicans, democrats or populists are in power in Washington? He knows that he has a business that gives him independence, and with its expansion and growth will come wealth and leisure and the highest educational opportunities for his children. Oh, for a thousand men with the force of character and common sense to begin on such a foundation!

It is not alone the mere matter of the negro learning this or that trade for which I plead, but through the trade, the industry; out from the trade or industry I want to see evolved the full-fledged, unhampered, unfettered man. I plead for industrial development, not because I want to cramp the negro, but because I want to free him. I want to see him enter the great and all-powerful business and commercial world.

By the side of every church I want to see the factory. Surrounding every school house I want to see a hundred farms. By the side of your certificate of church membership I want to see you place the bank book. If you give a promise to carry a torch in the political parade, secure a promise that you will be permitted to march in the labor parade with dinner bucket in hand the next morning and every day in the year.

It is far from my purpose to advocate a mere theory. Most that I have sought in this address to emphasize I have tried to live by and practice.

If for a brief moment you will excuse me for the seeming egotism I will tell you what a set of devoted colored men and women have done at Tuskegee, Ala., during the past nineteen years.

Beginning in 1881 with absolutely no property the Tuskegee Institute now owns 2,500 acres of land. Of this amount about [7]oo acres are this year under cultivation. There are upon the school grounds forty-eight buildings, and of these all except four have been wholly erected by the labor of the students. Students and their instructors have done the work, from the drawing of the plans and making of the bricks to the putting in of the electric fixtures. There are fifty wagons and buggies and [6]oo head of live stock. The total value of the real and personal property is $300,000. If we add to this our endowment fund of $165,000, the total property is $465,000, and if we add to this the value of the 25,000 acres of public land recently granted to this institution by Congress, the total property of this institution is $590,000. The students earn by work at their trades and other industries, about $56,000 a year. The total annual expenditure for carrying on this work is about $90,000.

The total monthly expenditure is nearly $7,500. The total daily expenditure is not far from $250.

Beginning with thirty students, the number has grown until at the present time there are connected with the institution a thousand and more students from twenty-four states, Africa, Jamaica, Cuba, Porto Rico and other foreign countries. In all of our departments, industrial, academic and religious, there are eighty-eight officers and teachers, making a total population on our grounds of about 1,200 people.

During the nineteen years the institution has been in existence hundreds of students have finished the academic and industrial courses, and if we add to this number about 2,000 students who were not able to remain and get a diploma or certificate, who, nevertheless, got the spirit of the institution and a knowledge of an industry to such an extent that they are doing good work as teachers, as farmers, as tradesmen, as leaders of thought, industry, thrift, morality and religion, the number can safely be placed at nearly 2,500.

Not a single one of our graduates has even been convicted by any court of crime.[2] Not a single one of our graduates has ever been charged with the crime of attempting an assault upon a woman.

At least half of these students are working in part or wholly at the trades or industries which they learned at Tuskegee. Whether they are working at the immediate trade which they learned or not, all have the spirit of industry and thrift that makes them valuable citizens. The Tuskegee Institute does not confine its work to the industrial training. Along with industrial training goes thorough mental and religious training. We keep in constant operation at which the various students receive training twenty-eight industries. All of these are industries at which our students can find immediate employment as soon as they leave the institution; in fact, we cannot begin to supply the demand for our graduates, and a large portion of these demands come from southern white men and women. We can now erect a building of any size without going off of the school grounds to employ a single outside workman.

This industrial development leads me in a logical order to the discussion of the most delicate part of my subject, that of the permanent residence of the negro, the relation of the two races and the question of citizenship.

Whether our habitat is to be in the south, the north, or west, the islands of the sea, or in Africa, I think you will agree with me that the elements of strength to which I have referred will be most valuable qualities for us as a race. My own belief is that we are to remain permanently in this country and the great bulk of us at the south, and until those who advocate a return to Africa prove their faith by their works, I shall judge them by their actions, and believe that they agree with me, that this is the better country to live in because they are most careful to reside here themselves.

Nearly all opportunities and privileges rest upon an economic or industrial basis, and when I say this I mean every time that this economic and commercial basis must be fortified and surrounded by mental development and religion. But there is the foundation. This granted, I do not believe, with all her fault[s] and wrongs, you can find a habitable portion of the globe where there is such opportunity for business, for commercial development, as the negro has open to him in our southern states. The black man who cannot succeed in business in the south cannot succeed out of it. But you suggest that commerce, mere dollars, is not all of life; there is something higher and beyond mere visible accumulation. In this I agree with you, but the history of all races and nations shows that they came into the enjoyment of those higher things through the economic gate. This is a great historic and economic fact, which we cannot change, and in the words of another, "When we cannot make our theories agree with the facts we had better change our theories."

In our present mental, economic and moral condition the same difficulties will confront us, no matter to what portion of the globe we go, in equal numbers. With economic development will come protection to property, security to life and the right of trial by jury in all cases.

There is no reason for despondency. The negro in the south is in a more hopeful condition than the serfs of Russia, has brighter prospects than the peasants of France and throughout the United States exercises more influence and control in government than any equal number of white people in the same material condition that can be found anywhere in Europe. We may have to struggle for decades and centuries before we get upon our feet, but out of the struggle we will gain a strength and confidence that we can secure in no other way. We shall get more out of struggle than out of contentment.

Place today every desire of the heart at our feet and within a few centuries our usefulness, strivings and ambitions will disappear.

Now I come to that part of the discussion upon which you and I are most likely to disagree — that of the relation of the races. In this matter I favor the negro taking an absolutely impregnable position, a position away up on high ground; a position where in future years there will be nothing to regret and nothing to explain. I want to see the negro be greater if possible, in sympathy than the white man. No race or individual can cherish hatred or practice injustice and cruelty against another race or individual without growing weak and narrow, without the conscience becoming seared and blunted to all the higher and sweeter things in life. If for no higher reason, in self-defense, we should learn to love instead of hate.

I want to see the black man take his place on high ground, away up in the atmosphere of usefulness, generosity, love and forgiveness.

If any white man would be mean, let us be good; if any white man would be little, let us be great; if any white man would push us down, let us help push him up. If others can excel us hating, let us excel them in loving. If others can excel us in the acts of cruelty, let us excel them in acts of mercy. You may call this cowardice; if so, it is the kind of cowardice that the Christ taught and practiced, and it is the kind of cowardice that in the long run will win our cause.

In plain words, the negro must learn to do what the white man does, what every other race does, and that is, make constant effort in every manly, straightforward, honorable way, not by crouching or debasing himself to make a friend of the man by whose side he lives.

This is the policy that the white man from the north pursues; this is the policy that the white man from Europe pursues. This is the policy that the black Cuban pursues in reference to the white Cuban. This is the policy that the negro in Jamaica pursues in reference to the white man in Jamaica.

While in national politics I am a republican, and expect to remain such till I can discover something better, yet I am free to say that there is little reason why in the future we should pursue the policy of arraying ourselves in all local matters solidly in politics against the men whose interests are mutually our own, and to whom we go naturally for assistance and advice.

The negro in the south has as much right to consult the interests of his immediate employer in regard to his voting as has the laborer in New York or Ohio. I have little faith in the negro who abuses the southern white man in public and goes in the dark to beg the southern man for money to help him out of difficulty. Let us be manly and straightforward. In the future, more than in the past, it should be the policy of the best representatives of the two races in the various communities to come together in small meetings, to come face to face, to shake hands and talk as brother to brother concerning the problems that surround us. Since the negro is the weaker race, in most cases he must take the initiative.

During recent weeks we have heard many mutterings as to the citizenship of our race. The south's material prosperity is in a large degree bound up in the negro. There are hundreds of counties in the south which if deprived of the black man's presence and toil would soon be howling wildernesses. The south cannot afford to jeopardize its prosperity by any practice that keeps alive in the negro a spirit of unrest, of fear, of suspicion; a feeling that life and property are not safe, a feeling that opportunities for education may be removed and he eventually deprived of his citizenship.

All this tends to keep the negro shifting from one portion of the country to another, and, worst of all, results in his leaving the large plantation districts of the south, where his labor is needed, for the cities, where his labor is not, as a rule, needed.

In these latter days we hear much about a new method of settling this problem, that of removing from our fundamental law, that great sheet anchor of our faith, the precious magna charta of our citizenship, the fifteenth amendment. Whether wisely or unwisely, this guarantee of our rights was placed in the Constitution by the ripest thought of the nation at the time it was enacted; it was placed there as a result of the sacrifice of a million heroic lives, as the result of the expenditure of millions of dollars, and there, in my mind, at the behest of the conservative and patriotic opinion of both the south and the north, it will remain while the Constitution itself stands.

Why divert attention and force from something that can be done, to something that can not be done?

In saying what I have, I would not convey the impression that a mere law can make one individual equal to another. No law can make ignorance equal with intelligence. The feet do not rule the head, simply because there are two of them. What the negro does ask is equality of opportunity, that the door which rewards and encourages virtue, intelligence, thrift, economy, usefulness, the possession of property, be kept wide open to the humblest black man from one shore of this continent to the other.

Close this door against a negro now, and within a few years the temptation will be to close it against a class of white men.

The minute you recognize a law which taxes a negro for support of government and denies him the opportunity to make his wishes felt at the ballot box, that minute you begin to undermine our whole theory of government and throw to the winds the principles for which the revolutionary war was fought.

The minute you deprive one-eighth of the population of the right of franchise, by reason of the accident of birth and race, that minute this country ceases to be a republic.

I stand today where I have always stood, advising my race that in their present condition it is a mistake for them to enter actively into general political agitation and activity; but when the foundation of our citizenship is attacked I think I have a right to speak, and I speak here in the same spirit that I have already spoken in the heart of the south.

It is to the interests of the southern white that there shall not be one law which can be made to apply to the white man, and another to the negro. Take away from any class of people in a free government the hope of reward, that the use of the ballot holds, and you produce a state of stagnation, ignorance, crime, corruption. A people thus deprived of hope of reward becomes an eternal millstone about the neck of the body politic.

Any subterfuge, any makeshift in the form of law that gives the ignorant white man a right to express his wants at the ballot box and withholds the same privilege from the ignorant negro, is an injustice to both races. In most cases such laws give the negro the incentive to prepare to become a voter by getting property and intelligence, but says to the white man in so many words, remain in ignorance and poverty, and a way will be found for you to exercise the franchise. No question is ever settled till settled right, till settled by the absolute immutable laws of justice.

In this matter there is but one way out of our difficulties in the south, and that is for each state that finds it necessary to change its constitution to make an election law, excepting possibly the soldiers who fought on both sides in all wars, that shall be based on intelligence, or poverty [property], or both, that shall apply every day in the year, honestly, squarely, fearlessly to both races.

Surely if the negro is willing to meet this test the white man should not shrink from it.

In closing, may I repeat a thought with which I began. It is my faith that the matchless combination of the northern white men and southern white men and black Americans who during three centuries have exhibited virtue, patience, wisdom, skill, physical power and perseverance enough to clear the forests, build the railroads and highways, tunnel the mountains, plant the cities, defeat foreign foes and establish a system of schools and churches, that has made ours the most inviting country known to man, I say the forces that could achieve these results will not be baffled or defeated in the settlement of our race problem.

No, there will be no race war. Race wars have been predicted in this country for three centuries, and the first has not occurred.

The main weapons of defense used by the negro have been the hoe, the shovel, the plow, the pick, the school, the church, kindness, forgiveness, meekness, his foreday prayers, his midnight groans, his songs and an inherent faith in the justice of his cause.

The Caucasian in the south needs the negro, the negro needs the Caucasian. The black man has gotten much from the white man. The white man has gotten much from the black man.

We must teach the white man to judge us by our best and not by our worst. We must judge the south by the best types of her white manhood, not by her worst.

This is not an age for pessimism, doubt and halting and prediction of disaster. The world is going forward, not backward. The accumulated and accelerated momentum of the universe for 4,000 years is in favor of giving men everywhere more liberty, more opportunity, more intelligence; is in favor of more sympathy and more brotherly kindness, and [the] trend in this direction can no more be resisted in any part of the country, than we can stay the life-giving influence of the rays of the daily sun.

The stormy billows are high; they progress. What to us seems defeat is with God triumph. When the hour seems darkest, when help seems farthest, let us repeat often with the psalmist, though "The stormy billows are high; their fury is mighty, but the Lord is above them and almighty and almighty."

Washington *Colored American*, May 26, 1900, 9, 13.

1 BTW spoke under the auspices of the Bethel Literary and Historical Association. The next day he gave this address in Columbus, Ohio, before the General Conference of the A.M.E. Church. He also used it as the basis of his remarks before the Afro-American Council in Indianapolis on Aug. 31, 1900. An edited version, entitled "The Storm Before the Calm," appeared in the *Colored American Magazine*, 1 (Sept. 1900), 199-213.

2 BTW modified this when he spoke at Columbus. "Of all the graduates from Tuskegee Institute," he said, "only one has been since sentenced to the penitentiary...." He added that "less than half a dozen" students in southern black institutions had been convicted of felonies. (See An Account of a Speech in Columbus, Ohio, May 24, 1900, below.)

An Account of a Speech in Columbus, Ohio

[Columbus, Ohio, May 24, 1900]

GREAT TRIBUTE TO WASHINGTON

More Than 6000 Persons Hear Noted Negro Educator and Sociologist

2 HUGE MEETINGS

Thousands Turned Away from Memorial Hall — Address at St. Paul A.M.E. Church

Columbus paid a wonderful tribute yesterday to the intellectual powers of Booker T. Washington, the noted negro educator, a living example of what education and training will do for the negro, when more than 6000 persons attended meetings at Memorial hall and St. Paul A.M.E. church. Racial prejudices were cast aside and silk-gowned white women rubbed elbows with less richly clad negro women as they walked up the broad marble stairs to Memorial hall. White professional men in broadcloth sat alongside colored men clad in coarse garments, with gnarled hands soiled by labor. Both classes joined in spontaneous applause when the noted economist stepped on the platform, the whites expressing their admiration for the wonderful struggle the man has made, and the negroes their appreciation for his up-lifting work in their behalf.

Every seat in Memorial hall was occupied an hour before the program was scheduled to begin. People began to file into the auditorium at 1:30 p.m. The aisles were filled after the seating capacity was exhausted. Then the stairways rapidly filled up and finally the doors in the east and west sides of the auditorium were thrown open and several hundred crowded into the areaway around the auditorium and heard the speaker.

THOUSANDS TURNED AWAY

Thousands still filed down Broad street to the hall and vainly sought admission while the big hall was jammed. The disappointment was so keen outside that overflow meetings at the Y.M.C.A. and St. Paul A.M.E. church were held yesterday afterward. Large congregations heard Dr. Washington at both meetings.

Dr. Washington made a powerful plea for more Biblical teaching among his race. He said many persons are worrying without cause about the racial question, because in a few years America will have no racial question if the people continue to spread the gospel among the negroes. He decried the impatience of some over the negro's slow progress and told them they were measuring his people by too exasperating a yard stick.

"Consider," he said, "a few centuries or even decades ago my people were led from the wilds of Africa and suddenly dropped into the very highest type of civilization. Pray don't measure us by your civilization and then kick us down because we don't measure up to requirements. If we were measured by certain Asiatic civilizations the comparison would not be so unfair. Just remember that in the race to come abreast with the white man, history shows there is no other ahead of the negro."

Near the close of his address the speaker, inspired by love for his people and the apparent justice of his plea, dramatically called upon the audience to remember that one man can't keep another down in the ditch without being in the ditch himself. He climaxed the plea by announcing that so long as any one portion of the country is submerged, other classes will, to a certain extent, be the under dog with them, and that the negro will bring many up with him when his race is finally abreast of the white man.

EXEMPLAR OF FORCE OF CHARACTER

Dr. Washington's physique, his face, head and gestures typify the indomitable will and strength that carried him from a position of abject slavery to a commanding position in the nation as a missionary, looked to by negroes as a Moses of their race. The phrenologist at a glance can see the lines that make him a successful president of Tuskegee institute, the largest colored school in America. Although born under conditions that would make the ordinary man a humble citizen, he is today accepted as a power among leading white educators.

Dr. Washington walked on the stage at Memorial hall with a firm, confident tread, as one sure of his ground. His shoulders are broad and his six feet of stature gives the strength and poise to command respect. His hair is close cut and gives him the aspect of a war dog with all its tenacious fighting spirit. The eyes, however, gleam with kindliness and they temper the appearance of the latent fighting forces. The man's forehead is broad, high and shapely, with enough space to contain a plentiful supply of reasoning powers. His lips are thin, drawn tight across his molars. They show strength of character. His jaw has the firmness of one who has the courage to stand by his convictions.

"It's easy to see how that man suceeds," whispered a delegate to the Bible students' conference after looking at the speaker.

JOHN R. MOTT[1] PRESIDES

John R. Mott, general secretary of the student movement of North America, presided at the afternoon meeting at Memorial hall. He introduced Thornton B. Penfield,[2] head of the theological department of the Bible student movement, who thanked the local brotherhood for the hospitality shown during the Bible Students' convention. President Beebe of the local brotherhood responded.

Mr. Mott announced Dr. Washington's subject as "The Place of the Bible in the Uplifting of the Negro Race." Dr. Washington began his address after a quartet sang. He first spoke of the 91 Y.M.C.A. organizations for colored youths; of the 5000 colored men studying the Bible, and of the 640 Bible students at Tuskegee, and pointed these as living examples of the progress of the negro. He pleaded for two more secretaries to teach the Bible in the Southland and thus lift the negro from the chain gang.

"The men doing the vital things of life are those who read the Bible and are Christians and not ashamed to let the world know it," said he. "The negro who does the shooting is uneducated and without Christian training. The negro without a home, who wanders about from community to community, fills the workhouses today.

ONLY ONE BLACK SHEEP

"Of all the graduates from Tuskegee institute only one has been since sentenced to the penitentiary, while of the hundreds of graduates from the 15 old colored institutions of the South, less than half a dozen have been convicted of felonies. So the work today is to make religion the vital part of the negro's life. But this is a stupendous task, as there is a nation of negroes with a nation of whites, the negro population of the United States is nearly twice as large as the population of Canada.

"Just remember that the negro came out of Africa a few centuries ago, half naked, with rings in his nose and ears and chains upon his ankles and wrists. He came out of that, clothed according to civilized customs with a hammer and saw in his hands and a Bible in his hands. No man can read the Bible and be lazy. Christianity increases a man's wants, and therefore increases his capacity for labor. The negro doesn't run from the Bible, either."

Unidentified clipping Con. 977 BTW Papers DLC.

1 John Raleigh Mott (1865-1955) was student secretary of the YMCA's international committee from 1888 to 1915, and general secretary from 1915 to 1931.

2 Thornton Bancroft Penfield (b. 1867) was general secretary of the YMCA's international committee from 1900 to 1914.

From Emily Howland

Sherwood, N.Y. May 24, 1900

Dear friend, Your letter of the 4th inst. would have been answered more promptly but for the unusual press of affairs which this season brings. I do not quite understand it supposing that I had made good all my pledges to Tuskegee. I have no doubt that you are correct but that I did not get the true meaning. Your letter says that I pledged $400. toward a relief fund, and that one half has been paid. I paid $500. in Feb. 1898, and $500. in Jan. 1899, besides the $1000. later. Where do you get the $200. p.d. from? Was $400. each year considered my regular contribution and the surplus $100. each year considered a payment on the relief fund? The $1000. was also for the temporary endowment I judge from the Circular letter yours enclosed. Is it so? I had supposed it was for a permanent fund. I am sorry to trouble you to explain, but I cannot act blindly. The Convention in Montgomery from the little I hear voiced nothing new nor wise. All this uprising to re-vamp constitutions to make them proscriptive etc. proves that the dominant race fears the progress that the other is making, not his ignorance, there was no problem in their minds until the colored race began to rise. The colored race and the women are on trial now, the parallel between the talk about the defects & limitations of both is striking, while both are steadily disproving all the charges against them, and proving that they are important factors in the industrial world as well as in civilization.

As soon as I can act understandingly I will remit what is proposed. Respectfully

Emily Howland

Kind regards to Mrs. Washington.

ALS Con. 175 BTW Papers DLC. Written on stationery of the Cayuga County Political Equality Club, of which Howland was president. The club was auxiliary to the New York State Woman Suffrage Association.

From Charles Octavius Boothe

Selma, Alabama, 5. 26. 1900

My Dear Friend: Since the "Conference" in Montgomery I have been trying to think over our real civil status in this country and of what we may do to better our condition. I confess that still for the most part the subject lies in mystery. However, I am impressed with what seems to me to be apparent *aspects* of the case. These views however, may after all be mere phantoms.

1. Our poverty a source of our ruin. The great majority of the human race are in absolute bondage to their animal wants. A city with a starving population would hardly give much attention to matters of religion — to matters of the higher nature. What will man — as a rule — *not* do for food and raiment? How small as compared with the total number of the human race, must be that class of persons whose activities rise only out of regard for truth.

And, where comes the hope for mental culture in that man whose toil brings to him only enough returns to satisfy the immediate wants of the body?

How often — when a boy toiling all day for bread till the sun had disappeared — have I tried in vain to "get my lesson." Sleep, weariness, closed my eyes upon my book. And it was the same "drop out," when I kneeled to pray.

Nor can the "poverty stricken" man command the respect of his neighbors. He may excite our *pity* — he can never command our *respect*. And too it is simply folly to think of a people in such a state as capable of legislating for the highest good of a civilized and civilizing government. For such a people to claim equil political rights with a people not thus enslaved by physical wants, is to excite in this people feelings of fear and opposition.

The attitute of our white neighbors toward us — while its manifestations are often extreme and oppressive — is not wholly unreasonable. Were we in their stead we would be as they are. But, what can be done?

(1) The great majority of our people are laborers on the farms of the south. Often these land owners see only the business side of the tenant's association with his stock and lands. That is to say he sees only the immediate results in bushels and bales. Cannot some-

thing be done by the leading men among us to induce the land owners to seek the betterment — material and otherwise — of his tenants? Suppose such a tho't could be started (and it can be) would it not pay in every way? Large land owners could affect not only the material condition of the people, but their educational and religious conditions as well. Is this not worth undertaking?

(2) Northern men who have money to invest, could buy large plantations in the south, or large bodies of land in the west, and encourage their tenants to purchase the land by allowing easy terms of payment.

(3) We have the most race friction where there are the largest bodies of colored people. The practical suggestion here is that we need to scatter more widely over the country. Thus we may hope to take from the white man his fears of negro "domination," and thus make a start toward reducing race-prejudice to its *minimum*.

2. Our lack of practical information.

We are not practical.

Perhaps our want on this line, occupying the greatest prominence, is our lack of skill in labor — the lack of skill in the "bread-and-butter" affairs of life. I say *"perhaps"* this is true. But our want of practical knowledge on *all* the lines of active life, is appalling. We are not *practical*, in our domestic relations, nor in our political relations, nor in our social relations, nor in our church relations. Everywhere, we move without order and end without results. This may be due to our want of clear — of proper — views of life, or it may be due to our want of will force — of power to enter into the good we see. Whatever may be the cause of our universal disorder the fact, with all its fearful consequences, is upon us.

What can be done.

(1) The *practical, sensible* men among us — to the extent of their ability — should place and hold conferences with the leaders of the people, (teachers and preachers say), in the different centers of influence with regard to the practical aspects of the various lines of life. The people — the *whole* people — the race, must be placed ahead of our little, selfish denominational organizations. The *spirit* and *principles* of Christianity *must* be made to appear to be more important than its mere formal manifestations.

(2) An effort should be put on foot to improve the local school facilities throughout the entire country.

547

The people, taken as a whole, must find their best & only school advantages in the little home-school house. If some persons might be engaged to act on the lines suggested, at least *some* improvement of our conditions may be hoped for. I wish I might give myself — at l[e]ast what little remains of me — to the good of the *whole* people. We *must* — we *must* bestir ourselves to a more general and more united movement for the elevation of the *bulk*, body, of the Negro life in this country. Hoping that you and yours are well, I remain   Yours sincerely,

C. O. Boothe

ALS   Con. 167   BTW Papers   DLC.

From Timothy Thomas Fortune

New York, May 31, 1900

My dear Mr. Washington: I am very glad to have your letter of the 26th instant today. I am very glad indeed to have you say I was of service in getting the Washington address in shape, because I was in a terrible state of nervous disorganization in Washington, complicated with the blamed stomach, so that I was as touchy as a cat. But you made a great hit in Washington and I am glad I had some share in it. And I feel that my suggestion as to conserving your voice will work infinitely to your advantage in the future — not only in saving you but in the effect on the auditors. You made the impression all right in Washington, I know, and I am pleased to have you say you struck the brethren right at Columbus.

Murphy? He will get in line with us, or I will do what I can to kill him and the Southern Society. The fast and loose business don't go with me on the race question.

I was in bed yesterday with my stomach. I shall have soon to leave New York or go to bed.

The Page people have not sent the check, and I [am] almost crazy over small debts I can't pay on that account, but it will all come right in the end, I hope.

I am sick but cheerful. Yours truly

T Thomas Fortune

ALS   Con. 172   BTW Papers   DLC.

From Timothy Thomas Fortune

New York, June 1, 1900

Dear Mr. Washington: Your letter of the 29th ult. was received.

Yes; I got the letter of the Pages, addressed to you, saying they would send me a check on receipt of signed contract, but up to this writing no check has reached me. I hope it will reach me in the morning, because I need the money Saturday badly; and I am very sorry that you have had to be bothered about it.

Your book from the Nichols people came this morning. It is to be regretted that so fine a book should be spoilt by such execrable white paper and such unaccountable ignorance in the typographical make up. Turn to pages 74, 302 and 402 for instance. No where outside of a country job office would a blank page be left in a book. The running of three cuts together (pp. 413-4-5) is also vile. Indeed, the book is chock full of typographical and aesthetic blemishes. But perhaps no one but a practical printer will note these.

As I had not seen the paragraph concerning myself in the Ms. I turned to it and *was very much taken* aback by the generosity with which you speak of Scott and me.[1] I appreciate it very much I can assure you.

You should see to it that Calloway has a copy of the book in his Paris collection.

My nerves are steadier, but my stomach is still in rebellion.

When are you coming North?

I am thinking of going to Atlantic City the last of next week and of remaining there until after the Philadelphia Convention. If I can raise the cash I shall.

Mrs. Fortune is sick abed with a heavy cold. Yours truly

T Thomas Fortune

ALS Con. 172 BTW Papers DLC.

[1] In February Fortune read the manuscript and wrote to BTW that he had received a "cold shock" when he "realized that you had finished the record of your life and work without deeming it necessary to mention my name as your good friend of eight years. . . ." (Feb. 3, 1900, Con. 172, BTW Papers, DLC.)

From Alonzo Homer Kenniebrew

Tuskegee Ala, June 1–1900

Prof B T Washington   I hereby submit the following report of the Health Division for the term ending May 31–1900.

Glad to say that we were so fortunate as to not have a single death from sickness during the term.

The five from ptomaine poisoning last summer "99" (Toxic fever) are not included in this report.

We were successful in keeping small pox out of the School although we might have had an epidemic from one suspicious case in November but being discovered before it developed and was moved out and quarantined & there developed small pox. The epidemic came within 3 miles of the school.

Miss S. May Smith[1] — Head Nurse was employed by school 1st Sept. "1899" and has come up to expectations very well indeed.

During the term we treated in the hospitals   Teachers 5   boys 459   girls 309   total 773 (4 students treated in families). Teachers treated in their rooms on the grounds & not sent to hospital Ladies 23   Men 21. Those treated off the grounds who do not board in the hall 10 total in all   Teachers 59   Students 772   "*831 in all* for the term by Resident Phys.

As to disease, I will name only the most important ones. Many of the others are of little importance & minor ailments.

	Males	Females
Bronchitis	8	3
Catarrh Jaundice	3	
Chron. Gastric inflamation	1	1
Pleurisy	3	2
Peritonitis	1	0
Appendocitis	1	0
Bright's disease	1	1
Dysentery	21	14
Pneumonia	3	3
Malarial fever	30	14
Fractures (broken bones)	2	One of colarbone the

other of Upper & lower arm & had to be amputated

1   Injury from laund[r]y M.

Abdominal Abcess	1	0
Cystitis	2	0
Retention of urine	1	1
Tetanus (lock-jaw)		1 result of injury

from laundry machinery — patient never recovered

Paralysis of vocal cords	1	0
Ureamic convulsions	1	0
Consumption	2	(one teacher)
(sent home)		
Venereal diseases	1	1 sent home

There were 6,689 meals served at hospital.

When school closed six patients were in boys hospital *none serious*. I wrote 6,612 prescriptions & saw 5182 patients (Students and Teachers) in my office.

The only professional help called in was to help in amputating Fred Blakely's[2] arm — and to see two of my patients while I was away in B'ham Ala two days, Dr Johnson[3] was called.

Mary Ella Holloway[4] was fatally injured by the machinery at laundry Oct. 14–"99" from which Tetanus (lock-jaw) was developed in a short while and she died Oct. 21st "99."

Wm Arrington[5] was the boy which was drowned April 29th in King's Creek.

The Nurse Training school has made great efforts this year towards advancement — more so than in the past. The work & teaching have been more thorough and satisfactory. As much so as the present conditions will allow.

The class at begining of term numbered 15 — (12 young ladies 3 young men) 2 probationers were droped after trial month as not suitable material and one girl & boy were dismissed from school. 3 young ladies finished the course but on account of academic class only one received certificate.

Account of the very limited time given us — we are compelled to have class for nurses every afternoon of the week & lectures twice per week.

The city physician's calls for nurses during past year were beyound our supply — but when possible Senior nurses were allowed to go.

The outlook of the Training school is very encouraging.

We have succeeded in getting the promise of Dr L. W. Johnson and practically of Dr Smith[6] to give lectures to the class next term and Dr Magruder[7] has not as yet decided. If in the above we succeed it will be of great help to us.

The putting of the boys in more comfortable quarters last winter had quite a noticeable effect of the sickness among them. We had only 2 serious cases of pneumonia where last year we had 7 and the other ailments due to exposu[r]e & want of better quarters were in likewise decreased.

In comparing records we notice that the sickness among the girls was much greater than in past year — & greater comparitively speaking than that of the boys. A very great proportion of their ailments which caused their admittance to hospital — was of simple, preventable ailments which they could have easily taken care of, had they been taught how — as they were in their monthly health talks in past terms. This was especially true of the new girls, as only a very few of the older ones had to go to hospital. And too the most serious cases among them was Pneumonia (3) and as they had never before had such diseases since I have been physician here I took special paines with assistance of the "head nurse" to find the cause, as in all cases possible, & two of them were due directly to the *use of corsets* irregularly during the winter months. That is — having them on three days of the week and off *two days* for gymnastics. It is a dangerous practice & finally Sylvia Hensly[8] was sent away from School acc't broken health first of May — due to this agency. I spoke to you about it during Winter, but as I heard no more about it — I thought that you overlooked it.

I suggest

That those large rooms w[h]ere 15 to 30 boys room be divided into smaller apartments as soon as possible — for physical as well as moral effects.

That the girls either quit the use of the corset, which is by far the best thing to do, or the gymnastics. In the interest of the girls' health a[t] school I beg that this recieve close attention.

That the girls have monthly talks on health, how to preserve it &c, as the boys have.

That as soon as practicable the Nurse Training division be made a regular Training School for Nurses, separate from the academic dept and grant a diploma. This would be productive of more good and many *well educated young* woman would then take the training, where as now they either don't do it or a few go to some place where the training is designated under a "Training School and Hospital.["] And such young women would be encouraged to come here.

The division has grown to that standard now where it demands very forcibly — better & larger buildings as a *hospital*. Our present ones are condemnable for great need of repairs & rooms. A modern hospital building in which to house the Training div. and patients would supply a *much needed* demand. We must have an operating room to teach surgical & obstetrical demonstrations, & to somewhat help out — we bid for the two room cottage near the hospital for hospital use. This we hope will meet your *immeadiate approval*. So that we might get them in *order* by school opening. Yours for health

A. H. Kenniebrew

ALS   Con. 177   BTW Papers   DLC.

1 S. May Smith was head nurse at Tuskegee Institute from 1899 to 1903.

2 Probably Frederick Blakely of Eufaula, Ala., who was a night-school student in the sub-C preparatory class during the 1899-1900 school year, rather than Fred David Blakely of Beaufort, S.C., who was a member of the A preparatory class in the 1900-1901 school year, and who advanced to the B middle class by 1903.

3 L. W. Johnston, born in Alabama in 1864, was a white physician residing in Tuskegee.

4 Not listed in the school catalogs.

5 William Arrington of Alligator Lake, Miss., was in the C preparatory class in the 1899-1900 school year.

6 Milton Smith was a white physician living in Tuskegee. He was born in Alabama in 1852.

7 William B. Magruder, another white physician in Tuskegee, was born in Alabama in 1862.

8 Sylvia Hensley of Birmingham, Ala., was a member of the A preparatory class during the 1899-1900 school year.

From Giles Beecher Jackson[1]

Richmond, Va. June 1st. 1900

Dear Sir: Referring to the brief consultation we had with the Hon. Judson W. Lyons and T. Thomas Fortune, at the Southern Hotel in Washington, D.C. on the 22nd. of May, relative to the proscriptive laws enacted by the Southern States against our race, I will say that I agree with your idea of having some one to make a quiet canvass among those who sympathize with us for the necessary funds to pay the Lawyer's fees who shall intercede to get these laws reviewed by the Supreme Court of the United States which I think should be done at the earliest practical moment. For if these laws are unconstitutional, then get the Court to say so; if not we have no other appeal except that before the bar of public opinion which amounts to but very little in our behalf in the Southern States. This whole matter was discussed yesterday before the National Council of the Constitutional Rights Association that assembled in this City for the purpose of preparing an address, which they did, and I will send you a copy as soon as they are printed, as I think it meets every argument against us.

Now again referring to our consultation I will say that after laying the whole matter before our board I have consented to accept your proposition to canvass the Country and raise the money necessary to pay the Lawyers, including the one you mentioned who said that he would win the case for $7,000. I think he should be retained at all hazzards. You mentioned that you could make arrangements with the railroad Companies for transportation. Please inform me to what extent you can arrange it and through what sections of the Country. I think the North and the West will prove a better field for the purposes indicated.

We would like very much to have you endorse our address, but for fear that it might embarrass you somewhat among your Southern friends, we did not call upon you, but after reading a copy of it and you decide it worthy of your endorsement, we would respectfully solicit it or any other aid and assistance you can give the Association which is organized for the purpose of contending for our rights guaranteed to us by the Constitution of the United States, especially since they are being systematically and gradually taken away from us by constitutional amendments and Legislature enactments by the Southern States until as recent as last month the Governors and ex-Governors of the Southern States decided in a Convention held in the State of Alabama that the 14th. & 15th. amendments to the Constitution ought to be repealed; from this it is quite evident that the South as a unit will cast its vote for the repealing of these amendments which brought us into existence; this being a fact, it only remains for them to secure enough States in the North or West to get a majority to decide with them which is required to repeal the said amendments; this may not be done next year or year after, but if the attitude of the white man continues to change towards the Negro with the same rapidity as it has in the last 2 or 3 years, it seems to me that it will be a question of not many years before the resolutions of the Alabama Convention will find supporters enough in the North or West to repeal these amendments, unless we as a race shall cease to surrender our rights without contention as a man who is struck and refuses to strike back generally gets whipped at the first blow. Therefore our organization is intended to do everything necessary to place our cause properly before the world and before the bar of public opinion who shall judge for us, and before every Court having jurisdiction until our every rights shall be sustained.

Pardon this lengthy communication. Awaiting your reply, I am your humble servant,

> Giles B. Jackson
> Secretary of the National
> Council of the Constitutional
> Rights Association of the
> United States.

TLS Con. 176 BTW Papers DLC.

1 Giles Beecher Jackson (1853-1924) was a leading black lawyer, businessman, and journalist in Richmond. Born a slave in Goochland County, Va., he moved to Richmond after emancipation and found employment as a house servant. Later he became a clerk in the law office of W. H. Beveridge, who encouraged him in the study of law. Jackson owned and edited the weekly *Negro Criterion*. He also owned a prosperous bakery in the same building as his law office. It was through his post as Grand Attorney of the Knights of the True Reformers that he became a director of the order's bank in Richmond. He was one of the first vice-presidents of the NNBL and was instrumental in bringing its annual convention to Richmond in 1902. He was a leading promoter of the Negro Department of the Jamestown Exposition in 1907 and helped to obtain a grant from Congress for the exposition. Jackson generally practiced a conciliatory race policy combined with efforts to promote black solidarity and mutual help, in the Tuskegee tradition, but just as BTW did, he occasionally resorted to direct challenge to segregation. With BTW's encouragement, Jackson opposed the Virginia Jim Crow car law in 1901, fought the discriminatory features of the Virginia Constitution of 1902, and joined with J. C. Napier of Nashville in an effort to overturn Tennessee's Pullman-car segregation law.

From Henry Sylvester Williams

London, 1.6.1900

Dear Mr Washington, The Pan African Conference is naming its proposed session which will occur on the 23, 24 & 25th July. We are anxiously expecting you to take a part in the proceedings, and therefore it is necessary for us to know when you will arrive in London. Several delegates have already arrived, and it is sincerely hoped that all the Members of the African Association including the Patrons will contribute to render the occasion memorable in history. With kindest wishes, Believe me   Yours truly

H. S. Williams

ALS Con. 187 BTW Papers DLC.

From Winfield Henri Mixon[1]

Montgomery, Ala., June 8, 1900

My dear sir: Some weeks ago the race problem was discussed in this City by some of the most prominent white divines and eloquent orators from all portions of this country. This discussion lasted a week and attracted the attention of the world. Since this Conference the leading newspapers of this country have analyzed this subject in long articles and editorials, but nowhere have we a record of what the leading spirits and thinkers of the negro race itself think upon this subject.

The discussion of this question, so recently held here, will be a matter of history upon this subject in the future. It is, therefore, very appropriate and of the utmost importance, at this juncture, in order that the history of this discussion be made more complete for the future, that the leading negro thinkers of this country should also hold a Conference in the very same place (Montgomery) and give expression, from the negro's standpoint, to their views upon the same high plane and in the same laudable spirit.

Accordingly, a Committee upon the conduct of a National Race Conference of Negroes has been organized and established and it has been arranged for this Conference to be held at Montgomery, Alabama for three days, July 25, 26 and 27: and you are earnestly requested to give your views in an address to the Conference upon this subject.[2] It is to be hoped you will regard this request seriously, as it is a matter of vital importance to our race. Some of the leading thinkers of our race have consented to be here and we desire your co-operation and trust to hear from you favorably.

Please give answer at once and address communications to Yours respectfully,

W. H. Mixon

Chairman

TLS Con. 179 BTW Papers DLC.

[1] Winfield Henri Mixon was born near Selma in Dallas County, Ala., in 1859. He was one of the first black men to engage in journalism in Alabama as editor of the *Dallas Post*, where he championed educational opportunities for blacks. Mixon was also a schoolteacher and was ordained a minister of the A.M.E. Church in 1879. He was well known in his church work for his oratorical powers and his organizing skills. Leaving editing behind, he rose in church ranks in Selma and later Montgomery. He was a member of the board of trustees of Wilberforce University for many years and was a founder of Payne Institute in Selma. His motto, which appeared with his signed portrait in Penn's *The Afro-American Press and Its Editors* (1891), was "Ignorance must die."

[2] BTW opposed Mixon's race conference from its inception. He urged Edgar Gardner Murphy, the leader of the white Montgomery Race Conference, to have a frank talk with Mixon and persuade him not to hold the conference. "Mr. Mixon is a thoroughly good man & means well," BTW wrote Murphy, "but he has no organizing, or business ability. I am afraid our cause will be hurt if such a Conference should be held at this time." BTW asked Murphy not to use his name because Mixon might interpret this to mean that BTW was "jealous of the movement, which as you will know is not true." (BTW to Murphy [copy in E. J. Scott's hand], ca. June 10, 1900, Con. 179, BTW Papers, DLC.)

J. W. Adams, a black Montgomery dry-goods merchant, wrote BTW that Mixon was naming BTW as one of the prime movers of the conference. Adams counseled BTW to have nothing to do with the conference. He wrote: "I have talked with a number of leading colored men of Montgomery and I haven't found one who is in favor of such a conference. . . ." In light of the recent conference of whites, Adams thought that Mixon's plan "looks like aping." (June 11, 1900, Con. 166, BTW Papers, DLC.)

Mixon continued to urge BTW to come to the conference, even after BTW had flatly refused to participate. "This race conference," said Mixon, "is going to be a power for good among our people, as well as our white friends." Mixon wrote BTW, "Your presence will add much dignity and importance to this great conference. . . ." He reported that other prominent blacks such as William H. Councill and P. B. S. Pinchback would attend. (June 16, 1900, Con. 179, BTW Papers, DLC.)

Mixon held his National Negro Race Conference as scheduled in July 1900. Overall attendance was good despite sparse attendance at the opening sesson, but no black leaders of national prominence appeared. At the opening session, on July 26, with only fifty persons in the hall, Mixon still insisted that BTW, W. H. Councill, and Bishop Turner would attend. Councill, who was on the program, failed to appear, at the last minute sending a telegram of regrets. Bishop Henry M. Turner also stayed away, citing ill health as the reason. Speaking for Turner was Dr. J. A. Brackett, who remarked: "Bishop Turner desires me to say to you that the negro has no manhood future in this country and he is better off in hell for the devil will not allow any discrimination on account of race or color in that hot clime. This is all I can give you from him." One white speaker, Rev. William D. Gay of the Adams Street Baptist Church in Montgomery, arose to speak, stating that he was denied the right to speak at the white conference because he was considered a crank. His solution to the race problem was "soap, soup, and salvation," and "if the negro had Jesus Christ in his soul he was the brother of the white man." (Montgomery *Advertiser*, July 27, 1900, 1.)

From Jefferson Manly Falkner[1]

Montgomery, Ala., June 9, 1900

Personal.

Dear Sir: I have been thinking a great deal about your school, about the Race Problem, and concerning all the comments that have been made. I have read your report with a great deal of interest.

I attended the Commencement of Paterson's Normal School at this place a few days ago, of which I am one of the Trustees, and at the conclusion I made a few minutes talk, in which I said "whenever it was decreed that the negro should leave this country, I proposed to take the train the day before they left." I have been trying to solve the problem, if there is a problem, and I believe that the work you are doing and some other work that can be done, will accomplish that end. I have no misanthropic ideas on the subject myself. I believe that God himself is working out a great problem in the Negro race, and that all will be well in the end.

I have not hesitated to encourage the discussion of the Race Problem, as by discussion we arrive at truth, and in that way something is always evolved, which generally proves to be the correct idea.

The first convenient opportunity I want to talk to you on certain lines. The Negro race in this country, at least, may be truly said to be a race of farmers, and it is along this line that I want to talk to you, as I think I can make certain suggestions by means of which all the seed that you have sown will grow and prosper, and in the end will work for the good of the people, both white and black, and to their entire satisfaction. If this can be done, you will certainly be entitled to the plaudits of all good people.

I am not sure that all my ideas are fully matured, but I feel confident that I have some suggestions to make to you at the proper time which can be formulated into a plan and which will work out very beneficially.

There is no haste about the matter in any way, but at your convenience, when you are in Montgomery, I would like to talk to you. Yours truly,

J. M. Falkner

TLS   Con. 172   BTW Papers   DLC.

1 Jefferson Manly Falkner, born in Randolph County, Ala., in 1843, was a lawyer and Baptist minister who owned a plantation and stock farm near Montgomery. In 1890 he became an attorney for the Louisville and Nashville Railroad in Alabama and the most prominent railroad lobbyist in the state. Falkner's law partner and associate in railroad matters was Thomas Goode Jones, former governor of Alabama, for whom BTW secured a federal judgeship in 1901. Falkner was active in the Montgomery Race Conference and often used his considerable influence in behalf of BTW and Tuskegee.

From Alice J. Kaine

[Milwaukee, Wis.] June 10, 1900

Dear Mr Washington, I confess I was sorry to leave Tuskegee without saying good by to you and Mrs Bruce but as you were in Council meeting I did not feel that I ought to disturb such a meeting. Please explain if you will to Mrs Bruce whom I learned to respect very highly and would not like to be misunderstood by her.

My visit was a great pleasure in many ways and I came away feeling that the School had made great strides in the four years of my absence.

You may be interested in some things I have written Mrs Washington about the part the Georgia women took in the Federation which I will not repeat here.

One thing is certain that they handled the Federation so far as the color question is concerned and Mrs Lowe[1] has been compelled to show her hand. At different times during the convention you and your wife were mentioned with praise by Southern women on the platform but at the same time it was plain that no recognition in the Federation would be granted if they could prevent it, which they did.

Some of us feel that it is a very serious matter and it looks like concerted action with the Southern men who are working to disfranchise the Colored men. We pray not. Mrs Ruffin[2] can tell you all that I know. Sincerely —

Alice J. Kaine

ALS Con. 177 BTW Papers DLC.

[1] Rebecca Douglas Lowe, born in Georgia, was president of the General Federation of Women's Clubs from 1898 to 1899. Earlier she was a leader in the club movement in the South and was founder of the Atlanta Women's Club in 1896, and president of the Georgia State Federation of Women's Clubs in 1897. The widow of William Bell Lowe, an Atlanta businessman, she married the magazine publisher George Gunton in 1904, and worked for better working conditions and increased wages for women.

[2] Josephine St. Pierre Ruffin (1842-1924) of Boston, a prominent black clubwoman, was the widow of George Lewis Ruffin (1834-86), an 1869 graduate of Harvard Law School who became the first black man appointed to a judgeship in New England. Josephine Ruffin did war relief work during the Civil War. She founded the Kansas Relief Society, which sent aid to black migrants to Kansas after the Civil War, and she was also an editor, for a time, of the Boston *Courant*, a black newspaper. Described as being of French, English, American Indian, and African descent, she was active in the white New England Women's Club that had been founded by Julia Ward Howe.

In 1894 Josephine Ruffin founded the black Woman's Era Club with the assistance of her daughter Florida, a Boston schoolteacher. The club became prominent among black women's organizations, and Ruffin served as its president until 1903 and also edited the club's magazine *Woman's Era*.

In 1895 several independent developments in black women's clubs, led by Josephine St. Pierre Ruffin, Margaret Murray Washington, and Mary Church Terrell, led Ruffin to call for a national meeting in Boston which resulted in the merger of several organizations in 1896 to form the National Association of Colored Women (NACW). After a brief rivalry with Mary Church Terrell for the presidency of the NACW, Ruffin became one of seven national vice-presidents, and her magazine, *Woman's Era*, became the official journal of the NACW for a time.

In 1899 the Woman's Era Club became a member of the white Massachusetts State Federation of Women's Clubs. The next year Ruffin sought membership in the white General Federation of Women's Clubs, which rejected the club's petition at their biennial convention in Milwaukee, although the white conferees agreed to seat Ruffin as a delegate if she claimed she represented a white club. This incident precipitated a bitter feud between white and black women's clubs that lasted for many years. Ruffin refused to accept the terms of the General Federation and left Milwaukee in protest against the racial segregation. Returning to Boston, she continued to be active in civic affairs and club work and was a founder of the Boston branch of the NAACP.

An Interview in the Knoxville *Journal Tribune*

Nashville, [Tenn.] June 16 [1900]

Booker T. Washington, the negro educator, passed through the city today en route from Tuskegee, Ala., to Cincinnati, and visited the colored institutions of Nashville. In reference to the organization of a national negro party and the connection of his name as a vice presidential candidate, he said:

"I am not in politics and have never been. I am simply an educator. I do not believe that I have any political preference. My friends and the friends of the negro are of all parties and religions.

"The mention of my name as a candidate for vice president on the colored peoples ticket is both ludicrous and ill-advised. I am neither a candidate nor a politician.

"What do I think about the organization of the negro party? Well, I think a little less politics and a little more work will have a salutary effect upon the negro. Politics not only 'makes strange bedfellows,' but enemies of those who are prone to be our friends.

"A colored man's party would go forth with a chip on its shoulder, and what we want is peace with the white man, and not war.

"Let the colored people devote their attention to the census enumerators who are now among them. The record of the advancement of the negro rests entirely with what they are to tell the census man. Whatever they have acquired will appear to the good of the race. Let us have more to tell the census enumerator and less to tell the politicians."

Knoxville *Journal Tribune*, June 17, 1900, 3.

To Emily Howland

Grand Union Hotel. New York, June 19th, 1900

My Dear Miss Howland: I am rather late in replying to your kind letter of June 8th containing Two hundred dollars ($200) as payment on the Relief Fund. We thank you sincerely for this.

I find that I must speak on the 11th of August in Cuba, N.Y. I am not quite sure as I have not a map whether this is anywhere near you or not. At any rate I shall keep your kind invitation in mind, and if I can possibly do so during the Summer I shall visit you. I enjoyed very much my visit to your home four years ago.

I am glad that you take such a far sighted and philosophical view of the Montgomery Conference. I believe that the whole movement is going to do good rather than harm. The world is going forward not backward. People cannot much longer resist the forward movement of civilization. There was some very mean things said at this conference about the Negro, and at the same time there was some good and brave things said. More addresses were made favorably to the Negro than were made against him, although, some of the latter I regret were not reported very fully.

Now that some of these people have said the very worst they can say I feel that future meetings are going to be more encouraging. It is a great thing to have a meeting in the midst of the Southern white people where the women could be present. I am quite sure that many Southern white women for the first time in their lives heard a colored man called "Mister," and providentially it seems that almost every speaker who referred to an individual Negro called him "Mister."

In the August Number of the Century there will be a short article written by me upon this conference. I should so much like to have the opportunity of talking the whole matter over with you. These are rather serious and in some respects trying days for our people, and I have to give a great deal of my time and sympathy to correspondence with the different elements throughout the country.

If this Montgomery Conference continues as it is likely to do the time will come when it will be compelled by force of public sentiment to put the Negro on the programme. I don't doubt this.

I am watching with a great deal of concern the outcome of the Constitutional Convention in Virginia. Yours truly

Booker T. Washington

TLS   Emily Howland Papers   NN-Sc.

From Warren Logan

Tuskegee, Ala., June 19, 1900

Dear Mr Washington: Our worst fears regarding Mrs H.'s[1] condition have been realized. She now admits that the physicians' diagnosis is correct and that she is pregnant. Weston[2] is the man in the case, just as we suspected.

Mr Calloway[3] has gone to Atlanta to-day to see if Mr Weston will marry Mrs H. If he consents, he will is to return with Mr Calloway and we will have the thing over to-night or tomorrow morning. I am just this minute in receipt of a telegram from Mr Calloway stating that Weston will come, so that I suppose we will be able to carry out this plan. I shall see that they leave Tuskegee as soon as possible. It will be necessary for the school to furnish the money to get them away.

With your approval and the consent of the mother, I will arrange to keep the two elder children at the school. Very truly yours,

Warren Logan

ALS   Con. 177   BTW Papers   DLC.

1 Altona Lillian Hamilton, the widow of Robert H. Hamilton, was in charge of the Tuskegee Institute sales room.

2 Edward H. Weston. See above, 4:379.

3 James Nathan Calloway.

To the Editor of *Century Magazine*

Grand Union Hotel. New York, June 20th, 1900

Dear Sir; Enclosed I return the proof of my article. I call your attention to two things. The first I am not quite sure I spelled Gov.

Mac Corkle's name correctly. You will note in my Manuscript that I spelled "Negro" with a capital "N" the way [the] word "Indian" is invariably printed with a capital "I." It seems that there is equally good reasons for using the capital "N" for Negro. Yours truly,

Booker T. Washington

TLS *Century* Collection NN.

From Warren Logan

Tuskegee, Ala., June 20, 1900

Dear Mr Washington Mrs Hamilton and Mr Weston were married last night by Mr Penney. They will leave Tuskegee in a few days or as soon [as] Mrs W. is able to travel.

We have arranged to take the house and lot for the school allowing $600.00 for it. Of this we will have to pay $350.00 in cash the other going to discharge the mtge. and pay open acct.

There seems nothing left for us to do but to take the two older children. This I shall arrange to do if you don't object. Very truly yours,

Warren Logan

ALS Con. 177 BTW Papers DLC.

From Robert Underwood Johnson[1]

New York June 21, 1900

Dear Mr. Washington: Thank you for the return of your proofs.

We find on referring to authorities that you have spelled Governor MacCorkle's name correctly. In spelling the word *negro* with a small *n* we have followed our usage. The word *Indian* is spelled with a capital because it is derived from the name of a proper place. However, we should defer to you in the matter were it not that we are in great haste to close the August number and cannot delay to make the changes. Yours sincerely,

R. U. Johnson
Associate Editor

TLS Con. 176 BTW Papers DLC.

1 Robert Underwood Johnson (1853-1937) was on the staff of *Century Magazine* from 1873 to 1913. He was the author of several books of poems and also was U.S. ambassador to Italy from 1920 to 1921. Johnson occasionally sent BTW articles regarding race matters for his criticisms before publication. (See BTW to Johnson, Feb. 27, 1900, *Century* Collection, NN.)

From Emmett Jay Scott

Tuskegee, Ala., June 21, 1900

Dear Mr. Washington: I think on the whole that the visit to New Orleans was a profitable one and your wisdom in seeking first an investigation as to the status of matters there has been fully vindicated. I had a conference while at New Orleans with Colonel James Lewis, Dr. Scott, Dr. Henderson and Rev. Mr. Reynolds and two other of the more prominent ministers. Whatever is to be done will be done by these men and without the aid of the offensive class of politicians who do more harm than good always when they co-operate with any effort.

The Wright case about which you have been written is a case of rape and the facts in the matter are substantially as follows: he was convicted and sentenced to be hung and was even on the gallows when a lawyer named Gussman[1] sought an appeal to save him. Gussman is himself a man of little weight and prestige and without any substantial standing in the community, except that of a respectable member of the community. He, I understand, years ago, was an influential member of the New Orleans bar, but has really outlived his usefulness. Colonel Lewis and others do something to keep him in food and clothing. He is an earnest man, but of course not such an one to take such a case as is in mind. It was simply out of humanity's impulse that he took the case of Wright. In this conference it was very thoroughly determined that it would not be well to risk the cause of the race in pressing the Wright case because of its character and also because of the fact that the constitution's validity is not directly involved therein. These men at New Orleans say that they are perfectly willing to go ahead with the case, but their point is that they do not know what kind of a case to bring. They ask that you consult with your friends in the North, those who are reputed as constitutional lawyers, and request of them a statement as to the kind of case to bring. They aver that they will not hesitate to have such a case brought as is suggested.

Colonel Lewis was appointed to see a man, who is undoubtedly the leader of the New Orleans bar and request of him a brief as to the possibility of attacking the law. He promises to write you about the matter as soon as he has seen the man. In this connection I may say that they consider the amount of $7000 named by Gussman as out of all proportion to the service which the lawyer would be called upon to render. I impressed as forcibly as I could your suggestion that an especial effort be made to raise a specified amount of money at once. I was unable to get any positive statement as to the amount they thought they could raise, but they outlined a course which they will pursue in raising the money and say that they will not relax their efforts until they have succeeded in raising as much as possible. They feel as you do, that the weight of the responsibility should rest upon them and I believe that they are so much in earnest now since you are willing to co-operate with them, that they will do a great deal more than has ever been done there anyway. They feel as I do, and as I am sure you do that the real needs of the case are, first, that a lawyer be secured who will command proper respect at the bar in New Orleans and one who will at the same time be sufficiently interested as to do all that lies within his power to secure favorable judgment.

I had with me the letter from the Texas colored lawyer and they read his brief with care and feel that perhaps it would be well to have a man of this character co-operate if the matter can be properly arranged so that every interest may be carefully guarded.

Recurring again to the financial matter, they have drafted a statement similar to the enclosed one issued by the National Afro-American Council and will confine their efforts particularly to churches and beneficial organizations among which they think they can succeed in raising a great deal of money. I did not call to see Mr. Gussman after the very frank talk with these men, as they thought that nothing was to be gained. They say that he took the Wright case of his own volition, but as soon as he found that there was a probability of co-operative effort he named the price of $7000 for his services. This would of course completely rehabilitate him personally but they do not feel that with his standing and ability the cause could be in any way advanced.

I trust that I have made the result of my visit clear to you. In personal conversation and otherwise I sought to impress the folks with the necessity of positive action at the earliest possible moment.

Will you undertake to write Mr. Henderson, whose address is, 2323 Bienville St., New Orleans, or Dr. Scott, or Colonel Lewis as to the kind of case that should be brought. This with them right now is the matter about which they are completely in the dark.

I called at the office to see Col. Falkner, but he was not in Montgomery and for that reason I could not have a conference with him as to his plans as outlined in his letter of June 9th to you. Mr. Murphy was also out of the city.

The colored people have had a meeting in Montgomery and are antagonizing the Mixon conference, but Mixon has told them that he intends holding the conference whether their assistance is given or not. I am sending you to-day a copy of the Montgomery Evening Journal, which has a reference to the antagonism of the black people. Mr. Adams states that he feels that no good can be done by such a conference at this time. Mixon still continues to advertise, as in last Sunday's paper, that you are to be one of those to be present and speak. You have, of course, written him to the contrary and I do not understand why he should continue to advertise your coming when he is positively advised that you are not to be there.

I am writing today to New Orleans to each of the persons at the conference to urge them to proceed at once in the work which is before them.

Trusting this is satisfactory and with all good wishes, I am, Yours very truly,

Emmett J. Scott

TLS Con. 182 BTW Papers DLC.

1 Anthony Leopold Gussman was a white lawyer and real estate dealer in New Orleans. The 1900 census reported his age as sixty-four.

To Emmett Jay Scott

Grand Union Hotel. New York, June 24th, 1900

My Dear Mr. Scott: I have received your letter and thank you for it. I think your letter covered the Louisiana cause pretty fully, and I shall try to bring the matter to some definite head before long.

I certainly hope that Mixon will be induced to give up the idea of holding his conference, I have both written and telegraphed him to this effect.

I see that our people in all parts of the country advertise that I am to be at this or that meeting without any authority from me. I do not know whether or not there is any way to stop it.

I want you to be very careful in handling that Louisiana matter to see that my name does not in any way appear. I shall wait before going further until I have heard from Colonel Lewis in regard to the Brief that he is to get from the leader of the New Orleans Bar. This is very important I wish you would write Colonel Lewis to have this Brief sent me at once.

I wish you would send me a copy of the address which I used at the Slater Meetings two years ago. I think the Charleston papers perhaps have the fullest account. I wish also that you would remind Mrs. Washington to revise her address. I think I put in your hands sometime ago some memoranda which I used in delivering these addresses, I wish you would send me them also.

Please also send me the name and address of the young lady who visited Tuskegee during the Commencement from Pensacola. She is a dressmaker. Yours truly,

Booker T. Washington

TLS Con. 186 BTW Papers DLC.

James Lewis to Emmett Jay Scott

New Orleans, La., June 25, 1900

Dear Sir: This will acknowledge receipt of your very kind favor. The Lithograph of Prof. Booker T. Washington and college grounds; I am pleased to learn that your stay was pleasant and your safe return home. Yes, I fully agree with you regarding the money feature of our committee. The need of that is being felt now. We have now before the State Legislature a separate or "Jim Crow" street car law, which must be met, and if nothing more, a protest should be made. I am pleased to say that the better class of our citizens are opposed to it, but when poor white trash is in power, the negro is made to suffer, as the bottom dog in the fight.

I shall head a delegation for Baton Rouge in a few days, as to the Louisiana Constitution Suffrage clause, it will not hold water, a change in the white republican leaders here, will bring about this result. I shall write you from time to time and keep you posted as we progress.

You will remember me kindly to the little Cuban boys. I have been too busy to reply to their letter. Remember me to Prof. Washington and believe me, truly yours,

James Lewis

TLS   Con. 178   BTW Papers   DLC.

From Henry Sylvester Williams

Common Room, Gray's Inn [London] 29-6.00

Dear Sir, Thanks for yours of recent date. The Pan African Conference Committee regrets the cause hindering your presence at the greatest gathering our race as a people has ever witnessed. We certainly would like to press you, but as you know best the circumstances referred to I am instructed to ask that you contribute a paper "On the industrial development of the people in the light of current history to meet the exigencies of an adapted civilisation." This will be read & given due publicity.

You will be pleased to learn that M. Benito Sylvain of Abyssinia will be present. Had a letter to that effect from him this week. The papers here have taken up the cause rather cogently and an undoubted success is possible.

It is hoped you have influenced many who are coming over to support the project. The singular & most effective thing about the

Conference is it is organised & worked by us purely. We are receiving slight opposition from "The Aborigines Protection Society" — (keep this to yourself as yet) but despite it many distinguished friends have signified their intention to be with us. "We must do for ourselves in order to demand and ultimately gain the respect of the other races."

With best regards to Mrs Washington, Believe me, Yours truly

H. S. Williams

Wrote this at the above place, to catch post — we are holding all meetings at 139 Palace Chambers.

ALS   Con. 187   BTW Papers   DLC.

To J. E. MacBrady[1]

[Tuskegee, Ala.] July 3, 1900

My dear Sir: My attention has just been called to your book, "A New Negro for a New Century."[2] I was very glad to be of some assistance to you in the way of counsel, etc. in connection with its publication, but I do not remember to have authorized you to use my picture on first page of cover nor to publish my name in connection with the matter which I wrote for you. On the contrary my remembrance is that I advised that it would not be possible for me to grant the latter matter even if I promised as to the first. If you will be kind enough to send me a copy of letter granting such permission I shall be most grateful.

The book as re-printed shows up well, but I find myself represented as the author of it on your cover when of course this is not true. It was also understood by me that I was to contribute 32 pages to your publication at the rate of $3 a page. I notice, however, that the matter when set up makes 72 pages. I understood that I should hear from you again as soon as you set the matter up as to the balance of matter if it was accepted and printed by you. Yours very truly,

[Booker T. Washington]

TLc Con. 179 BTW Papers DLC.

¹ J. E. MacBrady was president of the American Publishing House in Chicago. The firm specialized in subscription books and the sale of Bibles.

² Emmett J. Scott called BTW's attention to the design of the book and actually wrote this letter, which he forwarded to BTW for his signature. He advised BTW that the book was actually a reprint of N. B. Wood's *The White Side of a Black Subject* (1896) and that, the way it was now designed, BTW appeared to be the author. (July 3, 1900, Con. 182, BTW Papers, DLC.) BTW's name appeared much bolder on the title page than those of the other contributors, N. B. Wood and Fannie Barrier Williams. Despite the flattering comments that MacBrady wrote about BTW in the introduction, calling him "masterful" and an "authority," BTW tried to stop publication of the book. (See BTW to E. J. Scott, July 25, 1900, below.) He eventually let the matter drop, however, when his friend and lawyer Samuel Laing Williams, husband of Fannie Barrier Williams, advised that BTW did not have a strong legal position in the matter. (See Williams to BTW, Aug. 27, 1900, below.) Even though he had misgivings about the book, Scott, who was editor of the *Tuskegee Student*, included a warm review of it in the official Tuskegee organ, which referred to the work as "finely gotten up." (*Tuskegee Student*, 13 [July 14, 1900], 3-4.)

From Clara Johnston

Malden, West. Virginia. July, 3, 1900

Dear Uncle Booker: I hope this letter will find you well, and getting along nicely.

Please give me your advice, about what I'm going to ask you. That is this. I want Mother to borrow some money from the building association and have a house build in Slab Town. It is one mile from Charleston. The Town is just building up now, and we can get land very cheap.

She can buy, build and move there. And do good work at raising poultry.

It will be a great deal better for her health. The doctor has said she will be an invalid in four or five years, if she keeps going at the rate she [is] going now.

I suppose Mamma has told you she keeps restuarant. And she has over worked her self. She never gets any more then four hours sleep, and at times not that much. Her home is going to rack. If she moves she can be right in her home all the time.

Malden has gone down so much to what it was when I was here.

I never like to think of going to school, and leaving the children here.

Papa keeps sick often. He suffers with cramps. Some times when he has them he is unconscious. I think it is caused from plowing when the ground is very wet.

Now Uncle Booker, I hope you will decide the subject in my favor.

Dont think Mamma cant raise chickens, for she can. She has raised them before. Spring chickens are selling in Charleston for twenty five and thirty five cents. Mamma said did you get her last letter? It has been one week to day.

All are well and sends love. With much love.

Clara Johnston

P.S. Please tell Mamma not to go to Kelley Creek.

ALS   Con. 176   BTW Papers   DLC.

To Emmett Jay Scott

Roslindale, Mass., July 8th, 1900

Dear Mr. Scott: I enclose matter from your Press Syndicate. I think you will have to take charge of this the best you can. I think it best that you make a skeleton of the article that is sent with whatever information you can in addition to that contained in the printed circular. I want it understood that this organization[1] is for the colored people who are engaged in the most humble business as well as those engaged in what is call[ed] the higher business or trade.

You might also bring out the point that very few people understand how many successful colored people there are in business who are in remote towns and succeeding in a quiet way, but not often heard of. The object of this organization is to get hold of all such people, and give them such advice, encouragement and inspiration as will enable them to do more and better business.

I wish you would get hold of the photographs of such men as Mr. J. H. Lewis,[2] Washington Street, Boston, Mass., Peter J. Smith,

Jr., 45 Greenwich Street, Boston, Mass., who is to be Secretary of the local Committee, and such men in the South who have promised to attend or are likely to be present. Pettiford[3] would be a good man to get hold of. In making up the skeleton I should give them as much information as possible concerning such men who are doing business successfully. Send them as large a number of photographs as you can get. This will have to be done in time to reach them to be of any service to them.

I find that you will have to push this matter through the Press in order to make it successful. Keep notices constantly in the Student regarding it.

I wrote to Prof. Lee[4] some days ago to send me the street address of the persons who have promised to attend. I hope he has secured more promises by this time. I think you can follow the suggestions I have given in the matter. Yours truly,

Booker T. Washington

TLS   Con. 186   BTW Papers   DLC.

1 The NNBL.

2 J. H. Lewis, born in Heathsville, N.C., ran one of the largest tailor shops in Boston and was one of the wealthiest black men in America. He was a tailor in Concord, Mass., in the 1870s and then moved to Boston, where he began his own business with a capital of $100. By 1896 he was doing $150,000 worth of business annually. He became well known for manufacturing bell-bottom trousers. Most of the customers and employees at his fashionable shop were white. Lewis retired from business about 1912. He was among the first to suggest the creation of an organization of black businessmen as early as 1891, and he was one of the sponsors of the organizing meeting of the NNBL in 1900.

3 William Reuben Pettiford.

4 John Robert E. Lee.

An Address before the
National Educational Association[1]

[Charleston, S.C. July 11, 1900]

THE PROBLEM OF THE SOUTH

Ladies and Gentlemen: We stand tonight on historic ground. Charleston and South Carolina have made history — history that will always occupy a prominent place in the annals of our country. But South Carolina was never greater or prouder than tonight, when, with open arms and generous hospitality, she extends a welcome to the educators of America, regardless of race or color. The world is moving forward, not backward. Under the shadow of Fort Sumter we find ourselves tonight. If history be true, I think that it was nearly forty years ago that a little company of men, moved by a different spirit, clad in different uniforms, armed with different weapons, came to this vicinity to bring cheer, comfort, food, and reinforcement to an endangered, suffering, and starving garrison. The army that comes into Charleston today comes with guns beaten into plowshares, and swords into pruning-hooks. It comes with no special regalia. Already we find that Fort Sumter has surrendered and Charleston is ours. It is in this spirit and with this object we come to you — to bring relief, the relief that comes from the spreading of education and intelligence, kindness and brotherly love, among all nations and all classes. It is when we witness such scenes as this that our belief in the ability of our country to work out all its problems becomes stronger, and that the education of all the people, in heart, head, and hand, will be the solution of all the trying problems that surround and confront this southland, where both races have had difficulties to contend with which no other people have ever met.

When we disarm ourselves of prejudices and passions, we must acknowledge that the white South owes much to the Negro, and that the Negro owes much to the white South. The Negro has a right to cherish love for the South. It was here that we came centuries ago in our heathenism, and here we were taught the religion of Christ; here we came without a language, and here we were taught the Anglo-Saxon tongue; here we came without habits of thrift, and here we were taught industry and economy. The Negro has a right to cherish memories of the South. In a large degree it has been the brawn and muscle of the black man that have cleared the forests, opened the mines, and built the railroads; that have grown the rice and cotton and the sugar-cane; that have made the South rich and prosperous.

In all discussion and legislation bearing upon this subject we must keep in mind that the Negro has a peculiar claim upon the conscience, the intelligence, and the hearts of the American people. You must remember that you are dealing with a race not only forced to come into this country against its will, but in the face of its most earnest protest. These people have a claim upon your intelligence and your sympathies that perhaps no other people can have. And, now that we are here, the great problem that is confronting us is how to solve this problem in justice to southern white men, among whom the Negro must live, and in justice to the Negro himself.

During the last thirty-five years quite a number of suggestions have been made looking to a solution of this problem. A few years ago some six hundred of our people sailed from Savannah, Ga., bound for Liberia, and people said all at once: "We have found a way to solve this problem; our people have sailed for Africa, and the problem is solved." But those people forgot that on this same morning, here in the black belt of the South, perhaps before breakfast, about six hundred more black children came into the world.

I have a good friend in the state of Georgia who is very earnest in his belief that the way to solve this difficulty is to set aside some territory in the far West and put the Negro in it, and let him grow up there a distinct race. There is difficulty in that way. In the first place, you would have to build a wall about that territory to keep the black man in it, and, in the second place, you would have to build a wall about it — and I suspect a much higher one — to keep the white man out of it.

I was on the train not very long ago with a gentleman who had a third suggestion. He contended that the problem was solving itself, because the Negro was so fast becoming a part of other races that there soon would be no Negro race in this country. There is difficulty about that. If it is proven that a man has even 1 per cent. of African blood, he becomes a Negro every time; the 99 per cent. of Anglo-Saxon blood counts for nothing — the man always falls to our pile in the count of the races. It takes 100 per cent. to make a white man, and 1 per cent. will make a Negro every time. So, you see, we are a stronger race than the white race.

This problem will not be solved in any of these ways. There is only one way to solve it — by treating the Negro with humanity and justice, just as I find the people of Charleston treating the black man today. When you go still farther in the study of this question, you will find that the Negro is the only race that has ever had the rare privilege of coming to America by reason of having a very special and very pressing invitation to come here. The unfortunate white race came here against the protests of the leading citizens of this country in 1492 and later; while, for some reason, we seem to have been so important to the business prosperity of this country that we had to be sent for, and sent for at great cost and inconvenience on the part of our white friends. And now we have the reputation of being rather an obliging and polite race; after having put our white friends to so much trouble, expense, and inconvenience to get us here, it would be rather unkind and ungracious on our part not to stay here. Now, my friends, that we have got the white men of the North and the white men of the South face to face, I want to make one request of them, and I want to do it in the form of a story:

At one time an old colored man in South Carolina sold a hog to a white man for $5. The white man paid his money, took the hog, and went on his way. When he got about half way home the hog got out of the pen and went back home to the old Negro, Uncle Zeke. About noon another white man came along and wanted to buy a hog; and Uncle Zeke sold him the same hog for another $5. The second white man went on his way home, and met the first coming back to Uncle Zeke's house for his hog. He said, "Mister, where did you get that hog? Uncle Zeke sold me that hog this morning for $5, and he got away from me and went back." "Well," said the other, "he sold him to me this afternoon." "How are we going to settle this thing?" said the first purchaser. "Let's go back and see Uncle Zeke about it," said the other. They went back to Uncle Zeke's, and the first one said: "How about this hog? Didn't you sell him to me this morning for $5?" "I sure did," said Uncle Zeke. "Didn't you sell him to me this afternoon for $5?" said the other man. "I sure did," said Uncle Zeke. "Well, how about this thing?" they said, "we don't understand it." Uncle Zeke said: "Fore Gawd, can't you white people go settle that thing among yourselves?"

Now, for thirty-five years, my friends, you white people of the North and of the South have been contending as to which one of you is responsible for bringing the black man into this country. Now that you are here face to face, I want you to get together and settle this thing among yourselves.

But I assure you, my friends, I am not here this evening to plead for education merely in behalf of the Negro. Those of you who understood slavery and what it meant will agree with me when I say that slavery wrought almost as much permanent injury to the white man during its existence as to the black man. And those of you who understand conditions as they are today in the South will agree with me that so long as the rank and file of our people are in poverty and ignorance, so long will there be a millstone about the neck of progress in the South. So I plead, not for the Negro alone, but in a higher spirit, that you will remove the burden of poverty and ignorance from both races thruout the South.

In a larger degree, if we would work out our problem as black people, we have got to consider the immediate needs that surround and confront us as a race; and in a brief, earnest manner get down to the bottom facts of our conditions.

At one time, in Alabama, an old colored man, teaching a Sunday-school class, was trying to explain to the class how the children of Israel were able to cross the Red Sea without getting wet, and how the forces of Pharaoh got into the water. He said: "It was this way: When the first party came along it was early in the morning, and it was cold, and the ice was hard and thick, and they had no trouble in crossing. But when the next party came along it was 12 o'clock in the day, and the ice had begun to melt, and when they went on it it broke and they went down." There was in the class a man who had been going to school, and he said: "I don't understand that kind of an explanation. I have been studying that kind of thing, and my geography teaches me that ice does not form so near the equator." The old minister said: "I was expecting just that sort of a question. The time I am speaking 'bout was before they had any gografys or 'quators there." That old minister, in his straightforward way, was simply trying to brush aside all the artificiality and get to the bedrock of common-sense; and that is what we have to do to lift our people up.

I claim that, in the present condition of our people, industrial education will have a special place in helping us out of our present state. We find that in many cases it is a positive sin to take a black boy from an agricultural district and send him to a school or a city where he is educated in everything in heaven and earth that has no connection with agricultural life, with the result that he remains in the city in an attempt to live by his wits. And again, my friends, you will find that in proportion as we give industrial training in connection with academic training, there go with it a knowledge and a feeling that there is a dignity, a civilizing power, in intelligent labor. And you will find at those institutions where industrial education is emphasized, and the student enabled to work out his own expenses, that the very effort gives him a certain amount of self-reliance or backbone he would not get without such effort on his own part. When the Bible says, "Work out your own salvation with fear and trembling," I am tempted to believe it means about what it says. I believe it is largely possible for a race as well as an individual to work out its own salvation, and in the South we are to work out our salvation in a large measure in the field, in the college, in the shop, and with the hammer and the saw.

Once, in the South, an old colored man was very anxious to have turkey for his Christmas dinner, and he prayed for it night after night: "Lord, please send this darkey a turkey"; but no turkey came. So one night, when it got near Christmas time, he prayed: "Lord, please send this darkey *to* a turkey"; and he got it that same night. I don't know how you white people get hold of turkeys, but, my friends, we don't get hold of very much, as a race or as individuals, unless we put forth something of the kind of effort that old black man put forth. There are three things as a race we have to learn to do if we want to get on our feet. We have got to learn to put skill and dignity and brains into all our occupations. A few days ago a gentleman asked me in what way the North could protect the Negro in the exercise of his rights in the South. I answered, as I say to you tonight: Make the Negro the most useful man in the community. It will constitute his most lasting and most competent protection, whether in the North or in the South. Help him to do things so well that no one can do them better. Help him to do a common thing in an uncommon manner, and that will in a large measure help to solve our problem.

The black man, in connection with all this, has to learn that we have to pay the price; that a race, like an individual, must pay the price for anything that it gets. No individual or race can get hold of something for nothing, it has got to pay the price — starting at the bottom, and gradually, earnestly, thru a series of years, working up toward the highest civilization. One of the hardest lessons for a race, like an individual, to learn is that it will grow strong and powerful in proportion as it learns to do well the little things about its doors. The race that learns this lesson may be retarded in its upward progress, but it can never be defeated. In a larger measure thruout this country the black man should seek to make himself, not a burden, but a helper to the community in which he lives; not a receiver, but a giver; not a destroyer, but a producer in the highest sense. I want to see the Negro put that intelligence into labor which will dignify it, and lift it out of the atmosphere of sloth and drudgery into that atmosphere where people will feel that labor is glorified and dignified.

A short time ago I was in the state of Iowa, and I saw a white man out there planting corn, and this white man was sitting down upon some kind of a machine. All the work this white man seemed to do was to hold back two fine spirited horses and keep them from working themselves to death. He was not only sitting down planting corn, but he had a big red umbrella hoisted over him. When it went over the ground, I think that machine plowed up the ground, and I think it made all the furrows; I am sure it dropped the corn in the furrows and covered the corn. I was in one of our southern states later, and I saw a black man planting corn. I saw him competing in the market with this white man in Iowa. He had a mule going about a mile an hour. He had a pole on the plow. The mule would go a step or two and stop, and he would get the pole and hit him to make him start again. He would go on again and stop, and the old fellow would go and get a stone and knock the old plow together. He would go on a little farther, and then the old fellow would have to stop and fix up the harness — made partly of rags and partly of leather. He would go on a little farther, and have to stop and fix his "galluses" before he got to the end of the row. He was what we call a "one gallus farmer" — had only a strap across one shoulder. He would go on in that fashion and plow up the ground, and another black man, with the same kind of mule, would come behind him and lay off the furrows; another would come behind him and put in the corn, and a fourth would come behind and cover the corn. Under no conceivable circumstances is it possible for that black man, following that mule in the South, to compete with that white man in Iowa sitting under that red umbrella. You are going to buy your corn every time from the individual who can produce it cheapest, no matter what his color; all you want is the cheapest and best corn. My object in emphasizing industrial education is to help give the Negro boy in the South so much brain and skill that he can sit under a red umbrella and raise corn just as that white man does in Iowa; and we have got to do the same kind of a thing for the poor white boy — go and take him from that mule and put him under that umbrella, so as to make the forces of nature in a large degree work for him. When that is done we shall cease to buy our corn, and to compete as we do now in so large a degree with the West and the North. We will free the poor white boy and free the poor black boy in the South at the same time.

I was in Boston some time ago, and I saw a white man washing shirts; and, as usual, this white man was sitting down. You don't see a white man doing much work unless he is sitting down. But he "gets there" — he gets results, and results are what the world is looking for. When it wants corn and cotton, it does not care whether it is made by a black man standing up or a white man sitting down; all it wants is the best and cheapest corn and cotton. You must put brains and skill into all these common but important occupations if we would hold our own as a race in this country.

All this pertains to the material side, and not to the ethical, higher growth of the Negro, you say. I do not overlook or undervalue that side of our development. But show me a race that is living from day to day on the outer edges of the industrial world; show me a race living on the skimmed milk of other people, and I will show you a race that is a football for political parties. The black man, like the white man, must have this industrial, commercial foundation upon which to rest his higher life. The black man in the South is very emotional; but, my friends, it is hard to make a Christian out of a hungry man, whether black or white. I have tried that, but always failed. In proportion as the black man gets into habits of thrift and industry, in the same proportion he improves in his moral and industrial life. Would you think the average black man can feel as much in ten minutes as the white man can in an hour? In our religion we feel more than you do. When the black man gets religion he is expected to shout and jump around. If he does not, we get skeptical, and we say he has the white man's religion. This emotional side of our nature puts us in awkward circumstances sometimes. Some time ago a good old colored woman in some southern city went to the Episcopal church and they gave her a seat in the gallery. When the good preacher got warmed up in his sermon, the old woman got "happy" and got to groaning and singing. One of the officers of the church heard her going on and went to her. "What is the matter?" he asked; "why do you disturb us?" She said: "I am happy; I got religion." "Why," he said, "this is no place to get religion."

But gradually thruout the South, as we watch the influence of this industrial education as it strikes the rank and file of our people in the corners of the South, it not only changes them into habits of industry, but it is helping them in that moral and religious life. Some time ago I met an old colored man going to camp meeting. I asked: "Where are you going?" "I am going to camp meeting," he said. "I haven't been in eight years, and now I am going. I heard you tell us some time ago to buy land and stop mortgaging crops. I followed your advice. I ain't been to camp-meeting in eight years, but I am going now, sure. I bought fifty acres of land, and I done paid the last dollar on it. I got a house on it with four rooms, all painted, and I [am] going to camp-meeting this year. Do you see this wagon? I done paid the last dollar on it — ain't no man got a mortgage on it, and the wagon got a right to go to camp-meeting too this year. Do you see these two big mules? They belong to Sam. I paid the last dollar on them, and they got a right to go to camp-meeting. Do you see this bread in this basket? My old woman cooked the bread; I raised it, and the old woman cooked it. We are going to camp meeting, and are going to shout and have a big time. We have food in our stomachs and religion in our hearts."

Gradually we are changing the moral condition of the colored people thruout the South. We are making progress in the settlement of these problems. The black man is gradually buying land and teaching schools in every part of the South. The Negro is not only getting an education, but is fast converting the white man to believe in the education of the black man thruout this country. And in proportion as we can convince the white men in every part of the South that education makes black men more useful citizens, in the same proportion will our problem as a race be solved. And I want you all to remember that when you hear of crime being committed in the South, this crime is not being committed by the educated black men of the race. It is very seldom, if ever, that any-one has heard of a black man who has been thoroly educated in industrial schools or in colleges committing any of these heinous crimes so often charged up against our race. In a larger degree you must learn to judge the Negro race as you do other races, by the best that the race can produce, and not by the worst. You must judge us by those in the schoolroom, and not by those in the penitentiary; by those who are in the field and in the shop, not by those on the streets in idleness; by those who have bought homes and are taxpayers, not by those in dens of misery and crime; by those who have learned the laws of health and are living, not by those who are breaking the laws of health and are dying out. Keep the searchlights constantly focused upon the weaker elements of any race, and who among them can be called successful people? You judge the English by Gladstone, the Germans by Bismarck, the French by Loubet — by those who have succeeded, not by those who have failed.

We are making progress in another direction, and the Negro is not unappreciative of the opportunity the South gives him in this respect. Go out here about a mile from the center of this city, and I will show you a spectacle that perhaps no other city, in the North or West, can present — the spectacle of the white South giving to the black boy and the black girl an opportunity to work in a cotton factory. In proportion as we get these business opportunities, in the same proportion shall we go forward as a race.

At one time, in a certain part of the South, there was a white man who wanted to cross a river, and he went to a colored man near by and asked him to lend him 3 cents to pay his way across the ferry. The colored man said: "Boss, how much money have you got?" The white man replied: "I haven't got any today. I am broke and in bad circumstances, and I want to borrow 3 cents to pay my way across the ferry." "Boss," said the colored man, "I know you are a white man, and I expect you got more sense than this old 'nigger,' but I ain't going to loan you no 3 cents. The man that ain't got no money is just as well off on one side of the river as on t'other." Now, in reference to our race, I would say that a race that is without bank accounts, or property, or business standing, is just as well off on one side of the river as on the other. Whether we live in the North or the South, we have got to enter into the industries and enterprises of the community in which we live. And in proportion as we do that the whites will respect us more, no matter where we live.

Whenever a black man has $500 to loan there is never any trouble getting a white man to borrow it from him. I never heard of any such thing. A short time ago one of our men at Tuskegee tried to find how many bushels of sweet potatoes he could produce on a single acre of land. He got a yield last year of 266 bushels. The average production in that community before had been forty-nine bushels. When he produced those 266 bushels, you should have seen the white men coming to see how he did that thing. They forgot all about the color of his skin; they did not have any prejudice against those potatoes; they simply knew there was a Negro who by his knowledge of improved methods of agriculture could produce more potatoes than they could. Every white man there was ready to take off his hat to that black man. Put such a black man in every community in the South, and you will find that the race problem will begin to disappear.

In discussing this problem further, I thank God that I have come to a point in the struggle where I can sympathize with the white man as much as I can sympathize with the black man. And I thank God further — and I make a statement here which I have made in our northern cities — that I have grown to the point where I can sympathize with even a southern white man as much as I can with a northern white man. To me "a man is a man for a' that and a' that." And in extending this sympathy I believe as a race, we shall strengthen ourselves at every point; for no race, black or white, can go on cherishing hatred or ill-will toward another race without itself being narrowed and drawn down in everything that builds character and manhood and womanhood. I propose that no race shall drag down and narrow my soul by making me hate it. I propose that the Negro, if possible, shall be bigger in his sympathies than even the white man, and if the white man in any part of this country would hate us, let us love him; if he would treat us cruelly, let us extend to him the hand of mercy; if he would push us down, let us help to push him up.

No race has ever made such immense progress, under similar

conditions, as the black race of this country. You must not, however, measure us by the distance we have traveled so much as by the obstacles we have overcome in traveling that distance.

In conclusion, my friends of the white race, this problem concerns nearly ten millions of my people and sixty millions of yours. We rise as you rise, fall as you fall. Where we are strong you are strong. There is no power that can separate our destiny. No member of your race in any part of this country can harm the weakest member of mine without the proudest and bluest blood in your civilization being degraded. I believe the time has come in the history of this problem when the culture, the education, the refinement of the white South is going to take hold and help lift the black man up as it has never done before. No race can oppress or neglect a weaker race without that race itself being degraded and injured. No strong race can help a weaker race without the strong race being made stronger. Oppression degrades, assistance elevates. But you as white people and we as black people must remember that mere material, visible accumulation alone will not solve our problem, and that education of the white people and of the black people will be a failure unless we keep constantly before us the fact that the final aim of all education, whether industrial or academic, must be that influence which softens the heart, and brings to it a spirit of kindness and generosity; that influence which makes us seek the elevation of all men, regardless of race or color. The South will prosper in proportion as with development in agriculture, in mines, in domestic arts, in manufacture there goes that education which brings respect for law, which broadens the heart, sweetens the nature, and makes us feel that we are our "brother's keeper," whether that brother was born in England, Italy, Africa, or the Islands of the Sea.

National Educational Association, *Proceedings and Addresses, 1900* (Washington, D.C., 1900), 114–23. An autograph version is in Con. 959, BTW Papers, DLC, but it does not contain some of the anecdotes recorded in this stenographic version.

1 BTW drew the largest crowd at the convention, according to the Montgomery *Advertiser*, July 12, 1900, 1. An item from the Charleston *News and Courier*, reprinted in the *Tuskegee Student*, described BTW's platform style at the convention: "There is no educator here who is more conspicuous than this colored man. He is a typical colored man. He is broad shouldered, young and apparently full of strength and earnestness. When a colored speaker becomes an orator, he most frequently takes a front rank, and President Washington is of this type. He talks plainly, distinctly

and out spoken. He gestures frequently, folds his hands before and behind his body and talks with entire ease. He used no manuscript, spoke with earnestness and soon caught and kept the entire audience." (*Tuskegee Student*, 13 [Aug. 11, 1900], 1, 4.)

From a Well-Wisher

Charleston S.C. July 12, 1900

Dear Sir: I heard you with much pleasure last night at the Auditorium.

I made up my mind then to write you this. You are too useful a man to your country and race, not to feel it your bounden duty to prolong your usefulness so far as it may be possible. You are singularly gifted as a speaker. Your earnestness carries conviction with it, and your art is artlessly artful — those stories you tell are most luminous and appropriate.

Now, then, what I wish to say is this: If you do not go to some voice-trainer and learn how to make the best use of your voice in speaking, the *almost certainty* is that in a few years, you will destroy your voice. It is true that you may not often be obliged to speak in so large a hall or to so great an audience as you did last night, but it is also true that you have no idea how to manage or take care of your voice. You speak from your throat entirely and get your effects by main force. This is all wrong. Your voice and your oratorical powers are gifts of God, and should be respected as such. So long as you are young and strong, you may not appreciate the immense importance of conserving your vocal energies. After awhile (perhaps when too late) you will wake up to the fact that you have squandered God's gift.

I am no crank — only your well-wisher. I could name to you men of distinction & usefulness, who have had to renounce public life, *because they had ruined their voices.*

Go to the best voice-trainer in your reach. Learn how to *breathe* and how to *throw your voice* without effort. Excuse this unasked advice & believe me   Sincerely Your

Well-wisher

ALS Con. 184 BTW Papers DLC. Docketed: "This is a well-meant letter. I hope it be appreciated in this spirit! EJS."

From Henry C. Davis

South Yarmouth, Mass., 13th. July, 1900

My dear Mr. Washington: I have just re-read the letter you had from Mr. Hawk,[1] of the Coosa Mfg. Co. of Piedmont, Ala. and enclosed to me in yours of 7th. ulto. If under the guise of that Co., you can establish at, or new [near] you, such a Mill as would suit your wants as a means of instructing colored operators, it strikes me as a good step in the direction we are aiming for and without the responsibility of raising the necessary money and assuming the risks of operating. Have you heard further from him. A visit from his Managers could do you no harm and might interest some of them directly in your work.

I am getting along finely and feel equal to almost anything today. Yours very truly.

Henry C. Davis

TLS Con. 170 BTW Papers DLC.

1 John W. Hawk, a forty-six-year-old white man, was reported in the 1900 census as secretary and treasurer of a cotton mill in Piedmont, Ala.

Portia Marshall Washington to the Editor of the Boston *Transcript*

Normal School, Tuskegee, Ala. [ca. July 14, 1900]

To the Editor of the Transcript: Most of the readers of the Transcript have heard of the great industrial institute at Tuskegee, Ala., for the Negro. Perhaps they know of the many trades being taught there constantly by competent instructors of the same race. This institution is really a small village, composed of nothing but Negroes. The object of Principal Washington is to make it an object-lesson, or model community for the masses in general.

Just across the street from the institution there are many attractive residences, owned and rented by those of the faculty who have families. Some are more spacious than others, according to the means or position of the instructor. It seems that these pretty, well-built homes, all put up and owned by Negroes, go to prove that the Negro is learning to some extent at least the value of home training and home ties. Let us, for instance, compare this neat, well-kept avenue of these "gens de couleur," with streets occupied by these same people at the North — there, with few exceptions, we find filth and immorality of every description, dirty, ill-managed children, using still fouler language; everything showing ignorance and depravity. Yet this is the cultured North. Some claim that the chances of the Negro for wealth and education are greater at the North, but it seems to me that Northern competition is just a little too much for the Negro at present. It is better for him to remain at the South, where his chances to make a home for himself are just as great. At present there are many avenues open for his education at the South. There is no need of his going North to educate his children.

Most of the Negroes around Tuskegee own their homes and send their children to school. The Institute has an excellent training school which most of the village children attend. The influence of this great school is further shown by the work of Mrs. Washington among the women and girls in the town. She has rented two large rooms over a colored grocery store. Here every Saturday during the school term she holds her meetings. The women meet in one room and listen to her good, sensible talks about their homes and habits of living. In the adjoining room young girls are receiving lessons in housekeeping, cooking and sewing. With such scant facilities Mrs. Washington is doing a very helpful work. Most of these women are from the heart of the country, where their chances of refinement are few. If it were not for these meetings, many of the women would be hanging around the streets talking and laughing in a very coarse manner. As it is, they are taught to see the wrong in such actions. Mrs. Washington has also established a free public library on one of the principal streets of the town. This library is patronized by both white and colored. Everything under the care of the school has a thoroughly wide-awake, business-like appearance. The influence of the school is felt everywhere. Those who have given so freely towards aiding Mr. Washington in his splendid work need never feel any dis-couragement; for every penny is wisely used — and we know that

God is on our side helping us to lift our people to a higher degree of civilization, and we feel that our efforts for the sake of humanity are not in vain.

Portia M. Washington

Boston *Transcript*, July 14, 1900, 20. This letter also appeared in the *Tuskegee Student*, 13 (Aug. 25, 1900), 1.

From Emmett Jay Scott

Tuskegee, Ala., July 19, 1900

Dear Mr. Washington: I beg to hand you herewith and attached letter from the Secretary of the Charleston Exposition Company. It conveys notice of your election as Director-in-Chief of the Colored Department of said Exposition. Please accept my congratulations!

If you accept this place I think you may be able to do much to help not only the race in a very large measure, but I think you will be able to so arrange so as not to seriously interfere with your work here at Tuskegee. *Of course,* I shall be glad to do whatever I can to assist you. I need hardly tell you that. By the paper submitted to the gathering of colored men it is announced that *you alone* are to appoint the *Secretary-Treasurer.* I am not self-seeking but I have thought if you should accept this place I can render signal service not only to you but to the Exposition too if this place should be assigned me. I am very sincere in saying that my only desire would be to be in a position so as to personally look after *your* interests, considering in all events that you accept the place. But the work at Tuskegee is first to be considered and if you think best that I represent you here I shall continue to do so willingly. I shall not be disappointed whatever your decision. I simply wish to do what is for the best. Yours very truly

Emmett J. Scott

ALS   Con. 181   BTW Papers   DLC.

To Emmett Jay Scott

Roslindale, Mass., July 21st, 1900

Dear Mr. Scott; I have received the Conservator and also a copy of your letter sent to the Editor.[1] The Editorial in the Conservator is written by Miss Wells. The Editorial has really I think helped the League Meeting, as I have found that several of the colored papers have taken up the matter strongly in my defence.

Miss Wells is fast making herself so ridiculous that every body is getting tired of her. Yours truly,

Booker T. Washington

TLS   Con. 186   BTW Papers   DLC.

[1] On July 7, 1900, the Chicago *Conservator* ran an editorial entitled "Booker T. Washington's New Movement" which questioned why BTW would want to launch a new national organization when the Afro-American Council was already in existence. Ida B. Wells, the author, wrote that BTW failed to attend a single meeting of the council when it met in Chicago, even though he was in the city at the time. "Here he had ample opportunity," she wrote, "to suggest plans along business lines and Prof. Du Bois, the most scholarly and one of [the] most conservative members of the Council, who is chairman of the Business Bureau would have been glad to receive Mr. Washington's cooperation." Wells thought that the time of meeting of the NNBL in Boston, scheduled just a few days before the Afro-American Council meeting in Indianapolis, would hurt the work of the council. She speculated that BTW's lack of cooperation with the council was because he "will not go anywhere or do anything unless he is 'the whole thing.' He can't be 'all in all' in the Council for there are others who are as anxious as he is to find the right, and equally anxious to do it." Wells concluded that in BTW's new organization he would be "president, moderator and dictator." (Chicago *Conservator*, July 7, 1900, Clipping, Con. 1032, BTW Papers, DLC.) Scott responded to Wells's editorial by pointing out that the NNBL was not in opposition to any group then in existence. He erroneously suggested that BTW was not interested in leadership of the new organization. Scott argued that the race had "no time for internal bickerings." (Scott to the editor of the Chicago *Conservator*, July 14, 1900, Con. 182, BTW Papers, DLC.) Since only scattered issues of this newspaper are available, it is not clear whether the *Conservator* ran Scott's letter. He wrote BTW on July 25: "They did not print my rejoin[d]er in their issue this week and will not I am sure." (Con. 183, BTW Papers, DLC.)

The *Conservator* later acquiesced somewhat in the matter of the NNBL. On Sept. 8, 1900, the paper ran a long public-relations article praising the NNBL meeting as the most outstanding black convention yet held in America. Albreta Moore Smith, prominent black clubwoman in Chicago and a vice-president of the NNBL, wrote the article. (Chicago *Conservator*, Sept. 8, 1900, Clipping, Con. 1032, BTW Papers, DLC.)

From Edgar Gardner Murphy

Montgomery, Ala., July 23, 1900

Dear Mr. Washington: You have probably seen by the press reports that Mixon is proceeding with his conference plans in spite of the best counsel of the wiser men of both races. I have pointed out to him that a constitutional convention in Alabama is inevitable, and that if there ever was a time in the history of the state when our colored people should not irritate unnecessarily the dominant white population, that time is with us now. I have also pointed out that the conference would work grave injustice to our local Negroes because it will be impossible to control the speakers. Men will come here who would not think of saying inflammatory things in their own towns, they will make statements which will excite the antagonism of our white people, and then they will take the train the following day and leave the colored people of Montgomery to "face the music." Moreover, what could be so unwise as to associate the cause of the colored man with Susan B. Anthony,[1] as Mixon is doing? Her appearance has been broadly heralded in the local press. The influence of such action in the South — the most intensely conservative section of our country — can well be imagined. I enclose to you two clippings — one from the Montgomery Evening Journal, and one from the Advertiser.[2] You probably know the relative standing of the papers.

I have written direct to Councill upon the subject, and I am assured by those who know him here that he has no idea of attending. One of the speakers selected for the program is a man whose reputation was so odious, that his own colored congregation ousted him under the gravest charges of immorality only a few years ago. All in all, the proceeding is most unfortunate for the colored race. I have done my utmost in every wise and practicable way to point this out to them, and yet I fear that my counsel has been attributed to motives other than the real ones. If the matter assumes any importance whatever in the general press, I earnestly advise that solely in the interest of your own people you will give the Associated Press an interview upon the subject. If the whole plan had been deliberately constructed in order to prejudice the interests of the colored people in the South, it could hardly have been more neatly fitted to that end.

I hope to see you while I am North this Summer, and you may address me after August 8th at the St. Cloud Hotel, 42nd St. & Broadway, New York City. I am, with kindest regards, Sincerely and Cordially,

Edgar Gardner Murphy

TLS Con. 182 BTW Papers DLC.

1 Susan B. Anthony did not attend Mixon's conference.
2 Emmett J. Scott wrote on the letter that no clippings were enclosed.

To Emmett Jay Scott

Roslindale, Mass., July 25th, 1900

Dear Mr. Scott: Please let me know what answer you have received from the American Publishing House in Chicago. The fraud which they have perpetrated is outrage[ou]s. I am going to take some means to have the circulation of the book stopped, at least, in its present form. Yours truly,

Booker T. Washington

TLS Con. 186 BTW Papers DLC.

From Emmett Jay Scott

Tuskegee, Ala., July 25–1900

Dear Mr. Washington: Please note how the Supreme Court Decision as regards Negro jurors[1] is working in Texas. These clippings are from Texas newspapers.[2] Our people in all sections of the South have recourse to this decision if they but knew it. Some movement should be put afoot to make it known throughout the country, as we are confessedly at all times the victims of narrow and prejudiced decisions from purely white juries. Perhaps it is too much to say

591

always, but nearly so at any rate. The race owes Wilford H. Smith of Galveston a debt of gratitude which it will never pay, as it pays none of those who labor & sacrifice in its behalf. Note the announcement of Judge Brooks of the Texas court of Appeals.[3] Yours Sincerely

Emmett J. Scott

ALS   Con. 1   BTW Papers   DLC.

1 Seth Carter *v.* Texas.

2 The unidentified clippings, both dated June 30, reported a reversal of the conviction of a black man, Robert Smith, who had been found guilty of murdering a white woman, on grounds that blacks had been excluded from the jury-selection process.

3 One of the clippings accompanying Scott's letter reported the remarks of Judge M. M. Brooks of the Texas Court of Criminal Appeals, who stated that his opinion in the Smith case had not changed, but he was compelled to follow the decision of the U.S. Supreme Court.

From Isaac Fisher

The Fabyan House, Fabyan, N.H., Aug. 7, 1900

Dear Mr. Washington: Our collection at the Twin Mountain House last night was only $6.58.

Atlanta University must be given credit for making her engagements at the most desirable places ahead of us. We seem to be following in the footsteps of the two young men who represent that school.

It seems pretty hard that fine young men — fairly respectable — working in a worthy cause, should give an entertainment for a school and receive $12, while *one* Negro, representing in every particular, the minstrel type, working for himself alone should receive for acting the fool and servile Negro the handsome sum of $40. That happened at this hotel. But it doesn't stop here. Every day we are made to understand that if there was less refinement about us and more fool, we would do better.

This fact often discourages my boys to such an extent that they are often willing to forget who they are and what they represent, and sing and act in accordance with the public demand so that they may compete with others who seem to be reaping a financial harvest. I have not allowed and will not allow this to be done. Do not think that I do not try to please the people. But when I have about three persons ask for the Plantation Songs and about four score ask that we dance and sing songs which tell of Negroes stealing chickens, I make no pretensions to try to please.

I want to express to you, here and now, my admiration of your happy faculty of working on amid so many discouragements, and further for your belief, not only in the philanthropic people of the country, but in the white race as a whole. I wish I could share that belief with you.[1] I take it, however, that that very belief on your part has differentiated you from the average Negro and contributed in no small degree to your success. You have my best wishes. Very friendly,

Isaac Fisher

ALS Con. 272 BTW Papers DLC.

[1] Fisher's discouragement surfaced early in the summer tour when he discovered that many northern hotels refused to accommodate the Tuskegee Singers. "I may be wrong," he wrote to Warren Logan from Connecticut, "but it seems that the people here are becoming more intolerant and out of patience with Negroes than formerly." He complained that it used to be hard to find accommodations for the singers in private homes but now the difficulty extended to hotels as well. "Notwithstanding previous engagements of rooms which I have made at hotels," he wrote, "five times already, I have been compelled to plead for accommodations on humanitarian grounds." He told Logan that on three occasions he was refused meals in dining rooms and had been asked to eat in the kitchen, which he refused to do. (June 23, 1900, Con. 172, BTW Papers, DLC.)

From Edgar Gardner Murphy

Chattanooga, Tenn., Aug 7 1900

Dear Mr. Washington: I have just read your N.A. Review article and I thank you for it. It is wise in spirit and admirable in matter and in statement.

The Negro Conference at Montgomery made a great deal of "fuss" locally, and locally did some harm, but I am glad it attained no national importance or significance. Councill approved it at first but as soon as he understood the situation he took an effective stand against it. I am sure it will do no permanent injury to the Negro or to the South.

I should like to have an informal and confidential conference with Mr. Ogden, Mr. Baldwin, yourself, and one or two others while in New York in reference to the impending Constitutional Convention in Alabama. My address is the St. Cloud Hotel, 42nd St. and Broadway. I shall be near New York from Aug. 12 to Sept. 15. Very Cordially

Edgar Gardner Murphy

ALS Con. 272 BTW Papers DLC.

An Interview in the Boston *Journal*

Boston, Aug. 11, 1900

Mr. Booker T. Washington, the Principal of Tuskegee Normal and Industrial Institute, in speaking to a Journal reporter about the approaching session of the National Negro Business League in Boston, said: "Those who are promoting this business league do not overlook the importance of seeing that the negro does not give up the struggle for retaining his citizenship. They are against the repeal of the 15th Amendment. They believe that the election laws throughout the country should be made to apply with equal justice to white and black alike. Thus if the franchise is restricted in any State there should be no loophole by which the ignorant white man can vote, and the ignorant negro be prevented from voting. While those who are at the head of this enterprise hold these views, at the same time they recognize the fact that in order to maintain citizenship and the respect of the nation, there must go along with these demands for equal justice, tangible indisputable signs of our progress. In a word, that deeds and words must go together. They believe that helping the negro along commercial lines will assist in settling his political status.

"This meeting is to be purely a business one, and not a political affair. Politics and other general matters are dealt with in the National Afro-American Council which meets in Indianapolis. It

594

would be a mistake to have the two bodies take up the same line of work. Both of these organizations are working in perfect harmony."

Boston *Journal*, Aug. 11, 1900, 4.

From Alexander Walters

Jersey City, N.J., 8–14 1900

My Dear Friend: Your kind letter has been received. I was glad to hear from you. I regret my inability to be present at the meeting of the Business League. I leave Saturday for Fon[d] du Lac Wisconsin where I hold conference next week. I shall remain there until I go to Indianapolis. I wish the cause success. Dont think for a moment that I believe you disloyal to our cause. There can be no conflict between the Afro-American Council and yourself. You are contending for the industrial development of the Negro, while we are contending for his civil and political rights. I am with you in your work and I believe you are with us in ours. We understand that you would take the same stand that we are taking but for your school. I am delighted to know that you expect to be with us at Indianapolis. The outlook for a large and profitable meeting is splendid. I desire to be remembered to your Madam. Wishing you health and *great* prosperity   I remain   yours Sincerely

A. Walters

ALS Con. 186 BTW Papers DLC.

From Charles L. Mitchell[1]

Port of Boston, Mass., August 16th 1900

Dear Mr. Washington— I am just in receipt of your letter postmarked Bar Harbor, Aug. 15th. Agreeable to instruction, I have enclosed cut, &c. to Mr. Taylor,[2] Editor of *Boston Post*.

Rain to-day? Yes! I do not wonder that even the elements are

595

moved to emotional tears at the perfidy of the self-laudation mal-
contents in council assembled.[3] However, their pop-gun boom-a-
rang missils can do harm to no one but themselves.

Keep the Old Ark of Progress "a-moverin," friend Washington.
It seems as if these birds of prey would never soar above the mist
of the low lands.

Practical Work, not *Visionary Theory* is the need of the hour.
Fraternally yours,

Chas. L. Mitchell

P.S. Mrs. Mitchell[4] will send the names of her selections to your
agent, Mr. P. Smith. *Will you see that she is properly advertised
and programed?*

ALS   Con. 179   BTW Papers   DLC.

[1] Charles L. Mitchell, a black man born in Connecticut in 1830, was reported in
the 1900 census as a clerk in the Boston customs house.

[2] William Taylor.

[3] A meeting at the A.M.E. Zion Church in Boston on the evening of Aug. 16, 1900,
saw a clash between pro- and anti-Bookerites. William Monroe Trotter led the anti-
Bookerites in condemning the founding of the NNBL. Trotter maintained that what
was needed was an organization to fight for black political rights, not a league of
businessmen. (Boston *Advertiser*, Aug. 17, 1900, 5; Boston *Herald*, Aug. 17, 1900, 7.)

[4] Nellie B. Mitchell, born in New Hampshire in 1850.

From J. Francis Robinson

Boston, Aug 17th 1900

My Dear Mr Washington: Our cause will not suffer an iota, because of the diabolical meeting of last night at Zion Church, by the
sore heads and Namby, Pamby, political scullions who have never
done a thing but shoot off their cheap talk, and resolved to dis-
solved. I return to Norwich to-day and expect to be here at the
opening of your meeting with two or more delegates. They will
stop with me. I hope you are well and prospering. Faithfully &
Enthuiastically Yours,

J. Francis Robinson

ALS   Con. 182   BTW Papers   DLC.

From Emmett Jay Scott

Tuskegee, Ala., August 18, 1900

Dear Mr Washington: We have all heard with sincere regret of Mr. Huntington's death. When the telegram came from Mr. Miles asking to be present at the Huntington funeral I sent same to you at Roslindale by wire & also sent a note to the Advertiser. Doubtless you saw the item as marked on first page of paper. I sent it to you. Today I am glad to note that you were at the Funeral. The Advertiser makes note of your presence in headline. On first page you will also note the wire from Paris giving summary of awards & that Tuskegee gets one of the first prizes for Industrial Education Exhibit. This is gratifying & to you especially I am sure. With reference to Mr. Huntington's will I suspect we'll hardly be represented since he has done so much for the school lately. Even if he shouldn't remember us we all know how interested in our work he was & that he gave to it splendidly during his lifetime.

With reference to the Charleston matter about which you are kind enough to write, beg to say that I feel as I expressed to you in my other letter that I only wanted to serve *you* best, and I really have *no desire* either way, tho' now, since I have thought about it more, I rather suspect I shall prefer to remain here no matter what *your* decision, as to acceptance of place offered *you*. With best wishes for your health during this heated season & for the success of the League, I am, Yours sincerely

Emmett J. Scott

ALS   Con. 181   BTW Papers   DLC.

From Luella Linegar[1]

Creal Springs, Ills. Aug. 19–1900

Dear Sir: Having read much of the grand work you & your noble wife are doing for your race makes me feel that I must tell you of something that will help them more than anything on earth.

I am told that you take no interest in politics but I hope that is

597

not true. While the old parties are corrupt — too corrupt for any christian to support, there is a new one that proposes to change the competitive system which is an incentive to almost every form of corruption, into the co-operative system under which all people will be ennobled & uplifted, for it will mean the "brotherhood of man." We are all brothers white, black, or any other color.

This new party is the Social Democratic party. E. V. Debs[2] is ca[n]didate for president on this ticket. He was misunderstood by many in the Pul[l]man strike who have since learned to honor him. In the last 2 years he has lectured before the students of many of the leading universities of the U.S. He is a wonderful man but socialists are not man worshipers because they believe that while man is fallible, principles are eternal. Hero worship is a striking feature of the old parties. It is easier to do that than study into new things for benefit of humanity.

My father was an intimate personal friend of President Lincoln. In '60 he campaigned Southern Illinois as a republican candidate for congress, in joint debate with Gen. Jno. A. Logan who then declared that he would suffer his right arm to wither & die at his side before he would raise it against the South.

My father was always in public life. I know enough about politics to know that if any one has religion there is no better place to put it than in politics.

I received a sample copy of the "Social Age" which announced that you would contribute to it. I am sorry to say I have not seen your contribution. This periodical contained a number of socialistic articles, not all so labeled — but truly socialistic. I hope you & Mrs. Washington will investigate socialism & espouse it. You surely would if you knew how uplifting & ennobling it is.

I know that you have much reading & work to do but I implore you, if you have not already done so, to read Bel[l]amy's two famous books "Looking Backward" & its sequel, "Equality." These books give a word picture of what life would be under socialism — gives the socialists ideal.

"Socialism from Genesis to Revelations," by Sprague is fine, also, Grülund's "Co-operative Commonwealth" & H. D. Lloyd's "Wealth vs. Commonwealth." These books make a fine foundation to a socialist library. I have read dozens & consider them the best. There is a little 10c. pamphlet, published "Uncle Sam in Business" by

Kerr & Co., Chicago, which is very fine. It tells how to make the transformation.

I write this letter to you because you are a leader among your people & I believe with the highest purposes in your soul you mean to lead them to the highest human attainments & I believe you have great power to do so. You will find socialism the wholesale method of doing the highest & best possible things. It has the advantage, too of being a world wide movement. "Equality" speaks of the negro under socialism.

By this mail I send you some socialist papers & pamphlets which I hope you will read & induce as many others to read as possible. I hope you will not only subscribe for the "Appeal," but will take subscriptions for it. The remuneration is good. Also induce others to do so. I have no more financial interest in this paper than you have.

Under socialism there could be no such thing as deserving poor.

The 2nd chapter of Acts is full of socialist texts generally evaded by preachers who do not preach the full gospel. Yours for the uplifting of your race & mine,

(Miss) Luella Linegar

P.S. Skilled labor is highly satisfactory but under competition it will fall to the present price of unskilled when it becomes universal.

I am not a "party slave." I turn my coat as often as I find it on the wrong side. I intend to be a socialist until I find something better.

ALS Con. 178 BTW Papers DLC.

1 Luella Linegar of Creal Springs, Ill., was a single white woman, age thirty, who lived with her widowed mother and sister.

2 Eugene Victor Debs (1855-1926), American socialist and labor leader, organized the Socialist Democratic Party of America in 1897, and was Socialist candidate for president five times beginning in 1900. While Debs publicly championed equal opportunity for black workers, his mild racism was evident in his fondness for dialect jokes about blacks. When Debs announced the formation of the American Railway Union in 1893, its constitution stated that the union was for whites only.

Debs took a dim view of BTW's way of solving the race problem. "Mr. Washington is backed by the plutocrats of the country clear up, or down, to Grover Cleveland," Debs wrote. "They furnish the means that support his institute, and if it were conducted with a view to opening the Negro's eyes and emancipating him from the system of wage slavery which robs him while it fattens his masters, not another dollar would be subscribed for the Negro's industrial education." Debs also objected to Washington's meekness and humility, and asked: "When did he ever advise his race to stand erect, to act together as one, to assert their united power, to hold up their heads like self-reliant, self-respecting men and hew out their way from the swamps of slavery to the highlands of freedom?" (Quoted in Cleveland *Gazette*, Sept. 12, 1903, 1.)

From Thomas Junius Calloway

Paris, August 23, 1900

Dear Mr. Washington; The International Jury of Awards has announced its medals, and to the Tuskegee Institute is awarded a gold medal, and to yourself personally a silver medal.

There were a total of fifteen awards that came within the scope of the Negro Exhibit, of which one was a "Grand Prix" upon the entire collection. Very truly,

Thos. J. Calloway
Special Agent Negro Exhibit

TLS Con. 168 BTW Papers DLC. Written on stationery of the U.S. Commission to the Paris Exposition of 1900.

A Speech before the
National Negro Business League

[Boston, Mass., Aug. 23, 1900]

Ladies and Gentlemen of the Convention: I feel almost ashamed to occupy any portion of your valuable time in any general remarks this morning. Whatever degree of success may attend this meeting will be very largely due to the loyal and faithful work of the Local Committee in the city of Boston, who have stood by for a number of days, and for more nights, planning the work of this organization; and I am sure that you join with me in giving this Local Committee the most hearty thanks. (Applause.)

In the first place, the programme which is before you is far from perfect. It is perhaps far from satisfactory. It is not possible to have all the states represented on the programme. It is not even possible to have many important organizations represented that we should like very much to have represented. It is not possible to have as many persons speak from the platform as the committee desired to have speak; but I am sure that all of you will feel that in the first meeting it is hardly possible to have that degree of acquaintance with the individual members of the convention which would enable us to have the most perfect programme.

I very much hope that each one who speaks will understand it is very necessary that the addresses, the papers, be short; that they be just as compact as possible. I hope also that there will be no restraint; that you will speak out plainly and openly regardless of rhetoric, and regardless of mere grammatical forms. There is a story to the effect that the Boston people never have a public hearing of any bad grammar; that whenever a stranger comes to Boston with some bad grammar attached to him, that when he speaks the winds very softly and gently waft his language out into the harbor and the words return to the Boston audience perfectly purified. (Laughter and applause.)

One object of this organization of business men and women, as I understand it, is to bring together annually those of our race who are engaged in various branches of business, from the humblest to the highest, for the purpose of closer personal acquaintance, of receiving encouragement, inspiration and information from each other. The other object is to originate plans by which local business organizations will be formed in all parts of our country, where such organization can be made to serve the best interest of the race.

This organization does not overlook the fact that mere material possessions are not, and should not be made, the chief end of life, but should be made as a means of aiding us in securing our rightful place as citizens, and of enlarging our opportunities for securing that education and development which enhance our usefulness and produce that tenderness and goodness of heart which will make us live for the benefit of our fellow-men, and for the promotion of our country's highest welfare.

I have faith in the timeliness of this organization. As I have noted the conditions of our people in nearly every part of our country, I have always been encouraged by the fact that almost without exception, whether in the North or in the South, wherever I have seen a black man who was succeeding in business, who was a taxpayer, and who possessed intelligence and high character, that individual was treated with the highest respect by the members of the white race. In proportion as we can multiply these examples North and South will our problem be solved. Let every Negro strive to become the most useful and indispensable man in his community. (Applause.) A useless, shiftless, idle class is a menace and a danger to any community. When an individual produces what the world wants, whether it is a product of hand, head or heart, the world does not long stop to inquire what is the color of the skin of the producer. (Applause.)

This meeting will prove a great encouragement to our people in all parts of the country, bringing together, as it does, the men and women of our race who have been most successful in life. The most humble black boy will be made to feel what you have done he can do also.

We must not in any part of our country become discouraged, notwithstanding the way often seems dark and desolate; we must maintain faith in ourselves and in our country. No race ever got upon its feet without a struggle, trial and discouragement. The very struggles through which we often pass give us strength and experience that in the end will prove helpful. Every individual and every race that has succeeded has had to pay the price which nature demands from all. We cannot get something for nothing. Every member of the race who succeeds in business, however humble and simple that business may be, because he has learned the important lessons of cleanliness, promptness, system, honesty and progressiveness, is contributing his share in smoothing the pathway for this and succeeding generations. For the sake of emphasis, I repeat that no one can long succeed unless we keep in mind the important elements of cleanliness, promptness, system, honesty and progressiveness.

In conclusion, may I add that we shall succeed in our purpose in this organization just in proportion as each individual member is able to forget himself, to hide himself behind the great cause which has brought us together. Let us not lay too much stress upon "points of order" and useless parliamentary machinery, which often occupies valuable time and prevents our accomplishing the real purpose for which organizations are formed.

I want to congratulate you upon the fact that thirty-five years after our freedom so large a body of representative business men and women of the race have assembled in the city of Boston, a city dear to every Negro in all parts of our land. I want to congratulate you that we find ourselves in the home of Garrison, Phillips (applause), Shaw, George L. Stearns and a host of others, and I believe that on this sacred soil, guided and encouraged by the memory of those who have lived and died for us, we shall form an organization which will prove potential in the lifting up of the race in all parts of our country. No matter under what conditions we may find ourselves surrounded, may we ever keep in mind that the law which recognizes and rewards merit, no matter under what skin found, is universal and eternal, and can no more be nullified than we can stop the life-giving influence of the daily sun.

Having a notice from the Local Committee, I will now proceed to introduce the next speaker on the programme, who is a successful real estate dealer, who comes to us from the state of Virginia. I have great pleasure in introducing Mr. Giles B. Jackson of Richmond, Va., who will speak upon the subject of real estate.

NNBL, *Proceedings, 1900* (Boston: J. R. Hamm, 1901), 24–27. An autograph draft is in Con. 961, BTW Papers, DLC.

The Closing Address before the
National Negro Business League

[Boston, Mass., Aug. 24, 1900]

Ladies and Gentlemen: At this late hour it would be a decided imposition for me to make any extended remarks. That, I promise you, I shall not do. I simply rise for the purpose of emphasizing the thanks of this organization to the citizens of Boston for their very generous hospitality, and especially I thank the members of the Local Committee, who have stood by this effort by night and by day and have made it the success which has attended it; and I am sure that this whole audience, including not only the delegates, but the visitors, joins with me in extending a hearty unanimous vote of thanks to Mr. Louis F. Baldwin,[1] who has stood at the helm of this convention as the Chairman. (Applause.) I am sure that we shall go away from here with it in our minds that we for once have seen a model chairman of a meeting (applause), and we are grateful to Mr. Baldwin and to you that we have not heard a single "point of order" from the beginning to the end of the meeting. It is sometimes said that the Negroes cannot come together; that they cannot unite in praiseworthy effort and hold meetings as we have tried to hold these during the last two days. This has been a demonstration of the fact that it is possible for colored men to come together and conduct themselves in a fitting and praiseworthy manner. (Applause.) The thing that has given me most encouragement, and I may add most surprise, from the beginning to the ending of this meeting, is the manly, straightforward tone which all of you have used in the description of your work and in the description of the communities where you live. We haven't heard a single "baby cry" from the beginning to the ending of this meeting. We haven't heard any complaints; we haven't heard any man asking for quarter because of his color or because of his location. All that has been said here has been straightforward, manly and praiseworthy.

My friends, I must not detain you longer, but I must make a single request, and that is that you take the spirit of this meeting into your homes, to your immediate localities; that you take the resolutions which you will find printed and distributed, plenty of them here, to your own homes; that you take the spirit of this meeting, the suggestions that the committee have put in print, and that in each community you try to plant the spirit to form an organization that will result in the employment of the colored people where you live. I believe that the spirit of this meeting will go into every portion of our country, and where there has been disunion, and where there has been lukewarmness, in the future there will be union and a hearty support for all these efforts that look forward to the upbuilding of our people. Let us in our communities come together and throw aside this spirit of jealousy. Let us, no matter what business we are engaged in, meet the brother from across the street — meet and shake hands together and stand together in the community. I believe that next year you will come with larger numbers, with stronger reports; and I believe that through this organization will be put on foot a spirit that shall make us feel that notwithstanding color we can succeed; that we can grow and be a people right here in America. (Applause.) We must not grow discouraged, my friends; we must keep up our spirits; and I hope you will teach to your boys and girls, when you return home, that right here about them are opportunities through which they can rise to manhood and womanhood. As Mr. Garrison[2] said last night, "Who will take the job of keeping down, repressing such an audience as this?" There is no force on earth that can keep back a people continually getting education, light, intelligence, property and Christian character. In our efforts to rise we may for a while have obstacles cast in our pathway; we may be inconvenienced, but we can never be defeated in our purpose. (Applause.)

I thank you, ladies and gentlemen, again for your interest in this meeting, for your hearty support, and the citizens of Boston for their generous hospitality. (Applause.)

NNBL, *Proceedings, 1900* (Boston: J. R. Hamm, 1901), 213–14.

1 Louis F. Baldwin, born in Massachusetts in 1865, was a real estate broker residing in Cambridge.
2 Francis Jackson Garrison.

To Emmett Jay Scott

Boston Mass   8/24 1900

Meeting overwhelming success beyond expectation every-one pronounced it best race conference ever held three hundred delegates present & from thirty states most greateful to you & Mr Lee

Booker T. Washington

HWSr   Con. 540   BTW Papers   DLC.

To the Editor of the New York *Tribune*

Tuskegee, Ala., Aug. 26, 1900

Sir: Since the death of Collis P. Huntington, I have been much interested in reading what has been said about his life.

For more than ten years it was my privilege to know Mr. Huntington and to come in close contact with him. Perhaps because I was a member of another and unfortunate race, who had no claims upon him, gave me an opportunity to really know the higher and better life of the man better than some others. The first time I saw Mr. Huntington he gave me $2 for our school at Tuskegee; the last time I saw him he gave me $50,000 toward the endowment of our school. Mr. Huntington not only aided our school at Tuskegee financially, but he took a deep and personal interest not only in the Hampton and Tuskegee schools, as well as others, but in the entire negro race.

Many times when I have met him at his home or at his office I have wondered how a man who was burdened with such tremendous responsibilities could find the time to talk with me at so great a length about the welfare of our school and the race. Often I have gone to his office in the midst of his most busy days, and he would spend an hour in getting information and giving advice regarding the elevation of the negro race. He not only did this, but I received from him many long letters, in which he took the greatest pains to point out the best way for the conduct of our school and the education of the race. When travelling in the South, in his private car, he could always be approached by the most humble black man.

To me his heart always seemed as tender as that of a child, and I never went to him for anything that he thought our school at Tuskegee needed that he did not assist in securing. Only a short while before he died he learned in some way that the work at Tuskegee would be made more efficient if we could secure an additional boiler and engine. As soon as he learned this he told me that he wanted to provide these for us. In order to be sure that we secured just what was needed, he gave his personal attention to seeing that the proper boiler and engine were bought and shipped to us.

At another time, when I called to see him at his country home, when he learned that I had walked from the station to his house, he had his carriage got ready, and drove me himself to the station when I returned. So I could continue relating incident after incident that to me showed the greatness and goodness as well as the simplicity of this rare man.

It does not cost much effort or goodness of heart to treat well those who are our equals in wealth and social standing, but it seems to me the true test of the man comes when he is thrown in contact

with those who are his inferiors. In the death of Collis P. Huntington my race has lost a great, wise and true friend.

Booker T. Washington

New York *Tribune*, Aug. 31, 1900, 9.

An Address Honoring Washington

Boston Mass. Aug. 26th 1900

My Dear and Kind Sir — It becomes my pleasant duty and it is an
honor for me to present you a token[1] that in silent tones bespeaks
not only the appreciation of the Alabama Delegation but which
bespeaks the appreciation of the American people, North, South,
east and West.

We revere and adore you for the manly, wise and determined
position that you have taken in the world to lead your people from
that low and despised position and condition to a plane of moral
elevation, industrial elevation, intellectual elevation and religious
elevation which are essentials to all progressive, successful and eminent people.

We stand to-day a pillar under your arms to support you, stand
by you, revere and honor you: so long as you continue in the common sense line of leader-ship, that you have so long and nobly
followed. We support you, not after trying to kill you. Jealousy often arises in rivalry. It has arisen in yours. You were forced to the
front by the people, because of the natural, common sense and that
indominable will power of yours, which are also essentials to all
worthy and true leaders.

You stand to-day in the brilliant rays of natural beauty and lus-
ter — guiding, directing the course of the American Negro, and
may this little token be the crowning feature of the National Negro
Business League, and when God in his Alwise Providence, sees fit to
call you from labor to reward, may Angles in the presence [of] God
witness the erection of that super-Natural mon[u]ment; that material mon[u]ment to your honor as a leader, statesman, educator
and liberator of an oppressed, but magnificent race.

L. L. Burwell,[2] MD

AMS   Con. 167   BTW Papers   DLC.

1 A gold fountain pen.

2 Lincoln Laconia Burwell, born on a farm in Marengo County, Ala., graduated from Alabama Baptist Normal and Theological School (Selma University) in 1886 and from Leonard Medical College of Shaw University three years later. Returning to Selma to practice medicine, Burwell established a drugstore so that blacks would have a place to buy medicine and meet socially. During the Spanish-American War he raised a small contingent of men for the 3rd Alabama Volunteers. He was a member of the board of trustees of Selma University and a founder of an infirmary for blacks.

From Samuel Laing Williams

Chicago, Aug. 27th 1900

My dear Mr. Washington: I have received all of your notes with enclosures since I last wrote you. I now have in hand what I believe to be the full correspondence that passed between the American Publishing House and yourself in relation to the book in question.

After studying the correspondence quite thoroughly it is my judgement that the most you can insist upon are some of the changes indicated in my last letter.

I had quite a long conference with the attorney on the other side and he assured me that these can be made, except your picture on the outside of the book. In fact the Company already has ordered new dies for the back of the book so that your name is not used as the sole contributor. Their attorney has further assured me that the chapters will be so arranged as to show exactly where your contribution begins and ends. They are not willing to take your picture from the outside of the book, and from your letters giving your consent to the use of your picture "in" the book, I am afraid you could not legally compel them to yield this point. While your picture on the outside of the book does give you a great deal of prominence as having something to do with the publication, your letters do not show that you prohibited its use in this way. Your consent to the use of your picture seems to be without positive restrictions and their contention is that it was done with deference to your popularity just as the pictures of prominent men have been used on other publications.

It occurs to me that the picture on the outside is of less importance as bearing on the question of authorship than the entitling. If they make the other changes I have suggested and insisted upon, I believe that you have gained all that it would be possible to get by a law suit.

The Nichols people came in to see me, but I was out. He left a note and I sent to him the letter from you to me which he wanted.

I did not think it advisable to show him all of your correspondence. The letters to the American Publishing House dated Nov. 29th—1898 and Jan. 16th—1899 might be construed by them as not sufficiently regardful of your contract with them.

Permit me to further advise you that if you write a letter which may be used by the Nichols Co. with their agents, that it is so worded as to show just the facts of your connection with "The New Negro For A New Century." The use of such terms as "To deceive the public" and criticisms of their method of publishing the book after changes have been made may involve you in some difficulties.

I have already told Mr. Hertel to be careful about this, for your protection and I shall further caution him.

I will write again in a few days after I have had a further conference with the Attorney on the other side. Very sincerely yours

S. Laing Williams

TLS Con. 187 BTW Papers DLC.

From Peter Jefferson Smith, Jr.

Indianapolis, Ind., Aug 28th 1900

My dear Mr Washington Here I am. I have seen Fortune and placed in his hands $40.00 forty dollars.

Things seem to be going along smoothly so far and I hope will so continue. White, Lyons, Pledger Col Lewis of New Orleans Dancey, Bishop Walters Clinton,[1] Harris[2] and other great Negroes are here and so a hot time is expected. Many inquirers after you. Fortune says keep away from here, by all means.[3] Scarborough is. There is talk of running White from North Carolina for President of the Council. What think you? I think it will be hard to defeat him (I mean Walters). I am with Fortune on the Com. on Address to the Country and resolutions and we are to receive resolutions before they are read to the meeting. Now Mr Washington I am oblige to ask you to send me not less than $25.00 as I find I can not possibly get through with what you gave me; in reckoning you seem to have forgotten that there are other expenses beside traveling. As for instance sleeping car travel and hotel bill even ½ rate over those roads on which I have rates it cost $28.25 so you see I have not enough left to get my return ticket to say nothing of the $5.00 which [I] had to pay to be admitted to the floor.

I shall use economy and judgment in the use of funds.

Please send to me here at once. So that I may not have that [to] worry about. Faithfully yours

P. J. Smith Jr

ALS   Con. 184   BTW Papers   DLC.

¹ George Wylie Clinton.

² Cicero Richardson Harris, an A.M.E. Zion bishop, was born in Fayetteville, N.C., in 1844. He taught at Livingstone College from 1882 to 1886. He was business manager of the *Star of Zion* (1882-84) and general secretary of the A.M.E. Zion Church (1882-88).

³ BTW addressed the Afro-American Council meeting on Aug. 31, 1900, but kept his remarks and his visit brief. (See John Coburn to BTW, Sept. 3, 1900, below.)

To the Editor of the New Orleans *Times-Democrat*

Tuskegee, Alabama, August 29th, 1900

Dear Sir: In the discussion of the change of the course of study in the Colored Public Schools of New Orleans, I think my own position in regard to the education of our people is somewhat misunderstood.

I believe thoroughly in hand training or industrial education for the masses of our people, but at the same time there should go along with industrial training the most thorough training of the heart and head. No race can be made safe and useful until its mind is awakened and strengthened. Manual or industrial training is now being introduced into the public schools of all the large cities throughout the North and West; at the same time there goes with this kind of training the proper training of the mind. The South has nothing to fear from the thoroughly educated Negro. Those who give trouble in many cases are those who have received merely a smattering of book education. There are very few examples of where a black man has been given a thorough education and that he has been guilty of committing crime or inciting riot. In fact, in most every case it has been the calm, self-controlled, conservative, educated leaders who have exercised a wise control of the element given to crime and notorious conduct.

Ignorance in the end is always more costly to the State or Nation than intelligence.

Intelligence and morality combined with a spirit of thrift and industry, is what is wanted, it seems to me. While the child is being given book education at the same time, let him be given such manual training, when practicable, that he will not only be able to earn his living, but will get that spirit in him which will make him love labor and despise idleness, and the individual will not become a loafer on the public streets.

Since the colored people are going to be educated, it is far better that it should be done in the public schools, controlled by the State and City authorities, than that they be left almost wholly to be educated by means supplied from a distance. It is always wiser, it seems to me, to let the colored people feel that in a large measure they are indebted to their own state and community for their education than to have them feel that they are wholly obligated to foreign money and foreign influences.

Referring to another subject, I note that many occurrences in connection with the recent race riots in New York City have been exaggerated and unwarranted conclusions have been drawn.[1] I happened to be in New York during these riots, and they were largely inspired by the most ignorant and degraded element, very largely foreigners; and these riots no more represent the sentiment existing towards the Negro in New York by the educated and property-holding element in that city, than that the best element of white people of New Orleans were responsible for the race riots in that city.[2]

In my opinion, the outbreak in New York City was one of those periodical occurrences which must take place in a population that is so mixed and complex as is that of the United States.

Booker T. Washington

TLSr Con. 187 BTW Papers DLC. The letter was addressed to the New Orleans *Times*, even though the *Times* had merged to become the *Times-Democrat* in 1881. It was not published.

1 The Tenderloin district of New York City exploded into racial violence on several nights in mid-Aug. 1900. Spurred by an incident in which a recent black migrant to the city had killed a policeman, mobs of whites roamed the streets beating blacks. The police force, mostly Irish, often did little to protect black citizens, and in some cases policemen actually led the mobs in their search for victims. While the worst was over by Aug. 16, tensions ran high for weeks and hardly a day went by in the district without some racially inspired fight. (See Osofsky, *Harlem*, 46-52.)

2 On the night of July 25, 1900, white lynch mobs roamed the streets of New Orleans in search of blacks to avenge the death of two New Orleans police officers who were killed two days earlier by a black man. Several blacks were wounded and four were killed before racial tension subsided. (New Orleans *Picayune*, July 26, 1900, 1, 7, 9; New Orleans *Times-Democrat*, July 26, 1900, 1, 9.)

An Article in the *North American Review*

[August 1900]

EDUCATION WILL SOLVE THE RACE PROBLEM
A REPLY

"Will Education Solve the Race Problem?" is the title of an interesting article in the June number of The North American Review, by Professor John Roach Straton,[1] of Macon, Georgia. My own belief is that education will finally solve the race problem. In giving some reasons for this faith, I wish to express my appreciation of the sincere and kindly spirit in which Professor Straton's article is written. I grant that much that he emphasizes as to present conditions is true. When we recall the past, these conditions could not be expected to be otherwise; but I see no reason for discouragement or loss of faith. When I speak of education as a solution for the race problem, I do not mean education in the narrow sense, but education which begins in the home and includes training in industry and in habits of thrift, as well as mental, moral and religious discipline, and the broader education which comes from contact with the public sentiment of the community in which one lives. Nor do I confine myself to the education of the negro. Many persons, in discussing the effect that education will have in working out the negro question, overlook the helpful influence that will ultimately come through the broader and more generous education of all the race elements of the South. As all classes of whites in the South become more generally educated in the broader sense, race prejudice will be tempered and they will assist in lifting up the black man.

In our desire to see a better condition of affairs, we are too often inclined to grow impatient because a whole race is not elevated in a short time, very much as a house is built. In all the history of mankind there have been few such radical, social and economic changes in the policy of a nation as have been effected within thirty-five years in this country, with respect to the change of four million and a half of slaves into four million and a half of freemen (now nearly ten million). When all the conditions of the past are considered, and compared with the present, I think the White South, the North and the Negro are to be congratulated on the fact that conditions are no worse, but are as encouraging as they are. The sudden change from slavery to freedom, from restraint to liberty, was a tremendous one; and the wonder is, not that the negro has not done better, but that he has done as well as he has. Every thoughtful student of the subject expected that the first two or three generations of freedom would lead to excesses and mistakes on the part of the negro, which would in many cases cause moral and physical degeneration, such as would seem to the superficial observer to indicate conditions that could not be overcome. It was to be anticipated that, in the first generation at least, the tendency would be, among a large number, to seek the shadow instead of the substance; to grasp after the mere signs of the highest civilization instead of the reality; to be led into the temptation of believing that they could secure, in a few years, that which it has taken other races thousands of years to obtain. Any one who has the daily opportunity of studying the negro at first hand cannot but gain the impression that there are indisputable evidences that the negro throughout the country is settling down to a hard, common sense view of life; that he is fast learning that a race, like an individual, must pay for everything it gets — the price of beginning at the bottom of the social scale and gradually working up by natural processes to the highest civilization. The exaggerated impressions that the first years of freedom naturally brought are giving way to an earnest, practical view of life and its responsibilities.

Let us take a broad, generous survey of the negro race as it came into the country, represented by twenty savages, in 1619, and trace its progress through slavery, through the Civil War period, and through freedom to the present moment. Who will be brave enough to say that the negro race, as a whole, has not increased in numbers and grown stronger mentally, morally, religiously, industrially, and in the accumulation of property? In a word, has not the negro, at every stage, shown a tendency to grow into harmony with the best type of American civilization?

Professor Straton lays special stress upon the moral weakness of the race. Perhaps the worst feature of slavery was that it prevented the development of a family life, with all of its far-reaching significance. Except in rare cases, the uncertainties of domicile made family life, during two hundred and fifty years of slavery, an impossibility. There is no institution so conducive to right and high habits of physical and moral life as the home. No race starting in absolute poverty could be expected, in the brief period of thirty-five years, to purchase homes and build up a family life and influence that would have a very marked impression upon the life of the masses. The negro has not had time enough to collect the broken and scattered members of his family. For the sake of illustration, and to employ a personal reference, I do not know who my own father was; I have no idea who my grandmother was; I have or had uncles, aunts and cousins, but I have no knowledge as to where most of them now are. My case will illustrate that of hundreds of thousands of black people in every part of our country. Perhaps those who direct attention to the negro's moral weakness, and compare his moral progress with that of the whites, do not consider the influence of the memories which cling about the old family homestead upon the character and aspirations of individuals. The very fact that the white boy is conscious that, if he fails in life, he will disgrace the whole family record, extending back through many generations, is of tremendous value in helping him to resist temptations. On the other hand, the fact that the individual has behind him and surrounding him proud family history and connections serves as a stimulus to make him overcome obstacles, when striving for success. All this should be taken into consideration, to say nothing of the physical, mental and moral training which individuals of the white race receive in their homes. We must not pass judgment upon the negro too soon. It requires centuries for the influence of home, school, church and public contact to permeate the mass of millions of people, so that the upward tendency may be apparent to the casual observer. It is too soon to decide what effect general education will have upon the rank and file of the negro race, because the masses have not been educated.

Throughout the South, especially in the Gulf States, the great bulk of the black population lives in the country districts. In these districts the schools are rarely in session more than three months of the year. When this is considered, in connection with poor teachers, poor school-houses, and an almost entire lack of apparatus, it is obvious that we must wait longer before we can judge, even approximately, of the effect that general education will have upon the whole population. Most writers and speakers upon the subject of the negro's non-progressiveness base their arguments upon alleged facts and statistics of the life of negroes in the large cities. This is hardly fair. Before the Civil War the negro was not, to any considerable extent, a denizen of the large cities. Most of them lived on the plantations. The negro living in the cities has undergone two marked changes: (1.) the change from slavery to freedom; (2.) the change from country life to city life. At first the tendency of both these changes was, naturally, to unsettle, to intoxicate and to lead the negro to wrong ideas of life. The change from country life to city life, in the case of the white man, is about as marked as in the case of the negro. The average negro in the city, with all of its excitements and temptations, has not lived there more than half a generation. It is, therefore, too soon to reach a definite conclusion as to what the permanent effect of this life upon him will be. This, I think, explains the difference between the moral condition of the negro, to which Professor Straton refers, in the States where there has been little change in the old plantation life, as compared with that in the more northern of the Atlantic States, where the change from country to city life is more marked.

Judging from close observation, my belief is that, after the negro has overcome the false idea which city life emphasizes, two or three generations will bring about an earnestness and steadiness of purpose which do not now generally obtain. As the negro secures a home in the city, learns the lessons of industry and thrift and becomes a taxpayer, his moral life improves. The influence of home surroundings, of the school, the church and public sentiment will be more marked and have a more potent effect in causing him to withstand temptations. But, notwithstanding the shortness of the time which the negro has had in which to get schooled to his new life, any one who has visited the large cities of Europe will readily testify that the visible signs of immorality in those cities are far greater than among the colored people of America. Prostitution for gain is far more prevalent in the cities of Europe than among the colored people of our cities.

Professor Straton says that the negro has degenerated in morals since he became free; in other words, that his condition in this respect is not as hopeful as it was during the early period of slavery. I do not think it wise to place too much reliance upon such a view of the matter, because there are too few facts upon which to base a comparison. The bald statement that the negro was not given to crime during slavery proves little. Slavery represented an unnatural condition of life, in which certain physical checks were kept constantly upon the individual. To say that the negro was at his best, morally, during the period of slavery is about the same as to say that the two thousand prisoners in the State prison and the city penal institutions in the city of Boston are the most righteous two thousand people in Boston. I question whether one can find two thousand persons in Boston who will equal these two thousand imprisoned criminals in the mere negative virtues. During the days of slavery the negro was rarely brought into the court to be tried for crime; hence, there was almost no public record of crimes committed by him. Each master, in most cases, punished his slave as he thought best, and as little as possible was said about it outside of his little plantation world. The improper relations between the sexes, with which the black race is now frequently charged in most sections of the South, were encouraged or winked at, under the slavery system, because of the financial value of the slaves. A custom that was fostered for three centuries cannot be blotted out in one generation.

In estimating the progress of a race, we should not consider alone the degree of success which has been actually attained, but also the obstacles which have been overcome in reaching that success. Judged by the obstacles overcome, few races, if any, in history have made progress commensurate with that of the colored people of the United States, in the same length of time. It may be conceded that the present generation of colored people does not compare favorably with the present generation of the white race, because of the reasons I have already given, and the further reason that on account of the black man's poverty of means to employ lawyers to have his case properly appealed to the higher courts, and his inability to furnish bonds, his criminal record is much worse than that of the white race, both in the Northern and Southern States. The Southern States, as a whole, have not yet reached a point where they are able to provide reformatories for juvenile offenders, and consequently most of these are sent to the State prison, where the records show that the same individuals are often committed over and over again, because, in the first instance, the child prisoner, instead of being reformed, becomes simply hardened to prison life. In the North, it is true, the negro has the benefit of the reformatories; but the unreasonable prejudice which prevents him from securing employment in the shops and the factories more than offsets this advantage. Hundreds of negroes in the North become criminals who would become strong and useful men if they were not discriminated against as bread winners.

In the matter of assault upon white women, the negro is placed in a peculiar attitude. While this vile crime is always to be condemned in the strongest language, and should be followed by the severest legal punishment, yet the custom of lynching a negro when he is accused of committing such a crime calls the attention of the whole country to it, in such a way as is not always true in the case of a white man, North or South. Any one who reads the daily papers carefully knows that such assaults are constantly charged against white men in the North and in the South; but, because the white man, in most cases, is punished by the regular machinery of the courts, attention is seldom attracted to his crime outside of the immediate neighborhood where the offense is committed. This, to say nothing of the cases where the victim of lynch law could prove his innocence, if he were given a hearing before a cool, level-headed set of jurors in open court, makes the apparent contrast unfavorable to the black man. It is hardly proper, in summing up the value of any race, to dwell almost continually upon its weaker element. As other men are judged, so should the negro be judged, by the best that the race can produce, rather than by the worst. Keep the searchlight constantly focused upon the criminal and worthless element of any people, and few among all the races and nations of the world can be accounted successful. More attention should be directed to individuals who have succeeded, and less to those who have failed. And negroes who have succeeded grandly can be found in every corner of the South.

I doubt that much reliance can safely be placed upon mere ability to read and write a little as a means of saving any race. Education should go further. One of the weaknesses in the negro's present condition grows out of failure, in the early years of his freedom, to teach him, in connection with thorough academic and religious branches, the dignity and beauty of labor, and to give him a working knowledge of the industries by which he must earn a subsistence. But the main question is: What is the present tendency of the race, where it has been given a fair opportunity, and where there has been thorough education of hand, head and heart? This question I answer from my own experience of nineteen years in the heart of the South, and from my daily contact with whites and blacks. In the first place, the social barrier prevents most white people from coming into real contact with the higher and better side of the negro's social life. The negro loafer, drunkard and gambler can be seen without social contact. The higher life cannot be seen without social contact. As I write these lines, I am in the home of a negro friend, where in the matter of cleanliness, sweetness, attractiveness, modern conveniences and other evidences of intelligence, morality and culture the home would compare favorably with that of any white family in the neighborhood; and yet, this negro home is unknown outside of the little town where it exists. To really know the life of this family, one would have to become a part of it for days, as I have been. One of the most encouraging changes that have taken place in the moral life of the negro race in the past thirty years is the creation of a growing public sentiment which draws a line between the good and bad, the clean and unclean. This change is fast taking place in every part of the country. It is one that cannot be accurately measured by any table of statistics. To be able to appreciate it fully, one must himself be a part of the social life of the race. The significance of it is all the more important when it is remembered that, only a few years ago, the colored woman who sustained immoral relations with some white man was envied and looked upon as a social leader. There are now few communities in the South where such a woman is recognized in the social life of the best colored people. This change is yet far from complete, but the tendency is strongly in this direction, and is growing and broadening. In a few more years the moral life of the negro will be greatly strengthened by that education which comes from the force of public opinion.

As to the effect of industrial education in the solution of the race problem, we should not expect too much from it in a short time. To the late General S. C. Armstrong, of Hampton Institute, in Virginia, should be given the credit, mainly, for inaugurating this system of education. When the Hampton Institute began the systematic, industrial training of the negro, such training was unpopular among a large class of colored people. Later, when the same system was started by me at the Tuskegee Normal and Industrial Institute, in Alabama, it was still unpopular, especially in that part of the South. But the feeling against it has now almost completely disappeared in all parts of the country; so much so, that I do not consider the opposition of a few people here and there as of material consequence. Where there is one who opposes it there are thousands who indorse it. So far as the colored people are concerned, I consider that the battle for this principle has been fought and the victory won. What the colored people are anxious about is that, with industrial education, they shall have thorough mental and religious training; and in this they are right. For bringing about this change in the attitude of the colored people, much credit should be given to the John F. Slater Fund, under the wise guidance of such men as Mr. Morris K. Jesup and Dr. J. L. M. Curry, as well as to Dr. H. B. Frissell, of the Hampton Institute. That such institutions for industrial training as the Hampton Institute and the Tuskegee Institute are always crowded with the best class of negro students from nearly every State in the Union, and that every year they are compelled to refuse admission to hundreds of others, for lack of room and means, is sufficient evidence that the black race has come to appreciate the value of industrial education. The almost pathetic demand of the colored people for industrial education in every corner of the South is added evidence of the growing intelligence of the race. In saying what I do in regard to industrial education, I do not wish to be understood as meaning that the education of the negro should be confined to that kind alone, because we need men and women well educated in other directions; but, for the masses, industrial education is the supreme need. I repeat that we must not expect too much from this training, in the redemption of a race, in the space of a few years.

There are few institutions in the South where industrial training is given upon a large and systematic scale, and the graduates from these institutions have not had time to make themselves felt to any very large extent upon the life of the rank and file of the people. But what are the indications? As I write, I have before me a record of graduates, which is carefully compiled each year. Of the hundreds who have been trained at the Tuskegee Institute, less than ten per cent. have failed, and less than five per cent. have failed because of any moral weakness. These graduates, as well as hundreds of other students who could not remain to finish the course, are now at work in the school-room, in the field, in the shop, in the home, or as teachers of industry, or in some way they are making their education felt in the lifting up of the colored people. Wherever these graduates go, they not only help their own race, but, in nearly every case, they win the respect and confidence of the white people.

Not long ago, I sent a number of letters to white men, in all the Southern States, asking, among others, this question: "Judged by actual observation in your own community, what is the effect of education upon the negro?" In asking this question, I was careful to explain that by education I did not mean a mere smattering, but a thorough education of the head, heart and hand. I received about three hundred replies, and there was only one who said that education did not help the negro. Most of the others were emphatic in stating that education made the negro a better citizen. In all the record of crime in the South, there are very few instances where a black man who has been thoroughly educated in the respects I have mentioned has been even charged with the crime of assaulting a woman. In fact, I do not know of a single instance of this kind, whether the man was educated in an industrial school or in a college.

The following extracts from a letter written by a Southern white man to the *Daily Advertiser*, of Montgomery, Alabama, contains most valuable testimony. The letter refers to convicts in Alabama, most of whom are colored:

"I was conversing not long ago with the warden of one of our mining prisons, containing about 500 convicts. The warden is a practical man, who has been in charge of prisoners for more than fifteen years, and has no theories of any kind to support. I remarked to him that I wanted some information as to the effect of manual training in preventing criminality, and asked him to state what per cent. of the prisoners under his charge had received any manual training, besides the acquaintance with the crudest agricultural labor. He replied: 'Perhaps about one per cent.' He added: 'No; much less than that. We have here at present only one mechanic; that is, there is one man who claims to be a house painter.'

" 'Have you any shoemakers?'

" 'Never have had a shoemaker.'

" 'Have you any tailors?'

" 'Never have had a tailor.'

" 'Any printers?'

" 'Never have had a printer.'

" 'Any carpenters?'

" 'Never have had a carpenter. There is not a man in this prison that could saw to a straight line.' "

Now, these facts seem to show that manual training is almost as good a preventive for criminality as vaccination is for smallpox.

We can best judge further of the value of industrial and academic education by using a few statistics bearing upon the State of Virginia, where graduates from the Hampton Institute and other schools have gone in large numbers and have had an opportunity, in point of time, to make their influence apparent upon the negro population. These statistics, based on census reports, were compiled mainly by persons connected with the Hampton Negro Conference:

"Taking taxation as a basis, the colored people of the State of Virginia contributed, in 1898, directly to the expenses of the State Government, the sum of $9,576.76, and for schools $3,239.41 from their personal property, a total of $12,816.17; while, from their real estate, for the purpose of the commonwealth there was paid by them $34,303.53, and for schools $11,457.22, or a total of $45,760.75 — a grand total of $58,576.92.

"The report for the same year shows them to own 987,118 acres of land valued at $3,800,459, improved by buildings valued at $2,056,490, a total of $5,856,949. In the towns and cities, they own lots assessed at $2,154,331, improved by buildings valued at $3,400,636, a total of $5,554,976 for town property, and a grand total of $11,411,916 of their property of all kinds in the commonwealth. A comparative statement of different years would doubtless show a general upward tendency.

"The counties of Accomac, Essex, King and Queen, Middlesex, Mathews, Northampton, Northumberland, Richmond, Westmoreland, Gloucester, Princess Anne and Lancaster, all agricultural, show an aggregate of 114,197 acres held by negroes in 1897, the last year accounted for in official reports, against 108,824 held the previous year, an increase of 5,379, or nearly five per cent. The total valuation of land owned by negroes in the same counties for 1897, is $547,800 against $496,385 for the year next preceding, a gain of $51,150, or more than ten per cent. Their personal property, as assessed in 1897, was $517,560, in 1896, $527,688, a loss of $10,128. Combining the real and personal property for 1897, we have $1,409,059, against $1,320,504 for 1896, a net gain of $88,555, an increase of six and one-half per cent.

"The records of Gloucester, Lancaster, Middlesex, Princess Anne, Northumberland, Northampton, King and Queen, Essex, and Westmoreland, where the colored population exceeds the white, show that the criminal expense for 1896 was $14,313.29, but for 1897 it was only $8,538.12, a saving of $5,774.17 to the State, or a falling off of forty per cent. This does not tell the whole story. In the first named year twenty-six persons were convicted of felonies, with sentences in the penitentiary, while in the year succeeding only nine, or one-third as many, were convicted of the graver offences of the law."

According to these returns, in 1892, when the colored people formed 41 per cent. of the population, they owned 2.75 per cent. of the total number of acres assessed for taxation, and 3.40 per cent. of the buildings; in 1898, although not constituting more than 37 per cent. of the population (by reason of white immigration), they owned 3.23 per cent. of the acreage assessed, and 4.64 per cent. of the buildings — a gain of nearly one-third in six years.

According to statistics gathered by a graduate of the Hampton Institute, in twelve counties in Virginia, there has been in the part of the State covered by the investigation an increase of 5,379 acres in the holdings of colored people, and an increase of $51,150 in the value of their land. In nine counties there has been a decrease in the number of persons charged with felonies and sent to the penitentiary from twenty-six in 1896 to nine in 1897.

I do not believe that the negro will grow weaker in morals and less strong in numbers because of his immediate contact with the white race. The first-class life insurance companies are considered excellent authorities as to the longevity of individuals and races; and the fact that most of them now seek to insure the educated class of blacks is a good test of what these companies think of the effect of education upon the mortality of the race.

The case of Jamaica, in the West Indies, presents a good example by which to judge the future of the negro in the United States, so far as mortality is concerned. The argument drawn from Jamaica is valuable, chiefly because the race there has been free for sixty-two years, instead of thirty-five, as in our own country. During the years of freedom, the blacks of Jamaica have been in constant contact with the white man. Slavery was abolished in Jamaica in 1838. The census of 1844 showed that there were 364,000 negroes in the Island. In 1871 there were 493,000, and in 1891 there were 610,579. In a history of Jamaica written by Mr. W. P. Livingston, who spent ten years studying the conditions of the Island, we find that, immediately after emancipation in the Island, there was something of the reaction that has taken place in some parts of our country; but that recently there has been a settling down to real, earnest life on the part of a large proportion of the race. After calling attention to certain weak and unsatisfactory phases in the life of the Jamaica negro, Mr. Livingston says:

"This, then, is the race as it exists to-day, a product of sixty years of freedom; on the whole, a plain, honest, Anglicized people, with no peculiarity except a harmless ignorance and superstition. Looking at it in contrast with what it was at the beginning of the period, one cannot but be impressed with the wonderful progress it has made; and where there has been steady progress in the past, there is infinite hope for the future. * * * The impact of Roman power and culture on the northern barbarians of the United Kingdom did not make itself felt for three hundred years. * * * Instead of dying off before civilization, he (the negro) grows stronger as he comes within its best influences."

In comparing the black race of Jamaica with that of the United States, it should be borne in mind that the negro in America enjoys advantages and encouragements which the race in Jamaica does not possess.

What I have said, I repeat, is based largely upon my own experience and observation, rather than upon statistics. I do not wish to convey the impression that the problem before our country is not a large and serious one; but I do believe that in a judicious system of industrial, mental and religious training we have found the method of solving it. What we most need is the money necessary to make the system effective. The indications are hopeful, not discouraging; and not the least encouraging is the fact that, in addition to the munificence of Northern philanthropists and the appropriations of the Southern State Governments from common taxation, with the efforts of the negro himself, we have now reached a point at which the solution of this problem is drawing to its aid some of the most thoughtful and cultured white men and women of the South, as is indicated by the article to which I have already referred, from the pen of Professor John Roach Straton, a representative of the best element of the South.

North American Review, 171 (Aug. 1900), 221–32.

[1] John Roach Straton (1875-1929), a Baptist clergyman, was a member of the faculty of Mercer University in Macon, Ga., at the time of this document. From 1903 to 1905 he taught at Baylor University in Waco, Tex. After preaching in the South, Straton moved to New York in 1918 and became nationally known as a fundamentalist preacher. He was active in the Anti-Saloon League in the 1920s and was a staunch opponent of drinking, dancing, and prizefighting. He was an outspoken champion of William Jennings Bryan in the 1925 Scopes trial.

Straton's article appeared in the *North American Review*, 170 (June 1900), 785-801. A social Darwinist, Straton thought that blacks would eventually die out if forced into contact with Anglo-Saxon civilization. He believed that education only hastened the process and led to increased crime among blacks. Following the thesis of Frederick L. Hoffman's *Race Traits and Tendencies of the American Negro* (1896), Straton assumed that blacks had a "tendency to immorality and crime." He wrote that crime was lowest, and black life was best, where blacks were illiterate and lived more closely to the style of the slave period such as in Mississippi and other deep South states. Praising BTW as "that great and good man," Straton argued that in dustrial education was the best temporary policy to follow and urged support for BTW. He cautioned, however, that industrial education would not help improve the "ethical condition of the negro."

An Article in *Century Magazine*

[August 1900]

THE MONTGOMERY RACE CONFERENCE

Within the last half-century at least two gatherings of national importance have assembled in Montgomery, Alabama. The first was the Confederate Congress, in 1861, which was a result of measures which had been taken to dissolve the relations existing between the Southern States and the rest of the Union. The second was the Southern Conference for the Discussion of Race Conditions and Problems in the South, held in May, 1900, thirty-nine years later.

Few movements in the country in recent years have caused so much discussion as this conference. As it is likely to be a permanent organization, it is important to understand from the promoters and organizers themselves something of the object and scope of the organization. Personally I have no connection with this conference, but I have known the promoters and officials of it for years, and believe that they have in view nothing but the permanent elevation and highest good of both races in the South. I differ widely and radically with many of the views of individual members of the conference, and with those of several of the speakers, but I think it only fair to deal with the organization itself as we should with an individual, and judge it by its public expression until it proves itself unworthy of confidence. The conference was started by some of the most eminent white citizens of Montgomery, Alabama, including the leading clergymen, and its president is the Hon. Hilary A. Herbert of that city, formerly Secretary of the Navy.

According to its constitution, it is non-partizan, being composed of Democrats, Republicans, Populists, and Prohibitionists. Any movement that brought merely the friends of the negro together would mean little in the way of distinct gain. The conference is pledged not to commit itself to any special policy affecting the race problem. For example, the Hon. Bourke Cockran advocated in his address before the conference the repeal of the Fifteenth Amendment, as a partial solution of the race problem, but the conference itself was not responsible for Mr. Cockran's views, any more than it was for the views of ex-Governor MacCorkle, who opposed such repeal in the strongest and most eloquent terms. In other words, the conference is an organization composed of Southern white people, that serves as a medium for free and open discussion of the race problem by such persons as are invited to speak before it. On this point I quote a clause of the constitution:

"The object of this society shall be to furnish, by means of correspondence, publications, and partly through public conferences, an organ for the expression of the varied and even antagonistic convictions of representative Southern men on the problems growing out of the race conditions obtaining in the South, and thus to secure a broader education of the public mind as to the facts of the situation, and a better understanding of the remedies for existing evils."

When we consider that thirty-nine years after the secession of the Southern States, at Montgomery, this conference is called by Southern white people, I do not believe that there is any reason for those interested in the progress of both races to grow discouraged, even though we cannot agree with all of the opinions expressed. In my opinion, the greatest value of the conference is in the opportunity which it furnishes in the heart of the South for free speech. Both the North and the negro have criticized the South for not always encouraging freedom of expression and debate. If this first session was not all that might be desired by some in this regard, it should be borne in mind that no great movement can reach perfection at once. While some very strong things were said in favor of the negro, and some strong things against him, it was a noteworthy and most encouraging fact that every speaker, no matter what his views, was received with the greatest respect and consideration. That some views were more heartily applauded than others was to be expected.

I consider that this conference represents in a large measure the "Silent South." For years we have heard the voice of the North, the voice of the negro, the voice of the politician, and the voice of the mob; but the voice of the educated, cultivated white South has been too long silent. No matter what our own individual feelings and wishes may be, when it comes to a consideration of hard cold facts we must agree that the Southern white man is an important factor in any settlement of the race problem.

The program presented at the first meeting of the conference occupied three days. There were nineteen speakers, all Southern men except two. Of these not more than four made speeches that any one could consider antagonistic to the highest interests of the negro. There was but one speaker who seemed to oppose the education of the negro. There was a difference of opinion as to the exact form, and perhaps the amount, of education that should be attempted, but that the negro should be educated in some manner there was virtual agreement among all who took part in the conference; and on the subject, "The Duty of the Nation and the South to Educate the Negro," the Hon. J. L. M. Curry, a Southern man, an ex-slaveholder and an ex-Confederate, delivered one of the most eloquent addresses that it has ever been my privilege to hear. To have given the opportunity for this address alone, in the Black Belt of the South, it seems to me was worth the holding of the conference. On the subject of religion, of course, there was virtual unanimity. Every one is in favor of salvation for the negro in the future world; it is only the salvation of his mind and body in this world that causes disagreement.

Upon one other subject the conference appeared to be well-nigh unanimous — that the negro should and would remain in the South.

The two speakers who dealt with the subject of lynching both argued that in all cases of crime the law should be allowed to take its course. In fact, I was told that no white man of any standing in the South could be found to speak in favor of lynching.

The subject of the franchise naturally excited the keenest interest. The Hon. Bourke Cockran and ex-Governor W. A. Mac-

Corkle, the opposing speakers, both claimed that they had nothing but the highest good of the negro in view. Aside from Mr. Cockran's plan for the repeal of the Fifteenth Amendment, his speech consisted mainly of a plea for the highest justice to the negro. Ex-Governor MacCorkle, a Southern man and a Democrat, argued in the most eloquent terms that absolute justice and equality should be accorded the negro at the ballot-box, by means of property and educational tests that should be applied to both races.

The only address delivered during the whole conference which seemed to take anything like a hopeless or dismal view of the future of the negro came from Dr. Paul B. Barringer of Virginia. I would say of Dr. Barringer's expressions, as I would of others, that if persons have feelings that are antagonistic to what we should consider the best interests of the negro it is better that these views be expressed than repressed; and herein, again, is shown the value of these conferences. The man who speaks out truly and frankly is not a person to be feared; it is the one who smothers and represses his real feelings that does injury. In Dr. Barringer's speech of over an hour he gave the most discouraging views I have ever listened to regarding the present and the future of the negro, industrially, physically, mentally, and morally, and as I sat through it I wondered what would be its effect on the Southern audience. This question was soon answered. When the proper time came, ex-Secretary Herbert, the chairman of the meeting, and an ex-slaveholder, in the most courteous language, firmly dissented from many of Dr. Barringer's discouraging views. This incident proved that the Southern white people who have known and lived with the negro for three centuries could not pass over in silence a speech in which the negro as a freeman was not given credit for having even one redeeming quality. Many of the misleading statements which in some way Dr. Barringer has been led into making are going to serve a good purpose. For example, in arguing that industrial education would not solve the problem, he claimed authority for the statement that out of twelve hundred students educated at industrial schools only twelve were farming and only three were working at trades. This statement put a number of Southern white people to thinking, and, best of all, to investigating, and they soon discovered that in the city of Montgomery alone, almost within hearing of Dr. Barringer's voice, there are fifteen of our graduates or ex-students working at trades or industries learned at Tuskegee; and it was further discovered that in one county in Alabama there are thirty-five graduates and ex-students of the same institution who are engaged in farming or working at trades.

On the whole, I cannot but feel convinced that this conference is going to serve a good purpose, and that in future meetings, more than in the first one, the wisdom of the movement will be demonstrated. Among other things likely thus to be accomplished is a larger measure of first-hand investigation of the negro's real condition. The negro suffers very often in reputation because few of those who make damaging statements have ever taken the trouble to visit him in his place of business, his home, his school, and his church, where the higher and more encouraging side of his life may be seen. More and more the American people must come to judge the negro much as they do other races — by the best types, and not by the worst.

Century Magazine, 60 (Aug. 1900), 630–32. An undated typed draft is in Con. 959, BTW Papers, DLC.

From John Coburn[1]

Indianapolis, September 3rd 1900

Dear Sir, I expected to see you & talk to you when you attended the Convention here. But you came so late that I could not see you before you spoke — I fear you made a mistake in not giving us your full address.[2]

That was & will be held to have been a memorable Convention: possibly as much for what was not done, as for what was done.

Your speech I could not hear; having got in too late for a favorable place on the floor. But I read what was published in the Journal.

That was, every word, to the purpose & excellent. Strongly suggestive to the men of color of how to take life, in earnest, with a steady practical purpose; how to climb; how, in the long run, to dominate.

But the tacit admission that the race was *practically* a failure, was not exactly made but, by many readers, was read between the lines. Not by me; for I am an unshaken believer that the every day life of the colored toiling millions must lead to strength and elevation of character; and to the ultimate recognition of a manhood and a womanhood, such as the world never saw; coming to the top from the slave ship, the slave pen, the overseer's lash, the unrequited toil of a downtrodden people.

It will be a social and a political miracle; but in the providence of God, it must yet come.

Must they have seperate public schools? I think not. Must they sit on juries? I say yes. Yes side by side with white men. Must they have the right to hold offices? I say yes. Must they have the right to vote? I say yes. A thousand times yes.

Strike down the right of suffrage and you put a lever under free government that will lift it up and crack the structure till it tumbles down and must be reconstructed.

The sacred basis of our nation is the free and fair right to vote. It cannot rest upon any other.

The man at the plow; in the factory; with the sledge hammer; on the locomotive; holding the musket; ramming the cannon in the field, or on the slippery, bloody deck; white or black; is the bed rock of the United States of America.

May God almighty hold you in the hollow of his hand till your great work is triumphantly done. Yours very truly

John Coburn

ALS Con. 168 BTW Papers DLC.

1 John Coburn was a black lawyer in Indianapolis.

2 BTW, attempting to keep his appearance before the council brief, arrived in Indianapolis from New York just thirty minutes before he was scheduled to speak. The Indianapolis *Sentinel* reported that he was received with a "storm of applause" when he entered the room. T. Thomas Fortune introduced BTW to the delegates. (Indianapolis *Sentinel*, Sept. 1, 1900, 3.) BTW's address was a condensed version of his speech before the Metropolitan A.M.E. Church in Washington, D.C. (See above, May 22, 1900.) Apparently he had planned to discuss southern assaults on the Thirteenth, Fourteenth, and Fifteenth amendments, a topic that had kept the convention delegates agitated all week. But BTW failed to utter a single word on the subject, much to the chagrin of many of the delegates. One newspaper reported that several delegates believed that BTW left out any discussion of politics to avoid further controversy at the convention. Later that evening at the Occidental Hotel, while being questioned on southern politics by a reporter, BTW said: "I would be delighted to give an interview on that subject if I felt it advisable to talk, but I must decline.

I cannot see my way clear to giving you anything which I did not utter in my speech to the council." The reporter asked if BTW had originally planned to discuss politics, and BTW declined to answer. (Indianapolis *Journal*, Sept. 1, 1900, Clipping, Con. 1032, BTW Papers, DLC.)

From Richard W. Thompson

Washington, D.C., Sept. 3, 1900

Dear Mr. Washington: Your friends here are highly pleased over the successful outcome of the Boston Business League, and a prosperous career is predicted for it by many who have heretofore been doubtful as to the utility of Negro organizations. There is, as yet, no branch league here, but I am under the impression that Mr. Hilyer[1] is formulating a plan to get up something that will not only awaken interest in the Negro's commercial status, but be of financial benefit to those who must purchase commodities. Mr. Hilyer as you know is a very earnest man — industrious, thorough and honest.

While it is felt here that the Afro-American Council did not accomplish a great deal of good in a general way, we are glad you attended and took occasion to make a speech that tempered a highly aggravated condition. It served the further purpose of disarming the little band of cheap critics who professed to believe that the National Business League was designed to overshadow or supplant the Council. The pleasant result of your visit to Indianapolis was well worth the time and expense that it entailed.

I am a little at sea journalistically. Partially because of poor health, due to a long nervous strain, and more particularly because of Cooper's unreliability in a number of ways I have resigned the associate editorship of "The Colored American." There is no open rupture, but the situation is such that I do not feel like sacrificing my time and strength for meager results and less appreciation. I wish you would advise me, however as to how I can best serve your interests. You have been so very kind to me that when I dip into ink I take pleasure in trying to hold up your hands, and I recognize with you, the value of The Colored American's influence throughout the nation in pushing the work along. I have arranged to furnish a regular letter for The Freeman — for a moderate compensation — but have carte blanche to say what I please, without being back-capped. I shall not slight Tuskegee nor the Business League. What would you suggest with reference to the American? A special department, over my own signature, or that you arrange with Cooper to have me look after your interests as they may come up? Of course, I make no charge for any thing I can do for you, and it is hardly worth while for me to make a financial deal with Cooper, for he will not keep his word except when he is obliged to do so to keep things moving — and especially now that I am drawing a "fabulous" salary from the government. These points are confidential, and any advice you may give will be likewise confidential, as it is my wish that all forces be kept in working order. My health is greatly improved, and the approach of cooler weather and rest will put me in trim again.

Our section is working hard with correspondence to farmers asking that omissions in crop reports be supplied. Picked men are on this work, and the bauble of promotion is being held out for "proficiency" or "efficiency." They are reaching our people for the $1,000 rate, and several of the proteges of influential men have been raised. Two went up on Sept. 1. I am under the impression that I am entitled to an increase, and also that you are entitled to ask further recognition as to salary, since you have made no heavy demand here for places. I think my record is satisfactory, and if attention is especially called something may be done on the 15th. I would suggest that you write a letter to Mr. L. G. Powers, Chief Statistician in Charge of Agriculture, noting my case, and urging promotion if my record is consistent therewith. If you think best, a similar letter might also be sent to Gov. Merriam. I hope I am not greedy, but since the Census will not last forever, hay must be made while the sun shines. I shall be grateful for any boost you think proper to give, and advice that may prove of mutual advantage. All matters confidential. Wishing you continued success, I am, Very truly yours

R. W. Thompson

ALS   Con. 185   BTW Papers   DLC.

1 Andrew F. Hilyer.

From Beno von Herman auf Wain[1]

Berlin NW., the 3rd of Septemb. 1900

Dear Sir, Referring to my to-day's cable and to our conversation in Roslindale Mass. of August 13th, I take pleasure in informing you that the company to whom I referred your propositions after my arrival has agreed to everything and wishes me to ask you to have the great kindness to select for us two negro-cottonplanters and one negro-mechanic who would be willing to come over to said company's land in the colony of Togo in West-Africa to teach the negroes there how to plant and harvest cotton in a rational and scientific way. The company is perfectly willing to have one of the men married if you think it better or if you cannot find 3 unmarried men. The company will in that case pay the fair to and from Togo also for the wife in question. If it is possible the company should like the 3 men (and one woman if necessary) to leave New-York by the Hamburg-American-Line, steamer "Patricia" on October 27th; they would get there tickets 2nd class at the Lines Office Broadway 35, New-York, where the agent would be informed of their coming and would help them in every way, so that they would get safely to Hamburg. There they would again be received by an agent of the company, would be shown round the city and taken care of till they would have to leave Hamburg on November 11th, for Togo on another German steamer. Arriving in Togo they would again be received by an agent of the company (who of course all speak English) and would be helped to get to their place of destination about 60 miles in land from the sea-port Lome.

As you suggested the salary for each of the 3 men would be 100 dollars a month or a little less than that if the company would give them 50% of the cotton harvested the first year for their personal benefit so as to induce them to plant and raise as much and as good a cotton as possible.

The contract with the 3 men would be for one year with the prospect of being prolonged for more years if the results of the plantations are good and if the company is satisfied with the work and behaviour of the men. Should one of the men disbehave inside of the first year, the company would have the right to break the contract and to send him back to America at his own expense. As to the actual form and wording of the contract I expect though your propositions as you have promised me to send them in Roslindale.

The company has already a small plantation of about 30 acres in cotton and the first task for your men would be to harvest that cotton which is expected to be ripe in November and December. For this purpose it would be necessary for the men to bring two different kinds of hand gins and one press. The seed of that plantation could instantly be used again for part of next years' experiments and the cotton after being pressed would be transported by already existing cars on a good road to the sea-coast about 60 miles distance and would be shipped from there to Europe to be examined by cotton experts. After this the two planters would go round the country under the advice of the Head official of the company to select the land which they would consider best for two different experiment-farms. There they would prepare the soil and put up the necessary buildings with the help of the natives so as to be ready for planting when the raining-season begins in the month of April.

The plow is as yet unknown in that colony the natives doing all the little work they do with the hoe, but if your planters bring the plows, cultivators etc. which are used for cotton planting in America, they will find small horses and oxen which will partly have been broken to harness and which will be ready for plantation-work. It seems to me that for the present it would only be necessary for your planters to bring the most necessary machines and instruments as they will have time from the end of November until beginning of April (when the raining- and planting-season begins) to communicate through the company with you and suggest what kind of machinery etc. and how many they will think necessary for their experiment-farms.

I enclose some maps of Africa and the Togo colony, further some statistics about analysis of soil, temperature, rainfall etc. by which the chief of your agricultural departments will be able to suggest what kind of seed, what kind and how much furtilizer should be used on the experiment-farms. The company would then be thankful if your institute would provide for the cotton-seed, whereas the furtilizer would be purchased in Germany and shipped to Togo as soon as the necessary quantity and quality is known.

The company is perfectly willing that your planters should try diversified farming although she thinks that for the present the cotton-planting would be safest and most profitable, but if your planters bring some seed to plant for their own use and for the local-market corn, sweet potatoes, peanuts, bananas etc., which are cultivated there in a rough way by the natives, they will find time and help to make some small experiments in these crops. The company wishes however to have the first year already as much cotton planted as possible, so much more so as it would surely be good to experiment with a few different American varieties of cotton besides the above mentioned native grown cotton. The population being very dense, horses and oxen to be had as much as required, the two plantations could be made as large as the necessary control of the work by your planters would allow it. I speak of two plantations as it seems to be best to take two different localities not very far apart from each other with different soil and to give each planter the whole responsibility of the work and the result of his plantation. This would involve as it seems to me a healthy competition between the two men to do the best they can.

As you kindly promised in Roslindale I expect to receive from you before long a list of all the instruments and machineries necessary for a cotton-plantation giving also the prices for each implement. The company would look the list over and return it to you, as you so very kindly offered to have all the machinery etc. bought through your institute.

As all lists would mean a certain amount of expenses, will you kindly give the company the address of your banker to whom the money could be remitted in advance.

The company would also ask you to kindly notify her by cable to the above telegram-address, day and name of steamer, when the planters definitively leave New-York.

Some members of the company have certain misgivings whether your negro-planters might find some difficulties in starting and developing their work in Togo, in finding the necessary authority towards the native population and in having at the same time the necessary respect towards the German government official who of course would try to help them as best they could in their work.

Do you think that it might be necessary to send out with them a man of highest education, who would help them in organising the whole work and who would do the scientific work of examining the soils, keeping the books, paying out the accounts etc. etc. This of course would involve much larger expenses and perhaps you could tell us how much such kind [of] other man would expect to be paid and where he could be found.

Thanking you again for your great kindness and help in this matter and hoping to hear as soon as possible from you   I am very truly   Yours

Baron Herman

I send you by special cover one large map of Africa and a book of Togo, which will give you through its picture an idea of the colony.

TLS   Con. 177   BTW Papers   DLC.

1 Baron Beno von Herman auf Wain (b. 1862) was royal councillor, court chamberlain, and chief forester of the King of Württemberg. He represented the Kolonial Wirtschaftliches Komitee (KWK) in its negotiations with BTW to secure several persons to engage in a cotton-raising experiment in Togo. The KWK was a private German organization with close ties to the German government that sought to advance economic development of the German colonies. Herman was the author of *The Commerciograph, a New Means to Study Commercial Geography and the Trade of the World* (1900). (See Harlan, "BTW and the White Man's Burden," 442-47.)

To Samuel Y. Taylor[1]

Tuskegee, Ala., Sept. 9, 1900

Dear sir: School opens next Tuesday and we are expecting a good number of students.

Owing to the present state of feeling in the town we have decided that it will be wise to absolutely prohibit any of our students from visiting the town for some time and we hope that you will assist us in enforcing this rule.

Our students have never gotten into trouble in the town and we do not want to run any risks in this direction now.

Thanking you for all your kindness   I am   Yours truly

Booker T. Washington

ALS Copy   Con. 20   BTW Papers   ATT.

1 Samuel Y. Taylor, born in Alabama in 1851, was the town marshal of Tuskegee.

To Timothy Thomas Fortune

Tuskegee, Ala., Sept. 11, 1900

Dear Mr. Fortune: I presume this letter will find you in New York. I hope you had a conference with Mr. Hanna and that something good came out of it.

In regard to sueing the Nichols people I hardly think it will pay to bother with them so far as the cash gotten out of it is concerned. I think, however, it will help matters to scare them a little. Mr. Scott is going to Chicago within a few days and I am going to make an effort to have the American Book Co. pay what is still due you for that manuscript.

I think before long that we ought to get twelve or fifteen of the strongest and most influential Negroes in the country and have a private conference lasting two or three days if necessary and in that way get hold of the whole situation and determine what are the proper efforts to be put forth to help and improve conditions as they now exist.[1] Matters have got to get better or worse soon. Yours truly,

Booker T. Washington

TLS Con. 172 BTW Papers DLC.

1 BTW postponed this meeting, and lack of funds forced him to postpone it again in 1903. After the Boston Riot dramatized the struggle for black leadership, however, BTW secured funds from Andrew Carnegie and William H. Baldwin, Jr., for a private conference of representative black spokesmen of diverse views. This was the Carnegie Hall Conference, Jan. 6-8, 1904, BTW's final attempt to achieve harmony with the militants on his terms.

From John Elmer Milholland

London, September 13th, 1900

My Dear Mr. Washington, Why did you mar that fine tribute you paid Huntington in the "Tribune" by permitting yourself to talk about "inferiors?"[1] Don't you know that such expressions grate upon plain people like the undersigned, for example, who try to see things as they are in this world? And don't you know that they encourage erroneous thinking on the part of those with whom we are laboring? You should not do it. You should avoid all such expressions. They are wrong. They have no place in such connections at all.

Do you know what to me is perhaps the most interesting contribution to the Montgomery Conference? You would not guess in a week. Well, I'll tell you. It was when that presiding officer in gushing over you wound up by asking the assembly if any one present would welcome you as a guest to his household; and such was the cowardly, disgraceful spirit of the audience at the time that no one stood up to answer in the affirmative. I would have cheerfully given a thousand dollars to have been present just at that time. It was an opportunity for the stupidest man that ever faced an assemblage to score a point. I need not tell you, because you know it already, that there are thousands and hundreds of thousands who, like myself, consider themselves honored by your presence and social relationship; a relationship that knows no limit whatever on account of race, color, birth, or previous conditions; but that it should be possible for an audience of American citizens to get together and have such a question debatable is an incident over which the future student of social progress and civilization will meditate, as we do now upon the times when men and women were burnt on account of witchcraft and religious intolerance.

I have the liveliest and the pleasantest recollections of our little chat at the Tribune Building on that stormy night last winter, and I hope that we may supplement it when I get back to New York a little later on.

That outbreak in the Tenderloin was outrageous. I read the reports in Switzerland, and immediately wrote a note to the "Herald," a copy of which I enclose. I also wrote to the Republican National Committee, and am sending a contribution to Moss[2] today to help bring the rascals to justice.

But there are no mistakes in history, and all these things are helping on the better day. A reaction is inevitable, and I think we will be well abreast of public spirit when we come to propose a National Franchise Law. This is my notion now of practical effort. How does it strike you? In fact almost everything in the situation, national and international, is going to tell in favor of the Negro in the near future. The forty years in the wilderness are drawing to a close. Sincerely yours,

Jno. E. Milholland

TLS Con. 1 BTW Papers DLC.

1 See To the Editor of the New York *Tribune*, Aug. 26, 1900, above.

2 Probably Frank Moss (1860-1920), a prominent New York lawyer who was counsel for the Society for the Prevention of Crime beginning in 1887. In 1897 he was president of the board of police commissioners in New York City.

To Timothy Thomas Fortune

Tuskegee, Ala., Sept. 15, 1900

Dear Mr. Fortune: I received your telegram and am glad to hear that matters are going so smoothly. In addition to the matter which I mentioned yesterday, I hope you will be very careful to keep on smooth terms with Mr. Hanna and all who are in authority. It will pay you to bite your tongue very often and sit down upon dignity in order to accomplish the ends which we have in view. If you can go through the campaign and keep on smooth terms with all concerned and impress the authorities with your value I am sure that we can secure a handsome reward for you at the close of the campaign. Yours truly,

Booker T. Washington

TLS Con. 172 BTW Papers DLC.

To Beno von Herman auf Wain

[Tuskegee, Ala.] Sept. 20, 1900

Dear Sir: I take pleasure in writing you further according to promise made in my last letter. This is a more full answer to yours of Sept. 3d.

I am very glad that your Company has agreed to the suggestions which you made to it. We have already selected three of our best men[1] to go to Togo. Two of them have had training in farming at this institution and the third is a mechanic, able to do all kinds of woodwork and certainly to some extent able to work in metals. Of course the two farmers understand the planting and harvesting of cotton, though I should very much hope that your Company will not make the same mistake that has been made in the South among our people, that is, teach them to raise nothing but cotton. I find that they make much better progress financially and otherwise where they are taught to raise something to eat at the same time they are raising cotton.

All three of the men are unmarried.

Since your last letter came we have been considering carefully the suggestion that you made of having a stronger, older and much better educated man accompany these three young men. Our officers are convinced that such a plan would be wise, and I should say that if the man goes with them whom we have in mind it would leave nothing untried to make the experiment a success, that is I mean to say that if this fourth man could not make it a success I do not believe that it would be possible to do so under the circumstances. The name of the man that we recommend to take the lead is Mr. James Nathan Calloway. Mr. Calloway is a man about 40 years old, has a college education, has studied German, and besides all this has had for a number of years the practical care of a large farm of 800 acres belonging to the school. He understands farming both in a practical and scientific manner. Mr. Calloway has volunteered his services to accompany these men to remain with them for at least a year if the Company thinks that his services are needed for so long a time. He volunteers to go in a perfectly disinterested spirit, his only ambition being to have the young men who go out from here succeed. He would not disconnect himself with this institution, but in case it is necessary we have voted to give him a leave of absence for twelve months. He is a man of great tact and full of resources and I believe that it would pay your Company to have him go. If he found that he could get the young men well started off within a shorter period than twelve months he would wish to return with the consent of your Company before the end of twelve months, but of course if the Company desired him to remain the full twelve months he would do so. He would expect pay at the rate of two hundred dollars ($200) per month, the salary to take effect on the date of sailing from New York and remain in effect until he reached New York on return. In order for Mr. Calloway to get ready to accompany the other three men it would be necessary for you to cable me whether or not you wish to engage him.

I do not think in any case that there will be much if any difficulty in the men who go from here treating the German officials with proper respect. They are all kindly disposed, respectful gentlemen. I believe at the same time they will secure the respect and confidence of the natives.

We shall plan to have the party leave New York by the Hamburg-American Line steamer "Patricia" on October 27th. You do not say anything about the providing of the cost of getting the party to New York from Tuskegee. This will be not far from $30 for each man. If we do not hear from you about this before the men sail we shall advance this money and charge it to the account of the Company.

The head of our Agricultural Department will give the men before they leave here full instructions as to the kind and amount of fertilizers to use on the experiment farm. We shall also provide for the cotton seed as you suggest.

The name of our bank is the Macon County Bank, Tuskegee, Alabama, U.S.A.

We have received the map and book together with the various charts giving an analysis of soil, etc., which the head of our Agricultural Department finds quite valuable.

Since re-reading your letter of Sept. 3d I find that you suggest that our men take with them only such machinery as will be necessary for harvesting the cotton crop which is now already growing. If I do not hear to the contrary I shall have them carry out this plan and that will of course necessitate their taking a smaller number of implements, altho I think that it will be wise for the men to take with them the carpenters tools and some of the other tools on the list which I sent you. Without the carpenter's tools of course the mechanic would be practically idle after he got there for some period of time.

After making a careful inquiry I find that there is no hand gin now manufactured or used in America. The nearest to it is a gin run by horse power. This will get out about two bales of cotton a day. The gin itself will cost about $100 and what is called the "power," that is the machinery etc. necessary to gear it up, will cost about $100 additional. The cheapest and I think the best thing in the end would be to buy a small portable steam boiler and engine which would cost about $500. This would get out about ten bales a day. But I shall not take the liberty of getting the steam engine unless I get further instructions from you. Yours truly,

Booker T. Washington

TLpS   Con. 282A   BTW Papers   DLC.

1 The first three Tuskegee graduates to go to Africa were Shepherd Lincoln Harris (see above, 4:211), John Winfrey Robinson, and Allen Lynn Burks. Robinson, an 1897 graduate of Tuskegee, was the most persistent in trying to make growing cotton work in Togo. In 1905 he opened a school to teach African farmers how to grow cotton, and within a year he had 200 pupils. Robinson was drowned in Togo in 1909 while crossing a swift river in a canoe. Burks, a 1900 Tuskegee graduate, spent at least two years in Africa before returning to America. Between 1901 and 1909, nine Tuskegee students went to Africa as part of the cotton-raising experiment. Four died in Togo, including two who were drowned in the surf before they could get ashore, and five others spent just a few years each in Africa. (Harlan, "BTW and the White Man's Burden," 444-45.)

To John A. Hertel

[Tuskegee, Ala.] Sept. 22, 1900

Dear Sir: In addition to the written application which my secretary, Mr. Scott, made to be placed before your company at its next meeting, I wish to say that so far as the mere letter of the law is concerned I feel quite sure I could go ahead and publish the Reminiscences and be sustained in doing so, but it has been my rule to deal frankly and sympathetically with my publishers as well as others with whom I have dealings, and I not only want to obey the letter of the law but have your frank and sympathetic consent in anything that I do, in other words I want to work with you and not in opposition to you and I want you to do the same thing with me.[1]

I am quite sure that, as Mr. Scott stated to you, the two publications will not in any way clash with each other since, in the first place, they are to be on different lines and to be sold in an almost wholly different section of the country and sold by the trade instead of by subscription. I believe that what I have planned to do for the other people will help your book since you know that anything that keeps my name before the public will assist in increasing the sale of your book.

And finally I urge as the strongest point that the work which I am to do for the other people will have for its main advantage the bringing of this institution before a class of people who have money and to whom I must look for money for endowment and other purposes. In proportion as I can get money from these people and keep this institution in a prosperous condition, in the same degree will there be a sale for your book. If this institution were to go down tomorrow, your book would at once become dead property on your hands, so you see it is important that we work wisely and sympathetically together.

I shall hope in the future to do more business with you in regard to publishing books; I don't want this to be the last by any means. This is another reason why I want to keep in close and sympathetic touch with you.

I hope you will put what I have stated in this note and what Mr. Scott has stated before your company and that you will comply with my request. If Mr. T. Thomas Fortune happens to be in Chicago on the day your board meets I have asked him to go to Naperville to confer with you and the board if you think it best. Yours truly,

Booker T. Washington

TLpS   Con. 282A   BTW Papers   DLC.

1 Hertel replied that Nichols and Co. had no objection to BTW doing another book as long as it met certain conditions. The proposed book, Hertel suggested, should be entirely different from *The Story of My Life and Work*, and the title of the book should be such as would not be confused with *Story*. Furthermore, the book "must be sold only to the trade and not to subscription book houses," and BTW was forbidden to write on Negro-related subjects "for any other subscription book publishers or allow his name to be used on the title page of any other subscription book during the life of his contract with us." (Oct. 9, 1900, Con. 182, BTW Papers, DLC.)

To David A. Graham[1]

[Tuskegee, Ala.] Sept. 24, 1900

Dear Sir: Please excuse me for intruding upon your valuable time. From one or two things I have seen in the newspapers from time to time I have gotten the impression that my name has been used or is being used in connection with the discussion of a change of studies in the New Orleans colored public schools in a way to give the impression that I favor only industrial or manual education and not the literary training of our people. If at any time you have occasion I wish you to make it known that while I earnestly advocate the importance of industrial and manual training that at no time on any occasion have I ever advised the lowering of the standard of academic education. I believe that with industrial education there should go the severest and most thorough form of mental drill as well as moral training. Industrial education without being accompanied by severe and systematic mental training will not accomplish what is expected from it. As I note the progress of our graduates after they have gone out into the world I find that those who have most thoroughly mastered their academic branches are those who are succeeding most admirably in following their trades or industries for which they were fitted while here at Tuskegee. The two forms of training, academic and industrial, should go hand in hand. Yours truly,

[Booker T. Washington]

TL Copy   Con. 171   BTW Papers   DLC.

1 David A. Graham, pastor of the St. James A.M.E. Church in New Orleans, was born in Indiana in 1861.

From William Henry Baldwin, Jr.

N.Y. [City] Sept. 27th, 1900

Dear Mr. Washington: Your letter of the 17th, referring to the book of the story of your life. I had read this book before. I did not know about it until this summer, when I took a copy and read it all through. I think that it is rough in some respects, but undoubtedly appeals to the colored people particularly, and it will do them a world of good if they will read it. It is not as good as you can do, and some of the illustrations are a little rough. I thank you very much for the copy which you sent me, and shall prize it highly. Very truly yours,

W H Baldwin Jr

TLS   Con. 792   BTW Papers   DLC.

To Hollis Burke Frissell

Tuskegee, Ala., Sept. 29, 1900

Dear Dr. Frissell: I have a letter from Mr. Baldwin suggesting that we apply to Mr. Jesup for money from the Slater Fund for which to pay the cost of making the exhibits in Montgomery, Atlanta and Birmingham. What do you think of the idea? Of course I would not apply unless Hampton would agree to apply for money in the same direction. I do not know how Dr. Curry would take it. It might be wiser to make the application through Dr. Curry in case we made it at all.

We have got to do something in this part of the South to keep up the interest of the Southern white people in the common schools among our people and notwithstanding the fact that we have no money in sight for the purpose I think it is the proper thing under the circumstances for us to make the exhibit in the three Southern cities named and shall plan to do so. I think it important that we give more attention to the education of the white people in the South, in the direction of believing in Negro education.

I want to see you or hear from you regarding the matter of public meetings in the North during the winter. I think it well that we arrange matters so that there shall be no conflict. Yours truly,

Booker T. Washington

TLS   BTW Folder   ViHaI.

From Lyman Abbott

New York   October 1, 1900

My dear Mr. Washington: I have read with great interest the first pages of your Autobiography, which I return to you herewith. I do not think there is any danger that you will go too much into detailed facts. The pictorial side of your life, the experiences through which you have passed, the incidents which you have seen, out of which your own generalizations have grown, will be of the first interest and the first value to our readers. I, for example, would like very much to know more of your boyhood life in the slave days, if it were possible for you to give it. Did you have any sports, any education, any work to do before emancipation? Probably all this lies back of your recollection, but if it did not, it would be of great interest; and the answer to the same questions within the range of your recollections and after emancipation, would be almost as interesting.

So would your personal recollections of the Reconstruction period and of the way in which that period looked to the just emancipated slave. It is generally looked upon wholly from the white man's point of view, sometimes the Southern white man's, sometimes the Northern white man's. How did it seem then to the Negroes, how does it seem now to one who has the interest of his race at heart and sympathizes with their point of view?

As to style, I have the impression that this manuscript has been dictated, and that if you were to go over it carefully, you would condense it somewhat by cutting out some repetitions. I have hinted at some of these with my own pencil, and I have made a few verbal alterations which I am sure you would approve, & suggested a change in the order of incidents. In order to get this manuscript into The Outlook the first week in November, we ought to have a good instalment in hand by the last of this week, or the first of next week at the latest. Yours sincerely,

Lyman Abbott

TLS   Con. 188   BTW Papers   DLC.

From Amanda Ferguson Johnston

Malden, W Va   Oct. 2 1900

my Dear Brother   the death of Aunt Sopha was a Shock to me. James Wright[1] was down Sunday & said She was as well as usal Thursday I got the Phone   Sh was dead. The money yu sent I sent eight dollars to Cousing Sallie & two dollars to the white Preacher for His Ser[v]ises at the grave as there was no Colord one Heare. the men are all gone out to work up the river   She died Happy.

Brother I Lost my Cow Last night   dont know what Caused Here deth[2]   She seemed Crazy   it is a Heavy Lost to me   I got the Pitchure Of mrs. washington   I Caried it all eaveing showing to the whites   tell Dr. W. F. Shirkey[3] is Looking for His Pitcure. Love to all from your sister

Mrs Johnson

ALSr Con. 176 BTW Papers DLC. "Mrs Johnson" is in another hand, perhaps added later at Tuskegee.

[1] James Wright, according to the 1900 census, was a twenty-two-year-old coal miner who boarded in the home of BTW's cousin Sallie Agee Poe.

[2] BTW had apparently sent his sister the money to purchase the cow as she had requested in Mar. 1900. (Johnston to BTW, Mar. 4, 1900, Con. 176, BTW Papers, DLC.)

[3] Wilbur F. Shirkey of Malden, W.Va., was a white physician, born in West Virginia in 1858.

From Jesse Lawson

Washington, D.C., Oct. 3, 1900

My dear Sir: Your very kind favor, of recent date, was duly received, and contents noted.

Did I make it plain that Mr. Birney[1] is to work up the case from the beginning? Start it in Louisiana and take it through the U.S. Supreme Court. He wants $500 as retaining fee.

I have heard nothing from Mr. McGhee[2] as yet. I understood you to say, when we were in Indianapolis, that you had received $100 from parties in the North to assist in the matter of testing the validity of the Louisiana constitution of 1898, and I wrote suggesting that that money be either turned over to me, as secretary of the committee in charge of the fund, or that it be paid directly to Mr. Birney, who has charge of the case.

The National Council, aside from our committee, has done nothing in the matter, but talk. The registration books in La., will close pretty soon, and then we shall have to wait two years before we can get a case, and in that time the people will have lost confidence in us, and justly so.

Mr. Birney went to work on the case according to our request and agreement, and we are in duty bound to keep our part of the contract.

On account of the great work you are doing for our people at the South, and the delicate position which you occupy in connection with that work, I think it best for you to keep in the background in matters like the Louisiana case. Your real friends appreciate your position, and will do nothing that is calculated to embarrass you in that work, or jeopardize your standing before the public.

You are a man of good sense, and will appreciate the following quotation: "A man is known by the company he keeps."

Your address at Indianapolis was in excellent taste, and I thank God that you did not fall into the trap that had been set for you.

I sent you The Star containing an interview relative to the Indianapolis convention.

Mrs. Lawson desires to be kindly remembered to Mrs. Washington and Mrs. B. K. Bruce. Yours truly,

Jesse Lawson

TLS Con. 178 BTW Papers DLC.

1 Arthur Alexis Birney (1852-1916), grandson of the abolitionist James Gillespie Birney, was an assistant U.S. attorney in the 1870s. Beginning in 1880 he helped reorganize the law department of Howard University and lectured there for many years. Birney was U.S. attorney for the District of Columbia from 1893 to 1897. He and his father, William Birney (1819-1907), were law partners. At the time of this letter Birney was a partner in the Washington, D.C., firm of Birney and Woodward.

2 Fredrick L. McGhee (1863-1912) was a black lawyer in St. Paul, Minn., a civil rights activist in Minnesota in the 1890s, and a leader in the Afro-American Council. BTW turned to McGhee on several occasions that involved secret civil rights activities. In 1904 BTW used McGhee, who was a Democrat and a Catholic, to attempt to persuade Cardinal Gibbons in Baltimore to oppose disfranchisement in Maryland. Even though McGhee worked for BTW, he was not a loyal Bookerite. He pre-

ferred a more militant stance on the civil rights issue. In 1905 he was a founder of the Niagara Movement, and is generally credited with the original idea for the movement. McGhee served as head of the Niagara Movement's legal department. (Meier, *Negro Thought*, 241-42.)

To Arthur Ulysses Craig

[Tuskegee, Ala.] 10, 5, 1900

Mr. Craig: Please arrange my telephone so that persons cannot call me up directly. Carry out the idea which you mentioned to me of having another telephone for Mr. Scott so that I can call persons up but that they cannot call me up directly.

B. T. W.

TLI   Con. 194   BTW Papers   DLC.

From Giles Beecher Jackson

Richmond, Va. Oct. 5th. 1900

Dear Sir: Yours of the 1st. to hand in which you said that you was a little disappointed at not hearing from me as to the result of the New England work and how much money had I in hand to be used in the Louisiana matter.

In reply I will say that upon my return from Boston, I found myself confronted with a large amount of professional work which necessarily absorbed every minute of my time; then again on the 1st. Tuesday in September the Grand Fountain of the United Order of True Reformers assembled here in convention which continued for a whole week; then on the 12th. of September, the meeting of the National Baptist Convention convened here which continued its session for a week; my presence and attention was demanded at both of these Conventions during their deliberations; for this reason you will see that I have had comparatively no time at all from the time I arrived home from Boston until now to give to the Louisiana and other matters pertaining to the disfranchisement of our race; I am now head and Soul in a local fight arising here in the City of Richmond from an effort on the part of the City Council to pass a "Jim Crow Car" ordinance providing for separate street cars in the City of Richmond; as you will see from an address and protest we have entered and made, a copy of which is here enclosed that you may see and understand the fight we have before us, and I am in the front of this battle which has absorbed almost all of my time; and I will say that I am confident that my efforts will be crowned with success. I have changed the sentiments of some of the newspapers in this City and succeeded on Monday night October the first in getting an indefinite postponement of the said ordinance; I merely mentioned these facts that you may see the reason why I have not communicated with you as frequent as in the past; for the matters and things complained of demands the strictest attention of every race leader and lover, and surely you are one of these; now referring to the Louisiana matter I will say that my interview with Mr. Pillsbury while in Boston caused a change of plans as Mr. Pillsbury had himself partly investigated the fighting grounds and thinks that a test case should not be made from the Louisiana Constitution and advises us to select the North Carolina or Mississippi constitution; in fact he thought it possible we would have to carry up more than one of the States to get a final and effective decision which would render the obnoxious constitutions ineffective in all of the States wherein they have been adopted.

Now in reference to the money necessary I will say that our Association is now entirely without funds and I am contributing out of my own means for the entire expense we are going and have gone to in testing the constitutionality of the Jim Crow Car Law which is now pending in the Supreme Court of the United States which we hope will be argued or set for hearing this month. We have not raised but $8.25 outside of the State of Virginia for this cause, as you know our Association started out to use all of its efforts in defeating the operation of the "Jim Crow Car Law"; but they have since agreed to unite with you and the other gentlemen who met in Washington, in raising the money to test the constitutionality of the "Grandfather Clause" of the several Southern State Constitutions; and this we will proceed to do at once; in the meantime however I would like to have another conference with you. Could you not come to Richmond that we may confer? From there we can proceed to Washington and complete the plans of operation; I know a plan by which we can raise all the money necessary but that will have to be done through you and myself and you need not then be publicly known; if you will come this way I will make it worth your while by getting up a big meeting for you to lecture in the interest of the National Business League, at which meeting we will form a branch league for the City of Richmond; it will hardly be necessary for me to promise you a good audience as I have always been fortunate in getting a big meeting in this City whenever I sign my name for that purpose. I have several letters and communications with Mr. Pillsbury outlining the work and suggesting the way in which it is to be done which I will send you to read should you not decide to come this way as indicated. Now I ask you to pardon me for not have written you for so long since our wonderful success in Boston. Hoping to hear from you by return mail I am   Very Respectfully Yours,

Giles B. Jackson

(Dict'd.)

TLSr   Con. 176   BTW Papers   DLC.

From Jesse Lawson

Washington, D.C., October 8, 1900

My dear Sir: Your letter enclosing postal order for $100 was received by me, this morning, and I sincerely thank you for the same. I also received, on Saturday, a letter from Mr. McGhee informing me that you had requested him to draw on the National Treasurer for the sum of $250 to be paid to the lawyer whom we had engaged. He also enclosed a type-written blank form in which the name of the lawyer should be inserted. I answered his letter immediately returning the blank filled in as requested. This he is to indorse, and forward to Bishop Walters for his signature, and Bishop Walters is to forward the same for the signature of Mr. J. Frank Blagburn[1] who resides at Des Moines, Ia., then back to Bishop Walters in Jersey City, who, in all probability, will be away from home for about three months, and we may get the money, if there be any in the treasury, about the beginning of next year, or sometime during the spring.

Mr. Birney is going right on with the work. He is in correspondence with a lawyer in Louisiana who has given the case considerable study, and this lawyer is a U.S. Senator. Lawyer Birney has received a letter from Mr. Pillsbury to the effect that the said Pillsbury will not be able to render any service in preparing the case, but will argue the subject before the U.S. Supreme Court when the case is brought there for action. Mr. Birney thinks that the most important thing to do is to get the case before the Court in the proper form and on the proper grounds, and that the verbal argument is a thing of less import, and I fully agree with him. Mr. Birney is to have charge and supervision of the case both in Louisiana, and at Washington, but he wants the best legal talent associated with him in Louisiana, and at Washington, and I have agreed to allow him to select that talent.

I have informed Congressman White and Register Lyons of every step taken, and they are in full accord with me on the matter.

Now concerning the money received: I send you herewith receipt for one hundred dollars ($100) on our printed form.

I have received money for nothing else except for the testing of the validity of the Louisiana law. Will also send receipt to the parties contributing the money, if you so desire.

The hundred and fifty dollars from New Orleans, promised in your telegram of to-day will just make out the other $250 due Mr. Birney, and will be sufficient to meet our present demands.

You promised to be responsible for $200. We shall need $500 more for Mr. Birney individually, but I am not advised as yet as to the amount that will be required for the lawyers associated with him. Mr. Birney is thoroughly professional, and in every way trustworthy, and you may communicate with him feeling assured that the public will never learn from him anything about your connection with the matter.

Mr. Lyons is fully aware of the needs of the situation. I shall try to arrange a conference with him for to-morrow.

Thanking you again for your good work in behalf of the race, and for the advancement of humanity, I remain, Yours truly,

Jesse Lawson

P.S. Mr. Pillsbury is rated as being a great lawyer, and we are quite fortunate in having him connected with the case, and we must be prepared to satisfy his financial demands for service rendered. He has given us no figures as yet.

J. L.

TLS Con. 178 BTW Papers DLC. Enclosed was a form receipt to BTW for a $100 contribution to the National Afro-American Council.

1 J. Frank Blagburn, born in Iowa in 1868, was a black pharmacist.

To Lyman Abbott

[Tuskegee, Ala., ca. Oct. 8, 1900]

My dear Dr. Abbott: I have received your kind letter together with the manuscript.

I am grateful to you for the suggestions which you make. I think you will find that the rest of the manuscript will be in better condition as to compactness, &c. I think you will find that most of the incidents which you suggest that I bring out more fully are covered in the later manuscript. The matter about which I am most anxious how ever to have an understanding is the order of treatment. When I talked with you and your son[1] I got the impression that you did not care for some of the rather stereotyped styles of autobiographies which as a rule are divided into the periods, of childhood, youth, &c, with each period exhausted before another is begun. This I have sought to avoid not only because I thought you desired it but also because it is in keeping with my own method of writing.

My general plan is to give the *first place* to facts and incidents and to hang the generalizations on to these facts — taking for granted that the average reader is more interested in an interesting fact than in a generalization based on that fact, and for this reason I have sought not to use too many generalizations and when they are used to have them well sugar-coated with some interesting incident.

I think you will find that all my facts are given in chronological order and that the generalizations based upon these facts only go beyond the natural order. For example in giving my experience in entering the Hampton Institute, I describe my first contact with general Armstrong. From this I go on and describe the general influence of general Armstrong — speak of his coming to Tuskegee 18 years later &c. In a word while I am at it I say nearly every thing that I intend saying about general Armstrong. This is the order of treatment in which I feel that I can do my best work. Still I want to be guided by your wishes.

This explanation together with the additional manuscript will enable you to give suggestions for my future work. I fear that you could not get a very correct idea of what I am trying to do from the small amount of man[u]s[c]ript which I sent you. By this mail I send you an additional installment. From this I think you can get a pretty correct idea of what to expect. If after you have gone over this you still feel that the order of treatment is not what you desire, I would suggest one of two things: that you have some one in your office rearrange it or if there is time you return it to me for rearrangement. Yours truly

[Booker T. Washington]

ALd Con. 166 BTW Papers DLC. Corrections and rearrangement instructions in Emmett J. Scott's hand.

1 Lawrence F. Abbott.

From John Elmer Milholland

London, Oct. 9th, 1900

Personal

My Dear Mr. Washington, I will take pleasure in discussing, for practical purposes, the two suggestions contained in your letter of Sept. 27th, which has just arrived, when I get to New York.

I refer to the farm experiment, and the proposed dis-franchisement case before the Supreme Court.

I am arranging now to sail on the "Oceanic," which leaves Wednesday of next week. That will give a chance to do a little something in the campaign for McKinley.

I have been trying to make the National Committee see the powerful argument there is in exposing the hypocrisy of that Democratic solicitude for the Philippine Islanders, ten thousand miles away, while it deliberately attempts to put back nine millions of American citizens into a condition of practical slavery. The President, you notice, touched on it very gingerly in his Letter of Acceptance. In that only, I hope, he exemplified the present materialistic, dough-faced, short-sighted leadership of the Republican Party.

In a letter the other day, I told him frankly that were it not for my faith in him, and not the party leadership, I would like to see a Republican defeat, by way of punishment for the cowardly desertion of its faithful Negro allies, who, if they had been fairly dealt with, would have placed the Solid South in the archives of history long ago.

For handling this entire matter I have a general plan worked out, a comprehensive, rational plan, and I think one that will prove successful in its results. I want to talk it over with you, and then we will talk it over with some other people and get to work at once.

I am carrying big burdens now, but I am going over to the United States expecting to translate some of them into cash. If I succeed in this I don't think we shall have to worry about funds for our campaign of equal rights, common sense and imperative Justice. We should start immediately.

But I am tired of these spasmodic, ill-considered efforts, which have made the Afro-American crusades little more than things of shreds and patches. We must organise in a thorough manner. We must unite, so far as possible, the various elements of strength, and place the whole thing under the direction of a strong resolute, intelligent committee, whose members care nothing whatever for individual positions or personal aggrandisement, but seek only solid accomplishment.

However, I need not elaborate this point, you understand I am sure what I am after.

By this mail goes another letter to the New York "Herald," which if published, will tend to keep matters alive until after the election, and then we must be prepared to take hold of this issue with a grip of steel and the tenacity of the bull dog —

> "Stick to our aim. The mongrel's hold will slip,
>   But only crowbars loose the bulldog's grip.
> Small though he looks, the jaw that never yields
>   Brings down the bellowing monarch of the fields."

My address in New York will be the Manhattan Hotel. Write me there, telling me when you will be in the City. Arrange to spend the entire evening. Dine with me, and we can talk the whole matter over fully. There are some things that require deliberation. Once in a while you get a subject that justifies you in crossing your legs, lolling back in your chair, and talking it out. This is one of that kind. Sincerely yours,

Jno. E. Milholland

TLS   Con. 1   BTW Papers   DLC.

From Richard Price Hallowell

Boston, Oct. 10, 1900

Dear Mr. Washington: I have received from Mr. Smith[1] your draft of the appeal which you wish me to sign and publish in the Boston Evening Transcript. After making a few verbal and other slight amendments, I have submitted it to Mr. Clement of the Transcript and he has consented to publish it. No doubt he will also give it editorial attention. I do not believe it will secure any large subscriptions. It ought to be signed by a more influential person or persons. If you could bring yourself to consent to the public use of your name, I am very sure the money asked for could be easily raised. As soon as the appeal is published I will send it to you. You will note that I agree not only to receive and receipt for, but also to *account* for whatever may be sent to me. In order to [do] this it will be necessary for you to give me a list of the names of your committee in Washington, and said committee must send to me in detail an account of disbursements. Very truly yours,

R. P. Hallowell

TLS   Con. 174   BTW Papers   DLC.

1 Peter J. Smith, Jr.

A Statement Written for Richard Price Hallowell

Boston. [ca. Oct. 10, 1900]

It is now evident that something should be done to secure a decision of the Supreme Court of the United States upon the validity of such election laws as have been recently passed in such States as Louisiana & North Carolina. Justice demands this not only in the interest of the Negro but in the interest of the Northern States which are being done a great injustice growing out of the fact that certain Southern States have virtually disfranchised a large part of the Negro population and others notably Virginia and Alabama are planning to do so, and still retain their full quota of Congressmen and members of the electoral college.

The Negro in the South does not object to any property or educational test provided the same test is applied honestly to both races. A company of responsible colored men in Washington have engaged lawyers who are now engaged in preparing a case to be brought before the United [States] Supreme Court, the colored people themselves have raised about $1500 towards the expens[e]. The total expenses in connection with the case will be about $5000.

I will be pleased to receive and receipt for any amount that any one may desire to contribute towards this cause.

Rich P. Hallowell

HdSr Con. 175 BTW Papers DLC. Written in BTW's hand. The item appeared, slightly revised, in the Boston *Transcript*, Oct. 10, 1900, 14.

To Emily Howland

Tuskegee, Ala., Oct. 15, 1900

Dear Miss Howland: I have received your kind letter and thank you for your encouraging words as well as for your check.[1] I agree with you fully that we must not suffer ourselves to be drawn aside on side issues but always keep in mind that education and property are the main forces by which we are to be elevated. I think however, that the violation of our constitutional rights is so flagrant in many of the recent laws that it will help us before the world if it be known that we are not sleeping over our rights.

Mrs. Washington asks to be remembered to you. I very much wish that you might come to our Conference in February. Yours truly,

Booker T. Washington

TLS   Emily Howland Papers   NN-Sc.

1 Howland sent BTW $10 toward the defense fund and wrote that she was "glad that the colored men are rousing to contest the proscriptive laws in the highest Court. . . ." She said, however, that she was mainly interested in supporting Negro education, which she believed would be the "righteous solution" of racial problems. (Oct. 7, 1900, Con. 703, BTW Papers, DLC.)

From George Bryant McCormack[1]

Birmingham, Ala. Oct 25th.,1900

Dear Sir: I have your letter of Oct. 21st. and your letters to the other officers of the company have also been handed to me. When the contract with the Birmingham Grate Coal Mining Company[2] was by me submitted to the governing committee of this company it had very careful consideration and received the approval of the governing committee only because we believed we could thus give the Negroes a chance to show whether or not they could under favorable circumstances make a success of operating a coal mine. The contract was one which we would not under any circumstances have made with anyone else. We believe we have been a friend to your people in very many ways and we were interested in seeing them make this experiment hoping that they would succeed and that it might be a step forward for them. At the same time I, knowing the coal field which they desired to develop, warned them that they were likely to meet with many disappointments and urged upon them the necessity of the use of economy and judgment in spending their money. The co-operative plan upon which they started does not appear to have been successful and they, as I believe unwisely, began borrowing money in quite large sums, paying no doubt high rates of interest and spending the money in many cases without proper regard for conditions and circumstances. We have been exceedingly lenient. We have furnished them the land and the houses with which to make the experiment in the business of coal mining. We have not even had from them the small rent promised to be paid us for the houses nor have we had from them the promised royalty on the coal mined from our land and sold to our regular customers. We are not complaining about our loss of rents and royalty. We feel that the experiment has been worth something to your people and what we may lose by it we shall lose willingly and uncomplainingly. We do not believe, however, having furnished the land and houses free of any charge, that we should be expected to do anything more. The experiment has not been a success and we regret to say that we doubt its being made a success even with the expenditure of more money. Feeling as we do about it and having the report of our engineers on the property, we believe that it is a kindness to Messrs. Pettiford and Walker to tell them that we are so firmly convinced that their mine cannot be made a success that we cannot extend them further assistance in any way. What you ask for them is for us to give them a class of contract which will be salable by them. In other words we are asked to give something of value to them, and to us, to relieve them from personal liability. I do not think it would be fair to the owners of the Tennessee Coal, Iron and Railroad Company for us to do that. Although we have the right under our contract to call for the greater part of their output at a fixed price we have not called for a ton of it but have on the other hand helped them to sell their coal to one of our regular customers, thus reducing the amount of coal which we could sell, to that customer. In that way we have contributed quite largely to the earnings of the Birmingham Grate Coal Mining Company and reduced our own profits. I have endeavored to write you fully so that you may understand the whole situation. In declining to accede to your request we believe that we are doing your people a kindness. Yours truly,

G. B. McCormack
General Manager

TLS Con. 185 BTW Papers DLC. Written on stationery of the Tennessee Coal, Iron and Railroad Co.

1 George Bryant McCormack (1859-1925) was general manager of the Tennessee Coal, Iron and Railroad Co. from 1895 to 1902. With a partner, Erskine Ramsay,

he also invested in real estate and coal lands around Birmingham, eventually forming the Pratt Consolidated Coal Co. He was president of the Alabama Coal Operators
Association from 1908 to 1921.

2 The Birmingham Grate Coal Mining Co. was probably the only black-owned
and -operated coal mine in the country when it was organized in 1899. The president
of the company was T. W. Walker of Birmingham, a forty-seven-year-old black minister. William Reuben Pettiford, a black minister and banker, was the general manager. The company operated a mine, "The Helena," at Tacoa, twelve miles outside
of Birmingham, and also operated a coal yard in the city. The 150 stockholders of
the company were all black, including the forty workers at the mine, most of whom
held shares. The mine was actually owned by the Tennessee Coal, Iron and Railroad
Co., a large employer of black miners, which leased it along with 2,000 acres of land
to the black operatives. The company produced its first coal in Sept. 1899, but was not
in full operation three months later when Max Bennett Thrasher visited the site.
(New York *Evening Post*, Dec. 2, 1899, 17.) At the first meeting of the NNBL in Aug.
1900, T. W. Walker gave a talk on the operation of the mine, and he seemed to be
a harbinger of the growth of black capitalism in the South, but the experiment
failed despite BTW's urging that the Tennessee Coal, Iron and Railroad Co. should
supply additional support.

An Editorial in the Washington *Colored American*

[Washington, D.C., Oct. 27, 1900]

MR. WASHINGTON NOT A POLITICIAN

Some papers are claiming that Booker T. Washington is a Democrat. This is not true. Mr. Washington, in a speech in Washington, D.C., last May said very positively: "I am not a politician, but
I am a republican." President McKinley and Mr. Washington are
close friends and the former showed his warm sympathy with the
latter's educational work sometime ago by paying a visit to Tuskegee and delivering an address, teeming with commendation of
the wonderful results being wrought for the race by the industrial
propaganda. Mr. Washington is not a politician and his silence
during the campaign is in accord with good sense. He here sets an
example for educators and ministers, that could be followed to
splendid advantage.

Washington *Colored American*, Oct. 27, 1900, 8.

From Charles Waddell Chesnutt

Cleveland, O. Oct. 29, 1900

My dear Mr. Washington, Your favor of recent date, inviting me to visit Tuskegee in February next, was duly received. I think I can safely accept your invitation, with the proviso that if I should come before that time, I would not be unwelcome. I am writing a novel which may require me to visit the South sooner than February, in which event I might visit Tuskegee & kill two birds with one stone. If I decide to come earlier, I will let you know, & try to time my visit so as to catch you there. I am sure I shall enjoy the visit.

I hope you will see my new novel, "The House Behind the Cedars," which runs along the "color line." My next book on the subject will be square up to date, & will deal with the negro's right to live rather than his right to love.

Mrs. Chesnutt joins me in regards to you, & I remain, Cordially yours,

Chas. W. Chesnutt

ALS   Con. 170   BTW Papers   DLC.

A Poem by Paul Laurence Dunbar

[October 1900]

BOOKER T. WASHINGTON

The word is writ that he who runs may read.
What is the passing breath of earthly fame?
But to snatch glory from the hands of blame,—
That is to be, to live, to strive indeed.
A poor Virginia cabin gave the seed,
And from its dark and lowly door there came
A peer of princes in the world's acclaim,
A master spirit for the nation's need.
Strong, silent, purposeful beyond his kind,
The mark of rugged force on brow and lip,
Straight on he goes, nor turns to look behind

Where hot the hounds come baying at his hip;
With one idea foremost in his mind,
Like the keen prow of some on-forging ship.

New England Magazine, 23 (Oct. 1900), 227.

A Statement on Southern Politics

[Tuskegee, Ala., ca. October 1900]

THE INTOLLERENCE OF THE SOUTH

Politically speaking there are at least one fourth [of] our states that might be designated as the "submerged fourth." Politically they are dead states. From now until the second Tuesday in November in every part of the union outside of the South, there will be public speaking torch light processions &c that will reach the remotest corner of each state. Besides this political documents by the thousand pounds will be sent into these states. No one can fail to see that the opportunity to hear and see some of the greatest statements and most eminent speakers and to be constantly in receipt of political literature is in the long run a great education. But the South receives no such education and [appears] to not want to receive it. It prefers to remain politically dead. In Georgia, Alabama, Mississippi, Lou[i]siana, Floridia, North Car[o]lina, South Car[o]lina, Virginia, there will be no discussion of the great national issues upon which the campaign is being fought. There will be in these states personal squabbles for the party nominations in which as a rule nothing but local matters are discussed and personal abuse often dealt in, but no broad generous discussions of the great questions of the day. There will be no torch light processions, no great speakers, hardly a dozen pounds of literature will be sent by either party into these states.

We have been told year by year that it was the Negro that kept the South politically dead. Let us see, the Negro has been practically out of politics in Miss. and South Carolina for *ten* years by reason of the new Constitutions adopted in these states, and yet Mississippi, and South Carolina are in exactly the same political condition as the other Southern States.

Our Southern friends may say that Mass., New Hampshire, and Vermont are politically solid, yes, but there is free vote and a fair count in these states and there is political discussion in every one of these states thr[ou]gh out the campaign. Neither Mr. Bryan nor Mr. Roosevelt will think of going into the South during the campaign. Both know that it is useless.

It is not the Negro that keeps the South in its present dead political condition. It is the intollerence of the Southern white man. It is the determination not to permit freedom of speech and freedom of action. It was this intollerance that ran the Tolberts[1] out [of] South Carolina a few months ago simply because they did not agree with their neighbors politically. There is no more opportunity for Negro rule in Mississippi, South Carolina, Louisiana under their new Constitutions than there is in Massachusetts and yet these states prefer to remain politically dead simply because the people have not learned and seemingly will not learn to shake off their old spirit of intollerance.

The way that Mr. Bryan and other party leaders treat the South ought to be an insult to the South. To secure the votes of the other states there must be hard earnest work. The vote of the South they know will always be cast in a certain way no matter what the issues are and no matter whether an effort is made in the South or not. All this is not complimentary to the South, but it will never be changed till the South makes up its mind to permit free speech and free action. The intollence of the old South must go.

AMd   Con. 18   BTW Papers   ATT.

[1] R. R. Tolbert, a white Republican candidate for Congress in South Carolina, and his brother, T. P. Tolbert, set up a special voting box outside the regular polling place in Phoenix, S.C., and urged blacks who were refused the right to vote to drop in an affidavit. When the Tolberts' scheme was challenged by the Democratic candidate, violence erupted, resulting in the shooting death of the Democrat and the wounding of Tolbert, who fled for his life. Later a white mob attacked and wounded R. R. Tolbert's uncle and a nephew, who were unaware of the earlier events. Turning its wrath from the Tolberts to blacks, the mob roamed widely in Greenwood County, murdering and lynching several people. Senator Benjamin R. Tillman blamed the Tolberts for the whole affair because they had encouraged blacks to vote, but he cautioned the white citizens of Greenwood to stop the violence or federal authorities might intervene. He told the whites to leave blacks alone and "go and kill the Tolberts. . . ." R. R. Tolbert's political career was ended and he left the state. (Tindall, *South Carolina Negroes*, 256-58.)

From Frederick H. Christensen[1]

Beaufort, S.C., November 2, 1900

Dear Sir   Some years ago, while a student in the Brookline High School, I had the pleasure of listening to an eloquent address delivered by you to the school. I can not say that I then became interested in the subject of industrial education among your people, for coming from the South, and belonging to the South, I had ever been interested in this, and had heard much of your institution. For this reason I was even more interested in your address than the others, realizing how much good your work may do.

My mother,[2] who is now in Brookline Mass., writes me that she has written to you or Mrs. Washington urging that a young man be sent here from Tuskegee, to start such a work here, on a small scale. She requests me to write to you explaining something about the conditions existing here.

Recently I read a book entitled "Stephen the Black," which doubtless you have seen. If the obstacles he met and had to contend against are a fair sample of the conditions existing among the whites and blacks through out the South, then this immediate section is in many respects far ahead of the South as a whole.

This is the "Black County" of the state. Often I ride into the country in the morning, ride for eight or ten hours and return to town in the evening without having seen a white face outside of the town. There are very few white farmers on this, Port Royal Island. The "Cracker" is utterly unknown here in this part of the county, save when court or similar events draw them from distant parts of the county.

Never-the-less the colored farmers are much more prosperous than those described in the book referred to. Most of them live on small farms that they own themselves — farms of from five to fifty acres. Most of them about 10 acres. Some have two-story houses, but most of them live in two room frame houses or log cabins, some of the former ceiled inside, and occassionally boasting a shed on back, containing a kitchen. Some of the less energetic live in one room log cabins.

The tenant system, which I understand is a curse to many places, is unknown here. Any man who is willing to work for it can buy his place, on easy terms.

Despite these advantages there is room for a great deal of improvement. Farming, if it can be dignified by that name, is done in a very primitive way. This year crops planted in low lands were "Drowned out," because the lands were not properly drained, while those on high ground suffered during the dry weather, which followed the wet, because not properly tended.

Some of the white farmers make as much as forty bushels of corn to the acre; and I believe the land capable of much more, yet the average colored farmer does not make more than one fourth of that amount.

Of course improvement in matters of farming would only be means to an end. The prosperous man with a comparatively large income would be anxious to improve his home and mode of living.

Very few of the colored farmers can either read or write, or have been farther from home than Savannah or Charleston. When one is fortunate with his crop and gets some cash on hand, instead of building barns, fencing in his land or buying more acres, he lays out his earnings on a buggy, or something else equally unnecessary.

Though we have not the tenant system as in parts of the South the credit system is a curse to both farmer and merchant. The merchant sells ploughs etc. in the Spring, to be paid for in the fall, the farmer giving chattel mortgages as security. Groceries and other things which he needs, or thinks he needs, are bought in this way. The merchant is obliged to charge more than if selling for cash. If this crop is poor the merchant suffers, realizing this he tries to insure himself against loss by increasing the price of the goods. The farmer of course is sure to lose by such a transaction. Yet I venture to say that if they only raised their own food stuffs, and knew how to manage, a great deal of this credit business could be done away with. I assure you the merchant would be as glad of it as the farmer.

The climate and soil are particularly well adapted to market gardening. Several crops can be raised on the same land each year. Very little of this is done by the colored farmers.

Certainly no young man working for the betterment of his people on Port Royal Isld would be hampered by the opposition of the whites. On the contrary when they became convinced that he was sincere, and that he was made of the right stuff to command respect he would receive much encouragement, and material help from this part of the population.

I don't want to paint in too vivid colors, or give a wrong impression, but yet I don't see how one engaged in your work could find a section in which he could work to better advantage than right here.

Compared with other parts of the South that I read of, the colored farmers here are more prosperous, but they don't know how to get one fourth out of the land that they should, nor how to save and use what they do make.

Here we have great hopes for Beaufort and Port Royal. Some day our harbor may become one of the greatest shipping points on the whole coast. Shall this city of the future be surounded by an ignorant, happy go lucky, semi civilized population; or shall we draw on a self-respecting, prosperous, law abiding, thrifty, people for our bone and sinew with which to build up this great city.

I am informed that a church which gives $100.00 for two scholarships at Tuskegee wishes that the two students might be sent from Port Royal Isd. The church committee having the matter in charge having requested mother to name two young men who would be likely to make the most of such a privilege. Kindly let me know whether this $50.00 covers anything more than tuition, and what chances a student would have to earn his board and lodging. What other expenses would he have to meet?

If there is any other information you would like to have which I can give, I should be glad to furnish it. Respectfully

Frederick H. Christensen

ALS Con. 169 BTW Papers DLC.

1 Frederick H. Christensen was born in South Carolina in 1878. The 1900 census reported his occupation as a salesman. He probably worked for his father Neils Christensen, who ran a hardware store in Beaufort, S.C. His brother, Neils Christensen, Jr., was an active promoter of schools in the Sea Islands and was a founder of the Port Royal Industrial School.

2 Abbie H. Christensen.

From Osceola Edward Jones[1]

Alcala P.I. Nov. 4–1900

Dear Principal: It affords me no little degree of pleasure to give you an idea of what the few Tuskegee students who inlisted in the U.S.V. are doing, and how they are getting along. There are four including myself in my Reg't. (The 49th U.S.V.).

We are stationed in Luzon and are scattered over the entire Island.

Two Batallions of us are in the northern part of Luzon and one on the south line. I am in company "C." We are stationed in a little Town to ourselves. The town is Alcala, on the "Rio Grande" /Spanish "Grand river"/English.

It is a very nice situation and we have not had any trouble with the Insurectors until here of late. We had a little fight in which we killed 30, captured 5, and wounded several. We were lucky in not loosing a man. Myself and two other young men of Tuskegee are non-comissioned Officers. Soldiering in Luzon is very hard, we have so much scouting to do and it keeps us always on the tramp, but we have stood it a year now and it is not long before we will be home again. I have learned a great deal of a soldier's life and what he has to undergo in a country like this.

It is rainy season here now and it is very hard on the soldiers, for mud and water is all you can see.

Mr. Washington, I would [like] so much to get a student[2] now and then, and find out what is going on at old Tuskegee.

Here is something for the student Mr. Washington if you find it interesting enough.

My Experience in Luzon

Many read and hear but none know the sorrows and afflictions of the American Soldier in The Phillipines but those who served in ranks. I have often read of the hardships undergone by the American soldier and of all of them none exceed my experience in this place. I have been out on 50 and 100 mile scouts when the thermometer regestered about 90, 5 and 6 miles from any shade or water and where it was too hot to stop or even walk slowly. Many times have we hiked all day long without any thing to eat more than two or three old hard tacks, and out in a country where there was nothing you could buy to eat, not even in the Towns.

One of the great reasons of so much scouting and hardships is due to the fact that we had nothing to fight.

Such soldiers as the Philipino, I say soldiers such scrubs are not fit to live. Attack them if you dare they fire one volley and are gone and away we go after them across that extremely hot country in pursut of flying Ladrones, for rogues is all they are. Ignorant half starved, half armed savages roming and plundering the country for what they could find and that was nothing more than trash.

In my estimation of these people and I think it is a very lenial one for I have traversed the entire Luzon on foot and have taken special notice as to the intelligence and industrous qualities of the Philipino, and he is in my estimation on a whole 100 years behind the simi civilized people of the world. He has no pride, no self respect, eats any thing that he can get, filth of numerous kinds is his delight. A person who comes to the Islands, stops in Manila and there by judges the remainder is vastly mistaken for the contrast is equal to that of day and night. All of this savagery makes life a burden for the civilized American soldier. In the rainy season which lasts nearly six months the Islands at most times is a perfect bog almost impassable yet we had to tramp it on foot, through mud and water knee deep, still hot mutilated and completely exhausted but with that ambition with which an American soldier conqueres though he falls we continue our weary march until we have reached our destination or some reconoitering place, where we can gain new strength and vigor. Luzon is made up entirely of mountains and vast naked plains or deserts uninhabited and with out growth of any kind.

The months of April, May and June in which we did the most of our scouting and the hotest of the year on the Islands. The Thermometer has registered [*blank*] in cool places imagine how it was with a soldier packing 100 and some times 200 rounds of amunition with 5 and 6 days rations across plains and naked mountains where shade and water was at times 6 and 7 miles apart. Returning to our well located quarters on the Rio Grande in the little villiage of Alcala I shall Always remember the old ma[ho]gony log on which we used to sit and talk over our scouts and encounters with the Phillipino soldier. Many an old familiar tune has been played off in that lonesome country on the little old guitar our company had while in Alcala.

Many a worried and homesick heart has left the old log for his bunk, there to lie and think of mother, sweet heart and home and long for those happy days to come again.

We have been on the Islands some time now and we have been steady going so some of us are very tired now and long for relief. The days are not so gay now as they seemed while steering into the harbor at Manila a year ago. They have become more solemn and discharge their duty with firmness and no play.

The products mostly produced on the Islands are rice corn, tobacco and hemp. The natives in general are very lazy and insolent, and the real strength is seldom obtained from the extremely furtil soil. These people are very peculiar in their mode of religion, all of them are religious and yet all of them gamble curse and use all manner of profane language publicly and regard it as perfectly correct.

There are some very intelligent people among the Phillippino's but they are few and far between.

One peculiarity about them they all strive to be merchants and all have something to sell. Sunday is their great market day.

Corporal O. E. Jones Co. "C" 49th U.S.V.

Give my best regards to the teachers and students. Ans. soon, Your obedient servant and student,

Osceola E. Jones

ALS Con. 176 BTW Papers DLC.

1 Osceola Edward Jones (1878-1930), of Meridian, Miss., was a member of the B middle class at Tuskegee from 1897 to 1899. He served with the 49th Regiment, U.S. Volunteer Infantry, from Sept. 1899 to June 1901. Later he moved to Chicago, where he worked as a bricklayer, a trade he had learned at Tuskegee.

2 *Tuskegee Student.*

Extracts from an Address at a Dinner for Oliver Otis Howard[1]

Waldorf-Astoria, New York, November 8, 1900

Within the last few hours I have traveled nearly one thousand miles and would gladly have traveled an additional thousand if necessary in order that I might be here to assist Bishop Gaines in bringing the greetings and the gratitude of nearly ten millions of my people to this occasion and to the man whom it honors.

No word or act of mine can add to General Howard's greatness, but I am most grateful for the privilege of reminding General Howard and the promoters of this fitting tribute, how deep and sincere is the gratitude in the heart of every member of the Negro race from one shore of this country to the other, for what he has done for and been to us. I am glad to add my word of praise while the General is with us in the flesh and strength of life. Too often it is our custom to curse men while they live and to praise only when they are dead. Howard is a name that the Negro keeps tenderly folded in his bosom by the side of that of Garrison, Phillips, Lincoln and Grant. The Negro is not and will never prove himself ungrateful for what you did. But you will agree that this occasion is too great, too sacred, for mere personal eulogy. The individual is the instrument — national virtue the end.

The great question that concerns General Howard and the rest of this company is, has it all paid? Are the tangible, visible results in the progress of the Negro in keeping with the priceless sacrifice of life, limb, health, and treasure, sustained by the Howard type of man? Are the Negroes justifying the faith which you have placed in them?

Some thirty-five years ago when General Howard was in Atlanta and asked of the school boys in Atlanta University what message he should take from them back to the people in the North, you remember the story immortalized by Whittier of how one little barefooted boy arose and exclaimed, "Tell 'em we're risin'." That once barefooted boy, Richard Wright, who in a sense is a type of the race, has been "rising" ever since until he is now honored president of one of the largest and most prosperous colleges in the South, and only a few months ago received a visit at his college from the President of the United States. And so when I left the South to attend this meeting, I asked our boys and girls our men and women, what message I should bring to General Howard to cheer and comfort him on the anniversary of his seventieth birthday, and with united voice the answer came, "Tell General Howard that we are still rising; tell him that the sacrifice has not been in vain; tell him that up from the depths of ignorance and poverty we are coming, by habits of thrift, economy, by the way of the industrial school and college we are coming. We are crawling up, working up, yea, bursting up. Often through oppression and prejudice, but through them all we are coming up and with proper habits, intelligence, and property, there is no power that can permanently stay our progress."

As great as is the honor extended to General Howard tonight around this festal board by his friends and fellow soldiers, I believe the greater tribute is being paid him in the cotton, rice and sugar fields of the South by the struggles and sacrifices of a race to justify all that has been done and suffered for it.

The work which General Howard so well began in the dark past is not yet complete, though almost miraculous progress has been made. Those of us who are strong in body, strong in purse, and young in years must, with General Howard's assistance while he remains, complete this work. This task must be completed in public school, industrial school and college, and most of all in the efforts of the Negro himself; in efforts to withstand temptation, to economize, to exercise thrift, to disregard the superficial for the real, the shadow for the substance; to be great and yet small, learned and yet simple, in efforts to be patient in the laying of a firm foundation to grow so strong in skill, knowledge and possessions that he will be recognized everywhere by reason of his intrinsic worth as a race.

TM Con. 955 BTW Papers DLC. Interspersed in the text are notes in BTW's hand to remind him to pause for anecdotes and jokes, for example: "Half Negro," "the changeless laws," and "Pig story." An autograph draft is in Con. 175 and an early typed draft is in Con. 182, BTW Papers, DLC.

1 Max Bennett Thrasher wrote Emmett J. Scott that "Mr. Washington's address last night at the Waldorf was a notable success in every way." "The boxes," Thrasher continued, "were largely filled with magnificently dressed ladies, satins, silks, laces, diamonds, and more bare shoulders and arms than one is apt to see outside the Waldorf-Astoria." He wrote Scott that he had never heard BTW do better, that "he

was almost constantly interrupted by applause, much more and h[e]artier than any one else got." As a result of his performance, BTW was invited to speak at the exclusive Lotos Club. Thrasher thought this was "a *very* great compliment." (Nov. 9, 1900, Con. 185, BTW Papers, DLC.)

To Emmett Jay Scott

New York, Nov. 9 1900

Dear Mr. Scott: The banquet last night was a great thing[,] the greatest one that I have attend[ed] for a long while. My address made a greater impression than any I have delivered for a long while. I send you a marked copy of the World.[1] New York news papers are vile. You can not depend upon them to do justice to any decent occasion.

As a result of my address I have been invited with Mark Twain to address the Lotus club[2] Saturday night. This is said to be the most select and aristocratic club in America.

Every one openly remarked last night that my address was *the* address of the occasion. I am rather glad I came. Yours Sincerely

Booker T. Washington

ALS   Con. 86   Emmett J. Scott Papers   MdBMC.

[1] An account of the O. O. Howard dinner appeared in the New York *World*, Nov. 9, 1900, 6. The article listed the guests and even mentioned that BTW's talk was the hit of the evening because of its wit and earnestness. BTW was perhaps disappointed that the paper did not reproduce his speech, or report the affair in more depth.

[2] The Lotos Club, founded in 1870, was a New York club composed of journalists, artists, musicians, and members of the city's business elite. Many famous persons spoke at the club over the years. Among them were Henry M. Stanley, Ulysses S. Grant, and Oliver Wendell Holmes. Probably the club members that BTW knew best were John E. Milholland and Charles Francis Adams, Jr.

From Charles Waddell Chesnutt

Cleveland, O., Nov. 10, 1900

My dear Mr. Washington: Your favor of Nov. 3d is at hand. I shall try to regulate my visit to Tuskegee so as to meet you there, as it would otherwise be like seeing the play of Hamlet with Hamlet left out. In one sense, at least, you are Tuskegee; as Page says in his new magazine "Every successful industrial or financial combination is built on a strong personality," and so is every other great enterprise, Tuskegee included.

I read the first of your Outlook serial with great interest and pleasure, and look forward to reading them all with similar profit. I am pleased to know that you read "The Sway-backed House" & hope you may see my new novel, which is already winning golden opinions. Sincerely yours,

Chas. W. Chesnutt

ALS Con. 170 BTW Papers DLC.

From Theodore Roosevelt

State of New York Executive Chamber   Albany   Nov. 10th, 1900

My dear President Washington: Your telegram gave me peculiar pleasure.

Now, when you come up North next I particularly want to see you. I have had some long talks recently with my friend Lewis[1] of Harvard. There are points where I do not entirely agree with him and I want to consult you about them. Faithfully yours,

Theodore Roosevelt

TLS Con. 174 BTW Papers DLC. Docketed in Emmett J. Scott's hand: "You have him sure!"

1 William Henry Lewis.

From Allen Ralph Griggs[1]

Dallas, Texas. 11/16/1900

PERSONAL & PRIVATE,
    CONFIDENTIAL
Dear Brother: On the 28th inst. I am to meet, at Chattanooga, Tennessee, a committee of five, appointed by the National Baptist

Convention, at Richmond, Va., to confer with a like committee from the Home Mission Board of the Southern Baptist Convention, to discuss plans of cooperation between the Southern White Baptist and the Negro National Baptist Convention; as I understand it.

The Southern White Baptist, in my judgement, are seeking a channel through which to enter into a closer relationship with the Negro Baptist of the South in the expenditure of benevolent funds for the moral religious and intellectual development of the race. As I regard you one of the leaders of our people and one of our foremost thinkers I write you for an opinion as to what in your judgement would be the best organized channels and plans for cooperative work among our people, and along what lines of Christian work do you think the money, they have to spend, would reach the greatest number in the production of the greatest possible good for the race and denomination.

I mention here a few things I have heard discussed:

1. That the Southern White Baptist should help support theological teachers in a great theological seminary wholly under the control of colored people and *distinctively Negro.*

2. That they the Southern Baptist should devote the major part of means and energies to the development of the Fortress Monroe Compact entered into in 1893, between the American Baptist Home Mission Society and the Southern Baptist Convention, known as the New Era Institute work.

3. That the Southern Baptist Convention (White) should help support about four general district missionaries and educational agents to organize the colored people through out the south for earnest, active, aggressive and cooperative work in concentrating missionary and educational forces wholly under the control of the Negro.

Now does either of these plans suit you, or can you suggest to me a better one?

I hope you will regard this letter as strictly private and confidential until you hear from me after the Chattanooga meeting on the 28th.

I hope to hear from you in a few days and to have the privilege of using at that meeting any thing you may say for the good of our race, or I will agree to keep it to myself, your name and opinion or either as you may direct. Respectfully,

A. R. Griggs

TLS Con. 173 BTW Papers DLC.

1 Allen Ralph Griggs was born in slavery in Georgia in 1852. He was a student at Virginia Union University in Richmond and was ordained as a Baptist minister in 1874. Serving in Texas, he was responsible for the organization of about 500 churches. He was active in the National Baptist Convention, serving a three-year term as president, and was a member of numerous Baptist conventions, both black and integrated, in America and Europe. He also helped organize several schools in Texas and edited the *Western Star* in Houston, Tex.

From Mary Fletcher Mackie

Newburgh [N.Y.]—Nov. 21—1900

My dear Booker — On my way home from church I was stopped by one of the ministers of a neighboring church — whom I have known for 35 years who said "Miss Mary I want to congratulate you on having gone onto the roll of honor.["] I knew at once that he had been reading the Outlook. I had not read the last number and so I laughed and said "yes I have heard that Mr. Washington has immortalized me by giving credit as I feel far beyond my deserts but I have not read his eulogy." And now I do want to tell you how much I am enjoying your autobiography. It is beautifully written and sets forth more graphically than any article that I have read the transition life from slavery to freedom. It reads like a romance. I have smiled m[an]y times over the inspiration which guided you in your choice of a surname. The more I think of it I feel you were wisely *guided* in your choice and if he who has made the name honored to us as the "Father of his country" you too by your earnest, wise, unselfish life are adding fresh laurels to the same name which future generations shall blend together as belonging to a name which all Americans both white and colored, shall honor as leaders of the two races which make our commonwealth. I feel quite sure "George" would be proud to grip hands with our Booker in recognition of the honored place he has made for himself in this country. I never realized until now how many beautiful unwritten histories lay all around us in that H. work, but we were too busy in other ways to draw them out of the students. How little I realized the burdens you were all carrying. My heart condemns me now that I did not read better between the lines and do more than I did for your comfort. I for one feel greatly indebted to Mrs. Ruffner for training me so good a janitor. I often picture to myself how you used to come in and drop down a perfectly tremendous load of blankets — more than enough really for two men — while the perspiration rolled down your face. I have truly not the slightest recollection of that remarkable examination you give me credit for — but I do want to say I have thanked God many times that I was ever allowed the privilege of contributing in a small degree to the preparation of so noble a life work as yours. You have honored all your teachers in the noble use you have and are making of your life. May God spare you for many years yet that you may see as your noble Gen. and leader did the abundant fruits of an unselfish devoted life to the good of others.

Has this autobiography ever been printed in book form or is it something new you are writing for the Outlook? I was told last summer as I understood it, that you *had* published an autobiography, perhaps I got it wrong, that you were to do it. Now I have a favor to ask of you. Don't you want to send me some time a good photograph of yourself. This picture which goes with the story is such a caricature I do not like to have our girls associate it with your name. My sister Miss Mackie is reading the story to our girls every Sunday night and I want them to know you do not look like that picture — then I shall value it myself very much.

When I saw in the So. Letter a year ago last spring that some of your friends had sent you to Europe I determined to write you at once if only to tell you how much I was enjoying with you your trip — but like many such plans I failed to carry it out at once and so you never got it. The truth is I have more or less rheumatism all the time in my hands and there are days when it is hard for me to use even a pencil. I have many friends that I send only one letter a year to; the fact is I seldom write a letter but I love my friends just as well as I ever did — and my Hampton pupils are among my dearest friends. I often wish Booker I could do something for your work; to be very straight forward we have been very much cramped during the past few years. Our boarding School has grown very small — last year we had 6 — this year 8 — where we used to have 35 pupils. The day school is large but that is not remunerative — and as we are entirely self supporting we have to live very economically as far as we are ourselves concerned. I am not unhappy over it except that I have been obliged to cut off some of the little outside helps it used to be a great pleasure to make.

I wish sometime when you are in our neighborhood you would come and see us. We should all enjoy having you do so and I would like to have our School girls meet you. If this finds you at Tuskegee please give my love to all my old pupils. I often think of them all — Mr. Logan — Mr. Green — Mr. Palmer and I suppose you have still others. I always think of them as boys. I wondered as I read today which one it was who pushed the Gen. in his rolling chair up the hill. I always read with great pleasure anything which comes from your pen. The last was "Education *will* solve the race question" to which I say amen. Miss Charlotte and I are planning if all goes well to go to Hampton in the Spring to spend Easter — if you do I hope you will either be going to or from Tuskegee and so can take in Hampton that we may have the pleasure of meeting you there on the spot so dear and now sacred to us all.

Please remember me kindly to Mrs. Washington whom I should like to meet sometime. With love for you   Sincerely your friend,

M. F. Mackie

ALS   Con. 212   BTW Papers   DLC.

An Interview in the New York *Times*

Boston, Nov. 22, 1900

Booker T. Washington said to-night regarding the recent lynching of a negro in Colorado that the same class of people who begin to break the law by lynching a negro will soon learn to break the law by lynching a white man.

"I think," said Mr. Washington, "that the Colorado lynching emphasizes the fact that the only way to stop such outbreaks is in the first place to bring about such general education, not only in books, but in industry and thrift, as will make such acts as that which provoked the lynching fewer, and then to educate public sentiment up to the point where the people in all parts of the country will see that we can only have the highest civilization if the law is enforced regardless of race or color.

"Wherever people begin to lynch for one kind of offense they are soon led into the temptation of lynching for any other kind of offense. Aside from the injustice that is perpetrated upon the individual put to death without a legal trial, we must bear in mind that there is a permanent degradation which comes to the individual who takes part in and witnesses such an outrage as occurred in Colorado."

When asked his opinion of the disfranchisement of the Southern negroes Mr. Washington said:

"My attitude regarding the restriction of the ballot is well known by the white and colored people in the South. More and more I am settling down to the idea that no special law can permanently hold the colored people back; neither can any special law push them forward in any large measure. We have got to depend upon the slow but sure forces of education in head, hand, and heart for our development."

New York *Times*, Nov. 23, 1900, 2. The interview appeared as a news item in the Montgomery *Advertiser*, Nov. 24, 1900, 1.

To Emmett Jay Scott

Crawford House, Boston, Mass. Nov. 23, 1900

Dear Mr. Scott: You will notice that a man by the name of Hammond[1] has introduced into the lower house of the Alabama Legislature House Bill No. 218 which has for its object the separation of white and colored passengers in sleeping cars. I wish you to go to Montgomery at once and see Col. Falkner and try to get him to use his influence against the passage of this bill.[2] I think if you talk to him in the right way that he will become interested and will bring about its defeat. I wish you to attend to this matter at once.

If he cannot defeat the bill I hope you will urge upon him to have its passage delayed until I can have an opportunity of going before the committee that has the bill in charge. Please deliver the enclosed letter to Col. Falkner.

I wish you to watch very closely the Alabama papers and Georgia papers and notify me at once by telegram if necessary if any race legislation is introduced into either house of either Legislature. Yours truly,

B. T. W.

TLI   Con. 187   BTW Papers   DLC.

1 Burwell Pope Hammond, a lawyer and a Democrat, was born in Alabama in 1868 and served as a representative from Etowah County in the Alabama General Assembly of 1901.

2 See Scott to BTW, Nov. 27, 1900, below.

From Alice Bradford Wiles[1]

Chicago, November Twentythird [1900]

Mr. or Mrs. Booker Washington, Dear Sir or Madam, The public press has reported you both, as saying publicly that in your opinion the time had not come when the admission should be urged of a club of colored women to the General Federation of Women's Clubs. May I ask if this is correct and if you are willing that I should so quote you?[2] I will use only your own language in so quoting you, if you will give it to me in the form of a letter or a telegram (sent at my expense).

I am exceedingly anxious to hear from you by Tuesday night or early Wednesday morning next November Twentyeighth, for on the afternoon of Wednesday, the Chicago Woman's Club takes up the question, and an effort will be made to protest against the action of the executive board in last June postponing action upon the admission of a club of colored women. Your opinion or that of your wife (or husband) would have immense influence.

I am the daughter of a Boston abolitionist, who was the warm friend of Garrison, but I believe the admission of a club of colored women would disrupt the National Federation, because of the prejudices of southern white women, which they have not yet had time to outgrow. Such disregard of their feelings I think would increase the bitterness and misunderstanding following the war, and would therefore be really a great national calamity, and I believe it would not help the negroes one bit, but rather postpone the time, we all long for, when a better relation shall exist between the Whites and the Blacks.

I deeply deplore the apparent disregard of the feelings of black women who wish to join us, but I believe they are very very few, whereas there are thousands of our members already among the southern white women — six thousand in Georgia alone.

I want to be right on this question, and take the side which promises the widest good to our country as a whole. Your opinion will be welcomed. That you may know that you are writing to one having her little share of influence in women's clubs, may I be excused for telling you that I have been chairman of the education department of the Chicago Woman's Club, and president of the Illinois Federation of Women's Clubs. Yours very sincerely,

Alice Bradford Wiles

A telegram will *surely* reach me in time.

ALS   Con. 187   BTW Papers   DLC.

1 Alice Bradford Wiles was born in Massachusetts in 1855. She resided in Chicago with her husband, Robert H. Wiles, a patent lawyer, and two children.

2 BTW and his wife received several letters from leading clubwomen in Illinois and other states seeking their advice on the issue of the integration of the General Federation of Women's Clubs. The General Federation had refused to admit black delegates and turned the controversial matter over to the various state federations. On Dec. 6, 1900, Clara M. T. Larson, a former president of the Illinois State Federation of Women's Clubs, wrote BTW that she saw no reason for "excluding the intelligent colored women from our counsels," but that her opinion had been countered by others who insisted that BTW was opposed to integration of the federation. (Con. 178, BTW Papers, DLC.) Clara Kern Bayliss, of Springfield, Ill., wrote BTW that she hoped the race issue could be sidestepped by proposing an educational requirement for admission, "thus making the barrier one which the colored delegates may hope to surmount and which will be a spur to their ambition, rather than an utterly insurmountable one for whose existence they are in no way responsible." She urged BTW to give her "the arguments which should be given most emphasis." ([1900], Con. 190, BTW Papers, DLC.) It is not certain whether BTW answered the inquiries or developed a clear-cut position on the matter of integrated clubs. In 1901 several clubwomen again asked BTW for his advice. He apparently replied to one that he did not want to be drawn into the controversy, for Mrs. J. Lindsay Johnson of Rome, Ga., replied: "Yours received, I feel you are right to a great extent

because it would not do to be drawn into this and that. . . ." (May 20, 1901, Con. 201, BTW Papers, DLC.) In 1902 Emmett J. Scott wrote to Mrs. M. F. Cummings, a clubwoman in Ypsilanti, Mich., that "Mr. Washington very scrupulously avoided any discussion of the matters coming before the Federation, though importuned to do so from every conceivable source." (July 18, 1902, Con. 272, BTW Papers, DLC.)

To Emmett Jay Scott

Crawford House, Boston, Mass. Nov. 24, 1900

Dear Mr. Scott: I have just sent a letter to the Atlanta Constitution dealing with the bill which is now before the Legislature and indirectly with other matters relating to the cutting off of the public school appropriation from the colored schools. As soon as the Atlanta Constitution prints this letter I want you if possible to get the Advertiser to copy it; in order to do this you will have to go to Montgomery. If the Advertiser will not copy it in full I think you had better get the Journal to print it. I do not know whether the Advertiser will do it because there is some feeling between the Constitution and the Advertiser, still if you work the matter right the Advertiser may publish it.

I am sending also to you the letter to the Advertiser regarding a Negro reformatory which I wish you would send direct to the paper.

I wish you would send a copy of "Tuskegee" to each one of our Northern and Eastern Trustees, also send copy to Mr. J. W. Adams. Yours truly,

Booker T. Washington

TLS Con. 182 BTW Papers DLC.

To the Editor of the Montgomery *Advertiser*[1]

[Crawford House, Boston, Mass.] 11-24-00

THE NEED AND VALUE
OF A REFORMATORY FOR
NEGRO YOUTHS

At this period of our civilization it is hardly necessary to attempt to advance any argument in favor of the necessity of a Reformatory for young Negro Criminals. The most important thing that I can say in favor of such an institution is that no state or nation that has ever tried the reformatory system has ever abandoned it. I have visited personally a large number of state reformatories in the North and West, and I have not found a single instance where the state officials would be willing to abandon the reformatory for the old method of simply punishing criminals with little idea of reforming them.

The State of Virginia has within a few years established a Reformatory for Negroes and the results so far are satisfactory. I know of other instances where Negro youths have been permanently cured of crime through the influence of a well conducted reformatory.

Some may argue that a reformatory will not help the Negro criminal. Certainly it can not hurt him. The habit which is now largely practised of necessity in this state of placing mere children in some cases in prison by the side of old and hardened criminals, is something that few of the best people in Alabama endorse. The result of placing children by the side of old criminals, is that the child's nature is soon hard[en]ed and blunted and instead of being reformed or even punished (for he is too young to appreciate punishment) he comes out of prison worse than when he went in. Whether one believes that the reformatory will help Negro children or not; for the sake of humanity I believe that all will agree that the present system should be changed.

Many of the Negro children now in the convict camps are there for stealing apples, ban[a]nas, chickens &c.

I have consulted freely Col. S. B. Trapp of the Penitentiary commission on this subject. Col. Trapp has wide experience in dealing with crim[i]nals and has had opportunity of observing the results brought out in reformatories in many other states and [I] have his permission to say that he will endorse any wise movement for a reformatory of young Negro criminals.

[Booker T. Washington]

ALd Con. 20 BTW Papers ATT.

To the Editor of the Atlanta *Constitution*

Tuskegee, Alabama   Nov. 26, 1900

Editor Constitution: A few days ago in New York I heard Dr. Truman H. Backus,[1] a famous educator of that state say in a public address in discussing the Negro in the South that [there] was no instance [in] history where the former owners of an enslaved race had ever done so much immediately after emancipation to assist their former slaves, materially educationally and religiously and had on the whole shown them [so] much kindness and sympathy as is true of the white people in the South in their dealings with their former slaves since the war. Before I heard this remark by Dr. Backus I had never thought of the matter in this way. Since I have made some investigation and notwithstanding many things that have taken place in the South which both races regret, I find that history supports Dr. Backus statement. This is a record which every white man and woman and every Negro should be proud of. Some times I know we think we have had pretty rough times, but [when] we take a broad generous view of the history of the South during the last forty years I think that both races have great reason to congratulate themselves that things are in as good condition as they are.

At the present time I do not believe that there [are] any two southern states where the two races are getting on so well and peacefully as in Georgia and Alabama. It seems to me that it is to the interest of both races that the present good and helpful relations continue. I regret to see that a bill is pending before the Georgia legislature which I am told has for its object the cutting off of a large proportion of the public school fund that is now going to the colored schools. Such legislation or agitation not only serves to stir up and unsettle the colored people and make [them] discontented and restless, but it proves a direct loss to the Southern white people who depend upon Negro labor for their income in the farming districts. When ever the Negro in the country districts is made to feel that the school privileges for his children are going to be cut off, he at once begins to prepare to move to a city where he knows that he can keep his children [in] school eight or nine months in schools that are maintained by missionary funds or by special taxation. The white land owner is left without a tenant ·and with great scarcity of labor in the seasons when the Negros labor is most valuable. I repeat that efforts at such legislation hurts both races. It causes the Negro to come to the cities where he does not as a rule do as well as he did in the country because of the severe competition and many temptations, and it causes the white man to lose in dollars because the white man is without sufficient tenants and laborers.

While I am on this subject I might as well add that the aggition [agitation] of all legislative measures which the Negro considers oppressive results in making many of the most valued colored people leave the farms for the cities of the South or the Northern States. I am told on pretty good authority and the white news papers bear out the statement that thousands of the best colored people have left the farming districts of the State of North Carolina within the last few months and that many of the white farmers have met with great financial loss because of the scarcity of Negro farm labor. ~~Lynching is~~ It is always the white man who lives in the country or who owns land in the country that is one of the main suffer[er]s when the Negro is stirred up and made dis[s]atisfied. Some of the counties of Georgia I think have recently experienced what it means to get the Negroes so stirred up that they move by car loads to other sections even though by moving they did not help themselves. I repeat that the Southern white people have shown much generosity to the colored people in the matter of their education, [and] in other directions but I do not believe that there is a single white man in the South today who is the poorer because of any [of] his money that has gone into the public schools. I do not believe that there is a Southern white man who would take back a single act of kindness that he has ever done for a Negro.

If we can just let matters alone for a while, cease stirring [up] all these questions that excite and embitter the races so that the people will have more time to give to their material & educational development I believe that the South will be a glorious country for both races.

Georgia and Alabama are in the lead in helpfulness to the Negro as well as in the helpful friendly feeling prevailing between the two races and I pray God that nothing may be done to disturb these relations.

Booker T. Washington

ALdS Con. 18 BTW Papers ATT. The letter appeared in the Atlanta *Constitution*, Nov. 28, 1900, 6, and in the Montgomery *Advertiser*, Dec. 5, 1900, 6.

[1] Truman Jay Backus (1842-1908) organized a school for blacks in Richmond, Va., at the close of the Civil War. In 1867 he joined the faculty of Vassar College and was instrumental in the development of education for women. He was president of Packer Collegiate Institute in Brooklyn from 1883 until his death.

In a speech on Negro education before the American Missionary Association in Oct. 1900, Backus argued in favor of limiting black education to the three Rs. He believed this was sufficient to prepare blacks for citizenship. He urged that missionary money be spent on small neighborhood schools where the teachers also played the role of moral leaders of the community. (Brooklyn *Eagle*, Oct. 25, 1900, 4.)

From William Henry Baldwin, Jr.

N.Y. [City] November 26, 1900

Dear Washington: I saw William E. Dodge today.

He spoke of the great pleasure he had in reading your life in "The Outlook." He thought it told it in a simple, straightforward way, and it was very attractive.

I want to speak to you again about the Montgomery matter. You must bear in mind if it ever becomes known that the colored people are willing to hire or retain anyone to defend any bills which may be introduced against their interest, that there will be a great many bills introduced for the purpose of getting your fees. It is a two-edged sword you are playing with, and you must watch it carefully. Very truly yours,

W. H. Baldwin, Jr.

TLSr Con. 792 BTW Papers DLC.

From Emmett Jay Scott

Tuskegee, Ala., Nov. 27, 1900

Dear Mr. Washington: I returned from Montgomery last night. I went at once to see Colonel Falkner and had a very satisfactory and pleasant interview with him. He is certainly a most remarkable man and one that we must tie to. I found him especially interested in your matter. He said, however, that it had not escaped him and that as soon as he noticed any reference to the introduction of the bill he had it smothered beyond resurrection. He said all of this in the most jubilant way and seemed especially delighted that he had done so without having you mention it to him. At the same time, however, he seemed very glad to learn that you keep so well advised as to the trend of events.

He must be the power so far as the Alabama Legislature is concerned, because there must have been from five to eight men waiting to see him during the hour that I myself was compelled to wait. All of these men I learned from the employees of the office, were interested in one way or another in legislative matters.

I feel quite sure that you received my telegram with pleasure. With reference to the exhibit, I can say that it is the feature of Montgomery just now. The three days that I was there, Friday, Saturday and Monday, it was simply crowded during the whole time.

Not only are the white men of the city taking an interest in the exhibit, but the white women as well. They seemed delighted in being shown around and I believe that your judgment in carrying it there has been admirably vindicated.

Most of the Legislature are visiting the exhibit in parties of twos, threes and singly. I met any number of them myself and took great pleasure in showing them around.

All of the matters about which you have written recently, have had my attention. Yours very truly,

Emmett J. Scott

TLS   Con. 183   BTW Papers   DLC.

686

From William Torrey Harris

Washington, D.C. December 3,1900

My dear Professor Washington: I have read four chapters of your new autobiography "Up from Slavery" and I am anxious to tell you how much pleasure it gives me to say to you that you have made one of the great books of the year. I predict for your book a wide sphere of influence. It will be a great blessing not only to your people but also to all the other part of the Nation, for it will help to guide the Nation out of its difficulty.

Mrs. Harriet Beecher Stowe wrote "Uncle Tom's Cabin" and thereby produced a civil war in the Nation. You have written a book which I think will do more than anything else to guide us to the true road on which we may successfully solve the problems left us by that civil war. I have always admired your work and looked upon you as a benefactor both to white and to colored people, but I think that in writing this autobiography you have come upon a method by which you can increase your usefulness tenfold and a hundredfold by revealing in a book the spirit of your methods.

I congratulate you for what you have done and for what your book will do. Very sincerely yours,

W. T. Harris

TLS   Con. 261   BTW Papers   DLC.

From Mary Thorn Lewis Gannett[1]

Rochester, N.Y. December 4th 1900

My dear Mr. Washington, I cannot tell which is most deeply interested in the story of your life, coming out in The Outlook, our children, to whom I've been reading it, or their mother — but I want to tell you what an immediate influence it had on our nine year old boy. He showed me with great pride, the other day, a rack for his jimlets[2] he'd been making of hard wood, and said "I'd never have got that more than half done, mother, if I hadn't kept thinking all the time how Booker Washington made up his mind he'd *do*

687

things!" So you see your story has already helped one small boy.

My heart throbbed and my eyes filled as I read your tribute to General Armstrong. It was my great privilege to meet him more than once and I'm so glad I realized at the time that it *was* a wonderful privilege.

Mr. Gannett & I went to Fort Monroe on our Wedding Journey & spent most of the three days there at that blessed Hampton.

Blessed is Hampton and so is Tuskegee & so are their children and those who are making them what they are.

Pray do not let this letter (which was meant to be a short note) lay on you the burden of acknowledging it. I know too well what that means to a busy man. With high regard & honor I am sincerely yours

Mary Thorn Lewis Gannett

ALS Con. 198 BTW Papers DLC.

1 Mary Thorn Lewis Gannett of Philadelphia married the prominent Unitarian clergyman William Channing Gannett in 1887. In 1889 the Gannetts moved to Rochester, N.Y., where Rev. Gannett was pastor of the Unitarian church, a position he held until 1908.

2 Gimlets.

From Timothy Thomas Fortune

New York, Dec. 4, 1900

Dear Mr. Washington: I have been as blue as indigo all day. The supreme court has affirmed the right of a State to enact and enforce Separate Car legislation.[1] We have got to find a way out of this thing. We must get an amendment to the Inter State Commerce law that will cover the case. We must do something. The Supreme Court cannot be left to have things its own way. Yours truly,

T Thomas Fortune

ALS Con. 172 BTW Papers DLC.

1 In Chesapeake and Ohio Railway Co. *v.* State of Kentucky, 179 U.S. 388-95, the Supreme Court upheld the Kentucky law that provided for separate coaches for blacks. The railroad had argued that the requirement of separate cars was an im-

pediment to interstate commerce. On Dec. 3, 1900, the Supreme Court made its ruling without dealing directly with the issue of interference with interstate commerce. Justice Henry Billings Brown gave the majority opinion, which said there would be sufficient compliance with the law if a separate coach was added for local black passengers as the train passed through Kentucky. Justice John Marshall Harlan's dissenting opinion was that the law violated federal control of interstate commerce and that Kentucky had no right to differentiate between citizens on the basis of color.

From John A. Hertel

Naperville, Illinois, 12/6/00

Dear Sir: I have been looking over your Autobiography in the "Outlook" and I am really surprised to learn that this is to be an autobiography pure and simple. It appears to me, Mr. Washington, that this is doing us a great injustice.

Now you will remember when this question came up when you sent your private secretary, Mr. Scott, here that we hesitated considerably, but when we were assured that you were going to write a series of sketches entitled "Reminiscences" and that the subject matter and *title* was to be entirely different from that of our book we consented. We stated very specifically that the title should be such that this book could not be confused with your Autobiography, "The Story of My Life."

I do not know what you can or intend to do about it now, but I wish simply to say that we are not making a howl about nothing. You can count on us always for doing the fair thing. We want to be liberal and just to you and to every one concerned but we wish simply to enclose you a letter that we have just received from one of our customers in the East — you can see what effect this new Autobiography is having on the sale of "The Story of My Life." Of course, publishers whom we have succeeded in inducing to sell this book are very much surprised to think that we would put money in a book of this kind and then permit the author to repeat it in a monthly paper.

I might add that your Autobiography is having an excellent sale. We are putting lots of money and energy into it and we are now planning to get out another 10,000 edition which we shall do unless the Autobiography in the "Outlook" interferes materially.

I should like to know at an early date what you have to say about this. Yours very truly,

J. A. Hertel

TLS   Con. 182   BTW Papers   DLC.

To Mary Thorn Lewis Gannett

Tuskegee, Ala., Dec. 7, 1900

Dear Madam: I wish to tell you how greatly I appreciate your kind word, advising as to the interest of yourself and children in the narrative of my life which is appearing in the Outlook. I hope that the subsequent numbers will prove as interesting.

Of course you know I appreciate to the fullest extent all you say regarding General Armstrong. He was one of the most wonderful of men and was in every way one of God's noblemen. I am glad that you were permitted to know him. Yours very truly,

Booker T. Washington

TLSr   Con. 16   William Channing Gannett Papers   NRU.   Signed in Emmett J. Scott's hand.

From Mary Fletcher Mackie

Newburgh. [N.Y.] Dec. 9. 1900

My dear Booker — Thank you for the excellent photograph which stands now on my bureau beside Gen. Armstrong's balanced on the other side by that of Gen. and Mrs. Marshall. It was very good of you to send it so promptly when you have so many so important requests constantly to meet. On the back of it I have pasted those lines of Paul Dunbar's which I think are fine — not only because true but because he has put so much in such few words. I hear nothing but praise, on every side, of your articles in the Outlook.

Every letter from every old friend I receive who knows you speaks of the autobiography in the highest terms and adds "It is wonderful how widely it is being read." My daily prayer for you is that your life may long be spared to carry on the work you have so nobly begun. Be warned by Gen. Armstrong's fate and do not go too far beyond your daily strength. The world needs you for many years to come.

Always with the deepest and truest interest   Your friend

M. F. Mackie

How do people generally address you? I know you have received some degree but just what I do not know. I want to give you all the *respect* the world so justly accords you — but as I dont really know I shall have to call you Prof. Your own name is what future generations will honor.

ALS   Con. 179   BTW Papers   DLC.

From Ernest Lewis Ruffner

Buffalo, N.Y., Dec 9 1900

My dear Mr Washington, I see by the papers you have consented to address the Independent Club of our City.

Mrs Ruffner & I would consider it a pleasure to have you a guest in our home during your stay in Buffalo.

If possible for you, we would enjoy having you spend the Sunday previous, or if not, any length of time agreeable.

Grandma speaks of you so often, we would enjoy meeting you. Sincerely,

Ernest Lewis Ruffner

ALS   Con. 182   BTW Papers   DLC.

From Martha Calhoun

Cambridge [Mass.], Tuesday 18th Dec. [1900]

My dear Mr Washington   I heard you speak last evening — at least I heard half your speech, for I had to go out early, with a little sleepy maiden.

Now, no one living, can have the well-being and growth of the whole human family, more at heart, than I have — and no one living, feels more keenly the wrongs my race have inflicted upon yours, than I feel!

But — with all my well-wishes and all my natural hopefulness, I see slavery in one way, perhaps even in a more cruel way, just as pronounced as ever. Therefore when you tell an audience that the barber shop has been taken from the colored man, I see nothing in it, to make an audience laugh — on the contrary, everything in it, to weep for. It is not really because of improved methods that the white man has wrested this honorable and lucrative occupation from his colored brother. It is because he is the ~~stronger~~ popular one, and in the majority and because he feels a cruel hatred to his once prosperous colored brother in the trade. No man living, is more facile, and more quick to learn, & to take up improved methods than the colored man. It doesn't need Tuskegee to teach him, at least how to shave with intelligence. The white man who has dethroned him didn't learn his new methods at any school.

And with the old-time white-washer, let us hope that he has not been dethroned because he couldn't learn the new methods, but because he isn't given a chance to learn them. I remember away, away back, long before you were born, a dear old white-washer, who each spring and autumn came to whiten up our house; and he left just as much love and brightness in our childish hearts, as he left freshness and brightness in the rooms. "Uncle Cyrus" was our friend, and each day when he went home with his arms full of treasures for his dear old wife, my mother used to say, "Children if you will grow up into the saintship of that man, you will be sure of the same eternal rest that he is sure of — there is no color line beyond the stars; no low-down occupations there." That the good old "Uncle Toms" are deprived this one occupation, by reason of the suspicion that they cant reach to the newer, and better methods in it, is — pardon me — an insult to one of the most apt, and quick-learning races of the world! To tell the audience before which you stand the real truth — that the white man is jealous of the dark man, and will not permit him to forge ahead where he can help it — is, let us hope to set the audience thinking of the great injustice: and thinking in a right direction, always brings good. A colored man doesn't need a school to tell him how to drive a car, or collect fares on it; nor does colored man or woman, need more than the ordinary education to be clerk or accountant in a store. Yet who employs them? I went to a factory in Nashua a couple of years ago, knowing they wanted help, to get employment for two young men — educated, and refined, earnest and honest. The superintendent laughed at my proposition, and said "Why the french Canadians wouldn't work an hour beside colored people." Are these things nothing to talk of? Will educating a few ever open the eyes of Americans to the fact, that they the Americans are the most monstrously unjust people in all the world? ~~No!~~ They want the cruel fact that millions of their fellow citizens are handicapped in the poor life race, set graphically and constantly before them. They want to be told that such handicapping is a danger, as well as a stupid injustice to helpless people; and that crime naturally *must be the result.* We can't be saints, if we are always hungry; nor can we feel any thing but bitterness towards those who forbid us work, that we may *not* be hungry. You say every one knows all these conditions — but I find it astonishing how little people *do* know. Even teachers and preachers give no heed to the subject: they don't care that restaurant, hotel, theatre, even church, are closed to colored people — *every where* except in Boston; and I confess I find no *real* liberty there. I would like to take an earnest young student friend to dine with me, betimes, here, where I take my meals; but I cant; the boarders would object. A colored lady came here in Cambridge, once, with the Christian Endeavorers. Not a house would take her in!! Do we wonder that thinkers become infidels in view of such things?

Mr Shaler[1] said last evening, there was really a *raison d'être* for slavery. Tropical people were needed to work in a new tropical country. Very likely: but why pay them for their work in bondage and stripes rather than in gold? "God ordered all this," &c. A queer God, to demand that thousands of his own dear children, have

693

hearts & backs broken, that other thousands no better — or, because of the stain not half as good — live in idle luxury!

Do you stay hereabout, long? Come over some afternoon; and
over a cup of tea let us talk about it all. Only let me know when,
that I may surely be at home. Very faithfully I am   Yours

Martha Calhoun

ALS   Con. 169   BTW Papers   DLC.

1 Nathaniel Southgate Shaler.

From Robert Leon Campbell[1]

Tuguegarao Luzon P.I. Christmas Eve 1900

Dear Sir: I received your letter dated Oct 19th 1900 and to express
my thoughts and pleasure would be very difficult. I am proud to
have the honor of getting a letter from you Sir, and will do all I
can to uphold your teachings. I have been benefitted beyond measure, by my connection with Tuskegee and under the influence of
your wise counsel and I am desirous of pursueing my studies at
Tuskegee when I am through with this service.

I only wish I was in circumstances so that I might help to build
up Tuskegee.

The young men who are in the Regiment from Tuskegee are
doing very well and express a desire to return and resume their
studies as soon as possible. It seems as if we have been from home
a very long time, and we are anxious to return to our people.

The natives of this section of the country are not half so ignorant
as they are represent[ed] to be in all of my experience with them
I have not found one who could not read and write in his or her
own language and some of them can do fairly well with English,
and it is a common every day occurrence to see them read and write
Spanish, they are not as far behind as one might expect after hearing accounts of them from those who are narrow minded and not
desirous of giving all peoples their dues.

There are wild tribes in the mountains fastness which we have
never seen they are not hostile to the Americans alone but to all

mankind who intrude in their domain, the[y] are mostly of the dwarf type of man, and are call Negritos, and some other names I dont remember.

Taking the civilized native as he stands, looking at him through an unprejudiced eye and he will compare favorable with other races who have been under Spanish rule.

I did not receive the first letter you sent me but I am hoping to get it in a few days.

I am satisfied that any young man who has been so fortunate as to come over here safe, and keeps his health and gets back safe will profit greatly by his trip, there are some of the greatest historical scenes to be found in Manila and surroundings as any other place in the eastern hemisphere.

I do not regret my trip, but I have no intention to go in the army again. I think any man who has any humanity about him at all will make a mistake to fight against such a cause as this. I believe these people are right and *we* are wrong and terriblely wrong. I am in position to keep from bearing arms against them and I will try and keep myself in such position until we are mustered out, of course if I am order[ed] to fight I will obey orders as a soldier should, but I am expressing my opinion privately to you Sir.

Mr. Washington believe me to be one of Tuskegee's most ardent admirers and were I able (financially) I would be one [of] Tuskegees most enthusiastic supporters, and as I am I will never fail to give and assist all I can towards its success.

Please write to me when ever you find it convenient and believe me, Yours very respectfully

Robert L. Campbell

Clerk Q.M.D. Headquarters 49th Infty.

ALS Con. 193 BTW Papers DLC.

1 Robert Leon Campbell, of Athens, Ga., was a member of the B middle class at Tuskegee before he enlisted in the 49th Regiment, U.S. Volunteer Infantry, in 1899. Serving two years in the Philippines, he rose to the rank of sergeant before mustering out in 1901. Campbell returned to Tuskegee in 1901 in the A middle class and continued his studies as a machinist. At commencement in 1903 he was awarded a prize for his patented invention of a reversing valve.

An Article in the *International Monthly*

[December 1900]

The American Negro and His Economic Value

Within the last two months I have had letters from the Sandwich Islands, Cuba, and South America, all asking that the American Negro be induced to go to these places as laborers. In each case there would seem to be abundant labor already in the places named. It is there, but it seems not to be of the quality and value of that of the Negro in the United States.

These letters have led me to think a good deal about the Negro as an industrial factor in our country.

To begin with, we must bear in mind that when the first twenty slaves were landed at Jamestown, Virginia, in 1619, it was this economic value which caused them to be brought to this country. At the same time that these slaves were being brought to the shores of Virginia from their native land, Africa, the woods of Virginia were swarming with thousands of another dark-skinned race. The question naturally arises: Why did the importers of Negro slaves go to the trouble and expense to go thousands of miles for a dark-skinned people to hew wood and draw water for the whites, when they had right about them a people of another race who could have answered this purpose? The answer is, that the Indian was tried and found wanting in the commercial qualities which the Negro seemed to possess. The Indian would not submit to slavery as a race, and in those instances where he was tried as a slave his labor was not profitable and he was found unable to stand the physical strain of slavery. As a slave the Indian died in large numbers. This was true in San Domingo and in other parts of the American continent.

The two races, the Indian and the Negro, have been often compared to the disadvantage of the Negro. It has been more than once stated that the Indian proved himself the superior race in not submitting to slavery. We shall see about this. In this respect it may be that the Indian secured a temporary advantage in so far as race feeling or prejudice is concerned; I mean by this that he escaped the badge of servitude which has fastened itself upon the Negro, and not only upon the Negro in America, for the known commercial value of the Negro has made him a subject of traffic in other portions of the globe during many centuries. Even to this day, portions of Africa continue to be the stamping-ground of the slave-trader.

The Indian refused to submit to bondage and to learn the white man's ways. The result is that the greater portion of American Indians have disappeared, and the greater portion of those who remain are not civilized.

The Negro, wiser and more enduring than the Indian, patiently endured slavery; and the contact with the white man has given the Negro in America a civilization vastly superior to that of the Indian.

The Indian and the Negro met on the American continent for the first time at Jamestown, in 1619. Both were in the darkest barbarism. There were twenty Negroes and thousands of Indians. At the present time, there are between nine and ten millions of Negroes and fifty-eight thousand eight hundred and six Indians. Not only has the Indian decreased in numbers, but he is an annual tax upon the government for food and clothing to the extent of $12,784,676 (1899), to say nothing of the large amount that is annually spent in policing him. The one in this case not only decreased in numbers and failed to add anything to the economic value of his country, but has actually proven a charge upon the state.

Let us see how it is with the other. For a long time our national laws bearing upon immigration have been framed so as to prevent the influx into this country of any classes or races that might prove a burden upon the taxpayers, because of their poverty and inability to sustain themselves, as well as their low standard of life which would enable them to underbid the American laborer. The effect has been, then, to keep out certain races and classes. For two centuries and more, it was the policy of the United States to bring in the Negro at great cost. All others who have come to this country have paid their own passage. The Negro was of such tremendous economic value that his passage was paid for him. Not only was his passage paid, but agents were sent to force him to come. This country had two hundred and fifty years in which to judge of the economic value of the black man, and the verdict at the end was that he was constantly increasing in value, especially in the southern part of the United States.

Would any individuals, or a country, have gone to the expense during so many years to import a race of people that had no economic value?

The Negro seems to be about the only race that has been able to look the white man in the face during the long period of years and live, not only live, but multiply. The Negro has not only done this, but he has had the good sense to get something from the white man at every point he has touched him; something that has made him a stronger and a better race.

As compared with the Malay race, the Negro has proven his superiority as an economic factor in civilization. Take for example the Malays in the Sandwich Islands. Before the Sandwich Islanders came into contact with the white race, they had a civilization that was about equal to that of the twenty Negroes who came to Jamestown in 1619. Since their contact with the white man they have constantly decreased in numbers, and have so utterly failed to prove of economic value that practically the industries of the Islands are now kept in motion by other races, and a strong effort has recently been made to induce a large number of black Americans to go to these Islands as laborers.

The industries that gave the South its power, prominence, and wealth prior to the Civil War, were mainly cotton, sugar-cane, rice, and tobacco. Before the way could be prepared for the proper growing and marketing of these crops, forests had to be cleared, houses to be built, public roads and railroads to be constructed. In all of this, no one will deny that the Negro was the chief dependence.

The Negro was not only valuable as a common workman, but reached a degree of skill and intelligence in mechanics that added a large per cent to his money value. Indeed many of the most complicated structures at the South to-day stand as monuments to the skill and ability of the Negro mechanic of ante-bellum days.

In the planting, cultivation, and marketing of the cotton, rice, sugar-cane, and tobacco, the black man was about the sole dependence, especially in the lower tier of the southern states. In the manufacture of tobacco, he became a skilled and proficient workman and at the present time, in the South, holds the lead in this respect in the large tobacco manufactories.

Not only did the black American prove his worth in the way of skilled and common labor, but there were thousands of Negroes who demonstrated that they possessed executive ability of a high order. Many of the large plantations had a Negro overseer to whom the whole financial interests of the masters were very largely intrusted. To be able to plan months ahead for planting and harvesting of the crop, to reckon upon the influence of weather conditions, and to map out profitable work for scores of men, women, and children required an executive ability of no mean order. In very few instances did the black manager prove false to his trust.

Without the part which the Negro played in the physical development of the South, it is safe to say that it would be as undeveloped as much of the territory in the Far West.

The most valuable testimony that I have seen upon the subject that this article covers is from the pen of Prof. N. S. Shaler, Dean of the Scientific School of Harvard University, which appeared recently in *Appleton's Popular Science Monthly*.[1] My readers, I am sure, will forgive me for using a rather long quotation from Professor Shaler's article. I do it for the reason that Professor Shaler is not only a recognized scientist, but for the further reason that he is a southern man and has had abundant opportunity to secure valuable testimony. Professor Shaler says:

"The Negroes who came to North America had to undergo as complete a transition as ever fell to the lot of man, without the least chance to undergo an acclimatizing process. They were brought from the hottest part of the earth to the region where the winter's cold is of almost arctic severity; from an exceedingly humid to a very dry air. They came to service under alien taskmasters, strange to them in speech and in purpose. They had to betake themselves to unaccustomed food and to clothing such as they had never worn before. Rarely could one of the creatures find about him a familiar face of friend, parent, or child, or an object that recalled his past life to him. It was an appalling change. Only those who know how the Negro cleaves to all the dear, familiar things of life, how fond he is of warmth and friendliness can conceive the physical and mental shock that this introduction to new conditions meant to them. To people of our own race, it could have meant death. But these wonderful folk appear to have withstood the trials of their deportation in a marvelous way. They showed no peculiar liability to disease. Their longevity or period of usefulness was not diminished, or their fecundity obviously impaired. So far as I have been able to learn, nostalgia was not a source of mortality, as it would have been with any Aryan population. The price they brought in the market and the satisfaction of their purchasers with their qualities show that they were from the first almost ideal laborers.

"If we compare the Algonquin Indian, in appearance a sturdy fellow, with these Negroes, we see of what stuff the blacks are made. A touch of housework and of honest toil took the breath of the aborigines away, but these tropical exotics fell to their tasks and trials far better than the men of our own kind could have done. . . . Moreover, the production of good tobacco requires much care, which extends over about a year from the time the seed is planted. Some parts of the work demand a measure of judgment such as intelligent Negroes readily acquire. They are, indeed, better fitted for the task than white men, for they are commonly more interested in their task than whites of the laboring class. The result was that before the period of the Revolution slavery was firmly established in the tobacco planting colonies of Maryland, Virginia, and North Carolina; it was already the foundation of their only considerable industry. . . . This industry (cotton), even more than that of raising tobacco, called for abundant labor which could be absolutely commanded and severely tasked in the season of extreme heats. For this work the Negro proved to be the only fit man, for while the whites can do this work, they prefer other employment. Thus it came about that the power of slavery in this country became rooted in its soil. The facts show that, based on an ample foundation of experience, the judgment of the southern people was to the effect that this creature of the tropics was a better laborer in their fields than the men of their own race.

"Much has been said about the dislike of the white man for work in association with Negroes. The failure of the whites to have a larger share in the agriculture of the South has been attributed to this cause. This seems to be clearly an error. The dislike to the association of races in labor, is, in the slaveholding states, less than in the North. There can be no question that if the southern folk could have made white laborers profitable they would have preferred to employ them, for the reason that the plantations would have required less fixed capital for their operation. The fact was and is, that the Negro is there a better laboring man in the field than the white. Under the conditions, he is more enduring, more contented, and more trustworthy than the men of our own race."

So much for the Negro as a financial factor in American life before the Civil War. What about his value as a free man?

There were not a few who predicted that as soon as the Negro became a free man he would not only cease to support himself and others, but he would become a tax upon the community.

Few people in any part of our country have ever seen a black hand reached out from a street corner asking for charity. In our northern communities a large amount of money is spent by individuals and municipalities in caring for the sick, the poor, and other classes of unfortunates. In the South, with very few exceptions, the Negro takes care of himself and of the unfortunate members of his race. This is usually done by a combination of individual members of the race, or through the churches or fraternal organizations. Not only is this true, but I want to make a story illustrate the condition that prevails in some parts of the South. The white people in a certain Black Belt county in the South had been holding a convention, the object of which was to encourage white people to immigrate into the county. After the adjournment of the convention, an old colored man met the president of the meeting on the street and asked the object of the convention. When told, the old colored man replied: "Fore God, boss, don't you know that we Niggers got just as many white people now in this county as we can support."

The fact is often referred to that the Negro pays a very small proportion of the taxes that support his own schools. As to whether or not this is true depends a good deal on the theory of political economy that we follow. Some of the highest authorities on political economy contend that it is the man who rents the house that pays the taxes on it, rather than the man who simply holds the title to it. Certain it is that without the Negro to produce the raw material in the South from which a large proportion of the taxes are paid, then there would not be a very large tax paid by any one.

Reliable statistics concerning the economic progress of the Negro are difficult to be obtained, owing to the fact that few of the states keep a record separating the property owned by Negroes from that owned by white people. The state of Virginia and one or two southern states do keep such a record. Taking the matter of taxes as a basis for indicating the Negro's value Prof. J. W. Cromwell, of Washington, D.C., gave the following statistics bearing upon the colored people of the state of Virginia, at a recent conference at the Hampton Institute:

"The colored people contributed in 1898 directly to the expenses of the state government, the sum of $9,576.76, and for schools $3,239.41, from their personal property, a total of $12,816.17; while from their real estate for the purposes of the commonwealth there was paid by them $34,303.53, and for schools $11,357.22, or a total of $45,760.75; a grand total of $58,576.92.

"The report for the same year shows them to own 978,118 acres of land valued at $3,800,459, improved by buildings valued at $2,056,490, a total of $5,856,949. In the towns and cities they own lots assessed at $2,154,331, improved by buildings valued at $3,400,636, a total of $5,554,967 for town property and a grand total of $11,411,916 of their property of all kinds in the commonwealth. A comparative statement for different years would doubtless show a general upward tendency.

"The counties of Accomac, Essex, King and Queen, Middlesex, Mathews, Northampton, Northumberland, Richmond, Westmoreland, Gloucester, Princess Anne, and Lancaster, all agricultural, show an aggregate of 114,197 acres held by Negroes in 1897, the last year accounted for in official reports, against 108,824 held the previous year, an increase of 5,379, or nearly five per cent. The total valuation of lands owned by Negroes in the same counties for 1897 is $547,800 against $496,385 for the year next preceding, a gain of $51,150 or more than ten per cent. Their personal property as assessed in 1897 was $517,560, in 1896, $527,688, a loss of $10,128. Combining the real and personal property for 1897, we have $1,409,059 against $1,320,504 for 1896, a net gain of $88,555, an increase of six and a half per cent."

The greatest excitement and anxiety has been recently created among the white people in two counties in Georgia because of the fact that a large proportion of the colored people decided to leave. No stone has been left unturned to induce the colored people to remain in the county and prevent financial ruin to many white farmers.

Any one who has followed the testimony given recently before the United States Industrial Commission will see that several white men from the South have stated in the most emphatic language, that the Negro is the best laborer that the South has ever had and is the best that the South is likely to get in the future. Not the least part of the Negro's worth at the present time (and this is going to be more apparent in the future than now) is that he presents a conservative, reliable factor in relation to "strikes" and "lockouts." The Negro is not given to "strikes." His policy is to leave each individual free to work when, where, and for whom he pleases.

The cotton crop of the South has increased many fold since the beginning of freedom. Of course the Negro is not the only labor element to be considered in the production of cotton, but all will agree that the black man is the chief dependence in this country for that purpose. In order to be more specific I give some figures that will indicate the difference between the number of bales of cotton produced by slave and free labor:

SLAVE LABOR		FREE LABOR	
Year	Bales	Year	Bales
1845	2,394,503	1890	8,652,597
1850	2,233,781	1899	8,900,000

While there are several factors, among them increase in population, entering into these figures, still I think they show clearly that freedom has not destroyed the economic value of the Negro.

What I have thus far stated, relates mainly to the common Negro laborer before and since the war. But what about the educated Negro?

Reference is often made to the large proportion of criminal and idle colored men in the large cities. I admit that this class is much larger than it should be, and in some cities it is beginning to present a rather serious problem. Two things, however, should be kept in mind when considering the younger generation of colored people: First, that the transition from slavery to freedom was a tremendous one; that the Negro's idea of freedom for generations had been that it meant freedom from restraint and work; that the Negro mother and father had little opportunity during slavery to learn how to train children; and that family life was practically unknown to the Negro until about thirty years ago. Secondly, the figures relating to criminality among all races in all countries show that it is the younger people, those between the ages of sixteen and thirty-five, that are given to crime and idleness.

Notwithstanding these facts, I want to present some testimony showing that the young, educated Negro is not failing to prove his worth.

Some time ago, I sent letters to about four hundred white men scattered throughout the southern states in which these three questions were asked:

1. Has education made the Negro a more useful citizen?

2. Has it made him more economical and more inclined to acquire wealth?

3. Has it made him a more valuable workman, especially where thought and skill are required?

Answers came from three hundred of my correspondents, and nine tenths of them answered the three questions emphatically in the affirmative. A few expressed doubts, but only one answered the questions with an unmodified "No."

In each case, I was careful to ask my correspondents to base their correspondence upon the conditions existing in their own neighborhood.

The Negro is gradually branching out in nearly all lines of business. To illustrate this remark, I give a few statistics representing typical cases in different portions of the South. These statistics were gathered by Dr. Du Bois of the University.

NEGRO BUSINESS MEN

Birmingham, Ala.

Grocers	8
Barbers	6
Banks and Brokers	5
Druggists	4
Tailors	4
Miscellaneous	5

Montgomery, Ala.

Grocers	6
Undertakers	2
Drug-stores	2
Butcher	1

Vicksburg, Miss.

Saloons	2
Jewelers	2
Clothiers and Tailors	2
Drug-stores	2
Newspapers	2
Dry-goods	2
Undertaker	1
Confectioners	2
Upholsterer	1
Butcher	1
Fish and Oysters	1
Miscellaneous	3

Nashville, Tenn.

Contractors	9
Grocers	6
Undertakers	2
Saloons	2
Drug-stores	2
Second-hand Stores	2
Livery-stables	2
Publishers	2
Tailors	2
Coal and Ice	1
Produce Merchant	1
Furniture	1
Transfer Wagon	1
Restaurant and Grocer	1
Grocer and Saloon	1
Second-hand Furniture	1
Miscellaneous	9

Houston, Tex.

KINDS OF BUSINESS	YEARS IN BUSINESS	CAPITAL INVESTED
Grocery	4	$1,500
Grocery	3	1,000
Grocery	5	2,000
Grocery		1,000
Real Estate Dealer	15	10,000
Real Estate Dealer	18	50,000
Contractor	12	10,000
Contractor	12	8,000
Barber	20	1,000
Barber	19	1,200
Barber	16	1,000
Saloon	14	4,000
Hair Dressing	20	1,000
Real Estate Broker	3	6,000
Real Estate Broker	20	40,000
Real Estate Broker	30	75,000
Grocer	5	350
Grocer	15	1,200
Contractor, Builder	6	7,000
Grocer	3	200
Contractor, Builder	30	5,000
Grocer	10	3,000
Grocer and Real Estate Broker	10	15,000
Grocer	4	500
Grocer	3	500
Barber	10	2,000
Barber	15	3,000
Real Estate Broker	10	14,000
Dairyman	14	2,000
Real Estate	6	7,000
Real Estate	8	4,000
Tailor	6	5,000
Huckster	12	2,000
Barber	9	2,500
Contractor and Real Estate	15	12,000

KINDS OF BUSINESS	YEARS IN BUSINESS	CAPITAL INVESTED
Wood Dealer	10	900
Saloon Business	3	6,000
Caterer	15	1,000
Blacksmith and Wheelwright	12	1,800
Pawn Broker	8	3,500
Saloon	17	5,000

Richmond, Va.

Insurance and Banking	$75,000
Insurance and Banking	135,000
Fish Dealer	3,000
Fish Dealer	2,000
Dry-goods Store	2,000
Insurance Society	1,000
Undertaker	2,000
Undertaker	10,000
Photographer	1,500

Mound Bayou, Miss.

KINDS OF BUSINESS	YEARS IN BUSINESS	CAPITAL INVESTED	ASSESSED REAL ESTATE
General Merchandise . . .	10	$5,000	$3,000
Merchandise and Ginning . .	8	1,000	2,000
General Merchandise . . .	2	300	500
General Merchandise . . .	8	150	800
General Merchandise . . .	3	750	
Merchandise and Blacksmith .	7	150	800
Merchandise and Sawmill . .	10	1,000	10,000

Americus, Ga.

KINDS OF BUSINESS	YEARS IN BUSINESS	CAPITAL INVESTED
Grocery and Farming	14	$1,500
Grocery and Restaurant	10	1,200
Grocery	9	1,500
Druggist	5	1,000

KINDS OF BUSINESS	YEARS IN BUSINESS	CAPITAL INVESTED
Grocery	2	225
Grocery	6	300
Furniture	7	3,000
Grocery	4	300
Grocery	10	270
Grocery	8	300
Grocery	8	375
Grocery	5	300
Grocery	12	1,000
Restaurant and Barber Shop	9	500
Market	7	1,000
Wood Yard	22	1,000
Grocery	9	500
Cigars and Tobacco	4	500

Tallahasse, Fla.

KINDS OF BUSINESS	YEARS IN BUSINESS	CAPITAL INVESTED	SALES PER YEAR
Groceries and Dry-goods	—	$1,500	$6,000
Meat Market	—	1,000	4,680
Meat Market	—	250	832
Groceries	—	400	1,500
General Merchandise	—	150	

Seattle, Wash.

KINDS OF BUSINESS	YEARS IN BUSINESS	CAPITAL INVESTED
Real Estate	5	$10,000
Stock Broker	3	2,500
Hotel	2	1,500
Club House	2	700
Barber	6	3,000
Saloon	2	1,000
Barber	3	500
Restaurant	4	900
Restaurant	9	1,000
Newspaper	6	2,000

From all the foregoing facts, I think we may safely find ground for the greatest hopefulness, not only for the Negro himself, but for the white man in his treatment of the Negro. In the South, especially, the prosperity of the one race enriches the other, the poverty of one race retards the progress of the other.

The greatest thing that can be done for the Negro at the present time is to make him the most useful and indispensable man in his community. This can be done by thorough education of the hand, head, and heart, and especially, by the constant instilling into every fibre of his being the thought that labor is ennobling and that idleness is a disgrace.

International Monthly, 2 (Dec. 1900), 672–86.

1 Nathaniel S. Shaler, "The Transplantation of a Race," *Popular Science Monthly*, 56 (Mar. 1900), 513-24.

BIBLIOGRAPHY

T<small>HIS</small> <small>BIBLIOGRAPHY</small> gives fuller information on works cited in the annotations and endnotes. It is not intended to be comprehensive of works on the subjects dealt with in the volume or of works consulted in the process of annotation.

Alabama. *The Code of Alabama, Adopted by Act of the General Assembly of the State of Alabama, Approved February 16, 1897.* Vol. 1. Atlanta: Foote and Davis Co., Printers and Binders, 1897.

Bailey, Hugh C. *Edgar Gardner Murphy: Gentle Progressive.* Coral Gables, Fla.: University of Miami Press, 1968.

Buckle, Henry Thomas. *History of Civilization in England.* 2 vols. London: J. W. Parker and Son, 1857-61.

Chase, Edna Woolman. "Fifty Years of *Vogue.*" *Vogue,* 102 (Nov. 15, 1943), 35-37.

Crofts, Daniel W. "The Warner-Foraker Amendment to the Hepburn Bill: Friend or Foe of Jim Crow?" *Journal of Southern History,* 39 (Aug. 1973), 341-58.

Dabney, Charles William. *Universal Education in the South.* 2 vols. Chapel Hill: University of North Carolina Press, 1936.

Du Bois, William Edward Burghardt. *The Autobiography of W. E. B. Du Bois: A Soliloquy on Viewing My Life from the Last Decade of Its First Century.* New York: International Publishers, 1968.

———. *The Philadelphia Negro: A Social Study.* Philadelphia: University of Pennsylvania, 1899.

Edmonds, Helen G. *The Negro and Fusion Politics in North Carolina.* New York: Russell and Russell, 1951.

Ellison, Rhoda Coleman. *History of Huntington College 1854-1954.* University: University of Alabama Press, 1954.

Filler, Louis, ed. *Mr. Dooley, Now and Forever, Created by Finley Peter Dunne.* Stanford, Calif.: Academic Reprints, 1954.

Fox, Stephen R. *The Guardian of Boston: William Monroe Trotter.* New York: Atheneum Publishers, 1970.

Fullinwider, S. P. *The Mind and Mood of Black America.* Homewood, Ill.: Dorsey Press, 1969.

Gatewood, Willard B. *Smoked Yankees and the Struggle for Empire: Letters from Negro Soldiers, 1898-1902.* Urbana: University of Illinois Press, 1971.

Georgia. *Acts and Resolutions of the General Assembly of the State of Georgia, 1899.* Atlanta: George W. Harrison, 1899.

Harlan, Louis R. *Booker T. Washington: The Making of a Black Leader, 1856-1901.* New York: Oxford University Press, 1972.

————. "Booker T. Washington and the National Negro Business League." In *Seven on Black: Reflections on the Negro Experience,* ed. William G. Shade and Roy C. Herrenkohl, pp. 74-91. Philadelphia and New York: J. B. Lippincott Co., 1969.

————. "Booker T. Washington and the White Man's Burden." *American Historical Review,* 71 (Jan. 1966), 441-67.

————. "The Secret Life of Booker T. Washington." *Journal of Southern History,* 37 (Aug. 1971), 393-416.

————. *Separate and Unequal: Public School Campaigns and Racism in the Southern Seaboard States, 1901-1915.* Chapel Hill: University of North Carolina Press, 1958.

Harris, Joel Chandler. *The Chronicles of Aunt Minervy Ann.* New York: Charles Scribner's Sons, 1899.

Herbert, Hilary Abner. *The Abolition Crusade and Its Consequences: Four Periods of American History.* New York: Charles Scribner's Sons, 1912.

Hoffman, Frederick L. *Race Traits and Tendencies of the American Negro.* New York: American Economic Association, 1896.

Humes, Dollena Joy. *Oswald Garrison Villard: Liberal of the 1920s*. Syracuse, N.Y.: Syracuse University Press, 1960.

Love, John L. *The Disfranchisement of the Negro*. Occasional Paper No. 6. Washington, D.C.: American Negro Academy, 1899.

MacCorkle, William Alexander. *The Recollections of Fifty Years of West Virginia*. New York: G. P. Putnam's Sons, 1928.

————. *Some Southern Questions*. New York: G. P. Putnam's Sons, 1908.

Mackintosh, Barry. *General Background Studies: The Burroughs Plantation 1856-1865*. Washington, D.C.: National Park Service, 1968.

Mathews, Basil Joseph. *Booker T. Washington, Educator and Interracial Interpreter*. Cambridge, Mass.: Harvard University Press, 1948.

Meier, August. *Negro Thought in America, 1880-1915: Racial Ideologies in the Age of Booker T. Washington*. Ann Arbor: University of Michigan Press, 1963.

Merrill, Horace Samuel, and Marion Galbraith Merrill. *The Republican Command, 1897-1913*. Louisville: University of Kentucky Press, 1971.

Miller, Kelly. *A Review of Hoffman's Race Traits and Tendencies of the American Negro*. Occasional Paper No. 1. Washington, D.C.: American Negro Academy, [1897].

Mooney, James E. *John Graham Brooks, Prophet of Social Justice: A Career Story*. Worcester, Mass.: Davis Press, 1968.

National Educational Association. *Proceedings and Addresses, 1900*. Washington, D.C., 1900.

National Negro Business League. *Proceedings, 1900*. Boston: J. R. Hamm, 1901.

Neyland, Leedell W., and John W. Riley. *The History of Florida Agricultural and Mechanical University*. Gainesville: University of Florida Press, 1963.

Osofsky, Gilbert. *Harlem, the Making of a Ghetto: Negro New York, 1890-1910*. New York: Harper and Row, 1966.

Proctor, Henry Hugh. *Between Black and White: Autobiographical Sketches*. Boston: Pilgrim Press, 1925.

Render, Sylvia Lyons, ed. *The Short Fiction of Charles W. Chesnutt*. Washington, D.C.: Howard University Press, 1974.

Roosevelt, Theodore. *The Rough Riders*. New York: Charles Scribner's Sons, 1899.

Scott, Emmett Jay, and Lyman Beecher Stowe. *Booker T. Washington: Builder of a Civilization*. Garden City, N.Y.: Doubleday, Page and Co., 1917.

Smith, Charles Spencer. *The Race Question Reviewed*. Nashville, 1899.

Spear, Allan H. *Black Chicago: The Making of a Negro Ghetto, 1890-1920*. Chicago: University of Chicago Press, 1967.

Straton, John Roach. "Will Education Solve the Race Problem?" *North American Review*, 170 (June 1900), 785-801.

Thornbrough, Emma Lou. *The Negro in Indiana: A Study of a Minority*. Indiana Historical Collections, Vol. 37. Indianapolis: Indiana Historical Bureau, 1957.

——. *T. Thomas Fortune: Militant Journalist*. Chicago: University of Chicago Press, 1972.

Tindall, George Brown. *South Carolina Negroes, 1877-1900*. Columbia: University of South Carolina Press, 1952.

Villard, Oswald Garrison. *Fighting Years: Memoirs of a Liberal Editor*. New York: Harcourt, Brace and Co., 1939.

Virginia. *Biennial Report of the Superintendent of Public Instruction of the Commonwealth of Virginia, with Accompanying Documents, School Years 1897-98 and 1898-99*. Richmond: J. H. O'Bannon, Superintendent of Public Printing, 1899.

Washington, Booker T. *Education of the Negro*. Nicholas Murray Butler, ed. Monographs on Education in the United States, No. 18. Albany, N.Y.: J. B. Lyon Co., 1900.

Washington, E. Davidson, ed. *Selected Speeches of Booker T. Washington*. Garden City, N.Y.: Doubleday, Doran and Co., Inc., 1932.

Wood, Norman Barton. *The White Side of a Black Subject; Enlarged and Brought Down to Date. A Vindication of the Afro-American Race. From the Landing of Slaves at St. Augustine, Florida, in 1565, to the Present Times.* Chicago: Donohue, Henneberry and Co., 1896.

Wreszin, Michael. *Oswald Garrison Villard: Pacifist at War.* Bloomington: Indiana University Press, 1965.

INDEX

NOTE: The asterisk indicates the location of detailed information. This index, while not cumulative, does include the major identifications of persons annotated in earlier volumes of the series who are mentioned in this volume. References to earlier volumes will appear first and will be preceded by the volume number followed by a colon. Lyman Abbott's annotation, for example, will appear as: *3:43–44. Occasionally a name will have more than one entry with an asterisk when new information or further biographical detail is presented.

Valdes, Julian, 199–202, *203
Valdes, Luis Delfin, 199–202, *203
Vance, James J., *389; opposes lynching, 389–90
Vanderbilt, Consuelo, 104
Vanderbilt, Cornelius, III, 157, *158, 219
Van Wyck, Augustus, 231
Vassar College (N.Y.), 685
Venable, William H.: letter from, 508–*9
Victoria (Queen of England), 157, 166, 253; tea with BTW, 170
Villard, Helen Frances Garrison (Fanny), 255
Villard, Henry, *4:273; 255
Villard, Oswald Garrison, *255, 439, 447; helps plan BTW's vacation, 68; letter from, 254–55; praises BTW, 255; relationship with BTW, 255
Virginia Polytechnic Institute, 489
Virginia Union University, 675
Vogue, 103, 104

Wabash Railroad, 464
Waddell, Alfred Moore, 441, *442–43, 476, 507; racial views, 508
Walker, Dayse D., 132, *133, 411
Walker, T. W., *660
Wallace, William James, 231
Walters, Alexander, 122, *123, 138, 179, 187, 193, 197, 203, 295, 457, 609, 651; defends BTW before Afro-American Council, 175; letter from, 595
Wanamaker, John, 249
War Camp Community Service, 133
Ward, William Hayes, *4:248–49; 186, 223
Warner, Charles Dudley, 505, *506; opposes higher education for blacks, 507
Warren, Charles A., *500
Washington, Booker Taliaferro, 3; accused of lies and slander, 188; accuses American Missionary Association of falsehood, 209; admonishes school physician, 224–25; advice to students, 501–4, 520; adviser to Gov. Theodore Roosevelt, 673; advises against black migration to Europe, 132; advises T. T. Fortune on Afro-American Council matters, 203; advises T. T. Fortune to restrain himself during political campaign, 639; aids cotton-growing

experiment in Togo, 633–36, 639–42; apprehensive about speaking in Huntsville, 206, 212; attends reception in London, 144–47; borrows from J. F. B. Marshall, 86; cancels speaking engagement, 228–29; cautioned not to become discouraged, 208; compared with W. E. B. Du Bois, 207; compares black-white educational expenditures, 282; compares Europe to American South, 132; complains of treatment by book publisher, 570, 571, 591; complimented by A. H. Grimké, 152; compliments southern whites on interest in blacks, 215; condemns discrimination against H. M. Turner, 403–5; congratulates A. H. Grimké on protest of lynching, 126; contract with M. B. Thrasher, 59–60; cooperation sought for 1900 census, 247–48; denies affiliation with insurance company, 416; denies discouragement over race conditions, 216; describes building of Tuskegee, 86–87; describes founding of Tuskegee Negro Conference, 95–101; describes meeting in Boston, 7; discriminated against in Denver hotel, 424; discriminated against in Indiana hotel, 448; discusses land bill strategy, 42–44; discusses salary with J. B. Bruce, 197; disturbed over lynching, 172; endorses M. B. Curry, 104–5; endorses W. W. Thompson as land agent, 43–44; eulogy of C. P. Huntington, 605–7; has tea with Queen Victoria, 170; invites W. E. B. Du Bois to join Tuskegee faculty, 245; involvement in search for D.C. school superintendent, 450, 452, 458–59, 460–61, 462–63, 465, 466, 471–74; makes poor speech in Boston, 58; makes recommendation for librarian of Congress, 26, 27; meets H. M. Stanley, 148; negotiations with publisher, 642–43; on board *S. S. Friesland*, 112, 113–14; open letter to Louisiana constitutional convention, 355–58; opinion sought on colonization of blacks, 17–18; opposed to black race conference in Montgomery, 557, 568; opposes racial division of school funds, 683–85; optimistic about Montgomery Race

DATE DUE

HIGHSMITH 45-220